Fodor's see it™

new york
CITY

FODOR'S TRAVEL PUBLICATIONS
NEW YORK • TORONTO • LONDON • SYDNEY • AUCKLAND

WWW.FODORS.COM

Contents

KEY TO SYMBOLS

- ✚ Map reference
- ✉ Address
- ☎ Telephone number
- ⊘ Opening times
- ✋ Admission
- Ⓢ Subway station
- 🚌 Bus number
- 🚉 Train station
- ⛴ Ferry/boat
- 🎫 Tours
- 📘 Guidebook
- 🍽 Restaurant
- ☕ Café
- 🏬 Shop
- 🚻 Toilets
- ① Number of rooms
- 🅿 Parking
- 🚭 No smoking
- 🏊 Swimming pool
- 🏋 Gym
- ▷ Cross reference

How to Use this Book

Understanding New York is an introduction to the city, its geography, economy and people. **Living New York** gives an insight into the city today, while **The Story of New York** takes you through its past.

For detailed advice on getting to New York—and getting around once you are there—turn to **On the Move**. For useful practical information, from weather forecasts to emergency services, turn to **Planning**.

New York's key attractions are listed alphabetically in **The Sights** and are located on the maps on pages 58–61. The key sightseeing areas are described on pages 62–66 and are circled in blue on the map on the inside front cover.

Turn to **What to Do** for information on shops, entertainment, nightlife, sport, health and beauty, children's activities, and festivals and events. Entries are listed by these themes, then alphabetically. Shops are located on the maps on pages 160–163 and theatres on the maps on pages 186–189. The top shopping areas are described on pages 164–168 and circled in green on the map on the inside front cover.

Out and About offers ten walks around New York and two excursions that encourage you to explore further afield.

Eating and Staying gives you selected restaurants and hotels, listed alphabetically. Restaurants are located on the maps on pages 266–269 and hotels on the maps on pages 294–297.

Map references refer to the locator maps within the book or the street atlas at the end. For example, Empire State Building has the grid reference 60 E19, indicating the page on which the map is found (60) and the grid square in which the building sits (E19). Grid squares remain the same whatever page the map is on.

UNDERSTANDING NEW YORK

New York City is an international center for entertainment, fashion, creative arts and finance. It has great shopping, dynamic theater, superb concert halls and clubs, world-class museums, gorgeous parks and gardens, and sports events all year long. The variety and quality of restaurants is incomparable.

As a world financial center, it soars and plummets with the fluctuations on Wall Street. New Yorkers move fast, talk fast and are passionate about politics and style. They come in all shapes, sizes, colors and ethnicities; the city's multiculturalism is part of its charm. Although known for being brusque, New Yorkers are often surprisingly warm. Sometimes infuriating, the city is never dull. And chances are, with its vibrant whirl of activity, it's nothing like home.

NEW
YORK
■

THE MANHATTAN LAYOUT

Manhattan is just one of five boroughs that comprise New York City. The others, sometimes known as the Outer Boroughs, are the Bronx, Brooklyn, Queens and Staten Island.

Manhattan is the long, narrow island jutting southwest off the mainland and is the smallest borough at 13.5 miles (22km) long and 2.25 miles (3.5km) wide. On the east side of the island is the East River. On the west is the Hudson River. To the north is the Harlem River. Upper New York Bay—the city's fine harbor—is to the south.

In Manhattan, most streets are numbered and laid out in a grid. The exception to this is Lower Manhattan, south of 14th Street, which grew up before the grid system was established. On the grid, "avenues" run from north to south, and "streets" run east and west. Broadway, a chief exception to this rule, cuts across town diagonally from northwest to southeast. First Avenue is on the eastern side of town, while Twelfth Avenue is on the western side. Fifth Avenue divides the city into the East Side and the West Side (except south of Washington Square, where Broadway becomes the east–west divide).

No matter where you are in Manhattan, if you are heading north you're going "uptown" and if you're heading south you're going "downtown."

If you want to travel east to west or west to east, you want to go "crosstown."

CLIMATE

From January to March, New York can be very cold, and occasional blizzards can obliterate your view of skyscrapers. But cheaper air fares and hotel rooms can make it worth your while to visit then—and sometimes the weather can be temperate. The best times to visit are in late April and May, when temperatures are generally no lower than 61°F (16°C), and attractions are crowded only at peak times, and in September to early November, when temperatures range from 50°F (10°C) to 77°F (25°C). The city is hot and humid in July and August, with extremes of 95°F (35°C) or higher, but the pleasures of Central Park, open-air concerts and ferry rides are compensations, and almost everything is air-conditioned.

STREET LIFE

Walking is the best way to fully appreciate the city, with its architectural splendors, intriguing sculptures, pretty fountains, beautiful parks and iconic landmarks. The street life is entertaining and colorful. New Yorkers speak Spanish, Chinese, Russian, Yiddish, Korean, Greek and English, to name just a few of the languages you will hear on the streets.

MANHATTAN NEIGHBORHOODS AT A GLANCE

Financial District Oldest part of the city and nexus of the securities industry anchored by the New York Stock Exchange and Wall Street.

TriBeCa It means *Tri*angle *Be*low *Ca*nal and is defined by Canal and Barclay streets and Broadway and the Hudson River. A mixed-use neighborhood of gritty warehouse lofts, loft-style restaurants and low-end retail.

Chinatown Stretching over about 30 blocks, from Kenmare and Delancey streets to East Broadway and Worth Street, and from Broadway to Allen Street. Throngs of people shop for fish, meat, vegetables and herbal remedies or dine in the many affordable restaurants.

Little Italy Consists largely of Mulberry Street, lined with tourist-oriented restaurants, plus one or two genuine delis and pastry stores.

SoHo An ultra-expensive, chic shopping mall that is crowded with non-residents on weekends.

Lower East Side From 14th Street to Fulton and Franklin and from the East River to Broadway,

Take the Staten Island Ferry for one of the best views of the Manhattan skyline

the area takes in Chinatown, Little Italy and the East Village neighborhoods. Haunt of young professionals and artists.

Greenwich Village/West Village Stretches from 14th Street to Houston and from the Hudson River to Bowery and Fourth Avenue. Boutiques line the west end of Bleecker Street.

Noho Between SoHo and Greenwich Village (from Houston to Eighth streets and Mercer to Bowery/Third Avenue), this youth-oriented neighborhood has plenty of fashionable shopping, bars and restaurants.

East Village Filled with restaurants, bars and a youth-oriented street scene.

Union Square/Flatiron District Hot neighborhood south of the Flatiron Building on 22nd Street and around Madison Square with plenty of bars, restaurants and clubs. From 14th to 23rd streets and Park Avenue to Sixth Avenue.

Chelsea Center of the gay community. Numerous warehouse/garage galleries along 24th Street, and a lively club and restaurant scene. Stretches from 14th to 30th streets and from Sixth Avenue to the Hudson River.

Hell's Kitchen The latest neighborhood undergoing gentrification (from Eighth Avenue to the Hudson River between 30th and 59th streets).

Midtown Commercial heart of the city between 34th and 59th streets on the West Side and from 40th to 59th streets on the East Side.

Times Square/Theater District The area around 42nd Street and Broadway is now occupied by major corporations and national chain stores, as well as new hotels, clubs and theaters.

Upper East Side From 59th to 96th streets and from Fifth Avenue to the East River. Madison Avenue is the ultra-chic shopping street.

East/Spanish Harlem From 96th to 142nd streets between Park Avenue and the East River. A mixed neighborhood of Italians, African-Americans and Hispanics.

Upper West Side Broadway cuts right through this section that extends from 59th to 125th streets between the Hudson River and Central Park West.

Harlem Stretching from 110th Street to the Harlem River and from Fifth to St. Nicholas avenues, Harlem is the city's most famous black community.

The Bronx North of and linked to Manhattan by bridges and subway. Home of the New York Botanical Garden, the Bronx Zoo and Yankee Stadium.

Brooklyn Southeast of Manhattan and connected by bridges, a tunnel and subway, it is New York's most populous borough. Take in great views of Manhattan from Brooklyn Heights.

Queens A 20-minute subway trip east from Manhattan takes you to Queens, one of New York's fastest-growing and most ethnically diverse areas.

Staten Island The most southerly and least populous borough, with attractions such as Historic Richmond Town. Good views of Manhattan and the Statue of Liberty from the ferry.

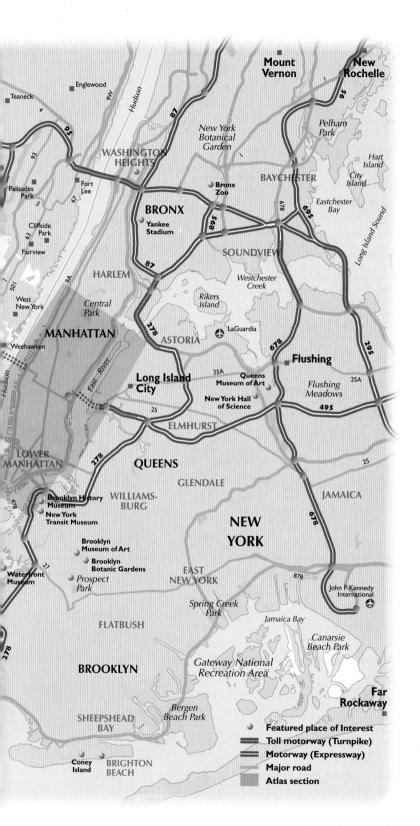

Teaneck

Englewood

9W

Hudson

87

Mount Vernon

New Rochelle

95

Palisades Park

93

95

WASHINGTON HEIGHTS

New York Botanical Garden

Pelham Park

Hart Island

City Island

Fort Lee

Bronx Zoo

BAYCHESTER

5

67

BRONX

Eastchester Bay

Cliffside Park

63

Yankee Stadium

895

678

695

Fairview

SOUNDVIEW

Long Island Sound

9A

501

HARLEM

87

Westchester Creek

West New York

Central Park

Rikers Island

LaGuardia

278

295

Weehawken

MANHATTAN

ASTORIA

678

East River

Long Island City

25A

Queens Museum of Art

Flushing

Flushing Meadows

25A

New York Hall of Science

25

ELMHURST

495

LOWER MANHATTAN

278

QUEENS

25

GLENDALE

JAMAICA

478

Brooklyn History Museum

WILLIAMS-BURG

NEW YORK

New York Transit Museum

678

Brooklyn Museum of Art

Brooklyn Botanic Gardens

EAST NEW YORK

878

21

Waterfront Museum

Prospect Park

John F Kennedy International

Spring Creek Park

FLATBUSH

Jamaica Bay

Canarsie Beach Park

278

BROOKLYN

Gateway National Recreation Area

Far Rockaway

SHEEPSHEAD BAY

Bergen Beach Park

Coney Island

BRIGHTON BEACH

Featured place of Interest

Toll motorway (Turnpike)

Motorway (Expressway)

Major road

Atlas section

THE BEST OF NEW YORK

BEST PLACES TO SHOP

B & H Photo (▷ 184) The professional place for cameras, video equipment and film, all at great prices.

Barneys (▷ 176) For cutting-edge fashion. Don't miss the handbag department.

Bloomingdale's (▷ 176) A department store that's so very New York.

Century 21 (▷ 177) For seriously discounted designer wear and a crowd scene worthy of the annals of shopping.

Dean & DeLuca (▷ 177) Everything in this fancy food emporium is absolutely the best of its kind. A sensuous browsing and tasting experience.

Tiffany's window displays on Fifth Avenue are worth a peek

FAO Schwarz (▷ 184) The ultimate toy store, as seen in the film *Big* with Tom Hanks.

J & R (▷ 179) Audiophiles and technophiles can satisfy every craving for audio components and CDs, computers and peripherals, cameras and other gadgets at good prices.

Jeffrey (▷ 171) The shoe department at this expensive clothing store is stellar, and the best place to see high-designer selections in a single location.

Sherry-Lehmann (▷ 178) An education; the inventory of international wine selections is worth $10 million.

Tiffany (▷ 183) Superb silver, crystal and other luxury gifts are the attraction at this famous American name, in the jewelry business since 1837.

Big names on the bags: Barney's (top left) and FAO Schwarz (above)

BEST MUSEUMS AND GALLERIES

American Museum of Natural History (▷ 68–72) Not only for dinosaur fossils and moon rocks, but also a planetarium complex that is out of this world.

Frick Collection (▷ 100) A large collection of masterpieces by Rembrandt, Vermeer, El Greco and Goya housed in Henry Clay Frick's splendid mansion.

International Center of Photography (▷ 101) More than 60,000 photographs by top names.

Metropolitan Museum of Art (▷ 114–119) 5,000 years' worth of art from around the world.

Museum of Modern Art (▷ 125) Now doubled in size after architect Yoshio Taniguchi's expansion, MOMA displays masterworks of modern sculpture and painting.

Barosaurus at the American Museum of Natural History

BEST OUTDOOR SCULPTURES

Alice in Wonderland (▷ 82) by José de Creeft (1959). In Central Park Alice perches on a giant mushroom while the March Hare holds out a watch and the Mad Hatter looks on.

Bronze Bull by Arturo Di Modica (1989). Reminds many stock-market traders who pass by daily that better times are ahead. At Bowling Green (▷ 73).

The Immigrants (▷ 73) by Luis Sanguino (1973). A heart-rending sculpture evoking the hardships of early immigrants. In Battery Park.

Prometheus by Paul Manship (1934). Rockefeller Center's (▷ 128) famous gold-leaf and bronze statue overlooks the ice-skating rink.

The Sphere (▷ 73) Fritz Koenig's 22-ton symbol of global peace, rescued from the plaza between the twin towers after 9/11, is now a memorial to the victims. In Battery Park.

Statue of Liberty (▷ 136–137) America's symbol of freedom, by Frédéric-Auguste Bartholdi (1885). Take the ferry to Liberty Island for a close-up look.

The gilded figure of Prometheus at the Rockefeller Center

BEST PLACES TO EAT

Babbo (▷ 271) Mario Batali's flagship is the place to sample his lusty cuisine.

Le Bernardin (▷ 280) Everything about this seafood specialist is perfect—the service, the flowers and the exquisitely refined, thoughtful cuisine.

DB Bistro Moderne (▷ 275) Eating at one of Daniel Boulud's restaurants is a must for every food-loving visitor. This is the most relaxed and joyous of them all.

Four Seasons (▷ 277) Even though it has been around since 1959, it remains supremely modern and the darling of the city's movers and shakers. Christian Albin's cuisine is another bonus.

Jean-Georges (▷ 279) All of Jean-Georges Vongerichten's restaurants (Jo Jo, Vong, 66, Mercer Kitchen and Spice Market) showcase his brilliance, but this is his flagship.

Nobu (▷ 283) Nobu Matsuhisa's sushi is inspirational.

Per Se (▷ 284) Thrilling cuisine by Thomas Keller, of French Laundry, Napa Valley fame. Currently the city's most coveted reservation.

Restrained elegance, in decor and cuisine, at Jean-Georges

Tabla (▷ 288) Seductive neo-Indian cuisine by master spice blender Floyd Cardoz.

BEST BARS

Flute (▷ 214) A luxury subterranean retreat serving 20 champagnes by the glass. Perfect for pre- or post-theater.

King Cole Bar (▷ 215) Where the Bloody Mary was invented. Maxfield Parrish's mural adds vibrant color. In the St. Regis Hotel.

MO Bar (▷ 303) Romantic hot spot in the Mandarin Oriental Hotel.

P. J. Clarke's (▷ 218) A beloved New York saloon, home to a rakish crowd.

Pen Top Bar (▷ 216) Who can resist a rooftop bar in Midtown?

Pravda (▷ 216) Sixty-five vodkas, plus caviar and Russian snacks at this trendsetter.

Rainbow Grill Bar (▷ 216) The bartenders mix a great cocktail at this romantic only-in-New York locale.

Top of the Tower (▷ 217) A nostalgic 26th-floor piano-bar overlooking the East River.

The bar scene lasts till dawn in the city that never sleeps

BEST PLACES TO STAY

Carlyle (▷ 299) The city's most discreet retreat.

Four Seasons (▷ 301) Legendary for its service and its immense bathtubs.

Library (▷ 303) A book-lovers' haunt notable for its hip minimalist design and good service.

Marcel (▷ 304) and the **Metro** (▷ 304) Chic on the cheap (by New York standards).

Le Parker Meridien (▷ 302) Very French uptown hotel with hip downtown style. Pool with a view and a rooftop jogging track.

Ritz Carlton (▷ 306) The opulent Central Park star offers superb service, the latest techno amenities and the only La Prairie spa in the United States.

St. Regis (▷ 307) A gilded Beaux-Arts beauty just off Fifth Avenue.

Soho Grand (▷ 307) First of the hip downtown hostelries. Pets get the red-carpet welcome.

Trump International Hotel and Tower (▷ 308) Enjoy breathtaking views of Central Park from this stylish hotel.

The art deco Carlyle Hotel (above); welcome to the St. Regis (right)

BEST BUILDINGS AND SKYSCRAPERS

Ansonia Hotel (2101 Broadway) The Upper West Side's largest Beaux-Arts apartment-hotel. Soundproof partitions between floors attracted musicians and singers, many of them now famous.

Cathedral Church of St. John the Divine (▷ 67) It dates from 1892 and still isn't finished, but the mix of architectural styles inside is amazing.

Chrysler Building (▷ 85) An art deco masterpiece, a shrine to the Chrysler automobile.

Flatiron Building (▷ 87) New York's first skyscraper got its nickname from its triangular shape.

Guggenheim Museum (▷ 110–111) Frank Lloyd Wright's only New York building, a whirling wonder both inside and out.

42nd Street/Times Square (▷ 236–237 and 138–140) Architecture as performing art, with luminous facades of pulsating color. Best at night.

New York Public Library (▷ 127) Archetypal Beaux-Arts magnificence.

City icons: the Guggenheim (left) and the Chrysler Building

BEST FREE SIGHTS

Central Park (▷ 78–83) New York's green lung and Frederick Law Olmsted's masterpiece of landscape architecture.

Hispanic Society of America (▷ 101) An extraordinary collection of paintings, sculpture and decorative arts. See El Grecos, Goyas and an exceptional collection of works by Joaquin Sorolla y Bastida. The 100-year-old buildings are architectural treasures too.

Parades (▷ 324) A festival of color and the city's best people-watching. There are many every year.

Staten Island Ferry (▷ 54) A trip across the harbor. Just hop on.

Whitney Museum of American Art at Philip Morris (▷ 148–151) A branch of the Whitney with wonderful exhibitions by living artists and a charming sculpture court. Worth a stop if you're in the Grand Central neighborhood.

Rockefeller Center and Grand Central Terminal (▷ 128–130 and 102–104) Two architectural gems worth a self-guided tour.

Outdoor New York: Staten Island Ferry (left) and Central Park

BEST EXPERIENCES

Empire State Building (▷ 94–96) The Observation Deck offers a panoramic view of all Manhattan, which is very romantic at sunset.

A Broadway show Seeing one is a quintessential New York experience and various discount pricing schemes make it more affordable.

M4 bus to the Cloisters (▷ 48) A great trip past Columbia University (▷ 77) and through some colorful neighborhoods.

Bronx Zoo (▷ 157) Always entertaining—the people are sometimes as interesting as the animals.

Waldorf-Astoria Hotel (▷ 309) A study in opulence. Ogle the amazing floral displays in the lobby.

A walk across the Brooklyn Bridge (▷ 74–75) A terrific view of the skyscrapers in Lower Manhattan and the East River.

Allow a day to visit the Bronx Zoo (left), and an hour or two for the Empire State Building

Living
New York

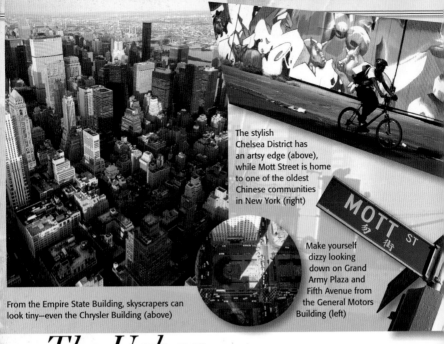

The stylish Chelsea District has an artsy edge (above), while Mott Street is home to one of the oldest Chinese communities in New York (right)

Make yourself dizzy looking down on Grand Army Plaza and Fifth Avenue from the General Motors Building (left)

From the Empire State Building, skyscrapers can look tiny—even the Chrysler Building (above)

The Urban Landscape

Commuting on the subway is part of daily life (above), as is taking a break in the park (below)

Manhattan is only 13.5 miles (22km) long and 2.25 miles (3.5km) wide. Geologically it consists of bedrock made of gneiss, marble or mica schist. These two factors, plus population density, have played major roles in shaping the city's land- and streetscape, making it more vertical than most. Tall buildings line the streets, and people think nothing of riding elevators to their 50th-floor offices. Daily the population swells as commuters pour into Manhattan from the suburbs, creating a crowded environment that throbs with energy. Commuters access the city via ferry, tunnels and bridges, the most graceful of which are the Brooklyn (1883) and George Washington (1931) bridges. North of 14th Street the streets are laid out in a grid. There are few open spaces or green parks to provide relief— only one or two squares, such as Union, Washington and Madison, or small pockets of asphalt with benches, statues and fountains. Instead, there is one vast park, Central Park, separating East and West Sides uptown. It functions as the city's playground.

The grid and the warren

Most visitors to New York City quickly grasp the logic of the streetscape north of 14th Street. A series of broad north–south avenues is crossed by east–west streets, numbered logically. Below 14th Street things get more complicated. Here the narrow streets twist and turn, reminiscent of a medieval city, and have names rather than numbers. This came about because the city grew haphazardly and there were only a few long arteries connecting farms and villages. So in 1811 an orderly grid of 12 broad avenues and 155 streets was established, subdivided into lots measuring 25 by 100ft (7.5 by 30m). It was thought that traffic would be heaviest on the east–west routes, so more streets than avenues were planned. This pattern remains.

Central Park (right) is great for recreation: You can walk, jog, cycle, roller-blade, sail model boats or just take a picnic and chill

With only one major park in the city, every possible space is turned into an outdoor haven (right); street vending (left); locally made produce (bottom)

Underground city

First-time visitors to Manhattan often notice the rooftop water towers, fire hydrants, potholes and, weirdest of all, steam-belching funnels. The last give an inkling of what lies below—a multi-level network of electric and telephone cables, plus steam, water, gas and sewage pipes, all laid above the subway. A large water tunnel under the subway supplies the city's drinking water. The subway alone has 660 miles (1,062km) of track and 490 stations. There's 100 million miles of telephone cable. City water comes from upstate New York reservoirs, and the 1,500 million gallons a day is delivered by more than 6,000 miles (9,654km) of tunnel and water mains. Installed before 1930 and made of cast iron, they can rupture, which causes chaos. When the piped gases build up, they cause man-hole explosions. The steam-belching funnels help to relieve the pressure and stop the 60,000 manholes from erupting.

Robert Moses—New York's Baron Haussmann

Robert Moses (1888–1981), who served on the Parks and Planning commissions, had a huge impact on the city's overall design. Between 1924 and 1968, he transformed the city, building 17 parkways, 14 expressways (including the Brooklyn–Queens Expressway), the FDR and Harlem River drives, the Triborough and Verrazano bridges, Lincoln Center and Stuyvesant Town. In the process he destroyed whole neighborhoods, tearing down slums and relocating residents in dehumanizing public housing in Harlem, the Lower East Side, the Bronx and Brooklyn. The citizens got angry. And when he moved to route cars through Washington Square and put parking lots in Central Park they mobilized to preserve the small scale of their neighborhoods. Still, Moses left a gigantic imprint on the city.

Waking up to the waterfront

For years New York City's 580 miles (920km) of waterfront lay blighted, the site of rusting piers, crumbling warehouses and refuse-strewn lots. Suddenly it's as if the city has woken up to its potential pleasures, as citizens go kayaking, fishing and sailing. A 28-mile (45km) bike path now encircles Manhattan, and the waterfront has been converted into a park with promenade and gardens from the Battery to 58th Street. It's hard to pinpoint when it began. In the 1980s, South Street Seaport, Battery Park City and Chelsea piers were important beginnings, followed by Riverbank State Park (1993). The rest has followed, culminating in Stuyvesant Cove Park (2002) and Hudson River Park (2003).

Urban gardens

New York City has one large park and only two major botanical gardens, so resident horticulturists create their own gardens in unlikely corners. If you look up at the residential buildings you might see green fronds peeking out from the roofline. Some of these roof gardens are luxurious indeed, planted with trees and flowers and decorated with urns and statues. In contrast are the hundreds of community gardens, usually created on vacant city-owned lots, which serve as neighborhood social centers. The impetus for such gardens can be traced to 1972 and a garden at Bowery and Houston tended by the Green Guerrillas. Mayor Giuliani sought to destroy such gardens and battled with neighborhood activists, but Mayor Michael Bloomberg has moved quickly to make peace.

THE URBAN LANDSCAPE 13

You can play a game of softball on the Great Lawn in Central Park anytime

Shoe-shining outside Grand Central

Formal suit, fun transportation— New Yorkers like to be different

A New York cop

Peruvian celebrations in Bryant Park, Midtown (above)

The People

Playing chess in Chinatown (above); many waiters earn most of their money from tips (below)

New York City is a city of immigrants. Between 1892 and 1924, 16 million immigrants poured through Ellis Island, many heading to the Lower East Side. Today, the gateways are Kennedy and Newark airports, and the immigrants' destinations are often the ethnic mosaics of Brooklyn and Queens, where such high schools as New Town have students who speak 30 different languages, and where the Central Library caters to a population that speaks nearly 40 languages. The Dutch, of course, were the first immigrants. They were interested in talent and enterprise and opened the city to immigrants of all sorts—Huguenots, Jews, Germans, Africans (slave and free) and the English, Scottish, French and Irish. At the turn of the 20th century, large numbers of Jews, Italians and Russians arrived, and after 1965, people from the Caribbean, Central America and Asia. The percentage of foreign-born has always fluctuated. At 40 percent, it is today at its highest. The lowest was in 1970 (18 percent). The population is 8.2 million, of which 35 percent are white, 27 percent Latino, 25 percent black and 10 percent Asian.

International express—the number 7 train

In the census of 2000, Queens had the fastest-growing population, having risen by 11 per-cent in the preceding decade. Much of that rise can be attributed to the arrival of new immigrants from all over the globe— Indians, Colombians, Ecuadorians and Peruvians in Jackson Heights; Dominicans, Colombians and Mexicans in Corona; Chinese, Koreans and Vietnamese in Flushing. Queens is the city's new melting pot—the new gateway to America. A ride on the number 7 train will confirm this. The first few stations (40th to 61st streets and Queens Boulevard) are in Sunnyside and Woodside, where the most recent influx of Irish immigrants has settled. It then proceeds along Roosevelt Avenue, stopping in Jackson Heights (74th Street), Corona (111th Street) and, finally, Flushing.

The Polish Day parade (left) takes place every October

A bright mural covers a wall in Chinatown (above); many early settlers were Jews, and there is still a large Jewish community in New York

Cool clothing for a steamy New York summer's day (left)

Hispanics—second in strength

The 1961 movie *West Side Story* depicted the struggle of Puerto Ricans, the city's first Hispanic community. Today, joined by nationals from Cuba, Ecuador, Colombia, El Salvador, the Dominican Republic and Mexico, Hispanics are the city's largest minority, representing 27 percent of the population. The Hispanic influence can be seen everywhere, from media and music to politics and cuisine. Turn on the TV and you'll find Telemundo and Univision offering Spanish talk shows and steamy soap operas. Scan a stand for newspapers *El Diario/La Prensa, Hoy, El Nacional* and *El Tiempo*. Baseball teams are peppered with Latin names; the Latino music craze continues, as more artists cross over in the footsteps of Ricky Martin; and chefs deliver the latest Spanish and Latino cuisine at such hot spots as Bolo and Casa Mono.

Bollywood on the Hudson

Before 1965 only a few South Asian students lived in the city, but after 1965, the Indian, Pakistani, Bangladeshi, Sri Lankan and Nepalese presence increased noticeably. Gradually Asian cuisine, music and culture registered on the consciousness of New Yorkers. Now even fusion is occurring. Witness Panjaba MC and Jay-Z's hit *Beware of the Boys*, in which hip-hop meets British *bhangra*. In the 1970s more Asian professionals settled in Queens. Jackson Heights became the commercial center, with Sam and Raj opening in 1976 on 74th Street. Here are stores selling saris, South Asian DVDs, music and cooking staples. There are also several Hindu temples. And Madison Square Garden headlines Bollywood entertainers. And it's not uncommon to walk past venues like Madison Square Garden and see top Bollywood entertainers headlining their marquees.

Tracing African-American heritage

A scholar interested in the black experience would begin at the Schomburg Center on 125th Street. Documents here chart the growth of the community from 14,000 in 1830 to 1.96 million today, along with the lives of such famous black New Yorkers as abolitionists Henry Highland Garnet and Alexander Crummell, and civil rights leaders Adam Clayton Powell and Malcolm X. A casual visitor might start at the African Burial Ground at Broadway and Duane. Here, from 1712 to 1794, 10,000–20,000 black people were buried as they were excluded from the Trinity Church graveyard. Few traces remain of Manhattan's 19th-century black communities, but much is found in Harlem: the church where Adam Clayton Powell, Sr. and Jr. preached, at 138th Street; the mosque associated with Malcolm X; and many Harlem Renaissance sites.

Understanding Yiddish

Every New Yorker knows what *chutzpah, mensch* and *kvetch* mean, and what the difference is between *shlep, shlemiel* and *schmozzle*. New York has the largest Jewish community outside Israel, but it's not its size so much as its spirit that counts. The greatest number of Jews came in the late 19th century, fleeing pogroms in Russia and Eastern Europe and settling on the Lower East Side. Their story is told in Irving Howe's history, *World of Our Fathers*. A tale of struggle rewarded by success and assimilation, it's a journey seen in the contrast between Woody Allen's Jewish outsider and Jerry Seinfeld's totally assimilated incidental Jew. Successful Jews moved from the Lower East Side and Brooklyn to the Upper West Side and the suburbs. They became financiers, doctors, lawyers, stand-up comedians and schoolteachers, and passed along Yiddish.

The 1959 Guggenheim Museum (right) was designed as a flowing building to please the eye

Brooklyn Bridge was the world's first steel suspension bridge (below)

The 1902 Flatiron Building (above) is barely a skyscraper, measuring only 285ft (87m)

The New York skyline, now without the World Trade Center (above); Lee Lawrie's *Wisdom* at the G. E. Building (right)

New York Architecture

Beyond signature skyscrapers

Yes, the Empire State and the Chrysler buildings are two stunning skyscrapers, but they're not alone. The Bayard Condict Building (1898) on Bleecker Street is the only example of Louis Sullivan's work in the city. Later skyscrapers often incorporated elements from earlier eras, as did Daniel Burnham's Renaissance Revival Flatiron Building (1902). Raymond Hood's Radiator Building is a beauty—black brick and blue-green tiles with gold ornamentation. The Seagram Building on Park Avenue, by Mies van der Rohe and Philip Johnson, is a good example of 1950s modernism. Architects are still building the skyscrapers of tomorrow—Daniel Libeskind's design was chosen for the new complex to be built at the site of the former World Trade Center.

There are so many great buildings in New York that it can be overwhelming. Many great buildings have also been lost to redevelopment, and that too is overwhelming, but not surprising, given the city's commercial nature. Skyscrapers dominate the island of Manhattan, a building style made possible by the confluence of several factors—the geological bedrock, the availability of steel, and the techniques of engineering. City governments had always emphasized growth and innovation, which helped create such real-estate moguls as John Jacob Astor, William Zeckendorf, Harry Helmsley and Donald Trump. Zoning laws arrived only in 1916 and conservation came even later. Robert Moses razed whole neighborhoods, and between 1900 and 1965 many architectural gems were replaced with inferior substitutes. New Yorkers finally woke up in 1965, after Penn Station was demolished and replaced with the sorry station there today. A Landmarks Preservation Commission was founded, but it still had to be re-affirmed by the Supreme Court in 1978 when Grand Central Station was threatened.

The Chrysler Building, with its gleaming stainless-steel spire, is a 1930s art deco masterpiece

Brownstones in TriBeCa (left inset); the Empire State Building (right)

Tenements with their fire escapes clearly visible (below left); vast columns decorate the former U.S. Custom House (right); a quirky statue in SoHo (below)

Brownstones and tenements

Besides skyscrapers there are plenty of other building types to appreciate. Brownstones —named after the sandstone from the banks of the Connecticut and Hackensack rivers—line the streets of Greenwich Village, Chelsea and other districts. Today they make elegant residences. In the mid-19th century, cast iron was used for the facades of factories, shops and warehouses, many in SoHo. They seem to be carved in stone, but are in fact some of the first pre-fabs ever made. The most spectacular examples are at Nos. 260–561 Broadway and Mercer Street in SoHo.

Humble tenements with fire escapes are also city trademarks. Built to house the 19th-century immigrants, they were narrow, cramped and unsanitary, but cheap— $2–$3 per month. Examples still line the streets of the Lower East Side and East Village. Today the rent is 500 times more.

Mews, and other nooks and crannies

Visitors soon discover Midtown's pocket parks and plazas, but if you wander farther you'll find more charming oddities. Pomander Walk (West 94th and 95th streets), for example, is 16 two-story Tudor-style cottages. Sniffen Court, 150–158 East 36th Street, is a beguiling collection of brick carriage houses now used as residences. The Village has several oddities. The enclaves of Patchin Place (1848), West 10th Street, and Milligan Place (1852), on Sixth Avenue between West 10th and 11th streets, were originally built to house Basque waiters, who worked at the Brevoort House on Fifth Avenue. Later residents were more famous—among them e e cummings. Along Bedford Street, between Morton and Commerce, stands the narrowest house in the city—it's only 9ft (3m) wide and was home to Edna St. Vincent Millay in 1924.

Sculptors and painters help to gild the lily

Visitors often focus on the number and size of Manhattan skyscrapers, failing to notice the many embellishments created by famous and not so famous stonemasons, sculptors and painters. Daniel Chester French adorned the U.S. Custom House with monumental portraits of Asia, America, Europe and Africa. Reginald Marsh painted the interiors, celebrating the maritime wealth of the city. The lower facades of the art deco Rockefeller Center are encrusted with sculptures and bas-reliefs. Lee Lawrie's *Wisdom* hovers above the entrance to the G. E. Building, while inside José María Sert's mural, *Man's Conquests,* covers the walls. Portraits of Mary Pickford and Ethel Barrymore by Alexander Stirling Calder grace the Miller Building at West 46th Street and Seventh Avenue. French artist Marc Chagall adorned the Metropolitan Opera House.

Cass Gilbert

Cass Gilbert stands out as the designer of some of the city's most beautiful and luxuriant buildings. Go into the Woolworth Building (1910–1913) at 233 Broadway, for example. Woolworth, who paid the $15.5 million price tag in cash, certainly got his money's worth. The exterior soars 792ft (240m) without a setback. The interior is stunning. The vaulted lobby is swathed in veined marble, gold leaf and mosaic, and decorated with humorous sculptures, including one of Cass Gilbert himself holding the building and another of Woolworth counting his dimes. Gilbert's other great building is the U.S. Custom House (1907), a suitably grand repository for the wealth of the early city. He also contributed the New York Life Insurance Building (1907) at 51 Madison Avenue, between 26th and 27th streets, and the Federal Courthouse on Foley Square (1936).

You can visit some famous graves in Trinity Church (above); a choir sings out loud and proud in Harlem (left)

Katz's Deli (above) serves Jewish deli food; hot dogs and bagels are part of the NYC experience

New York Way
of Life

Thousands of commuters pass through Grand Central Station every day

Most New Yorkers are not born in the city. They come to it. They come for many reasons, most of which involve dreams of success and the money, power and fame that follow. So the city is full of competitive people trying to make it on stage, in music, in real estate, on Wall Street, Madison Avenue or in any other arena. Even though many citizens are in "success overdrive," there are other factors that affect the rhythms of city life. New York is not monolithic. It's a cluster of neighborhoods, each with a different ambience and energy. The West Village wakes up late and operates at a slow pace; the East Village wakes up very late and parties very late; Washington Heights is loud and moves to a Dominican rhythm; Beekman Place is always subdued. The city may stay open 24 hours, but each neighborhood plays its own rhythmic variation.

A hot dog with mustard and ketchup—lunch on the run

Worship at your choice of altar

Many visitors are surprised to learn how religious New Yorkers are and how many people attend religious services. From its founding it has offered an array of religious options, when Anglicans, Presbyterians, Quakers, Anabaptists, Jews, Catholics and Lutherans co-existed. Today, Christians, Buddhists, Hindus, Sikhs, Jews and Muslims all have a place to worship in the city. If you want to understand a culture, attend a religious service. In New York, head to Harlem and hear the gospel choirs raising the roofs of the Baptist churches, or go to West 113th Street to the Mosque of Islamic Brotherhood. Take the train to the Hindu temples or Sikh gurdwaras in Queens, or drop in to one of the Buddhist temples in Chinatown. Or visit St. John the Divine or St. Patrick's.

Yellow cabs (above) first hit the streets in 1907

Sex and the City's four sirens of singledom: Kim Cattrall, Kristin Davis, Sarah Jessica Parker and Cynthia Nixon (below)

Doing weights at the gym is much more interesting with the Manhattan skyline to look at (above)

Roller-blading is a speedy and healthy option (right)

Convenience greases the daily wheels

To the average New Yorker, speed and convenience take precedence over everything else. Time is, after all, money. So meals on the run are habitual. Workers en route to their offices, the women sporting Adidas, stop for an Egg McMuffin at McDonald's or coffee and a danish at Starbucks. At lunch, New Yorkers "order in" a sandwich or salad and soft drink, instead of going out for a leisurely meal. Or if they have a corporate cafeteria they go there. Some of these are extraordinary, the most famous being the Philippe Starck version at Condé Nast. If workers do go out, it will often be to "brown bag it," taking a sandwich to a pocket park.

At night, they may go home and order take-out from one of the many neighborhood menus that they keep by their phone—Thai, Chinese, Mexican, Indian, Italian or Japanese.

Exercise, exercise!

Although a recent study reported that 35 percent of New Yorkers are overweight or obese, you would not know it from the frequent sightings of earnest New Yorkers pumping iron or running on treadmills. Keeping fit is a serious business. Most executives receive a standard gym membership and many have personal trainers, who show them how to work the machines and set their fitness goals. Of course, the Old Guard have always had their clubs, where they go to swim, exercise or get a massage—The Knickerbocker, the Union, the Colony or the Harmonie are just some examples. After these come luxury gyms like the Sports Club/L. A. Average New Yorkers are more likely to join Bally Fitness or Crunch and take some aerobics classes. It's all part of the endless New York regimen of health and beauty.

Yellow cabs—love or hate?

The average New Yorker rides the bus or the subway, but many prefer to hail a cab, one of around 13,000 licensed to roam the city streets. You can't miss the yellow chariots. They have been in business since 1907. Early operators were so corrupt that in 1923 a Taxi and Limousine Commission began issuing licenses. LaGuardia sold the first medallion for $10 in 1937. Today they cost as much as $379,000. Every immigrant group has driven cabs—initially Jewish settlers, Italians and Irish and more recently people from Russia, Africa, Haiti and South Asia. They often receive only 24 hours of instruction. Some cabs perform some wild maneuvers to grab passengers. The bulletproof partitions separating passenger from driver were installed in 1967. Most recently, required touch-screen GPS units have caused strikes and much contention.

New York solutions to singledom

There are 100 million "singles" in the United States. Several million of them live in New York, and many are looking for the perfect mate, supporting a veritable marriage market industry. Even in the 1860s, matrimonial brokers' ads ran in the press. For example, John Johnson and Co. offered services to "ladies wishing agreeable and wealthy husbands," and to men desiring "beautiful, rich and accomplished wives." If you scan the ads in the local media, you'll find little has changed. Now, though, individuals advertise themselves, posting photographs in such publications as *New York Magazine*, revealing their most intimate data online at itsjustlunch.com, or signing up for TV shows such as "Perfect Partner" and "Boy Meets Boy." There are singles groups of all kinds, from speed-dating specialists to one for tall people only.

The
Metro-
politan
Opera
House
stages
excellent
performances
(right); one
of a series
of Jackson
Pollock's
modern, some
say aggressive,
pieces (below)

Everything from
ancient Egypt to
Van Gogh is in
the Metropolitan
Museum of Art
(above); the all-
singing, all-dancing
1980s musical
42nd Street has
been revived (right)

The Arts

New York City leads the nation in arts and entertainment. It's the world's center of contemporary art, and also has a phenomenal collection of performing arts companies in dance, music and theater. The city's cultural groups have also led the way in finding innovative ways to fund their endeavors. For years, although they have received some funding from government, city cultural institutions and groups have developed their own funding resources—private donors, memberships, bookstores and other ancillary profit centers. The arts scene is constantly evolving. There is an uptown mainstream scene and a downtown more experimental scene, and within each shifts are always occurring—SoHo galleries migrating to Chelsea, for example. Don't worry, whatever excites you in the arts can be found in New York.

Thoroughly Modern Millie is a big, bright, upbeat story of a young girl from Kansas arriving in New York in 1922 (above); modern art in SoHo (below)

Culture and money

Wealthy dynasties have always served as patrons of the arts, and New York's are no different. Mayor Bloomberg donates a large part of his fortune to cultural institutions, as do many in the Social Register. Today, the money is likely to be dispensed by the 525 city-based foundations, which control $82 billion. These cultural donors are copying earlier magnates whose names still resonate throughout the city—Astor, Carnegie, Morgan, Rockefeller, Vanderbilt and Whitney. John D. Rockefeller gave away $1.5 million annually and launched the Rockefeller Foundation in 1913 with $100 million. His son, John, Jr., founded Rockefeller University and donated the Cloisters, Fort Tryon Park and the site for the United Nations building. John Jacob Astor left $400,000 for a library, which Brooke Astor, the wife of his great-great grandson, still supports.

New York and jazz are synonymous (above); this huge red cube (right) by Isamu Noguchi is on Church Street; unmissable house number outside 9 West 57th Street (below)

Martin Scorsese's movie is about Irish immigrants in 1863 (above)

New York, New York, it's a helluva town

The film industry may have moved from New York to Hollywood after World War I, but it is still a film town, thanks to the renovation of old studios and the encouragement of the Mayor's Office of Film. Film-makers have long conducted a love affair with the city, sometimes using fake studio backdrops, as they did in *King Kong*, and other times filming the reality on location. The directors most associated with New York are Martin Scorsese, Paul Mazursky, Sidney Lumet, John Cassavetes, Spike Lee and Wes Anderson (*The Royal Tenenbaums*). But the love affair goes back a long way to such films as *Miracle on 34th Street* (1947), *The Naked City* (1948) and *On the Waterfront* (1954).

If you want an architectural tour of New York plus an insight into its collective unconscious, treat yourself to any Woody Allen film.

They still make Steinways in New York

The name Steinway signifies the best pianos in the world, and it has done so since 1853, when Henry Steinweg started the company. The company was so successful that by 1873 the family was able to build a company town in Astoria, Queens, complete with factory, housing, a school and other amenities. At one time, the company made 6,000 grand pianos a year, but the industry collapsed in 1927 with the introduction of radio and the phonograph. The company survived, although the family sold it in 1972. Today it continues to operate with 450 workers, who handcraft about 2,000 grand pianos (and 500 uprights) a year, which cost from $25,000 to $147,000. Even though the eight-month process is the same, each one has a different musical personality, depending on the wood and other subjective factors.

Chelsea—new center of contemporary art

Although the acclaimed Dia Center for the Arts has closed its Chelsea gallery and is looking for a new home, in the late 1980s and early 1990s it made Chelsea the new vortex for contemporary art, surpassing SoHo and 57th Street. Since then, the area between 19th and 29th streets and 10th and 11th avenues has grown into a large gallery district with more than 200 spaces. All the former big names in SoHo and Uptown are now represented here— Matthew Marks, Larry Gagosian, Mary Boone, Pace Wildenstein, Paula Cooper, Robert Miller, Barbara Gladstone, Holly Solomon and Sonnabend. Some galleries have hangar-like spaces large enough to accommodate massive works by such artists as Richard Serra. In some cases entire buildings (529 West 20th Street and 526 West 26th Street, for example) now house multiple galleries.

The challenge of Broadway

Every year Broadway is reported teetering on the edge of economic disaster and accused of abandoning serious theater for warmed-over revivals. It's tough to make money on Broadway. Back in 1866, *Black Crook*, a musical melodrama, ran for only 475 performances and took in $1.1 million, easily recouping the $24,000 investment. Today a musical costs on average $8 million to put on, and the show has to run for at least 520 performances just to break even. When producers have to rely on tourists to fill the seats, it gets really tough. Success then depends on low costs, good press, a Tony Award and lots of luck. Few shows meet the test. In fact, about 80 percent of Broadway shows fail to recoup their investments. So producers of serious theater turn to Off- and Off-Off Broadway, where costs are lower and they can afford to nurture new playwrights.

THE ARTS 21

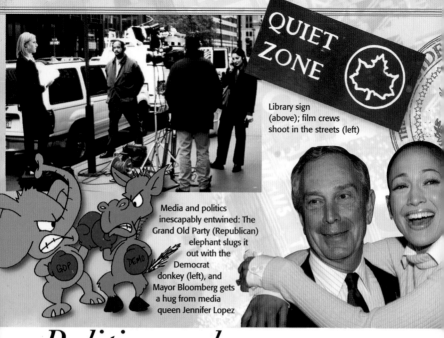

Library sign (above); film crews shoot in the streets (left)

Media and politics inescapably entwined: The Grand Old Party (Republican) elephant slugs it out with the Democrat donkey (left), and Mayor Bloomberg gets a hug from media queen Jennifer Lopez

Politics and Media

Summarizing New York City politics is difficult. It's a complex city divided into five boroughs—Manhattan, Brooklyn, the Bronx, Queens and Staten Island—populated by 8 million people of different races and religions, and diverse socio-economic interests. As a consequence, city politics are often contentious, with ethnic rivalries playing a large part in the political process. The municipal employee unions—police, fire, teachers, sanitation and transit—also play a major role in city politics and can make the city a more, or less, pleasant place to live and work. As far as national politics goes, New York City is firmly Democratic, even though it has voted for two Republicans in the last three mayoral elections. Only Staten Island votes pretty solidly Republican. The print media cut across party lines. The *New York Times*, the *Daily News* and *Newsday* lean toward the Democratic Party while the *Wall Street Journal*, the fledgling *New York Sun* and Rupert Murdoch's *New York Post* take a more Republican tack.

For some, the alternating political processes are nothing but a failure

WILL WORK FOR FOOD MAY GOD BLESS YOU PEOPLE!

Who's in charge?

It's hard for outsiders to determine who is in charge. Under the federal system, the responsibilities are divided among the federal, state and municipal governments. Although there have been many powerful mayors—LaGuardia, Koch, and Giuliani in particular— their power is limited by the state governor, the state assembly and senate, the borough presidents and the city council, to name the major challengers. Currently, for example, even though Mayor Bloomberg presides over a city containing 38 percent of the state's population, he is battling Governor Pataki over the redevelopment of Lower Manhattan and the building of a water filtration plant. The city lives under a tough set of fiscal rules imposed by the state 30 years ago, with four agencies monitoring city finances. If the city fails to balance the budget or pay its debt, the state will assume financial control.

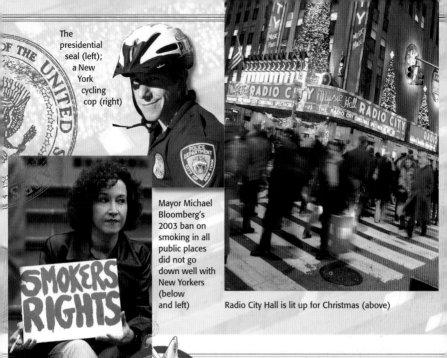

The presidential seal (left); a New York cycling cop (right)

Mayor Michael Bloomberg's 2003 ban on smoking in all public places did not go down well with New Yorkers (below and left)

Radio City Hall is lit up for Christmas (above)

SMOKERS RIGHTS

Education is the topic of the day

From the 1960s to the early 1990s crime and race dominated the headlines, but under Mayor Guiliani crime dropped dramatically and although race continued to play a divisive role, it diminished as a headline issue. Today, education is such a compelling issue that among the wealthy even getting into the "right" nursery school matters. Although there are top-notch schools (Stuyvesant, Bronx Science), the public (state) school system is in crisis. It educates 1.1 million students in 1,200 schools, many of which are in disrepair, require students to pass through metal detectors, and have truancy problems. Bloomberg has staked his reputation on reforming it by streamlining the bureaucracy and imposing a standard curriculum.

The smoking edict

Mayor Giuliani disciplined New Yorkers for such "bad behavior" as jay-walking, panhandling, staging scatological art shows, squeegeeing and sleeping on, or occupying, two seats on the subway. New Yorkers grumbled, but came to appreciate the improvement in the quality of life that followed. When Bloomberg tried the same, he ran into resistance, particularly when he banned smoking from all public spaces, including bars. Bar and nightclub owners, libertarians and dedicated smokers were irate. A few years on, everyone has calmed down. In fact smokers even admit to enjoying smoke-free interiors and the camaraderie of smoking outside with others. Business has not been adversely affected.

Gossip

Gossip has a high profile in New York City because power, money, sex and celebrity drive society and gossip helps keep score on who's in and who's out. Gossip may have begun with Mrs. William Astor and her 400 and continued on the zebra-striped banquettes at El Morocco and at Walter Winchell's table at the Stork Club, but now it's everywhere. It's not confined to the tabloids, either. They may not be called a gossip columns, but that's what they are: The New York Times has "Boldface Names;" New York Magazine has "The Intelligencer;" The New Yorker calls it the "Talk of the Town" and Town & Country insists that it's "Parties." Tina Brown leavened Vanity Fair with it. Everyone has to read the New York Post's Liz Smith, Cindy Adams and Page Six. And it's becoming even more center stage, as the Star moves into Manhattan and gossip drives the content of glossies U.S. and People.

Madison Avenue

Madison Avenue may be the Golden Mile of designer retailing, but it is also synonymous with one of the largest and most important city industries. In 2002, a massive $117 billion was spent on advertising, plus $6.8 billion on focus groups alone. With consumer spending accounting for 60 percent of the national economy and 22,000 new packaged products being launched annually, advertising plays a huge marketing role. New York City remains the advertising capital, because all the TV networks and publishing companies have their headquarters or offices here. Although the advertising companies are not necessarily on or near Madison Avenue anymore—Saatchi & Saatchi is at 375 Hudson in the West Village—they do need to be near the media buyers and sellers, so that they can easily participate in the seasonal media buying frenzy.

Alan Greenspan (above) became Chairman of the Federal Reserve Board in 1987, a post he held for more than 18 years

Nasdaq and Wall Street are familiar names in the world of money

The New York Stock Exchange is the heart of financial America

Commerce and
Finance

New York City has always been a money-making city. John Jacob Astor made his fortune in real estate, J. P. Morgan in banking, Cornelius Vanderbilt in transportation and John D. Rockefeller in oil. Today wealth is still made in finance, real estate and commodities, but the new money is in technology and communications and less in manufacturing and trade. Manufacturing has moved South or to Mexico and to Asia, while the once mighty port business has shifted to New Jersey. New York is still the financial capital of the world, the global center of banking and insurance (more than 70 banks had their headquarters here in the mid-1990s), even though some have moved, like Goldman Sachs, to New Jersey. The securities industry is vital to the city's economy. When it is booming, the city flourishes and when it declines, the city does too. When the dot-com bubble burst in March 2000 and was followed a year and half later by the tragedy of 9/11, the city suffered and by fall 2002 the city had a projected deficit of $5 billion. Under Mayor Bloomberg the city has staged a remarkable economic recovery.

Seventh Avenue hangs on

From the 1930s to the 1950s, the garment industry was the biggest in the city. Cutters, pattern-makers and sewing-machine operators and button and zipper makers jammed the blocks between 36th and 38th streets between Madison and Eighth Avenues. (Seventh Avenue is also called Fashion Avenue between 23rd and 42nd streets.) Today the only evidences of the trade are the racks being pushed along the sidewalks and the "seconds" bins. Most manufacturing has gone to low-cost countries like China. What remains is on the Lower East Side, and in Chinatown and Queens, where Chinese, Thai and Dominicans staff sweatshops. The Garment Industry Development Corporation is working to reinvigorate the industry.

The NYSE, Amex and Nasdaq—the three pillars

The New York Stock Exchange, whose 1,366 seats are for sale by auction, is the most prestigious of the three. The first seats sold in 1868 for $4,000; in October 2002 a seat sold for $2.3 million, though the current average is $300,000. Only the most carefully scrutinized companies—about 2,800 of them—are listed on the NYSE, which has a global market capitalization of $23 trillion and trades an average 1.6 billion shares every day.

Those who could not afford to join the NYSE started the Amex, on Trinity Place. It lists only 696 companies. It was originally called the Curb Market because the brokers did their business at the curbside.

In 1971 the National Association of Securities Dealers Automated Quotation (Nasdaq) was launched as the world's first electronic stock market. It lists 3,300 mostly high-growth companies.

The Story of New York

Early Colonial Days

In the 16th century the area now known as Manhattan was a land of natural beauty, populated by wild animals and Native American tribes. Early explorers' engravings and vellum maps depict the hilly terrain and early settlements, including the Indian longhouses near Coney Island. In the early 16th century, Giovanni da Verrazano, a Florentine navigator and merchant working for the French, attempted to find the supposed Northwest Passage, a more direct route between Europe and Asia. Instead, he found himself sailing into the wonderful natural harbor that is now New York Harbor on April 17, 1524, and was greeted by the astonished native Algonquians.

However, not much exploring went on until the arrival in 1609 of Henry Hudson, an English navigator working for the Dutch East India Company. He sailed up the river that now bears his name and reported back on the abundance of

otter, beaver, mink and wildcat and on the possibilities of the fur trade. The Dutch, recognizing the potential, went into business and brought traders to settle the area. One farm belonged to Jonas Bronck, whose name has stuck firmly to the area known today as The Bronx.

Native Algonquian (left); Giovanni da Verrazano (right) gave his name to the Verrazano Narrows Bridge

Native Americans

During the early colonial days, the Algonquians were often at war with each other and with the Iroquois. To protect themselves, the tribes lived in tight-knit groups under strong chiefs.

In the beginning, the Algonquians were a friendly people and showed the Dutch colonists where to hunt, farm and fish. The Native Americans enjoyed trading just as much as the Dutch, but then, as the colonists tried to take land away, fighting broke out. The Dutch attacked two encampments, killing 80 Native Americans, and started a very bloody war. Reports of this fighting got back to Holland, discouraging emigration to the New World.

1500 uw Amsterdam op de Manhatans.

Manhattan (right) was named New Amsterdam after the Dutch took control; the trial of John Peter Zenger (below) ended in victory for the press

Dutch colony

Peter Minuit bought Manhattan Island in 1626 for a cool $24 worth of kettles, axes and cloth. However, the Native Americans he paid did not share his concept of land ownership and didn't understand the sale; furthermore, the transaction was made with the Canarsie tribe, who were merely passing by on that day. Dutch garrisons built a windmill, a fort, a barracks, a jail, a church, a tavern and a governor's house. There were about 120 houses by 1656, and about 300 four years later. Merchants and traders ran the municipal government and everyone was happy until the Dutch governor tried civilizing the rowdy populace.

Peter Minuit purchased Manhattan illegally for next to nothing (below)

Peter Stuyvesant

The early colonists were a fairly lawless lot, and drunkenness and violence were common. Then, in 1647, the one-legged Peter Stuyvesant stepped in as governor. Under his strict control, law and order were established, along with a school, hospital, prison and post office. But Stuyvesant was not popular, and he eventually surrendered to English attackers, then returned to Holland in 1665 to defend himself against charges of misconduct. In 1667, he came back to his New York farm, the *bouwerij* that has given its name to New York's Bowery. Stuyvesant died in 1672 and was buried on his farm, now the site of St. Mark's Church-in-the-Bowery (▷ 131).

Peter Stuyvesant's lack of a limb never held him back (below)

The English

In 1664, with 8,000 unhappy Dutch colonists living on the island, now known as New Amsterdam, Colonel Richard Nicolls easily seized the territory from the Dutch on the orders of King Charles II of England. The king's brother, the Duke of York, took control and changed the colony's name to New York. The terms of the surrender were generous, and not a single Dutch resident took Nicolls up on his offer to repatriate them. Nicolls became governor and was both efficient and popular. In 1673, when a war between Holland and England broke out, New York returned to Dutch control, but it bounced back to the English in 1674 under the Treaty of Westminster.

King of New York: Charles II of England (below)

Freedom of the press

German immigrant John Peter Zenger became the editor of the *New York Weekly Journal* in 1733 and quickly grew unpopular with Governor William Cosby. His opposition to the governor's arbitrary acts gained support from lawyers, merchants and others of independent spirit. In 1734 he was arrested for seditious libel. His lawyer, Andrew Hamilton, refuted the libel charge on the basis that the offensive article was not actually false. The court disagreed, stating that whether or not the publication was true was irrelevant and that merely publishing such wicked words about the government was enough to convict.

However, Hamilton's eloquent appeal to the judge and jury resulted in Zenger's acquittal and a victory for freedom of the press, setting a precedent against judicial tyranny in libel suits and leading eventually to the First Amendment to the Constitution.

1750

A view of the early settlement of New York (above)

Revolutionary Period

King's College, now Columbia University (▷ 77), was established in 1754 by royal charter of King George II with the twin aims of preventing the growth of republican principles and promoting the teachings of the Anglican Church. As the American colonies grew more independently minded, students such as Alexander Hamilton emerged to become America's patriot leaders.

In 1765 a Stamp Act passed by Parliament in London taxed marriage licenses, playing cards, newspapers and 40 other necessities of life, and infuriated the colonists. Leading opposition to the Stamp Act, New York sent a formal protest to the king; 28 delegates from nine colonies attended the Stamp Act Congress in New York. After protests that included the virtual suspension of all port activity for nearly two weeks, Parliament repealed the Act in March 1766. New York joined the fight against taxation that eventually led to the American Revolution. Although New York did not see a great deal of action, it was Britain's military headquarters and was the only city occupied by the British throughout the conflict. When the war ended, many loyalists left America for the West Indies or Canada and the population dwindled to 12,000. But within six years of the British departure, New York had become America's most vibrant city.

You'll find Alexander Hamilton (left) on a $10 bill; the Stamp Act imposed by London (right)

British occupation

The city's Tories, who supported the British Crown, were jubilant when British troops entered New York in June 1776. Patriots surrounded the city, denying the British easy communications with other colonies. Under military occupation, the city suffered terrible fires and loss of life and property. A fire on September 21, 1776 destroyed a quarter of the city, including Trinity Church (▷ 142–143). On August 3, 1778, 100 houses burned. The guerrilla war between the two opposing sides involved cattle-rustling, abductions and deliberate burning of crops. American prisoners of war were either incarcerated in a crowded, appalling dungeon on Liberty Street or in ships anchored in the harbor. Almost 11,000 soldiers perished in the horrendous conditions.

1750

The impressive entrance to the library at prestigious Columbia University (above)

Raging fires in New York in 1776 claimed many lives and destoyed parts of the city (right)

Defeat on Long Island

After forcing the British General William Howe to evacuate Boston in March 1776, General George Washington arrived in Manhattan on April 13. Knowing that he would meet General Howe's army again, forts were built in Brooklyn Heights and Lower Manhattan. On July 2, Howe's force landed on Staten Island. On July 9, the Declaration of Independence was read to Washington's soldiers on Bowling Green. The delighted soldiers and civilians tore down the statue of King George III and melted it down to make bullets—42,088 of them. Meanwhile, Howe's army moved to the south of Brooklyn, where his 20,000 British regulars surprised Washington's 7,000 militiamen. The Battle of Long Island, a terrible defeat for Washington, left 2,000 Americans dead.

Benedict Arnold

In today's United States, the name Benedict Arnold is synonymous with traitor. After Arnold had fought for General Washington against the British at Lake Champlain and in Connecticut, he was placed in command of Philadelphia in 1778. But he became disillusioned with Congress after he was overlooked for promotion. He knew British General Clinton was bribing Americans to desert and he began a treasonable correspondence with Clinton. He was in the process of making plans to surrender West Point, the military academy then under his command, to the British when the plot was revealed. Arnold managed to escape and became a leader of British troops in New York. After the British surrendered, he and his wife moved to England, where they were deeply unpopular.

From general to president

On November 25, 1783, General Washington made his ceremonial entry into New York and gave a farewell address to his troops in front of Fraunces Tavern at 54 Pearl Street, then returned to his home at Mount Vernon in Virginia. On February 4, 1789, he was unanimously chosen as president of the new United States in Philadelphia.

On April 30, 1789, Washington took the oath of office on the balcony of L'Enfant's Federal Hall, on the site of today's Federal Hall National Monument (▷ 97). Thousands lined Murray's Wharf at the end of Wall Street as he arrived by ceremonial barge. The cheering crowds, waving their hats, then followed him on his route through the downtown streets.

The Tea Party

The British Parliament approved the Tea Act in 1773, giving the British East India Company a monopoly on all the tea sold in the colonies. The angry Manhattan Sons of Liberty encouraged the public to repel the tea ships; New Yorkers boycotted all establishments offering East India tea. On December 16, 1773, the Boston Tea Party, a protest in which a group of men masquerading as Mohawks dumped 342 cases of East India tea into Boston Harbor, further fueled radicalism in New York. Britain passed the Intolerable Acts which closed Boston's port, alarming New Yorkers. On April 22, 1774, New York had its own Tea Party and dumped 18 boxes of tea into the bay. This led to the establishment of the revolutionary government in New York State.

The hero of the piece—George Washington (left)

Benedict Arnold (left) played a large part in the shaping of New York

1800

Troops were employed to escort the stamped paper for the 1765 Stamp Act to City Hall (below)

The inauguration of the United States' first president, George Washington, on the balcony of Federal Hall (above)

Commercial *Growth*

The first half of the 19th century brought New York conflict, epidemics and disaster, as well as an explosion of commerce and riches. During the War of 1812 between the United States and Britain, New York's port was blockaded. Ten years later, a yellow fever epidemic broke out in Front Street, and in 1832 a cholera epidemic killed 4,000. The Great Fire of 1835 gutted 700 buildings in a 17-block area below Wall Street; in 1845, another fire destroyed 300 buildings in Lower Manhattan.

The achievement that brought growth, prosperity and international commerce to the city was the building of the Erie Canal in 1825, a project of Governor DeWitt Clinton. In following years, powerful men went from rags to riches practically overnight. Cornelius Vanderbilt (1794–1877), an uneducated Staten Island farm boy, became one of the wealthiest men in America when he took control of much of the shipping business in the harbor and along the Hudson River to Albany.

The swelling city needed news. William Cullen Bryant, whose name is now associated with Bryant Park, became editor of the New York *Evening Post* in 1829. In 1834 Horace Greeley founded the *New Yorker*, a weekly literary and news journal unrelated to the modern magazine. In 1841, he became the founding editor of the *New York Tribune*, while other newspapers also flourished.

1800

Knickerbocker

The word knickerbocker was a literary invention of author Washington Irving (1783–1859) in his *Diedrich Knicker-bocker's History of New York* (1809). A satire on pedantry, manners, politics and history told by an imaginary Dutch colonist, Knickerbocker, it won Irving much acclaim in the United States and Europe. New Yorkers of Dutch descent, and by extension the entire city, became known as Knickerbockers. The group of writers including Irving, novelist James Fenimore Cooper and poet William Cullen Bryant was known as the Knickerbocker Group.

Writer Washington Irving (left) and editor William Cullen Bryant (above) left their mark

This was how New York appeared in 1849, looking south from Union Square

Parts of the city were left in ruins after the Great Fire on December 16 and 17, 1835 (above)

John Jacob Astor

By 1808, John Jacob Astor—who emigrated to America from Germany in 1783—had amassed a fortune in the fur trade and was the sole owner of the American Fur Company. When he grew fat and his health deteriorated, he sold the company and took up real estate. After he invested in farmland north of New York City, in what is now the heart of Manhattan, the city's rapid expansion turned his farmland into a goldmine. Astor House, the biggest hotel in the world at the time, stood on what is now City Hall Park (▷ 77) and was the first building to bear the family's name. The Astor Library, which he bequeathed to the city, is now part of the New York Public Library (▷ 127).

John Jacob Astor was the richest man in the world when he died

Grid system

New York City's grid system of streets was devised in 1811, at a time when the population was increasing rapidly. In need of new streets for the undeveloped land north of Washington Square, city officials accepted the plans put forward by engineer John Randel, Jr. The commissioners dismissed the idea of ovals, circles or stars and opted for the economy of straight lines and right angles. The Commissioner's Plan called for 2,000 long, narrow blocks, disregarded the contours of the land, and provided for neither parks nor open spaces.

Erie Canal

The Erie Canal, connecting the Hudson River and the Great Lakes, made New York the only eastern port with a waterway route to the farmlands of the Midwest, and instantly turned the city into America's center of commerce. It was New York governor DeWitt Clinton who oversaw the $7 million project, which skeptics at the time called "Clinton's Folly." The 10-day canal trip from New York to Buffalo meant that goods from around the world could be transported via New York to the interior of the New World. There was an explosion of new office space and warehouses along the harbor, and New York began its career as a major world trading center.

Artist and inventor

By 1825, many of the most respected American painters were living in New York—that is the ones who stayed in the country and did not flee to Paris. A significant artist of the Romantic School and a successful portrait painter, Samuel F. B. Morse is best remembered as the inventor of the Morse Code. He moved permanently to New York in 1824 and became a founder of the National Academy of Design in 1826. *The House of Representatives* (1822–23), one of Morse's most notable paintings, includes more than 80 portraits of politicians. By the early 1830s, he was more interested in electrical experiments than in painting, and in 1844 he tapped out in code the famous message, "What hath God wrought?"

DeWitt Clinton (above) was a governor with invaluable foresight

1850

The first barges arrived from Buffalo along the Erie Canal (above)

City Hall, finished in 1812, gave the city a venue for meetings and events

Social Unrest and *Reform*

By 1875 more than a million people lived in New York. The poor, many of them recent immigrants, lived in tenements that bred hatred, violence and disease, especially tuberculosis. Jacob Riis published a book of photographs, *How the Other Half Lives* (1890), which called the public's attention to the atrocious living conditions. As a result, reformers like Theodore Roosevelt and Frances Perkins joined a crusade to rid the city of these inhumane dwellings.

The enormous task of transportation in the growing city was a major problem. In 1858, about 35 million passengers used horse-drawn trams to move around. In the 1860s, trains were a welcome improvement. Washington Bridge, opened in 1889, made it easier to go from Manhattan to the Bronx. Commissioner George Waring reorganized the sanitation system, and in 1893, New York began chlorinating its drinking water. Progressive reformers brought education to immigrant children and they were offered free medical examinations in 1895. The changes came too late for many immigrants, but at last something was being done to improve their lives.

Immigrants poured into the city in the second half of the 19th century (right); Dr Elizabeth Blackwell was the first woman on the British Medical Register (far right)

Elizabeth Blackwell

Elizabeth Blackwell came from Bristol, England, to New York in 1832 to train as a doctor. She applied to eight medical schools before being accepted at Geneva Medical School. Graduating in 1847, she was ostracized by the profession because she was a woman. With great determination, she opened a dispensary for the poor in the slums of the Lower East Side. In 1857 she founded the New York Infirmary for Indigent Women and Children (the New York Infirmary). In 1868, after creating a training school for nurses, she founded the Women's Medical College of the New York Infirmary. In 1910, she died in Hastings, England.

ELIZABETH BLACKWELL M D 1849

1850

A pictorial railway ticket (above); the elevated railway on Third Avenue (right)

Slavery

By the middle of the 18th century, New York had the highest concentration of slaves north of Virginia. They were sold at the slave market at the foot of Wall Street until slavery was abolished in New York State in 1827. But slavery was to continue, especially in the South, for another 38 years. New York provided a pivotal stage for its demise. On February 27, 1860, Abraham Lincoln arrived in New York City to give his celebrated antislavery address in the Great Hall of the Cooper Union Foundation Building on East 7th Street, now a designated historic landmark. His eloquent defense of the Constitution and the call for the freedom of slaves helped him secure the Republican presidential nomination.

The famous features of President Abraham Lincoln

Tammany Hall

In 1850 William Marcy Tweed organized a volunteer fire department, a move which made him popular enough to get elected to city and state posts. In the 1860s and 1870s, under Tweed's direction, corrupt politicians at the Democratic Party headquarters, Tammany Hall, ran the party by bribery, coercion and vote rigging. Having swindled the city at every opportunity, Tweed was finally caught after the Tweed Ring reneged on a deal with the sheriff, who went to the press. *The New York Times* revealed the facts, and on November 19, 1873, Tweed was sentenced to 12 years in prison.

Draft riots 1863

A dearth of volunteers for the Civil War led to conscription in 1862. In New York, as in other places, the draft met with great opposition and bounty hunters found substitutes for men who could pay. Others with $300 in their pocket could pay to be exempt. The cost of living in New York had doubled and the mostly Irish dock workers had gone on strike for higher wages; they were furious when 'scabs' were brought in to work. Under the circumstances the Irish could see no reason to fight for black freedom and bitterly resented conscription. Four days of rioting in scorching heat ended on July 17, 1863, but not before 120 men had died, mostly African-Americans killed by Irish immigrants.

Jewish immigrants

The first Jewish people, 27 of them, arrived in New York in 1633. But the pogroms in Russia and Eastern Europe resulted in the great influx of Jewish immigrants at the turn of the 19th century. In 1892, around 81,000 Jewish people arrived at Ellis Island (▷ 90–93) and 258,000 more between 1905 and 1906. They crowded into the tenements on the Lower East Side (▷ 109), alongside the Irish, who had come earlier and who resented the newcomers. Given that many of the police officers of the day were Irish, it is not surprising that Mayor McClellan's police commissioner claimed that 50 percent of the city's crimes were committed by Jewish people. The outraged Jewish community forced him to make a public retraction.

A cartoon satirizing William Marcy "Boss" Tweed (1823–78), the corrupt politician who defrauded New York City of $30 million

1900

The building on Ellis Island that was the first sight of New York for most immigrants (above)

Ulysses S. Grant, the Union and Republican President, tans the hides of Confederate generals and his electoral opponents (left)

World's Second-Largest City

By 1900 Greater New York had a population of 3.5 million and was the world's second-largest city after London. In Manhattan, 42,700 tenements housed the 1.5 million poor in dire conditions. By the 1920s a campaign to restrict immigration resulted in legislation that brought a decline in the number of newcomers from Poland, Russia and Italy. The great metropolis experienced terrible disasters and celebrated remarkable triumphs. In 1901, a heatwave killed nearly 100 New Yorkers in just 24 hours. The first skyscrapers went up, starting with the Flatiron Building in 1902, symbolizing the city's wealth and hopes for the future. Meanwhile, Prohibition drove New Yorkers to illegal speakeasies. Many went uptown to Harlem for nights of pleasure. Then, on October 24, 1929, the New York stock market collapsed, bringing the Roaring Twenties to a sudden halt. A loudspeaker attached to a dirigible above the skyscrapers cried out to the employed, "Give until it hurts." Books like Theodore Dreiser's *Sister Carrie* (1900), and F. Scott Fitzgerald's *This Side of Paradise* (1920) and *The Great Gatsby* (1925) depicted a New York that had lost much of its sparkle.

The Empire State Building is a powerful symbol (left); at the Cotton Club (right) whites were entertained by blacks, who were banned from watching

Harlem

Jazz flourished in Harlem in the 1920s and 1930s as white New Yorkers discovered establishments such as the Cotton Club, famous for its "Colored Revues" and as the home of Duke Ellington, the Great Orchestrator of Jazz. Ellington's band, the Washingtonians, and his arrangements dominated big-band jazz for three decades. In 1932, he wrote a song whose title served as a slogan for the next 10 years: *It Don't Mean a Thing If It Ain't Got That Swing*. Cotton Club owner Owney Madden, a gangster and bootlegger, strictly enforced segregation. The Depression took the swing out of these Harlem night-spots, and the Cotton Club moved down-town to West 48th Street, eventually closing in 1940.

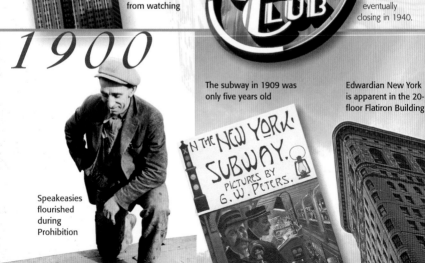

1900

Speakeasies flourished during Prohibition

The subway in 1909 was only five years old

IN THE NEW YORK SUBWAY. PICTURES BY G. W. PETERS.

Edwardian New York is apparent in the 20-floor Flatiron Building

THIS WAY TO SPEAKEASY

Triangle Shirtwaist Fire

Sweatshops in the Lower East Side at the beginning of the 20th century employed immigrant families in dreadful conditions at very low wages. Wages were increased after a series of strikes, but the tragedy of the Triangle Shirtwaist Fire in 1911 was to bring improvements in safety standards. The factory, on the top three floors of a 10-story building at the corner of Washington Place and Greene Street, employed 600 workers, mainly young women. They were ready to go home when the fire broke out. Many doors to the fire escapes were locked, as was common during working hours, and 146 workers perished, some leaping to their deaths. Public outrage brought new legislation for safety in the workplace.

Tin Pan Alley

By 1900 New York was the place to be for the young, ambitious songwriter. Theaters were flourishing and music publishers needed as many songs as they could get their hands on. Hundreds of composers and small publishing firms crowded into the abandoned brownstones on 28th Street, between Fifth Avenue and Broadway, and the area became known as Tin Pan Alley because of the cacophony coming from the open windows. Two of the great songwriters of this era were George and Ira Gershwin, sons of Russian immigrants. At 15 years old, George was the youngest song demonstrator. The brothers' many hits included the classics *I Got Rhythm*, *Embraceable You* and *Somebody Loves Me*. George died of a brain tumor in 1937 at the age of 38.

The subway

The elevated railways, financed by Jay Gould, Russell Sage and J. P. Morgan in the 1860s, improved public transportation, but were already inadequate by 1900. It was time to go underground. The Interborough Rapid Transit Company was born. The first line, 22 miles (35km) long, opened in 1904, carrying 600,000 passengers each day. It was a huge success and the profits enabled the city to expand the system. In 1921, New York and New Jersey joined forces to create the Port of New York Authority to develop and operate transportation. Delightful Coney Island, with its family entertainment, vaudeville and exhibitions, became accessible to everyone, thanks to New York's subways, which now total 660 miles (1,062km) in length, across 25 lines.

Organized crime

Just before Mayor William O'Dwyer, first elected as New York's mayor in 1946, began a re-election campaign, the *Brooklyn Eagle* published some very damning news about the mayor's connection to organized crime in the city. The newspaper charged that policemen and judges were being paid off in return for protection for 4,000 bookies. The mayor fled to Florida "for health reasons." In the hope of avoiding prosecution, more than 110 policemen resigned. In August 1950, the mayor also resigned. Subpoenaed and left with little choice, O'Dwyer admitted he knew about the corruption and that he too had associations with mobsters. Yet for a lack of hard evidence of willful wrongdoing, he went unpunished.

George Gershwin (far left; 1898–1937) wrote the classical *Rhapsody in Blue* (1924), while Irving Berlin (left; 1888–1989) gave the world *White Christmas*, among other classics, before living as a recluse in Manhattan

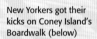

New Yorkers got their kicks on Coney Island's Boardwalk (below)

1950

Although America entered World War II in 1941 (below), New York City was physically unaffected

The Stock Exchange (above) is still a powerful financial institution

The Late 20th Century

The years between 1950 and 2000 swung back and forth between economic booms (1950s, 1980s, 1990s) and financial crisis (1970s), and Wall Street struggled and soared with the times. New York's Abstract Expressionist painters inspired the art world in the late 1940s and 1950s; the Pop Artists shocked and thrilled the public from the late 1950s to the 1970s. Music and theater got a big boost when the Lincoln Center was built in the 1960s. The number of Asian and Hispanic immigrants swelled, with Hispanics overtaking the African-American population as the city's largest minority group. In 1989 the city elected its first black mayor, David Dinkins, who beat Rudolph Giuliani. Crime soared in the 1970s and 1980s, and vandals defaced landmarks with graffiti. After Rudolph Giuliani was elected mayor in 1994, the number of recorded crimes dropped from 430,460 per year in 1993 to 161,956 in 2001, and the city had bright hopes for the future.

The Vietnam Veterans' Memorial is a moving display of letters written home by the troops

Mayor David Dinkins

Greenwich Village

By the 1950s, New York was America's cultural marketplace and Greenwich Village, with its cheap rents and bohemian flair, attracted America's finest artists and writers. Cedar Street Tavern at 24 University Place was the favorite Village hang-out for Abstract Expressionist painters Jackson Pollock, Willem de Kooning and Franz Kline. Regulars at the San Remo bar on the corner of Bleeker and MacDougal streets included writers James Agee, James Baldwin, Allen Ginsberg, Jack Kerouac and William Burroughs. It was here that the word Beatnik entered the language. Writers Dylan Thomas and Norman Mailer preferred the White Horse at Hudson and West 11th Street. Mailer's disregard for the Beats produced the Hip Generation.

1950

OUR NATIONAL
4,075,551.5
YOUR *Family share* $
THE NATIONAL DEBT
NATIONAL DEBT INCREASE PER
1992 INTEREST COST - $29

Nonconformist Greenwich Village (above); counting the national debt (right)

Sweet success

In 1962, astronaut John Glenn, the first American to orbit the earth, arrived in New York and jubilant throngs lined Broadway for a tickertape parade, an honor bestowed only on visiting heads of state, generals, victorious baseball teams, athletes and great politicians. New Yorkers flung 3,474 tons of tickertape, more than anyone had ever seen before, from office buildings and skyscrapers along the route.

In 1969 the New York Mets rose from ninth place in the National League, defeating the Baltimore Orioles in the World Series and ending up with their first victory pennant. But they only received a tickertape flurry compared to the blizzard that welcomed John Glenn (below).

Andy Warhol

Pop Art changed the art scene when Andy Warhol (below) opened his Factory in 1963. His Coca-Cola bottle, Campbell's Soup cans and multicolor silk-screen images of icons Marilyn Monroe, Elvis Presley and Jackie Kennedy were as astonishing at the time as the openly gay lifestyle he confidently espoused in an era when "homophobic" wasn't even a word. As a movie director he filmed *Kiss* and *Blow Job* in friends' apartments on the Lower East Side and in Greenwich Village. He lived as a recluse for the last 13 years of his life at 57 East 66th Street and died in 1987 rather bizarrely after routine gallbladder surgery.

Woody Allen

Allan Konigsberg changed his name when he started out as a comedian in Greenwich Village comedy clubs. He went on to make about a movie a year after 1965, most of them about New Yorkers. In 1977 for *Annie Hall* the brainy, scrawny actor and director won Oscars for Best Director and Best Screenplay. He sometimes shows up on Monday night at the Cafe Carlyle (35 East 76th Street at Madison Avenue) to play clarinet with the resident jazz band. His 1992 affair with and later marriage to the adopted daughter of his partner Mia Farrow shook his fans and damaged his career.

Ed Koch

The Big Apple was in such dire financial straits in the 1970s that it seemed only a miracle could prevent a collapse. In October 1975, for instance, the city was only 53 minutes from defaulting on its almost $477 million debt. After the Federal government proved unwilling to extend a hand, money from teacher pension funds inched the city back from the brink of disaster. When Ed Koch ran for mayor, he vowed to restore prosperity. He kept his promise after winning the 1977 election, and was re-elected by a landslide victory in 1981. His tax cuts, along with changes to investment banking, restored corporate America's confidence in New York.

Ed Koch, Ronald Reagan and a large U.S. Treasury check

Andy Warhol

2000

Public safety officers are on hand in Times Square, although it's a lot tamer than it used to be

The New Millennium

New York City's financial situation was not rosy at the start of the millennium. Mayor Rudolph Giuliani had cut taxes by $3 billion, and the city was heavily in debt. Then came the terrorist attack on September 11, 2001, that killed nearly 3,000 people, destroyed 25 million square feet (2.25 million square meters) of office space and closed the Stock Exchange for four days. Mayor Giuliani's courage and compassion immediately after the attack was admired by all. For plain-speaking Michael Bloomberg, elected mayor in 2002, Giuliani has proved a hard act to follow. The Republican billionaire businessman spent $70 million on his first election campaign. The city has largely recovered from the economic impact of 9/11 and slowly New Yorkers have come to appreciate Bloomberg.

Crime

In 2003, New York happily boasted that it was America's safest large city, and given its history of disturbing crime statistics, this is good news. New York was ranked 160th in total crime among 205 American cities. The 15-year trend of crime reduction, with homicides at a 40-year low, is continuing. It was the controversial, aggressive policing during the Giuliani years that helped to cut crime by 62 percent. The mayor beefed up the police force with 4,000 new officers and sent them out to tackle jaywalking, sleeping on subways, defacing property, and other petty crime and quality of life issues. Mayor Bloomberg has continued to fight crime.

Cleaning up

Between the 1960s and 1980s, the district from 40th Street to 53rd Street between 6th and 8th avenues was a sleazy area overrun by hookers, pimps and gamblers. In the 1970s and 1980s a strategy of implementing noise abatement laws and health statutes helped to close down brothels, gambling joints and massage parlors. A new zoning law banned "adult entertainment" from within 500ft of a residential district. In the 1990s Mayor Giuliani's tough policies made the area more desirable. His reputation as a reformer led to a strong bid for the US presidency in 2007–08.

Grand Central Terminal (below); Mayor Giuliani (below left)

2000–today

Messages and prayers were everywhere after 9/11 (right)

Neon and color are de rigueur in Times Square (below)

On the Move

ARRIVING

ON THE MOVE

Arriving by Air

You can fly direct to New York from most major European cities and from many other destinations around the world. International carriers fly into John F. Kennedy International Airport, 15 miles (24km) from Manhattan, on Jamaica Bay, and Newark Liberty International Airport, 16 miles (26km) west of town. LaGuardia Airport handles mainly domestic flights and is 8 miles (13km) from Manhattan in the borough of Queens.

John F. Kennedy International Airport (JFK)

JFK has nine passenger terminals, though Terminal 5 is currently closed as it integrates with Terminal 6. Terminal 7 handles all British Airways flights, jetBlue uses Terminal 6, and Virgin Atlantic Terminal 4.

There are information desks, restaurants and concession stands in all terminals. An AirTrain links the airport and the New York

	JOHN F. KENNEDY INTERNATIONAL AIRPORT (JFK)	LA GUARDIA AIRPORT (LGA)
TRANSPORTATION FROM MAJOR AIRPORTS		
Distance from Manhattan:	15 miles (24km).	8 miles (13km).
Journey time to Manhattan:	Taxi 45–60 minutes, Subway 60–100 minutes.	Taxi 20–35 minutes, Bus 40–50 minutes.
Ground transportation information:	Baggage claim level of all terminals.	Baggage claim level of all terminals.
Transport	**Shuttle/subway** • A free yellow, white and blue Long-Term Parking Lot shuttle bus runs to the Howard Beach Station, where you get the A subway train to Manhattan. • The free shuttle runs every 10 to 15 minutes during rush hour, every 20 minutes at all other times. • The subway costs $2 but you will need to buy a MetroCard (▷ 43). **AirTrain** • Buy your ticket ($5 each way) at the station, or from a vending machine in the airport. • These connect to the LIRR at Jamaica station, subways at Howard Beach/JFK Airport station and Sutphin Blvd.-Archer Ave./Jamaica station, and local bus lines.	**Bus** • Follow the "Ground Transportation" signs out of the terminal. You will see the M60 bus stop sign at the curb. • The fare is $2, but you save on the transfer if you use a MetroCard (▷ 43). • Take the M60 to 106th Street at Broadway. • Get off at Lexington Avenue to catch the 4, 5 and 6 subway trains; at Malcolm X Boulevard for the 2 and 3 trains; at St. Nicholas Avenue for the A, B, C and D trains; at 116th Street-Columbia University for the 1 train. • The bus runs daily between 4am and 1am, leaving every 30 minutes. • For more information, visit www.mta.nyc.ny.us/nyct

subway, local bus lines and the LIRR.

LaGuardia Airport (LGA)

Most domestic flights go through LaGuardia Airport, with United Airlines and Continental Airlines operating the lion's share. If you need assistance, look out for the Customer Service Agents in their red jackets or go to the information desk between concourse C and D on the departure level. There's a selection of restaurants in the USAir and Delta terminals, which are accessible via a free shuttle service.

TIP

● Avoid airport hustlers offering taxi services. City cabs and car services are a better option and equally convenient—they wait outside terminals in designated areas.

Newark Liberty International Airport (EWR)

Major carriers that fly into this airport include Virgin Atlantic, British Airways, Lufthansa and Continental Airlines. All passenger terminals—A, B and C—have restaurants on the concourse level, and the Information desk is in Terminal B, lower level. The AirTrain system links the airport with the subway, NJ Transit, Amtrak and LIRR, and makes for a quick and cheap way of getting into the city.

LEAVING THE AIRPORT

After collecting your bags and going through Customs, you can get into the city in several different ways.

TAXI

You will easily find taxi stands outside airport terminals. Dispatchers work during peak hours at JFK and LaGuardia, and 24 hours a day at Newark. For more information about

USEFUL TELEPHONE NUMBERS AND WEBSITES

John F. Kennedy International Airport (JFK)
718/244-4444
www.panynj.gov

LaGuardia Airport
718/533-3400
www.panynj.gov

Newark Liberty International Airport
973/961-6000
www.panynj.gov

taxis, ▷ 51. Tip your drivers 15 percent to 20 percent.
● At JFK, you are charged a flat rate of $45, plus round-trip tolls.
● At LaGuardia, you pay by the meter ($24–28), plus tolls.
● At Newark, dispatchers ask you where you are going. Give an address and you will be quoted the fare ($40–$75, plus tolls and a $15 surcharge).

ON THE MOVE

NEWARK LIBERTY INTERNATIONAL AIRPORT (EWR)	ADDITIONAL INFORMATION

16 miles (26km).

Taxi 35–50 minutes,
Airtrain 30 minutes.

On the baggage claim level.

AirTrain
• This modern speedy monorail/rail link operated by NJ Transit and Amtrak is comfortable and fast, and also easy, provided you do not have a lot of baggage.
• Follow signs to the AirTrain from any Newark arrivals terminal.
• Buy your ticket at the station (NJ Transit trains $14/children under 5 free) or from a vending machine in the airport or at the train station.
• These take you to Penn Station at Eighth Avenue and 31st Street in Manhattan.
• Do not get off at Newark's Penn Station if you want to go to Manhattan—stay on board until the next stop to reach New York's Penn Station. From there, you can easily catch a cab, the subway or a bus to your hotel.
• NJ Transit trains run two to three times an hour during peak travel times, once an hour off-peak.
• It is easy to make connections to destinations beyond Manhattan from the Newark International Airport Station. For details, phone NJ Transit 800/626-RIDE or visit www.njtransit.com or phone Amtrak 800/USA-RAIL or visit www.amtrak.com

Telephone contact
The Air-Ride number, 800/247-7433, describing transportation to and from all three airports, is answered by an operator Monday to Friday between 8am and 6pm; at all other times you get recorded information.

NYC and Co.
810 Seventh Ave., New York, NY 10019
212/484-1200
www.nycvisit.com
Contact NYC and Co. to order the *Official NYC Guide* listing hotels, restaurants, theaters, attractions and events. The visitor's kit also includes a map, brochures, a newsletter and information on services.

PRIVATE TRANSPORTATION FROM MAJOR AIRPORTS

New York Airport Service express bus
Tel 718/875-8200
www.nyairportservice.com
Follow the "Ground Transportation" signs to the pick-up point outside the terminal.

From JFK

This service runs between 6.15am and 11.10pm, and travel time is 45 to 65 minutes, longer during rush hour. The trip to the Port Authority Bus Terminal, at 42nd Street and Eighth Avenue, costs $15 ($27 round-trip). The journey to Grand Central Terminal at Vanderbilt Avenue and 42nd Street or to Bryant Park costs $15 ($27 round-trip), or $33 round-trip to hotels between 31st and 60th streets. The service to New York's Penn Station costs $15 ($27 round-trip).

From LaGuardia

This service runs between 7.20am and 11pm, and travel time is 30 to 45 minutes, longer during rush hour. The journey costs $12 ($21 round-trip) to Port Authority Bus Terminal at 42nd Street and Eighth Avenue or Grand Central Terminal at Vanderbilt Avenue and 42nd Street or Bryant Park, and $27 round-trip to hotels between 31st and 60th streets. From Grand Central there are onward connections from the 30-minute journeys to Penn Station (also $21 round-trip from LaGuardia).

SuperShuttle

Tel 800/451-0455 or 212/315-3006
www.supershuttle.com
Go to the Ground Transportation desk and dial SuperShuttle on the courtesy phone in the baggage claim area of JFK, LaGuardia or Newark airports. Vans run 24 hours a day, throughout all five boroughs of New York City. Reservations are not required. The fares range from $15 to $19.

Coach USA

Tel 877/8-NEWARK (639275)
www.coachusa.com
Operating only out of Newark Airport, Coach USA takes passengers to Penn Station, at 34th Street and Eighth Avenue; to Grand Central Terminal, at Vanderbilt Avenue and 42nd Street; to the Port Authority Bus Terminal, at Eighth Avenue and 42nd Street; and to Chinatown and Lower Manhattan. The bus leaves every 15 minutes to Midtown and every 30 minutes to Lower Manhattan and costs $14 ($25 round-trip); children under 12 ride free.

SECURITY AT CUSTOMS

Since 9/11, security has been stepped up at airports, tunnels, bridges and train stations. To facilitate departure, do cooperate. Do not carry sharp items on your person or in your carry-on bags.

Empty your pockets before walking through the security detection scanner. Be prepared to open bags or remove your shoes for inspection or to allow a security officer to scan your body with a hand-held scanner.

Arriving by Road

Driving into Manhattan is not for the faint-hearted and once you've got into the city, you then have the problem of finding somewhere to park. Expect lengthy delays on the bridges and tunnels that cross to the island of Manhattan, especially on the bridges that cross the East River (repairs are ongoing). It is best to avoid the morning, lunchtime and evening rush-hour traffic.

Arriving by Rail

Most commuter trains from Connecticut and the suburbs north of the city serve Grand Central Station (on 42nd Street at Park Avenue). Amtrak's long-distance trains from across the United States pull into Penn Station at 31st Street and Seventh Avenue and for journeys to and from Long Island and New Jersey, the Long Island Railroad and New Jersey Transit are the trains to catch, also operating out of Penn Station.

A New York Airport Service express bus

GETTING AROUND

The best way to see Manhattan is on foot. Streets in most Manhattan neighborhoods are safe both by day and after dark. However, walking takes time, and if you want to visit several museums or neighborhoods, or if the weather is bad, the subways are a better option. They are easy to use, inexpensive, and relatively clean and safe. Buses are more pleasant than subways because you get a chance to see street life as you travel, although you need to pay with correct change, and during rush hour traffic slows your progress—sometimes it's faster to walk.

OPTIONS

If you will be in New York for seven days or more, buy a MetroCard to save money on transit fares. You swipe the card at the subway turnstile or as you get on the bus, and you do not have to worry about having the correct change. Taxis are the quickest way for many to travel but the most expensive. When you take a cab, don't forget to tip the driver 15 percent or more.

Driving your own car in New York is not usually the best option. Besides the traffic, you will need to park on the street, and garages are expensive. If you do arrive in New York by car, the best course is to leave your car in a garage until you are ready to leave town (head for the eastern or western fringes of Manhattan if saving money matters more to you than convenience).

WALKING IN NEW YORK
- Always use crosswalks; jaywalking is against the law.
- Stay to the right as you would when driving.
- When the light changes and you are about to cross, check the intersection to make sure that no drivers or bicyclists have decided to make a dash through the light. This is not uncommon.

METROCARD

What is it?
A magnetically encoded card that debits the fare when you swipe it through the turnstile in the subway or the fare box on a bus.

What about transfers?
When you use a MetroCard for a trip, transfers between subways and buses within a 2-hour period are free.

Where can I buy one?
From staffed subway booths (cash only), special vending machines in most subway stations (cash, credit cards, debit cards), drugstores like Rite Aid, Hudson News at Penn Station and Grand Central Terminal, or at the Times Square Visitors Center at 1560 Broadway between 46th and 47th streets (cash, credit cards, debit cards). Many hotels sell them, too.

What's the cost?
Pay-Per-Ride MetroCard: $10 buys 6 rides, $20 buys 12 rides. These can be swiped four times

MetroCard Vending Machines

At This Station

Pay with credit card, ATM/debit card or cash.

in succession, so are good for up to four people traveling together. Just swipe, walk through, and hand the card to the person behind you, who swipes, walks through, and hands it to the person behind. You can refill these cards—that is, put more rides on them—in the vending machines located in most subway stations. Just put the card in, indicate how much money you want to spend, and insert your credit card or cash.
Unlimited Ride MetroCard: $7 buys a 1-Day Fun Pass, $24 buys a 7-Day Card, $76 buys a 30-Day Card. These can't be used by

more than one person—an 18-minute interval must elapse between successful card swipes at the same station. These cards go into effect the first time you use them, not the day you buy them.

Can I get a discount?
Seniors and visitors with disabilities can get reductions; phone 718/243-4999.

How do you use a MetroCard?
When you swipe your card, the turnstile indicator shows how much money is left on the card. If you swipe the card too fast or too slowly, the indicator asks you to swipe it again. If this happens, swipe it again. Do not go to a different turnstile, as you may end up paying twice.

Where can I get more information?
Phone 800/METROCARD or 212/638-7622, from Monday through Friday between 9 and 5 or visit **www.mta.nyc.ny.us/metrocard**

Subways

The Metropolitan Transit Authority (MTA) runs the subway system. **It runs 24 hours a day, seven days a week. Rush hour is roughly between 7.30 and 9.30am and again from 4.30 to 6.30pm Monday through Friday except holidays. The subway is quick, inexpensive, efficient, generally safe, and fairly easy to figure out.**

Fares are $2 ($1 for seniors and people with disabilities); children under 44 inches (1.13m) ride free. The best way to pay is by MetroCard (▷ 43).

A campaign promotes polite behavior, and posters ask passengers to give their seats to the elderly and infirm, to move to the center of the train so as not to block the doors, and to walk rather than run.

Stations are clearly marked

TIP
● New Yorkers refer to subway lines as trains. "Take the A train" means "Take subway line A."

UNDERSTANDING THE SUBWAY MAP

MTA maps are free and easy to understand. You can get them in any subway station, at information centers and in hotel lobbies.

The map (▷ 45) shows each line as a different color, but it is the number or letter that you need to know. No one refers to trains by color.

Solid black circles on the colored lines indicate stops for local trains, which make more stops than express trains.

Black and white lines connecting white and black circles indicate free subway transfers.

White circles on the colored lines indicate express train stops. Express trains skip about three stops for every one they make.

Below the name of every stop, the letters or numbers of the lines that stop there are indicated. Boldface type, for example **B**, indicates that the line offers a full-time service. Lightface type, for example B, indicates a part-time service. At 72nd Street, you see B, **C**, indicating part-time service on line B and full-time on C.

ON THE MOVE

- The Lower East Side and the East Village are not well served by subways. If you are traveling to or from these areas at night, it is best to take a taxi.

SUBWAY HELP
- Station clerks are very helpful, and many subway stations are manned.
- For help in English, call 718/330-1234, 24 hours a day.
- For help in other languages, call 718/330-4847, between 7am and 7pm.

FINDING A SUBWAY
- In the station look for the signs with colored circles showing the subway line letter (A, B, C, etc.) or the subway line numbers of the trains that stop there.
- If you need help finding a subway station, ask a policeman or step into a hotel lobby, museum or store to ask. Most people working in such places are used to helping tourists but even regular New Yorkers on the street do so quite happily.

FINDING THE RIGHT SUBWAY LINE
- After you have paid and walked through the turnstile, look for the colored circles. Find the line you want, and follow the signs. Above the platform edge, signs indicate the trains that stop there, their destinations and hours of operation. Changes to the line's service are usually posted, but signs are not very large, so you need to look carefully.
- Uptown or downtown? If you want to go north of where you are, no matter where in the city you happen to be, you want an uptown train. If you want to go south of where you are, you want a downtown train. Some stations are Uptown Only or Downtown Only—clearly marked at street level. If you find the color circle

A MetroCard ticket machine

HOW TO USE THE SUBWAY

- Although the New York subway once had a bad reputation for safety, trains are now safer and cleaner. However, pickpockets and beggars are perennial, so keep a close eye on your bags. Keep your money well hidden and do not wear expensive jewelry or even jewelry that looks expensive.

- Do not wait for trains near the edge of the platform; stand back a bit.
- If there are few people on the platform or if you are alone, stand under the yellow

sign "During Off Hours Trains Stop Here." When the train stops, the conductor sticks his or her head out the window from a middle car, which is where he or she rides, and you should, too.

- Let passengers off first before getting on.
- Stay out of empty cars.
- After 11pm or midnight, take a taxi until you know your way around in the subway.
- If you find yourself on an express train speeding past your destination, get off at the next stop and either take the same line back to where you got on or ask the station clerk for directions. Be prepared to pay an extra fare to re-enter the platform; at some stations, you may need to exit the station, cross the street, and re-enter the station on the other side to catch the train that's going in the right direction for you.

with the number or letter you want and know that you want to go north, for example, do not go into a subway entrance marked Downtown Only—any train you catch there will take you in the opposite direction. Trains headed in the right direction are nearby—the entrance is usually across the street.

● On the front and side of every train, the route number or letter is displayed. Make sure you look for this before getting on the train to be sure it is the one you want.

● If you really want to be sure, stand in the middle of the platform, halfway between the two ends of the train, and when the train rolls into the station, look for the conductor leaning out of a window in the center car—he or she can tell you definitively where the train is headed.

KNOWING WHEN TO GET OFF

● Conductors make announcements before each stop. On new trains, these are recorded.

● Every subway car has a map posted on the wall by a door, so you can make sure you are traveling in the right direction and can see how many stops you need to go.

● Look for signs on the station walls as you pull into the station.

LEAVING THE SUBWAY

After you get off the train, go upstairs (usually a stairway, but

sometimes an escalator). You have to go through the turnstiles to exit the station, but you do not need to use your MetroCard again. Make sure you choose the right exit for your destination.

DISRUPTIONS

● Subway lines are occasionally closed or re-routed for maintenance or construction work. Weekly service advisories for all lines are posted on the MTA website and alternative directions are given (www.mta.info/nyct/service/advisory.htm).

● Weekend service is sometimes altered on some lines to allow for maintenance. Announcements are posted in the affected stations.

IN CASE OF EMERGENCY

● Look for a police officer. The

Passengers travel way above a Harlem street on an elevated section of the subway

Transit Bureau Police patrol the subways.

● Look for a telephone and call 911. This is a free call.

● Go to the station clerk in the booth.

● On the subway train, make your way to the middle of the train to find the conductor or to the front of the first car to find the operator.

TRAVELERS WITH DISABILITIES

Not all subways are wheelchair accessible. You can find information on the 30 or more stations that are by visiting www.mta.nyc.ny.us

TRAINS MOST USEFUL FOR VISITORS	
4, 5 and 6	The trains run up and down the east side of Manhattan, to the Bronx and to Brooklyn.
1, 2, 3, A, B, C, D, E and F	The trains run up and down the west side of Manhattan, to the Bronx and to Brooklyn.
N, R, Q and W	The trains run from Brooklyn and Queens in and out of Manhattan.
S	The train runs between Times Square and Grand Central Terminal, operating as a shuttle.
L	The train runs across 14th Street to Brooklyn.

Lexington Avenue subway

Buses

The Metropolitan Transit Authority (MTA) runs the city's buses, and fares are the same as for subways (▷ 44–47). You can use your MetroCard or exact change to pay for your ride. Bus drivers do not give change, so travel with plenty of quarters if you do not buy the more practical and economical MetroCard. Buses are slower than subways. Buses run 24 hours a day on most routes but less often at night, and on weekends. Drivers are helpful, so if you need advice, don't be afraid to ask.

FINDING A BUS
● Go to a designated bus stop, recognized by the yellow-painted curb and blue-and-white sign.
● Look at the posted Guide-A-Ride boxes, showing the route map and service schedule.
● Most major avenues have their own bus routes, running north or south.
● Crosstown buses, running east and west, are strategically located on major streets across Manhattan.

GETTING ON AND OFF
Board buses at the front. Swipe your MetroCard or pay in exact change. Leave seats in front for the elderly, the infirm and adults with small children. You will notice a tape strip above and beside the windows. To indicate to the driver where you wish to get off, push on this about one block before your stop. Front doors open automatically; to exit by the back, wait for the green light to go on above the doors, then press the yellow tape on the doors to open them.

WHICH BUS TO TAKE
The routes given here are the ones most used by visitors for the main attractions. If you need further guidance, see the Bus Buster Chart opposite, or pick up an MTA bus map from any visitor center (▷ 324), subway station or hotel lobby.

ADDRESS LOCATOR
To locate the cross street of an address on an avenue:
● Drop the last digit of the street number.
● Divide by 2.
● Add or subtract the number given below.
● The answer is approximately the nearest number cross street (for example 54th Street).

AVENUES

A, B, C, D, First, Second		add 3
Third, Eighth		add 10
Fourth		add 8
Sixth		subtract 12
Seventh		add 12
Ninth		add 13
Tenth		add 14
Amsterdam		add 60
Broadway	(23rd to 192nd St)	subtract 30
Fifth	up to 200	add 13
	up to 400	add 16
	up to 600	add 18
	up to 775	add 20
	up to 1286	drop last digit and subtract 18
	up to 1500	add 45
	above 2000	add 24
Central Park West		divide by 10 and add 60
Columbus		add 60
Lexington		add 22
Madison		add 26
Park		add 35

Bus routes criss-cross the city

North–South buses
● **M1, M2, M3** and **M4** basically run north up Madison and south down Fifth. These buses take you to the museums along Fifth Avenue, also called Museum Mile; M4 travels as far north as The Cloisters in Fort Tryon Park (▷ 252).
● **M5** runs from Houston Street north along Sixth Avenue, then up Riverside Drive and Broadway to Washington Heights.
● **M6** runs from Central Park South down Broadway to South Ferry, through Times Square, Union Square, Greenwich Village, SoHo and the Financial District, then back up Sixth Avenue.
● **M7** runs between Union Square and West 146th Street/Malcolm X Boulevard. It runs up

The Coach USA sign

Sixth Avenue, over Broadway, up Amsterdam Avenue, and across Central Park North, then up to 146th Street. On the return, it travels south on Columbus, Seventh Avenue and Broadway back to Union Square.

- **M9** runs from Union Square to Battery Park along Manhattan's Lower East Side.
- **M10** runs from West 31st Street/Seventh Avenue (Penn Station) to West 159th Street/Frederick Douglass Boulevard. It travels up Central Park West, stopping at the American Museum of Natural History, and is a good bus for getting to Central Park.
- **M11** runs along the west side of Manhattan, north on Tenth Avenue/Amsterdam Avenue right up into Harlem.
- **M15** runs from South Ferry, north along the East Side to Second Avenue/East 126th Street.

- **M60** runs from West 106th Street/Broadway to LaGuardia Airport.
- **M100** runs from West 220th Street/Broadway to East 127th Street/Second Avenue.

Crosstown buses
- **M8** runs from Avenue D to West Street through the East Village and Greenwich Village.
- **M14A** and **M14D** run from the Chelsea Piers to the Lower East Side.
- **M27** runs between West 41st Street/Eighth Avenue (Port Authority Bus Terminal) and East 42nd Street/First Avenue.
- **M34** runs from Jacob Javits Convention Center at Eleventh

BUS BUSTER CHART

CHANGE AT OR WALK TO/FROM:

▨ Union Square   ▨ Times Square   ▨ Broadway and East 8th/9th Streets
▨ Central Park South   ▨ South Street
w = walk   F = South Ferry from South Street

Use this chart to find out which buses will take you to your chosen destination. Follow the rows of squares horizontally and vertically from the name of the destinations until they meet. This square contains the number(s) of the bus(es) you'll need to catch. Bus numbers on white squares are direct. Numbers in shaded squares show that you have to change buses or take a bus some of the way and walk the rest. Start out on the first bus listed, then change to the second bus. Look at the key to find out where you must change buses or walk to/from. Note that the bus stop may be a few minutes' walk away from the destination.

Routes change regularly, and often differ on Sundays, so check an up-to-date timetable or bus map before setting out.

Destinations (diagonal labels): AMERICAN MUSEUM OF NATURAL HISTORY, BROOKLYN BRIDGE, CENTRAL PARK, EAST VILLAGE AND NOHO, ELLIS ISLAND MUSEUM OF IMMIGRATION AND HISTORY CENTER, EMPIRE STATE BUILDING, GRAND CENTRAL TERMINAL, GREENWICH VILLAGE, GUGGENHEIM MUSEUM, LINCOLN CENTER, METROPOLITAN MUSEUM OF ART, ROCKEFELLER CENTER, SOHO, SOUTH STREET SEAPORT, STATUE OF LIBERTY, TIMES SQUARE/BROADWAY, TRINITY CHURCH, WHITNEY MUSEUM OF ART

MAIN TOURIST BUS ROUTES

Certain bus routes link key attractions. All routes shown are circular (north to south section of M15 shown only). Start and end stops are given as well as stops near to main attractions.

M1

Jewish Museum, Cooper Hewitt, National Academy of Design, Guggenheim
Metropolitan Museum of Art
Central Park
Frick Collection
Rockefeller Center
Grand Central Terminal, Chrysler Building
Morgan Library
Whitney Museum

Harlem, Malcolm X Blvd./146 St.
Fifth Ave./Central Park North
Fifth Ave./96–97 Sts.
Fifth Ave./84 St.
Fifth Ave./E79 St.
Fifth Ave./E72 St.
Fifth Ave./60 St.
Fifth Ave./49–50 Sts.
Fifth Ave./41 St.
Park Ave./E39 St.
Madison Ave./E43 St.
Madison Ave./E72St.
Harlem, Malcolm X Blvd./W147 St.

M6

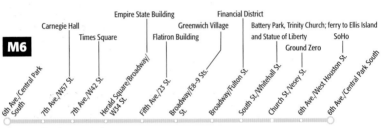

Empire State Building
Carnegie Hall
Times Square
Financial District
Greenwich Village
Flatiron Building
Battery Park, Trinity Church; ferry to Ellis Island and Statue of Liberty
SoHo
Ground Zero

6th Ave./Central Park South
7th Ave./W57 St.
7th Ave./W42 St.
Herald Square/Broadway/W34 St.
Fifth Ave./23 St.
Broadway/E8–9 Sts.
Broadway/Fulton St.
South St./Whitehall St.
Church St./Vesey St.
6th Ave./West Houston St.
6th Ave./Central Park South

M7

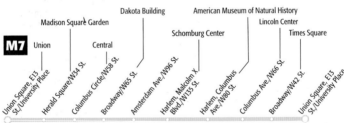

Dakota Building
Madison Square Garden
American Museum of Natural History
Schomburg Center
Lincoln Center
Union
Central
Times Square

Union Square, E13 St./University Place
Herald Square/W34 St.
Columbus Circle/W58 St.
Broadway/W65 St.
Amsterdam Ave./W96 St.
Harlem, Malcolm X Blvd./W135 St.
Harlem, Columbus Ave./W80 St.
Columbus Ave./W66 St.
Broadway/W42 St.
Union Square, E13 St./University Place

M15

Little Italy
Gramercy Park
East Village
Chinatown, Brooklyn Bridge
South Street Seaport
City Hall
Wall Street
Jewish Heritage Museum, Battery Park; ferry to Staten Island

East Harlem, 2nd Ave./E126 St.
2nd Ave./E23 St.
2nd Ave./E9 St./St. Marks Place
Allen St./Delancey St.
Center St./Park Row
St James Place/Madison St.
Pearl St./Fulton St.
Water St./Wall St.
South Ferry

Avenue/West 34th Street to the Ferry Terminal at East 34th Street.
● **M42** runs along 42nd Street from Circle Line Pier to the United Nations Headquarters.
● **M72** runs from the Upper West Side to the Upper East Side from West 68th Street/Freedom Place to East 72nd Street/York Avenue.
● **M79** runs from West 79th Street/Riverside Drive to East 79th Street/East End Avenue.

SAFETY
Buses are safe throughout the day and the early hours of the night, but after 10pm it is best to take a taxi rather than wait for a bus on a deserted street. If a beggar asks you for money, just shake your head and do not get embroiled in conversation.

TRAVELERS WITH DISABILITIES
Buses are equipped with wheelchair lifts, and drivers can make the buses "kneel" by lowering the front step of the vehicle for people who have difficulty getting on.

Taxis and Car Services

New York's official taxicabs are licensed by the Taxi and Limousine Commission (TLC). They are easily recognizable; they are always yellow, always display the rates on the door, and always have a light on the roof and a flat bronze medallion on the hood. Do not get into any other taxi; only yellow cabs with the distinctive markings are legally licensed. Car services operated by private companies are available at an hourly rate and must be arranged in advance; they are not allowed to pick up passengers who hail them. Limousines are also available to rent.

A distinctive yellow New York taxi

HOW TO GET A TAXI

You can hail a taxi on any street by holding out your arm at the curb. When the light on the roof is turned on, the taxi is available. If the light is turned off, it is occupied. Usually you don't have to wait long before getting one, but it sometimes takes a while—after the theater, in the theater district and just about anywhere with the approach of rush hour time (4pm). Try to hail a taxi in the direction you would like to travel, which saves travel time and money. The best way to direct the driver is by giving the cross street and the avenue—for example, 42nd Street and Fifth Avenue. As you get closer to your destination, you can let the driver know the exact address. Many taxi drivers do not have a great command of the English language, so speak clearly and not too quickly when giving addresses or asking questions.

HOW MUCH IS THE FARE?

● As soon as you get into the cab, the meter is turned on; this flag-drop fare is $2.50.
● After that, it's 40 cents for every one-fifth mile (0.3km) or 20 cents per minute in stopped or very slow traffic.

● Tolls at tunnels and bridges cost extra. The driver may ask you for the toll money as you approach or may pay it himself then charge you at the end of the journey. Tolls range from $2 to $6. For more information on toll charges, visit www.panynj.gov
● Between 8pm and 6am, you pay a night surcharge of 50 cents; during weekday peak hours from 4 to 8pm the surcharge is $1.
● Tip your driver between 15 percent and 20 percent on the fare excluding tolls.
● Note down the taxi driver's four-digit medallion identity number, which is posted on the divider behind the driver's head and ask for a receipt. These will be useful if you accidentally leave one of your possessions in the taxi or if you want to make a complaint.
● There is no extra charge per passenger, but taxis cannot take more than four people. There is also no extra charge for luggage.

KNOW YOUR RIGHTS

Drivers are required by law to:
● Be polite.
● Take passengers anywhere in the five boroughs, to Westchester and Nassau counties, and to Newark Airport.
● Provide air conditioning.
● Turn off the radio if asked.
● Refrain from smoking while a passenger is in the taxi.

For full information on the Taxi Rider's Bill of Rights, call the 24-hour Consumer Hotline 212/NYC-TAXI or visit www.nyc.gov/taxi

Some visitors choose to arrive at their hotel by taxi

● Fasten your seatbelt. All taxis are required by law to provide them and passengers in the front seat are required to wear them.

TRAVELERS WITH DISABILITIES

Taxis are required to carry passengers with folding wheelchairs, as well as those with guide dogs and therapy dogs.

CAR SERVICES

Most car services have a two-hour minimum rental period and rates start at $35 per hour. Try Allstate Car and Limousine Service (tel 212/741-7440), Carmel (tel 212/666-6666) or Dial 7 (tel 212/777-7777). The Yellow Pages has a complete listing. Alternatively, you can contract with a car service, through a concierge. It might be possible to agree a pre-set rate for a specific trip.

Driving

Driving in New York City is not for everyone. Garage parking runs to $25 a day or more, and finding on-street parking is nearly impossible; restrictions are designed to discourage drivers from using their cars. Plus tow trucks are out in force, and to get your car back if it's towed, you have to pay a hefty fine—in cash, often in a neighborhood you would rather not visit. Traffic is taxing during rush hours, between 7.30 and 9.30am and again from 4.30 to 6.30pm. Drivers are aggressive, unpredictable, or both.

DRIVING CUSTOMS AND LAWS

● Most streets in New York are one-way. Newcomers from Britain and Australia need to remember to drive on the right.
● No right turn is permitted on red lights in New York City.
● Drivers must wear seatbelts. By law, front-seat passengers and children aged 4 to 10 in the back seat must also wear them. Children under 4 ride in child safety-seats.
● Passing (overtaking) is permitted on the inside and outside lanes of Interstate Highways.

PARKING

● Check street parking signs carefully. For street cleaning, parking is prohibited on alternate sides of the street on different days.
● For on-street parking you may need to feed the parking meter with change, sometimes on an hourly basis. In Midtown, look for Mini Meters, kiosks that dispense timed parking chits to leave locked inside your car, visible to parking inspectors.
● Do not park within 15ft (4.6m) of a fire hydrant.
● Never leave anything inside a

Nose to tail on Madison Avenue

SPEED LIMITS	
Major streets	30mph (48kph)
Residential areas	25mph (40kph)
Major expressways (in New York City)	50mph (80kph)
Highways in rural areas out of town	55mph (88kph)

ROAD SIGNS

Regulatory information appears on signs with a white background. Warning information appears on signs with a yellow background.

Left reverse turn ahead

Sharp curve to the right

Intersection within curve

Give way to other traffic

Intersection lane control

Y intersection ahead

T intersection ahead

Give way to other traffic ahead

High occupancy vehicle lane ahead

Divided highway

Divided highway ahead

Stop ahead

Advisory speed on deceleration lane for exit

Exits are clearly signed (above). Traffic policeman (below).

parked vehicle, not even in the trunk (boot). Even an empty shopping bag can provoke a thief's curiosity—and yield a broken window or locks.

● Parking garages are easy to find but expensive, in the range of $15 for the first hour to $40 a day, with special rates if you arrive before 10 or 11am. Midtown is the priciest area; to save money, park closer to the rivers.

CAR RENTAL COMPANIES		
NAME	**TELEPHONE**	**WEBSITE**
Alamo	800/462-5266	www.alamo.com
Avis	800/331-1212	www.avis.com
Budget	800/527-0700	www.budget.com
Dollar	800/800-3665	www.dollar.com
Hertz	800/654-3131	www.hertz.com
National	800/227-7368	www.nationalcar.com

CAR RENTALS

Car rental companies are at all three major airports and at various locations around the city. Prices vary considerably, but as a general rule, a one-day weekday rental costs between $75 and $100, weekly rates run between $210 and $300, and weekend rates run around $65 for one day to $175 for two days.

If you require a specific type of car then make sure the rental company is aware of your needs because in a lot of cases you will be reserving the rental rate and not an actual car model when you make your booking. When working out costs, remember to consider the 13.63 percent tax in addition to the quoted price and remember that rates are calculated using the 24-hour clock. Most rental companies will offer various insurance packages which may include Collision Damage Waiver (CDW), Loss Damage Waiver (LDW), Physical Damage Waiver (PDW) or Additional Liability Insurance (ALI) in their cover. Another

charge to look out for is the "dropping off" charge levied when you want to leave the car in a different place to where you collected it. This charge is usually minimal but can be quite high if you decide to journey interstate. Most car rental companies have a stock of childrens' car safety seats but these need to be requested when you make your initial booking.

TIPS

To rent a car you must:
● Be 25 years old to rent a car from most companies (and be aware that some companies may have an upper age limit, too).
● Have a valid driver's license bearing your photo.
● Produce a major credit card and, if you're not an American citizen, your passport.
● Have your own insurance or purchase maximum insurance from the rental company.
● Return the car with a full tank of fuel or the company will fill it up and add the cost to your bill.

Alternatives

Depending on where you want to go, your trip can be a travel experience.

FERRIES
Ferries offer a comfortable ride with spectacular views. The free Staten Island Ferry has been running since 1905; it gives you a great view of the Statue of Liberty and New York Harbor. Boats depart from Whitehall Terminal 1 (Whitehall Street, tel 718/727-2508, www.nyc.gov) and operate from Staten Island to Manhattan round the clock, except on holidays, roughly every 30 minutes during the day and hourly at night. Vehicles are not allowed on the ferry at the present time. The trip, 5.2 miles (8.4km), takes 25 minutes. Listed below are only some of the ferry commuter services available. For sightseeing cruises, ▷ 260.

NY Waterway (tel 800/53-FERRY, www.nywaterway.com) operates commuter ferries from New Jersey to points in Manhattan and from Manhattan to Yankee Stadium and Shea Stadium using several piers:

Midtown at West 39th Street, Pier 11 at Wall Street, and the World Financial Center. Ferries run between 6am and 9.30pm, depending on location. Harbor sightseeing cruises are also available.

New York Water Taxi (tel 212/742-1969, www.nywatertaxi. com) runs a shuttle between several piers around Manhattan, including Chelsea Piers on West 26th Street and at Pier 45 at Christopher Street.

Circle Line operates sightseeing cruises (▷ 260).

NYC Department of Transportation (tel 311) can give you information on all New York City ferries.

PEDICABS
On weekends and evenings in Greenwich Village, SoHo, Times Square, Midtown and the East Village, consider a pedicab for a unique view of town. Some drivers are licensed NYC tour guides. Most fares from Manhattan Rickshaw (tel 212/604-4729, www.manhattan-rickshaw.com)

are from $15–$30 and upwards, depending on the distance. Consult a driver or contact the company by telephone. Pedicabs may be hailed in the street; there are no stands.

CARRIAGES
A good old-fashioned carriage ride around Central Park can be an idyllic experience. Carriages stand at Fifth Avenue and Central Park South. Most charge $40 for 20 minutes. For specific information call Central Park Carriages (547 West 37th Street, tel 212/736-0680, www.central parkcarriages.com).

Pedicab and driver

New York Water Taxi

LEAVING NEW YORK

If you want to sample life away from the metropolis for a day then head out to the boroughs. If you have more time then travel north into the beautiful Hudson Valley, with its pretty towns and historical buildings, or go south to Philadelphia or Washington, D.C. Trains and buses serve all major routes out of town if you decide not to take to the road yourself.

BY RAIL

New York has two train stations: Grand Central Terminal on the east side and Pennsylvania Station on the west.

● Local Metro-North commuter trains run in and out of Grand Central Terminal to New York and Connecticut suburbs. Information: 212/532-4900 or 800/METRO-INFO; www.mta.info/mnr

● Long Island Railroad (LIRR) runs commuter trains to and from Long Island. Information: 718/217-5477; www.mta.info

● PATH connects Manhattan to many New Jersey cities. Information: 201/216-6000 or 800/234-7284; www.panynj.gov/path

● Amtrak's high-speed Acela trains serve Penn Station as well as Boston, Philadelphia and Washington, D.C. Amtrak also has a daily service to cities throughout the US. Information: 800/872-7245 or 212/630-6400; www.amtrak.com

BY ROAD

Long-distance and commuter buses, as well as airport buses, operate from the Port Authority

Travel by Greyhound bus is quick and comfortable

Bus Terminal (625 Eighth Avenue, tel 212/564-8484), which is New York's main bus station.

Greyhound® buses travel to cities and towns across the US. Information: 800/231-2222; www.greyhound.com

---

BUS VERSUS TRAIN

All prices are based on prebooked one-way tickets. To ensure availability, bookings should be made at least 24 hours in advance. Some train journeys involve transfers; contact Amtrak for information.

ALBANY–HUDSON RIVER VALLEY
Train 2 hours 30 min. $59
Coach 2 hours 49 min. $43.50

HARTFORD
Train 2 hours 45 min. $33
Bus 2 hours 20 min. $29.50

BOSTON
Train Acela Express 3 hours 30 min. $101
Bus 4 hours 20 min. $35

PHILADELPHIA
Train 1 hour 30 min. $43
Bus 2 hours. $21

WASHINGTON, D.C.
Train 3 hours 15 min. $117
Bus 4 hours 20 min. $27

CHICAGO
Train 19 hours, reservations only. $126
Bus 17 hours 15 min, reservations only. $54

ATLANTA
Train 18 hours, reservations only. $186
Bus 18–22 hours. $54

The mileages given on the chart below represent recommended driving routes and are not the shortest distances between cities.

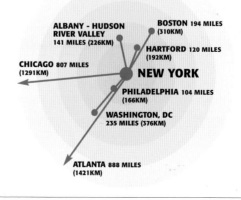

ALBANY - HUDSON RIVER VALLEY 141 MILES (226KM)

BOSTON 194 MILES (310KM)

HARTFORD 120 MILES (192KM)

CHICAGO 807 MILES (1291KM)

NEW YORK

PHILADELPHIA 104 MILES (166KM)

WASHINGTON, DC 235 MILES (376KM)

ATLANTA 888 MILES (1421KM)

VISITORS WITH A DISABILITY

Thanks to the Americans with Disabilities Act, New York City is a fairly accessible place for wheelchair users. Most streets are level with curbs, cut at corners. Buses have lifts for wheelchairs, and taxis are required to pick up those with folding wheelchairs or guide dogs.

ON THE MOVE

GETTING ABOUT

All three airports serving New York are wheelchair accessible and have restrooms for travelers with disabilities as well as TDD telephones in all terminals.

Most subway stations provide elevators and ramps, and there are tactile and audio features on ticket vending machines. If you use a wheelchair, alert the station clerk, who will collect your fare and buzz you through the entry gate near the turnstile; customers can enter the subway with a special Autogate MetroCard (▷ 43).

The MTA buses are equipped with wheelchair lifts that are at the rear of most vehicles and are operated by the bus driver. Once on board, the driver makes sure that the wheelchair is secure. The buses are also fitted with a device that lowers the front of the vehicle so that people with impaired mobility are able to board and alight safely.

The car rental companies Avis and Hertz have some hand-operated cars for rent (▷ 53). There are car rental desks at each airport.

Many theaters offer discounts to people with disabilities, and most cultural events are sign-language interpreted. Museums are accessible, but some old buildings have not yet been converted.

USEFUL CONTACTS

If you have accessibility concerns and require information on visiting sights, contact individual venues or any of the following:

Mayor's Office for People with Disabilities (tel 212/788-2830; www.nyc.gov/mopd) will send the free book *Access New York* to people who phone in a request. This large-type book provides resources and reviews.

Metropolitan Transit Authority (tel 718/596-8585, TTY 718/596-8273; 718/330-3322 for subway maps in Braille; 646/252-5252 for Access-a-Ride) provides information on New York's public transportation system.

Gray Line Air Shuttle (tel 212/445-0848) provides transportation between the three major airports and area hotels with 24-hour notice.

Travel Information Center for Hearing Impaired Visitors (tel TTY 718/596-8273) can help.

Society for Accessible Travel and Hospitality (SATH; tel 212/447-7284; www.sath.org) gives information on travel worldwide.

Big Apple Greeter (tel 212/669-8159, 212/669-3602, TDD 212/669-8273; www.bigapplegreeter.org) provides free tours of New York's neighborhoods with native New Yorkers. If you wish, you may ask for a volunteer guide with a disability. Reserve at least a week in advance.

Scoot Around (tel 888/441-7575; www.scootaround.com) provides wheelchairs and scooters for rental.

Hospital Audiences (tel 212/575-7676, 888/424-4685, TTY 212/575-7673; www.hospitalaudiences.org) arranges seats at theaters, concert halls and other venues.

Hands On Sign Interpreted Performances (tel 212/740-3087; www.handson.org) can tell you where you will find sign language interpreters at exhibitions, performances and film screenings citywide.

New York City Sports Commission (tel 877/NYC-SPORTS; www.nyc.gov/sports) gives information on accessible sports leagues and venues.

AT&T Relay Operator (tel voice 800/421-1220, TTY 800/662-1220; www.consumer.att.com/relay). Operators act as interpreter between a TTY user and a voice telephone user. The operator reads the TTY user's typed message back to the other party.

This section is divided into three parts: Sightseeing Areas, consisting of five areas (circled in blue on the map inside the front cover) highlighting what to see; A–Z of Sights, an alphabetical listing of places to visit in New York City, all located on the maps on pages 58–61; and Farther Afield, which describes attractions outside New York City (see map on pages 6–7).

The Sights

B

American Academy,
Columbia University,
The Cloisters,
Cathedral Church of St John the Divine,
Hispanic Society of America,
Riverside Church,
General Grant Nat Memorial

C

West 95th Street
West 94th Street
West 93rd Street
UPPER WEST
West 92nd Street
SIDE
West 91st Street
West 90th Street
West 89th Street
West 88th Street
West 87th Street
West 86th Street
86th Street
West 85th Street
West 84th Street
West 83rd Street
West 82nd Street
West 81st Street
West 80th Street
West 79th Street
79th Street
West 78th Street
West 77th Street
West 76th Street
West 75th Street
West 74th Street
Ansonia Building
West 73rd Street
West 72nd Street
72nd Street
West 71st Street
West 70th Street
West 69th Street
Freedom 69th Street
West 68th Street
West 67th Street
66th Street Lincoln Center
West 66th Street
Juilliard School
West 65th Street
West 64th Street
Lincoln Center
West 63rd Street
West 62nd Street
West 61st Street
West 60th Street
West 59th Street
West 58th Street
WEST 57TH STREET
West 56th Street
West 55th Street
West 54th Street
West 53rd Street
De Witt Clinton Park
West 52nd Street
West 51st Street
West 50th Street
West 49th Street
West 48th Street
West 47th Street
West 46th Street
West 45th Street

D

Cent
Par
Reser

86th S
CENTR
PARK

81st Street
Museum of Nat Hist

**American Museum
of Natural History**

79th street Trans
Cen
Turtle

**New-York
Historical Society**

San Remo
Apartments
The
Lake

The Dakota

72nd
Street
Strawberry
Fields

The
Sheep
Meadow

Tavern
on the
Green
65th

**Museum of
Biblical Art**

64th Street
63rd Street
61st Street

59th Street
Columbus
Circle
**COLUMBUS
CIRCLE**
Central

57th
Street

**Carr
Hall**

50th
Street
49th
Street

BROADWAY

Riverside Park
Hudson River
Riverside Park

HIGHWAY 9A

RIVERSIDE DRIVE

WEST END AVENUE

AMSTERDAM AVENUE

BROADWAY

COLUMBUS AVENUE

CENTRAL PARK WEST

12th Av
11th AVENUE
10TH AVENUE
9th Avenue
8th Avenue
7th Avenue

West 59th Street
West 48th Street

13
14
15
16
17

SIGHT LOCATOR

58

B

Intrepid
Sea, Air and Space
Museum
West 46th Street

C

D

60

Harlem,
Museo del Barrio,
seum of the City of New York,
dio Museum in Harlem,
omburg Center for
earch in Black Culture

E

F

G

Mill Pock
Park

East 95th Street
East 94th Street
East 93rd Street
Jewish Museum
East 92nd Street
East 91st Street

Cooper-Hewitt National
Design Museum
National Academy
of Design

East 90th Street
Guggenheim
Museum

East 88th Street
East 87th Street
86th
Street

Neue
Galerie

East 85th Street
East 84th Street
East 83rd Street
East 82nd Street

The Metropolitan
Museum of Art

East 81st Street
East 80th Street
East 79th Street
East 78th Street
East 77th Street
77th
Street
East 76th Street

Whitney Museum
of American Art

Conservatory
Water

East 75th Street
East 74th Street
East 73rd Street
East 72nd Street

Frick
Collection

East 71st
Street

Asia Society
and Museum

East 70th Street
East 69th Street
68th Street
Hunter College
East 68th Street
East 67th Street
East 66th Street
East 65th Street
East 64th Street

Ice
Rink

FIFTH AVENUE

Lexington Avenue
63rd Street

East 63rd Street
East 62nd Street
East 61st St

Mount Vernon Hotel
Museum and Garden

The
Pond

East 60th Street

5th
Avenue

59th
Street

HIGHWAY 25

QUEENSBORO
BRIDGE

East 59th Street
East 58th Street
WEST 57TH STREET EAST 57TH STREET
Trump
Tower

West 56th Street
West 55th Street

Museum of
Modern Art

Museum of
and Design
Paley Center
for Media

Seagram
Building

St Patrick's
Cathedral
Municipal
Art Society

Radio City
Music Hall

G E Building

Rockefeller
Center

DIAMOND
DISTRICT

MIDTOWN
MANHATTAN

United Nations
Headquarters

59

East Harlem area labels and street grid continue across map.

Gracie
Mansion

Carl
Schurz
Park

ROOSEVELT
ISLAND

Roosevelt
Island
Main
Street

13

14

15

16

17

FIFTH AVENUE
PARK AVENUE
Lexington Avenue
3rd Avenue
2nd Avenue
1st Avenue
York Avenue
FRANKLIN DELANO ROOSEVELT DRIVE

West 15th Street   East 15th St
UNION SQUARE
WEST 14TH STREET   EAST 14TH STREET
EAST 14TH STREET SERVICE DRIVE
14th Street Loop

West 13th Street   East 13th Street   EAST 13th Street

West 12th Street   East 12th Street   EAST 12th Street
Forbes Magazine
Galleries

West 11th Street   East 11th Street   EAST 11th Street
Grace Church
St Mark's-in-the-Bowery

West 10th Street   East 10th Street   EAST 10th Street
Jefferson
Market
Library

West 9th Street   East 9th Street   EAST 9th Street

8th Street   Wanamaker Place
EAST VILLAGE   EAST 8th Street
Tompkins Square Park

Washington Mews   Astor Pl   Saint Marks Place   EAST 8th Street

WASHINGTON SQ NORTH   Astor Place   East 7th Street   EAST 7th Street

Washington Square Park   East 6th Street   EAST 6th Street
Ukrainian
Museum

NOHO   East 5th Street   EAST 5th Street

WASHINGTON SQUARE SOUTH   West 4th Street   East 4th Street   EAST 4th Street
Merchant's
House Museum

West 3rd Street   East 3rd Street   EAST 3rd Street

Bleecker Street   East 2nd Street
House of Oldies
Rare Records   60   EAST 1st Street

2nd Avenue   EAST HOUSTON STREET

HOUSTON STREET   EAST HOUSTON STREET

Broadway-Lafayette Street
St Patrick's
Old Cathedral

New Museum of
Contemporary Art

SOHO
Little
Singer
Building

Haughwout
Building

LITTLE ITALY
Lower East Side
Tenement Museum   LOWER EAST SIDE   23
New York City Fire
Department Museum

Seward
Park

CANAL   Holland Tunnel

LOWER MANHATTAN
Museum of Chinese
in the Americas

CHINATOWN

TRIBECA   24

US
Courthouse

City Hall and
Civic Center

BROOKLYN BRIDGE
Avenue of the Finest
Mills Road

Woolworth
Building
Church of
St Peter   East River
25

St Paul's Chapel   BROOKLYN BRIDGE
World Trade
Center
Ground
Zero
BATTERY PARK CITY
American
Numismatic
Society
Federal
Reserve
Bank

Fulton Street
Market
South Street Seaport

Federal Hall
National
Memorial

Trinity
Church

Museum of American
Financial History   WALL ST
26

Rectory of
the Shrine
of Elizabeth
Ann Seton   New York City
Police Museum

Museum of
Jewish Heritage   Frraunces Tavern
Museum

Battery Park
E   F   G   61

Around Museum Mile

🚌 M1, M2, M3, M4
🚇 4, 5, 6

Several of New York's finest museums are on the stretch of Fifth Avenue going north from 79th Street—an area known as Museum Mile.

This chic part of town, once known as Millionaires' Row, is also called the Carnegie Hill Historic District. Running from 86th to 98th streets between Fifth and Lexington avenues, Carnegie Hill is home to a concentration of imposing mansions by some of New York's most prestigious architects. Today's museums are housed in what were the great mansions of wealthy industrialists, who turned their attentions to this part of town in the 1890s. Central Park runs along the western edge, and provided stunning views for the former residents.

THE SIGHTS

The Guggenheim Museum is a Frank Lloyd Wright masterpiece

MAIN SIGHTS
From 79th Street going north the main museums are the Metropolitan Museum of Art, the Guggenheim Museum and the Jewish Museum, but there are several others that are also worth a visit.

Metropolitan Museum of Art
The Great Hall of this enormous museum, the third-largest in the world, is one of the city's great public spaces. It costs nothing to walk in and spend a few minutes admiring it; the splendid collections could keep you awestruck for weeks (▷ 114–119).

Guggenheim Museum
To fully appreciate Frank Lloyd Wright's unsurpassable 1940s swirl, step inside, go to your right and look up. The fine collection and special exhibitions are ranged along a spiral walkway and are more than worthy of the setting (▷ 110–111).

Jewish Museum
This Loire Valley-style chateau, designed by Charles P. H. Gilbert, was completed in 1908 and was the home of financier Felix Warburg. Now it houses a museum of Jewish art and culture and offers an in-depth look into the lives of 19th- and 20th-century European and American Jewish communities (▷ 109).

OTHER PLACES OF INTEREST
Cooper-Hewitt National Design Museum
Completed in 1902 to a design by the architectural firm of Babb, Cook & Willard, this 64-room Georgian mansion was originally the home of industrialist Andrew Carnegie and his wife Louise until his death in 1919. Now owned by the Washington, D.C.-based Smithsonian Institution, the industrialist's splendid home displays a superb design collection assembled by the Cooper and Hewitt families (▷ 77).

National Academy of Design
This museum, also a school of fine art founded in 1826, owns a large collection of 19th- and 20th-century American art painted by its members (▷ 124).

Neue Galerie
Built in 1914 in the style of a place des Vosges mansion, and once the home of Mrs Cornelius Vanderbilt III, the top society hostess of her time, the

Go to the Great Hall of the Metropolitan Museum of Art to pick up information for your visit

residence was designed by Carrère & Hastings. Today it displays 20th-century German and Austrian works of art and design (▷ 124).

WHERE TO EAT
Sarabeth's
Delicious breakfasts and filling lunches (▷ 286).

TIP
● The Whitney Museum of American Art (▷ 148–151) and the Frick Collection (▷ 100) are not far south along Fifth Avenue.

Map labels:

Jewish Museum — East 92nd Street
Cooper-Hewitt National Design Museum — East 91st Street
East 90th Street
National Academy of Design
0 100 m
0 100 yds
Guggenheim Museum — East 88th Street
Central Park Reservoir — East 87th Street
East 86th Street — 86th Street
86th Street Transverse Road
Neue Galerie — East 85th Street
Central Park — East 84th Street
East 83rd Street
The Metropolitan Museum of Art — East 82nd Street
East 81st Street
East Drive
5th Avenue
Madison Avenue
PARK AVENUE
Lexington Avenue
E13 F13 F14 E14

Around St. Patrick's Cathedral

HOW TO GET THERE

🚌 M1, M2, M3, M4, M5, M6, M7

🚇 B, D, E, F, V

When St. Patrick's Cathedral was built in 1878, architect James Renwick, Jr. must have had a premonition of the skyscrapers to come. Everything in this tightly packed area of Midtown Manhattan reaches to the heavens.

Unlike Lower Manhattan, where the streets tend to have names, Midtown is all numbered streets and avenues, which makes navigating easier for the visitor. Get caught up in the fast pace of life and you can easily spend an entire day here as there is so much to see and do. Aside from the sights, this is one of New York's main shopping districts, with the flagship store of the venerated national chain Saks Fifth Avenue.

The double-spired, Roman Catholic St. Patrick's Cathedral

MAIN SIGHTS

St. Patrick's Cathedral is right in the middle of this area, encircled by entertainments at Rockefeller Center, the museums of Modern Art, of Arts and Design and the Paley Center for Media, and the stunning Seagram Building.

St. Patrick's Cathedral

The twin towers and ornate white spires, reaching to 330ft (100m), remain impressive and are still often photographed, though dwarfed now by taller neighbors. The windows and stonework are beautiful and the space impressive (▷ 131).

Museum of Modern Art

The city's premier collection of contemporary art recently doubled its size. Go to see the great Impressionist and Post-Impressionist art and to relax in the serene sculpture garden (▷ 125).

Seagram Building

The plaza of this bronze and glass giant, built in 1958, offers Midtown workers a place to soak up the sun over lunch (▷ 141).

Trump Tower

The ultimate in shopping malls and decadence, with its many pricey shops, waterfalls and acres of marble and brass (▷ 144).

Paley Center for Media

Access to nearly 100 years of TV and commercials through theaters, screening rooms and consoles. A good shop is the icing on the cake (▷ 126).

Rockefeller Center

This city within a city is home to entertainment, shopping, dining, an ice-skating rink in winter and NBC's "Today" show. Some of New York's finest public sculptures, murals and friezes are here (▷ 128–130).

OTHER PLACES OF INTEREST

Museum of Arts and Design

Huge exhibition of 20th-century crafts from America and around the world (▷ 123).

Saks Fifth Avenue

Flagship store (▷ 176).

Takashimaya

The New York branch of Japan's department store (▷ 176).

Trump Tower is about as ostentatious as it gets

WHERE TO EAT

Oceana

French-Asian cuisine and lots of wines by the glass (▷ 283).

'21' Club

A former speakeasy frequented by such figures as Humphrey Bogart and F. Scott Fitzgerald (▷ 289).

TIPS

● Shop at Saks Fifth Avenue, Thomas Pink or Cartier could liven up a visit.

● Try and catch a show at the Radio City Music Hall or at the TV studios.

THE SIGHTS

The Flatiron District, Union Square and Gramercy Park

HOW TO GET THERE
🚌 M1, M2, M3, M5, M6, M7
🚇 4, 5, 6 or N, Q, R, W

These three overlapping neighborhoods stretch east of Sixth Avenue (Avenue of the Americas) between 15th and 28th streets, south of Midtown Manhattan.

Each has managed to retain something of its historic charm. The Flatiron District has its early 20th-century classic skyscrapers around Madison Square Park, while Gramercy Park Historic District has leafy squares and fine old brownstones, and Union Square some of the first theaters. The area also provides some of New York's hottest restaurants (there's loads of choice) and hip, trendy shops like Emporio Armani and Diesel.

The Flatiron was built for the Fuller Construction Company

MAIN SIGHTS
The Flatiron District, Gramercy Park, Theodore Roosevelt Birthplace and Union Square form a cluster of sights centered on the Flatiron Building.

Flatiron Building and District
When Daniel Burnham's triangular, steel-framed skyscraper went up in the city's most prominent site on Madison Square in 1902, it was dubbed "the Flatiron" because it was shaped like an iron (then called a flat iron). Painters and photographers have made it into one of the city's enduring symbols (▷ 87).

Gramercy Park Historic District
Only residents around this lovely little park, or guests of the few hotels that front it, are allowed to enter the park; the gates are kept well locked. But you can see it well enough from the other side of the fence. Fine 1840s row houses line the west and south sides (▷ 101).

Theodore Roosevelt Birthplace
The house is not the actual birthplace of Teddy Roosevelt, the 26th president, but a 1923 reconstruction. It was built for the Women's Roosevelt Memorial Association. Roosevelt is the only native New Yorker to have become president (▷ 141).

Union Square
If you arrive at the Lincoln Statue in Union Square Park at 2pm on a Saturday, you can join a free walking tour of this neighborhood—a thriving theater, shopping, dining and entertainment area. If you go on Monday, Wednesday, Friday or Saturday you will find one of the best of the city's green markets—farmers' markets that inspire New York's ambitious chefs and delight New York food lovers (▷ 145).

OTHER PLACES OF INTEREST
Little Church Around the Corner
In 1870, when a minister of a nearby church refused to conduct an actor's funeral service, he suggested that mourners try "the little church around the corner" (▷ 109).

Metropolitan Life Insurance Tower
Designed in 1907 by Pierre Le Brun to be the world's tallest building, the Met Life skyscraper, at 700ft (214m), was soon

The National Arts Club in Gramercy Park Historic District

overshadowed by the Woolworth Building. A four-faced clock is its most prominent feature (▷ 120).

WHERE TO EAT
Eleven Madison Park
International menu and stylish interior (▷ 276).

Veritas
Plenty of wines to choose from, and a tasty menu (▷ 289).

TIP
● The Empire State Building (▷ 94–96) is only a few blocks north, at East 33rd Street and Fifth Avenue.

SoHo and Little Italy

HOW TO GET THERE

🚌 M1, M5, M6
🚇 4, 5, 6 or N, Q, R, W

In these adjacent neighborhoods, some of the best galleries display works by innovative contemporary artists from around the world, and there are also many historic landmarks.

SoHo, between Broadway and Sixth Avenue and West Houston and Canal streets, became of particular interest when mid-19th-century Italianate and French Second Empire cast-iron-fronted buildings were discovered. Its former manufacturing buildings are now apartments, and its artists' studios are still thriving, although today they're for wealthy artists only. Chic boutiques and restaurants ensure that the area is mobbed on weekends.

Little Italy, next door to SoHo to the east and bordered by East

Shopping for the unusual in SoHo's unique shops

Houston and Canal streets and Broadway to the Bowery, has at its heart Mulberry Street, once almost entirely inhabited by Italians, but now also home to a large Chinese community. Since the shrinking of Italian influence, trendy shops and restaurants have tended to move just north of Little Italy, to an area known as NoLita (North of Little Italy).

Even so, Little Italy still boasts a couple of *salumerias* (delicatessens) worth seeking out—Di Palo's, 206 Grand Street at Mott and the Italian Food Center at 186 Grand Street at Mulberry.

MAIN SIGHTS

Aside from the many galleries that dot the streets in SoHo, St. Patrick's Old Cathedral is an early 19th-century landmark.

St. Patrick's Old Cathedral

This Gothic-style landmark has a grand interior with cast-iron columns supporting a timber roof. Construction began in 1809 on what is now the oldest Roman Catholic church in the city. In 1866, after suffering severe fire damage, it was restored. In 1879, after a new cathedral was built on Fifth Avenue, this building was renamed St. Patrick's Old Cathedral and it was demoted to parish church status (▷ 131).

OTHER PLACES OF INTEREST
New York City Fire Museum
At 278 Spring Street in a Beaux Arts-style firehouse this collection shows how firefighting developed from the 18th to the 20th centuries (▷ 124).

Haughwout Building
This building, on the corner of Broadway and Broome Street, is a classic example of the restored cast-iron buildings in SoHo, completed in 1857 (▷ 242).

Little Italy still exists but is also home to a Chinese community

wood-fired ovens at this cozy storefront (▷ 284).

Nyonya
A favorite for Malaysian cuisine (▷ 283).

WHERE TO EAT

Bread
Soups and salads (▷ 273).

Peasant
Rustic Italian cuisine from

TIP

● Little Italy's Feast of San Gennaro in September is 10 days of colorful festivities. Vendors offer tempting foods.

The Financial District

HOW TO GET THERE

🚌 M9, M15

🚇 2, 3, 4, 5, 6 or J, M, Z

The oldest part of Manhattan, the Financial District grew from the 1800s into a global focus for trade and commerce.

It is packed with historic landmarks, grand neoclassical buildings and contemporary high-rise steel and glass skyscrapers, and it's one area no visitor should miss. Come on a weekday to appreciate its vitality and robust flavor.

MAIN SIGHTS

Wall Street has been synonymous with high finance since the days of Dutch governor Peter Stuyvesant, and here too are the Federal Hall National Monument and Museum of American Financial History. Trinity Church provides a peaceful sanctuary from all that money.

George Washington surveys the New York Stock Exchange

Wall Street

The skyscrapers lining this old, narrow street cast a shadowy gloom even on sunny days. But the passion for creating wealth that suffuses the offices overlooking this 'canyon' makes this little superhighway the city's most famous street. With many American flags waving overhead, it's a sight to see. The New York Stock Exchange is also on Wall Street (▷ 146–147).

Federal Hall National Monument

As you stroll along Wall Street, you can't miss the imposing bronze statue of the country's first president, George Washington, on the steps of the Federal Hall National Monument across the street from the New York Stock Exchange. On this site, Washington took the oath of office. Inside is an exquisite rotunda, among the finest Greek Revival rooms in the city. There are free exhibits, including the Bible on which Washington placed his right hand during the swearing-in (▷ 97).

Trinity Church

At the west end of Wall Street is Trinity Church. Do pause for a look at this 1846 landmark's beautifully carved front doors, white marble altar and wooden vault. At 280ft (85m), Trinity Church was Manhattan's tallest building from 1846 to 1890 (▷ 142–143).

Museum of American Financial History

The museum moved from its Broadway location to a new home, the previous base of the Bank of New York on Wall Street in January 2008. This Smithsonian affiliate displays some surprisingly interesting coins, documents and artifacts, and the interactive financial news terminals keep children amused (▷ 120).

OTHER PLACES OF INTEREST

Fraunces Tavern Museum

On this site in 1783 General George Washington bade farewell to his officers at the end of the American Revolution. Fires in the 19th century all but destroyed the original building; what was left of it was bought by the Sons of the Revolution in 1904, who renovated it in Colonial Revival style. The tavern is now a museum and restaurant (▷ 99).

Beautiful stained-glass windows adorn Trinity Church

New York City Police Museum

The New York Police Department is proud of its achievements. This museum offers a glimpse into the arrest records of famous criminals, a look at police weapons, and an introduction to forensic science (▷ 124).

WHERE TO EAT

Mark Joseph Steakhouse
A steakhouse for the power brokers (▷ 281).

TIP

● Century 21 is a designer discount heaven (▷ 177).

THE SIGHTS

Battery Park City Esplanade is popular with the city's joggers

Detailed carvings front the Cathedral of St. John the Divine

AMERICAN ACADEMY AND INSTITUTE OF ARTS AND LETTERS

Off map 58 C12 • Broadway at 155th Street 10032 ☎ 212/368-5900 🕐 Mon–Fri 9.30–5 🚇 M4, M5 🚊 1, C
www.artsandletters.org

One of America's first planned cultural centers, the Renaissance Revival complex,now known as the Audubon Terrace Historic District was the brainchild of Archer M. Huntington, the son of Collis P. Huntington, builder of the Central Pacific Railroad, who founded the Hispanic Society of America in 1904 (▷ 101). The American Academy of Arts and Letters gives grants and prizes to artists and holds two month-long special exhibitions of works by member artists, composers or authors (in April and mid-May to mid-June).

AMERICAN MUSEUM OF NATURAL HISTORY

See pages 68–72.

AMERICAN NUMISMATIC SOCIETY AT THE FEDERAL RESERVE BANK OF NEW YORK

61 F25 • 96 Fulton Street 10038 ☎ 212/571-4470 🕐 Mon–Fri 10–4 🚹 Free 🚇 M1, M6, M15 🚊 2, 3, 4, 5, A, C, J, M, Z
www.numismatics.org

This society "advances the study and appreciation of coins, medals and related objects of all cultures." Housed in the magnificent Florentine palazzo-style bank building, the society has a huge collection of coins, estimated at around 800,000 items, as well as maps and photographs. Exhibitions documenting the heritage of US coins and medals and the history of money are held nearby at The Federal Reserve Bank of New York, 33 Liberty Street.

ASIA SOCIETY AND MUSEUM

59 F15 • 725 Park Avenue at 70th Street 10021 ☎ 212/288-6400 🕐 Tue–Sun 11–6, Fri 11–9 🚹 Adult $10, under 16s and members free, Fri 6pm–9pm free for all 🚇 M1, M2, M3, M4, M30, M66 🚊 6 📷 ♿ 🚻
www.asiasociety.org

Founded by John D. Rockefeller III in 1956 to promote relations between America and Asian countries, the society mounts exhibitions, lectures, conferences, concerts and workshops. A $30-million renovation of the 1981 building completed in 2001 doubled the exhibition space. The collection is based on Rockefeller's donation of acquisitions from all over Asia, and ranges from 11th-century BC Chinese ceramics to Japanese prints and Cambodian sculptures to 19th-century objects.

BATTERY PARK

See page 73.

A 14th-century Nepalese sculpture on display in the Asia Society and Museum

BATTERY PARK CITY

61 E25 • Southwest tip of Manhattan 🚇 M20, M22 🚊 1, 2, 3, M1, M6, M9, M15, E, N, R
www.batteryparkcity.org

From Pier A to Chambers Street, the $4-billion, 92-acre (37 ha) Battery Park City development was created using the earth excavated in the 1970s during construction of the World Trade Center. It's a great place for a stroll along the waterfront, or for watching the boats on the Hudson River. Cesar Pelli's World Financial Center (1987) sits amid residential plazas, plazas and parks. The Gardens of Remembrance were planted here two months after 9/11.

BROOKLYN BRIDGE

See pages 74–75.

CARNEGIE HALL

See page 76.

CATHEDRAL CHURCH OF ST. JOHN THE DIVINE

Off map 58 C12 • 1047 Amsterdam Avenue at 112th Street 10025 ☎ 212/316-7540 🕐 Daily 7.30–6 🚹 Fee for tour 🚇 M3, M4, M7, M11 🚊 L1, B, C 📷 Tue–Sat 11, Sun 1; $5. Vertical tours by reservation Sat 12, 2 🚻
www.stjohndivine.org

Seat of the Episcopal Diocese of New York, the cathedral is the largest Gothic church in the world. Building began in 1892 and has stopped and started many times, as funds dried up; the end is still not in sight. Besides the dizzying scale and contrasting architectural styles, admire the Mortlake Tapestries, woven from a design by Raphael in 1623, and the Barberini tapestries. Chapels around the cathedral are dedicated to other world faiths; memorials pay tribute to victims of genocide and racism, and to those who died on 9/11.

American Museum of Natural History

36 million specimens, from dinosaur fossils to moon rock, and state-of-the-art exhibitions.

The main entrance to the museum on Central Park West

Biology and evolution of humans on Earth

Hanging around the Hall of Biodiversity

SEEING THE AMERICAN MUSEUM OF NATURAL HISTORY

There are three entrances to the museum: the main entrance on Central Park West, where you will see the impressive bronze statue of President Theodore Roosevelt on horseback; the Columbus Avenue entrance onto West 77th Street; and an entrance on West 81st Street into the Rose Center for Earth and Space, a planetarium with a narrated history of the universe. The museum has grown over the years and now has 40 grand exhibition halls, so you will have to decide what interests you most and save the rest for other visits. A good way to start a visit is to join one of the free Highlights Tours; you will hear about some of the museum's prized treasures and get orientation on the layout of the exhibits. Ask at the information desk inside the main entrance, where the tour begins. The tour guides are friendly, well informed, usually very entertaining and easy to spot: They hold up a yellow flag as they proceed through the museum. You can join in along the way.

HIGHLIGHTS

ROTUNDA

Inside the main entrance is the Rotunda, a city landmark, where colorful murals depict great accomplishments of Theodore Roosevelt, the first New Yorker to become president of the United States. The *Barosaurus* in the middle of the Rotunda is the tallest mounted dinosaur in the world at 50ft (15m). The real bones are stored elsewhere; the ones you see here are casts.

RATINGS	
Good for kids	●●●●
Historic interest	●●●●
Specialist shopping	●●●●
Value for money	●●●●

TIPS

● Go on a free Highlights Tour.
● On the first Friday of every month top jazz musicians entertain for free at 5.30 and 7.15. Tapas and drinks are available.
● Purchase a CityPass (▷ 317), good for nine days, to save money and avoid standing in line for tickets.
● The gift shop has a wide range of jewelry, pottery, metalwork and glasswork from all over the world.

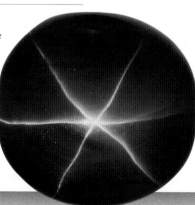

The 563-carat Star of India sapphire in the Hall of Gems (left); the Barosaurus in the Rotunda (far left)

The gorilla diorama (top); the Hall of Northwest Coast Indians

Totem poles dominate the Native American exhibition

The Hall of the Universe, on the lower level of the Rose Center

ROSE CENTER FOR EARTH AND SPACE
Hayden Sphere
Part of the four-story, $210-million Rose Center for Earth and Space, opened in 2000, which occupies a glass cube designed by James Polshek, the great Sphere contains the planetarium. Take a 30-minute virtual ride through the Milky Way and find out about distant planets and superclusters elucidated through the fascinating commentary and stellar special effects. The spiral Cosmic Pathway winds down around the course of the Sphere.

FIRST FLOOR
Dzanga-Sangha Rainforest (Hall of Biodiversity)
The full-size rainforest diorama, 90ft (27m) long, 26ft (8m) wide and 18ft (6m) high, re-creates a forest in the Central African Republic. Visitors can go behind the glass into a world where high-resolution imagery, video, sound and smell take you into a rainforest experience. On the forest floor, insects, reptiles and small mammals scuttle through the saplings, shrubs, herbs, ferns and leaf litter; a stream runs past, and in the distance you may get glimpses of elephants moving about, while birds and primates hang around in the tangle of overhead vines, branches and trunks.

Blue Whale (Hall of Ocean Life)
One of the museum's favorite exhibits, the 94ft (31m) model of a blue whale dominates the state-of-the-art Hall of Ocean Life. Video projection screens and interactive computer stations help you to understand marine environments across the world.

Discovery Room
Designed to interest children between the ages of 5 and 12, the Discovery Room has puzzles, games, scientific challenges and investigations to explore.

SECOND FLOOR
Elephant Diorama (Akeley Hall of African Mammals)
This venerable diorama, constructed in the 1930s, set the standard for natural history museum displays. The group of

A decorative mask

GALLERY GUIDE

KEY TO MAIN ROOMS

FOURTH FLOOR
1: Research library
2: Vertebrate origins
4: Advanced mammals
5: Primitive mammals
7: Ornithischian dinosaurs (*Stegosaurus* and *Triceratops*)
9: Saurischian dinosaurs (*Tyrannosaurus* and *Apatosaurus*)

THIRD FLOOR
1: Pacific peoples
2, 3: Plains and Woodlands Indians
4: Primates
5: North American birds
6: New York State mammals
7: New York City birds
8: African mammals
9: Reptiles and amphibians (including the world's largest lizard, the 10ft/3m Komodo dragon)
10: Hayden Planetarium Space Theater

SECOND FLOOR
1: South American peoples
2: Mexico and Central America
3: Birds of the world
4: Asian peoples
5: Asian mammals
6: Main entrance and Rotunda
7: Oceanic birds
8: Scales of the universe
9: Cosmic pathway
10: Big Bang
11: African mammals
13: African peoples

FIRST FLOOR
1: Ross Hall of Meteorites
2: Spitzer Hall of Human Origins
3: Discovery Room
4: New York state environment
5: North American forests
6: Hall of Biodiversity
7: Theodore Roosevelt Memorial Hall
8: Hall of Planet Earth
9: Cosmic pathway
10: Rose Gallery (space show boarding)
11: North American mammals
12: Hall of Ocean Life
14: Northwest Coast Indians
15: IMAX theater
19, 20: Gems and minerals (Star of India sapphire)

THE SIGHTS

BASICS

🏛 58 D14 • Central Park West at 79th Street 10024-5912

☎ 212/769-5100

🕐 Daily 10–5.45 (Rose Center open to 8.45 first Friday of the month). Space shows Sun–Tue, Fri–Sat 10.30–4.30, Wed 11–4.30, first Fri 10.30–7 every half hour (tickets can sell out, so buy in advance online or phone 212/769-5200)

💵 Museum and Rose Center suggested donation: adult $15, child $8.50. Admission and Space Show suggested donation: adult $22, child $13. Additional charge for IMAX and some special exhibitions

🚌 M7, M10, M11

🚇 B, C

🎧 Rose Center audiotours at desk near the Planetarium shop on the lower level, free. Hour-long guided Highlights Tour on the hour 10.15–3.15, free. Free thematic Spotlight Tours change each month

🍴 Museum Food Court on the lower level (daily 11–4.45); Starlight Café on the fourth floor (usually 10–5); Café on One on the first floor (daily 11–4.45); Tapas Bar on the lower level (Fri 5.30–8)

🏛 🛍

www.amnh.org
Comprehensive information to help you plan your visit, including a map of the area and tips on parking. There's a floor plan, a guide to current exhibitions, and the facility to book advance tickets.

The Rose Center glass cube is made up of 736 panes of glass

elephants is set amid vegetation typical of their natural habitat. Other dioramas in the hall show more of Africa's stunning wildlife.

THIRD FLOOR

Passenger pigeon (Hall of New York City Birds)
Two centuries ago, the passenger pigeon was one of the most abundant birds in North America. Now extinct, the bird's life is traced through vivid displays.

FOURTH FLOOR

Stegosaurus and *Triceratops* (Hall of Ornithischian Dinosaurs)
These two huge dinosaurs were vegetarians, protected from rapacious attacks by massive bony jaw plates. Begin with a visit to the Wallach Orientation Center for an overview of the six fossil halls. Did you know that the word dinosaur means "terrible lizard"?

Tyrannosaurus and *Apatosaurus* (Hall of Saurischian Dinosaurs)
You may feel very small when you enter the Hall of Saurischian Dinosaurs and meet the giants displayed here. *Tyrannosaurus rex* is an awesome sight, with the horrendous teeth of a meat-eater.

BACKGROUND

Increasing interest in natural history and the discovery of fossils, particularly of dinosaurs, across the United States provided the inspiration for this great museum, founded in 1869 by Albert S. Bickmore. Originally the museum was in the Arsenal building in Central Park. Construction on this site began in 1874, to plans conceived by Calvert Vaux and J. Wrey Mould. President Ulysses S. Grant laid the cornerstone, and President Rutherford B. Hayes formally opened the museum in 1877. Additions in many architectural styles have expanded the museum since. The Theodore Roosevelt Memorial Hall, finished in 1936, was designed by John Russell Pope. Roosevelt, a keen hunter and collector, donated specimens from his many expeditions, including a bat and the skull of a red squirrel. The museum also includes a research center with numerous laboratories, teaching and other facilities, and a library that has the largest collection of natural history books in the Western hemisphere. The collection of dinosaurs and other fossils is the largest in the world, and many of those on view are real, not cast reproductions.

Heading for the relative peace and quiet of Battery Park

BATTERY PARK

Spectacular views take in New York Bay to the south and the Financial District skyscrapers rising to the north.

These 21 acres (8.5ha), at the southern tip of Manhattan, are the site of Castle Clinton, a national monument, where you can buy tickets for the ferries to Liberty Island (▷ 136–137) and Ellis Island (▷ 90–93). The park's meandering paths are scattered with large, poignant memorials to more than 200 years of war dead. With its terrific view of the harbor, it is a pleasant place to get away from the busy, skyscraper-packed Financial District. Once a rocky ledge, Battery Park was created with landfill to protect the island from British attack in 1811, and it was named for the cannons that stood here.

CASTLE CLINTON

Castle Clinton was built between 1807 and 1809 for defense. In 1823 the U.S. government ceded it to the city, and it became a center for theatrical and musical entertainment, hosting such events as the triumphal 1850 appearance of the Swedish soprano Jenny Lind. From 1855 to 1890 almost 8 million newly landed immigrants passed through Castle Clinton, when it was the immigration processing center, recalled by the statue in front of the castle, *The Immigrants* by Luis Sanguino. In 1889 immigration processing moved to Ellis Island. From 1896 to 1911, Castle Clinton was home to New York's first aquarium, now at Coney Island. Dioramas in the small museum depict Castle Clinton's history.

THE HARBOR

At the south end of Battery Park is the terminal for the Staten Island Ferry. From here, looking out across the city's harbor, you have a magnificent view of the Statue of Liberty, Ellis Island, Governors Island, and the Verrazano Narrows Bridge with the Atlantic Ocean beyond. Just past Slip 6 is a sculpture by Marisol, the *American Merchant Mariners Memorial*, dedicated to all merchant mariners who have served the United States since the Revolutionary War. Throughout the park vendors sell everything from T-shirts to ice cream.

Artturo Di Modica's bronze bull—Financial District landmark since the 1980s

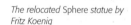

The relocated Sphere *statue by Fritz Koenig*

RATINGS	
Good for kids	●●●○
Historic interest	●●●●●
Photo stops	●●●●
Walkability	●●●●●

BASICS

✚ 344 E26 • Southwest tip of Manhattan on the Hudson River
🚌 M9, M15, M20, M22
🚇 1, 4, 5, N, R

TIP

● If you enter the park from Bowling Green subway station, you will pass the damaged 22-ton bronze *Sphere,* which once stood between the twin towers of the World Trade Center. It was recovered and placed temporarily in the park as a memorial to the victims of the 9/11 attack.

Brooklyn Bridge

**A walk across Brooklyn Bridge yields a memorable view of
Lower Manhattan and New York Harbor.
A symbol of true pioneering spirit.**

*The bridge has been described as the crowning glory of an age
memorable for great industrial achievements*

*The walkway is a good place to
enjoy the cityscape*

RATINGS	
Historic interest	●●●○
Photo stops	●●●●○

BASICS
✚ 61 G25 • From southern Manhattan over the East River to Brooklyn
🎫 Free
🚌 M9, M15, M103
🚇 2, 3, 4, 5, 6, N, R

TIP
● Walk across the bridge at dusk on a summer evening as the sun slowly sets behind Liberty Island and the city lights begin to twinkle.

This remarkable feat of 19th-century engineering, designed by John
Roebling and built between 1867 and 1883, was the world's first
steel suspension bridge. It spans a mile (1.6km) across the East
River, roughly between Cadman Plaza in Brooklyn and Park Row
in Manhattan.

CONSTRUCTION CASUALTIES

The construction of the bridge cost several lives, including that of the
chief engineer. While doing the final survey for the bridge, John
Roebling suffered a severe injury to his foot. He survived the
amputation of his toes, but died on July 22, 1869, of the resulting
tetanus infection. His son, Washington Roebling, an engineer with the
Union Army during the Civil War, took over as chief engineer. Working
underwater on the caissons one day in 1872, Washington surfaced
too quickly and was partially paralyzed by the resulting attack of the
bends, also known as decompression sickness. He carried on,
directing construction from his window in Brooklyn Heights with the
aid of a telescope, while his wife Emily marched back and forth
delivering his instructions to workers. Of the 600 laborers who
worked on this project, 20 lost their lives in construction accidents.

When the bridge opened in May 1883, the public marveled at the
Gothic-inspired span with its stone pylons and web of steel cables.
Roebling's understanding of aerodynamic stability was very advanced
for the time and he was the first to introduce radiating stays extending
from the tops of the towers to the lower end of the suspender cables.
It is estimated that 150,000 people walked across Brooklyn Bridge on
opening day—but not Roebling, who refused to come after a bitter
dispute with the company that financed the project. Disaster struck days
later. A woman stumbled and fell while walking across. As people tried
to see what was happening, there was much pushing and shoving.
It was Memorial Day, a national holiday commemorating American
servicemen killed in action, so there were great crowds on the bridge.
A rumor started that the bridge was about to collapse, and everyone
panicked and rushed toward land. Twelve people were trampled to
death and many were injured. On a cheerier note, in 1884 the great
circus entertainer P. T. Barnum led 21 elephants across the bridge,
which bore the weight without incident.

THE BRIDGE TODAY

As you walk along the wooden pedestrian walkway, you will come to a viewing spot where a bronze plaque gives information about the Roeblings. Take a look at the map etched in metal alloy, so that you know which skyscrapers loom ahead.

American poet Walt Whitman described the bridge and the views as the best medicine his soul had ever experienced. He might balk at the number of skyscrapers, and probably at the number of bicycle-riders, roller skaters and joggers racing across it today, but they have their own lane so pedestrians can stroll at their own pace and in safety.

The twin Gothic arches tower 277ft (84m) above the East River. The bridge was repainted in 1973, in its original beige and light brown. The walkway was reconstructed in 1983. In 2009, work starts to paint the bridge and strengthen the approaches at a cost of $725 million.

Jogging across the one-mile (1.6km) span of the bridge is a popular way to keep in shape

Many famous conductors have appeared on this great stage, conducting music by names like Gershwin and Stravinsky

CARNEGIE HALL

The outstanding acoustics of this world-famous concert hall attract the world's most gifted musicians.

This superb Italian-Renaissance-inspired concert hall took seven years to build, opening in 1891. With 2,804 seats and excellent acoustics, it remains one of New York's most highly prized music centers. The Rose Museum on the second floor (daily 11–4.30 and available to concert patrons in the evenings; free) has archival treasures relating to the history of the building and famous figures who have performed here.

EARLY HISTORY
Late 19th-century New York was an important place but it did not have a concert hall. When the steel magnate Andrew Carnegie heard this, he put up the $2 million needed to construct the building, on the condition that the city provide the land on which to build it: At that time New York was a stretch of vacant lots, coal yards and row houses. Chief architect William B. Tuthill was a gifted amateur cellist, so was determined to get the acoustics right. Tchaikovsky opened the hall, making his American conducting debut in 1891. In the years since, the world's greatest musicians, including Rachmaninoff, Horowitz, Stravinsky, Ravel and George Gershwin, have all performed here. The New York Philharmonic orchestra made this its home until moving to the Lincoln Center (▷ 112–113) on the Upper West Side in 1962.

The second building, added in 1894, housed famous musicians, architects, dancing classes and agencies. In 1894 the green mansard roof of the main building was removed to build the studio floor. There is a small recital hall within the original building and an elegant auditorium, which was a movie theater until 1997.

THE HALL TODAY
In the 1960s, Carnegie Hall was saved from demolition largely by violinist Isaac Stern. So it is for good reason that the main auditorium is named after him. The Weill Recital Hall features singers and chamber groups; Zankel Hall offers contemporary innovative programming. Between 1981 and 1990, Carnegie Hall underwent a $50-million renovation. The modern 60-story office tower next door, sensitively designed by Cesar Pelli, was built in 1990.

The distinctive red-brick exterior of Carnegie Hall

RATINGS

Good for kids	●●
Historic interest	●●●●
Value for money	●●●●

BASICS

✚ 58 D17 • 156 West 57th Street at Seventh Avenue 10019

☎ 212/247-7800

🎦 For performance schedule, check website or phone 212/903-9765

💷 Check website or phone 212/247-7800

🚶 One-hour tours Mon–Fri 11.30am, 2pm, 3pm, Sat 11.30, 12.30, Sun 12.30 when concert schedule permits

🚌 M6, M7, M10, M20, M30, M57

🚇 N, Q, R, W

🍴 🏛 👥

www.carnegiehall.org

The Civic Center dates from the 19th century

The Alma Mater statue, Columbia University

Painting by François-Xavier Fabre, Dahesh Museum of Art

CENTRAL PARK

See pages 78–83.

CHELSEA

🔳 60 D20 • Seventh to Eleventh avenues between 14th and 28th streets 🚇 M20 🚇 C, E 🍴 🛍 ♿

Galleries, studios and dance and media centers add the artsy edge to this now-stylish district. Before World War I the US movie industry developed in disused warehouses and theaters here before moving to California. The Kitchen, at 512 West 19th Street, has film, music and dance. Among the many galleries worth visiting are the Gagosian (555 West 24th Street, tel 212/741-1111) and Cheim & Read (547 West 25th Street, tel 212/242-7727). The Dia Center for the Arts (tel 212/989-5566; www.diacenter.org) has closed its Chelsea space pending a move to a new location. Meanwhile it stages exhibitions at the Hispanic Society of America (▷ 101) in Upper Manhattan.

West of the West Side Highway, a series of piers on the Hudson, known as Chelsea Piers, forms a sports and entertainment complex with ice skating, roller skating, swimming and restaurants.

CHINATOWN

See page 84.

CHRYSLER BUILDING

See page 85.

CITY HALL AND CIVIC CENTER

🔳 61 E25 • Broadway and Chambers Street 10007 ☎ 212/788-3000 🚇 M1, M6, M15 🚇 2, 3, 4, 6, N, R ♿ Tours by appointment, tel 212/639-9675

Built between 1802 and 1812 in the Federal style with French influence, City Hall is one of New York's most elegant buildings. The heart of the city's administration, it is where the City Council meets and where the mayor has his office. Tours are available on weekdays free of charge, only by reservation. The surrounding Civic Center area includes City Hall Park and Foley Square, several city, state and federal government offices and police headquarters, including the New York State Supreme Court, the U.S. Courthouse and the New York City Criminal Courts Building.

THE CLOISTERS

See page 86.

COLUMBIA UNIVERSITY

🔳 Off map 58 C12 • West 114th to 120th streets 10027 ☎ 212/854-1754 🚇 M4, M11, M60, M104 🍴 🛍 ♿ 🚻 ✉ Free guided tours weekdays www.columbia.edu

Founded as King's College in 1754 as a rival to the by then well-established Harvard and Yale, this was New York's first college and the fifth-oldest in the nation, and is among the Ivy League's wealthiest universities. Originally located in the schoolhouse of Trinity Church (▷ 142–143), the college has occupied several Manhattan locations. It moved to the current 36-acre (15ha) campus, originally the site of Bloomingdale's Insane Asylum, in 1897. The heart of the campus is the magnificent Low Library, inspired by the Pantheon in Rome; academic buildings are arranged around it. In 1934 the Low became the university's administrative center, and the library was moved.

COOPER-HEWITT NATIONAL DESIGN MUSEUM

🔳 59 E13 • 2 East 91st Street 10128-9990 ☎ 212/849-8400 🕐 Mon–Thu 10–5, Fri 10–9, Sat 10–6, Sun noon–6 🎟 Adult $15, under 12 free 🚇 M1, M2, M3, M4 🚇 4, 5, 6 🍴 🛍 🚻 www.si.edu/ndm

This elegant, 64-room, wood-paneled Georgian mansion, built from 1899 to 1902, was the home of the industrialist and philanthropist Andrew Carnegie. Designed by the architectural firm Babb, Cook & Willard, it was the first private residence in New York to have an Otis elevator, and also came with air-conditioning. Today it houses one of the largest design collections in the world, with more than 250,000 items. The collection, originally from the Cooper Union School for the Advancement of Science, was donated in 1967 to the Smithsonian, which moved it here. It includes a drawing by Michelangelo, furniture designs by Frank Lloyd Wright and industrial design drawings by Donald Deskey and Henry Dreyfuss.

DAHESH MUSEUM OF ART

www.daheshmuseum.org

Established in 1995, the Dahesh is the only museum in America dedicated to 19th- and 20th-century European academic art. Dr. Dahesh is in fact the Lebanese writer and philosopher Salim Achi; his collection of some 3,000 works of art was moved here from Beirut in 1975 to protect it from the civil war there. It includes paintings, sculptures, drawings, prints, photographs and books, ranging from landscapes to portraits, exotic Oriental themes and scenes of everyday life.

In 2007 the museum closed its Madison Avenue location and will acquire a new building for a permanent home. Through 2009 its works will be shown in several traveling exhibitions, both nationally and abroad. More than 200 works can also be seen online on the above website. Items from the popular museum shop, inspired by artworks in the collection, will also be available online.

THE SIGHTS

Central Park

New York's "great green lung," designed by Frederick Law Olmsted and Calvert Vaux in 1851. Enjoy 843 acres (340ha) of green space with woods, gardens, playing fields and a zoo. Great for birdwatching, cycling, rowing, ice skating, rollerblading, strolling or jogging along 58 miles (95km) of paths.

Softball games often take place on the Great Lawn

The city's 843 green acres are perfect for dog walking

Cyclists enjoy the park's car-free roads on the weekends

RATINGS

Good for kids	●●●●●
Historic interest	●●●
Photo stops	●●●●
Walkability	●●●●●

TIPS

- Don't stroll alone in deserted areas, and stay out of the park at night unless you are going to a play or concert. The park is now generally safe by day and after dark when there are crowds on hand. Police and park rangers patrol in vehicles, on skates and on horseback.
- Count on spending a half day or more here, depending on what you want to see.
- On the roads, watch out for bicycle traffic, and always look carefully when crossing.
- The park has 21 children's playgrounds. Many are state of the art and no two are alike.

SEEING CENTRAL PARK

Several entrances lead into Central Park from Central Park South (59th Street) at the southern edge and 110th Street at the northern. The most popular entrance is at Grand Army Plaza, at 59th Street and Fifth Avenue. From Fifth Avenue on the east side, you can enter at 66th, 72nd, 79th, 85th, 97th and 102nd streets. On the west side, from Central Park West, you can enter at 66th, 72nd, 81st, 86th, 96th and 100th streets. North of 96th Street, the park is more rugged and less suitable for visitors with disabilities. Because there are so many different access points, study the map before entering, read about the highlights, then decide on a route through the park. Many roads that cut through the park are closed to vehicular traffic on weekends in summer, which makes it perfect for joggers, bikers, rollerbladers and baby-strollers. There are bronze statues throughout the park, including monuments to Beethoven, Christopher Columbus, William Shakespeare and Mother Goose in the south end. At the entrance to the Delacorte Theater are lovely statues of Romeo and Juliet, and from Shakespeare's *The Tempest,* Prospero with his daughter, Miranda. Bring binoculars; especially in the Ramble or on the lake.

HIGHLIGHTS

SOUTH QUADRANT

The Pond is a lovely first impression of Central Park for visitors who come in at Grand Army Plaza. The gilded bronze statue of Civil War Union General William Tecumseh Sherman by sculptor Augustus Saint-Gaudens is one of the most distinguished equestrian groupings in Western art. Along Central Park South, drivers of horse-drawn carriages wait for passengers. Nearby, the wooded Hallett Nature Sanctuary juts into the Pond, which has an island inhabited by turtles and birds and a lovely waterfall.

The Wildlife Center fills 5.5 acres (2ha) just north of Grand Army Plaza. This state-of-the-art zoo (tel 212/439-6500; Apr–end Oct Mon–Fri 10–5, Sat–Sun 10–5.30; rest of year daily 10–4.30; adult $8, child (3–12) $3) is home to more than 130 species from three climate zones: monkeys, crocodiles and snakes in the Rain Forest, Asian and North American animals in the Temperate Territory, and polar bears, penguins and polar foxes in the Polar Circle. The sea lion pool in the central courtyard is very popular, especially at feeding times (daily 11, 2 and 4). Young children can feed goats, sheep and a cow in the Children's Zoo. There are also daily animal shows in the Acorn Theater. North of the zoo, the George Delacorte Clock plays a nursery rhyme every hour on the hour as miniature animals glide around the base playing musical instruments. There is a café.

Wollman Memorial Rink (tel 212/439-6900, www.wollmanskating-rink.com; Mon–Tue 10–2.30, Wed–Thu 10–10, Fri–Sat 10am–11pm, Sun 10–9; Mon–Thu adult $9.50, child $4.75, Fri–Sun $12, $5, respectively, skate rental $5) is filled with ice skaters in winter. With its classic New York views of the Midtown skyline and its terrace overlooking the rink, this is one of the park's gems. Lessons are available and there's a snack shop.

 The Dairy (tel 212/794-6564; Tue–Sun 10–5 year-round), a 19th-century building overlooking the Wollman Rink, has an exhibit about the history and design of the park. There's a 12ft (4m) model of the park.

Friedsam Memorial Carousel (tel 212/879-0244; May–Oct Mon–Fri 10–6, Sat–Sun 10–7; Nov–Apr Sat–Sun 10–dusk), in the middle of the park at 64th Street, is one of the largest carousels in the U.S., with 58 handcarved, painted horses. Every year about 250,000 people mount a steed for a magical ride.

Mature trees surround the lake in the Ramble

Dine at the Tavern on the Green, perhaps before the theater

Horse-drawn carriage rides are popular with visitors year round

BASICS

 58 D16–off map • Central Manhattan from 59th to 110th streets between Fifth and Eighth avenues

☎ 212/794-6564 or 800/201-7275

🕐 6am–1am

🚌 M1, M2, M3, M4 to Fifth Avenue (East Side) and M10 (West Side)

🚇 A, B, C, D, 1 to Columbus Circle (southwest corner)

ℹ Look for park lamp posts to find out where you are in relation to city streets. The first two digits on the lamp post are those of the nearest street. There are direct-line emergency phones throughout the park and a 24-hour Park Line (tel 212/570-4820) you can call from mobile phones.

🍴 The lavish Tavern on the Green ▷ 212/873-3200, reservations advised

🍽 The open-air Boathouse Café serves contemporary American cuisine from early spring to late October. Other cafés and food stalls throughout the park

📷 Guided Central Park Conservancy Walking Tours (tel 212/360-2726) and Central Park Bicycle Tours (tel 212/541-8759); horse-drawn hansom cabs (tel 212/736-0680)

🔲

www.centralparknyc.org
Excellent online tours include details of the park's highlights, maps and information on events and things to do.

There are plenty of places to stop for a snack or a drink

The park is a favorite with joggers (top); Bow Bridge (above)

MID-PARK QUADRANT

The Sheep Meadow is 15 acres (6ha) of grass where you can have a picnic, fly kites and sunbathe. Some 300 sprinkler heads now keep the grass green and lush. A flock of sheep grazed here until 1934; their sheepfold is now a restaurant, the Tavern on the Green. On the east side of the meadow is a patch of pavement where you can watch talented roller skaters practice their moves.

Bethesda Terrace, in Olmsted and Vaux's original design, was "the heart of the park." By the 1980s it had fallen into disrepair and was rebuilt. Stand on the Upper Terrace for a splendid view of the lake and the wooded area known as the Ramble. The fountain, *Angel of the Waters* (1870), was the work of sculptor Emma Stebbins.

Strawberry Fields was created in 1981 with funds provided by Yoko Ono, widow of musician John Lennon, after his murder in 1980 outside The Dakota (▷ 87), and named after his song *Strawberry Fields Forever*. Italian craftsmen made the black-and-white mosaic embedded in the path near the entrance at West 72nd Street, directly across the street from The Dakota apartment building where he was killed. It is centered around the word "imagine," recalling another of Lennon's most popular songs. Yoko Ono provides $1 million annually to the Central Park Conservancy for the upkeep of these 2.5 acres (1ha). Fans often stop to pay their respects and leave flowers or candles, and a huge crowd gathers every year on the singer's birthday (October 9) to sing, pray and celebrate his life and work.

Loeb Boathouse rents out rowboats and bicycles (mid-Apr to end Oct daily 9.30–5.30). Rowboats cost $10 for the first hour, $5 for each extra half hour; each boat takes up to five people. A $30 cash deposit is required. Renting a bicycle costs between $9 and $15 per hour, and you must leave a credit card, driver's license or a passport as a deposit. In June and August (weather permitting) another option is a gondola ride—not cheap at $30 per half hour, but memorable. A fast-food restaurant in the Boathouse offers cold drinks and snacks. The Boathouse Restaurant is a lovely spot, serving brunch and lunch year round, and dinner from April to November (reservations are a

Charles A Dana
Discovery Center

El Museo
del Barrio

Museum of the
City of New York

Jewish
Museum

Cooper-Hewitt
National Design
Museum

National
Academy
of Design

Guggenheim
Museum

Neue
Galerie

The Metropolitan
Museum of Art

American Museum
of Natural History

New-York
Historical Society

San Remo
Apartments

Ansonia
Building

The Dakota

Whitney Museum
of American Art

Frick
Collection

Asia Society
and Museum

Juilliard School

Lincoln
Center

Tavern on
the Green

Museum of
Biblical Art

Central Park
Reservoir

Central Park

CENTRAL PARK

UPPER WEST
SIDE

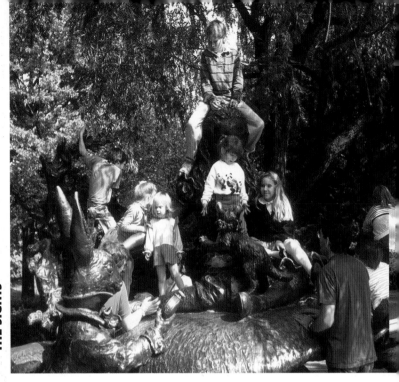

Children love to climb on the bronze Alice in Wonderland sculpture by Jose de Creeft, in Conservatory Water

must, tel 212/517-2233). Birdwatchers record their observations in the Bird Register, inside the Boathouse, and other visitors' sightings also make for interesting reading.

Conservatory Water is the park's famous pond. On Saturdays at 10am from spring through fall, the Model Yacht Club races its radio-powered craft. You can rent miniature boats. North of the pond is the delightful *Alice in Wonderland* sculpture and to the west is the Hans Christian Andersen sculpture; children climb up on it to sit on his lap, and there are story hours on summer Saturdays at 11am.

Belvedere Castle (tel 212/772-0210; Tue–Sun 10–5) was Olmsted and Vaux's folly, an open-air flight of fancy that served as an elaborate scenic lookout across the lake. But during an extensive restoration in the early 1980s windows and doors were put in and it is now the Henry Luce Nature Observatory. Here you will find interesting displays—telescopes, microscopes, skeletons, feathers—intended to help children understand how naturalists observe the world. The US Weather Bureau has been operating from here since 1919, and you can get up-to-the-minute weather reports on the second floor. Also on this floor is a tree loft with a wonderful collection of papier-mâché models of bird species found in the park.

The Delacorte Theater, built in 1962, is where Shakespeare in the Park performances delight large audiences in summer. Waiting in line for a free ticket is part of the experience. New Yorkers bring picnic baskets and books when they line up (starting around 10am) and make a day of it. The box office begins distributing tickets at 1pm. Tickets are also handed out at the Public Theater at 425 Lafayette Street on the day of the performance from 1 to 3pm.

RESERVOIR QUADRANT
The Jacqueline Kennedy Onassis Reservoir, named for the widow of President John F. Kennedy because of her fondness for the place and her contributions to the city, is noted for the 1.58-mile (2.55km) track around it. Joggers and walkers come here by the thousands every day. This 106-acre (43ha) body of water no longer supplies

Manhattanites with fresh water, but it still feeds the other ponds in the park. In spring glorious ornamental cherry trees blossom on the slopes.

NORTH QUADRANT

The Conservatory Garden is 6 acres (2.5ha) of formal gardens with lovely fountains in an area that has been landscaped in a more rustic, naturalistic style than the southern part of the park. If you enter from Fifth Avenue at East 104th Street, you will pass through giant Parisian wrought-iron gates from the mansion of Cornelius Vanderbilt II.

Harlem Meer, Dutch for "little sea," is a pretty pond, well stocked with about 50,000 fish. Catch-and-release fishing (Apr–end Oct Tue–Sun 11–5) is great entertainment for kids, big and small. Fishing rods can be rented at the Charles A. Dana Discovery Center.

SOUTH QUADRANT

The Arsenal (Mon–Fri 9–5), originally the New York State National Guard's munitions supply depot, was built between 1847 and 1851. Now a New York City Landmark, the Arsenal houses Olmsted and Vaux's original blueprint for Central Park, called the Greensward Plan. You can see it in a glass case on the third floor.

Looking across at the city from Bow Bridge in the Ramble

The park's waterways provide different ways to relax

The Chess and Checkers House is a magnet for children

Lasker Memorial Rink and Pool (skating; tel 917/492-3856; pool: Mon–Thu 10–3.45, Tue 8–10pm, Fri 10–10, Sat 1–10, Sun 12.30–4.30; adults $4.50, child (under 12) $2.25), built in the 1960s, is an ice-skating rink from November through March and a roller-skating rink for the rest of the year. Skate rental is available. Very popular in summer, the swimming pool opens on July 1 and closes after Labor Day.

BACKGROUND

In the 1850s, many New Yorkers felt that their growing city needed a park. A large central site was chosen, and a competition in 1858 attracted 33 entries. A farmer, Frederick Law Olmsted, and an architect, Calvert Vaux, won the $2,000 commission. Olmsted was appointed superintendent of Central Park. Jacob Wrey Mould took on the ornamental side and designed the bridges, the Belvedere and the terrace. Construction took 16 years and cost more than $14 million. Three thousand workers, mostly unemployed Irish immigrants, and 400 horses moved stone and earth and planted 500,000 trees, shrubs and vines. The park got its own police force to discourage lawlessness. In 1925, the first of 19 playgrounds, the Heckscher Playground at 61st Street and 7th Avenue, was constructed. Between 1913 and 1919, decay took its toll on some of the fine designs. By 1934 Vaux's Marble Bridge was beyond repair and had to be demolished. In 1934, when parks commissioner Robert Moses moved the sheep from Sheep Meadow to Brooklyn's Prospect Park, the sheepfold, designed by Mould, was turned into the restaurant that's now the Tavern on the Green. The addition of the Wollman Skating Rink came in 1951 and the Delacorte Theater in 1963. Many statues were added along the way. The 1970s brought another period of neglect and lawlessness and the park was for a while not a safe place to visit. But that changed after the Central Park Conservancy, headed by Elizabeth Barlow Rogers, took the initiative in the 1970s and 80s to clean up the park and raise funds to establish a safer and cleaner space. The Sheep Meadow, the first area to be restored by the conservancy, was reopened in 1981 and remains one of the safest, most pleasant areas of the park.

MID-PARK QUADRANT

The Dairy, a Gothic Revival cottage, was once a place where children could go for a glass of fresh milk. It now houses a visitors center (tel 212/794-6564; Tue–Sun 10–5) with video information terminals and a permanent exhibit on the history of the park. To the west of the Dairy is the octagonal Chess and Checkers (draughts) House, where you can test your skills at one of the 24 chess tables.

RESERVOIR QUADRANT

As you walk, or run, around the reservoir, note the three pedestrian wrought-iron bridges, called 24, 27 and 28. New Yorkers call Bridge 28 the Gothic Arch because of its lace-like quality.

NORTH QUADRANT

The Charles A. Dana Discovery Center, opened in 1993 on the northern shore of the Harlem Meer, is a visitor and community center with free educational exhibits relating to Central Park (tel 212/860-1370; Tue–Sun 10–5).

Signs are in Cantonese and English along the busy shopping streets

CHINATOWN

The largest Chinatown in the United States—colorful, noisy and exotic, with 300 restaurants.

Chinatown, northeast of City Hall and below Canal Street, has been home to generations of immigrants from China, Hong Kong, Taiwan, Korea, Vietnam and other Asian countries for more than 150 years. Now covering 3 square miles (8sq km), it has all but crowded out its neighbors, Little Italy and the Lower East Side. For cheap restaurants, bargain clothing, souvenirs, and exotic herbs and spices, no other Manhattan neighborhood compares.

The district occupied by today's densely populated Chinatown was dominated by the hog and cattle industry in the 17th and early 18th centuries; many streets were named for prominent local butchers (including Joshua Pell and John Mott). During the 1800s, the area was populated by Irish and German immigrants; some of New York's dirtiest and most crowded tenements were around the intersection of today's Mosco, Worth and Baxter streets, then known as the Five Points—the setting for Martin Scorsese's 2002 movie *Gangs of New York*. Chinese immigrants arrived in the late 1870s.

PLACES TO VISIT
Visit the Church of the Transfiguration, a Georgian church with Gothic windows at 25 Mott Street, built in 1801 by the English Lutheran Church and later the Zion Protestant Episcopal Church, and a Roman Catholic church in 1853. Columbus Park, created in 1897 at Mulberry Street and Baxter Street below Bayard Street, is popular among Chinese women, who bring their swords to practice tai chi in the morning, and senior citizens, who meet for Chinese chess or mah-jongg.

The Museum of Chinese in the Americas (▷ 123) is dedicated to the history and culture of the Chinese and their descendants in the Western world. The Kim Lau Chinese Memorial Arch, in Chatham Square, commemorates the Chinese-Americans who died in World War II. Facing the arch is a statue of imperial commissioner Lieutenant B. R. Kim Lau, who fought against the opium-smuggling that led to the Opium Wars. The 15ft (4.5m) statue of Confucius at Confucius Plaza on the Bowery has been a landmark since 1976. It was sculpted by Liu Shih, and a proverb inscribed on its base commends the virtues of a government that cares for the weak. The 1785 Edward Mooney House, at 18 Bowery, is the oldest townhouse in New York.

Street markets are an integral part of everyday life here

RATINGS	
Historic interest	● ● ○
Photo stops	● ● ○
Specialist shopping	● ● ●
Walkability	● ● ●

BASICS
✚ 61 F24 • Between Little Italy and the Lower East Side, bounded by Canal and Worth streets between Broadway and Bowery
🚌 M1, M6, M103
🚇 J, M, N, Q, R, W, Z, 6
🍴 Hundreds of restaurants
☕ Saint's Alp Teahouse, 20 Elizabeth Street 10013, tel 212/227-2880
ℹ️ Lower East Side Visitors' Center, 261 Broome Street between Orchard and Allen streets
🛍️ Dozens of souvenir shops; a few concentrate in the mini-mall at 15 Elizabeth Street

With its shining stainless-steel spire, the Chrysler Building is an icon

CHRYSLER BUILDING

New York's most stunning art deco skyscraper has a magnificent lobby with walls of African marble and steel.

The Chrysler Building's diamond-honed Enduro KA-2 steel is as incandescent today as it was in 1929. From the street, look up at the spire with its pattern of 30 radiating triangular windows. Note the 9ft (3m) pineapples on the spire and the mighty, gargoyle-like eagle heads at the corners of the building. Around the 30th floor, a brick frieze depicts hubcaps. Go inside to view the lobby's sumptuous walls of African marble and steel and the Parisian-style elevators. The elaborate ceiling was painted by Edward Trumbull.

Walter Chrysler, the third-biggest car manufacturer in America, spent $2 million of his own money to buy the skyscraper's site. Chrysler had been an automobile mechanic for most of his life and had very little formal education, but when it came to machines he was a genius. After saving General Motors a fortune with his new techniques, he moved to New York from Chicago at the age of 45. Already earning a million dollars a year, he produced his first line of Chryslers in January 1924. They appealed to the rich and were a symbol of wealth and luxury—they were the right product for the booming 1920s. For Chrysler, building a skyscraper more fantastic than anything anyone had ever seen was a challenge he could not resist.

THE TALLEST BUILDING IN THE WORLD
In late 1929, architect William Van Alen watched anxiously as the spire was raised above the 77-story structure to make it, at 1,048ft (320m), the world's tallest building, beating the Bank of the Manhattan Company Building at 40 Wall Street. It held the title for only a short time. Opened on May 1, 1931, the 1,250ft (381m) Empire State Building surpassed it. Securing an object at such a height had never been done before, and the job had been kept so secret that no reporters were around when it actually happened—probably on October 24, 1929, the day before the Wall Street Crash. The spire was as daring as it was ingenious and took the city by surprise. Many thought the building a crass bit of architectural advertising; today it is a symbol of an age when anything was possible.

In 1978, the Chrysler Building was designated a New York City Landmark. In 1997, Tishman Speyer Properties took it over and restored the art deco lobby. The lancet crown was first switched on in 1981.

The view from Lexington Avenue (above); the lobby (below)

RATINGS
Good for kids	●●
Historic interest	●●●●
Photo stops	●●●●●

BASICS
✚ 60 F18 • 405 Lexington Avenue at 42nd Street
☎ 212/682-3070
🕐 Mon–Fri 7am–6pm
🚌 M98, M101, M102, M103
🚇 4, 5, 6, 7, S

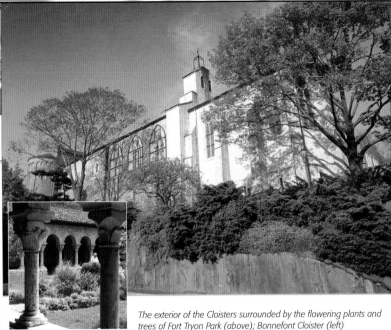

The exterior of the Cloisters surrounded by the flowering plants and trees of Fort Tryon Park (above); Bonnefont Cloister (left)

RATINGS

Historic interest	●●●●○
Photo stops	●●●●○
Specialist shopping	●●●○○
Walkability	●●●●○

BASICS

✚ Off map 58 C12 • Fort Tryon 10040
☎ 212/923-3700
🕐 Mar–end Oct Tue–Sun 9.30–5.15, rest of year Tue–Sun 9.30–4.45
💳 Adult $20, under 12 free. Ticket includes same-day admission to the Metropolitan Museum of Art
🚌 M4
Ⓐ A
🍴 The Trie Café on the lower level in the Trie Cloister; May–Oct Tue–Sun 10–4.15
🎧 Free guided tours Tue–Sun 3pm; audioguide adult $7, under 12 $5
📷 🚻
www.metmuseum.org

TIPS

● Take the subway ride if you are in a hurry. Get off at 190th Street and take the elevator to street level. Enter Fort Tryon Park and walk up the Promenade to the Cloisters.
● In summer there is a direct bus from the Metropolitan Museum of Art—more expensive than public transportation but quicker.

THE CLOISTERS

An outstanding collection of medieval art and architecture from Europe in idyllic Fort Tryon.

Perched high above the Hudson River, the Cloisters is in delightful Fort Tryon Park in Washington Heights, at the northern tip of Manhattan, with spectacular views across the river to the steep rock-faced cliffs known as the Palisades. The Cloisters opened in 1938 as a branch of the Metropolitan Museum of Art (▷ 114–119) and is devoted to the art and architecture of medieval Europe. The building, in the style of a fortified monastery, includes large sections transported from five 12th- to 15th-century cloisters in southern France and Spain.

The collection is based on medieval sculptures and segments of architecture acquired by American sculptor George Grey Barnard during trips to Europe, and includes 5,000 sculptures, tapestries, illuminated manuscripts, paintings, stained glass and other priceless objects. He brought them to New York and exhibited them in a brick building on Fort Washington Avenue. In 1925, John D. Rockefeller donated a large sum of money to the Met to purchase the Barnard collection. Then in 1930, Rockefeller gave his beautiful Fort Tryon estate to the Met, stipulating that the Cloisters be built to house a medieval collection.

HIGHLIGHTS

On the main floor is the Fuentidueña Chapel, whose 1160 apse comes from the Church of San Martín in Castile, Spain. The capital on the right side depicts Daniel in the Lions' Den, while the one on left shows the Adoration of the Magi. The Virgin and Child fresco in the semidome came from a small Catalan church in the Pyrenees. The Romanesque doorway in the nave of the chapel was carved in about 1175 in Tuscany. Also on this floor is the Saint-Guilhem Cloister, whose imposing covered walkway is from a Benedictine abbey near Montpellier, France. The columns have intricately carved capitals and date from the 12th to 13th centuries.

In the center of the main floor is the Cuxa Cloister, from a Benedictine monastery near Prades, France. The cloister was abandoned during the French Revolution and was later sold off in parts. Barnard managed to collect about half the original capitals, 25 bases and 12 columns. In the Nine Heroes Tapestries Room are some of the oldest surviving tapestries from a set dating from 1385.

Detail above the entrance of the Daily News Building

The Dakota Building was the city's first luxury apartment block

The distinctive triangular Flatiron Building was built in 1902

DAILY NEWS BUILDING

✚ 338 F18 • 220 East 42nd Street 10036 ⏰ Daily 9–5, lobby only 🚌 M42, M104 🚇 4, 5, 6, 7

Founder of the *Daily News*, James Patterson commissioned this modernist steel-and-concrete song of praise to popular journalism in 1925. It was one of the first skyscrapers in New York not built in Gothic style. On the ground floor, outside and in, abstract art deco ornamentation contrasts with the modernist strips on the upper facade. Inside, the lobby is still mostly original. Note the revolving globe, 12ft (3.5m) in diameter; the frieze representing the early days of the paper; and the clock that gives the time in 17 different time zones. The floor is laid out like a giant compass.

In 1995, the *Daily News* moved out and the building was renamed the News Building.

THE DAKOTA

✚ 58 D15 • 1 West 72nd Street 10023 🚌 M7, M10, M11 🚇 B, C

A vaguely Germanic Upper West Side landmark, this marble-floored, mahogany-paneled structure was the first luxury apartment block on Central Park.

Far beyond the city's bright lights or even the power supply, it seemed as far away from the city as the Dakotas when it opened; the name was a joke on its remoteness. It wasn't long before the city moved uptown, however. Prices soared, and the rich and famous moved in—among them musician Leonard Bernstein and actress Lauren Bacall. John Lennon was tragically shot dead on the sidewalk outside the door as he returned home one night, and his widow, Yoko Ono, still lives here.

No one can move into this building without the agreement of all the other inhabitants.

EAST HARLEM

✚ Off map 59 E12 • Fifth to First avenues, East 97th to East 125th streets 🚌 M15, M101, M102, M103 🚇 4, 5, 6

Above the Upper East Side is East Harlem, once known as Spanish Harlem and now as El Barrio (the neighborhood). Unlike Central Harlem, this area developed in the 1870s and 1880s. Its poor-quality working-class dwellings were home to immigrants—first the Irish and then, from the 1890s, Italians. As the Puerto Ricans moved on up the social and employment ladder, they began to move in and soon made the area their own. The city's Puerto Rican population numbered 45,000 by the 1930s and 600,000 by the 1960s; today more than a million Puerto Ricans live in New York, and Spanish is an unofficial second language. El Barrio has a vibrant Hispanic flavor, with family-owned stores and restaurants lining the avenues and a busy street scene.

EAST VILLAGE AND NOHO

See pages 88–89.

ELLIS ISLAND IMMIGRATION MUSEUM

See pages 90–93.

EL MUSEO DEL BARRIO

✚ Off map 59 E12 • 1230 Fifth Avenue 10029 between 104th and 105th streets ☎ 212/831-7272 ⏰ Wed–Sun 11–5 💷 Suggested donation: adult $6 (seniors free on Thu), under 12 free. Special exhibition rates apply 🚌 M1, M2, M3, M4 🚇 6 🏛 ♿
www.elmuseo.org

Growing out of a classroom display and opened in 1969, this is one of the few museums in the United States dedicated to Puerto Rican, Latin American and Caribbean culture and art.

There is a permanent display of hand-carved religious statuettes known as *santos de palo*, and another of artifacts from Caribbean cultures that welcomed Christopher Columbus to the New World.

Changing exhibits of Latin American and Caribbean art and crafts regularly eclipse the permanent displays. With its lectures and workshops, the museum is a cultural focal point.

EMPIRE STATE BUILDING

See pages 94–96.

FEDERAL HALL NATIONAL MONUMENT

See page 97.

FIFTH AVENUE

See page 98.

FLATIRON BUILDING AND DISTRICT

✚ 60 E20 • 175 Fifth Avenue at Broadway 10017 🚌 M2, M3, M5, M6 🚇 N, R

Squeezed into the angle where Broadway crosses Fifth Avenue, the Flatiron Building, at a mere 285ft (87m), never competed for New York's tallest-building status. Originally known as the Fuller Building, it was built to designs by architect Daniel Burnham in 1902. The unusual proportions and elaborate architecture have attracted the interest of photographers and the amazement of tourists for more than a century. Below 23rd Street, Fifth and Sixth avenues and Broadway were once the swankiest shopping district of New York, and this stretch of Sixth Avenue was called Ladies' Mile. Large department stores brought commercialism, a new style of architecture, and prestige to the area. Just northeast of the Flatiron Building is Madison Square Park.

East Village and NoHo

A funky area of vintage-clothing shops, ethnic diners, innovative restaurants and trendy clubs, with numerous historic sites.

The Joseph Papp Theater   *Hippy chic on St. Mark's Place*   *Music is a part of Village life*

RATINGS					
Historic interest	●	●	●	●	●
Photo stops	●	●	●	●	
Specialist shopping	●	●	●	●	
Walkability	●	●	●	●	●

Artists sell their wares along the sidewalk in the East Village

The East Village and NoHo (*North of Houston*) extend between 14th Street and Houston Street, between Broadway and Avenue B. Once farmland owned by Dutch governor Peter Stuyvesant, this area was home to Irish, German, Jewish, Ukrainian and Italian immigrants in the 1800s and 1900s. Today you can visit the Ukrainian Museum (▷ 144) to appreciate the culture of immigrants from the Ukraine.

New York's second-oldest church, St. Mark's-in-the-Bowery (▷ 131), on Second Avenue at 10th Street, is on land that was once part of the Stuyvesant farm; the old governor is buried in the churchyard. Poet W. H. Auden, who lived at 77 St. Mark's Place from 1953 to 1972, was a parishioner at the church.

In the 1830s the richest of the rich lived at 428–434 Lafayette Street, south of Astor Place, known as Colonnade Row. Among them were John Jacob Astor, some of the Vanderbilts, and the Delano family. Today only four of the original nine houses remain. Cooper Union, at 51 Astor Place, was founded by one of America's great engineering geniuses, Peter Cooper. Now a designated New York landmark, it was completed in 1859 and was where Abraham Lincoln made the antislavery speech that helped earn him the Republican Party's presidential nomination. In the 1870s, wealthy New York women attended services at Grace Church (▷ 99), by architect James Renwick, Jr., one of the finest examples of Gothic Revival architecture in the United States.

JEWS, RUSSIANS AND TURKS

At the beginning of the 20th century, Second Avenue between Houston Street and 14th Street became a center of Yiddish culture and came to be known as the Jewish Rialto. Edward G. Robinson and Walter Matthau got their start in the Yiddish theater here. Although the much-loved Second Avenue Deli has been driven out by rent rises, plaques in the sidewalk outside its old location at No. 156 honor Yiddish theater stars. The Christadora House, on the corner of 9th Street and Avenue B, was where George Gershwin gave his first public recital. On 10th Street, between First Avenue and Avenue A, the Russian and Turkish Baths (tel 212/674-9250) opened in 1892; unlike many similar establishments, it has survived to become a New York institution. Inside, the baths are not glamorous but poignantly evoke 19th-century New York.

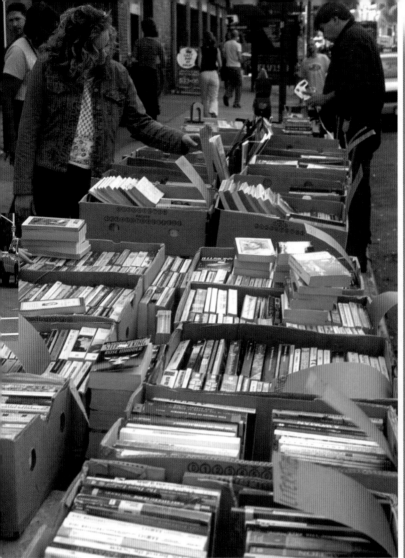

A BOHEMIAN DISTRICT

In the 1960s and 1970s, the East Village was a focal point of the American hippie culture. Anarchist Abbie Hoffman lived on St. Mark's Place and Allen Ginsberg, Timothy Leary, Andy Warhol and a motley collection of Hell's Angels, Hare Krishnas and political rebels frequented the area, often meeting for protest rallies and rock concerts in Tompkins Square Park. For years, until a 1990s restoration, the area attracted the homeless and drug-users. Today it is lovely by day, but still best avoided after dark.

The Joseph Papp Public Theater on Lafayette Street is one of the city's most famous off-Broadway theaters. Impresario Joseph Papp rescued the old Astor Library from demolition, and his theater opened in 1967 with the original production of the musical *Hair*.

The mix of ethnic restaurants in the East Village gives visitors a choice of great food at budget prices. For more stylish dining at higher prices, head for NoHo, the area around Lafayette and Broadway between Bleecker and 4th streets.

The farthest area east, known unofficially as Alphabet City because the streets are designated by letters not numbers, is less accessible by subway, so it's best to arrive and leave by taxi. The area has some chic shops and fashionable bistros.

BASICS

61 F22 • South of 14th Street, east of Bowery

M8, M15

4, 5, 6

TIPS

● Skip the area east of Avenue B—it's not really worth visiting and can be intimidating.
● Check local listings to find out what's on at theaters.
● Visit in late afternoon or early evening for a stroll and an inexpensive dinner.

Ellis Island Immigration Museum

A deeply moving memorial to the 12 million immigrants who arrived from distant lands between 1892 and 1924. Permanent exhibits include passports, clothing, baggage and family heirlooms donated by immigrants and their families.

BASICS

✚ Page 6 • Ellis Island, New York 10004 ☎ Information 212/363-3200, ferry 212/269-5755; audiotours, café and gift shop 212/344-0996

🕐 Daily 9.30–5, last outbound ferry departs 3.30. Extended hours in summer

💵 Museum free, including film. Ferry ticket: adult $11.50, child (4–12) $4.50. Audiotours $6

🚢 Buy tickets in Castle Clinton, Battery Park. Ferry runs approximately every 30 min daily 9–3.30, depending on season

🚌 M1, M6, M9, M15

🚇 1, 4, 5

🧭 Park Rangers periodically conduct tours; check schedules on arrival

🍽 Ellis Island Café serves burgers, pizza, sandwiches, soft drinks and beer and wine. Outdoor seating

📷

www.ellisisland.com
The museum's website, complete with practical details, island map and a virtual tour. It's a little confusing to navigate but packed with useful information and links.

www.ellisisland.org
Website of the family history facility (in the museum on the first floor), which has passenger records for immigrants arriving between 1892 and 1924. You can search these online.

SEEING ELLIS ISLAND

To reach Ellis Island, buy a ferry ticket at Castle Clinton in Battery Park (▷ 73). Boarding is on a first-come, first-served basis, so in spring and summer, catch the ferry early to avoid long lines. From Battery Park, take the Circle Line-Statue of Liberty ferry; en route you can stop at Liberty Island (▷ 136–137). Upon arrival at Ellis Island, walk under the glass-and-metal canopy from the ferry slip to the museum, an ornate Beaux Arts building with fanciful copper-domed turrets. The magnificent arched portals must have been both imposing and intimidating to the arriving immigrants. There are three floors with permanent and changing exhibits about the immigration process, the living conditions of the detainees, memorabilia and displays on the building itself and its restoration. Upon entering, collect your free ticket for the 30-minute film *Island of Hope, Island of Tears*. The audiotour is also well worth getting.

HIGHLIGHTS

FIRST FLOOR

The Peopling of America Exhibit, in the old railroad ticket office, provides statistical information on the history of immigration to the US from as early as the 17th century. Trace migration patterns since the 18th century on the 6ft (180cm) globe.

The American Family Immigration History Center helps anyone to research their ancestors using high-tech facilities. Visit the website at **www.ellisislandrecords.org**

SECOND FLOOR

The Registry Room is reached by climbing the stairs to the Great Hall, as every immigrant did, with doctors scrutinizing their walk for physical impairment. The voices of thousands of people speaking in many different languages filled this hall as inspectors and their interpreters questioned each adult and asked any child who looked old enough to give his or her name. The inspectors asked each immigrant up to 29 questions he or she had already answered on the ship's manifest. If the immigrants' answers did not match their previous answers, they were detained and questioned further. It was a harrowing experience for people who had traveled far, leaving family and possessions behind and enduring a long and difficult journey across the Atlantic. The railings that were here to keep the immigrants in orderly lines were removed in 1911 and replaced with benches. Today visitors pay tribute to the immigrants in this quiet space.

In 1916 the spectacular arched ceiling with Guastavino tiles and the red Ludowici tiled floor were added. During the 1980s restoration, only 17 of the 28,000 tiles needed replacing.

In the West Wing is an exhibit re-creating the step-by-step immigration process. In the East Wing, photographs and memorabilia explore the immigrants' hopes and expectations, fears and hardships. You can also listen to first-hand accounts of the process.

Study the moving portraits in Treasures from Home

THIRD FLOOR

Treasures from Home displays more than 1,000 objects, including clothing, jewelry, family heirlooms and photographs donated by immigrants and their descendants. There are touching reminders of the life each person left behind and of the bright future they were hoping to find. A wedding dress, a grandmother's bracelet, a child's teddy bear—all testify to the heartbreaking sacrifices made by people desperate to find freedom and hoping for prosperity.

IN THE GROUNDS

The American Immigrant Wall of Honor displays the names of over 500,000 immigrants whose descendants made donations to the Ellis Island Restoration Project. It serves as a memorial to all those who passed through here as they fled persecution and disease, poverty and hopelessness.

BACKGROUND

Dutch settlers named this 3-acre (1.2ha) island Oyster Island because of the abundance of oyster beds in the area. In the 1760s, after the execution of pirates on the island, it was known as Gibbet Island. It then came under the ownership of Samuel Ellis, and when the city of New York bought it after his death in 1807, it was renamed again. Expanded by landfill to 272 acres (110ha), it became home to Fort Gibson and housed munitions. The original wooden fort burned down in 1897.

IMMIGRATION

From 1892 Ellis Island replaced Castle Clinton as the inspection center for newly landed immigrants. The architectural firm Boring & Tilton designed its current Beaux Arts buildings. Until 1924, while the island was active, 70 percent of the immigrants to the US passed through the receiving facility; it served as a hospital, detention facility and transportation station. First- and second-class passengers were processed on board ship in more comfortable quarters, but steerage passengers were herded onto the island. Because it was assumed that these huddled masses came from countries with substandard hygiene, no one was allowed to

RATINGS	
Good for kids	●●●○
Historic interest	●●●●
Specialist shopping	●●●○
Value for money	●●●●●

TIP
● Allow at least three hours; the museum alone usually takes two to three hours. Add extra time to visit the gift shop if you are interested in immigration or genealogy.   ● Stop by the Information Booth to check the times of the daily free tours given by park rangers.

The Registry Room is where arriving immigrants would have their first taste of America

Immigrants arriving with all their worldly belongings

The Baggage Room is the first room you will see

The copper-domed turrets stand out from the water

MAKE A DAY OF IT

Your ferry ticket is also good for a visit to Liberty Island to see the Statue of Liberty (▷ 136–137). Since 9/11 the Statue of Liberty has been closed to the public, so call ahead. Even if you don't climb the 354 steps to the crown, you can walk around the island and see the statue up close.

sleep on a bed provided by Uncle Sam without first having a bath. Public Health Service doctors examined every person and if they detected signs of heart problems, mental problems or moral degradation, they would return the individual to their homeland. Eyes were examined for signs of trachoma, a highly contagious eye disease that led to blindness and even death; doctors, who came to be called "buttonhook men," used their fingers or a button-hook to turn eyelids inside out in search of redness caused by inflammation. Via translators, immigrants had to answer questions about their finances, their intended residence, and any waiting relatives. They had to prove they were strong, intelligent and able to find work. Fearful, many immigrants gave contradictory answers and corrupt immigration officers took advantage of many by accepting bribes when they gave a "wrong" answer. Inspectors questioned 400 to 500 individuals each day, spending only a few minutes with each. The bureaucracy was daunting, and Ellis Island became known as the Island of Tears, although most new arrivals received the landing card that allowed them to enter the US. Despite this, immigrants were often overcharged for their first train tickets in their new homeland so that many began their new lives in the poverty and squalor of New York City tenements.

AFTER WORLD WAR I

During World War I, the island came under US Army control and was used as a hospital. In 1924, after changes in legislation, prospective immigrants were checked in US consulates abroad and Ellis Island became a deportation center for illegal aliens. A new immigration building, a ferry house and a recreation building were added between 1934 and 1936 under the Public Works Administration. During World War II, the US Army used the island to detain enemy aliens. Between 1945 and 1954, the buildings were abandoned and deteriorated. In 1952, despite a proposal to convert the main building into a museum, it remained unused and was closed in 1954. In 1965, President Lyndon Baines Johnson designated the island part of the Statue of Liberty National Monument. In the 1980s, architects Beyer Blinder Belle led a massive restoration project. The museum opened in 1990.

The Circle Line-Statue of Liberty ferry passes Ellis Island

KEY TO MAIN ROOMS

THIRD FLOOR

17: Restoring a Landmark: photographs of the restoration
16: Silent Voices: large photographs of the abandoned building before restoration
15: Treasures from Home: immigrants' memorabilia
14: Ellis Island Chronicles: detailed models depicting the island's history 1897–1940
13: Dormitory Room: early 20th-century furnished room showing cramped conditions
12: Changing exhibits

SECOND FLOOR

11: Peak Immigration Years: photographs, memorabilia and recorded commentaries on immigration 1880–1924
10: Theater 2: shows *Island of Hope, Island of Tears* film, where immigrants tell their stories
9: Registry Room: the now empty great hall where immigrants were processed
8: Through America's Gate: 14 rooms with exhibits on the inspection process and the "Stairs of Separation"

FIRST FLOOR

7: Shop
6: Ellis Island Café
5: Theater 1: shows *Island of Hope, Island of Tears* film, where immigrants tell their stories
4: The Peopling of America: immigration patterns from 17th century to the present, and a Word Tree explaining the origins of words
3: Baggage Room: immigrants' suitcases and bags
2: Learning Center
1: American Family Immigration History Center

THE SIGHTS

WEST
EAST
MAIN ENTRANCE

Empire State Building

This New York City icon is the most famous skyscraper in the world. Millions of visitors a year go up to the 86th-floor Observation Deck for spectacular panoramas of the great metropolis.

BASICS

THE SIGHTS

✚ 60 E19 • 350 Fifth Avenue 10118
☎ 212/736-3100
🕐 Daily 8am–2am, last elevator ascends at 1.15am
🎫 Adult $18, child (12–17) $16, child (6–11) $12, under 5s free, military in uniform free. 102nd floor observatory $15 extra
🚌 M1, M2, M3, M4, M6, M7
🚇 6 to 33rd Street or B, D, F to 34th Street/Herald Square
🎧 Observatory audiotour $6, corresponds to signs on the Observation Deck so you know exactly what buildings you are seeing
🍴 🏛 🎦

www.esbnyc.com
Listen to an audiotour sample, take an online tour, buy tickets and shop online, get the lighting schedule and a list of special events, and information about the ESB in the news and in the movies.

TIPS

● To avoid waiting in line for tickets, buy them online, or in advance at the NYC & Company Visitor Center (tel 212/484-1200) at 810 Seventh Avenue between 52nd and 53rd streets.
● Come on a clear day and bring some quarters for the binoculars outside.
● The elevators carry only 16 people at a time, so be patient.
● Dusk is a popular time, so buy a ticket in advance if you can. Starry nights are magical and you can stay until closing time. There is no time limit on your visit.

SEEING THE EMPIRE STATE BUILDING

The main entrance is on Fifth Avenue. You pass through a security checkpoint similar to those at airports. There is no coat check (cloakroom), so you must carry your belongings. If you have not purchased a ticket in advance, take the escalator or elevator to the Concourse level and the Observatory ticket office. Signs indicate the waiting time and visibility. After buying your tickets, go back up the escalator to the main floor and follow the signs to the Observatory elevators on the second floor. Elevators let you out on the 80th floor, where staff direct you to the Tower elevator to the 86th floor. Viewing areas are indoors and outdoors.

HIGHLIGHTS

FIFTH AVENUE LOBBY

Interesting exhibits show off memorabilia from New York's museums, galleries and artists. The marble walls are stupendous and the metal relief sculpture of the building dazzling.

34TH-STREET LOBBY

Eight huge color panels by artists Roy Sparkia and Renee Nemerov depict the Seven Wonders of the Ancient World and the eighth wonder from the modern world. The tallest Wonder of the Ancient World is the 600ft (183m) Lighthouse of Pharos.

CONCOURSE LEVEL

In addition to the Observatory ticket office, there is a collection of photographs of famous people who have visited the Empire State Building, including Queen Elizabeth II and Fidel Castro.

SECOND FLOOR

Special exhibits about New York City and its museums, cultural institutions and tourist attractions are on this floor. NY SKYRIDE (tel 212/279-9777, www.skyride.com, daily 8am–10pm) gives a thrilling simulated tour of the city via the same simulator hardware that is used to train 747 commercial pilots.

86TH-FLOOR OBSERVATION DECK

On the outside deck you can get close-up views of the surrounding buildings and area using the high-powered binoculars. There is also an indoor, enclosed deck, which is useful if it's raining.

102ND FLOOR OBSERVATORY.

The highest observation deck on the 102nd floor reopened in November 2005. Separate admission tickets must be bought at the Observatory ticket office on the second floor, at an additional cost.

FLOODLIGHTS

Powerful floodlights illuminate the upper 30 floors between 9pm and midnight every night. Significant colors are used for special occasions —red, white and blue for Independence Day (July 4); green on St. Patrick's Day (Mar 17); red, black and green on Martin Luther King

Day (third Mon in Jun); yellow and white for Easter; lavender and white on Gay Pride Day (Jun). The stainless-steel window frames glimmer by day and night. In spring and fall during the bird migration season, the lights are turned off on foggy nights because the light shining through the fog confuses them.

THE TOWER

Broadcast cameras and microwave antennae on the east and west sides of the building monitor city traffic conditions for major TV and radio stations. The National Broadcasting Company (NBC) sent out the United States' first experimental transmission from the TV station here on December 22, 1931. Since 1965, FM radio has been transmitting from the tower, as has the New York Telephone Company.

The Empire State Building looks most dramatic at dusk (above); jostling for a good view on the 86th floor outside deck (inset left); the Fifth Avenue entrance lobby is dominated by the shining relief of the skyscraper (inset right)

STATISTICS

- The Empire State Building weighs 365,000 tons; took 7 million man-hours to build; and is made up of 60,000 tons of steel, 2.5 million ft (790,000m) of electrical wire, 10 million bricks, 62 miles (100km) of water pipes, 6,500 windows, 72 elevators, 7 miles (11km) of elevator shafts, 1,860 steps, and a foundation that extends 55ft (17m) below street level.

- The purchase price for the land, the site of the old Waldorf-Astoria Hotel, was $16 million; construction costs were $25 million. Construction time was an amazing 14 months. The building opened on May 1, 1931.

- With 102 stories, the Empire State Building stands 1,454ft (436m) tall. Eighty-six stories are usable office space. The Observation Tower is 16 stories.

- The TV antenna, installed in 1985, is 22 stories high.

- More than 3.8 million visitors ascend annually. The stupendous 360-degree view extends for around 80 miles (130km) on a clear day.

- The Fleet Empire State Building Run-Up Race, a New York Road Runners Club event, was first run in 1978 and is now held annually in February. Competitors run up 1,567 steps. The current record is 9 minutes 33 seconds.

BACKGROUND

In 1827, William B. Astor bought the farm where the Empire State Building now stands for $16,000 and erected the first Waldorf-Astoria hotel. In 1928 the hotel was sold for $20 million and demolished to make way for the present structure. Excavation began in 1930. The developer was General Motors' vice-president, John Jacob Raskob, who wanted to create the world's tallest structure as quickly as possible. As a result, designs to decorate the limestone facade and the chromium-steel windows were machine-stamped. Completed in 1931, and $5 million under budget, the Empire State Building replaced the Chrysler Building as the world's tallest building and held this title until surpassed by the World Trade Center in 1971. Since 9/11 it has again become the tallest building in New York City, but not the world.

The Depression and then World War II put an end to the city's prosperity and much of its office space stood vacant. The tallest building in the world was dubbed the Empty State Building. However, the Observation Deck was so popular that the income from admission charges paid the taxes on the building. In 1933 the thriller *King Kong* was released and the Empire State Building became a movie star for the first time. Concerns about the stability of the building were put to rest on July 28, 1945, when a U.S. Army B-25 bomber crashed into the 78th and 79th floors, killing 13 people and causing extensive damage.

Looking northeast toward the borough of the Bronx from the top of the Empire State Building

The present Federal Hall building dates from 1842

FEDERAL HALL NATIONAL MONUMENT

The site of the nation's first capitol, where the first president of the newly created United States, George Washington, took the oath of office.

As you approach the Federal Hall National Monument there's no escaping the massive bronze John Quincy Adams Ward statue of George Washington on the front steps. This Doric-columned, Greek Revival building resembles a simplified Parthenon, and looks a bit out of place among Wall Street's massive structures. Inside, the rotunda has 16 marble Corinthian columns, a domed ceiling and ornate bronze railings. One exhibit explores the Constitution. Another showcases the Bible used to administer the solemn oath to Washington.

A HISTORIC SITE
New York's first City Hall was built on this site in 1699 and petty offenders were flogged in front of the building. In 1789 it was reconstructed by Pierre Enfant, who later designed Washington, D.C., and the First Continental Congress met here to draft the Bill of Rights, guaranteeing the rights to freedom of worship, speech, press, assembly, keeping and bearing arms, trial by jury, and the right against unreasonable searches and seizures. April 30, 1789, the day Washington took the oath of office, was an occasion for massive celebrations. The building remained the nation's first capitol until 1790, when the "famed deal" between Thomas Jefferson and Alexander Hamilton moved the seat of government along the Potomac River.

Many other important historic events took place on this site. Newspaper publisher John Peter Zenger was imprisoned here for seditious libel in 1734; a brilliant defense by lawyer Alexander Hamilton secured him victory in court and was an important step towards freedom of the press (▷ 27). In 1765, the Stamp Act Congress assembled here to protest taxation without representation. In 1787, after the colonies won their independence, the First Continental Congress met here to establish procedures for the creation of new states. The state, war and treasury departments were established here, as was the Supreme Court. Customs stayed for 20 years before moving to Wall Street. The building became a National Historic Site on May 26, 1939, and a National Memorial to George Washington on August 11, 1955.

Doric temple on the outside and graceful rotunda on the inside

RATINGS	
Good for kids	● ● ●
Historic interest	● ● ● ● ●
Photo stops	● ● ● ●
Walkability	● ● ● ● ●

BASICS
✚ 61 E26 • 26 Wall Street 10005
☎ 212/826-6888
⏰ Mon–Fri 9–5
🎫 Free
🚇 M9
🚇 4, 5

Fifth Avenue—one of the most famous streets in the world

FIFTH AVENUE

One of New York's most fashionable avenues, with shopping, museums and a few landmark skyscrapers.

The Empire State Building was completed in 1931, on Fifth Avenue at 34th Street. From its 86th-floor Observation Deck all of Fifth Avenue stretches out below you. The avenue begins downtown in Washington Square Park. Nearby, at No. 47, the Salmagundi Club, in an elegant Italianate brownstone, is America's oldest club for artists, founded in 1871. At No. 62 are the Forbes Magazine Galleries (▷ 99). At 23rd Street is Manhattan's first skyscraper, the triangular Flatiron Building (▷ 87).

St. Patrick's Cathedral (▷ 131) is between 50th and 51st streets. At No. 645 is the Olympic Tower, the headquarters of the late Aristotle Onassis's empire, with shops, offices, apartments and a restaurant. These two landmarks are at the heart of a section famous for its luxury shopping, between 49th and 59th streets. Tiffany & Co., founded in 1837, is now at 57th Street. Along with Saks Fifth Avenue, between 50th and 51st, and Bergdorf Goodman, also at 57th Street, are the Disney Store and many other retailers. Beyond the Trump Tower (▷ 144), Central Park (▷ 78–83) spreads out on the west side.

MANSIONS AND MUSEUMS

In the 19th century, Fifth Avenue was the fashionable address for the very wealthy, such as coke-and-steel tycoon Henry Clay Frick, tobacco magnate James Duke and railroad baron Jay Gould, who built increasingly large mansions. Some of them were demolished in the 1920s to make way for luxury apartments, but many remain. The first one, at No. 998, built in 1912, was such a success that it became the model that hundreds copied in form and detail. The starched doormen are an indication of the wealth of the residents, who enjoy spectacular views of Central Park. Henry Clay Frick's mansion at 70th Street is now open to the public, displaying his outstanding collection of European art in a residential setting. Andrew Carnegie's 64-room home at 91st Street is now the Cooper-Hewitt National Design Museum (▷ 77). The Jewish Museum, at 92nd Street, occupies another fine old home. The stretch between 79th and 104th streets is also punctuated by museums and has become known as Museum Mile, with the Metropolitan Museum of Art (▷ 114–119), the Guggenheim Museum (▷ 110–111) and the Museum of the City of New York (▷ 123).

RATINGS

Historic interest	●●●●●
Photo stops	●●●●●
Specialist shopping	●●●●●
Walkability	●●●●●

BASICS

✚ 59 E16 • From Washington Square north to the Harlem River
🚌 M1, M2, M3, M4
🚇 4, 5, 6

TIP

● Be sure to catch a parade on Fifth. The St. Patrick's Day Parade on March 17 is the biggest, but there are others. Check the NYC & Company events calendar for details. Crowds are so thick on the sidewalks during parades that you will not be able to shop or sightsee.

The elegant facade of the Fraunces Tavern Museum

Ulysses S. Grant's tomb was completed in 1897

Gracie Mansion has a prime location by the East River

FORBES MAGAZINE GALLERIES

🞤 60 E21 • 60–62 Fifth Avenue 10011
☎ 212/206-5548 ⏰ Tue–Wed, Fri–Sat 10–4 💲 Free 🚌 M1, M2, M3, M6 🚇 1, 4, 5, 6, N, R, A, C, E, B, D ♿
www.forbesgalleries.com

Publishing magnate and adventurer Malcolm Forbes (1919–1990) had a passion for collecting, and the former home of the Macmillan publishing house, now the offices of *Forbes* magazine, includes a gallery that displays the result: old Monopoly games, model boats, whole battlefields with model soldiers, about 3,000 historical documents (including Abraham Lincoln's *Emancipation Proclamation*) and, among a display of objets d'art, a dozen of the fabled, bejewelled Easter eggs crafted for Russian czars by the house of Fabergé.
    Children enjoy the antique toy collection, the model boats and other watercraft.

FRAUNCES TAVERN MUSEUM

🞤 61 F26 • 54 Pearl Street 10004
☎ 212/425-1778; restaurant 212/968-1776 ⏰ Mon–Sat 12–5 💲 Adult $4, child (7–18) $3 🚌 M6, M15 🚇 4, 5 🍴 ⛪ ♿
www.frauncestavernmuseum.org

The 18th-century Queen's Head Tavern on this site, run by one Samuel Fraunces, was visited in 1783 by George Washington himself. Here, in the Long Room, now reproduced in the style of a dining room of the period, he met with fellow officers and gave his famous farewell address at the end of the American Revolution. The current structure is a 1907 reconstruction sponsored by the Sons of the Revolution and now, together with adjacent 19th-century buildings, contains a museum of

early American history and culture. Children can dress up in costume and try writing with quills. Separate from the museum is a restaurant busy all day serving all-American dishes to downtown workers.

FRICK COLLECTION

See page 100.

GENERAL GRANT NATIONAL MEMORIAL

🞤 Off map 58 C12 • Riverside Drive at West 122nd Street 10027 ☎ 212/666-1640 ⏰ Daily 9–5 🚌 M4, M5, M104 🚇 A, 1

Generally called Grant's Tomb, this may be the nation's largest and most impressive sepulcher. Rising dramatically 150ft (46m) next to the Hudson River, the squat, dome-topped granite building fronted by six Doric columns proclaims the importance of wildly popular Civil War general, and later president, Ulysses S. Grant (1822–1885).
    The design, chosen after a competition, was copied from the fourth-century BC tomb of Mausolus at Halicarnassus. Work began soon after Grant's death, with contributions from more than 90,000 people, many of them African-Americans, for whom Grant's achievements at the head of the Union army outweighed his less successful efforts as president.
    Inside the massive bronze doors, below the domed rotunda and set off by the gleaming white marble, two 9-ton polished black sarcophagi hold the remains of Grant and his wife, Julia.

GRACE CHURCH

🞤 60 F21 • 800 Broadway at 10th Street 10004 ☎ 212/254-2000 ⏰ Mon–Fri 10–4, Sun for services only 🚌 M1, M7 🚇 N, R, W, 6
www.gracechurchnyc.org

By the time James Renwick, Jr. began building churches, the Gothic Revival was in full swing. Renwick, like Richard Upjohn, who designed Trinity Church (▷ 142–143) on Lower Broadway, took up the style with enthusiasm. Grace Church, completed in 1846, was one result, another was St. Patrick's Cathedral (▷ 131), on Fifth Avenue at 50th Street.
    The church's original wood steeple was replaced by marble in 1888. It stands on the first bend of Broadway, so that it anchors the view up Broadway from downtown. The complex that surrounds the church includes Renwick's Grace House (1881) and the Rectory, and, on Fourth Avenue South, Renwick's Grace Memorial House.

GRACIE MANSION

🞤 59 G13 • East End Avenue at East 88th Street 10128 ☎ 311 or 212/639-9675 ⏰ Guided tour only–late Mar to mid-Nov Wed 10, 11, 1 and 2. Reservations required 💲 $7 🚌 M15, M31, M86 🚇 4, 5, 6

Nothing remains for long without modification in the city of permanent change, and Archibald Gracie's stately home is no exception. This fine example of Federal architecture has survived against the odds. A quiet country retreat overlooking the East River when it was built in 1799, it was enlarged in 1804. It was sold in 1823, when Gracie's shipping business went under. It then spent an ignominious period as a refreshment stand, before being bought by the city's Department of Parks in 1896 and converted into the Museum of the City of New York in 1924. In 1942, after renovation, it became the official residence of the mayor of New York, although Mayor Bloomberg declined to use it. Major restoration renewed it in 1985.

The Frick mansion was designed in 18th-century European style (above); Sir Thomas More (1527) by Hans Holbein (left)

FRICK COLLECTION

A striking collection of masterpieces tastefully displayed in Henry Clay Frick's luxurious mansion.

Henry Clay Frick (1849–1919) has gone down in history as a ruthless businessman, staunchly anti-union, obsessed with acquiring wealth—in other words, a master entrepreneur. Frick had his own successful business, the Frick Coke Company in Pittsburgh, when Andrew Carnegie made him his partner in the Carnegie Steel Company. Together they made the Carnegie steel empire one of the most important businesses in the country, and both men became multimillionaires. Frick's sole interest outside the world of steel and coke was art. He collected works painted by the world's masters from the 14th to the 19th centuries. At the age of 64 he had a palatial residence on Fifth Avenue built as his private home and gallery, to plans drawn up by Carrère & Hastings. Frick and his wife lived in the home until their deaths—his in 1919, hers in 1931. Frick, in an uncharacteristically generous move, bequeathed the house and paintings to the public.

After Frick's wife's death, the house was enlarged and became a museum in 1935. There is a reference library next door on East 71st Street, designed by John Russell Pope, the architect of the National Gallery in Washington, D.C. The house is set back from Fifth Avenue behind an elevated garden designed by Russell Page. As part of multimillion dollar improvements, the stone wall surrounding the site was replaced in 2002 and the wrought-iron fence was restored.

ARTISTIC HIGHLIGHTS

Through the 16 galleries, the paintings are not arranged by period or national origin, but in the way Frick would have had them displayed in his home. The Fragonard Room shows the large Fragonard paintings depicting *The Progress of Love* and contains 18th-century French furniture and porcelain. In the Living Room are paintings by Holbein, El Greco, Titian and Bellini. Through the Library, past Italian bronzes and Chinese vases, is the West Gallery, where there are landscapes by John Constable and portraits by Rembrandt and Velázquez. Especially delightful is the East Gallery, with works by Degas, Goya, Turner, Van Dyck and Whistler. After your visit, pause in the peaceful Garden Court (the enclosed Palm Court is the perfect oasis on a cold New York day), which occasionally hosts special exhibitions.

RATINGS

Historic interest	●●●●●
Value for money	●●●●●
Walkability	●●●●●

BASICS

➕ 58 E15 • 1 East 70th Street at Fifth Avenue 10021

☎ 212/288-0700

🕐 Tue–Sun 10–6; closed Mon; limited hours, 1–6, on Presidents' Day, Election Day and Veterans' Day

💵 Adult $15, no children under 10. Sun pay what you wish 11–1; ArtPhone audio guide free

🚌 M1, M2, M3, M4

🚇 4, 5, 6

🏬 Books, cards, CDs, videos and museum-inspired gifts

👬

www.frick.org

TIP

● Try to come for a chamber music concert (year round on occasional Sundays at 5pm). Check website for details.

The National Arts Club in Gramercy Park

Harlem's most famous club, now on 125th Street

A veteran aircraft in the Intrepid Sea, Air and Space Museum

THE SIGHTS

GRAMERCY PARK HISTORIC DISTRICT

⊞ 60 F20–F21 • Between Park Avenue South and Third Avenue from 18th to 21st streets 🚌 M1, M2, M3, M6, M7 🚇 N, Q, R, 6

Copied from elegant London squares by the developer Samuel Ruggles in 1831, Gramercy Park is the only private park in New York City and is still surrounded by the original high iron railings. The elegant area, full of attractive buildings, has long been favored by well-to-do citizens. At No. 16 Gramercy Park South the actor Edwin Booth, brother of Lincoln's assassin, lived in a superb brownstone. Booth's statue is inside the park. At No. 15, Samuel Tilden, Governor of New York from 1875 to 1877, installed steel doors and a tunnel to 19th Street in fear of the mob.

GRAND CENTRAL TERMINAL

See pages 102–104.

GREENWICH VILLAGE

See pages 105–107.

GROUND ZERO

See page 108.

GUGGENHEIM MUSEUM

See pages 110–111.

HARLEM

⊞ Page 7 • Fifth Avenue to Morningside Avenue north of 110th Street 🚌 M2, M3, M7, M10, M102 🚇 2, 3, A, B, C, D 🏛 Harlem Tourist Center and Gift Shop, 2224 Frederick Douglass Boulevard

Harlem is forever linked with the speakeasies and jazz of the Prohibition era. Today the bleak landscape that saw the departure of middle-class families in the 1960s has given way to housing renovation and a growing, upbeat population. There is much of

architectural interest, but many are attracted by the nightlife, jazz clubs and cultural attractions, including Manhattan's oldest residence, the Morris-Jumel Mansion Museum (65 Jumel Terrace, tel 212/923-8008, Wed–Sun 10–4, adult $4), and the Schomburg Center (▷ 131). After completing his second term as president, Bill Clinton opened an office in Harlem.

HISPANIC SOCIETY OF AMERICA

⊞ Off map 58 C12 • 613 West 155th Street at Broadway 10032 ☎ 212/926-2234 🕐 Tue–Sat 10–4.30, Sun 1–4 🎫 Free 🚌 M4, M5 🚇 1 ♿
www.hispanicsociety.org

This museum, described as one of the best-kept secrets of New York, is well worth the half-hour subway ride from Times Square. Audubon Terrace was the brainchild of philanthropist and Spanish scholar Archer Huntington. He founded the Hispanic Society in 1904 and commissioned his cousin to design the buildings. A little jewel devoted to the arts and culture of Iberia, the museum is a lavishly appointed showcase of all things Spanish, from Paleolithic tools to the masterpieces of Velázquez and Goya. It currently stages exhibitions with the Dia Center for the Arts.

INTERNATIONAL CENTER OF PHOTOGRAPHY

⊞ 60 E18 • 1133 Avenue of the Americas at 43rd Street 10036 ☎ 212/857-0000 🕐 Tue–Thu 10–6, Fri 10–8, Sat–Sun 10–6 🎫 Adult $12 🚌 M5, M6, M7 🚇 B, D, F, V ♿
www.icp.org

In the heart of Midtown Manhattan, the ICP is both a school and a museum. Temporary exhibitions are always on view, and the permanent

collection has 60,000 photographs ranging from old daguerreotypes to iris prints, mainly from American and European reportage and documentation from the 1930s to the present. There are photographs by such well-known names as Henri Cartier-Bresson, Elliott Erwitt and Harold Edgerton, along with an impressive collection of 13,000 original prints by Weegee, who photographed crime scenes and New York nightlife in the 1930s and 1940s.

INTREPID SEA, AIR AND SPACE MUSEUM

⊞ 58 B18 • Hudson River Pier 86, west end of 46th Street 10036 ☎ 212/245-0072 🕐 Closed until fall 2008. Call for details of opening 🎫 Adult $16.50, child (6–17) $11.50, child (2–5) $4.50, under 2/those on active duty with ID free 🚌 M16, M42, M50 🚇 A, C, E 🎫 Free tours
www.intrepidmuseum.org

The veteran aircraft carrier *Intrepid*, built in 1943 at a cost of $44 million, makes a fascinating museum. It is 898ft (275m) long, weighs 42,000 tons, and had a crew of 3,500. The Hangar Deck is divided into four exhibits: Pearl Harbor and World War II, Life Aboard an Aircraft Carrier, the Story of *Intrepid*, and Space Exploration, Satellite Communication and Weaponry. On the Flight Deck you can inspect aircraft apparently ready for take-off, including a Lockheed A-12 Blackbird, a Russian MIG and a Cobra helicopter. You can also tour the destroyer *Edson* and the submarine *Growler;* take a seven-minute SR-2 flight simulator ride; and rent a two-hour audiotour, during which veterans tell how they survived kamikaze attacks. The complex reopens on Veteran's Day (November 11) 2008 after renovation.

Grand Central Terminal

New York's most magnificent public space and one of the city's finest landmarks. Full of sophisticated shops and interesting places for a quick bite. Every day, trains running on 48 pairs of railroad tracks bring in half a million commuters from the northern suburbs.

Thousands of commuters use the station every day

The brass four-faced clock tells the time from all angles

Passengers make a beeline for the central information booth

SEEING GRAND CENTRAL TERMINAL

Enter Grand Central on 42nd Street at Park Avenue in order to experience the full impact and grandeur of the main concourse. As you enter, the feeling of space, sophistication and city bustle creates an awesome introduction to Manhattan. The careful $200-million renovation project that has restored its grandeur fills even cynical New Yorkers with civic pride. Notice the 75ft (29m) windows, the Tennessee marble floor, the brass clock over the central kiosk, and the gold-and-nickel chandeliers. Stroll around the arcades leading to Lexington Avenue and the lower level where you'll find restaurants and shops, including The Children's General Store, The Discovery Channel Store, Banana Republic and Godiva Chocolatier. Off the main concourse is the Grand Central Market, packed with fresh produce. The New York Transit Museum Annex & Store is worth visiting if you've got time. A maze of underground walkways links the terminal to surrounding streets; you can stay underground as far north as 48th and Park streets.

HIGHLIGHTS

THE MAIN CONCOURSE CEILING

With 59 electric stars replicating the zodiac constellations, in reverse, the design is based on an illustration from a medieval manuscript. It is not known whether the ceiling's French creator, Paul Helleu, was aware that depicting the heavens in reverse, or from God's point of view, was a common practice of medieval illustrators. The main concourse itself is 375ft long (114m) and 120ft wide (36m).

JULES ALEXIS COUTAN'S SCULPTURE

Mercury, the Roman god of travel and commerce, is the central figure of this 1935 sculpture over the south entrance. He is supported by Minerva and Hercules, representing mental and physical strength.

GRAND CENTRAL OYSTER BAR AND RESTAURANT

This restaurant, with its low-vaulted ceiling, is worth seeing. The tiles are by Guastavino. Order a bowl of clam chowder—either Manhattan (tomato-based) or New England (cream-based) style (▷ 278).

RATINGS

Good for food	●●●●●
Historic interest	●●●●
Photo stops	●●●●
Specialist shopping	●●●●

BASICS

⊞ 60 E18 • East 42nd Street at Park Avenue 10017

☎ 212/532-4900; for travel information 718/330-1234, or tours 212/340-2345

🕐 Daily 5.30am–1.30am

🎫 Free

🚌 M1, M2, M3, M4, M101, M102

🚇 4, 5, 6, 7, S

🎧 Excellent free tour by the Municipal Arts Society on Wed at 12.30. Meet at the information desk, under the clock, in the main concourse

🍴 Grand Central Oyster Bar & Restaurant on the lower level; Mon–Sat, tel 212/490-6650, www.oysterbarny.com. Michael Jordan's The Steak House N.Y.C. serves just that; tel 212/655-2300, www. theglazier-group.com. Métrazur serves Charlie Palmer's progressive American cuisine along with seafood and pasta; tel 212/687-4600, www.metrazur.com.

🏬 50 specialist shops on the mezzanine and lower levels

www.grandcentralterminal.com
Phone numbers for stores and shops, information about tours, menus and prices for all the restaurants, travel information and information on events.

Make time for a shoeshine (above); the famous Oyster Bar and Restaurant (above right)

TIPS

- Take one of the free area tours sponsored by Grand Central Partnership (GCP), one of the largest business improvement districts, every Friday at 12.30, rain or shine. Meet inside the Whitney Museum Annex at the Philip Morris Building at 42nd Street and Park Avenue.
- For lunch in New York, the food concourse on the lower level is fun, with its many interesting options from Cajun pizza to Vietnamese sandwiches. But go early—after 12.30 it's next to impossible to find a seat.
- Don't rush, take your time to enjoy the shopping, restaurants and most of all the architecture. This is not just a train station, it's a New York experience.
- When you leave the building, walk a couple of blocks south to 40th Street, then turn around and look back at Coutan's neoclassical sculpture over the south entrance.

THE CAMPBELL APARTMENT

This elegant (if pricey) cocktail bar was built by John Campbell as an office and pied-à-terre in the 1920s in the style of a 13th-century Florentine palazzo, with its stained-glass windows by Louis Comfort Tiffany and elegant dark paneling. Follow signs to the small staircase across from Michael Jordan's The Steak House off the west balcony.

NEW YORK TRANSIT MUSEUM GALLERY & STORE

Changing exhibits on the history, impact and future of public transportation (tel 212/878-0106, http://mta.info/mta/museum).

SPECIAL EVENTS

Exhibitions, food tastings, treasure hunts and concerts take place regularly. The Christmas Market in Vanderbilt Halt showcases the work of dozens of innovative regional craftspeople and retailers.

BACKGROUND

New York Central Railroad magnate Cornelius Vanderbilt ordered the construction of Grand Central Terminal. Built between 1903 and 1913, it replaced the 42nd Street Terminal, an iron and glass train shed dating from 1871. At the turn of the 20th century, this area was the northern edge of the city, but as the new station flourished, stores, hotels, restaurants and offices grew up around it. By the 1920s it had become a fine boulevard graced with luxury apartment buildings.

Grand Central is an outstanding example of Beaux Arts design, with triumphal arches filled with glass and steel, a grand waiting room, sumptuous concourse, superb vaulted ceiling and imposing sculptures of Roman deities. The innovative design, by engineer William Wilgus and architects Reed & Stem, included extensive tunnels, a ramp system instead of stairs to keep people moving, and upper and lower level concourses. Architect Whitney Warren, a Vanderbilt cousin, was responsible for the outstanding facades and interior. The public was delighted with this marvel, but by the 1970s, the station had acquired layers of grime and was not a place to linger. The steel was rusty, the asbestos was falling out and the stairways stank: It had become a symbol of decay.

A NEW LEASE OF LIFE

In 1978, a New York City developer proposed building a 55-story office tower on top of the station, obliterating the facade. After a series of legal challenges, a US Supreme Court decision sided with the New York City Landmarks law and saved it from this fate. Jacqueline Kennedy Onassis was a prime force in the battle against the tower. Restoration was completed in 1998 under architects Beyer Blinder Belle, who examined 4,500 of Warren's original drawings and blueprints. Over a period of four years, 80-year-old wiring and plumbing were replaced, air conditioning was installed and new entrances were built. All of this was done while the station continued to operate, and not a single train was late or delayed owing to construction.

Greenwich Village

A fascinating, once bohemian, now celebrity-studded area bursting with funky shops, unique bookstores, sidewalk cafés and cool clubs. Where famous artists, writers and radical thinkers lived and hung out.

George Segal's sculpture Gay Liberation *was installed in 1992*

Lively Bleecker Street has great shops and cafés

Chumleys' walls are lined with photos of its literary patrons

SEEING GREENWICH VILLAGE

Broadway divides Greenwich Village into the East Village (▷ 88–89) and the West Village. Bleecker Street is the main thoroughfare of the West Village and is full of cafés, restaurants and shops. Coffeehouses, music and poetry still thrive, and this definitely is a lively place for a late night out, whether you take in the bars and clubs, or just go for a stroll.

HIGHLIGHTS

CHRISTOPHER PARK

Bordered by Christopher Street, West 4th Street and Seventh Avenue, Christopher Park is home to George Segal's life-size sculpture *Gay Liberation*, which depicts a gay couple standing in front of a bench where two lesbians sit. Behind them is the Stonewall Bar & Grill, where riots in 1969 sparked the nation's Gay Liberation movement. Christopher Street is a focal point of gay life in New York City.

CHUMLEY'S

At 86 Bedford Street, near Grove Street, this former speakeasy is not easy to find—it has no sign outside and the number does not appear on the front of the building. Over time many New York writers, including John Steinbeck (1902–68), have found solace in a drop or two here. Photos of famous patrons decorate the interior walls. The bar has appeared in several movies, including Woody Allen's *Sweet and Lowdown*.

JEFFERSON MARKET LIBRARY

In 1885, a survey of architects found this Gothic building at 425 Sixth Avenue, designed by Calvert Vaux and Frederick Clarke Withers between 1874 and 1877, to be the fifth most beautiful building in the United States. The richly ornamented facades include a pediment depicting the trial scene from Shakespeare's *The Merchant of Venice*. The tower has been used as a fire watch, and originally the building housed a police court and a district court. After years of neglect, it was about to be demolished when local activists saved it and it became a branch of the New York Public Library in 1967.

RATINGS	
Historic interest	●●●●●
Photo stops	●●●
Specialist shopping	●●●●
Walkability	●●●●●

BASICS

✚ 60 D22 • From Broadway west to the Hudson River, between Houston Street to the south and 14th Street to the north

🚌 M1, M2, M3, M5–8, M20

🚇 A, C, E, F, N, R, V 1, 2, 3

🍴 A huge number of restaurants on Bleecker Street, Greenwich Avenue and streets in between provide a choice of international cuisines

🍽 Florent, 69 Gansevoort Street, tel 212/989-5779, open daily 24 hours, French-American cuisine and a full bar

🛍 Shops on Bleecker Street and Greenwich Avenue and many others

ℹ Information centers at Sixth Avenue and Christopher Street and at Astor Place Triangle, both Jul 1–Labor Day daily noon–6

TIPS

● Enjoy the outrageous costumes and partying up and down Sixth Avenue at the Village Halloween Parade.

● Stop at the Village Chess Shop at 230 Thompson Street, between Bleecker and West 3rd streets, for a friendly game of chess (www.chess-shop.com).

ADDRESS GUIDE

ARTISTS

24 University Place: The site of the Cedar Street Tavern, where Jackson Pollock, Franz Kline and Willem de Kooning shared ideas, along with Beat writers Allen Ginsberg and Jack Kerouac.

8 West 8th Street: The first address of the Whitney Museum of American Art (▷ 148–151).

Garrick Theater, Bleecker Street: Crowds flocked here for

Skyscrapers north of Washington Square Park

seven months to see Andy Warhol's movie *Flesh*, which premiered in October 1968.

WRITERS

145 Bleecker Street: Home to James Fenimore Cooper, author of *The Last of the Mohicans*, in 1833.

172 Bleecker Street: Where James Agee wrote the screenplay for *The African Queen*.

130–132 MacDougal Street: Louisa May Alcott stayed in this house and, it is believed, wrote *Little Women* here.

137 MacDougal Street: Home to the Liberal Club. Writers such as Upton Sinclair, Jack London, Theodore Dreiser and Sinclair Lewis regularly met in the house that once stood here.

85 West 3rd Street: Edgar Allen Poe lived on the third floor in 1845 (his was the last window on the right).

11 Commerce Street: Washington Irving wrote *The Legend of Sleepy Hollow* while living here.

14 West 10th Street: Home of Mark Twain when he moved to New York at the age of 65.

(Continued on page 107)

SHERIDAN SQUARE

Sheridan Square is at the point where Seventh Avenue, West 4th Street and Barrow Street intersect. Named after the Civil War general Philip Henry Sheridan, it is the site of the first protests that culminated in the Draft Riots of 1863 when 120 were killed, mostly African-Americans, by Irish immigrants (▷ 33). You can see the statue of General Sheridan in Christopher Park.

WASHINGTON MEMORIAL ARCH IN WASHINGTON SQUARE

Built in 1889 as the entrance to the park at the base of Fifth Avenue, the original triumphal arch commemorated the centenary of George Washington's inauguration. Architect Stanford White designed the first arch, which was made of wood, plaster and papier mâché. It was so successful that a fund to erect a permanent stone arch of the same design soon raised $134,000. The arch you see today, 30ft (9m) across and 77ft (23m) high, became the gateway to fashionable Fifth Avenue in the 1950s, when cars passed directly underneath it and the avenue cut through the park, and remains a treasured city icon.

Many artists have painted or drawn the arch, including Childe Hassam in his 1894 *Washington Arch, Spring*. Many New Yorkers feel that New York University's 12-story Helen and Martin Kimmel Center on Fifth Avenue at Washington Square North detracts from the magnificence of the arch.

WASHINGTON MEWS

As you approach Memorial Arch from Fifth Avenue, on your left is a lovely little cobblestone street called Washington Mews. Originally the houses here were the stables and servants' quarters for the elite town houses on Washington Square North, known as "The Row," a street lined with fashionable homes built in 1833 by John Jacob Astor and Cornelius Vanderbilt.

The delightful old houses lining Washington Mews have long been sought as residences by artists and painters, including Gertrude Vanderbilt Whitney, founder of the Whitney Museum of American Art (▷ 148–151). Members of the faculty of New York University have more recently taken up residence here.

WASHINGTON SQUARE PARK

Washington Square is the heart of Greenwich Village. In warm weather the park is alive with street musicians, students, skateboarders, rollerbladers, the occasional film crew and chess players (bring your own set), so this lively little park is great for people-watching.

Originally the site was marshland and a hunting ground; until the 1820s, criminals were hanged from the large elm in the northwest corner, and from 1797 until 1926 it was a potters' field, where paupers were buried. The remains of about 10,000 people rest here in peace, if not quiet. Washington Square was eventually acquired by the city, cleared, and laid out as a military parade ground. The Common Council then purchased more land, and the 9 acres (3.5ha) became the city's largest park in the 1840s. In 1963 the city closed the park to traffic, making it even more attractive to the students in the area. By the 1970s, alcohol and drug abusers had taken over. A clean-up over the past decade has left it the mellow, genial place you see today.

BACKGROUND

By 1700 Greenwich Village, named after a town in England, had grown to become a small village of wood-framed houses and tree-lined, mud streets north of the city. A single grand estate, Richmond Hill, built by a British paymaster-general at what is today the intersection of Varick and Charleston streets, was George Washington's headquarters during the attempt to defend New York in 1776 and was later home to vice presidents John Adams (1767–1848) and Aaron Burr (1756–1836). Burr sold much of the land to John Jacob Astor, who divided it up into 456 lots, which he leased for a tidy little profit.

The streets grew up, sometimes along former cowpaths, before the grid street plan was introduced in 1811. When yellow fever struck in the 1820s, half the population fled the city, and prominent families looking for fresh air settled in Greenwich Village, tearing down most of the original frame houses and rebuilding in brick. The Village was a fashionable residential area by July 4, 1826, when Washington Military Parade Ground (Washington Square) was officially opened to celebrate the 50th anniversary of the signing of the Declaration of Independence. African-Americans moved in after the Draft Riots in 1863 and soon Italian immigrants from Little Italy were spilling over into the neighborhood. Tenements and factories were built, and wealthy New Yorkers moved north.

In the early 1900s, social changes and new zoning laws created cheap housing, attracting artists looking for studio space and low

RADICALS

12 Charles Street: Home of suffragette Crystal Eastman and a suffragist gathering place.

91 Greenwich Avenue: Where *The Masses* was published. This left-wing publication backed the Communist Party and was a precursor to the counter-culture of the 1960s.

147 West 4th Street: John Reed rented a room in this house while he wrote *Ten Days That Shook the World*.

Regular jamming sessions still liven up the park

Pretty brownstone townhouses characterize the streets

Bustling markets fill the streets on Sunday mornings

rents. Intellectuals, writers and rebels took up residence, creating a bohemian enclave. Social critics, including suffragists, anarchists and Communist sympathizers turned the Village into a hotbed of disaffection. Writers such as Henry James, O. Henry, Mark Twain, Edgar Allen Poe and Stephen Crane all lived here. The Village's artist-residents, including Edward Hopper, Jackson Pollock, Franz Kline and Willem de Kooning, created a new American style. Today, the Village is one of the liveliest parts of the city, and maintains its artsy overtones, despite being a very expensive place to live and therefore also popular with wealthy professionals.

Memorial Arch provides a sedate backdrop to performances in Washington Square Park

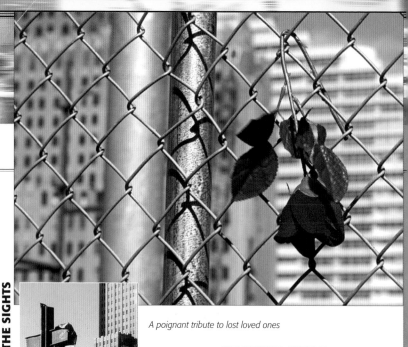

A poignant tribute to lost loved ones

GROUND ZERO

Ground Zero looks like nothing so much as a construction site. But seeing this corner of Lower Manhattan brings vividly home the horrors of 9/11.

The World Trade Center once filled seven buildings on the 16 acres (6.5ha) bordered by Church Street, Liberty Street, Park Place and West Street. The center's twin towers became the tallest buildings in the world in 1973, and for the next 28 years more than a million visitors visited every year, thrilling to the views from the open-air rooftop observation level. Then, on the morning of September 11, 2001, New Yorkers and the rest of the world watched with horror on their televisions as two hijacked commercial jets slammed into the towers. A total of 2,752 people were killed, 343 of them firefighters. When the towers collapsed, six buildings were destroyed and about 100,000 jobs were lost. Mayor Rudolph Giuliani was on the scene within minutes. Streets like Church and Vesey were completely enshrouded in thick white dust, people were in shock, and emergency crews and firemen rushed to the scene, hoping to find survivors, but there were very few. When the fires were eventually extinguished, Ground Zero was all that was left.

A symbol of hope and strength, the iron cross at Ground Zero

BASICS

✚ 61 E25 • Church to West streets, Liberty to Vesey streets

🚌 M6, M9, M20

🚇 1, E, N, R

www.projectrebirth.org
Excellent site with archive of articles, stories, photographs and films about the regeneration of Ground Zero.

LOOKING TO THE FUTURE

Within a year, clean-up crews had completed their gruesome task and workers had started rebuilding affected subway stations. The Lower Manhattan Development Corporation (LMDC) staged a design competition, inviting top architects around the world to create plans for the site. Six were unveiled in July 2002; all were rejected. Calling for more plans, the LMDC got responses from 406 teams of architects, and in March 2003 the governor and the mayor announced the winner: Daniel Libeskind, a Polish immigrant who arrived in the U.S. in 1960, aged 13.

An avant-garde architect, known for his commemorations of tragic events, Libeskind designed the Imperial War Museum in Manchester, England, and the Jewish Museum in Berlin. The heart of his underground memorial is the enormous slurry wall that kept the Hudson River from eroding the World Trade Center foundation. It surrounds the footprints of the two towers. Rising above is a symbolic 1,176ft (359m) tower with landscaped gardens. An elevated promenade allows visitors to view the memorial, and at ground level, a named marker will be put in the pavement for each rescue company that responded on 9/11. Commercial and cultural buildings are also planned.

A Culture and Continuity gallery in the Jewish Museum

Go to Little Italy for the flavors and colors of the Mediterranean

An interior display from the Tenement Museum

JEWISH MUSEUM

🚩 59 E13 • 1109 Fifth Avenue at 92nd Street 10128 ☎ 212/423-3200 🕐 Mon–Wed 11–5.45, Thu 11–8, Sat 11–3, Sun 10–5.45. Closed Fri 🎟 Adult $12, under 12s free 🚌 M1, M2, M3, M4 🚇 4, 5, 6 📅 💻 www.thejewishmuseum.org

A faux Loire Valley chateau, the former family home of banker Felix Warburg, this greystone mansion dating from 1908 contains the Jewish Museum's collection of Jewish ceremonial objects and works of art.

A generous philanthropist, Warburg died in 1938 and his widow left the house to the museum in 1944. The permanent exhibit, entitled Culture and Continuity: The Jewish Journey, is based on Warburg's personal collection of artifacts, covering an impressive scale and time-span.

In a re-created 1900s café, oral histories reveal Jewish life in Europe at that time and explore the immigrant experience in the U.S. Family workshops and other events celebrate Jewish culture, holidays and traditions.

LINCOLN CENTER

See pages 112–113.

LITTLE CHURCH AROUND THE CORNER

🚩 60 E19 • East 29th Street between Fifth and Madison avenues ☎ 212/684-6770 🕐 Daily 9–5 🚌 M2, M3, M4 🚇 1, 6, N, R, W www.littlechurch.org

The Episcopal Church of the Transfiguration is affectionately called the Little Church Around the Corner. Nothing could better demonstrate changed attitudes to all things theatrical than the way in which this charming little church acquired its nickname. In 1870, a nearby church declined to conduct funeral rites for actors, and directed one such request to

"the little church around the corner." It has been favored by theater folk ever since.

An English-style lychgate leads to the church, set back from the street in a quiet garden. The interior maintains the intimate, modest atmosphere with carved wooden pillars and beams.

LITTLE ITALY

🚩 61 F23 • Between Canal, Lafayette, and Houston streets and the Bowery 🚇 6 🚌 M1, M103

Once the overcrowded destination of Italian immigrants coming from Ellis Island, Little Italy is shrinking under pressure from New York's burgeoning Chinatown (▷ 84). A few blocks recall the friendly, festive area chock-a-block with Italian restaurants and grocery stores, where lavish displays of cheese, olives and salami entice visitors. Descendants of the initial immigrants still gather for family occasions. In mid-September the Feast of San Gennaro, patron saint of Naples, fills Mulberry Street, the main artery, from Canal Street to Spring Street. With gaudy lights and carnival booths, it's definitely a scene to see if you don't mind crowds.

LOWER EAST SIDE

🚩 61 G23 • East of the Bowery, south of East Houston to the East River 🚌 M9, M14A 🚇 F, J, M, V, Z

A slum tenement here was the next stop for most 19th-century immigrants after the ordeal of Ellis Island. The squalor, stench and disease in these overcrowded apartments during the area's heyday—from the mid-19th century until the 1920s—can barely be imagined today. Few of the original town houses survived the frenzied 19th-century building of tenement blocks, but most of these survived later rebuilding.

Today, although there is little to admire in the architecture, the area is thick with history. It is also one of New York shoppers' best bargain-hunting destinations, particularly on Sundays. Almost every day except Saturday (when stores are closed), the discount garment stores in the streets off Delancey and Orchard streets are crowded. Ethnic food shops in the area are wonderful; Essex Street Market (Mon–Sat) shows the changes in the ethnic mix of residents.

LOWER EAST SIDE TENEMENT MUSEUM

🚩 61 G23 • 90 and 97 Orchard Street, between Broome and Delancey streets ☎ 212/431-0233 🕐 Guided tours only; available from the Visitor Center. Times vary but normally every 30 or 40 min Tue–Fri 1–4, Sat–Sun 11–4.30. Interactive program Sat–Sun 1pm, 2pm, 3pm. Visitor Center Mon11–5.30, Tue–Fri 11–6, Sat–Sun 10.45–6 🎟 Adult $17, under 5 free. Advance tickets (advisable), tel 866/811-4111 🚌 M9, M14A, M15 🚇 F, J, M, V, Z 📅 🎒 🕐 Guided tours www.tenement.org

Four re-created apartments in a typical, five-story tenement dating from 1863 give a disturbing insight into how the other half lived, or at least managed to exist, in the overcrowded, unsanitary conditions common on the Lower East Side between the 1870s and 1920s.

Some 10,000 seekers of the American Dream and refugees from violent pogroms passed through this building over 70 years, as you learn on a guided tour. Fewer people go on each of these—never more than 15—than lived in a typical apartment. None of this is really for kids. For them, take in the interactive living history program, where they can try on period clothes and talk to "Victoria Confino," a Jewish teenager who lived here in 1916.

Guggenheim Museum
●

A masterpiece of modern architecture designed by Frank Lloyd Wright. Exhibiting one of the world's finest collections of modern and contemporary art.

The dramatic sweeping curves of the Guggenheim's exterior

Permanent exhibit Still Life: Flask, Glass and Jug by Paul Cézanne

Under the rotunda (above) the ramp spirals downward (right)

RATINGS

Photo stops
Specialist shopping
Value for money

BASICS

✚ 59 E13 • 1071 Fifth Avenue at 89th Street 10028
☎ 212/423-3500
🕐 Sat–Wed 10–5.45, Fri 10–7.45
💲 Adult $18, under 12 free, Fri 5.45–8 pay-as-you-wish
🚍 M1, M2, M3, M4
🚇 4, 5, 6
📖 Free *Guggenheim Guide* containing listing of exhibits and programs, available at admission desk
🍴 Daily 9.30–3
🍴 Sat–Wed 9.30–6.15, Thu 11–6, Fri 9.30–8.30
🎧 Free tours daily. Reservations are taken at the information desk from 1.30 Audio tours $5
www.guggenheim.org
Links to the Guggenheim's museums in Venice, Berlin, Bilbao and Las Vegas; online listings of exhibitions with detailed information about each piece of art; museum store with innovative contemporary collectables.

SEEING THE GUGGENHEIM

As you enter, to your right is the admission desk, where you can pick up a free exhibitions program with a floor plan. As you look up at the five levels above the low white walls bordering the ramp you see a tall empty atrium-like space so dramatic that it is easy to forget that you came here to see modern art. Frank Lloyd Wright designed this building with the belief that the eye should not be confronted with angles and sudden changes of form when viewing works of art. From a logistical point of view, the best way to see the works hung here is to take the elevator to the skylit top and meander down the spiral ramp. However, the exhibits are often hung with the opposite path in mind.

HIGHLIGHTS

PAUL CÉZANNE, *STILL LIFE: FLASK, GLASS AND JUG*

In this 1877 still life, Cézanne (1839–1906) perceived objects in space as being interrelated. He created an illusion of objects resting and flowing simultaneously, calling attention to the two-dimensional canvas. This painting, and others, made Cézanne the foremost precursor of Cubism.

PABLO PICASSO, *WOMAN IRONING*

Painted in 1904 at the end of his Blue Period, *Woman Ironing* is Picasso's (1881–1973) quintessential work of labor and fatigue, reminiscent of the years he spent among the Paris working class. His expressionist style, with strong angular contours and attenuated proportions, expresses the woman's movement poetically, making her the metaphor for the pathos of the working poor.

MAX ERNST, *ATTIREMENT OF THE BRIDE*

This 1940s Surrealist painting by Max Ernst (1891–1976) evokes late 19th-century Symbolist painting, while the sleek, round-bellied figures recall motifs of 16th-century German art. The background architecture indicates the strong influence of the Italian painter Giorgio De Chirico. Ernst's invented alter-ego, the bird-man on the left, depicts the artist with a symbolic phallic spear. The picture-within-a-picture shows the same bride walking amid overgrown Classical ruins, indicating the role of the bride throughout history. Garish colors and beastly figures suggest something violent about to happen.

BACKGROUND

The Solomon R. Guggenheim Museum, designed by Frank Lloyd Wright, opened on October 21, 1959. The inverted-ziggurat design, with its ramp encircling the walls, is as surprising today as it was when it was created. Solomon R. Guggenheim, a wealthy New Yorker whose father was a prominent 19th-century mining and smelting capitalist, used some of his wealth to buy works of art. He was content with Old Masters until 1927, when at the age of 66 he met baroness Hilla Rebay von Ehrenwiesen. The baroness favored European abstract art and introduced Guggenheim to such artists as Wassily Kadinsky, Fernand Léger and Robert Delaunay. It was she who suggested that Wright design a museum to house the great collection Guggenheim was amassing. Guggenheim died in 1949 and never saw the wondrous building, but Wright took on the job with enthusiasm and later pronounced it his "Pantheon."

Jeanne in a Yellow Jumper *by Amedeo Modigliani (1919)*

Lincoln Center

The Upper West Side's performing arts center offers the best in opera, classical music, chamber music, jazz, ballet and theater.

The Lincoln Center's fountains are dramatically lit at night

Take in a concert at Damrosch Park in summer

Colorful cafés line the Lincoln Center plaza

RATINGS

Good for kids	●●●
Photo stops	●●●●●
Specialist shopping	●●●●●
Value for money	●●●●●

BASICS

🞢 58 C16 • 70 Lincoln Center Plaza 10023-6583

☎ 212/546-2656 for main Lincoln Center

🚌 M5, M7, M10, M11, M66, M104

🚇 1

🎫 Guided tours of the Lincoln Center start from the tour desk below the lobby of the Metropolitan Opera House, daily 10.30, 12.30, 2.30, 4.30, adult $13.50 (reservations tel 212/875-5350); Metropolitan Opera House backstage tours weekdays at 3.30 from Oct–May only, Sun 10.30 adult $15 (reservations tel 212/769-7020)

🍴 Avery Fisher Hall: Panevino Ristorante, tel 212/874-7000, Mon–Sat for dinner, lunch on matinée days

☕ Avery Fisher Hall: Espresso Bar, 5pm–intermission nightly, opens at noon for matinées

🏪 Metropolitan Opera Shop, tel 212/580-4090; Avery Fisher Hall Shop, tel 212/580-4356; The Gallery at Lincoln Center, tel 212/875-5017 🛍

www.lincolncenter.org
Order tickets online, get visitor information about all events and performances.

With 14 venues offering everything from classical music to performances for children, the Lincoln Center is New York's premier center for performing arts. In the 1960s, a block of old tenements on the Upper West Side, where some of *West Side Story* was filmed, was demolished in a 12-block urban renewal project, and the Lincoln Center for the Performing Arts was built on the site. The initial investment for the Lincoln Center was more than $165 million. The state contributed the site and the rest of the money came from private contributions.

In 1962 the New York Philharmonic moved here from Carnegie Hall (▷ 76), which at the time was threatened with demolition. But the acoustics were never good, so in 1973 Avery Fisher donated $10 million to improve them. The hall closed for a time to undergo this work, but musicians and music-lovers were still not satisfied, so in 1992 the hall underwent further renovation.

OPERA, BALLET, THEATER, JAZZ

The New York State Theater is home to the New York City Opera and the New York City Ballet. The theater seats 2,700.

The Metropolitan Opera House, affectionately known as the Met, is home to both the opera company and the American Ballet Theater and seats 3,800. General manager Joe Volpe started as an apprentice carpenter and has worked his way up; he knows what attracts crowds and what doesn't.

The Guggenheim Bandshell in Damrosch Park, on 62nd Street near Amsterdam Avenue, hosts open-air concerts in summer.

The Lincoln Center Theater consists of the Vivian Beaumont Theater, with seating for 1,140, and the Mizi E. Newhouse Theater, an established Off Broadway venue.

Jazz, led by trumpeter and composer Wynton Marsalis, has moved to the massive new Time Warner headquarters at nearby Columbus Circle, after receiving a $10 million gift from the Coca-Cola Company. The $128-million jazz venue is the focal point of the building, with three main performance spaces (tel 212/258-9800).

THE JUILLIARD SCHOOL OF MUSIC

The Juilliard School of Music is the top music school in the United

States. The campus includes Alice Tully Hall, a wonderful venue for chamber music and solo recitals, and the Walter Reade Film Theater, where the New York Film Festival sends up sparks every fall.

FUTURE PLANS

There is currently a plan to tear down Philharmonic Hall and start again; it is estimated that renovation of the existing building will cost half the amount of the projected $325 million reconstruction. When the New York Philharmonic is not in residence, leading orchestras give concerts in the house.

There are also plans to turn West 65th Street into a broad boulevard, much like a central artery of the Lincoln Center. This will be the first step in the $150-million redesign of the public areas and the center's buildings and grounds. The avant-garde design team of Diller and Scofidio, who are described as "artist architects," and specialize in experimental installations, have been selected for the project. Other features of the plan include technologically sophisticated signs with information about events, a sweeping staircase into the plaza, and a new look to a number of the buildings.

Marc Chagall's murals are visible through the windows of the Metropolitan Opera House

TIPS
● There is a vast underground parking area, if you dare drive in New York.
● Special events take place all year, from summer's Mostly Mozart concert series and swing dancing to live jazz under the stars and the annual run of the Big Apple Circus, which pitches its tent in Damrosch Park at the beginning of November.

Metropolitan Museum of Art

•

A spectacular collection spanning 5,000 years.

The entrance to the museum is imposing from any angle

Mary Cassatt's Lady at the Tea Table *(1885)*

The Petrie European Sculpture Court is an idyllic spot for a rest

RATINGS	
Cultural interest	●●●●●
Good for kids	●●●
Photo stops	●●●●
Specialist shopping	●●●●●

SEEING THE METROPOLITAN MUSEUM OF ART

The grand main entrance, with its impressive neoclassical facade, is on Fifth Avenue at 82nd Street. Take a moment to look at the three-story banners announcing exhibits. As you enter the Great Hall inside the main entrance, go to the information desk to pick up a museum plan, which lists special exhibitions and new installations, and ask about the day's activities, including gallery talks. Allow plenty of time—there is much to see. The collections number more than 2 million items, with around 100,000 on display at any given time. It can be confusing if you simply wander around, so begin by deciding which galleries you want to see and go straight to them. You may wish to rent an audioguide; some focus on special exhibitions, others on selections from the permanent collection. Or join a free guided tour; sign up at an information desk in the Great Hall.

HIGHLIGHTS

GREEK AND ROMAN ART
Statue of a *Kouros*
With more than 35,000 works ranging from the Neolithic period to AD312, in beautifully renovated galleries, the Greek and Roman Art collection is one of the most comprehensive in North America.

In the center of the Steinhardt Gallery is the marble statue of a *kouros* (youth), one of the earliest of such statues of boys to survive complete. Carved in Naxian marble in Attica, the boy's rigid stance reflects the influence of Egyptian art. It is believed to have marked the grave of a young Athenian aristocrat.

Other Highlights
In the Belfer Court is a collection of terracotta pots, gemstones, figures and sculptures from the Neolithic period to the fifth century BC. There are interesting pieces from the Minoan Palace of Knossos in Crete and Roman copies of Hellenistic sculptures from classical Greece.

Upstairs are bronze mirrors from the sixth century BC, painted amphoras from the fifth century BC, Corinthian and Hellenistic pottery, and bronze reliefs from the Etrusco-Roman period.

Enter via the Great Hall, with its large ornamental flower planters

Take in the view from the Roof Garden, where a modern sculpture overlooks the museum's environs

BASICS

➕ 59 E14 • 1000 Fifth Avenue at East 82nd Street 10028-0198

☎ 212/535-7710

🕐 Tue–Thu, Sun 9.30–5.15, Fri–Sat 9.30–8.45

💲 Suggested donation (includes main building and same-day visit to The Cloisters) adult $20, under 12 with adult free

🚍 M1, M2, M3, M4 to 79th Street

🚇 4, 5, 6 to 86th Street

🎧 Audioguide to special exhibitions and selections from the permanent collection in English, Chinese, French, German, Italian, Korean, Portuguese, Russian, Spanish or Japanese: adult $7, under 12 $5. The Key to the Met Audio Guide provides commentary on selected works of art

🍴 Petrie Court Café, Balcony Café & Bar plus cafeteria on first floor behind Medieval Hall

🏛 The Met Store prides itself on being the largest museum bookstore in America and offers reproductions of the collection's jewelry, china and other objets d'art

🛍

www.metmuseum.org
Informative introductions to collections. View highlights of 3,500 works of art online, get information on current exhibits and shop online from the Met Store.

THE SIGHTS

EUROPEAN SCULPTURE AND DECORATIVE ARTS

Bacchanal: A Faun Teased by Children

With 60,000 exhibits ranging from the Renaissance to the early 20th century, European sculpture is one of the largest departments in the museum. In the Northern Renaissance and Florence galleries is a sculpture by Rome's Gian Lorenzo Bernini (1598–1680), which he created when he was only 18. Distinctive of his revolutionary style, it breathes life into the marble with profound emotional and spiritual intensity. The satin-like texture, strong accented lines and bacchic subject are typical Bernini.

Small Desk (Bureau Brisé)

In the Louis XIV Gallery, this little oak, pine and walnut veneered desk, engraved with tortoiseshell, brass, ebony and rosewood, is one of a pair made in France for Louis XIV. It was made to fit into the king's small study in the north wing of the Palace of Versailles by a little-known cabinetmaker by the name of Alexandre-Jean Oppenordt (1639–1715). On the closed top is a barely distinguishable engraved mask of Apollo above the crown, and inlaid Apollo lyres on the top's sides.

Other Highlights

In the English galleries are a rococo-style dining room from Kirtlington Park, Oxfordshire, and a lavish dining room from Lansdowne House, London. The French galleries include a Paris shopfront from 1775, a daybed made for Marie Antoinette in the boudoir of the Hotel de Crillon, and in the Louis XVI Gallery, the king's desk from his study at Versailles .

Petrie European Sculpture Court

Not to be missed is the beautiful Petrie European Sculpture Court. Fountains and greenery and a splendid view of Central Park and Cleopatra's Needle provide a peaceful setting for fine Italian and French sculptures. Cleopatra's Needle was a gift from the Pasha of Egypt.

THE AMERICAN WING

One of the Met's most popular areas, the American Wing has three floors and centers on the splendid Charles Englehard Court. Focusing on the development of art and design in America, the collection fills 25 rooms with period furniture and furnishings, more than 1,000 paintings by American artists, 600 sculptures, 2,500 drawings and numerous examples of the decorative arts.

Louis Comfort Tiffany Vase

This vase, one of the first pieces of American glass in the collection, came from Louisine and Henry Havemeyer in 1896. Tiffany (1848–1933) showed his talents as a colorist, designer and naturalist in this beautiful example of his Favrile glass peacock vases—the fan shaped like a peacock's outspread plumage, the eyes of sliced glass millefiori canes, and the graceful lines depicting each individual feather.

Emmanuel Gottlieb Leutze, Washington Crossing the Delaware

Painted in 1851 by the German-born painter E. G. Leutze (1816–68), this American icon depicts General George Washington's surprise

KEY TO MAIN ROOMS

SECOND FLOOR
1: Modern art
2: 19th-century European paintings and sculpture
3: Islamic art
4: Cypriot art
5: Ancient Near Eastern art
6–7: Asian art
8: Musical instruments
9: American Wing: American paintings, sculpture, decorative arts and period rooms
10: European paintings
11: Special exhibitions
12: Drawing, Prints, Photographs

FIRST FLOOR
14: 20th-century paintings
15: Sculpture and artifacts from Africa, Oceania and the Americas
16: Greek and Roman art from prehistoric to classical
17: Egyptian art, Sackler Wing and Temple of Dendur
18: American Wing: American paintings, sculpture, decorative arts and period rooms
19: Arms and Armor: European, Islamic and Japanese armor, weaponry from Ottoman Turkish and Mughal Indian courts
20: European sculpture and decorative arts
21: Medieval art
22: Robert Lehman Collection: Old Masters, Impressionist, Post-Impressionist paintings
23: Library

GROUND FLOOR
24: The Ruth and Harold D. Uris Center for Education
25: Costume Institute: Late 16th-century to present clothing and costumes
26: Robert Lehman Collection

THE SIGHTS

METROPOLITAN MUSEUM OF ART 117

attack on the Hessians at Trenton, New Jersey, on Christmas night 1776. Washington's physical stamina and indomitable spirit as he leads 2,400 men to victory is central. In attempting to mythologize, Leutze takes liberties with history and focuses attention on inaccuracies such as the flag, not adopted until six months after the crossing. Leutze painted three versions of this work: The original went to the Kunsthalle in Bremen, the second was made for engraving.

Hart Room

The earliest interior in the American Wing, the Hart Room is from the home of Thomas Hart of Ipswich, Massachusetts. Built sometime between 1639 and 1674, this is a typical example of homes of the early New England settlers. The post-and-beam construction, much used in England, was both simple and sturdy. The bed is a reproduction ash and pine frame. The handwoven and sewn wool hangings around the bed helped to keep drafts away from the sleeper.

Other Highlights

In the airy Charles Englehard Court, linger to study Tiffany's *Garden Landscape and Fountain* and the beautiful stained-glass *Autumn Landscape*. The former was inspired by the Byzantine churches Tiffany saw while traveling in Europe. Turn to the right to see Tiffany's extravagant loggia from Laurelton Hall. The dahlias at the top of the columns are in three stages of growth: bud, full bloom and seed pod.

The sculptures in this glass-enclosed garden are by American artists Augustus Saint-Gaudens, Frederick MacMonnies and Daniel Chester French. In Gallery 127 is the work of the world-famous architect Frank Lloyd Wright. *Living Room from the Little House*, a very modern design in 1912, was designed for Francis Little.

Paintings and sculptures by American artists on this floor include John Singleton Copely's *Midshipman August Brine*, *The Falls of Niagara* by S. F. B. Morse, James McNeill Whistler's *Arrangement in Flesh, Color and Black*, John Singer Sargent's *Madame X* (1884), Mary Cassatt's *Lady at the Tea Table* (1885), and from the Hudson River School Frederic Church's *Heart of the Andes*.

EUROPEAN PAINTINGS

Albrecht Dürer, *Virgin and Child with St. Anne*

Germany's greatest Renaissance artist portrays St. Anne with her daughter, the Virgin Mary, holding the infant Jesus. It is believed that Dürer (1471–1528) painted this in 1519, at the time he was becoming an ardent follower of Martin Luther. By including St. Anne, who was a much-venerated saint in Germany, the artist was perhaps questioning the veracity of a virgin birth.

Vincent Van Gogh, *Cypresses*

Painted in 1889 when Van Gogh (1853–90) began his year-long confinement in the asylum at St-Rémy, *Cypresses* was one of several paintings the artist produced of familiar landscapes during this time. The illuminating shades of the background contrast sharply with the tree's splash of black. The use of swirls evokes the unpredictability of weather and the possible threat of the unknown.

Claude Monet, *Terrace at Sainte-Adresse*

Painted in 1867 at a time when Monet (1840–1926) was exploring new ways of representing modern life, this painting shocked his contemporaries. The bold use of pure colors and strong contrasts combine to capture the blinding glare of the sun's reflection off the water, the paths and flowers. Giving balance and depth to the painting, the flags' movement gives the impression that the painter has caught a moment in time, like photographers would later be able to do with the camera.

Other Highlights

Among the many Italian masters' works are Raphael's *Madonna Enthroned with Child and Saints* (1505), Titian's *Venus and the Lute Player* (c1560), Tintoretto's *Finding of Moses* (c1550), Botticelli's *Last Communion of St. Jerome* (c1450) and Caravaggio's *Musicians* (1504). Early Dutch painters include a Rembrandt *Self-Portrait* (1660),

The marble statue of a youth, kouros, in the Steinhardt Gallery

Stroll among the statues in the Petrie European Sculpture Court

The Rocky Mountains, Lander's Peak, *by Albert Bierstadt (1863)*

Degas' The Dance Lesson *(c1879)*

Take an audiotour or a guided tour from the Great Hall

Vermeer's *Woman with a Water Jug* (1664) and works by de Hooch, van Goyen and others. French paintings include Poussin's *Rape of the Sabine Women* (c1635) and Jean Clouet's *Guillaume Budé*. Spanish works include El Greco's *View of Toledo* and *Grand Inquisitor Cardinal Don Fernando Niño de Guevara*. The English collection is represented by William Hogarth, Joshua Reynolds and Thomas Gainsborough.

European paintings of the 19th century include Millet's *Autumn Landscape with a Flock of Turkeys* (1872–73) and many Impressionist and Post-Impressionist paintings. Besides 100 works by Degas, there are paintings by Manet, Renoir, Seurat, Toulouse-Lautrec, Cézanne, Gauguin and Van Gogh. Worth seeing are one of Cézanne's best still lifes, *Still Life with Apples and a Pot of Primroses* (1895), and Monet's *Terrace at Sainte-Adresse* (c1867).

BACKGROUND

Members of New York's Union League Club—businessmen, artists and scholars—founded the Metropolitan Museum of Art in 1870. Originally at 681 Fifth Avenue, the museum moved to its present site in 1880. The original red-brick building, designed by Jacob Mould and Calvert Vaux, has been incorporated into the present museum and is visible in the Lehman Wing. The Richard Morris Hunt facade fronting Fifth Avenue was built in 1902. Beginning with a Roman sarcophagus, donations have continued over the years, but it was in 1904, when multimillionaire J. P. Morgan was elected president of the Board of Trustees, that world masterpieces became the main acquisitions. Morgan was not very interested in American art, nor in contemporary artists like Paul Gauguin and Henri de Toulouse-Lautrec, but preferred the Old Masters. A former Cypriot consul sold his collection of 6,000 objects to the museum, and Catherine L. Wolfe handed over 143 paintings of the Dutch and Flemish schools. Louis Comfort Tiffany's work was first presented in 1896 with 56 Favrile glass vases and in 1951 the Tiffany Foundation donated spectacular pieces from a private collection. In 2003, more than 100 works of art by Henri Matisse were given to the museum. The Met has also been running excavations for more than 30 years, and the finds are added to the collection.

TIPS

● To avoid long lines at the main entrance, enter at 81st Street, where there is a ticket and information desk.
● If you plan to visit the Cloisters (▷ 86) on the same day, it's best to visit the two sites on a Friday or Saturday, when the Met stays open later. Do the Cloisters in the morning and the Met in the afternoon.
● To avoid crowds, weekday mornings are optimal. Or plan a Friday or Saturday evening visit.
● Plan to take in the Roof Garden (May–end Oct). It's worth visiting not only for the splendid views of Central Park, the sandwiches and drinks, but also for the magnificent collection of sculptures.

The Metropolitan Life Insurance Tower stands proud

The elegant Ladies Parlour at the Mount Vernon Hotel

Stock-market ticker at the Museum of American Financial History

THE SIGHTS

MERCHANT'S HOUSE MUSEUM

➕ 60 F22 • 29 East 4th Street 10003
☎ 212/777-1089 🕐 Thu–Mon 12–5
💲 Adult $8, under 12 free 🚌 M1, M5, M6, M102 🚇 6, N, R 🅿 Tours every half hour Sat–Sun 🚻 ♿
www.merchantshouse.com

This museum is an 1832 time capsule, one of six Federal-style row houses with a charmingly gracious Greek Revival doorway. Bought by wealthy merchant Thomas Tredwell in 1835, the house was lived in by his daughter for 93 years. Renovated after her death in 1933, it was opened to the public as a museum in 1936 with the original furnishings intact, including personal family possessions. It is the only 19th-century house in Manhattan to be so completely preserved. Seven rooms on three floors and a secret garden are on view. Miss Tredwell is thought to have been the model for a character in Henry James' *Washington Square.*

METROPOLITAN LIFE INSURANCE TOWER

➕ 60 E20 • 1 Madison Avenue 🚌 M1, M3 🚇 4, 5, 6

Met Life's 1893 main building on 23rd Street stands on the site of the Madison Square Presbyterian Church, whose minister savagely attacked the corrupt politicians who ran the city in 1892. This 54-story tower, built in 1909, was their revenge. Planned as the tallest building in the world and a proud symbol of Met Life's promi-nence, it was soon overtaken by the Woolworth Building (▷ 144). The Met's campanile was 700ft (214m); in 1913, the Woolworth surpassed it by 92ft (28m).

In 1962, the tower was stripped of its original ornamen-tation, leaving the gold dome and the huge clock faces.

METROPOLITAN MUSEUM OF ART

See pages 114–119.

MIDTOWN MANHATTAN

See page 121.

MORGAN LIBRARY

See page 122.

MOUNT VERNON HOTEL MUSEUM AND GARDEN

➕ 59 G16 • 421 East 61st Street at York Avenue ☎ 212/838-6878 🕐 Tue–Sun 11–4; closed Aug 💲 Adult $8, child under 12 free 🚌 M15, M31, M57 🚇 4, 6, N, R,
www.mvhm.org

In this splendid hotel, eight of the rooms were filled with Federal period furnishings by the Colonial Dames of America when they bought the structure in 1924. In the Gentlemen's Tavern Room, you're welcome to sit down and read a newspaper from 1828, and don't miss the museum's delightful 18th-century gardens. To get a feel for the place, visit the website and take a tour. The museum was a house that once belonged to Abigail Adams, the daughter of US president John Adams and the wife of George Washington's aide, William Stephens Smith. The Smiths had to sell the property in 1798 before all the buildings were complete and so never lived here. In 1826 the building underwent conversion into a hotel. There are regularly scheduled events such as talks on American furniture of the early 19th century.

MUNICIPAL ART SOCIETY

➕ 59 E17 • 457 Madison Avenue 10022 ☎ 212/935-3960 reservations; 212/439-1049 for tours and meeting places 🕐 Mon–Sat 10–6 (Wed to 8), Sun 11–5 💲 Guided walking tours $15; some walking and bus tours are more expensive
www.mas.org
Founded in 1893, MAS is a non-profit, private, membership society aiming to promote a "more livable city." It advocates excellence in architecture, design and planning, public art and preservation of historic buildings, and believes sensible development is critical to the city's economic health and social well-being. It also organizes exhibitions and walking tours. The guides on these tours are highly qualified and give insights into the history and significance of the urban scene. Exhibitions are held at the headquarters, the Urban Center Galleries in one of the Villard Houses at the Helmsley Hotel, and are free and open to the public.

MUSEUM OF AMERICAN FINANCIAL HISTORY

➕ 61 E26 • 48 Wall Street 10005 ☎ 212/908-4110 🕐 Tue–Sat 10–4 🚇 2, 3 💲 Adult $8, child 6 and under free 🚻 ♿
www.financialhistory.org

On the site of Alexander Hamilton's law office, once the headquarters of multimillionaire John D. Rockefeller's Standard Oil Company, this four-room, Smithsonian Museum affiliate celebrates America's spirit of entrepreneurship with exhibits of coins, tickertape from the Wall Street Crash of 1929, curiously interesting photographs and murals of Wall Street and other documents and artifacts. Interactive financial news terminals help children understand the stock market. Special exhibitions have included informative displays about the history of the Dow Jones Industrial Average, banknote engraving and counterfeiting. The shop has interesting gifts for that person who has everything.

The view across town from the dizzying heights of the legendary Empire State Building

MIDTOWN MANHATTAN

Chic shopping, high-priced hotels, skyscrapers, landmarks and bright lights.

Midtown Manhattan stretches from 34th Street to 59th Street, with Fifth Avenue—where shopping is a big attraction—splitting it into east and west. Megastores have made it big in Times Square and the Theater District, while Fifth Avenue and 57th Street are lined with the most glamorous names like Gucci and Chanel. In the past few years, retailers Niketown, Banana Republic and Liz Claiborne have moved in, joining classic Saks Fifth Avenue, Tiffany & Co. and Bergdorf Goodman on the stretch of Fifth Avenue from 49th to 59th streets.

Midtown has New York's major train station, bus stations, the largest concentration of hotels, big stores and corporate headquarters. Midtown West includes the Garment District and the Theater District, with Times Square and New York's longest street, Broadway (▷ 138–140), at the heart of it.

Bryant Park is where tents are set up in September for New York's Fashion Week, no matter what the weather. Here there are museums like the International Center of Photography (▷ 101), Museum of Arts and Design (▷ 123), Paley Center for Media (▷ 126) and the Museum of Modern Art (▷ 125). Rockefeller Center (▷ 128–130) and the home of the Rockettes, Radio City Music Hall (▷ 129), are in Midtown. Along the Hudson River, there's the Intrepid Sea, Air and Space Museum (▷ 101).

LANDMARK SIGHTS
Architectural landmarks in Midtown East include the Chrysler Building (▷ 85), the Chanin Building and the Daily News Building (▷ 87). Nearby is Grand Central Terminal (▷ 102–104). At 301 Park Avenue is the famous Waldorf-Astoria Hotel (▷ 309), where kings, queens and presidents have stayed. Along Madison Avenue are the stunning Villard Houses, notable for their turn-of-the-20th-century extravagance, now part of the Helmsley Palace Hotel. At the east end of 42nd Street is Tudor City, with 3,000 apartments and its own restaurants, parks, stores and post office. The United Nations Headquarters (▷ 144) stands on the East River, not actually on U.S. land, but on international territory belonging to the member nations. It has a serenity that sets it apart here.

Broadway is synonymous with theater and entertainment

RATINGS	
Historic interest	●●●●○
Photo stops	●●●○○
Specialist shopping	●●●●●
Walkability	●●●○

BASICS
✚ 59 E18 • 34th to 59th streets
🚌 M1, M2, M3, M4, M6
🚇 1, 2, 3, 4, 5, 6, B, D, F, N, R, Q, V, W
🍴 Oyster Bar Grand Central Terminal lower level, tel 212/490-6650
🍽 Bryant Park Grill and Café, 25 West 40th Street (behind New York Public Library), tel 212/840-6500, in summer eating outdoors

The Adoration of the Magi, *from a choirbook executed in about 1540*

MORGAN LIBRARY

An astonishing collection of rare books, illuminated and literary manuscripts and drawings by the Western world's most creative geniuses.

The Morgan Library reopened in spring 2006 with twice the gallery space, an enlarged auditorium, a café, a bigger shop and more open public spaces, following three years of improvement work. The Reading Room is now better equipped and the storage areas are much improved.

By the end of the 19th century, John Pierpont Morgan was one of New York's wealthiest financiers. To fulfill his desire to match Europe's greatest libraries, he began his opulent private library of European cultural treasures: manuscripts, paintings, prints and furniture. His travels abroad resulted in this priceless collection of nearly 10,000 drawings and prints, including some by Leonardo da Vinci and Albrecht Dürer. In 1902, he commissioned Charles McKim to design the magnificent Renaissance-style building. Later additions include those by Benjamin Morris in 1928, the annex, which was Morgan's private residence, at 231 Madison Avenue, and the garden courtyard in the 1990s.

MORGAN'S STUDY

The West Room of the library remains as Morgan left it when he died in 1913. He used it as a study and his huge wooden desk is still here, along with the Italian Renaissance paintings lining the walls. From the study you pass green-veined marble columns as you proceed toward the rotunda and the East Room. The beautiful three-tiered, walnut and bronze bookcases are almost as amazing as the ceiling covered with frescoes and the signs of the zodiac. Notice the 16th-century Flemish tapestry above the fireplace. But it is the collection of letters and manuscripts that most intrigues.

Morgan acquired nearly 600 medieval and Renaissance manuscripts, including the 9th-century Lindau Gospels, a rare vellum copy of the Gutenberg Bible, and the medieval Dutch masterpiece *The Hours of Catherine of Cleves*. He also purchased handwritten scores by such composers as Beethoven, Mozart and Puccini, which are protected under glass. The collection also includes manuscripts by authors of the calibre of Jane Austen, Charles Dickens, Henry David Thoreau and Mark Twain.

The decorated facade of the Morgan Library

RATINGS	
Cultural interest	●●●●●
Historic interest	●●●
Specialist shopping	●●●●
Value for money	●●●●

BASICS

✚ 60 E19 • 225 Madison Avenue at 36th Street 10016

☎ 212/685-0008

◉ Tue–Thu 10.30–5, Fri 10.30–9, Sat 10–6, Sun 11–6

💷 Suggested admission: adult $12, under 12 with adult free

🚍 M2, M3, M4

🚇 4, 5, 6, 7

🍴 Morgan Court Café serves lunch and afternoon tea

📖 Bookshop closes 15 min before galleries

♿

www.morganlibrary.org

The Museum of Chinese in the Americas was founded in 1980

Modern and chic objects for daily use are on display in the Museum of Arts and Design

MUSEUM OF ARTS AND DESIGN

🚇 59 E17 • 40 West 53rd Street 10019 ☎ 212/956-3535 🕐 Daily 10–6, Thu until 8 💷 Adult $9, under 12 free, pay-as-you-wish Thu 6–8 🚍 M1, M2, M4, M5 🚇 E, V 🏛 🚻 www.americancraftmuseum.org

In this museum (formerly the American Craft Museum), the American Craft Council displays the nation's biggest exhibition of 20th-century American and international crafts. From jewelry to baskets, furniture to teapots, everything is carefully selected to represent the finest in form and function. Stimulating special exhibitions are chosen from the extensive, wide-ranging collections, augmented by loans from other collections, to illustrate contemporary trends in technique and design. It's all shown to great advantage in a spacious, three-story atrium. Past exhibitions have included a retrospective on U.S. design from 1975 to 2000 and another showcasing elaborate cake decorating.

MUSEUM OF BIBLICAL ART

🚇 58 D16 • 1865 Broadway at 61st Street 10023 ☎ 212/408-1500 🕐 Tue–Sun 10–6 (Thu until 8) 💷 Adult $7, child under 12 free 🚍 M5, M7, M11, M104 🚇 59th Street/Columbus Circle (A, B, C, D, 1) www.mobia.org

This museum aims to foster an understanding and appreciation of art inspired by the Bible. It opened its new building in 2005 with an inaugural exhibition of works by self-taught Southern folk artists. The museum evolved out of the American Bible Society (1816), which had amassed a huge collection of scripture, now on view behind a glass curtain wall in the main gallery. Exhibitions focus on the collection's highlights, such as the recent For Glory and for Beauty, which displayed 29 rare scriptures.

MUSEUM OF CHINESE IN THE AMERICAS

🚇 61 F24 • 70 Mulberry Street, 2nd Floor 10013 ☎ 212/619-4785 🕐 Tue–Sun noon–6 💷 Adult $2, free Fri and child under 12 🚍 M103 🚇 N, Q, R 🏛 🚻 www.moca-nyc.org

This museum exhibits photographs and other works of visual art, rare historical documents, musical instruments, clothing and artifacts that help to explain Chinese history and culture. MoCA's most moving core exhibit, Where is Home?, interprets themes such as migration, abandonment, customs, women and home. Temporary exhibits are equally interesting. Post 9/11, Recovering Chinatown displayed images, artwork and other materials documenting the experience of Chinatown residents during and after the attack on the World Trade Center. Gotta Sing Gotta Dance! offered insight into the world of Chinese-American performers from the 1930s and the 1940s.

MUSEUM OF THE CITY OF NEW YORK

🚇 Off map 59 E12 • 1220 Fifth Avenue 10029 ☎ 212/534-1672 🕐 Tue–Sun 10–5. 💷 Suggested admission: adult $9, child under 12 free, family $20 🚍 M1, M2, M3, M4, M106 🚇 6 📷 Highlights tour Sat noon 🏛 🚻 www.mcny.org

A neo-Georgian, colonial-style villa built in 1929 houses this museum devoted to New York's history and life. The collections here hold more than 1.5 million objects relating to the social and economic life of the city—paintings, photographs, costumes, toys, decorative arts and other artifacts. Some are world-class, like the silver collection and the collection on American theater; the photography, marine and costume collections are also outstanding. The museum has sometimes been criticized for taking a dull approach to display, but lively exhibitions such as those devoted to Glamor New York Style and Puerto Rican New York have helped to change that reputation.

MUSEUM OF JEWISH HERITAGE

🚇 61 E26 • 36 Battery Place 10280 ☎ 646/437-4200 🕐 Sun–Tue, Thu 10–5.45, Wed 10–8, Fri 10–5, eve of Jewish holidays 10–3; closed Jewish holidays and Thanksgiving 💷 Adult $10, under 12 free 🚍 M1, M6, M9, M15, M20 🚇 4, 5 📷 💻 🏛 🚻 www.mjhnyc.org

This museum, opened in 1996 and designed by Kevin Roche and John Dinkeloo in a hexagonal shape to represent the Star of David, houses an exhibition of 20th-century Jewish history and culture. Presenting the story of Jewish tragedy and suffering, survival and renewal, the museum has three main sections: Jewish Life a Century Ago, The War Against the Jews, and Jewish Renewal.

Displays take you back to the now-vanished worlds of a century ago, through the horror of industrialized mass murder, to the resurgence of hope in a world not yet free of hatred and intolerance. Film clips, interspersed with displays of physical objects, include testimonies from Spielberg's Survivors of the Shoah project and footage from the museum's own archives.

Statue of Diana the Hunter in the National Academy of Design

Christian Schad's Maika (1929) in the Neue Galerie

Nineteenth-century fire carriages at the New York City Fire Museum

MUSEUM OF MODERN ART

See page 125.

NATIONAL ACADEMY OF DESIGN

⊞ 59 E13 • 1083 Fifth Avenue 10128
☎ 212/369-4880 ◷ Wed–Thu noon–5,
Fri–Sun 11–6 🎟 Adult $10, child under
12 free 🚌 M1, M2, M3, M4 🚇 4, 5, 6
🎧 Docent tours Fri 2pm $5 🎫 Tue,
Wed–Thu 10–5, Fri 10–6, Sat–Sun 11–6
👫
www.nationalacademy.org

The National Academy of Design was founded in 1825 by a group of accomplished artists, architects, sculptors and engravers, including Thomas Cole and artist/inventor Samuel Morse.

It is both a museum and a school of fine art, and also owns the largest collection of 19th- and 20th-century American art in the country—an astonishing collection with more than 5,000 works ranging from portraiture of the Federalist period, landscapes of the Hudson River School, gritty realism of the Ashcan Movement, and paintings representing movements from Fauvism to photo-realism.

The building was the home of Archer Milton Huntington and his wife, the sculptor Anna Hyatt Huntington. In 1913, they expanded and remodeled the house and lived here until 1939, when they gave it to the National Academy of Design, who moved in three years later.

Tours covering the collection's highlights and Edith Wharton's New York are available.

NEUE GALERIE

⊞ 59 E13 • 1048 Fifth Avenue at 86th
Street 10028 ☎ 212/628-6200 ◷ Fri
11–9, Sat–Mon, Thu 11–6 🎟 Adult $15,
no children 🚌 M1, M2, M3, M4 🚇 4,
5, 6 🍴 🎫 👫
www.neuegalerie.org

This museum, dedicated to early 20th-century German and Austrian art and design, has a marvelous collection of fine paintings, decorative arts and other media, including works by Gustav Klimt, Paul Klee, Egon Schiele, Josef Hoffmann and Adolf Loos.

On Friday nights there are cabarets in Café Sabarsky, which serves Austrian fare, including delicious pastries.

Some of the furniture is by Adolf Loos, and lighting fixtures are by Josef Hoffmann. The 1914 Carrère & Hastings mansion housing the museum was built for Mrs. Cornelius Vanderbilt III, and is every bit as remarkable as the collection.

NEW MUSEUM OF CONTEMPORARY ART

⊞ 61 F23 • 235 Bowery at Prince
Street ☎ 212/219-1222 ◷ Wed–Sun
12–6 (Thu–Fri to 10pm) 🎟 Adult $12,
free Thu evenings, under 18 free
🚌 M103 🚇 J, M Z 🎫 👫
www.newmuseum.org

The museum has been inviting international contemporary artists to mount shows of experimental work since 1977. It presents several major exhibits each year as well as shows in a space dedicated to digital art, experimental video and sound works.

In late 2007 the museum moved into its new home in this stunning building designed by Tokyo-based architects SANAA.

In addition to purpose-built galleries it contains a theater, education floor, café, shop and a top-floor events space with roof terraces.

NEW YORK CITY FIRE MUSEUM

⊞ 61 E23 • 278 Spring Street at
Hudson/Varick 10013 ☎ 212/691-1303
◷ Tue–Sat 10–5, Sun 10–4
🎟 Contribution requested (adult $5,

child $1) 🚌 M10, M21 🚇 C, E
🎧 Tours by appointment 🎫 👫
www.nycfiremuseum.org

A former firehouse of Rescue Company No.1, built in 1904, this museum packs three floors with firefighting paraphernalia, the most comprehensive collection in the United States.

Equipment from the 1700s to the present includes buckets, pumps, horse-drawn fire engines, a fire hydrant and more equipment and there's an exhibit on fire safety. Firefighters are usually around to share stories.

This is one of the best places in the city to pay tribute to the 343 firefighters who lost their lives on September 11, 2001. You can also see exhibits relating to the disaster.

NEW YORK CITY POLICE MUSEUM

⊞ 61 F26 • 100 Old Slip 10005
☎ 212/480-3100 ◷ Mon–Sat 10–5
🎟 Suggested donation adult $5, child
(6–18) $2 🚌 M15 🚇 2, 3, N, R 🎫
👫
www.nycpolicemuseum.org

This small museum exhibits a collection of uniforms, ceremonial batons, New York Police Department (NYPD) shields, handguns, and even the machine gun used by Al Capone's gang to assassinate Frankie Yale, the first homicide in New York by such a weapon.

Visit a prison cell and see the display on vintage weapons and notorious criminals, which includes arrest records. Learn about fingerprinting and forensics, then view the NYPD Hall of Heroes, which now has a memorial to the 23 policemen and women who died in the attack on the World Trade Center. "Policing a Changed City" covers the way New York has become one of the wolrd's safest cities.

Among many fine works is Van Gogh's The Starry Night *(1889)*

MUSEUM OF MODERN ART

The world's greatest collection of painting and sculpture from the late 19th century to the present.

When MoMA opened in 1929 it occupied six rooms on 57th Street. Today, after a dramatic $425 million renovation by architect Yoshio Taniguchi, it offers an unparalleled collection of modern and contemporary art. The new MoMA opened in November 2004 to much acclaim. Taniguchi's redesign doubled the institution's space, allowing it to display much more of its superb collection. Visitors can now enter from 53rd or 54th streets to view the galleries, which are clustered around a 110ft tall (34m) atrium, which diffuses light throughout the building and gives great views of the sculpture garden, which features Aristide Maillol's *The River*, Henry Moore's *Family Group* and other works in an inviting outdoor setting.

COLLECTIONS AND EXHIBITIONS

The permanent collection, spanning art from the late 19th century to the late 1960s, is displayed on the fourth and fifth floors. The works are displayed in chronological sequence to create a comprehensive history of modern art. The 12 galleries on the fifth floor cover Post-impressionism, Cubism, Italian Futurism, Austrian and German Expressionism, Social Realism and Surrealism. Each boasts a string of masterpieces; Vincent Van Gogh's *The Starry Night* and Salvador Dalí's *The Persistence of Memory* are just two of the most celebrated examples. One gallery is devoted entirely to Matisse. Fourth-floor galleries present works from the late 1940s to the late 1960s and include works by such major artists as Willem de Kooning, Jasper Johns, Francis Bacon and Andy Warhol, as well as some splendid holdings of Jackson Pollock's work.

Contemporary works created since 1970 are shown in the second-floor galleries, which also include a dedicated media gallery. The collections of drawings, photography, architecture, and design are found on the third floor. The drawing collection contains 7,000 works from 1880 onward and the photography collection 25,000 works, which document the development of photography from the 1840s. The photograph collection ranges from Henri Cartier-Bresson to Diane Arbus, highlighted by William Fox Talbot's *Lace* and Paul Strand's *Fifth Avenue, New York*. With 19,000 films and four million film stills, the Film and Media Department is also impressive. The sixth floor is reserved for special exhibits.

Yoshio Taniguchi's new MoMA, from 53rd Street

RATINGS	
Good for kids	● ● ●
Historic interest	● ● ● ●
Specialist shopping	● ● ●
Value for money	● ● ● ●

BASICS

➕ 59 E17 • 11 West 53rd Street 10019

☎ 212/708-9400

🕐 Sat–Mon 10.30–5.30, Wed–Thu 10.30–5.30, Fri 10.30–8; closed Tue

💵 Adult $20, under 16 with adult free, free Fri 4–8; audioguide $5

🚇 Fifth Avenue/53rd Street (E, V), 47th–50th St/Rockefeller Center (B, D, F)

🚌 M1, M2, M3, M4, M5

🎧 Audio programs free

🍽 1 restaurant, 2 cafés

🏛 MoMA Design and Book Store at museum, tel 212/708-9700; MoMA Design Store, 44 West 53rd Street, tel 212/767-1050; MoMA Design Store SoHo, 81 Spring Street, tel 646/613-1367

🚻

www.moma.org

Indian, *at the New-York Historical Society*

The Gothic Revival interior of the Riverside Church

THE SIGHTS

NEW-YORK HISTORICAL SOCIETY

✚ 58 D14 • 170 Central Park West at 77th Street 10024 ☎ 212/873-3400 🅖 Museum: Tue–Sat 10–6 (Fri to 8), Sun 11–5.45. Library: Tue–Sat 10–5. Print Room by appointment only 🅖 Adult $10, Fri 6–8 free, child under 12 free 🚇 M10, M79 🅖 B, C 🎧 Audiotours 📶 👥 www.nyhistory.org

At Central Park West, this Upper West Side museum is a great place to spend a morning or afternoon. For nearly 200 years, the Society has been collecting, preserving and interpreting books, paintings, sculpture, photographs and newspapers. The fascinating Henry Luce III Center on the fourth floor displays lamps by Louis Comfort Tiffany, Hudson River School landscapes, a complete set of watercolors by John James Audubon for *The Birds of America*, George Washington's inaugural chair, and much more. The library is the oldest research library in the country.

NEW YORK PUBLIC LIBRARY

See page 127.

PALEY CENTER FOR MEDIA

✚ 59 E17 • 25 West 52nd Street 10019 ☎ 212/621-6800 🅖 Tue–Sun noon–6, Thu until 8, Fri theater programs until 9 🅖 Adult $10, under 14 $5 🚇 M1, M2, M3, M4 🅖 E, V 🎧 🍴 📶 👥 www.mtr.org

Formerly called the Museum of Television and Radio, the new name reflects the growing range of media in modern times. William S. Paley (1901–90), former chairman of CBS, donated the land for this 17-story building, erected in 1989, to a design by architects Philip Johnson and John Burgee. Theaters, screening rooms, three public galleries and individual viewing and listening consoles are your access to the museum's collection of tapes of 100,000 programs and commercials celebrating nearly 100 years. Thousands of new programs are added every year.

When you arrive, make a reservation to use the computer catalog on the fourth floor to locate what interests you, then reserve it and watch it in one of the museum's consoles. Or take in a show or two at one of the screening rooms or theaters.

RECTORY OF THE SHRINE OF ELIZABETH ANN SETON

✚ 344 E26 • 7 State Street ☎ 212/269-6865 🅖 Mon–Fri, ring bell for admission

From 1801 to 1803, this red-brick town house was the home of the New York socialite and mother of five, Elizabeth Ann Seton, the first American-born woman to be canonized by the Roman Catholic Church.

Born in 1774, she converted to Catholicism as an adult and became a spiritual leader and educator. She founded the first order of nuns in the US: the Sisters of Charity. Her legacy includes six religious communities with more than 5,000 members, schools, and social service centers and hospitals in the US and across the world. Pope Paul VI declared her a saint in 1975.

RIVERSIDE CHURCH

✚ Off map 58 C12 • 490 Riverside Drive 10027 ☎ 212/870-6700 🅖 Daily 7am–10pm Claremont Avenue entrance 🚇 M4, M5, M60, M104 🅖 1 🎧 Tour after Sun service, 12.15pm, free 📶 👥 www.riversidechurch.net

Philanthropist John D. Rockefeller, Jr. funded the construction of this 21-story, steel-frame Gothic Revival church. Designed to resemble Chartres Cathedral in France, and completed in 1930, it is an interdenominational, interracial and international church. Nelson Mandela, Martin Luther King, Jr., and the Children's Defense funder Marion Wright-Edelman have all spoken from the pulpit. The bell tower houses the world's largest carillon, with 74 bells, as well as a 20-ton brass bell. A viewing platform on the tower gives a view over the Hudson River (call to check when it's open). Inside are stained-glass windows and a cast of Jacob Epstein's *Christ in Majesty*. Another Epstein work, *Madonna and Child*, is on the lawn.

ROCKEFELLER CENTER

See pages 128–130.

ROOSEVELT ISLAND

✚ 59 G15 • In the East River between Manhattan and Queens 🚋 Tram fare $2 🚇 Q102 🅖 F

You can take the subway to Roosevelt Island, but the East 60th Street Heliport Aerial Tramway is a much more fun way to travel the 300 yards (274m) over the East River. Today there are 8,000 residents on the island, which is 2 miles (3.4km) long and only 800ft (250m) wide.

With its quiet streets, well-planned housing and great views of the Manhattan skyline, this is a much sought-after area. in which to live.

Up to the 19th century it was farmed by the Blackwell family, then it housed a prison, a mental health facility, the Octagon Building (1842), as well as the Smallpox Hospital (1854) and at the northern tip, a lighthouse (1872), both designed by James Renwick, Jr.

Looking down on the Main Reading Room, where the reading tables are often fully occupied

THE SIGHTS

NEW YORK PUBLIC LIBRARY

Fascinating exhibits of New York culture inside a grand and beautifully restored Beaux Arts building.

Some things in New York are surprises, and this amazing research library is one of them. The massive white marble building, one of the first major commissions of the firm Carrère & Hastings in 1911, is absolutely gorgeous. Half of its $9-million cost was donated by steel magnate and philanthropist Andrew Carnegie (1835–1918). The two lions at the foot of the staircase fronting the museum are New York icons affectionately named Patience and Fortitude by New York's 1930s mayor, Fiorello LaGuardia; in the gift shop they adorn tote bags, spoons, charm bracelets, bookends, paperweights and more.

Up the imposing staircase and through the triple-arched portico is beautiful Astor Hall, named after John Jacob Astor (1763–1848), whose private library, along with that of James Lenox, was the foundation of this great collection. (Former New York governor Samuel J. Tilden bequeathed the $2.4 million to combine the libraries and erect the building.)

WHAT TO SEE, AND WHERE

Upon entering, pick up a floor plan at the information desk and ask about free tours around the library. Gottesman Hall, straight ahead, displays temporary exhibits. The DeWitt Wallace Periodical Room, to the left, is embellished with Richard Haas murals of New York magazine and newspaper offices. At the top of the marble stairs is the McGraw Rotunda. The stupendous Main Reading Room, restored in 1998 so that the oak and brass gleam, is to your right. Across the hall is the Edna Barnes Salomon Room, where recent popular exhibitions have included New York Eats Out, Baseball at the Library, Prints of James McNeill Whistler (1834–1903) and The Charles Adams Mother Goose.

This is not a lending library, but there are more than 80 branches in Manhattan and the outer boroughs. Occasionally, you can see important items here from the vast collection, which include a Gutenberg Bible, a 1493 folio edition of a letter written by Christopher Columbus describing his discoveries in the New World, a first folio edition of Shakespeare's works from 1623, an early draft of Thomas Jefferson's Declaration of Independence, and much more.

One of two stone lions lounging on the front steps of the library

RATINGS	
Historic interest	● ● ●
Photo stops	● ● ●
Specialist shopping	● ● ● ● ●

BASICS

🕀 60 E18 • Fifth Avenue and 42nd Street 10018
☎ 212/930-0830, exhibition information 212/869-8089
🕐 Mon, Thu–Sat 11–6, Tue–Wed 11–7.30, Sun 1–5
💵 Free
🚌 M1, M2, M3, M4
🚇 B, D, F
🎫 Free tours Mon–Sat 11 and 2, Sun 2 from Astor Hall
🚻 ♿

www.nypl.org
The library catalog, Digital Library Collections, sections for teenagers, health information and an online exhibition.

Rockefeller Center

A vital urban enclave in the heart of Manhattan.
More than 100 art deco works by 30 artists, including Paul Manship's iconic
gilded bronze *Prometheus* and Lee Lawrie's *Atlas*.
Home of Radio City Music Hall, a spectacular art deco landmark and home of the Rockettes.

Gilded sculpture on the front of the center

New Yorkers frequently take time out at Rockefeller Center

Radio City Music Hall is used fo live concerts and film premiere

BASICS

⊞ 59 E17 • West 48th to West 51st streets, between Fifth and Sixth avenues

☎ 212/332-6868 or 632-3975; Radio City Music Hall 212/247-4777

🎟 Free

🚌 M1, M2, M27, M50

🚇 B, D, F, Q

📖 Free walking-tour brochure from the main information desk in the lobby of the G. E. Building

🍴 Many eateries and restaurants including Cucina & Co., Mendy's Kosher Deli, Hale and Hearty, Ben & Jerry's. The Rainbow Room, 65th floor of the G. E. Building, tel 212/632-5000, is famous for its art deco revolving dance floor

☕ Rockefeller Center Café, 20 West 50th Street, tel 212/332-7620

🎫 Rockefeller Center tour Mon–Sat 11, 1, 3, 5, Sun 11, 1, 3, adult $12, departs from NBC Experience Store (tel 212/664-3700)

🏛

www.RockefellerCenter.com
View artwork from Rockefeller Plaza online; links to restaurants and cafés, Radio City Music Hall, NBC Store and ice-skating rink.

SEEING ROCKEFELLER CENTER

To get a good sense of the place begin at Channel Gardens, on Fifth Avenue between 49th and 50th streets, which are six pools surrounded by pretty flower boxes running between the Maison Française and the British Empire Building (hence the name). Straight ahead as you face the Channel Gardens, with your back to Fifth Avenue, is Rockefeller Plaza, with its sunken garden, which is turned into an ice-skating rink in winter and a restaurant in summer. The gilded *Prometheus,* stealing the sacred fire from the Greek gods to give to man, rises ahead, while flags flutter around the plaza's perimeter. At the top of the steps down to the Lower Plaza a bronze plaque from multimillionaire and philanthropist John D. Rockefeller, whose fortune built Rockefeller Center, praises the virtues of hard work. On the southeast corner of the Lower Plaza is a branch of the Metropolitan Museum of Art Store, full of elegant souvenirs and gifts. As the complex is large, it is best to pick up a walking-tour guide from the information desk in the lobby of the G. E. Building to help you decide what to see and do.

HIGHLIGHTS

THE G. E. BUILDING

Over the east entrance of this prominent tower, the former RCA Building, is Lee Lawrie's limestone-and-glass frieze, *Wisdom*, inspired by William Blake's painting of the same name. The beautiful granite and marble east lobby is worth visiting; it houses José Maria Sert's sepia mural *Man's Conquests*, commissioned to replace one by Diego Rivera, which was rejected because it included an image of Joseph Stalin. The anticommunist Rockefellers had insisted that Rivera remove the offending portrait, but Rivera refused and his mural was destroyed. The signature clock on the 51st Street corner has projecting arms grasping electric bolts (RCA was a subsidiary of General Electric). The stylized figures at the building's crown have haloes of electric rays. The viewing platform is open to patrons of the elegant Rainbow Room restaurant on the 65th floor; for a drink and a view, stop in at the adjacent Rainbow Grill.

ICE-SKATING RINK

☎ 212/332-7654 ⓒ Mid-Oct to mid-Apr Mon–Thu 9am–10.30pm, Fri–Sat 8.30am–midnight, Sun 8.30am–10pm 💲 Adult $10 weekdays/$14 weekends, child $7.50 weekdays/$8.50 weekends, skate rental $8

When this ice rink in the Lower Plaza opened on Christmas Day 1933, it was a novelty made possible by new refrigeration technology. Today, a quarter of a million skaters test their blades here every year. The rink is small—only 122ft long (37m) and 59ft (18m) wide.

RADIO CITY MUSIC HALL

With about 6,000 seats, Radio City was the world's largest theater when it opened in 1932. Impresario Samuel (Roxy) Rothafel's original plans were for live entertainment, but movies soon became the main fare, with the high-kicking Roxyettes, later called the Rockettes, performing before each feature film. Donald Deskey was the interior design coordinator. The great arched proscenium in the form of a setting sun is an art deco masterpiece. The Grand Foyer's 24-carat gold-leaf ceiling, sweeping staircase and elegant chandeliers are breathtaking. Radio City was designated a New York City Landmark in 1979 and a National Historic Landmark in 1987. Intensive renovation in the late 1990s then won it a National Preservation Award in 2000.

TOP OF THE ROCK

☎ 212/698-2000 ⓒ Daily 8am–midnight (last shuttle 11pm) 💲 Adult $17.50, child 6–12 $11.25
www.topoftherocknyc.com

Sky shuttles whiz you to the top of 30 Rockefeller Plaza for a fabulous 360-degree view of New York from the three-tiered observation deck on the 67th, 69th and 70th floors. There is an unparalleled view of Central Park from above. There are enclosed and open terraces.

NBC STUDIO SHOWS

To get standby tickets to join the studio audience of "Late Night with Conan O'Brien," line up at 9am on the day of taping outside 30 Rockefeller Plaza on 49th Street under the NBC Studios awning. Or reserve tickets by calling 212/664-3056. You must be aged at least 16.

In winter skaters show off their flashier moves at the Lower Plaza ice-skating rink

RATINGS				
Good for kids	●	●		
Photo stops	●	●	●	
Specialist shopping	●	●	●	●
Walkability	●	●	●	●

TIPS

● If you're in town between early December and early January don't miss Rockefeller Center. An enormous Christmas tree is put up and decked with 20,000 tiny lights—a favorite New York tradition.

● Go early if you plan to ice-skate on the rink in the Lower Plaza. The rink can hold only 150 skaters at a time and it gets busy, especially at lunchtime. Skate rentals and rink fees are cash only—and not cheap.

● NBC Experience store, 49th Street and Rockefeller Plaza, offers one-hour tours of news and entertainment studios. See the "Saturday Night Live" set: Arrive before noon in the busy holiday and summer period to get tickets, which are on a first-come, first-served basis.

The gilded Prometheus heralds the entrance to the center

WISDOM AND KNOWLEDGE SHALL BE THE STABILITY OF THY TIMES

Lee Lawrie's relief over the entrance to the G. E. Building (above right); one of Jose Maria Sert's sepia murals (above)

Every weekday between 7 and 9am, hundreds of people crowd the blue police barricades at the corner of West 49th Street and Rockefeller Plaza, just outside the ground-level NBC studio of the long-running morning "Today Show." The lure is a glimpse of the anchors or national exposure for a greeting for the folks back home scrawled on a piece of cardboard. In good weather a segment or two may be presented outdoors on the street.

BACKGROUND

The land on which Rockefeller Center stands belonged to Columbia University at the beginning of the 20th century. The university rented the land to farmers, but eventually developers came along and put up brownstones. By the late 1920s, the area was noisy and unpleasant, with elevated trains rumbling down Sixth Avenue and many residents too poor to spend money on the upkeep of the buildings. During Prohibition, the area was known as the "speakeasy belt," and along 52nd Street police raids were common. When liquor regained its legal status, the area became a popular setting for jazz clubs, where great musicians like Count Basie and Harry James entertained.

In 1928, John D. Rockefeller leased 12 acres (5ha) from Columbia University in order to build a colossal new opera house for the Metropolitan Opera. Rockefeller had a 24-year lease, but the project was dropped when the stock market crashed in 1929. But the rent still had to be paid, so Rockefeller decided to build a commercial center. In all, 228 buildings were demolished to make way for 12 new buildings to be designed by Associated Architects, a group directed by Raymond Hood. Between 1932 and 1940, this "city within a city," to use Rockefeller's words, was built. The central tower, the former RCA Building (now the G. E. Building) was planned with dense concentration of facilities for the creation and broadcasting of sound, with a vision of television's bright future. Today NBC occupies 11 floors.

Building Rockefeller Center was the largest privately sponsored real-estate venture in New York City's history. The complex was an instant success, and seven more buildings were added between 1947 and 1973. Today, 19 buildings cover 22 acres (9ha), about 65,000 people work in the offices here, and many more visit daily.

Six pools surrounded by flower boxes lead to the entrance

St. Mark's in the Bowery's Greek Revival steeple dates from 1828

The St. Patrick's Cathedral spires were completed in 1888

The striking interior of St. Patrick's Old Cathedral

ST. MARK'S CHURCH-IN-THE-BOWERY

➕ 61 F21 • East 10th Street 10004
☎ 212/674-6377 🕐 Events only
🚌 M8, M15 🚇 6, N, R
www.stmarkschurch-in-the-bowery.com

Peter Stuyvesant, New Amsterdam's last Dutch governor, had a *bouwerij* (farm) in the quiet countryside north of the bustling settlement. As the city expanded and land values soared, Stuyvesant's grandson sold off plots for development. In 1779, a year after the Stuyvesant mansion was destroyed by fire, his great-grandson sold the site of Stuyvesant's private chapel to the Episcopal Church for a nominal dollar. And so it was that St. Mark's Church-in-the-Bowery was built and named. The original church was Federal-style; in keeping with the area's increasing affluence it later acquired a cast-iron portico. Stuyvesant and six generations of his descendants are buried in the graveyard.

ST. PATRICK'S CATHEDRAL

➕ 59 E17 • Fifth Avenue (between 50th and 51st streets) 10022
☎ 212/753-2261 🕐 Daily 6.30am–8.45pm 🚌 M1, M2, M3, M4
🚇 6, B, D, E, F, V
www.saintpatrickscathedral.org

Each year the largest Roman Catholic cathedral in the United States, seating about 2,200, welcomes more than 3 million visitors. Designed by James Renwick, Jr., this Gothic Revival cathedral was inspired by European originals, most notably Cologne Cathedral in Germany. The spire is 330ft (100m) above street level. The pietà inside is three times the size of the one in St. Peter's in Rome. Tiffany & Co. designed the beautiful St. Michael and St. Louis altar.

Work began on the church in 1853 and it was consecrated in 1879. The cathedral's arrival encouraged the rich and powerful to move north and contributed to the development of Fifth Avenue's many sumptuous mansions.

ST. PATRICK'S OLD CATHEDRAL

➕ 61 F23 • 260–264 Mulberry Street 10013 🚌 M15, M103 🚇 N, Q, R 🔗
www.oldsaintpatricks.com

French architect Joseph François Mangin had been busy with the building of City Hall until 1809, when he began work on this Gothic structure, the first Roman Catholic cathedral of New York. At 120ft long (36m) and 80ft (24m) wide, it opened in 1815, when the area was heavily populated by Irish immigrants. The work of enlarging the cathedral was well under way in 1866, when a fire destroyed it. Restored and completed by 1868, the cathedral remained the seat of the archdiocese until the dedication of the new St. Patrick's in 1879. At that time the old cathedral was demoted to the status of parish church. Now restored, the interior is grand and gloomy, the timber roof is supported on iron columns and the organ is one of only a handful of good organs in the city.

ST. PAUL'S CHAPEL

➕ 61 E25 • Broadway between Fulton and Vesey Streets 10007 ☎ 212/233-4164 🕐 Mon–Sat 10–6, Sun 9–6
🚌 M1, M22 🚇 4, 5 🔗 Classical music Mon1–2pm, free
www.saintpaulschapel.org

This church was one of the outbuildings of the wealthy Episcopalian parish of Trinity Church (▷ 142–143). Modeled on London's St. Martin-in-the-Fields, it was built of local stone

between 1764 and 1768, with the graceful spire added in 1796. In 1789 the inaugural prayer service for George Washington, the new nation's first president, was held here. Pierre l'Enfant, the soldier-architect who laid out the plan for Washington, D.C. as the new capital city and designed the Federal Hall, is credited with the altar. After his inauguration, Washington worshiped here regularly and his pew, together with Governor Dewitt Clinton's, is preserved. On Mondays at 1pm you can come for a marvelous hour of classical music—and it's free.

SCHOMBURG CENTER FOR RESEARCH IN BLACK CULTURE

➕ Off map 59 E12 • 515 Malcolm X Boulevard 10037-11801 ☎ 212/491-2200 🕐 Days and hours vary; see website 🕐 Free 🚌 M7, M102 🚇 2, 3
🔗 By appointment, tel 212/491-2207, free 🛈
www.schomburgcenter.org

A research library that serves a national and international constituency, the Schomburg Center was founded in 1925 as a special collection in a branch of the New York Public Library (▷ 127). Arthur A. Schomburg, a Puerto Rican black scholar and bibliophile, had collected 5,000 books, 2,000 etchings and 3,000 manuscripts, among other material on African-American culture, which was acquired by the library.

The collection now has more than 5 million items, including books, art, artifacts, photographs, prints, manuscripts, rare books, moving images and recorded sound.

The focus is on preserving and providing access to this important collection, documenting the lives of people of African descent throughout the world. Past exhibitions have included *The Art of African Women*.

THE SIGHTS

SoHo

Stylish boutiques and stores, fashionable restaurants, fascinating architecture and plenty of art galleries.

Chic stores in SoHo keep the designer fashions coming

The gilded Puck statue on the Puck Magazine Building

Shopping addicts should head for West Broadway

BASICS

✚ 61 E23 • Canal Street to Houston Street, between Sixth Avenue and Lafayette Street
🚌 M1, M6
Ⓜ C, E, N, R, 6
🍴 Rocky's, 45 Spring Street, tel 212/274-9756 ☕ Le Pain Quotidien, 100 Grand Street, tel 212/625-9009 🔲

BACKGROUND

This area *South of Hou*ston (pronounced *how-stun*)—which actually extends as far south as Canal Street, and runs from Sixth Avenue on the west to Lafayette Street on the east—started out in the 19th century as an industrial zone. Architects kept catalogues of cast-iron window frames, balustrades and columns then pieced together what they liked; an Italian Renaissance motif was very popular. Fashion moved uptown in the early 20th century, taking industry and business out of the area. Development stalled; nothing went up—but nothing came down, either. Rents plummeted, opening up opportunities for artists and sculptors in need of cheap accommodation and studio space. Preservationists caught wind of the phenomenon and soon all New York was singing the praises of SoHo.

Today, there are 50 cast-iron structures on Greene Street alone. The most admired include the Haughwout Building at the corner of Broome Street and Broadway, the Little Singer Building at 561 Broadway, and the St. Nicholas Hotel, where Mark Twain met his future wife, at 521–523 Broadway. Across the street at 504 Broadway, Harry Houdini worked as a tie-cutter before his career as an escape artist took off. It was in the Haughwout Building that Elisha Graves Otis installed his first passenger elevator; unfortunately it is no longer in the building. (▷ 242–243 for a walk around this neighborhood.)

SOUGHT-AFTER NEIGHBORHOOD

By the 1970s, SoHo was one of the most desired addresses in town, rents shot up and struggling artists left. But many dealers and galleries thrived, like The Leo Castelli Gallery, which exhibited Andy Warhol, Frank Stella and Roy Lichtenstein in the 1960s, at 420 Broadway.

By the end of the 20th century there were about 200 other art galleries, as well more photography galleries than anywhere else in New York. Today many of the galleries have moved to Chelsea (▷ 77) and, to a lesser extent, to TriBeCa (▷ 141), but some remain. The Peter Blum Gallery at 99 Wooster Street (tel 212/343-0441) exhibits artists working in a variety of media, including photographs, drawings, sculpture and cartoons. Nearby at 429 West Broadway, the Nancy

There are still many art galleries

Hoffman Gallery (tel 212/966-6676) specializes in contemporary paintings, sculpture, prints, drawings and photography. The innovative New York Earth Room (tel 212/473-8072; Wed–Sun), at 141 Wooster Street, displays 14 tons of soil, rather intriguingly.

Stores followed the galleries, pushing out both galleries and artists. But in the interim, many well-to-do New Yorkers moved into the loft spaces on the buildings' upper floors, attracting still other high-end retailers to SoHo, along with chic cafés and lots of bars and music venues. Rents for apartments here can rise to $15,000 per month.

No matter what the season, SoHo's streets offer the ultimate New York experience.

Fashionable places in which to eat and be seen eating are what SoHo is all about

South Street Seaport

A landmark district of historic buildings, a maritime museum, and more than 100 shops, cafés and restaurants on the waterfront.

Look out over the East River from South Street Seaport's Pier 17 sun decks

The inside areas at South Street have been attractively restored

TIP

● If you plan to take a harbor cruise, reserve in advance to avoid disappointment.

SEEING SOUTH STREET SEAPORT

This "museum without walls" is a 12-square-block landmark district at the eastern edge of downtown Manhattan on the East River. Buildings include the Fulton Fish Market, Pier 17 Pavilion, the South Street Seaport Museum and retail outlets on the surrounding blocks. Begin your visit at Pier 17, where the eateries and shops are concentrated. Pick up a visitors' leaflet from one of the many display racks at the entrance to the pier. The clear, well-labeled map and listing of the stores and restaurants will enable you to decide the route that appeals to you most.

HIGHLIGHTS

PIER 17

From this impressive three-story glass-and-steel pier, transformed into a shopping center with dozens of restaurants and eateries, you can enjoy the magnificent views of the East River from the outdoor terrace.

SOUTH STREET SEAPORT MUSEUM
Historic Ships

Berthed between piers 15 and 17, the collection of ships includes the 1911 *Peking*, a four-masted cargo vessel built by Blohm and Voss in Hamburg, Germany, which made several trips around Cape Horn. After numerous voyages between Europe and South America, then serving as a stationary school ship for the British, it came to New York in 1975. The *Pioneer*, an 1885 schooner, takes visitors on a 2.5-hour harbor cruise, including close-up looks at the Statue of Liberty and Governor's Island (call for hours and reservations tel 212/748-8786).

World Port New York

The museum's core exhibition, with 24 galleries on the upper floors of the renovated Schermerhorn Row and the A. A. Low Building, explores the history of the port from colonial times to the present.

THE TITANIC MEMORIAL LIGHTHOUSE

At the Water Street entrance to the seaport, this monument to the victims of the *Titanic*, which sank on April 15, 1912 on its maiden

Advertising the Titanic's *tragic maiden voyage to New York*

voyage from Southampton, England, to New York, was put up in 1913 overlooking the East River. It was moved to its present site in 1968. John Jacob Astor, owner of the Astoria Hotel, which stood on the site of the Empire State Building, was one of the 1,513 people who died.

BACKGROUND

The South Street Seaport Museum, at 207 Front Street, opened in 1967 and was the original draw to this then-neglected area, leading to a complete restoration project. Schermerhorn Row is the most significant historical landmark in the South Street Seaport complex. Nos. 191 and 193 Front Street were built in the 1790s by Peter Schermerhorn, a leading merchant from a prominent New York family. He built further groups of four-story Georgian and Federal-style warehouses and counting houses on Fulton Street in 1812. The stone warehouse at 167–171 John Street was built in 1849 for A. A. Low & Brothers. By the 1860s, the South Street area was no longer the hub of commercial port activity and only the Fulton Fish Market remained. In the 1980s the Rouse Company moved in to start restoring.

The collection of ships berthed between piers 15 and 17

BASICS

🚹 61 F25 • South of Brooklyn Bridge at Fulton Street

ℹ️ 12 Fulton Street, Apr–end Oct daily 10–6; rest of year daily 10–5; tel 212/732-7678 or 212/748-8600

☎ Museum: 212/748-8600

🕐 Most shops Mon–Sat 10–9, Sun 11–8. Museum: Apr–end Oct Tue–Sun 10–6; Nov–end Mar Fri–Sun 10–5, shops 12–5, Mon 10–5 Schermerhorn Row galleries only

💲 Museum: adult $8, child (5–12) $4

🚌 M15

Ⓜ 2, 3, 4, 5

🚶 Guided walking tours: Ask at the ticket booth across from Pier 17

🍴 15 restaurants and food outlets

🍽 Seaport Cafe on Pier 17, tel 212/964-1120; Skipper's Pierside Café, Pier 16, tel 212/349-1188

www.southstreetseaport.com Events calendar, complete list of restaurants and shops.

www.southstseaport.org Preview museum's permanent collection, information about exhibits and ships.

There is often some sort of street music or entertainment at South Street Seaport

Statue of Liberty

The city's most important landmark, in New York Harbor, recognized throughout the world as a symbol of freedom, a must-see for millions of visitors every year.

The statue is often affectionately referred to as Lady Liberty

Buy your very own statue headgear and wear it with pride

You can get up close on a ferry for a better look

RATINGS	
Good for kids	●●●●●
Historic interest	●●●●
Photo stops	●●●●●

A symbol of freedom and democracy, the Statue of Liberty was the first sight for millions of immigrants as they approached their new homeland. As you sail toward her today, it's easy to imagine how they felt.

A JOINT PROJECT

When the Statue of Liberty was unveiled on October 28, 1886, thousands of spectators were filled with awe. Nearly three times the height of the Colossus of Rhodes, one of the Seven Wonders of the World, this gift from the people of France was in recognition of the friendship established between the two countries during the American Revolution. The French statesman Edouard de Laboulay proposed that the statue be made in France, but that the pedestal be made by the Americans. Alexandre-Gustave Eiffel, who designed the Eiffel Tower in Paris, came up with the revolutionary support system of interlocking angle irons for the enormous statue, which was designed by Frédéric-Auguste Bartholdi.

Paying for the project was a problem for both nations and great effort was put into fundraising events, such as theatrical performances, art exhibitions, auctions and prize-fights. But the public showed little interest. Joseph Pulitzer, who established the Pulitzer Prize, criticized the rich in his newspaper *The World* for failing to help finance the pedestal construction. He also criticized the middle classes for expecting the rich to provide all the money. Donations then came pouring in and the pedestal was completed in 1886. The French shipped the statue to New York in June 1885; it took four months to assemble.

VITAL STATISTICS

Lady Liberty, as she is often affectionately called, came to Bedloe's Island, renamed Liberty Island, in 1956. By presidential proclamation the Statue of Liberty became a National Monument in 1924; the United Nations designated her a World Heritage Site in 1984. After almost 100 years, the statue needed some attention; an $87-million restoration project ended with fireworks to celebrate the statue's centennial, coinciding with Independence Day, on July 4, 1986.

Her measurements are impressive. She weighs 225 tons and measures 151ft 1in (46.05m) from the top of the base to the torch.

The statue provides an inspiring welcome to the city

Her hands measure a whopping 16ft 5in (5m) and even her nose is 4ft 6in (1.37m). Richard Morris Hunt's magnificent pedestal measures 154ft (46.9m).

VISITING LADY LIBERTY

She can be fully appreciated only up close so it's unfortunate that the Statue of Liberty has been closed to the public for security reasons since September 11, 2001. Only the grounds are now open to visitors.

Still, it's worth taking the trip across the harbor to peer up at this monolith to liberty. For a panoramic view of the harbor, you can climb to an observation deck on the 16th floor at the top of the pedestal. There's also a museum.

To visit Liberty Island, take the Statue of Liberty & Ellis Island Ferry from Battery Park. In advance, buy tickets online, by telephone or at the ticket office. In person, use the CityPass (▷ 317) or get your ticket from Castle Clinton ticket office (▷ 73). Lines are long during peak season so, as there are no reservations, arrive early. There is a Time Pass system (free) for visiting the museum and pedestal observation deck. During peak periods it's best to order tickets in advance and request a time pass from the ferry company (tel 1-866/782-8834, www.statuecruises.com).

The statue arrived in 350 pieces packed in 214 crates

BASICS

✚ Page 6 • Liberty Island in New York Harbor

☎ General information 212/363-3200, ferry tickets 212/269-5755

🕐 Daily 9.30–5, extended hours in peak season

🎫 Ferry tickets (good for a round-trip that includes a stop at Ellis Island) adult $11.50, child (4–12) $4.50. Free admission to Liberty Island and the Statue of Liberty

🚇 1, 4, 5 🚌 M1, M6, M15

🍴 Refreshments on ferries; café on Liberty Island 🚻 On ferries 🚹🚺

www.nps.gov/stli
History and statistics, museum exhibits and security updates.

Times Square and Broadway

New York at its flashiest.
Neon signs, huge billboards, live TV broadcasts, enormous stores and
gigantic family-friendly theme restaurants, not to mention theaters.

THE SIGHTS

RATINGS				
Good for kids	●	●	●	
Photo stops	●	●	●	
Specialist shopping	●	●	●	●
Walkability	●	●	●	●

BASICS

✚ 60 D18
ℹ Times Square Information Center, 1560 Broadway between 46th and 47th streets, daily 8–8 (on Seventh Avenue)
☎ Times Square Information Center 212/869-1890
🚌 M6, M7, M27, M42, M104
🚇 1, 2, 3, N, R
🚶 Free walking tour every Friday at noon from the Times Square Information Center
🍴 Broadway Joe's Steakhouse, 315 West 46th Street, tel 212/246-6513– steaks and seafood
🍴 Planet Hollywood, 1540 Broadway at 45th Street, tel 212/333-7827, serves burgers and other American favorites, but movie memorabilia and giant projection screens are the real stars
🛍 Times Square Information Center

www.timessquarenyc.org
Get the latest news, events and tourist information, take a video tour or post a message.

SEEING TIMES SQUARE AND BROADWAY

Begin your visit at the Times Square Information Center, originally the attractive landmark Embassy Theater and now dominated by a branch of McDonald's. Even if you don't need information, take a look at the grand foyer. Over time, many of the old theaters have been renovated and now have landmark status. A special security force patrols the streets, and the area is as safe as any crowded urban neighborhood can be. If your visit to New York happens to coincide with New Year's Eve and you don't mind dense crowds, join the throngs in Times Square to see the glass ball drop at midnight to ring in the New Year. It's a great New York tradition.

HIGHLIGHTS

ED SULLIVAN THEATER
1697–1699 Broadway between 53rd and 54th streets
Built by Arthur Hammerstein as a memorial to his father, Oscar Hammerstein I, this theater was formerly called the Hammerstein Theater. The neo-Gothic vestibules, lobbies and auditorium are unique on Broadway. Used as a dance hall for many years, it made history when it became a television studio. "The Ed Sullivan Show," the longest-running TV show in history, was broadcast from here during the 1950s and 1960s. Today it is perhaps even more famous as the home of the "Late Show with David Letterman."

LYCEUM THEATRE
149 West 45th Street ☎ 212/239-6200
The oldest New York theater, saved from demolition in 1939, it is Broadway's most imposing structure with its magnificent Beaux Arts facade and powerful neo-Baroque columns. Inside are marble walls with murals by James Wall Finn. Many of Broadway's highly acclaimed comedies and dramas have been performed here, as well as classics by the National Actors Theatre. Such famous names as Ethel Barrymore, Bette Davis, Joseph Cotton, Melvyn Douglas, Alan Bates and Lauren Bacall have all performed at the Lyceum.

NEW VICTORY THEATER
209 West 42nd Street
www.newvictory.org
Built by Oscar Hammerstein I in 1899 and once known as Minsky's, the New Victory was restored and remodeled in 1995 and is the city's first full-time family-oriented performing arts center.

PARAMOUNT THEATRE BUILDING
1501 Broadway
The tallest building in Times Square when it was completed in 1927, the Paramount is crowned by a four-faced clock with a glass globe, a focal point of the area that is visible for miles when it's illuminated. The World Wrestling Entertainment's 2,000-seat theme restaurant, WWE New York, whose sign boasts the latest in fiber-optic technology, is in the old theater space; a 30ft (9m) video screen and 110 monitors

Transformed from a run-down, seedy area in the 1970s, Times Square is now respectable and much cleaner

ensure that every diner can watch live broadcasts of shows like "Raw" and "Smackdown!", and appearances by WWE stars. Other entertainments vary from concerts to magic shows.

BACKGROUND

Called Heere Straat (Main Street) by Dutch settlers, Broadway is New York's longest and oldest street. As the city's population grew, seedy bars, brothels and gambling dens opened on both sides. Even in the early 1800s, it bustled with pedestrians and horse-drawn carriages; there were even traffic jams. In the 1860s a row of minstrel halls opened along Broadway, and by 1900 the area on and off Broadway around Union Square had become the city's theater district. In 1880, the advent of electricity began to turn Broadway between 14th and 34th streets into the Great White Way. In the 1890s, when Oscar Hammerstein built the Olympia Theater on Broadway between 44th and 45th streets, the city's theatrical entertainment moved to the area that is now Times Square; it was then known as Longacre Square and was renamed only in 1904, when *The New York Times* moved into Times Tower on 42nd Street. In 1928, 14,900 electrical lights were added to the four sides of the Times Tower, creating the first moving electrical sign.

After the subway came to the Theater District, beginning in 1900, the crowds poured in. By the 1920s, movies had taken over many theaters. After this, the theaters started showing pornography and the crowd turned seedy. Sex joints drove out reputable business, and by the 1970s the district was crawling with hookers, pimps and other dubious characters.

During the 1990s, an aggressive clean-up operation—which included legislation against noise, gambling and prostitution, as well as new zoning laws—transformed the area. There's no question that the current state of the square and surrounding area has been an amazing show of effective planning, and a great triumph for the city.

Broadway is by far New York's longest street

TV SHOW TICKETS GUIDE

Tickets for live tapings of TV shows are free but usually hard to obtain because of the high demand, especially the immensely popular "Late Show with David Letterman." If you are seriously addicted to a show and you know six months in advance that you'll be in New York, register your preferred dates online.

Many studios hand out stand-by tickets on the day of taping, but you have to get up early and stand in line. In the dead of winter, you stand a better chance, as snow and cold winds put some people off. For more information call NYCVB at 212/484-1222. You can also phone or check show websites for information on ticket availability, waiting lists and stand-by tickets. When you attend a show, take photo ID, as it may be required.

"Late Show with David Letterman"
Register at **www.cbs.com/latenight/lateshow** or telephone 212/247-6497 for stand-by tickets on the day of taping at 11am sharp. You must be 18 or over to attend. You can request two tickets (maximum) in advance by filling out the request form online, or in person at the theater. Tapings are held at the Ed Sullivan Theater, 1697 Broadway between W. 53rd and W. 54th streets.

"Total Request Live"
To get tickets for the 3.30 MTV taping of this highly popular pop-music show, turn up by 2pm (earlier if the day's guest is a major celebrity) outside the 1515 Broadway studio between 43rd and 44th streets. A producer often roams around asking trivia questions about musicians and hands out tickets to those who answer correctly. You have to be between 18 and 24 to attend. For more information see www.nytix.com

"Good Morning, America"
Visit **www.abcnews.go.com/GMA** and you may be lucky and get to join Diane Sawyer and Charlie Gibson in their street-facing studio on Broadway at 44th Street. The show runs Monday to Friday from 7am to 9am. Tickets can only be reserved online for individuals.

"Montel"
Tickets to join the audience to see the Emmy award-winning talk show host Montel Williams can be obtained by visiting **www.**montel show.com and by emailing the form there. Three shows a day are taped on Wednesdays and Thursdays.

The stratospheric Seagram Building, a fine skyscraper

Lucky commuters get to ride the Staten Island Ferry every day

An attractive promenade flanks the Hudson River Park in TriBeCa

SEAGRAM BUILDING

⊞ 59 F17 • 375 Park Avenue 10022
☎ 212/572-7000 ◎ Mon–Fri 9–5 🚻

Erected in 1958 with interiors by Philip Johnson, this is New York City's only Mies van der Rohe building and one of the finest International-style skyscrapers in the world. The decision to set it toward the back of the granite-paved plaza was daring at the time, especially given real-estate values, but it ignited a taste for pedestrian plazas that lingers in Manhattan to this day.

The building is also notable as the site of the esteemed Four Seasons restaurant, famed venue for power lunches, and of the bustling Brasserie restaurant.

SOHO

See pages 132–133.

SOUTH STREET SEAPORT

See pages 134–135.

STATEN ISLAND FERRY

⊞ 344 F27 • Whitehall Terminal, 1 Whitehall Street 10004 ☎ Dial 311 for ferry information ◎ Daily 6am–1am both ways, less frequently on weekends, holidays and off-peak
🚊 Free 🚌 M1, M6, M9, M15 🚇 1, 4, 5, N, R
www.nyc.gov/dot

These commuter craft, which shuttle Staten Islanders to and from jobs in Manhattan, are—for tourists—a free, hour-long, round-trip excursion in the harbor—past the Statue of Liberty (▷ 136–137), Ellis Island (▷ 90–93) and Governors Island, with the Verrazano Narrows Bridge in the distance. In good weather, try for one of the old orange and green boats. The white boats are newer and have no outside deck. To get the best view, sit on the right side. Avoid rush hours, and disembark at Staten Island. On your right as

you get off, look for the boat-loading sign, which directs you to the next loading dock.

STATUE OF LIBERTY

See pages 136–137.

STUDIO MUSEUM IN HARLEM

⊞ Off map 59 E12 • 144 West 125th Street between Lenox and 7th Avenue 10027 ☎ 212/864-4500 ◎ Wed–Fri, Sun noon–6, Sat 10–6 🚊 Adult $7, child $3, under 12 free 🚌 M2, M7, M10, M100 🚇 2, 3 🛒 🍴 🚻
www.studiomuseuminharlem.org

Specializing in 19th- and 20th-century African-American art, and 20th-century African and Caribbean art and artifacts, this small museum has a lot to offer. Rotating exhibitions, a full calendar of events, and the annual exhibition from their Artists-in-Residence program make this a museum well worth a visit.

Exhibitions have included *Challenge of the Modern: African-American Artists 1925––1945*, which examined the modernist concepts adopted by black artists in the US and the Caribbean; and *Harlem Postcards 2007*.

The small sculpture garden is charming. The tempting gift shop offers a good selection of books, postcards and other items.

THEODORE ROOSEVELT BIRTHPLACE

⊞ 60 E20 • 28 East 20th Street 10003 ☎ 212/260-1616 ◎ Guided tour only (30 min) Tue–Sat 9–5 🚊 Adult $3, under 17 free 🚌 M1, M6, M23 🚇 6, N, R
www.nps.gov/thrb

Theodore (Teddy) Roosevelt, the great outdoorsman and 26th president of the United States, was born in New York in 1858 and spent his first 14 years in a fashionable brownstone just off

Broadway. The house was demolished just before his death in 1919, but the lot where the house stood was acquired in 1923 by the Women's Roosevelt Memorial Association, which commissioned a female architect to reconstruct it as it had been in Roosevelt's youth.

Rooms are furnished with objects preserved from the original house. The "lion's room" is filled with hunting and outdoor memorabilia. Roosevelt was sickly as a child, and a small gym that was intended to build up his health adjoins the nursery. There is also an exhibition about his eventful life.

TIMES SQUARE AND BROADWAY

See pages 138–140.

TRIBECA

⊞ 61 E24 • Between Hudson River and Broadway, Chambers and Canal streets
🚌 M20 🚇 1, 2, 3, A, C, E

TriBeCa (pronounced *try-beck-a*), the *Tri*angle *Be*low *Ca*nal Street, is where artists went in the late 1970s after sky-rocketing prices made SoHo (▷ 132–133) unaffordable to all but the very rich. They converted cast-iron warehouses into loft apartments, and now, predictably, a wealthy group has moved in along with antiques shops, design shops and some very fine restaurants. Actor Robert De Niro brought the Tribeca Film Center to the area in 1989.

There are some notable buildings, especially 2 White Street, dating from 1809; the Fleming Smith warehouse at 451 Washington Street, home of long-established Capsouto Frères bistro; and the Corinthian-columned, cast-iron 47 Worth Street. The area was greatly damaged on 9/11, but returned to full swing remarkably quickly.

Trinity Church

A historic church tucked away among Lower Manhattan's skyscrapers, and the final resting place of a handful of great Americans.

Many famous names are buried in the churchyard

Figures from the Bible mark the entrance to the church

Gothic romance authors have used the church as a setting

RATINGS	
Historic interest	●●●○
Photo stops	●●●○
Specialist shopping	●●●○
Walkability	●●●●●

BASICS

✚ 61 E26 • Broadway at Wall Street 10006

☎ 212/602-0800

🕐 Mon–Fri 7–6, Sat 8–4, Sun 7–4

🚌 M1, M6

Ⓜ 4, 5, 2, 3

🎧 Free guided tours daily 2pm

www.trinitywallstreet.org

As you walk up Broadway, north of Bowling Green, you come to Trinity Church. Now dwarfed by the surrounding skyscapers, Richard Upjohn's 1846 rose-pink sandstone masterpiece, with beautiful stained-glass windows and an eight-sided, 280ft (85m) spire, was once the tallest building in New York. The church bell was presented to the church in 1704 by the Bishop of London. As you enter, notice the biblical scenes on the bronze doors, designed by Richard Morris Hunt and donated in memory of John Jacob Astor III. Look for the white marble altar, the wooden vault and the screen of the Chapel of All Saints. To the left, at the back of the church, is a small museum (Mon–Fri 9–5, Sat 9–3, Sun 1–3.45) selling postcards, pamphlets outlining the church's history, books and videos, and gifts. The 30-minute guided tours of the church start from this museum. Classical music concerts take place in the church every Thursday from 1 to 2pm (free). Men must remove their hats as a sign of respect, even in the dead of winter, or will be reminded to do so by one of the church's wardens.

THE FIRST CHURCH

In 1697, by royal charter, the Anglican parish of Trinity became one of the largest landholders in Manhattan, and the first church was put up the next year, only to burn in the great fire of 1776, when the British army occupied New York. You will find the original royal charter for the church on display in the museum. During the struggle for independence, Trinity Church was a Loyalist bastion, but when the revolution ended, so did the Loyalists' hold on the city. A second building on the same spot was structurally flawed and was torn down in 1839. British architect Richard Upjohn, together with James Renwick, Jr., were commissioned to build the third Trinity Church. In the process, Upjohn made his reputation and went on to design many more churches around the country.

Before you leave the church, stroll around the small churchyard, a green oasis that's now estimated to be worth several million dollars for its prime location. Here are the graves of steamboat inventor Robert Fulton, statesman Alexander Hamilton, killed in a duel with Aaron Burr, and Francis Lewis, a signatory to the Declaration of Independence. The large cross in the churchyard is dedicated to Caroline Webster Schermerhorn Astor, the queen of 1800s high society.

Looking down Wall Street toward the Gothic Revival Trinity Church, with its imposing spire (right)

The opulence of Trump Tower is the stuff of legend

A symbol of peace and unity—the United Nations headquarters

Washington Heights is dedicated to an American Revolution battle

THE SIGHTS

TRUMP TOWER

✚ 59 E17 • 725 Fifth Avenue 10022
☎ 212/832-2000 ⏰ 8am–10pm
🚌 M1, M2, M3, M4 Ⓜ E, N, R, V
🍴 🏛

Not to be confused with the older Trump Building, originally the Manhattan Company Building, or with other Trump structures about town, this one rose in the 1980s as a glass monument to affluent lifestyles. Upper floors contain 263 plush apartments. (Trump himself was one of the first to move in.) Below them, the interior is a six-story atrium with escalators, waterfalls and glittering boutiques surrounded by pink marble, mirrors and shrubbery. It's ridiculously ostentatious but still quite the sight.

UKRAINIAN MUSEUM

✚ 61 F22 • 222 East Sixth Street between 2nd and 3rd Avenues 10003
☎ 212/228-0110 ⏰ Wed–Sun 11.30–5
🎟 Adults $8, children under 12 free
🚌 M101, M102, M103 Ⓜ 6 🚇 🏛
www.ukrainianmuseum.org

Ukrainian immigrants came to America in the 19th century and many stayed in New York and lived in the tenements on the Lower East Side, not far from this museum. Committed to preserving the cultural heritage of Ukrainians, this museum displays folk art items, including traditional costumes, decorative brass and silver jewelry, decorated Easter eggs, ceramics and woven and embroidered ritual cloths used as talismans at important events. It also curates shows of works by important Ukrainian artists.

UNION SQUARE

See page 145.

UNITED NATIONS HEADQUARTERS

✚ 59 G18 • United Nations Plaza 10017
☎ 212/963-8687 ⏰ Daily 9.30–4.45;
closed Sat, Sun in Jan and Feb 🎟 Adult $13, child (6–14) $7, under 5 not admitted 🚌 M15, M27, M42 Ⓜ 4, 5, 6, 7
🚶 Tours every half-hour Mon–Fri 9.30–4.45, Sat and Sun 10–4.30
🍴 🚇 🏛
www.un.org

At the end of World War II John D. Rockefeller, Jr. donated $8.5 million to purchase this site for the United Nations complex. The 544ft (166m) Secretariat building that dominates the site opened in 1950. Alongside are the General Assembly building, the Conference building (fronting the river) and the Dag Hammarskjöld Library. Fittingly, architects from many countries contributed to the designs. A 45-minute guided tour covers the General Assembly Hall and Security Council Chamber. You can see donated exhibits such as stained glass by Marc Chagall, a replica Sputnik, and, in the park, sculptures by Barbara Hepworth and Henry Moore. Visit the landscaped grounds, with beautiful views. Arrive early at peak times.

UPPER WEST SIDE

✚ 58 C13 • Between 59th and 125th streets, west of Central Park 🚌 M7, M10, M11, M104 Ⓜ 1, 2, 3, A, B, C, D
🍴 🚇 🏛

The Upper West Side is a lively residential area with numerous historic districts, sumptuous landmark buildings, affordable hotels and excellent restaurants, and an affluent crowd that includes many actors, actresses, directors and musicians. The popular American Museum of Natural History (▷ 68–72) is here, as are the city's premier performing arts complex, the Lincoln Center (▷ 112–113), and the Cathedral Church of St. John the Divine (▷ 67). While you stroll, note the San Remo

Apartment Building at 145–146 Central Park West, and the Trump International Hotel/Tower on Columbus Circle.

WASHINGTON HEIGHTS

✚ Page 7 • 155th Street to Dyckman Street 🚌 M4 Ⓜ 1, A, C 🍴 🚇 🏛

At the northern tip of Manhattan, this neighborhood of Latinos, Dominicanos, Greeks and Armenians does not attract many visitors. Yet there are some excellent restaurants and interesting attractions, including the medieval collections at the Cloisters (▷ 86) in Fort Tryon Park, which has spectacular views of the Hudson River. Washington Heights was the site of one of the earliest battles of the American Revolution, fought on November 16, 1776; Washington's troops lost to the British, who named the fort after the colonial governor, Sir William Tryon. John D. Rockefeller acquired the Cloisters property in 1917 and the museum opened in 1938.

WOOLWORTH BUILDING

✚ 61 E25 • 233 Broadway 10007
🚌 M1, M6, M15 Ⓜ 2, 3, 4, 5, 6, N, R

F. W. Woolworth, the department store mogul, hired fashionable architect Cass Gilbert to build the tallest building in the world in 1913. At 792ft (242m), this terracotta-faced, neo-Gothic masterpiece held the record until the Chrysler Building was completed in 1929 (▷ 85). In the 1980s much of the terracotta cladding was replaced. Inside, the lobby is a marvel of Skyros marble, with murals of *Labor and Commerce* and plaster depictions of some of the builders, including Gilbert, with a model of the building and Woolworth himself counting his cash.

Relax in the shade under the trees in Union Square's gardens

UNION SQUARE

A focal point of the off-Broadway theater scene, with great restaurants, excellent art galleries and interesting museums.

On a sunny day, the park is a pleasant place to people-watch and relax. There are also sculptures of Washington (1856) and Lincoln (1866), both by Henry Kirke Brown, and Lafayette by Statue of Liberty sculptor Frédéric-Auguste Bartholdi. Nearby are the Center for Jewish History at 15 West 16th Street; the eclectic Forbes Magazine Galleries at 62 Fifth Avenue at 12th Street (▷ 99); and Theodore Roosevelt's reconstructed birthplace at 28 East 20th Street.

At last count there were some 100 restaurants in the Union Square area, including some of the city's top tables. In September, at a fundraiser called Harvest in the Square, you can sample signature dishes of top neighborhood chefs. Also in September, the free outdoor Manhattan Short Film Festival screens 14 of the world's best short films and gives new film-makers a chance to compete for prizes.

A VARIED HISTORY

Run down and with a threatening atmosphere in the 1970s, Union Square is thriving and proud today. Every Monday, Wednesday, Friday and Saturday, a green market—one of the best farmers' markets in the United States—draws New Yorkers from all over the city and inspires local chefs. The bright idea of Barry Benepe (director of the green market)—who saw it as a way to simultaneously help Hudson Valley farmers and improve the neighborhood—it encouraged other communities to set up similar markets.

Union Square went residential in the 1840s, and America's greatest concentration of theaters, nightclubs, restaurants, hotels and luxury shopping followed. Union Square Park was laid out for the wealthy residents. In the 1800s, Ladies' Mile—Broadway and Sixth Avenue between 15th and 24th streets—was the height of fashionable shopping, until the turn of the 20th century when wealth moved uptown and the area deteriorated. In the late 1800s, Union Square was the center for demonstrations and political protests. In the early 1930s the editorial offices of The New Masses and the offices of the Communist Party's Yiddish-language paper moved here. A renovation of the square in 1936 discouraged further demonstrations.

The best chefs in town swear by the freshness and quality of produce at the farmers' market

RATINGS	
Historic interest	● ● ●
Photo stops	● ● ●
Specialist shopping	● ● ● ●
Value for money	● ● ● ●

BASICS

✚ 60 E21 • From East 12th Street to East 20th Street, between Third and Fifth avenues

🚌 M2, M3, M6, M7

🚇 4, 5, 6, L, N, Q, R

🚶 Free walking tour Sat 2pm, meet at the Lincoln statue near the Pavilion Building in Union Square Park

🍴 Old Town Bar & Restaurant, 45 East 18th Street between Broadway and Park Avenue, tel 212/529-6732

www.unionsquarenyc.org

Wall Street

The heart of New York's financial center and the historic site of George Washington's inauguration.

Shopping center underneath Wall Street

Playing chess in the street is a popular pastime today

The Stock Exchange, on the corner of Wall and Broad streets

This symbol of wealth is in fact a narrow 18th-century lane running from Broadway to South Street. The New York Stock Exchange (closed to the public since 9/11) stands on the corner of Broad Street and Wall Street. At the west end of the street on Broadway, framed between towering office buildings, is the Gothic Revival Trinity Church (▷ 142–143)—an impressive sight, and a great photo opportunity, with the many U.S. flags waving from their perches on the buildings along the street. Stop in front of Federal Hall National Monument (▷ 97); a statue of George Washington marks the spot where the first president took the oath of office. The two skyscrapers at Nos. 40 and 55 Wall Street rise up 930ft (282.5m) and 951ft (290m) respectively. This is an area steeped in history, evidenced by the many historical plaques, cornerstones, markers and notices. Take a look at the Morgan Bank headquarters at No. 60. Its bold arcade vies for attention as one of the tallest skyscrapers in the Financial District. Visit the white marble lobby.

Wall Street was named for the northern wall erected in 1653 to defend New Amsterdam from Native Americans. North of this wall were the *bouwerijs* (farms). After the English defeated the Dutch, and New Amsterdam was renamed New York, the wall started to crumble and in 1699 it was torn down. The bastion stones from the Dutch wall were carted off and used in the foundation of City Hall (▷ 77).

THE FIRST TRANSACTION

In 1792, 22 brokers and merchants stood in front of a buttonwood tree on Wall Street and made their first trading agreement. They were actively trading government securities, seeking to establish fixed commissions on transactions and favoring brokers who were signatories. This "Buttonwood Agreement," as it was called, eventually gave birth to the New York Stock Exchange. Their open-air trading activities moved indoors, probably to taverns, until premises on William Street were acquired in the 1860s.

The telegraphic ticker, new in 1867, has been replaced by today's latest market information display technology. The adrenaline rushes as hundreds of brokers on the trading floor, the size of a football field, trade billions of shares in about 3,000 companies. Sadly, this frenetic trading cannot be viewed live, because it is closed indefinitely to visitors. Call 212/656-3000 for further information.

RATINGS

Historic interest	●●●●●
Photo stops	●●●●
Specialist shopping	●●
Walkability	●●●●●

BASICS

🔲 61 F26 • Financial District

🚌 M1, M6, M15, M22

🚇 2, 3, 4, 5

🎫 Free 90-min Wall Street walking tour every Thu, Sat noon; meet on the steps of the U.S. Customs House at 1 Bowling Green, tel 212/606-4064

🍴 John Street Bar & Grill, 17 John Street, tel 212/349-3278, daily 11am–2am

🍴 Mangia, 40 Wall Street, tel 212/425-4040, Mon–Fri 7am–4pm

www.downtownny.com
Up-to-date information on Lower Manhattan's buses, subways, attractions, shops, hotels and transportation

TIP

● As the Financial District is deserted on weekends, visit on a weekday when this little street becomes a superhighway for stockbrokers in dark suits.

Wall Street is most famous internationally for the devastating Wall Street Crash in 1929

Whitney Museum
of American Art

More than 11,000 works by 1,700 prominent 20th- and 21st-century American artists, including Georgia O'Keeffe, Jasper Johns, Edward Hopper, Mark Rothko and Jackson Pollock. Provocative works by innovative and often controversial American independent film-makers, video artists, multimedia artists and photographers.

Taking a break at the museum

SEEING THE WHITNEY MUSEUM OF AMERICAN ART

Before entering the museum on Madison Avenue, take a few minutes to look at the striking granite, modernist building by Marcel Breuer and Hamilton Smith. In a neighborhood of traditional brownstone, limestone and brick row houses, this Brutalist architecture attracts attention, and when it was completed in 1966, many people thought it too heavy and dreary. Today, it is generally esteemed as daring and innovative as it rises in a series of inverted stairs above a sunken sculpture garden. As you enter, the ticket desk is to your left. At the ticket desk and checkout counter there are free Whitney calendars with the current exhibition schedule and leaflets about the current and upcoming temporary exhibitions. The free audiotours can be picked up at the end of the checkout counter.

Start your visit with the permanent collection, either on the second floor, De Kooning to Today, or on the fifth floor, Hopper to Mid-Century. New exhibitions are also staged (in the past these have featured individual artists and themed shows).

Works by contemporary artists are displayed to good effect in the museum galleries

HIGHLIGHTS

FIFTH FLOOR: HOPPER TO MID-CENTURY

The Leonard and Evelyn Lauder Galleries, which make up part of this floor, contain more than 200 works from the first half of the 20th century. As you leave the elevator on this floor, you will see the Early 20th-Century Urban Realism Gallery, with several paintings by Robert Henri, including a lovely portrait dating from 1916 of the museum's founder, Gertrude Vanderbilt Whitney, donated by her granddaughter, Flora. If you have the free audioguide, listen to Mrs. Whitney's granddaughter's description of her. The portrait depicts a woman of leisure, which surprises the granddaughter who remembers her as an energetic woman always on the go. On the opposite wall is a fine painting by William J. Glackens, *Hammerstein's Roof Garden* (c1901), which depicts wealthy New Yorkers at the beginning of the 20th century enjoying watching tightrope walkers, acrobats and jugglers on a hot summer's evening at Hammerstein's on the corner of Seventh Avenue and 42nd Street.

The Machine Age and Geometric Abstraction Gallery houses a collection of paintings of American factories and skyscrapers in a style called Precisionism. The artists' creations are a response to the explosion of industry in the early 20th century.

In the Early American Modernism Gallery are several paintings by Georgia O'Keeffe, including several of her dazzling flower paintings and *Summer Days* (1936), one of her many cow-skull paintings. You will also find her gorgeous *Music Pink and Blue II* (1919) and *Black and White* (1930).

The superb collection in the Edward Hopper Gallery displays such favorites as *7am* (1948), and his earlier *Small Town Station* (1918–20) and *Italian Quarter From Gloucester* (1912), as well as his particularly haunting painting, *Early Sunday Morning* (1930).

RATINGS	
Good for kids	●●●
Historic interest	●●
Specialist shopping	●●●●
Value for money	●●●●●

TIPS

● Come Fridays from 6pm to 9pm. Admission is pay-what-you-wish and there are live musical performances.
● For a good cross section of the latest in American art and to see works by unknown but promising artists, visit when the Whitney Biennial is on (even-numbered years).
● There's a branch of the museum in the Altria Building at 120 Park Avenue (Mon–Wed, Fri 11–6, Thu 11–7.30; free).

GALLERY GUIDE
Floors 1, 3, 4: Temporary exhibits.

Floor 2: De Kooning To Today: Mildred and Herbert Lee Galleries include works by Jackson Pollock, Jasper Johns, Claes Oldenburg, Robert Rauschenberg, Roy Lichtenstein, Frank Stella, Robert Smithson, Alexander Calder and Paul Pfeiffer. Also temporary exhibits. Marisol's *Women and Dog* (1964) sculpture is four

Notice the curtains and blinds in the windows above the storefronts in this picture. By making each window different, some with yellow blinds and others with white curtains, he gives a sense that people live in each of these dwellings, and that something different is going on inside each one. Hold up your hands to block from your view the barber's pole and the fire hydrant, and notice how they give focus and balance to the painting.

The Realism in the 1930s Gallery has fine works by Thomas Hart Benton. *Poker Night* (1948) was a commissioned work based on the Broadway performance of "A Streetcar Named Desire."

In the Early Abstract Expressionism Gallery is a sculpture by Louise Bourgeois called *Quarantania* (1953). The artist produced this work when she was feeling very homesick for her native France while she studied in the United States. Her longing for her loved ones comes

The entrance lobby is a riot of modern lighting

The fourth-floor gallery was used for temporary exhibitions during the 2000 Whitney Biennial

sculptures of the artist. The one with the green skirt and pink blouse has her photo stuck to the head.

Floor 5: Hopper to Mid-Century: Leonard and Evelyn Lauder Galleries include works by William Glackens and Robert Henri; Machine Age and Geometric Abstraction Gallery has works in the Precisionist style; Early American Modernism Gallery includes Georgia O'Keeffe; Edward Hopper Gallery; Realism in 1930s Gallery displays Thomas Hart Benton, John Stuart Curry and Joe Jones; Early Abstract Expressionism Gallery includes Louise Bourgeois. Also temporary exhibits. *The Lord is My Shepherd* (1926), by Thomas Hart Benton, is a painting of a husband and wife who were the artist's deaf-mute neighbors on Martha's Vineyard.

out in this sculpture. The Surrealism in America Gallery contains Man Ray's *La Fortune* (1938), a statement about man's attempt to win at games.

SECOND FLOOR: DE KOONING TO TODAY
Roy Lichtenstein, *Little Big Painting*
In the Pop Gallery, *Little Big Painting* (1965) is a celebration of mass media and popular culture. The red, white and yellow with harsh black lines resemble an image of an abstract painting. With no trace of the artist's hand, no visible brushstroke, and the dot screen in the

Hail, Bright Aurora, *by an unknown artist*

background, Lichtenstein (1923–97) evokes mechanical printing, the culture of mass reproduction.

Alexander Calder, *Circus*
Calder's (1898–1976) fascination with the circus and his training as a mechanical engineer inspired him to create *Circus* (1926–31) and to breathe life into the tiny wire tightrope walkers, acrobats, weight-lifters and dancers in this mixed-media, miniature reproduction of an actual circus. The sculpture is accompanied by a continuous screening of a film of the affable ringmaster, Calder, in his studio with his wife, winding up the gramophone, as they performed for the Paris avant-garde in the 1920s.

Other Highlights
The Mildred and Herbert Lee Galleries, occupying almost all of this floor, display works by American artists after 1945. In the Abstract Expressionism Gallery, Jackson Pollock's *Number 27* (1950) is one of the many pieces he created by placing the canvas on the floor and drizzling paint on it in a very controlled and deliberate manner. The Life Is Art Gallery contains Jasper Johns's *Three Flags* (1958), which he viewed as a deconstruction of this potent symbol of America.

BACKGROUND

Gertrude Vanderbilt Whitney (1877–1942), the daughter of Cornelius Vanderbilt (1843–1899), studied sculpture at the Art Students League of New York and went on to become one of the country's most generous patrons of the arts. In 1914, she launched the Whitney Studio Club, at 8 West 8th Street in the West Village, next to her MacDougal Alley studio, to exhibit works of young, avant-garde American artists. She was particularly fond of revolutionary artists such as John Sloan, Everett Shin and George Luks, realist painters Edward Hopper and Thomas Hart Benton, and early modernist painters such as Max Weber and Stuart Davis.

In 1929, after years of collecting, Whitney offered her personal collection to the Metropolitan Museum of Art. When the Met refused it, she established the Whitney Museum of American Art in 1931 with 700 objects, many from her personal collection. Thus the museum became one of the few museums anywhere in the world to be founded by an artist. The Whitney moved to its present building in 1966.

BASICS
🞡 59 E15 • 945 Madison Avenue at 75th Street 10021
☎ 1-800-WHITNEY (944-8639) or 212/570-3676
🕐 Wed–Thu 11–6, Fri 1–9, Sat–Sun 11–6
💲 Adult $12, under 12 free ($2.25 per ticket service charge online or by phone), pay-what-you-wish Fri 6–9pm
🚌 M1, M2, M3, M4
🚇 6
📋 Free exhibition tours start at the lobby information desk, tel 212/570-3676. Free self-guiding audiotours available in the lobby. Family audioguide; Saturday family programs free with museum admission for children aged under 11, call 212/671-5300 for info (reservations required for some programs)
🏠
🍽 Sarabeth's (tel 212/570-3670), a café, serves lunch Tue 11–3.30, Wed–Fri 11–4.30 and weekend brunch Sat–Sun 10–4.30
🖼

www.whitney.org
Highlights of the permanent collection, plus the latest on programs and events, shopping online, and Whitney Biennial information.

Railroad Crossing, *by Edward Hopper*

Enjoying the last rays of the evening sunshine from the Brighton Beach Boardwalk in Brooklyn

The elegant Palm House in Brooklyn Botanic Garden

Farther Afield

THE SIGHTS

BROOKLYN

BRIGHTON BEACH

✚ Page 7 • Southern tip of Brooklyn
🚇 B1, B68 🚇 Q 🍴 🚻 🏛

The influx of Russian immigrants to this area on Brooklyn's Atlantic-pounded shore has earned it the nickname Little Odessa by the Sea. You'll appreciate why as you stroll along the ocean's-edge boardwalk and Brighton Beach Avenue. The dozens of supermarkets and delicatessens are stocked with caviar, knishes, vodka, sausages and foods you just don't see back home unless home is Russia. The nightlife recalls Las Vegas, with its scantily clad dancers crowned with elaborate plumage.

BROOKLYN BOTANIC GARDEN

✚ Page 7 • 1000 Washington Avenue, Brooklyn 11225 ☎ 718/623-7200
🕐 Mar–end Oct Tue–Fri 8–6, Sat–Sun 10–6; Nov–end-Feb Tue–Fri 8–4.30, Sat–Sun 10–4.30 🎫 Adult $8, under 112 free. Free to all Tue and Sat 10–noon 🚌 B41, B43, B47, B48, B71 🚇 Q to Prospect Park, 2, 3 to Eastern Parkway 📷 Guided tours weekends 1pm 🏛 🏛 🚻
www.bbg.org

These 52 acres (21ha), planted with more than 13,000 varieties from around the world, are a place for a quiet stroll when you've had enough of Manhattan. There are water-lily ponds, stately old trees and flowering shrubs, a local plantlife section and a conifer collection. The Cranford Rose Garden shelters more than 1,000 varieties of rose. The stunning Cherry Esplanade draws large crowds in May for the blooming season and the Japanese hill-and-pond garden is one of the best of its type in the country. The Palm House, designed by McKim, Mead & White in 1914, and the greenhouses added in 1987, offer additional spaces. You can see everything in two or three hours.

BROOKLYN HISTORICAL SOCIETY

✚ 345 H26 • 128 Pierrepont Street, Brooklyn 11201 ☎ 718/222-4111
🕐 Wed–Sun noon–5 🎫 Adult $6, members and under 12 free 🚌 B51 weekdays only 🚇 2, 3, 4, 5 📷 Guided tours available 🚻
www.brooklynhistory.org

The Brooklyn Historical Society is a museum, library and educational center dedicated to preserving and exploring Brooklyn's heritage. It occupies a landmark Queen Anne-style building (1881) designed by George B. Post, who embellished the interior with Minton tile floors, elaborately carved black ash, and stained glass by Charles Booth. Post applied bridge engineering techniques to create an open and dramatic two-story space in the center of the building. The museum has a collection of 9,000-plus objects relating to local history. They are used in shows such as Brooklyn Works, which traced the history of working people from early farming days through the industrial era (when Brooklyn was the fourth-largest city in the US) to today. The shows are accessible and include fascinating oral history. Prints and Dodger memorabilia are strong elements, too. The society also offers walking tours of Brooklyn neighborhoods and a boat tour of the working waterfront (prices vary). The library (open by appointment) has a premier collection too, including a first edition of Walt Whitman's *Leaves of Grass*.

CONEY ISLAND

✚ Page 7 • Southern tip of Brooklyn 11224 🚌 B36, B74 🚇 F, Q, W
🍴 🚻 🏛 🚻
www.coneyisland.com

Known as the Playground of the World, Coney Island's a New York treasure, though it's seen tough times. It lost its Thunderbolt roller coaster and Kensington Hotel in 2000; Steeplechase Park was closed in 1964; Astroland Park's fate for summer 2008 was unknown at this writing. In spite of this, the New York Aquarium (opened in 1957) is going strong, and Astroland—whatever it may become—still has its Cyclone roller coaster. The Mermaid Parade, a summer solstice staple, is a must-see."

An early employee time recorder at the Brooklyn Historical Society

(Continued on page 154)

The Peaceable Kingdom *(1840–45), by Edward Hicks*

BROOKLYN MUSEUM

The second-largest art museum in New York City, and one of the largest in the country, attracts half a million visitors every year.

The Brooklyn Museum is housed in a grand Beaux Arts building designed by McKim, Mead & White in 1897, with an addition by Polshek Partners completed in spring 2004. The new plaza has two water features.

THE COLLECTIONS
The museum prides itself on its fine collection of Egyptian, Classical and Ancient Middle Eastern Art. It holds the third-largest collection of Ancient Egyptian artifacts dating from predynastic times to the Roman conquest. The renovated Morris A. and Meyer Schapiro Wing contains objects from 1350BC, in the reign of Akhenaten and his wife Nefertiti, through to the time of Cleopatra. Jewelry, reliefs of major deities, decorated sarcophagi, coffins and a 2,600-year-old mummy are on display.

The Arts of Africa, the Pacific and the Americas galleries have astonishing collections. An ivory gong from the Edo people of Benin, works from Polynesia and Indonesia, and important textiles from the Andes are just some of the fascinating items. The Arts of Asia collection has objects from China, India, Iran, Korea, Japan, Tibet, Thailand and Turkey.

The collection of decorative arts, costumes and textiles features a 17th-century Dutch farmhouse and a 20th-century art deco library. The costumes of 19th-century America and Europe are a glimpse at finery we can hardly imagine today.

Paintings, sculptures, prints, drawings and photographs include works by Gilbert Stuart, Thomas Cole, George Caleb Bingham, Winslow Homer, Auguste Rodin, Edgar Degas, Camille Pissarro, Edward Steichen and Paul Strand, to name just a few.

EVENTS
First Saturdays of the month are enormously popular. A free program of art and entertainment, with food and drinks supplied, attracts thousands. For example, the entertainment may start with spoken-word artists and members of the Brooklyn Philharmonic in Shakespeare Live alongside a program of Hands-on-Art that allows you to create your own Egyptian-inspired necklaces.

A sculpture in the grounds

RATINGS	
Historic interest	● ● ●
Photo stops	● ● ●
Walkability	● ● ● ● ●
Value for money	● ● ● ●

BASICS

✚ Page 7 • 200 Eastern Parkway, Brooklyn 11238

☎ 718/638-5000

◷ Wed–Fri 10–5, Sat–Sun 11–6, first Sat of the month (except Sep) 11–11

🎟 Adult $8, under 12 free; 1st Sat each month free 5–11

🚌 B41, B69, B71

Ⓜ 2, 3

🎧 Audiotour of permanent collection, $3

🍴 Museum Café Wed–Fri 10–4, Sat, Sun and holidays 11–5

🛍 BMA Shop Wed–Fri 10.30–5.30, Sat–Sun 11–6, until 11pm on First Saturdays 👥

www.brooklynmuseum.org
Floorplan, information on permanent and temporary collections, events, schedule for First Saturdays, online shopping.

Fun on the Ferris wheel at Coney Island in Brooklyn

Henry Ward Beecher at the Plymouth Church of the Pilgrims

The Kennedy arch at the entrance to Prospect Park

(Continued from page 152)

Nathan Handwerker opened his hot-dog emporium here in 1916, and his famous hot dogs are now sold all over New York.

Keyspan Park is the $39-million home of the Brooklyn Cyclones baseball team. It is located behind Parachute Jump on the Boardwalk.

NEW YORK TRANSIT MUSEUM

✚ Page 7 • Boerum Place and Schermerhorn Street, Brooklyn 11201 ☎ 718/694-1600 ⏰ Tue–Fri 10–4, Sat–Sun noon–5 💲 Adult $5, child (under 17) $3 🚇 2, 3, 4, 5 🏛 Annex Gallery and Store at Grand Central, tel 212/878-0106 ♿
www.mta.info/museum

The New York Transit Museum occupies a decommissioned subway station in downtown Brooklyn. The permanent and temporary exhibitions explore the history of buses and trolleys in New York City.

Have a go at the exhibits at the New York Transit Museum

Highlights are the vintage subway and trolley cars.

PLYMOUTH CHURCH OF THE PILGRIMS

✚ 345 H26 • 75 Hicks Street, Brooklyn 11201 ☎ 718/624-4743 ⏰ Guided tour only (1hr 30 min) Mon–Fri 10–4, Sun 11–2, advance reservation required 💲 Phone for prices 🚇 2, 3, A, C
www.plymouthchurch.org

The Plymouth Church of the Pilgrims, built in 1849, was the first Congregational Church in Brooklyn and a focal point of the anti-slavery movement at the time. Abraham Lincoln worshiped here twice in 1860, and many eminent writers have spoken here. Elegant and beautiful stained-glass windows by Tiffany adorn this otherwise modest church, and in the courtyard next to it is a superb bronze statue of Henry Ward Beecher (1813–87) with slaves, sculpted by Gutzon Borglum (famous for his work on Mount Rushmore).

Beecher, the most famous preacher in America, preached from this pulpit for 40 years, often speaking out against slavery.

PROSPECT PARK

✚ Page 7 • Flatbush Avenue at Grand Army Plaza. Information: Prospect Park Alliance, 95 Prospect Park West, Brooklyn 11215 ☎ Information: 718/965-8999; Lefferts Homestead Historic House Museum: 718/789-2822 ⏰ Daily 5am–1am. Museum: Apr–Nov Thu–Sun 12–5 💲 Free 🚌 B41, B69, B71, B75 🚇 2, 3, F, Q 🛒 🍴 🏛 ♿
www.prospectpark.org

Designed by Frederick Law Olmsted and Calvert Vaux, the designers of Central Park (▷ 78–83), this 526-acre (213ha) park is a pleasant place to spend a day. At the main entrance at Grand Army Plaza are a triumphal arch and

a monument to President John F. Kennedy.

In Leffert's Homestead is a museum for children. A zoo, skating rink, boathouse and pond, playgrounds, and a lovely 1912 carousel (Apr–end Oct; $1.50) are very popular with children, too.

The northeast corner has a rose garden, Japanese gardens, a sculpture garden and the Brooklyn Museum (▷ 153). Entertainment events throughout the year draw large crowds.

The Audubon Center provides maps and guides for self-guiding tours, as well as free guided nature walks and other programs (tel 718/287-3400, Apr–Nov Thu–Sun 12–5; Dec–Mar Sat–Sun 12–4).

WATERFRONT MUSEUM

✚ Page 7 • 290 Conover Street at Pier 44, Brooklyn 11231 ☎ 718/624-4719 ⏰ Thu 4–8 💲 Free 🚌 77 🚇 F, G
www.waterfrontmuseum.org

An unusual museum in the last surviving railroad barge, the Waterfront stages a summer music series on Saturday nights in July featuring blues to swing and country artists, and a program of Circus Sundays in June. The barge was designated by the U.N. in 1998 as the Regional Craft of the International Year of the Oceans.

Day visitors learn about New York Harbor, barge history and how this barge was rescued.

QUEENS

NEW YORK HALL OF SCIENCE

✚ Page 7 • 111th Street, Flushing Meadows–Corona Park, Queens 11368 ☎ 718/ 699-0005 ⏰ Apr–Jun Mon–Thu 9.30–2, Fri 9.30–5, Sat–Sun 10–6; Ju–Aug Mon–Fri 9.30–5, Sat–Sun 10–6; Sep–Mar Tue–Thu 9.30–2,

Education through fun at the Hall of Science Playground

Staten Island's Conference House retraces American history

The Waterfront Museum is in the last old railroad barge

Fri 9.30–5, Sat–Sun 10–6 🎫 Adult $11, child (2–17) $8. Sep–Jun, free Fri 2–5, Sun 10–11 Science Playground (age 6 and up, with adult supervision, Mar and Dec, weather permitting $3) 🚌 Q23, Q58 🚇 7 to 111th Street Queens 🎧 Audio tours $2 🚻 ♿ 🚼
www.nyscience.org

In this hands-on, interactive museum of science and technology, with more than 225 exhibits, trained Explainers answer questions about topics ranging from color or sound and light to microbiology and quantum physics. You can surf the net in the Technology Gallery, discover the wonders of science by conducting your own experiments in the Biochemistry Discovery Lab, or peer at the World of Microbes and the Realm of the Atom.

The Science Playground outside has more than 30,000sq ft (2,790sq m) of giant slides, windmills, waterplay features, kinetic sculptures and a 3-D spider web, where children can have fun.

QUEENS MUSEUM OF ART

🏠 Page 7 • New York City Building, Flushing Meadows–Corona Park, Queens 11368 ☎ 718/592-9700 🕐 Wed–Fri 10–5, Sat–Sun 12–5 🎫 Suggested donation: adult $5, child (under 5) free 🚌 Q47 🚇 E, F, G, R, 7 to 74th Roosevelt Avenue
www.queensmuseum.org

A $15-million renovation in 1994 by Rafael Viñoly expanded this museum for ambitious exhibitions of contemporary art.

The permanent collection includes beautiful glassware from the Tiffany Studio, which was in Queens from 1893 to 1938, and the Panorama of New York City, an 18,000sq ft (1,674sq m) minutely detailed scale model of New York City, with every building in place. The largest architectural scale model, it was created for the

1964–65 World's Fair, and it is regularly updated to reflect the changes in New York buildings. The museum's Art Moderne building was erected to house the 1939 World's Fair and was used again during the 1964–65 Fair, for which the adjacent Unisphere was created. It is the largest globe in the world, built by U.S. Steel.

From 1946 to 1952 the museum building was home to the United Nations General Assembly.

The Unisphere outside the Queens Museum of Art

STATEN ISLAND

ALICE AUSTEN HOUSE

🏠 Page 6 • 2 Hylan Boulevard, Staten Island 10305 ☎ 718/816-4506 🕐 Mar–end Dec Thu–Sun noon–5 🎫 Adult $2, child free 🚌 S51 to Hylan Boulevard ♿ 🚼
www.aliceausten.org

This unique museum is the restored Victorian house and garden of Alice Austen (1866–1952), one of America's early female documentary photographers. A visit here is fascinating for the quality of Austen's photographs, but also for the idea it gives of what middle-class life was like at the turn of the 20th century. The house was declared a city landmark in 1971.

The photographs give you a glimpse into the world of a

well-traveled young woman, who taught herself to operate the camera, develop heavy glass plates and make prints.

Alice took her equipment with her everywhere when she traveled, despite it weighing as much as 50 pounds (23kg), and photographed the world around her, including New York street scenes, using costuming and satire to create the desired effect.

Exhibitions and events take place throughout most of the year and often feature works by other local artists.

Take the Staten Island Ferry from Manhattan, then catch the S51 bus to Hylan Boulevard.

CONFERENCE HOUSE

🏠 Page 346 • 7455 Hylan Boulevard, Staten Island 10307 ☎ 718/984-0415 🕐 Apr–mid-Dec Fri–Sun 1–4, guided tours only 🎫 $3 🚌 S78 to Craig Avenue
www.theconferencehouse.org

Originally called the Billop Manor House, Conference House was built around 1680.

On September 11, 1776, Benjamin Franklin, John Adams and Edward Rutledge (a South Carolina governor and signatory to the Declaration of Independence) came here for a meeting with Admiral Lord Howe, the Commander of Her Majesty's Atlantic Squadron. Howe hoped to persuade the colonists to give up their fight for independence and to return to fold of the Mother Country, but the meeting lasted no more than three hours. The visitors made it clear that they were not interested in his offer.

The two-and-a-half-story house has beautifully furnished period rooms and offers a look at life in colonial America. There are special events taking place throughout the year.

The Garibaldi Meucci Museum is dedicated to two Italians

Restoration is widespread at Historic Richmond Town

There are plenty of beautiful buildings at Snug Harbor

THE SIGHTS

GARIBALDI MEUCCI MUSEUM

➕ Page 6 • 420 Tompkins Avenue 10305 ☎ 718/442-1608
🕐 Tue–Sun 1–5 ✋ Adults $5
🚌 S52, S78
www.garibaldimeuccimuseum.org

The Italian national hero, and one of the founders of unified Italy, Giuseppe Garibaldi (1807–82) spent two years in this 1840s house after fleeing the conquering republicans in Italy. It was the home of one Antonio Meucci (1808–89), who in fact was the inventor of the telephone. He invented a prototype several years before Alexander Graham Bell got into the picture, but, as he failed to patent his idea, he never got the credit.

After Garibaldi died in 1884, a committee decided to commemorate his stay in Staten Island and a plaque was placed on the house. After Meucci's death, the house was given to the Italian community to preserve as a memorial to Garibaldi.

Today the house is owned and operated by The Order of Sons of Italy in America and displays artifacts about the lives of these two men. From the Staten Island Ferry, take either bus S78 or S52.

HISTORIC RICHMOND TOWN

➕ Page 6 • 441 Clarke Avenue, Staten Island 10306 ☎ 718/351-1611
🕐 Sep–Jun Wed–Sun 1–5; Jul–end Aug Wed–Sat 10–5, Sun 1–5 ✋ Adult $5, child (5–17) $3.50, under 5 free
🚌 S74 ☕ 🍽 🚻
www.historicrichmondtown.org

About 15 historic buildings are spread out over 100 acres (40ha) at this museum complex. It stretches across three centuries of daily life and culture on Staten Island, from its earliest days as a rural crossroad to its incorporation into Greater New York. The quaint atmosphere and helpful staff make the whole experience a very pleasurable day out.

Special events take place throughout the year, including summer fairs, concerts and costumed re-enactments.

JACQUES MARCHAIS MUSEUM OF TIBETAN ART

➕ Page 6 • 338 Lighthouse Avenue, Staten Island 10306 ☎ 718/987-3500
🕐 Wed–Sun 1–5 ✋ Adult $5, child under 6 free 🚌 S74 to Lighthouse Avenue 🚻 🍽
www.tibetanmuseum.org

This lovely museum is one of New York's best-kept secrets. The Dalai Lama, when he visited in 1991, attested to the likeness of the stone cottage on Lighthouse Hill to a Tibetan mountain temple, with its peaceful terraced sculpture gardens and an attractive fish pond.

The museum exhibits Tibetan, Nepalese and Mongolian art from the 17th to the 19th centuries. The Nepalese metalwork, encrusted with jewels, and the metal figures of deities and lamas, are exquisite. Informative explanations help you understand the significance of the jewelry, dance masks, ritual objects, incense burners, paintings and many other items from the world's Buddhist cultures. Special exhibitions and activities enhance a visit.

SNUG HARBOR CULTURAL CENTER

➕ Page 6 • 1000 Richmond Terrace, Staten Island 10301 ☎ 718/448-2500
🕐 Grounds daily dawn–dusk. Gallery Museum: Tue–Sun 10–5 ✋ Gallery adult $3, child (under 12) $2. Grounds: free 🚌 S40 ☕ 🚻 🏛 🍽
www.snug-harbor.org

Snug Harbor, a National Historic Landmark District, spreads out over 83 acres (34ha). Its 26 buildings, a fine collection of Greek Revival, Beaux Arts, Italianate and Victorian architecture, housed "decrepit and worn-out" old sailors during the 1880s. By the 1960s, the buildings had fallen into disrepair. After a vast restoration project, however, they are now a focal point of Staten Island cultural life, with art exhibitions in the Newhouse Galleries (Wed–Sun) and other activities. Be sure to see the Main Hall (Tue–Sun), the oldest building, and its lavish ceiling mural, towering skylight dome and gilded weathervane.

Preparing flax at one of the Historic Richmond Town restoration projects

Seals bask in the sun in their landscaped habitat at the Bronx Zoo

BRONX ZOO

The largest metropolitan wildlife park in the country, with more than 4,500 animals representing 55 species housed on 265 acres (107ha).

Plan to spend a whole day at this wonderful and hugely popular zoo, which has no fewer than three names—Bronx Zoo (unofficial), New York Zoological Park and International Wildlife Conservation Park. The animals, including endangered and threatened species, are well cared for and their surroundings are as near as possible to their habitats.

HIGHLIGHTS

One of the most impressive areas is the Wild Asia Complex, where you can see Indonesian tigers and Asian elephants, but only from the Bengali Express monorail. Jungle World's indoor re-creation of an Asian forest will envelop you, and it's home to leopards, lizards, tree kangaroos and white-cheeked gibbons, among other exotic wildlife from jungles around the world. In the Himalayan Highlands there are extremely rare snow leopards as well as red pandas.

The Congo Gorilla Forest is a 6.5-acre (9ha) re-creation of an African rainforest; among the treetop lookouts, wooded pathways and lush greenery are 400 animals, including western lowland gorillas, who can be entertaining. You'll also see okapi and red river hogs.

In the Butterfly Garden (Apr–end Oct) the size of some of the butterflies might surprise you, not to mention the enormous variety and beauty of these complicated insects.

The World of Darkness, as you might imagine, is devoted to the lives of nocturnal creatures, such as fruit-eating bats.

The Children's Zoo (Apr–end Oct) has wonderful activities—kids learn to see like an owl and hear like a fox—and a petting zoo.

The Bengali Express monorail (late Apr–end Oct) is a 25-minute narrated ride above the roaming Siberian tigers, Indian rhinoceroses, Asian elephants, and other animals of the Indian subcontinent. It's a good way to see a lot without wearing yourself out. Other rides include the Skyfari aerial tram, camel rides and the Zoo Shuttle (Apr–early Nov).

In summer it can get very crowded, and if it is a very warm day the animals retreat from open sunny positions and it can be hard to see some of them.

Good for kids	●●●●●
Photo stops	●●●●●
Specialist shopping	●●●●
Value for money	●●●●●

✚ Page 7 • Bronx River Parkway and Fordham Road, Bronx 10460

☎ 718/367-1010

🕐 Apr–Oct Mon–Fri 10–5, Sat–Sun 10–5.30; rest of year Mon–Fri 10–4.30, Sat–Sun 10–5

💵 Thu–Tue adult $14, child (2–12) $10, under 2 free; Wed suggested donation. Congo Gorilla Forest, Children's Zoo, Skyfari, Zoo Shuttle, Butterfly Zone, Bengali Express $3 each. Camel rides and monorail $5. Pay-One-Price ticket that includes admission and all rides except camel rides: adult $25, child $19

🚌 Bx11, tel 718/445-3100 for details

🚇 2 or 5 to Pelham Parkway or East Tremont Avenue

🎫 Tours by Friends of the Zoo, tel 718/ 220-5141

🍴 🛍 ♿ 👫
www.bronxzoo.com

● **From Madison Avenue you can take the Liberty Lines Bx11 express bus directly to the zoo.**

● **Eat early or late or bring a picnic and drinks. Lines for the food stands can be long and slow on a busy, hot afternoon.**

THE BRONX: BRONX ZOO **157**

The New York Yankees have won 26 World Series, more than any other American baseball team

YANKEE STADIUM

Cheer the New York Yankees in their home stadium.

RATINGS

Good for kids	●●●●
Photo stops	●●●
Specialist shopping	●●●●
Value for money	●●●●●

BASICS

✚ Page 7 • 161st Street and River Avenue, Bronx 10451

☎ 718/293-6000

📅 Baseball season Apr–Oct

🎟 Tickets for games $12–$400, tel Ticketmaster 212/307-1212 or visit www.yankees.com

🚌 Bx6, Bx13, Bx55

🚇 4, B, D

🚶 One-hour behind-the-scenes tour, tel 718/579-4531, visit the website or buy tickets from one of the five Clubhouse Shops in Manhattan on the day of the tour. Adult $15, child $7

🍽 Sidewalk Café on the Plaza next to Gates 4 and 6; snacks and drinks throughout the stadium

🎁 Gift shops are on the Field Level sections 24, 25, Yankees Team store at Gate 4. Yankee Clubhouse stores have five Manhattan locations. Get the location details and opening hours from the website 🛍

www.yankees.com

Yankee Stadium, America's first triple-decker stadium, has been home of the New York Yankees since April 18, 1923. The most famous player of them all, Babe Ruth, hit a three-run homer on that inaugural day in front of 74,200 fans and the Yankees were victorious (4–1). After that, the stadium quickly became known as The House That Ruth Built. The stadium got electric lighting in 1946 and the first electronic message board in 1959. After CBS became its new owner in 1967, the Yankees spent two seasons at Shea Stadium while their own stadium was renovated. Upon their return, the Yankees went on to host the World Series.

The stadium is used for other events, including football, soccer, religious conventions, political assemblies and concerts.

At Monument Park, on Field Level Section 36, you can see a special walk honoring players whose uniform numbers have been retired. Old Timers' Day, usually held in July, brings back the grand old players for a bow before their cheering fans.

SEEING A GAME

There are seven main entrances, so make a mental note of where you enter to avoid confusion when you leave. Make sure that you have no reason to leave once you are inside, because you cannot re-enter the stadium using the same ticket. Arrive an hour and a half before the game Mondays to Fridays, two hours ahead on weekends to watch the batting practice. It can take some time to get through the entrance, so allow plenty of time to see the beginning of the game.

To get a behind-the-scenes tour, which starts at the Press Gate, go to the Advance Ticket window or any of the Clubhouse stores on the day of the tour and you can find out more about Yankee history, get a good look at the field, the dugout area, the press box, the Clubhouse and Monument Park.

Alcohol is sold up until the seventh inning of each game, but drunkenness is not tolerated; you can ask to sit in an alcohol-free section when you buy your tickets. Other rules ban bottles, cans, coolers or containers, large bags and briefcases, noisemakers, laser pens, beachballs, firearms and knives; and there's no smoking.

This chapter gives information on things to do in New York other than sightseeing.

Shops and performance venues are located on the maps at the beginning of each section.

What to Do

SHOP LOCATOR

13

14

15

16

17

Hue-Man Bookstore

West 95th Street
West 94th Street
West 93rd Street
UPPER WEST SIDE
West 92nd Street
West 91st Street
West 90th Street
West 89th Street
West 88th Street
West 87th Street
West 86th Street
86th Street
West 85th Street
West 84th Street
West 83rd Street
West 82nd Street
West 81st Street
West 80th Street
West 79th Street
79th Street
West 78th Street
West 77th Street
West 76th Street
West 75th Street
West 74th Street
West 73rd Street
West 72nd Street
72nd Street
West 71st Street
West 70th Street
West 69th Street
West 68th Street
West 67th Street
66th Street Lincoln Center
West 66th Street
West 65th Street
West 64th Street
West 63rd Street
West 62nd Street
West 61st Street
West 60th Street
West 59th Street
59th Street Columbus Circle
West 58th Street
WEST 57TH STREET
57th Street
West 56th Street
West 55th Street
West 54th Street
West 53rd Street
West 52nd Street
West 51st Street
West 50th Street
50th Street
58th Street
49th Street
West 49th Street
West 48th Street
West 47th Street
West 46th Street
West 45th Street

West 40th Street

Zabar's

Kenneth Cole

American Museum of Natural History

81st Street Museum of Nat Hist

New-York Historical Society

San Remo Apartments

Ansonia Building

The Dakota

Applause Theatre and Cinema Books

Lincoln Center

Juilliard School

Museum of Biblical Art

Time Warner Center

COLUMBUS CIRCLE

Tavern on the Green

The Mys... Bo...

7th Avenue

BROADWAY

Hudson River

Riverside Park

HIGHWAY 9A

Riverside Drive

West End Avenue

BROADWAY

Amsterdam Avenue

Columbus Avenue

Central Park West

West

Drive

CENTRAL PARK

The Lake

Strawberry Fields

The Sheep Meadow

De Witt Clinton Park

Intrepid Sea, Air and Space Museum

12th Av

12TH AVENUE

11th Avenue

10TH AVENUE

9th Avenue

8th Avenue

7th Avenue

Freedom Place

Riverside Boulevard

West 69th Street

West 68th Street

Ce... P... Rese...

Cer

Tia...

79th Street Tra...

Central

BROADWAY

SHOPPING

They say that you can buy anything you want in New York City, and it's true. New York's shopping ranges from large opulent department stores to tiny one-room boutiques. Many visitors come to New York just to shop, especially pre-Christmas, uptown at the flagship designer stores that line Madison and Fifth avenues, or downtown at the cutting-edge designers in SoHo and NoLita. More moderately priced wares can be found at stores around Herald Square and 34th Street, or in the branches of national chains. There aren't any malls of note. Many stores open seven days a week (with late-night hours usually on Thursday). European visitors should note that American sizes differ from British and European sizes (▷ 315). Note too that the sales tax (added at the cash register) is 8.375 percent. There is no tax on clothing or footware. Credit cards are accepted virtually everywhere.

textiles, jewelry, bowls made from gourds, wooden stools and other artifacts from Africa are for sale. The Annex Antique Fair and Flea Market in the parking lots at Sixth Avenue and 26th Street (tel 212/243-5343) is very popular. Get there early for the best pickings (it opens at 5am). The Sunday Columbus Avenue market (between 76th and 77th streets) is also fun. In summer, expect small neighborhood street fairs at which people sell all kinds of bric-à-brac, clothing, CDs, food and books. Green markets have become very popular.

Objets d'art and other decorative items from Greene Street, SoHo

Vintage clothing for both sexes at Screaming Mimi's

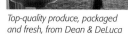
Top-quality produce, packaged and fresh, from Dean & DeLuca

SALES
The largest sales take place in January and July, and also around legal holidays—Presidents' Day, Memorial Day and Labor Day, for example.

To keep abreast of current and forthcoming sales check the relevant sections of *New York* magazine and *Time Out* or go online to www.dailycandy.com or www.nysale.com. Some of the best deals are found at sample sales, usually held in the spring and fall. Designers and manufacturers hold such sales to make space for their new design samples. Shopping fiends find out about them by subscribing

to S & B Report (tel 877/579-0222) or going online at www.lazarshopping.com. Online subscription is $75 a year. They are also listed at www.nysale.com. For visitors the best way to locate these sales is to go to a favorite designer or store and ask if they hold them. Or try walking around the Garment District, where people often give out flyers announcing them. Bring cash and note you may not be able to try items on. No refunds either.

MARKETS
Unlike European cities, New York has few outstanding markets, although one or two are worth visiting. At the African Market at 116th Street and Lenox Avenue,

The most storied is at Union Square (▷ 178), but there are smaller ones around town in Abingdon Square in the West Village or Tompkins Square in the East Village, for example.

Savvy New Yorkers also shop the thrift stores and consignment shops. Some of the best are: Housing Works, 143 West 17th Street (tel 212/366-0820) and 306 Columbus Avenue (tel 212/579-7566), Encore, 1132 Madison Avenue (tel 212/879-2850) at 84th Street, and the Salvation Army, 112 4th Avenue (tel 212/673-2741).

SoHo

HOW TO GET THERE

🚇 4, 5, 6, or N, Q, R, W
🚌 M1, M5, M6

SoHo has some of the hippest loft-style stores in the city. Concentrate on Mercer, Greene, Wooster, Prince and Spring streets, between West Broadway and Broadway. Many stores are open seven days a week, and the area can be crowded with non-residents on weekends.

Emerge from the subway at Broadway and Prince Street and you'll find three destination stores. **Dean & DeLuca**, on the southeast corner, is a landmark of New York for lovers of top-quality food. Displays are gorgeous creation , a café serves delicious pastries, and top-of-the-line cooking equipment is also for sale.

based **Eddie Bauer** sell casual wear, and the rapidly expanding Spanish chain **Zara International**, among other brand-name stores, sells fashion.

West along Prince Street look for more names. **Phat Farm** (No. 129) has plenty of stylish hip-hop wear.

On Mercer, look for **Marc Jacobs** at No. 163, the hottest fashion name of the moment, and **APC** at No. 131, south of Prince Street, which sells well-designed Parisian-style basics. **Kate Spade**, the famous bag designer, has a store at Mercer and Broome streets. On the same corner you'll find **Kelly Christy**, one of the city's bright young milliners, who makes hats in every fabric and style for men and women. At the corner of Mercer and Grand streets are the precise fashions of **Yohji Yamamoto**.

On Greene Street stock up on luxurious skin and hair care products at **SpaceNK** at No. 99 and **Kirna Zabete** at No. 96, shows fashions of the best of the current crop of international designers.

Turn off Prince Street and head south down Wooster, and you'll find **BCBG by Max Azria** selling individual women's fashions at No. 120, and **Eres** selling beautiful swimwear and lingerie at No. 98.

Check out Eres for the ultimate in swimwear and lingerie

Across the street on the north-west corner, the **Prada** store was designed by Dutch architect Rem Koolhaas; rows of mannikins wear the latest must-have designs from this fashion powerhouse.

On the southwest corner, **Victoria's Secret** sells romantic lingerie and swimwear. Farther down Broadway, **The Puma Store**, at No. 521, sells oodles of walking and running shoes. At No. 504 check out **Bloomingdales Downtown** and also **Pearl River Mart** at No. 477. Nearby, on Broadway, between Houston and Canal streets, branches of Seattle-

Prada's store on Broadway is worth a visit just to see the design of the interior

WHERE TO EAT

Cupping Room Café, 359 West Broadway between Broome and Grand streets (tel 212/925-2898), a fixture of SoHo, is casual and offers a menu of soups, burgers, salads and egg dishes.

At **Hampton Chutney**, 68 Prince Street between Crosby and Lafayette streets (tel 212/226-9996), tuck into southern Indian specialties—dosas, pancakes made with lentil flour, filled with both Indian and Western ingredients. You can get sandwiches on black, sourdough and other breads, too (▷ 278). **Fanelli's**, 94 Prince Street at Mercer (tel 212/431-5744), is reminiscent of the days when SoHo was a hang-out of artists. A good option for a burger or a plate of pasta, it also serves draft beer.

NoLita

HOW TO GET THERE

🚇 4, 5, 6
🚌 M1, M6, M21

NoLita stands for *North of Little Italy*. It is a warren of streets anchored by St. Patrick's Old Cathedral on Mulberry Street (between Prince and Houston streets), which was New York's original Roman Catholic cathedral. Dedicated in 1815, it was designed by Joseph Mangin, co-architect of City Hall. After a disastrous fire in 1866, the cathedral that stands on Fifth Avenue and 50th Street replaced it as the seat of the archdiocese.

The original congregation was largely Gaelic-speaking, poor Irish immigrants, and in those days the St. Patrick's Day parade terminated at the cathedral. At the turn of the 20th century, Italians

Pick up some unique accessories in NoLita's boutiques

formed the majority; today most of the congregation is Spanish-speaking.

Several members of the famous restaurant family, the Swiss Delmonico's, are buried in the crypt.

Pierre Toussaint, a Haitian slave who came to America in 1787, was buried in the cemetery. He attained his freedom, subsequently worked as a hairdresser and donated most of his wealth to various charities— orphanages, seminaries and hospitals.

The area developed as a shopping district when SoHo rents became too expensive for new designers and artists. Here, along Mulberry, Mott and Elizabeth streets between Kenmare and Houston streets are numerous small storefronts selling the latest fashions and accessories. From the Spring Street Station, walk east on Spring Street to Mulberry Street.

On Mulberry **Tracy Feith**, at No. 209, is famous for his ready-to-go party outfits. No. 257 used to be the Ravenite Social Club, a favorite John Gotti hang-out. Today, of course, it's a boutique.

Mott Street, between Prince and Spring streets, shelters **Resurrection Vintage**, one of the city's finest vintage clothing stores, plus **Zero** at No. 225, where Maria Cornejo crafts her own avant-garde line, and **Gas** at No. 238, which displays this French designer's jewelry, made with brilliant colored semi-precious stones. **Sigerson Morrison**, around the corner on Prince Street, sells some ultra-fashionable shoes at No. 28—they're almost as good as Manolos but at a fraction of the price. There are also more eye-catching boutiques on Mott Street between Prince and Houston streets.

Elizabeth Street is NoLita's main drag and has several

outstanding stores. **Me & Ro** at No. 239 are a duo who make some fun, inspired jewelry, often with Eastern motifs. North of Houston at 302 Bowery is **Patricia Field**, whose daring fashions were seen in *Sex and the City*.

Stores in NoLita tend to be one-of-a-kind rather than chains

WHERE TO EAT

Tiny **Bread**, at 20 Spring Street between Elizabeth and Mott streets (tel 212/334-1015), prepares soups, salads and Italian-inspired dishes. French-inspired **Café Gitane**, 242 Mott Street at Prince Street (tel 212/334-9552), serves good coffee plus salads, sandwiches and more substantial plates, such as couscous. Drop in to **Café Habana**, 17 Prince Street at Elizabeth Street (tel 212/625-2001), for some spicy tacos or a hefty Cuban sandwich.

You'll find designer jewelry aplenty in boutiques such as Me & Ro on Elizabeth Street

Fifth Avenue

After Madison Avenue, Fifth Avenue is the city's other famous shopping street, at least from 48th to 59th streets. Leave the subway stop at Fifth Avenue and 59th Street around the corner from the Plaza Hotel and stroll down Fifth Avenue.

Across the street looms the old General Motors Building. At the northeast corner of 58th Street **FAO Schwarz** is the city's legendary toy store. Farther down the Avenue are several of the city's great stores—**Bergdorf Goodman** at No. 754, **Henri Bendel** at No. 714, between 55th and 56th streets, and Japanese-owned **Takashimaya**, between 54th and 55th streets, with exquisite merchandise in

Jimmy Choo shoe

Go to Gap at No. 680 for practical, good-quality casuals

exquisite settings. Duck off Fifth Avenue east along 57th Street to the French classic, **Chanel**, and high-tech **NikeTown**, home of the swoosh.

As you progress down the Avenue, top-end designer showcases alternate with branches of national chains, making for sharp contrasts. At No. 720 **Fendi** sells its flamboyant, super-expensive accessories, while across the street a block farther south at No. 711, the **Disney Store** peddles character merchandise. **Gucci**, the premier Italian designer at No. 685, stands across from **Gap**, and a few blocks south at No. 666 is the **NBA Store**, which

stocks everything a basketball fan ever yearned for. **Tiffany** and **Cartier** are the two heavyweight jewelers on the Avenue, the first at No. 727, near 57th Street, and the second at No. 653 at 52nd Street. There are others, too—Bulgari, Van Cleef & Arpels, Harry Winston, and Wempe. **Jimmy Choo** displays his fantastic footwear at No. 645, at 51st Street. (**Manolo Blahnik** is just a few blocks away on 54th Street between Fifth and Sixth avenues.) At No. 640 **H&M** rolls out the designer knock-offs for the young shoppers, while at No. 626 **Banana Republic** concentrates its efforts on a more mature, more conservative audience. **Cole Haan** sells soft leather shoes and accessories at No. 620. At No. 626 **Saks Fifth Avenue** culls the best of the world's designers, including many you know and the most promising newcomers.

Well-cut, casual clothes for men and women at Banana Republic

In Rockefeller Plaza (between 49th and 50th streets), look for **J. Crew**, which caters to the college crowd, recent graduates and wannabes.

WHERE TO EAT

Wander the subterranean hallways under the G. E. Building where you will find numerous restaurants and cafés. **Au Bon Pain**, 1251 Avenue of the Americas (tel 212/921-5908), is a reliable standby for soups, sandwiches and pastries. Stylish **Morrells Café**, 1 Rockefeller Plaza (tel 212/262-7700), has a wide selection of wines to accompany its light fare.

Madison Avenue

HOW TO GET THERE

🚇 A, C, E

🚌 M1, M2, M3, M4, M5

Madison Avenue sells the crème de la crème of international fashion. From 53rd Street and the Fifth Avenue subway station, walk east to Madison Avenue and turn left (north) for a leisurely stroll.

At the northwest corner of 53rd, **Thomas Pink** sells beautifully cut shirts in rainbow hues. Across the street, **Talbots** at No. 525 sells comfortable, reasonably priced fashions to well-heeled women. Next door is an uptown branch of the casualwear favorite, **Gap**. Farther up the avenue at No. 543, **Lacoste** has complete wardrobes for cruising, golf and tennis. At No. 595 **Coach** sells attractive well-made bags and

*Map labels:*
East 72nd Street · Ralph Lauren · PARK AVENUE · Asia Society and Museum · East 71st Street · Frick Collection · Penhaligon · East 70th Street · Madison Avenue · Dolce & Gabbana · Alessandro dell'Acqua · 68th Street Hunter College · Donna Karan · East 68th Street · East 67th Street · Lexington Avenue · Central Park · East 66th Street · Giorgio Armani · East 65th Street · East 64th Street · Shanghai Tang · Lexington Avenue 63rd Street · FIFTH · East 63rd Street · AVENUE · East 62nd Street · Park Drive North · East 61st Street · Calvin Klein · DKNY · Lexington Avenue · The Pond · East 60th Street · Barneys · Ann Taylor · 5th Avenue · Tod's · 59th Street · Central Park South · East 59th Street · Crate & Barrel · PARK AVENUE · West 58th St · East 58th Street · Coach · Lexington Avenue · WEST 57TH ST · EAST 57TH STREET · Trump Tower · West 56th St · East 56th Street · 5th Avenue · West 55th St · East 55th Street · Lacoste · West 54th St · East 54th Street · Museum of Modern Art · Thomas Pink · Gap · Talbots · West 53rd St · 5th Avenue/53rd Street · East 53rd Street · Seagram Building · Paley Center for Media · 0 100 m · 0 100 yds

Bag from Coach

accessories. **Ann Taylor** caters to the young professional woman at No. 645, while the huge **Crate & Barrel** at No. 650 sells smart tableware, furniture and other items for the home. Italian shoemaker **Tod's** at No. 650 sells some of the most comfortable walking shoes ever made. Quintessential American designer **Calvin Klein**, who has lent his name to every conceivable wardrobe and houseware item, displays his talent at No. 654 at 60th Street. Designer Donna Karan has her **DKNY** store across the street at No. 655. **Barneys** is famous for its windows and for its highly selective range of all that's

cutting edge in international design. Between 62nd and 72nd streets, famous names tumble one after the other—**Shanghai Tang** displaying Asian-inspired fashions at No. 714 and **Giorgio Armani** (at 760 at 65th Street).

Farther up the Avenue are **Alessandro Dell'Acqua** at No. 818, **Donna Karan** at No. 825, **Dolce & Gabbana** at No. 816, **Penhaligon's** at No. 870 and **Ralph Lauren**, in a spectacularly renovated 19th-century town house at No. 867 at 71st Street—this store is worth seeing just for the architecture. Donna Karan's store is equally dramatic.

WHERE TO EAT

Brasserie, 100 East 53rd Street between Park and Lexington avenues (tel 212/751-4840), is a frenzied, streamlined, ultramodern space, where you can linger over lunch or grab a bite at the bar. The broad menu offers crepes, burgers, salads and bistro classics, as well as baguettes for a lighter snack (▷ 273). Food is served from early morning to late at night. **Pret à Manger**, 400 Park Avenue at 54th Street (tel 212/207-3725), is a branch of the British chain. It delivers freshly made sandwiches and wraps filled with appealing ingredients.

Shopping Directory

From large department stores and opulent designer stores to one-room boutiques, from diamonds to deckchairs and art supplies to zippers, you'll find it all in New York. Manhattan, though lacking the usual American city's bounty of malls, is itself like one huge open-air mall.

• ▷ 160–163 for shop locator maps
• ▷ 182–183 for chain stores chart
• ▷ 315 for clothing sizes

BOOKS

APPLAUSE THEATRE AND CINEMA BOOKS
Map 160 C15
211 West 71st Street between Broadway and West End Avenue
Tel 212/496-7511
www.applausepub.com
Books about Broadway, plays and playwrights, dance and film fill the shelves.
🕐 Mon–Sat 11–7 🚇 72nd Street (1, 2, 3) 🚌 M5, M7, M104

ARGOSY BOOKS
Map 161 F16
116 East 59th Street between Park and Lexington avenues
Tel 212/753-4455
www.argosybooks.com
This store, which has been operating since 1925, is one of the few remaining bookstores in the city for out-of-print and rare books. On its seven floors, it has an extensive stock of books, with particular strengths in Americana, contemporary first editions, and the history of science and medicine. It also sells prints, autographs, and antique maps.
🕐 Sep–end Apr Mon–Fri 10–6, Sat 10–5; rest of year Mon–Fri 10–6 🚇 59th Street (4, 5, 6) 🚌 M1, M2, M3, M4, M98, M101, M102, M103

BARNES & NOBLE
Map 162 E21
Union Square North at 33 East 17th Street between Broadway and Park Avenue South
Tel 212/253-0810
www.bn.com
Although not the original of this megachain with

branches all over the country, it is large and comfortable enough to be considered the flagship store. The rise of this chain from a small store near New York University into this behemoth is certainly quite a story. Like most branches, this store has a

Browsing for a good read in one of the city's many bookstores

café and comfortable chairs for reading, and sells music, software and magazines as well as books. The main college bookstore is at Fifth Avenue and 18th Street.
🕐 Daily 10–10 🚇 14th Street/Union Square (4, 5, 6, L, N, Q, R, W) 🚌 M1, M2, M3, M6, M7

BORDER'S BOOKS, MUSIC AND CAFÉ
Map 161 F16
461 Park Avenue at 57th Street (northeast corner)
Tel 212/980-6785
www.borders.com
The 'other' chain. It has a slightly more esoteric stock

and more personal feel than its competitor Barnes & Noble.
🕐 Mon–Fri 9am–10pm, Sat 10–8, Sun 11–8 🚇 59th Street (4, 5, 6), 59th Street (N, R, W) 🚌 M1, M2, M3, M4

HUE-MAN BOOKSTORE
Off map 160 D12
2319 Frederick Douglass Boulevard between 124th and 125th streets
Tel 212/665-7400
www.huemanbookstore.com
This bookstore stocks a large collection of classic and contemporary African-American fiction and non-fiction and holds author readings.
🕐 Mon–Sat 10–8, Sun 11–7 🚇 125th Street (A, B, C, D) 🚌 M10

KITCHEN ARTS AND LETTERS
Map 161 F13
1435 Lexington Avenue between 93rd and 94th streets
Tel 212/876-5550
www.kitchenartsandletters.com
You can find all of the classic cookery writers here—Julia Child, James Beard and M. F. K. Fisher—plus a host of others organized by category. Wonderful for rare and historic culinary volumes, too.
🕐 Mon 1–6, Tue–Fri 10–6.30, Sat 11–6 🚇 96th Street (6) 🚌 M98, M101, M102, M103

THE MYSTERIOUS BOOKSHOP
Map 1163 E24
58 Warren Street at Church Street, TriBeCa
Tel 212/587-1011
www.mysteriousbookshop.com
An essential stop for the compulsive mystery reader as well as the collector of first editions and rare volumes. Sherlock Holmes, Raymond Chandler, P. D. James and Patricia Highsmith are all here. Recommendations from owner Otto Penzler and staff are sure-fire winners.
🕐 Mon–Sun 11–7 🚇 Chambers Street (1, 2, 3, A, C, E) 🚌 M20, M22

POSMAN BOOKSELLERS
Map 162 E18
9 Grand Central Terminal (Vanderbilt Avenue and 42nd Street)
Tel 212/983-1111
www.posmanbooks.com
A general bookstore which offers a good selection of journals and sharp insightful staff recommendations.
Mon–Fri 8am–9pm, Sat 10–7, Sun 11–6 42nd Street (4, 5, 6) M1, M2, M3, M4, M42

RIZZOLI
Map 161 E16
31 West 57th Street between Fifth and Sixth avenues (north side)
Tel 212/759-2424
www.rizzoliusa.com
This gorgeous store has an excellent stock of art, design, and fashion books.
Mon–Fri 10–7.30, Sat 10.30–7, Sun 11–7 Fifth Avenue 59th Street (N, R, W), 57th Street (F) M1, M2, M3, M4, M5, M6, M7, M57

ST. MARK'S BOOKSHOP
Map 163 F22
31 Third Avenue between St Mark's Place and 9th Street on east side
Tel 212/260-7853
www.stmarksbookshop.com
The original counterculture bookstore of the same name thrived on St. Mark's Place in the 1980s and 90s. It offers political and alternative titles plus a good general stock of books.
Mon–Sat 10am–midnight, Sun 11am–midnight Astor Place (4, 5, 6) M101, M102, M103

SHAKESPEARE & CO
Map 163 E22
716 Broadway between West 4th Street and Washington Place
Tel 212/529-1330
www.shakeandco.com
One of the city's few surviving small independent book chains. As the name suggests, it leans toward literary and small press titles.
Sun–Thu 10am–11pm, Fri–Sat 10pm–midnight Astor Place (4, 5, 6), 8th Street (N, R, W), West 4th Street (A, C, E, F, S, V) M1, M5, M6

STRAND BOOKSTORE
Map 162 F21
828 Broadway at 12th Street
Tel 212/473-1452
www.strandbooks.com
New Yorkers come to this extraordinary bookstore to pore over the stacks and tables of publishers' review copies, sold at half price. Although you can browse, it's best to come with a title in mind, and ask the staff where to find it. The management claims to shelve 18 miles (29km) of books.
Mon–Sat 9.30am–10.30pm, Sun 11–10.30 14th Street/Union Square (L, N, Q, R, W, 4, 5, 6) M1, M5, M6

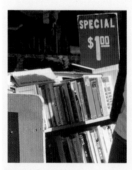

You can track down a bargain at Strand Bookstore

THREE LIVES
Map 162 D22
154 West 10th Street at Waverly Place (southwest corner)
Tel 212/741-2069
www.threelives.com
The proprietor of this store provides super customer service and stocks an amazing variety of titles given the size of the place. A real neighborhood store, and one of the last personal bookstores in the city.
Wed–Sat 11–8.30, Sun 12–7, Mon–Tue 12–8 Christopher Street (1), West 4th Street (A, C, E, F, V, S) M5, M6, M8, M20

APC
Map 163 E23
131 Mercer Street between Prince and Spring streets
Tel 212/966-9685
Atelier Production and Creation doesn't immediately suggest what you'll find here—good-looking, well-constructed Parisian-style basics. You can buy entire outfits, including cotton T's, turtlenecks, sweatshirts, dress shirts, leather jackets and very stylish jeans.
Mon–Sat 11–7, Sun 12–6 Prince Street (N, R, W) M1, M6

BCBG BY MAX AZRIA
Map 163 E23
#1B, 120 Wooster Street between Prince and Spring streets
Tel 212/625-2723
www.bcbg.com
Bon Chic, Bon Genre brings you great style and fine quality from designer Max Azria. The women's fashions are stylish and sexy, suitable for day or night. Eye-catching accessories too, all at fair prices. Also at 770 Madison Avenue.
Mon–Sat 11–7, Sun 12–6 Prince Street (N, R, W) M1, M6

BORRELLI
Map 161 E16
16 East 60th Street between Madison and Fifth avenues
Tel 212/644-9610
The ultimate Italian tailor favored by many a male film star offers exquisite shirts as well as a full line of beautiful suits, coats and sweaters, both custom-made and off the rack.
Mon–Sat 10–6.30, Sun 11–5 Fifth Avenue/59th Street (N, R, W) M1, M2, M3, M4, M30

DKNY
Map 161 E16
655 Madison Avenue between East 60th and 61st streets
Tel 212/223-3569
www.dkny.com
Donna Karan delivers what New York women want—

comfortable clothes that coordinate easily. Black used to be her favorite color, but the current inventory offers plenty of colorful blouses, dresses, miniskirts, combat jackets and accessories. This striking glass-wrapped boutique opened in 1998. Also at 420 West Broadway and Spring Street.
Ⓒ Mon–Sat 11–8, Sun 11–7 Ⓢ Fifth Avenue/59th Street (N, R, W) 🚌 M1, M2, M3, M4, M30

EMPORIO ARMANI
Map 163 E23
410 West Broadway at Spring Street
Tel 646/613-8099
www.emporioarmani.com
At this flagship of Giorgio Armani's less expensive line, you get the same great design at a fraction of the price.
Ⓒ Mon–Sat 11–7, Sun 12–6 Ⓢ Spring Street (C, E), Prince Street (N, R, W) 🚌 M1, M6

JEFFREY
Map 162 C21
449 West 14th Street between Ninth and Tenth avenues
Tel 212/206-1272
It took courage for former Barneys shoe buyer Jeffrey Kalinsky to open this giant industrial-chic boutique in the blighted Meatpacking District before it became so very hip. Naturally, the shoe department is stellar, chock full of Manolos and other designer names. You will also find fashions by such leaders as Fendi, Jil Sander, Celine, Prada, Gucci and Dolce & Gabbana. Service is gracious.
Ⓒ Mon–Fri 10–8 (Thu until 9), Sat 10–7, Sun 12.30–6 Ⓢ 14th Street (A, C, E) Eighth Avenue (L) 🚌 M11, M14

LACOSTE
Map 161 E17
575 Madison Avenue between East 54th and 55th streets
Tel 212/750-8115
www.lacoste.com
The alligator has been around since French tennis champion René Lacoste, nicknamed "alligator," sold his first polo shirt in 1933. Today, Christophe

Lemaire is re-energizing the company, adding fragrance, home fabrics, eyewear, underwear and footwear to the selection of golf, tennis and yachting sportswear.
Ⓒ Mon–Sat 10–7 (Thu until 8), Sun 12–5 Ⓢ Fifth Avenue/53rd Street (E, V), 51st Street/Lexington (6) 🚌 M1, M2, M3, M4

PATRICIA FIELD
Map 163 E23
302 Bowery between Bleecker and Houston streets
Tel 212/966-4066
www.patriciafield.com
Patricia Field's latest and largest shop sells camp fashions made of rubber, PVC, leather, spandex,

Coordinate in style at DKNY on Madison Avenue

plastic and feathers. Styles range from bustiers and garter belts to micro minis. Not for the faint of heart, accessories, wigs and cosmetics are equally outrageous.
Ⓒ Mon–Thu 12–8, Fri–Sat 12–9, Sun 12–7 Ⓢ 2nd Avenue (V, F), Bleecker Street (4, 5, 6) 🚌 M21, M103

PAUL STUART
Map 162 E18
Madison Avenue at East 45th Street
Tel 212/682-0320
www.paulstuart.com
This pricey haberdashery, which opened in 1938, feels like something from Savile Row. It sells fine-quality suits, Italian dress shirts, Irish argyles

and other good-looking traditional fashions for men. Women will find similar—silk cashmere turtlenecks, pinstripe pantsuits and leather jackets.
Ⓒ Mon–Wed, Fri 8-6.30, Thu 8–7, Sat 9–6, Sun 12–5 Ⓢ 42nd Street (B, D, F, V), 42nd Street/Grand Central (4, 5, 6, 7, S) 🚌 M1, M2, M3, M4, M5

PHAT FARM
Map 163 E23
129 Prince Street between West Broadway and Wooster streets
Tel 212/533-7428
www.phatfarm.com
A newer name on the hip-hop fashion scene, this line includes urban safari shirts and pants, scribble stitch jeans and jackets, plus hoodies, carpenter shorts and leather bomber jackets. Many bear the company logo.
Ⓒ Mon–Sat 11–7, Sun 12–6 Ⓢ Prince Street (N, R, W) 🚌 M1, M6

THE PUMA STORE
Map 163 E23
521 Broadway between Spring and Broome streets
Tel 212/334-7861
www.puma.com
Puma has made a dramatic return to the fashion scene, with shoes in olive and beige, as well as hot colors like canary yellow and lime green.
Ⓒ Mon–Sat 10–8, Sun 11–7 Ⓢ Prince Street (N, R, W)

SHANGHAI TANG
Map 161 E16
714 Madison Avenue between East 63rd and 64th streets
Tel 212/888-0111
www.shanghaitang.com
Asian cut and styling inform the youthful fashions at this store. Piping, clasps, and Chinese frog closures detail the women's jackets and blouses fashioned from pagoda prints. Kung fu and Fuji jackets with mandarin collars and knot buttons are favorites for men. Great home accessories too.
Ⓒ Mon–Sat 10–6, Sun 12–6 Ⓢ 59th Street (4, 5, 6), Lexington Avenue/53rd Street (F) 🚌 M1, M2, M3, M4

STEVEN ALAN

Map 163 E24

103 Franklin Street between West Broadway and Church Street

Tel 212/343-0692

www.stevenalan.com

Radical fashions for daring fashionistas. The store stocks the very latest international designers such as Vanessa Bruno, Alice Roi and Kateyone Adeli.

Mon–Sat 11.30–7 (Thu until 8), Sun 12–6 Franklin Street (1) M1, M6

THOMAS PINK

Map 161 E17

520 Madison Avenue between East 53rd and 54th streets

Tel 212/838-1928

www.thomaspink.com

This British store sells formal, business and casual shirts for men and women in strikingly beautiful colors and patterns, as well as cufflinks—pretty ones for her and elegant ones for him.

Mon–Fri 10–7 (Thu until 8), Sat 10–6, Sun 12–6 Fifth Avenue/53rd Street (E, V), 51st Street (6) M1, M2, M3, M4

WHAT TO DO

CLOTHING: DESIGNER

ALESSANDRO DELL'ACQUA

Map 161 E15

818 Madison Avenue between 68th and 69th streets

Tel: 212/ 253-6861

www.alessandrodellacqua.com

The Italian designer's clingy, sexy silk chiffon creations and revealing cuts are a hit with It Girls. His glamorous and sensual clothes were inspired by Italian films and leading ladies such as Anna Magnani and Sophia Loren, and are accompanied by shoes, bags and accessories with equal hot-chic appeal. There is also a line of high-fashion menswear.

Mon–Sat 10–6 68th Street-Hunter College (6) M66, M98, M101, M102, M103

ALEXANDER MCQUEEN

Map 162 C21

417 West 14th Street, between Ninth Avenue and Washington Street

Tel 212/645-1797

www.alexandermcqueen.com

The British fashion shock jock, who made his name at Givenchy and is now designing at Gucci, began his career on Savile Row and at theatrical costumer Angels and Bermans. His shows are famous for their theatricality and so are his fashions, which are fantastical but beautifully executed with whimsical details.

Mon–Sat 11–7, Sun 12.30–6 14th Street (A, C, E), Eighth Avenue (L) M11, M14

Mix with stars of stage and screen at Dolce & Gabbana

CALVIN KLEIN

Map 161 E16

654 Madison Avenue at East 60th Street

Tel 212/292-9000

The beloved Bronx-born American designer who re-made the American fashion industry in the 1970s has expanded beyond refined sportswear into shoes, accessories and home furnishings. He knows how to cut and he knows how to advertise. The boutique is a paragon of minimalism by British architect John Pawson, worth seeing in its own right.

Mon–Sat 10–6 (Thu until 7), Sun 12–6 Lexington Avenue/59th Street (N, R, W, 4, 5, 6) M1, M2, M3, M4

CHANEL

Map 161 E16

15 East 57th Street between Madison and Fifth avenues

Tel 212/355-5050

www.chanel.com

Coco Chanel created the little black dress and added slacks to a woman's wardrobe. Now Karl Lagerfeld designs the styles that will last forever and the accessories (including the quilted purse), shoes and scents to go with them. Two stores on Madison Avenue sell accessories and jewelry only.

Mon–Fri 10–6.30, Sat 10–6, Sun 12–5 Lexington Avenue/59th Street (N, R, W, 4, 5, 6) M1, M2, M3, M4, M57

DIANE VON FURSTENBERG

Map 162 C21

874 Washington Street at 14th Street

Tel: 646/486-4800

www.dvf.com

Famous for her signature Wrap dresses, Diane von Furstenberg encouraged women to "feel like a woman, wear a dress." Her DVF label now also includes a full line of sportswear, swimwear, accessories and cosmetics. Whether mini or maxi, free-flowing and casual or smart, figure-hugging dresses, the look is always elegant, feminine and flattering.

Mon–Sat 11–7 (Thu until 8), Sun 12–6 14th Street (A, C, E) Bus: M20, M14a, M14d

DOLCE & GABBANA

Map 161 E15

825 Madison Avenue between East 68th and 69th streets

Tel 212/249-4100

www.dolcegabbana.it

Domenico Dolce and Stefano Gabbana have dressed virtually every Hollywood and Broadway star in fashions that exude heat (distressed torn pants and shirts, lots of corset lacing). This spacious and beautiful store is their flagship.

Mon–Fri 10–6 (Thu until 7), Sun 12–5 68th Street (6) M1, M2, M3, M4

172 **SHOPPING**

DONNA KARAN

Map 161 E15

819 Madison Avenue between East 68th and 69th streets

Tel 212/861-1001

www.donnakaran.com

In the elegant and dramatic flagship of this very popular American designer, the floating staircase is worthy of Fred Astaire and Ginger Rogers.

🕐 Mon–Sat 10–6 (Thu until 7), Sun 12–5 🚇 68th Street (6) 🚌 M1, M2, M3, M4

EILEEN FISHER

Map 163 E23

395 West Broadway between Spring and Broome streets

Tel 212/431-4567

www.eileenfisher.com

New Yorkers love the easy-to-wear clothes designed by Ms Fisher –clothes that are versatile enough to take a woman through the day with minimal changes. This is the flagship store featuring her entire line, all made of natural fabrics. March and August sales are a big draw. Other stores are on Madison Avenue (at 53rd and 79th Streets) and Fifth Avenue (at 22nd).

🕐 Mon–Thu 11–7, Fri–Sat 11–8, Sun 12–6

🚇 Spring Street (C, E)

🚌 M1, M6

GIORGIO ARMANI

Map 161 E16

760 Madison Avenue at 65th Street

Tel 212/988 9191

www.giorgioarmani.com

The ultimate designer for men and women makes suits in understated fabrics with superb detailing.

🕐 Mon–Sat 10–6 (Thu until 7) 🚇 68th Street (6) 🚌 M1, M2, M3, M4

GUCCI

Map 161 E17

685 Fifth Avenue at East 54th Street

Tel 212/826-2600

840 Madison Avenue between 69th and 70th streets

Tel 212/717-2619

www.gucci.com

Tom Ford left Gucci in 2004

and now Frida Giannini has become creative director of womenswear and John Ray at menswear. Shop here for ultra-glamorous fashions.

🕐 Mon–Sat 10–7, Sun 12–6; Madison Avenue: Mon–Sat 10–6 (Thu until 7), Sun 12–5 🚇 Fifth Avenue/53rd Street (E, V), 68th Street (6) 🚌 M1, M2, M3, M4

ISSEY MIYAKE

Map 163 E24

119 Hudson Street at North Moore Street

Tel 212/226-0100

www.isseymiyake.com

This TriBeCa store, designed by Frank Gehry and his protégé Gordon Kipping, stocks all of

Superbly designed suits at Giorgio Armani

Miyake's lines including the A-POC ("a piece of cloth"), each item created from a seamless cloth. A Gehry metallic sculpture defines the loft space.

🕐 Mon–Sat 11–7, Sun 12–6

🚇 Franklin Street (1, 9) 🚌 M20

MARC JACOBS

Map 163 E23

163 Mercer Street between Houston and Prince streets

Tel 212/343-1490

www.marcjacobs.com

Marc Jacobs is one of the city's hottest designers, turning out luxurious, updated vintage designs in soft, feminine colors. He also has two stores on Bleecker Street, one selling

accessories (retro flats plus), the other his highly successful, less expensive Marc by Marc Jacobs line, which includes his must-have cargo pants.

🕐 Mon–Sat 11–7, Sun 12–6 🚇 Prince Street (N, R, W) 🚌 M1, M6

NICOLE MILLER

Map 161 E16

780 Madison Avenue between 66th and 67th streets

Tel 212/288-9779

www.nicolemiller.com

Nicole Miller's innovative, sexy and very wearable fashions attract a number of celebrity clients. She makes cowl-neck halter tops, distressed jersey tunics, bags and shoes, and simple evening gowns.

🕐 Mon–Fri 10–7, Sat 10–6, Sun 12–5 🚇 68th Street (6) 🚌 M2, M3, M4

PRADA

Map 163 E23

575 Broadway at Prince Street

Tel 212/334-8888

www.prada.com

Dutch architect Rem Koolhaas designed this $40-million store. The scooped-out ground floor is a performance space. Even the dressing rooms are high-tech. Of the designer's five stores in Manhattan, this is the one to see.

🕐 Mon–Sat 11–7, Sun 12–6 🚇 Prince Street (N, R, W) 🚌 M1, M6

RALPH LAUREN

Map 161 E15

867 Madison Avenue between East 71st and 72nd streets

Tel 212/606-2100

www.polo.com

Bronx native Ralph Lauren sells his distinguished cowboy and English country heritage looks in the Rhinelander Mansion, one of a handful of such turn-of-the-20th-century houses in Manhattan, renovated to gleaming splendor from its amazing hand-carved staircase to its Baccarat chandeliers and 19th-century oil paintings.

🕐 Mon–Wed 10–7, Thu 10–8, Fri–Sat 10–6, Sun 12–6 🚇 68th Street (6) 🚌 M1, M2, M3, M4

STELLA McCARTNEY

Map 162 C21
429 West 14th Street between Ninth and Tenth avenues
Tel 212/255-1556
www.stellamccartney.com
Since graduating from London's Central St. Martin's College of Art and Design in 1995, Stella McCartney began her rise to stardom at Chloe and continues in partnership with Gucci. In this store, which opened in 2002, fitting rooms are lined with marquetry or hand-printed fabric. Her full line of well-tailored but nicely draped fashions is for sale.
Ⓘ Mon–Sat 11–7, Sun 12.30–6
Ⓜ 14th Street (A, C, E), Eighth Avenue (L) 🚌 M11, M14

YOHJI YAMAMOTO

Map 163 E23
103 Grand Street at Mercer Street
Tel 212/966-9066
www.YohjiYamamoto.co.jp
Impeccable design and draping informs the fashions, often black and white, of this serene designer. The store itself is an aesthetic gem.
Ⓘ Mon–Sat 11–7, Sun 12–6 Ⓜ Canal Street (A, C, E, J, M, N, Q, R, W, Z, 6) 🚌 M1, M6

CLOTHING: TRENDY BOUTIQUES

ALIFE RIVINGTON CLUB (SHOES)

Map 163 G23
158 Rivington Street between Clinton and Suffolk streets
Tel 212/375-8128
The unmarked steel door opens onto a space paneled in cherry wood, where sneakers are treated as high fashion, and you can find limited-edition American, European and Japanese lines in fantastic colors.
Ⓘ Mon–Sat 11–7, Sun 12–6
Ⓜ Delancey/Essex (F, J, M, Z) 🚌 M9

ANNA

Map 163 G22
150 East Third Street at Avenue A
Tel: 212/358-0195
www.annanyc.com
Designer Kathy Kemp named her label after her grandmother, who taught her how to sew. Everyone from punk rock babes to Uptown trendies makes a beeline for her East Village boutique to check out her latest offbeat designs, which highlight the feminine form in fabrics that are cut to move.
Ⓘ Mon–Sat 1–8, Sun 1–7
Ⓜ 2nd Avenue (F), Essex Street (J, M, Z) 🚌 M15, M14a

Kirna Zabete stocks a range of avant-garde designs

JUSSARA LEE

Map 162 C21
11 Little West 12th Street between Washington Street and Ninth Avenue
Tel 212/242-4128
This Korean-Brazilian designer's clothes have an edge but are eminently wearable. Coats, dresses, tops, pants, skirts and bathing suits are elegantly displayed here and at her flagship store.
Ⓘ Mon–Sat 11–7, Sun by appointment 12–6 Ⓜ 14th Street (A, C, E) 🚌 M11, M14

KIRNA ZABETE

Map 163 E23
96 Greene Street between Prince and Spring streets
Tel 212/941-9656
www.kirnazabete.com
Beth Buccini and Sarah Hailes assemble their choice of the avant-garde designers at this pretty store. You might find mohair and lace cardigans, sweatshirts by Matthew Williamson, Cacharel T's, frayed and patchwork pieces by Jessica Ogden, plus such other hard-to-find designers as Clements Ribeiro and Hussein Chalayan. Accessories, too.
Ⓘ Mon–Sat 11–7, Sun 12–6 Ⓜ Prince Street (N, R, W) 🚌 M1, M6

LUCY BARNES

Map 162 D21
320 West 14th Street between Eighth and Ninth avenues
Tel 212/255-9148
Edinburgh-born Lucy Barnes has been collecting vintage materials for years and uses them beautifully either whole or in part to make her nostalgic, feminine clothes. The designs and colors are stunning and often feature gorgeous embroidery, beading and patchwork. Prices are excellent considering the quality of the materials and the beauty of the designs.
Ⓘ Mon–Sat 11–7, Sun 12–6 Ⓜ 14th Street (A, C, E) 🚌 M11

MARY ADAMS THE DRESS

Map 163 G23
138 Ludlow Street between Rivington and Stanton streets
Tel 212/473-0237
www.maryadamsthedress.com
Neighborhood pioneer Mary Adams, who moved in during the early 1980s, sells beautifully light evening dresses in pastel hues.
Ⓘ Wed–Sat 1–6, Sun 1–5
Ⓜ Delancey/Essex (F, J, M, Z) 🚌 M9, M15

MEMES

Map 163 F22
3 Great Jones Street between Broadway and Lafayette streets
Tel: 212/420-9955
www.memesnyc.blogspot.com
Red-hot street fashion from up-and-coming young designers from Japan, Europe and the USA. Jeans, jackets, trainers, shirts, Ts and more in this East Village boutique.
🕐 Mon–Sat 11–7, Sun 12–6
🚇 Bleecker Street (6) 🚌 M1, M5, M6

SHELLY STEFFEE

Map 162 D21
34 Gansevoort Street between Hudson Street and Ninth Avenue
Tel 917-408-0408
www.shellysteffee.com
The sign outside reads Design Studio and the clothes are displayed, in a museum-like fashion. The designs are sexy and fun. Capri pants have drawstrings at waist and calf; safari-style shirts are made from sheer material; and there are more tailored separates.
🕐 Tue–Sat 12–9, Sun 12–6
🚇 14th Street (A, C, E) 🚌 M11, M14

37=1

Map 163 F23
37 Crosby Street between Grand and Broome streets
Tel 212/226-0067
Jean Yu makes dresses, lingerie and separates of rich silks. The garter belts are to die for. Prices are up there.
🕐 Tue–Sun 1–6 🚇 Canal Street (N, R)
🚌 M1, M6

TRACY FEITH

Map 163 F23
209 Mulberry Street between Spring and Kenmare streets
Tel 212/334-3097
www.tracyfeith.com
Surf dude-turned-designer Tracy Feith dresses women in striking, playful, ready-to-party outfits. There's a gypsy glamour or ready-for-vacation air to all the clothes.
🕐 Mon–Sat 11–7, Sun 12–6 🚇 Spring Street (6), Broadway-Lafayette (F, S, V)
🚌 M1, M21

ZERO

Map 163 F23
225 Mott Street between Prince and Spring streets
Tel 212/925-3849
In this store you'll see capes, jackets and coats with an avant-garde look which Maria Cornejo sews in the back.
🕐 Mon–Fri 12.30–7.30, Sat–Sun 12.30–6.30 🚇 Prince Street (N, R)
🚌 M1, M6

CLOTHING: VINTAGE

EDITH MACHINIST

Map 163 G23
104 Rivington Street, between Ludlow and Essex streets
Tel: 212/979-9992
Everything from boots to ballet

Designer clothes from yesteryear at Resurrection Vintage

shoes, military-style jackets to furs, evening wear and jewelry comes through this Lower East Side shop, including designer names minus the high prices.
🕐 Mon–Fri 1–8, Sat–Sun 12–8
🚇 Delancey St (F), Essex St (J, M, Z)
🚌 M9, M14a, B39

FOLEY & CORINNA

Map 163 G23
114 Stanton Street between Ludlow and Essex streets
Tel 212/529-2338
www.foleyandcorinna.com
Fashionistas and celebrities flock here to see the famous silk and vintage lace butterfly blouses, mohair and cashmere knit coats and other

romantic hippie-chic fashions created by Dana Foley, who began her career at a city flea market. Partner Anna Corinna selects the vintage clothing and accessories.
🕐 Sun–Mon 12–7, Tue–Sat 12–8
🚇 Delancey/Essex (F, J, M, Z)
🚌 M15, M21

99X

Map 163 F21
84 East 10th Street between Third and Fourth avenues
Tel 212/460-8599
www.99xnyc.com
Most of the 60s to 80s fashions here come from the UK. Customers can pick up mod and rocker outfits, as well as punk stuff and even some slender Teddy Boy ties and pork-pie hats.
🕐 Mon–Sat 12–8, Sun 12–7 🚇 Astor Place (6) 🚌 M1, M8, M103

RESURRECTION VINTAGE

Map 163 F23
217 Mott Street between Spring and Prince streets
Tel 212/625-1374
www.resurrectionvintage.com
This store has great vintage designer clothes—Pucci slips, pieces by Miyake and Vivienne Westwood, and 80s-style skateboard clothes from Alva, Thrasher and other brands. The owners also offer their own line of skirts and tops.
🕐 Mon–Sat 11–7, Sun 12–7
🚇 Broadway-Lafayette (F, S, V) or Spring Street (6) 🚌 M1, M21, M103

SCREAMING MIMI'S

Map 163 F22
382 Lafayette Street between Great Jones and West 4th streets
Tel 212/677-6464
www.screamingmimis.com
The stock at this old-timer ranges from 1940s to 1980s. It's well displayed and in good condition. Cool and hip still, even though *Sex and the City* made it famous beyond a select circle of cognoscenti.
🕐 Mon–Sat 12–8, Sun 1–7
🚇 Broadway-Lafayette (F, S, V)
🚌 M1, M103

DEPARTMENT AND SPECIALTY STORES

BARNEYS
Map 161 E16
660 Madison Avenue between East 60th and 61st streets
Tel 212/826-8900, warehouse 212/450-8400
www.barneys.com
Barneys stocks only what's newest and hippest, so you'll find designers whose names everyone knows, as well as those known only to fashion cognoscenti—say, Proenza Schouler, Behnaz Sarafpour and Tess Giberson. The windows always make a statement, and people flock to the sales at the warehouse on 17th Street, between Seventh and Eighth avenues.
Mon–Fri 10–8, Sat 10–7, Sun 11–6 Fifth Avenue/59th Street (N, R, W), 59th Street (4, 5, 6) M30

BERGDORF GOODMAN
Map 161 E16
754 Fifth Avenue between 57th and 58th streets
Tel 212/753-7300
www.bergdorfgoodman.com
Some shoppers actually dress up to visit this luxurious store, which showcases classics and new talent. The store is beautifully laid out, the shoe department marvelous and the designer boutiques extraordinary. You'll find great accessories throughout. The men's store is just across the street.
Mon–Fri 10–8, Sat 10–7, Sun 12–6 Fifth Avenue/59th Street (N, R, W) M5, M30, M57

BLOOMINGDALE'S
Map 161 F16
Lexington Avenue at East 59th Street
Tel 212/705-2000
www.bloomingdales.com
Bloomingdale's, opened in 1879, is one of the most venerable names in Manhattan yet keeps up with every trend. It's an icon among its fans, and tourists and locals alike buy logo items emblazoned with the store's name or sobriquet,

"Bloomie's." On weekends locals come to schmooze.
Mon–Fri 10–8.30, Sat 10–7, Sun 11–7 59th Street/Lexington (4, 5, 6) M98, M101, M102, M103

HENRI BENDEL
Map 161 E17
712 Fifth Avenue at 56th Street
Tel 212/247-1100
www.henribendel.com
Henri Bendel is synonymous with sophistication and elegance. The inventory and the clientele are similar to Bergdorf's, but the displays reveal the store's élan. If you want to see works by the hottest new designers, check out the New Creators

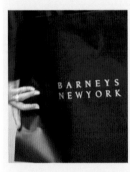

Head to Barneys for the hippest designs

boutique, which features such names as Michael Soheil, Peter Som, Alice Roi, Zac Posen and Behnaz Sarafpour.
Mon–Sat 10–8, Sun 12–7 Fifth Avenue/59th Street (N, R, W), Fifth Avenue/53rd Street (E, V) M5, M30, M57

LORD & TAYLOR
Map 162 E18
424 Fifth Avenue between 38th and 39th streets
Tel 212/391-3344.
www.lordandtaylor.com
This classic, established in 1826, targets traditional middle-aged shoppers, from Greenwich matrons to young working women. The Christmas

windows are a must-see.
Mon–Fri 10–8.30, Sat 10–7, Sun 11–7 42nd Street (B, D, F, V) M2, M3, M5

MACY'S
Map 162 D19
Herald Square at 34th Street and Broadway
Tel 212/695-4400
www.macys.com
Macy's calls itself the "world's largest department store." The Cellar stocks housewares and culinary delights, and clothing, generally mainstream, comes from a range of well-known names. The store has good seasonal sales, and sponsors the Thanksgiving Day parade and the July 4th fireworks.
Mon–Fri 10–9.30, Sat 9am–10pm, Sun 11–8.30 34th Street/Herald Square (B, D, F, N, Q, R, V, W) M6, M7, M34

SAKS FIFTH AVENUE
Map 162 E17
611 Fifth Avenue between 49th and 50th streets
Tel 212/753-4000
www.saksfifthavenue.com
Comfortable Saks offers a very fine selection of clothing by an excellent range of established and up-and-coming designers for men and women.
Mon–Fri 10–8 (Thu until 8), Sat 10–7, Sun 12–7 Fifth Avenue/53rd Street (E, V), 47th–50th streets/Rockefeller Center (B, D, F, V) M1, M2, M3, M4, M50

TAKASHIMAYA
Map 161 E17
693 Fifth Avenue between 54th and 55th streets
Tel 212/350-0100
www.takashimaya-ny.com
Step in to this beautiful branch of Japan's largest department store even if you're not a shopper. The flower shop on the sixth floor is a lovely retreat from Fifth Avenue. Look for gold-leaf cups, lacquer saucers and silk pillows.
Mon–Sat 10–7, Sun 12–5 Fifth Avenue/53rd Street (E, V) M1, M2, M3, M4, M5

WHAT TO DO

DISCOUNT OUTLETS

New York magazine's "Sales and Bargains" feature highlights current sample and stock sales. Online, www.nysale.com and www.dailycandy.com keep up to date with what's on.

CENTURY 21
Map 163 E25
22 Cortlandt Street between Broadway and Church Street
Tel 212/227-9092
www.c21stores.com
Customers do their trying on in the aisles at this resource for discounted designer fashions. Look for Prada, Armani and Jil Sander among other designers at 40 to 75 percent off or more.
🕐 Mon–Wed 7.45am–8pm, Thu 7.45am–10pm, Fri 7.45am–8.30pm, Sat 10–8, Sun 11–7 🚇 Fulton Street (4, 5) 🚌 M1, M6

INA
Map 163 E23
101 Thompson Street between Spring and Prince streets
Tel 212/941-4757
www.inanyc.com
The designer resale stock, discounted by 30 to 50 percent, changes daily, as models and the fashion set turn in their cast-offs. Look for Diane Von Furstenberg and Anna Sui. There's usually a fantastic array of Manolos, Pradas and Sigerson Morrisons, too.
🕐 Sun–Thu 12–7, Fri–Sat 12–8 🚇 Spring Street (C, E), Prince Street (N, R, W) 🚌 M5, M6, M21

LOEHMANN'S
Map 162 D21
101 Seventh Avenue at 16th Street
Tel 212/352-0856
www.loehmanns.com
This place has been a name on the discount shopping scene ever since Frieda Mueller Loehmann began selling well-priced skirts and blouses out of her Brooklyn home in 1920.

This flagship store has five floors of fashions to pick over. Discounts range from 30 to 65 percent.
🕐 Mon–Sat 9–9, Sun 11–7 🚇 14th Street (1, 2, 3) 🚌 M14, M20

FOOD AND WINE

CHELSEA MARKET
Map 162 D21
75 Ninth Avenue between 15th and 16th streets
Tel 212/243-6005
www.chelseamarket.com
When you stroll through the first floor of this building, you can put together an entire meal including table decorations. You'll find bakers, fishmongers, florists, wine

Dean & Deluca is a magnet for New York's gourmets

merchants, and such stores as Buon Italia, which sells superb cheeses, sausages, sauces, oils and other products from Italy. A good place to while away a rainy hour.
🕐 Mon–Sat 7am–9pm, Sun 10–8 🚇 14th Street (A, C, E) 🚌 M11, M14

DEAN & DELUCA
Map 163 F23
560 Broadway at Prince Street
Tel 212/226-6800
www.deandeluca.com
A wonderful place to browse. Absolutely everything here is top quality—pastries, cheeses, meats, fishes, chocolates and packaged products, plus the

baskets of hand-picked fruits and vegetables. There's also a coffee bar. There are two other branches in Manhattan.
🕐 Mon–Sat 9–8, Sun 10–7 🚇 Prince Street (N, R, W) 🚌 M1, M5, M6

JACQUES TORRES CHOCOLATE
Map 163 D23
350 Hudson Street at King Street
Tel 212/414-2462
www.mrchocolate.com
Former Le Cirque dessert chef Jacques Torres is still the best chocolate maker in the city. The gems at his factory/shop and cocoa bar are sublime. The chocolates contain no preservatives, colorings or additives, and he makes his own peanut butter, marzipan, walnut, praline and pistachio pastes. The pithiviers are heavenly.
🕐 Mon–Sat 9–7, Sun 10–6 💲$50 per pound ($110 per kilo) 🚇 Houston Street (1)

KAM MAN FOODS
Map 163 F24
200 Canal Street at Mott Street
Tel 212/571-0330
This large Chinese food hall overflows with exotic products, from live fish and edible birds' nests to ginseng priced at hundreds of dollars. It also sells inexpensive Asian cookware.
🕐 Daily 8.30am–8.45pm 🚇 Canal Street (J, M, Z) 🚌 M1, M103

MORRELL & COMPANY
Map 162 E17
1 Rockefeller Plaza
Tel 212/688-9370
www.morrellwine.com
Morrell, in business since 1947, is the other great wine shop in Manhattan after Sherry-Lehmann (▷ 178). It has its own wine bar and café next door.
🕐 Mon–Sat 10–7 🚇 47th–50th streets/Rockefeller Center (B, D, F, V) 🚌 M1, M2, M3, M4, M50

WHAT TO DO

SHERRY-LEHMANN
Map 161 F16
505 Park Avenue at East 59th Street
Tel 212/838-7500
www.sherry-lehmann.com
Even if you don't buy, this is a shop to browse. In business since 1934, it has a $10 million inventory of wines from every corner of the world, a spacious new flagship store, and a friendly, knowledgeable staff. Besides the premier cru Bordeaux and Burgundies, you'll find ice wines from Canada, Swiss and Lebanese varieties, and selections of sake, port and Madeira. Prices are good, too. Try to stop by for the Wednesday tasting from 3 to 6.
🕐 Mon–Sat 9–8 🚇 Fifth Avenue/59 Street (N, R, W), 59th Street/Lexington Avenue 4, 5, 6) 🚌 M1, M2, M3, M4, M30

UNION SQUARE GREEN MARKET
Map 162 E21
Union Square
Drop by this busy market to get a sense of the agricultural scene outside the city and to participate in a city happening.
🕐 Mon, Wed, Fri, Sat from 8am 🚇 14th Street/Union Square (L, N, Q, R, W, 4, 5, 6) 🚌 M2, M3, M5, M7

ZABAR'S
Map 160 C14
2245 Broadway between West 80th and 81st streets
Tel 212/787-2000
www.zabars.com
The countermen who wield the knives at this culinary landmark are legendary for their skills and their attitude. Look for exquisite smoked salmon and other smoked fish, terrific cheeses, and, upstairs, cookware and tableware at great prices.
🕐 Mon–Fri 8–7.30, Sat 8–8, Sun 9–6 🚇 79th Street (1) 🚌 M104

CASWELL-MASSEY
Map 161 F17
518 Lexington Avenue at East 48th Street
Tel 212/755-2254
www.caswell-massey.com
This apothecary, founded in 1752, provided perfume to George Washington and Dolly Madison and continues to produce a range of delicious floral scents such as freesia, lilac, rose, geranium and lily of the valley. You can find rosewater and glycerin soap, sandalwood massage oil and appealing gift sets.
🕐 Mon–Fri 8–7, Sat 10–6, Sun 10–5 🚇 51st Street (6) 🚌 M98, M101, M102, M103

Fresh produce is on sale at the Union Square Green Market

KIEHL'S
Map 163 F21
109 Third Avenue between East 13th and 14th streets
Tel 212/677-3171
www.kiehls.com
Now owned by L'Oréal, Kiehl's has been selling homeopathic remedies and natural cosmetics and treatment products since its inception in 1851. Natural herb-based moisturizers, cleansers, shampoos, eye creams, masques, scrubs, talc, lipsticks and toners line the shelves.
🕐 Mon–Sat 10–8, Sun 11–6 🚇 14th Street/Union Square (L, N, Q, R, W, 4, 5, 6), Third Avenue (L) 🚌 M101, M102, M103

L'OCCITANE
Map 162 E22
247 Bleecker Street between Sixth and Seventh avenues
Tel 212/367-8428
www.loccitane.com
The great range of beauty and body products sold here incorporates almond, honey, apricot, bergamot and other natural ingredients. The most irresistible product has to be shea butter hand cream, made from the shea, fruit of a tree that grows in Burkina Faso.
🕐 Mon–Sat 10–7, Sun 12–6 🚇 West 4th Street (A, C, E, F, S, V), Christopher Street (1) 🚌 M1, M5, M6

PENHALIGON'S
Map 161 E15
870 Madison Avenue between 70th and 71st streets
Tel 212/249-1771
www.penhaligons.com
Classic British style reigns at this wood-paneled emporium, the American outpost of the famous British perfumer, established in 1841. The seductive scents are handmade and have almost a cult following.
🕐 Mon–Sat 10–6, Sun 12–5. Closed Sun Jun to mid-Sep 🚇 68th Street (6) 🚌 M1, M2, M3, M4

SEPHORA
Map 162 D18
1500 Broadway between 43rd and 44th streets
Tel 212/944-6789
www.sephora.com
If you have ever been intimidated, or overwhelmed by the typical make-up counter, then you'll appreciate Sephora. This European chain, which arrived in 1998, has an efficient self-service orientation and sells more than 200 brands of beauty products, from Adrienne Vittadini to Philosophy. There's a scent-testing bar, and treatments are arranged by skin type.
🕐 Daily 10am–midnight 🚇 Times Square (N, Q, R, W, 1, 2, 3) 🚌 M6, M7, M10, M20

WHAT TO DO

SPACE.NK
Map 163 E23
99 Greene Street between Spring and
Prince streets
Tel 212/941-4200
www.spacenk.com
Soho is the perfect location for
the Stateside opening of
British founder Nicky
Kinnaird's must-have brand of
beauty products. This spacious
boutique is a temple of
temptation, stocked with her
lines in skin care and hair
products, carefully sourced
from specialists around the
world. You'll find the top
names and latest innovations
in moisturizers, masks, make-
up, fragrances, bath products
and more on the shelves.
You can also book facials and
other treatments.
🕐 Mon–Sat 11–7, Sun 12–7
🚇 Spring St (6), Broadway-Lafayette
(B, D, F, V) 🚌 M1, M5, M6, M21

HOME FURNISHINGS
ABC CARPET AND HOME
Map 162 E21
888 Broadway between 19th and 20th
streets
Tel 212/473-3000
www.abchome.com
Fabrics, furnishings and
interior design artifacts from
around the world are artfully
displayed on 10 floors.
Provençal armoires, Kashmiri
silks, gorgeously dressed beds
and Venetian chandeliers keep
company with rugs from India,
Nepal, Pakistan and China.
🕐 Mon–Fri 10–8, Sat 10–7, Sun 11–6.30
🚇 23rd Street (N, R, W) 🚌 M6, M7

BROADWAY PANHANDLER
Map 163 E22
65 East 8th Street between Broadway
and University
Tel 212/966 3434
www.broadwaypanhandler.com
Originally selling to
professional kitchens,
Broadway Panhandler now
offers the very best cookware,
tools, appliances and gadgets
to domestic cooks at decent
prices. There are hundreds of
different types of pots, pans

and skillets available—about
10,000 items in all. Special
weekend demonstrations
bring in the likes of Jean-
Georges Vongerichten, Eric
Ripert and Jacques Pépin.
🕐 Mon–Sat 11–7, Sun 11–6 🚇 8th
Street (N, R, W) 🚌 M1, M6

KATE'S PAPERIE
Map 163 F23
72 Spring Street between Crosby and
Lafayette streets
Tel 212/941-9816
www.katespaperie.com
Expensive but beautiful gifts
can be found at this elegant
store. Gorgeous stationery,
handsome journals and date
books, photo frames, alluring

*Professional cookware at
Broadway Panhandler*

wrapping papers and ribbons,
writing tools, and all kinds of
ingenious paper items are
attractively displayed.
🕐 Mon–Sat 10–8, Sun 11–7
🚇 Spring Street (N, R) 🚌 M1, M6

PEARL RIVER
Map 163 E23
477 Broadway between Broome and
Grand streets
Tel 212/431-4770
www.pearlriver.com
New Yorkers who have moved
out of town often return here
to browse the bargains—Asian-
style robes, embroidered silk
slippers, good-looking
ceramics, Asian cuisine
ingredients, paper lanterns, and

many other appealing objects.
🕐 Daily 10–7 🚇 Canal Street (N, R)
🚌 M1, M6

MUSIC
DISC-O-RAMA
Map 162 D22
186 West 4th Street at Jones Street
Tel 212/206-8417
http://discorama.com
From vinyl LPs to the latest CD
by top pop artists, you'll find it
here at a saving. Rock, pop,
R&B, hip-hop, country, jazz,
classical, reggae and more, as
well as DVDs, books and used
CDs and records. Other stores
at Union Square and NYU on
West 8th Street.
🕐 Mon–Thu 10am–11pm, Fri–Sat
10–midnight, Sun 12–8 🚇 W. 4th St-
Washington Square (A, B, C, D, E, F, V)
🚌 M5, M6

J & R MUSIC AND COMPUTER
WORLD
Map 163 E25
1-34 Park Row (one block south of
City Hall).
Tel 212/238-9000
www.jr.com
This store, opened in 1971,
stocks every conceivable brand
of audio, video, computer,
camera and cell phone, plus
software and household
appliances. Prices are excellent,
and the staff are knowledgeable
and helpful. The Music Store
has separate stores for jazz,
classical and pop.
🕐 Mon–Sat 9–7.30, Sun 10.30–6.30
🚇 Park Place (2, 3), City Hall (N, R, W),
Brooklyn Bridge/City Hall (4, 5, 6)
🚌 M9, M15

JAZZ RECORD CENTER
Map 162 D20
236 West 26th Street between Seventh
and Eighth avenues (8th floor, room
804)
Tel 212/675-4480
www.jazzrecordcenter.com
This store stocks all the great
jazz names and all the jazz
labels, plus books, videos and
ephemera. It specializes in rare
and out-of-print recordings.
🕐 Mon–Sat 10–6 🚇 28th Street (1)
🚌 M20

WHAT TO DO

SHOES AND ACCESSORIES

CARTIER
Map 161 E17
653 Fifth Avenue between 51st and 52nd streets
Tel 212/753-0111
www.cartier.com
Cartier opened in Paris in 1847 and has been famous for beautiful design ever since, creating such signature pieces as the three-band ring and the Portico Mystery Clock. Richard Burton went to Cartier for the diamond for Elizabeth Taylor. Today, it sells beautiful jewelry and watches, plus leather goods and other luxuries.
Mon–Fri 10–6, Sat 10–5.30, Sun 12–5 Fifth Avenue/53rd Street (E, V) M1, M2, M3, M4, M50

COACH
Map 161 E16
595 Madison Avenue between East 57th and 58th streets
Tel 212/754-0041
www.coach.com
This successful leather purveyor has a line of classics as well as seasonal collections. There are nine other branches in the city.
Mon–Sat 10–8, Sun 11–6 Fifth Avenue/59th Street (N, R, W), 59th Street (4, 5, 6) M1, M2, M3, M4, M57

COLE HAAN
Map 161 E17
620 Fifth Avenue at 50th Street
Tel 212/765-9747
www.colehaan.com
Nike now owns this maker of traditional, good-quality shoes and is jazzing it up with new ideas, colors and styles.
Mon–Fri 10–8, Sat 10–7, Sun 12–6 47th–50th streets/Rockefeller Center (B, D, F, V) M1, M2, M3, M4

DOLCE VITA
Map 163 G32
149 Ludlow Street between Stanton and Rivington streets
Tel 212/529-2111
http://shopdolcevita.com
High prices needn't freeze you out of fashionable footwear.

This acclaimed brand has all the coolest styles in boots, flats, heels, pumps, platforms and wedges at good prices.
Mon–Sat 12–8, Sun 12–7 Essex Street-Delancey Street (F, J, M, Z) M9, M14a, M15, B39

DOYLE AND DOYLE
Map 163 G22
189 Orchard Street between Houston and Stanton streets
Tel 212/677-9991
Doyle and Doyle offers some very alluring, historic estate jewelry in prime condition.
Tue–Sat 1–7 (Thu until 8), Sun 12–7 Lower East Side/Second Avenue (F, V) M9, M15

Accessorize to your heart's content at Eye Candy

ERES
Map 163 E23
98 Wooster Street between Spring and Prince streets
Tel 212/431-7300
www.eresparis.com
In 1968 Eres opened in Paris on place de la Madeleine, selling the ultimate swimwear—bikinis, suits and other one-pieces. Today it issues a cruise collection in November and a summer collection in January. Equally beautiful and flattering lingerie is offered as well now.
Mon–Sat 11–7, Sun 12–6 Prince Street (N, R) M1, M6

EUGENIA KIM
Map 162 D19
347 West 36th Street between 8th and 9th avenues
Tel 212/673-9787
www.eugeniakim.com
Former *Allure* editor Kim fell into her career when she fashioned a hand-feathered cloche for herself, went shopping, and attracted attention from shop owners. Her hats—many with a retro look—are dashing, flamboyant, beautifully crafted, and expensive, made of straw and cotton in cowboy, fedora, caps and other shapes, and trimmed with feathers, leather and ribbons. On the wild side.
Mon–Fri 9–6 34th Street-Penn Station (1, 2, 3, A, C, E) M11, M16, M20

EYE CANDY
Map 163 F22
329 Lafayette Street between Bleecker and Houston streets
Tel 212/343-4275
www.eyecandystore.com
The bags, costume jewelry and sunglasses here are the stuff of whimsical dreams.
Daily 12–8 Broadway-Lafayette (F, V, S) M1, M5, M6, M21

FENDI
Map 161 E17
677 Fifth Avenue between 53rd and 54th streets
Tel 212/759-4646
www.fendi.com
The flashy Fendi label conveys the message of money and glitz, and women wear Fendi for that reason. This flagship store sells the full line: handbags, shoes, accessories and furs.
Mon–Sat 10–7, Sun 12–6 Fifth Avenue/53rd Street (E, V) M1, M2, M3, M4, M57

GAS
Map 163 F23
238 Mott Street between Prince and Spring streets
Tel 212/334-7290
This outpost of the St. Tropez and Paris jeweler has lovely

inspirational handmade jewelry made with semi-precious stones.
🕐 Mon–Sat 11–7, Sun 12–6
Ⓜ Broadway-Lafayette (F, S, V)
🚌 M1, M103

JIMMY CHOO
Map 161 E16
716 Madison Avenue, between 63rd and 64th streets (west side)
Tel 212/759-7078
645 Fifth Avenue between 5th and Madison
Tel 212/593-0800)
www.jimmychoo.com
Velvet-quilted sofas and satin-covered chairs set the tone at this flagship store selling the exquisite shoes and purses by this legendary Malaysian designer, who cobbled for Princess Diana. His line offers a variety of styles from pony boots and evening slides to kitten heels, stilettos and sandals made in all kinds of materials and fabrics, which are decorated with beads, crystals or embroidery, or just beautifully colored.
🕐 Mon–Sat 10–6 (Thu until 7), Sun 12–5 Ⓜ 59th Street (4, 5, 6) or 68th Street (6) 🚌 M1, M2, M3, M4

KATE SPADE
Map 163 E23
454 Broome Street at Mercer Street
Tel 212/274-1991
www.katespade.com
The former *Mademoiselle* accessories editor, Kate started out in 1993, making handbags that emphasized utility, color and fabric. She opened her first store in 1996, and now sells a full line of exquisite nylon, leather and fabric bags, plus wallets, luggage, stationery, eyeglasses, fragrance and beauty products.
🕐 Mon–Sat 11–7, Sun 12–6 Ⓜ Prince Street (N, R, W) 🚌 M1, M6

KELLY CHRISTY
Map 163 E23
453 Broome Street at Mercer Street
Tel 212/965-0686
www.kellychristyhats.com
Kelly Christy makes eye-catching hats for men and women in all kinds of fabrics and in every conceivable style, from fedora to beret. Every hat is named to reflect a mood or character—recent examples are 'Miss Marple' and 'Let's skate'. Prices vary according to style and fabric and start at about $200.
🕐 Tue–Fri 12–6, Sat 12–5 Ⓜ Spring Street (6, A, C, E), Prince Street (N, R) 🚌 M21, M103

Jimmy Choo offers a range of exquisite footwear

KENNETH COLE
Map 160 D14
353 Columbus Avenue between West 76th and 77th streets
Tel 212/873-2061
www.kennethcole.com
Good, clean styling and quality for the money have made Kenneth Cole a major fashion player. He started with urban shoes, but has expanded to include such fashionable footwear as satin pumps with ankle straps, plus sportswear, handbags, fragrance and other accessories.
🕐 Mon–Sat 10–8, Sun 11–7 Ⓜ 79th Street (1) 🚌 M7, M11

LA PETITE COQUETTE
Map 163 E22
51 University Place between 9th and 10th streets
Tel 212/473-2478
This may well be the best lingerie store in the city. In a boudoir setting, it sells swimwear and sexy top-of-the-line, multi-hued lingerie (camisoles, corsets, garter belts and other scanties).
🕐 Mon–Sat 11–7 (Thu until 8), Sun 12–6 Ⓜ 8th Street (N, R, W) 🚌 M1, M3, M6

LE SPORTSAC
Map 163 E23
176 Spring Street between West Broadway and Thompson Street
Tel 212/625-2626
www.lesportsac.com
Fold-in-a-pouch bags made of rip-stop parachute nylon made this name famous after they were introduced in 1974. Today the brand continues to deliver practical, affordable totes, messenger bags and backpacks, now in fun prints and patterns including batik. A couture line features such materials as sheared mink and fox.
🕐 Mon–Sat 11–7, Sun 12–6 Ⓜ Spring Street (C, E) 🚌 M6

MANOLO BLAHNIK
Map 161 E17
31 West 54th Street between Fifth and Sixth avenues
Tel 212/582-3007
The sexy, strappy sandals, plain stiletto pumps, slingbacks and mules are beloved of the fashion and celebrity crowd, who pay $450 and up for these most glamorous accessories. They're fashioned from pony skin and other elegant materials in a brilliant palette.
🕐 Mon–Fri 10.30–6, Sat 10.30–5.30, closed Sun Ⓜ Fifth Avenue/53rd Street (E, V) 🚌 M5, M6, M7

WHAT TO DO

ME & RO

Map 163 F23
241 Elizabeth Street between Houston and Prince streets
Tel 917-237-9215
www.meandrojewelry.com
The collection of Michelle Quan and Robin Renzi uses precious and semi-precious stones in stackable rings, bangles, necklaces and other pieces with a lotus petal motif or Sanskrit and Tibetan calligraphy.
◷ Mon–Sat 11–7, Sun 12–6
🚇 Broadway-Lafayette (F, S, V)
🚌 M21, M103

MODELL'S

Map 163 E24
55 Chambers Street
Tel 212/732-8484
www.modells.com
Savvy New Yorkers come here to get the best deal on their running and athletic shoes (Adidas, New Balance, Reebok). The chain also stocks sports attire and gear, from treadmills and trampolines to baseball and yoga gear. Sports fans appreciate the reasonable prices on NFL, NBA and MLB souvenir stuff.
◷ Mon–Fri 8.30–8, Sat 10–7, Sun 11–6
🚇 Chambers Street (E), City Hall (R), Park Place (1, 2, 3) 🚌 M1, M6

OTTO TOOTSI PLOHOUND

Map 162 E20
137 Fifth Avenue between 20th and 21st streets
Tel 212/460-8650
Otto Tootsi Plohound offers a selection of very cool and stylish shoes both from their own line and from other European and American designers.
◷ Mon–Sat 11–8, Sun 12–7 🚇 23rd Street (N, R, W) 🚌 M2, M3, M5

CHAIN STORES

This chart tells you what to expect in many of the chain stores on New York's main shopping streets. Call the head office to find your nearest branch or check the website.

WHAT TO DO

NAME	Clothing	Fashion accessories	Souvenirs	Books and music	Outdoor sport	Shoes	Pharmacy and toiletries	Stationery	Food	Household and electrical goods	HEAD OFFICE CONTACT NUMBER
Abercrombie & Fitch	✔	✔			✔	✔					614/283-6500 or 888-856-4480
Ann Taylor	✔	✔				✔					212/541-3300 or 800-342-5266
Anthropologie	✔	✔					✔			✔	800-309-2500
Banana Republic	✔	✔				✔					888-277-8953
Bed Bath and Beyond	✔	✔								✔	800-462-3966
Benetton	✔					✔					800-535-4491
Bodyshop			✔				✔				800-263-9746
Brooks Brothers	✔	✔				✔		✔			800-274-1815
Club Monaco	✔	✔									212/886-2660
Crabtree & Evelyn			✔				✔		✔		860/928-2761 or 800-272-2873
Crate & Barrel										✔	847-272-2888 or 800-967-6696
Diesel	✔				✔						212/755-9200
Disney Store	✔		✔	✔							800-328-0368
Eddie Bauer	✔	✔			✔	✔					800-426-8020
Eileen Fisher	✔										866/512-5197
Gap	✔	✔				✔					800-333-7899
H & M	✔	✔									212/564-9922
J. Crew	✔	✔				✔					800-562-0258 or 800-932-0043
NBA Store	✔	✔	✔								877-622-0206 or 212/515-6244
Old Navy	✔	✔				✔					800-653-6289
Pier 1 Imports										✔	817/252-8000 or 800-245-4595
Talbot's	✔	✔				✔					781/749-7600 or 800-992-9010
Toys "R" Us				✔				✔			800-869-7787
Urban Outfitters	✔	✔				✔					215/564-2313 or 800-282-2200
Victoria's Secret	✔	✔				✔	✔				800-411-5116
Virgin Megastore				✔							877-484-7446
Williams-Sonoma									✔	✔	877-812-6235 or 800-541-2233

SIGERSON MORRISON
Map 163 F23
28 Prince Street between Mott and
Elizabeth streets
Tel 212/219-3893
www.sigersonmorrison.com
The shoes from this exciting
designer are not as pricey as
Manolos but are stunning
nonetheless. Colors range
across the spectrum from red
to lavender, and materials
include pony skin, suede, satin
and metallic leather. Styles
range from slingback stilettos
to flats and boots.
🕓 Mon–Sat 11–7, Sun 12–6
🚇 Broadway-Lafayette (F, S, V), Prince
Street (N, R, W) 🚌 M21, M103

SUAREZ HANDBAGS
Map 161 E17
450 Park Avenue at East 56th Street
Tel 212/753-3758
Here, copies of designer
handbags are on offer for a
fraction of the price.
🕓 Mon–Sat 10–6 🚇 59th Street (4, 5,
6) 🚌 M1, M2, M3, M4

TIFFANY
Map 161 E17
Fifth Avenue at 57th Street
Tel 212/755-8000
www.tiffany.com
Tiffany is famous for its superb
silver and crystal and its
beautiful design. Although
some items are astronomically
priced, it also displays more
moderately priced luxury
gifts—embossed note cards
($40 for 15) and singular silver
pieces. All are packaged in
the signature duck-egg blue
box tied with red or white
ribbon, which was introduced
when the store opened in
1837.
🕓 Mon–Fri 10–7, Sat 10–6, Sun 12–5
🚇 Fifth Avenue/59th Street (N, R, W),
57th Street (F) 🚌 M1, M2, M3, M4

TOD'S
Map 161 E16
650 Madison Avenue between East
59th and 60th streets
Tel 212/644-5945
www.tods.com

This Italian designer makes
ultra-comfortable shoes, plus
boots with equestrian styling.
They are relatively expensive,
but long-lasting.
🕓 Mon–Sat 10–6 (Thu until 7), Sun
12–5 🚇 59th Street/Fifth Avenue (N, R,
W) 🚌 M1, M2, M3, M4

SUPERSTORES
AVIREX
Map 163 F22
652 Broadway between Bleecker and
Bond streets
Tel 212/254-4000
www.avirex.com
Lusting for the bomber jacket
worn by Tom Cruise in *Top
Gun*? Head for Avirex, official
supplier of the U.S. Air Force's
A-2 leather flight jacket. It sells
unisex military fashions, biker
gear and varsity styles.
🕓 Mon–Sat 11–7, Sun 12–6
🚇 Broadway-Lafayette (F, S, V) 🚌 M1,
M5, M6

WHAT TO DO

LINE OF GOODS	WEB SITE
Stylish casual clothing for the American outdoors lifestyle	www.abercrombie.com
Elegant and casual women's fashion	www.anntaylor.com
Ethnically inspired clothing and eclectic housewares	www.anthropologie.com
Stylish fashion separates for men and women	www.bananarepublic.com
Everything and anything to go in the home	www.bedbathandbeyond.com
Contemporary fashions with Italian flair	www.benetton.com
Cosmetics and bath products made of natural ingredients	www.thebodyshop.com
Conservative and classic tailored fashions for men and women	www.brooksbrothers.com
Canadian chain selling chic basics and affordable high-fashion items	www.clubmonaco.com
Venerable British chain selling toiletries and British-oriented products like teas and jams	www.crabtree-evelyn.com
High-quality products for the home with a distinct West Coast style	www.crateandbarrel.com
Latest trends for kids from hip-hop style to surfer	www.diesel.com
Disney paraphernalia including clothes and furniture	www.disneystore.com
Casual stylish fashions with an outdoor orientation	www.eddiebauer.com
Casual, comfortable clothes for women	www.eileenfisher.com
The ubiquitous reasonably priced, casual clothing store	www.Gap.com
Low-cost versions of trendy youth-oriented fashion	www.hm.com
Casual preppy and collegiate fashions and affordable accessories	www.jcrew.com
Souvenir jerseys, posters, mugs and more for basketball fans	http://store.nba.com
Moderately priced high-street fashions for adults and children	www.oldnavy.com
Affordable, stylish home decor—from tableware to bed linens	www.pier1.com
Fine-quality, practical and affordable ladies' wear	www.talbots.com
Every toy imaginable plus a 60-foot (18m) Ferris wheel	www.toysrus.com
Practical casuals for the collegiate crowd	www.urbn.com
Sexy lingerie, sleepwear and swimwear are the staples at this famous chain	www.victoriassecret.com
Classical, pop and jazz CDs, including plenty of imports	www.virginmega.com
Upscale kitchen equipment, condiments and specialty ingredients	www.williams-sonoma.com

B & H PHOTO
Map 162 D19
420 Ninth Avenue between West 33rd and 34th streets
Tel 212/444-5000
www.bhphotovideo.com
Even if you're not in the market for a new camera, you might want to make a detour to this vast store to pick up inexpensive film in bulk. You'll also find every conceivable brand and type of camera, plus darkroom equipment and other accessories. Don't expect service—come knowing what you want to buy.
◷ Mon–Thu 9–7, Fri 9–2, Sun 10–5. Closed Sat ⊠ 34th Street/Penn Station (A, C, E) ⊟ M11

BED, BATH AND BEYOND
Map 162 E21
620 Sixth Avenue between West 18th and 19th streets
Tel 212/255-3550
www.bedbathandbeyond.com
It can be overwhelming to shop at this huge store, which sells absolutely everything for the bedroom, bathroom, kitchen and dining room, plus storage and cleaning accessories, lamps and window treatments.
◷ Daily 8am–9pm ⊠ 18th Street (1) ⊟ M5, M6, M7

CRATE AND BARREL
Map 161 E16
650 Madison Avenue at East 59th Street
Tel 212/308-0011
www.crateandbarrel.com
This chain sells affordable, good-looking designs for your home. The focus is on tableware (from linens to glasses). It also sells attractive outdoor dining stuff.
◷ Mon–Fri 10–8, Sat 10–7, Sun 12–6 ⊠ 59th Street/Fifth Avenue (N, R, W) ⊟ M1, M2, M3, M4, M5

DIESEL
Map 162 E21
1 Union Square West at University Place
Tel 646-336 8552
www.diesel.com
This Italian clothes house always keeps one step ahead

of the latest trends, whether it's hip-hop or surfer. Diesel jeans are de rigueur and so, too, are the shoes and bags. Also at 770 Lexington Avenue.
◷ Mon–Sat 11–9, Sun 11–8 ⊠ 14th Street/Union Square (L, N, Q, R, W, 4, 5, 6) ⊟ M2, M3, M5, M14

FAO SCHWARZ
Map 161 E16
767 Fifth Avenue between 58th and 59th streets
Tel 212/644-9400
www.fao.com
This famous store has been in Manhattan since 1876. It stocks everything: action figures, stuffed toys, books, games, dolls, science and

FAO Schwarz featured in the Tom Hanks movie Big

nature toys, and electronics, plus furniture and fashions.
◷ Mon–Wed 10–7, Thu–Sat 10–8, Sun 11–6 ⊠ 59th Street/Fifth Avenue (N, R, W) ⊟ M1, M2, M3, M4

HAMMACHER SCHLEMMER
Map 161 F16
147 East 57th Street between Lexington and Third avenues
Tel 212/421-9000
www.hammacher.com
Ingenuity meets the future. At this longtime innovator, which started as a hardware store on the Bowery in 1848, you will find such items as the upside-down tomato garden and the Roomba, a robotic cleaning device that navigates whole

rooms removing dust from carpet and floor.
◷ Mon–Sat 10–6 ⊠ 59th Street (4, 5, 6) ⊟ M57, M98, M101, M102, M103

PARAGON SPORTING GOODS
Map 162 E21
867 Broadway at 18th Street
Tel 212/255 8036
www.paragonsports.com
New Yorkers have been coming to this multilevel store for years to buy clothes and equipment for every conceivable type of sport or pastime. It stocks camping and hiking gear, binoculars for bird-watching, golfing gear, skis, snow and surfboards, tennis racquets and a terrific selection of brand clothing.
◷ Mon–Sat 10–8, Sun 11.30–7 ⊠ 14th Street/Union Square (L, N, Q, R, W, 4, 5, 6) ⊟ M6, M7

PEARL PAINT
Map 163 E24
308 Canal Street between Mercer Street and Broadway
Tel 212/431-7932
www.pearlpaint.com
You won't find a better place for fine arts supplies at discounted prices than this multilevel store. The selection of oils, acrylics and other mediums, brushes, easels, markers, pens, pastels, sketchbooks, photo frames, drafting and sculpting tools is superb.
◷ Mon–Fri 9–7, Sat 10–7, Sun 10–6 ⊠ Canal Street (N, R) ⊟ M1, M6

TIME WARNER CENTER
Map 160 D16
10 Columbus Circle
Tel 212/823-6000
This, the first luxury shopping mall in Manhattan, will be familiar to suburbanites. Here under one roof are such big-name stores as Coach, Cole Haan, Davidoff, Godiva, L'Occitane, Hugo Boss, Thomas Pink, and Williams-Sonoma.
◷ Mon–Sat 10–9, Sun 12–6 ⊠ 59th Street/Columbus Circle (A, C, B, D, 1) ⊟ M7, M10

ENTERTAINMENT

The city's performance scene reflects the diversity of the metropolis. Theater patrons will find an array of options. There are 39 or so Broadway theaters, plus 450 non-profit theaters operating in the city.

CINEMA

The city is a veritable cinema paradiso. Numerous art houses operate, frequently showcasing individual directors or focusing on particular themes or eras. First-run movies are shown all over town in grand movieplexes.

CLASSICAL MUSIC, DANCE AND OPERA

Musical riches abound, led by the Metropolitan and City Operas and Carnegie Hall and

There is plenty of classical music on offer

the New York Philharmonic. All kinds of smaller groups and orchestras, plus independent opera companies, play at diverse venues—museums, music schools and churches. The New York City Ballet and American Ballet Theatre lead the traditional dance scene, while Merce Cunningham, Mark Morris, Alvin Ailey, Paul Taylor and Martha Graham are the leading modern dance companies.

COMEDY, POETRY AND THE SPOKEN WORD

The spoken word can be heard throughout the city, as the

intellectuals and literary lights meet, greet and sign at bookstores, lecture at the 92nd Street Y, or deliver their poetry at poetry fests and St. Mark's-in-the-Bowery. And don't forget stand-up comedy, a unique American cultural contribution, celebrated in New York City clubs, which gave birth to such brilliant comedians as Jerry Seinfeld, Jay Leno, Woody Allen, Rosie O'Donnell and Joan Rivers.

CONTEMPORARY LIVE MUSIC

Cabaret is flourishing in alluring rooms at the Carlyle and the Algonquin hotels. Musically, uptown tends to be more traditional; downtown leans to the avant-garde. Indie rock clubs abound on the Lower East Side and in the East Village. Cool jazz and other exotica can be heard at the Knitting Factory and Tonic. Jazz continues to thrive as it has always in New York. The leading venue is still the Village Vanguard, now under the watchful eye of Lorraine Gordon, but it has been joined by the $140 million Jazz at Lincoln Center in the Time Warner building on Columbus Circle. World music programming is featured all over town at Town Hall, Zankel Hall at Carnegie, and Symphony Space.

THEATER

The Great White Way attracts the most visitors with its brightly lit marquees and gilded theaters named after such luminaries as Ethel Barrymore, David Belasco and Eugene O'Neill. The Public Theater and BAM are the shining lights of Off-Broadway. The first, founded by Joe Papp, also delivers free summer

Shakespeare in the Park, while BAM is famous for its New Wave Festival. Off-Broadway has nurtured many playwrights too, such as Wally Shawn, Lanford Wilson and Tony Kushner, and several Broadway hits have emerged from here, notably *Rent*, *Avenue Q*, *A Chorus Line* and the *Heidi Chronicles*. Off-Off-Broadway stages quirky experimental showcases in tiny theaters with less than 100 seats, but it has nurtured such players as Eric Bogosian and Laurie Anderson.

PRACTICALITIES

Most box offices open from

Jazz has always flourished in New York

Monday to Saturday, 10am to 8pm, and Sunday from 11am to 6.30pm. Tickets can be purchased here without paying a fee. Standing Room Only tickets, when available, go on sale on the day of the performance.

Tickets can also be purchased through Telecharge (tel 212/239-6200) and Ticketmaster (tel 212/307-7171).

Best performance listings are found in *Time Out, New York* magazine, the *Village Voice* and the Friday edition of *The New York Times*. A good website is www.timeoutny.com.

ENTERTAINMENT LOCATOR

B

C

D

13

14

15

16

17

Symphony Space, Leonard Nimoy Thalia

Cathedral Church of St John the Divine

Manhattan School of Music, Miller Theatre, Cotton Club, Smoke

Showman's Jazz Club, Aaron Davis Hall, Apollo Theater, Classical Theater of Harlem

West 95th Street
West 94th Street
West 93rd Street
West 92nd Street

UPPER WEST
SIDE

West 91st Street
West 90th Street
West 89th Street
West 88th Street
West 87th Street
West 86th Street
West 85th Street
West 84th Street
West 83rd Street
West 82nd Street
West 81st Street
West 80th Street
West 79th Street
West 78th Street
West 77th Street
West 76th Street
West 75th Street
West 74th Street
West 73rd Street
West 72nd Street
West 71st Street
West 70th Street
West 69th Street
West 68th Street
West 67th Street
West 66th Street
West 65th Street
West 64th Street
West 63rd Street
West 62nd Street
West 61st Street
West 60th Street
West 59th Street
WEST 57TH STREET
West 56th Street
West 55th Street
West 54th Street
West 53rd Street
West 52nd Street
West 51st Street
West 50th Street
West 49th Street
West 48th Street
West 47th Street
West 46th Street
West 45th Street

BROADWAY
Amsterdam Avenue
Columbus Avenue
Central Park West
West End Avenue
Riverside Drive
Highway 9A

Hudson River

Riverside Park

Central Park Reservoir

CENTRAL PARK

86th Street
79th Street Transverse
65th

86th Street

81st Street Museum of Nat Hist

Shakespeare in the Park (Delacorte Theater)

American Museum of Natural History

New-York Historical Society

San Remo Apartments

The Lake

The Dakota

Strawberry Fields

72nd Street

The Sheep Meadow

Tavern on the Green

Stand-Up New York

Beacon Theatre

Ansonia Building

72nd Street

Merkin Concert Hall

Makor

Juilliard School

Alice Tully Hall

Bruno Walter Auditorium

Film Society of Lincoln Center (Walter Reade Theater)

Vivian Beaumont Theater

Lincoln Center for the Performing Arts

New York Society for Ethical Culture

Mitzi Newhouse Theater

Avery Fisher Hall

Lincoln Center

Lincoln Plaza Cinemas

New York State Theater

Metropolitan Opera House

Museum of Biblical Art

Jazz at Lincoln Center

59th Street Columbus Circle

COLUMBUS CIRCLE

Central

57th Street

Carnegie Hall

Julia Miles Theater

Alvin Ailey American Dance Theater

Studio 54

De Witt Clinton Park

Irish Arts Center

August Wilson Theatre

Broadway

Chicago City Limits

Roseland Ballroom

Neil Simon

Iridium

Gershwin

Winter G

Circle in the Square

Caro on Broa

Ambassador Theatre

Eugene O'Neill

Walter Kerr

BROADWAY

Longacre

Brooks Atkinson Theatre

Biltmore Theatre

Ethel Barrym Theatre

Don't Tell Mama

Richard Roger

Imperial

Lyceu

Music Box

Marquis

Manha

Intrepid Sea, Air and Space Museum

B

C

D

↑ Lenox Lounge,
Schomburg Center for
Research in Black Culture

Jewish
Museum

East 93rd Street

East 92nd Street

East 91st Cooper-Hewitt
National Design Museum

National
Academy
of Design

East 90th Street

Guggenheim
Museum

East 88th Street

East 87th Street

86th Street

Neue
Galerie

East 86th Street

East 85th Street

East 84th Street

Grace Rainey
ers Auditorium
e Metropolitan
useum of Art)

East 83rd Street

East 82nd Street

East 81st Street

East 80th Street

East 79th Street

East 78th Street

Bemelmans Bar
& Café Carlyle

East 77th Street

East 76th Street

East 75th Whitney Museum
of American Art

East 74th Street

Conservatory
Water

East 73rd Street

East 72nd Street

Frick
Collection

Asia Society
and Museum

Asia
Society

East 71st Street

East 70th Street

East 69th Street

68th Street
Hunter College

East 68th Street

East 67th Street

East 66th Street

Kosciuszko Foundation

East 65th Street

Ice
Rink

East 64th Street

Lexington Avenue
63rd Street

FIFTH AVENUE

East 62nd Street

The
Pond

Café
Pierre

East 61st Street

Feinstein's
at the Regency

Lexington
Avenue

Dangerfield's

Chicago City Limits

Mount Vernon Hotel
Museum and Garden

East 60th Street

Florence Gould Hall

59th
Street

American Museum of
the Moving Image

HIGHWAY 25

QUEENSBORO
BRIDGE

Paris
Theatre

West 58th Street

West 57TH STREET   EAST 57TH STREET

Trump
Tower

West 56th Street

Central
Synagogue

West 55th Street

Museum of
Modern Art

York Theatre
St Peter's Church

West 54th Street

Museum of
and Design

Paley Center
for Media

YWCA Cine Club

West 53rd Street

Seagram
Building

West 52nd Street

Donnell Media Center
New York Public Library

io City
ic Hall

West 51st Street

St Patrick's
Cathedral

Municipal
Art Society

51st
Street

West 50th Street

G E
Building

West 49th Street

Rockefeller
Center

West 48th Street

DIAMOND
DISTRICT

Japan Society

West 47th Street

MIDTOWN
MANHATTAN

187

West 46th Street

West 45th Street

United Nations
Headquarters

92nd Street Y
(Kauffman Concert Hall)

ROOSEVELT
ISLAND

Gracie
Mansion

Carl
Schurz
Park

John Jay
Park

Roosevelt
Island

Mill Rock
Park

13

14

15

16

17

E   F   G

ENTERTAINMENT LOCATOR

189

Cinemas

Major cinema chains—AMC Empire, Cineplex Odeon, Loews and United Artists—have many theaters in the city showing first-run films. Those listed here screen more individual and varied fare. Most open around noon and operate continuously until late. You can get tickets in advance (for a surcharge) via websites such as fandango.com and movietickets.com. In the fall, the New York Film Festival is held at the Lincoln Center and other locations throughout the city. Spring is the time for the TriBeCa Film Festival.

AMERICAN MUSEUM OF THE MOVING IMAGE
Off map 187 G16
35th Avenue at 36th Street, Astoria, Queens
Tel 718/784-0077
www.movingimage.us
This museum in Queens, built on the site of the Astoria Studio, a former Paramount movie-production facility, hosts director festivals and retrospectives. Occasionally screenwriters answer questions at Friday and Saturday screenings. Take a look at how films are made in the core exhibition "Behind the Screen."
🎟 $10 🚇 Steinway Street (34th Avenue) (G, R, V), Broadway (N, W)

ANGELIKA FILM CENTER
Map 189 E22
Mercer and Houston streets
Tel 212/995-2000
www.angelikafilmcenter.com
This multiplex shows foreign films with subtitles, plusfilms by such artists as Atom Egoyan and other independent moviemakers. Pick up a latte at the café before or after the show.
🎟 $10–$11 🚇 Broadway-Lafayette (F, S, V), Bleecker Street (6) 🚌 M1, M5, M6, M21

ANTHOLOGY FILM ARCHIVES
Map 189 F22
32 Second Avenue at East 2nd Street
Tel 212/505-5181
www.anthologyfilmarchives.org
Shows new film-makers along with old and rare vintage pieces and occasional tributes to particular directors.
🎟 $8 🚇 Astor Place (6), Lower East Side/Second Avenue (F, V) 🚌 M15, M21

BAM ROSE CINEMAS
Off map 189 G25
30 Lafayette Street, Brooklyn
Tel 718/636-4100
www.bam.org
Screens at this house at the Brooklyn Academy of Music show contemporary first-run

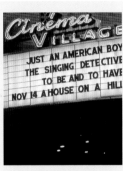

Cinema Village is one of the city's independent cinemas

films, and tributes to American and foreign cinema, often with discussions with the directors.
🎟 $11 🚇 Nevins Street (2, 3), Dekalb Avenue (B, D, Q, N, R)

CINEMA VILLAGE
Map 189 E21
22 East 12th Street between University Place and Fifth Avenue
Tel 212/924-3363
www.cinemavillage.com
Renovated in 2000, this independent cinema, housed in a former fire station, now has three screens. Documentaries and old movies are the staples.
🎟 $10 🚇 14th Street/Union Square (L, N, Q, R, W, 4, 5, 6) 🚌 M1, M2, M14, M101, M103

FILM FORUM
Map 189 E23
209 West Houston Street between Sixth Avenue and Varick Street (Seventh Avenue)
Tel 212/727-8110 or 212/727-8112
www.filmforum.com
The leading cinema for independent films, it also shows domestic and foreign documentaries, as well as revivals.
🎟 $10.50 🚇 Houston Street (1) 🚌 M5, M6, M20, M21

FILM SOCIETY OF LINCOLN CENTER
Map 186 C16
Walter Reade Theater, 165 West 65th Street
Tel 212/875-5600
www.filmlinc.com
This society hosts many different festivals—the New York Jewish Festival, Spanish Cinema Now, and Women in Film, for example.
🎟 $11 🚇 66th Street (1) 🚌 M5, M7, M66, M104

IFC CENTER
Map 188 E22
323 Sixth Avenue (on the west side of Sixth Avenue at West 3rd Street)
Tel 212/924-7771
www.ifccenter.com
The Independent Film Channel renovated this old movie theater, creating the ultimate space for independent film entertainment. It has three cinemas with comfortable luxury seating and high-def digital and 35mm projection. A short is shown before each feature and there are no commercials. The restaurant is also an appealing feature.
🕐 Daily show times vary (starting at noon, with late 11pm Sun–Thu)
🎟 $11 🚇 West 4th Street (A, B, C, D, E, F, V) 🚌 M5, M6

LANDMARK SUNSHINE CINEMA
Map 189 F23
143 East Houston Street between First and Second avenues
Tel 212/330-8182
www.landmarktheatres.com
This five-screener offers a medley of movies, from challenging documentaries such as *Bowling for Columbine,* foreign films and oldies, to first-run movies. Seating is raked and more comfortable than at other movie houses with similar programming.
$10.75 Second Avenue (F, V) M15, M21

LINCOLN PLAZA CINEMAS
Map 186 D16
1886 Broadway at 63rd Street
Tel 212/757-2280
www.lincolnplazacinema.com
A six-screener showing a select group of critically successful first-run movies and foreign films. For example, Gurinder Chadha's *Bend it Like Beckham* and Almodóvar's *Talk to Her* both played here.
$11 66th Street (1) M5, M7, M66, M104

MAKOR
Map 186 D15
1395 Lexington Avenue at 92nd Street
Tel 212/601-1000
www.92Y.org
This club, part of a Jewish community center, hosts different programs, including mainly documentaries and oldies. A new branch of the club opens in 2008 at 200 Hudson Street, between Vestry and Desbrosses streets (the telephone number is the same as above).
$9 86th Street (4, 5, 6) M1, M2, M86, M96, M101, M102

MOMA FILM
Map 187 E17
11 West 53rd Street
Tel 212/708-9480
www.moma.org
MoMA offers an ambitious film program of documentaries, historic retrospectives and director tributes.
$10 Rockefeller Center (B, D, F, V), 53rd Street/Fifth Avenue (E) M1, M2, M3, M4, M5, M6, M7

NEW YORK PUBLIC LIBRARY
Map 187 E17
Donnell Media Center, 20 West 53rd Street between Fifth and Sixth avenues
Tel 212/621-0609
Foreign films, shorts and documentaries, plus tributes to directors.
Free 53rd Street/Fifth Avenue (E, V) M1, M2, M3, M4, M5, M6, M7

PARIS THEATRE
Map 187 E16
4 West 58th Street between Fifth and Sixth avenues

Catch a film from northern Europe at Scandinavia House

Tel 212/688-3800
www.theparistheatre.com
The films that play here are mostly foreign.
$10–11 Fifth Avenue/59th Street (N, R, W) M1, M2, M3, M4, M57

QUAD CINEMA
Map 188 E21
34 West 13th Street between Fifth and Sixth avenues
Tel 212/255-8800 or 212/255-2243
www.quadcinema.com
This four-screen art house shows foreign and independent films and works by new directors.
$10 14th Street (F, V), 14th Street/Union Square (L, N, Q, R, W, 4, 5, 6) M2, M3, M5, M6

SCANDINAVIA HOUSE
Map 188 E19
Victor Borge Hall, 58 Park Avenue between East 37th and 38th streets
Tel 212/879-9779
www.scandinaviahouse.org
Scandinavia House shows films by directors and actors from Denmark, Finland, Iceland, Norway and Sweden.
$8 42nd Street/Grand Central (4, 5, 6) M1

SYMPHONY SPACE LEONARD NIMOY THALIA
Off map at 186 C12
2537 Broadway at 95th Street
Tel 212/864-5400
www.symphonyspace.org
Brilliant gems, like Fritz Lang's *Metropolis* and David Lynch's *Blue Velvet,* plus more recent independent films are shown here. There are also tributes to particular directors—Kurosawa, for example—and frequent double features.
$11 96th Street (1, 2, 3) M96, M104

TWO BOOTS PIONEER THEATER
Map 189 G22
155 East 3rd Street at Avenue A
Tel 212/591-0434
www.twoboots.com/pioneer
Opened in 2000 by the Two Boots pizza chain after they moved their East Village outlet to larger premises, this 100-seat house shows documentaries like *Bloody Sunday* and other foreign films, often followed by discussion sessions with the director.
$10 Lower East Side/Second Avenue (F, V) M14, M21

WHAT TO DO

Classical Music, Dance and Opera

CLASSICAL MUSIC

ALICE TULLY HALL
Map 186 C16
1941 Broadway on 65th Street between Broadway and Amsterdam
Tel 212/875-5050 or 212/721-6500
www.lincolncenter.org
This 1,096-seat hall is used for chamber music, vocal recitals, jazz and other musical events. The Chamber Music Society (tel 212/875-5788) resides here. Temporarily closed until winter 2008–2009.
 $27.50–$52 66th Street (1) M5, M7, M66, M104

AVERY FISHER HALL
Map 186 C16
10 Lincoln Center Plaza (Columbus Avenue at 65th Street)
Tel 212/875-5030 or 212/721-6500
www.lincolncenter.org or www.newyorkphilharmonic.org
Home to the New York Philharmonic, this hall seats 2,700. Many other groups perform here, including the American Symphony Orchestra, under Leon Botstein, and the summer Mostly Mozart Festival. During its season, the Philharmonic opens its morning rehearsals to the public (usually on Thursdays at 9.45 for $15).
 $25–$98 66th Street (1) M5, M7, M66, M104

BARGEMUSIC
Map 189 G25
Fulton Ferry Landing next to the Brooklyn Bridge
Tel 718/624-2083 or 718/624-4061
www.bargemusic.org
Anchored under Brooklyn Bridge, this old coffee barge-turned-125-seat concert hall is the brainchild of violinist Olga Bloom. A beguiling experience.
 $25–$40 High Street (A), Clark Street/Brooklyn Heights (2, 3)

BRUNO WALTER AUDITORIUM
Map 186 C16
The New York Public Library for the Performing Arts, 111 Amsterdam Avenue between West 64th and 65th streets
Tel 212/870-1630, 212/642-0142 (programs)
Lectures, seminars, concerts and films are the regular fare at this 212-seat hall. The library is a superb performing arts archive.
 Free 66th Street (1) M5, M7, M66, M104

CARNEGIE HALL
Map 186 D17
Seventh Avenue at West 57th Street
Tel 212/247-7800
www.carnegiehall.com
"Practice, practice, practice" is the answer to the old chestnut of a question, "How do you

Carnegie Hall has an illustrious past and superb acoustics

get to Carnegie Hall?" Many well-practiced conductors and artists have played in this famous hall, which was built with Carnegie money in 1891, from Tchaikovsky and Mahler to the Beatles and the Rolling Stones. Programming includes the great orchestras of the world, top-class instrumentalists, the New York Pops under Skitch Henderson, and performers of jazz, folk, pop and comedy. A small free museum on the second floor (tel 212/903-9629) displays associated memorabilia.
 Museum: daily 11–4.30; tours (tel 212/903-9765) Mon–Fri 11.30, 2 and 3, Sat 11.30, 12.30, Sun 12.30 $10–$102

 57th Street (N, Q, R, W) M6, M7, M57

CATHEDRAL CHURCH OF ST. JOHN THE DIVINE
Off map 186 C12
1047 Amsterdam Avenue at 112th Street
Tel 212/316-7540
www.stjohndivine.org
Stop by to admire the still-incomplete edifice, begun in 1892, and you may hear one of the sanctuary's five organs. The musical repertoire during arts events ranges from choirs singing Bach cantatas or chanting Tibetan monks to music made famous by Duke Ellington and Judy Collins.
 Varies Cathedral Parkway/110th Street (1) M4, M11

CENTRAL SYNAGOGUE
Map 187 F17
123 East 55th Street at Lexington Avenue
Tel 212/415-5500
www.92Y.org
Concerts at the synagogue often feature well-known or overlooked Jewish composers.
 Varies 51st Street (6) M98, M101, M102, M103

COOPER UNION
Map 189 F22
41 Cooper Square at 7th Street
Tel 212/353-4140
www.cooperunion.edu
Diverse array of musical performers and groups.
 Varies Varies 8th Street (N, R, W), Astor Place (6) M1

FLORENCE GOULD HALL
Map 187 E16
55 East 60th Street between Park and Madison avenues
Tel 212/355-6100
www.fiaf.org
Chamber groups, opera singers, pop and jazz artists, dance companies, and actors reading all entertain in this 400-seat auditorium associated with the Alliance Française.
 $30–$35 Fifth Avenue/59th Street (N, R, W) M1, M2, M3, M4, M5, M57

FRICK COLLECTION
Map 187 E15
1 East 70th Street
Tel 212/288-0700
www.frick.org
The recitals in this exquisite
museum are a must.
💷 Varies 🔲 68th Street (6) 🚌 M1,
M2, M3, M4, M72

GRACE RAINEY ROGERS AUDITORIUM
Map 187 E14
The Metropolitan Museum of Art, Fifth
Avenue at 82nd Street
Tel 212/535-7710 or 212/570-3949
www.metmuseum.org
Small musical groups and
individuals entertain in this
mid-size, 700-seat auditorium.
And the Met always has
chamber music in the Great
Hall Balcony on Friday and
Saturday evenings.
💷 $35–$55 🔲 77th Street (6) 🚌 M1,
M2, M3, M4, M79

JUILLIARD SCHOOL
Map 186 C16
144 West 66th Street at Broadway
Tel 212/769-7406 or 212/721-6500
www.juilliard.edu
This world-famous performing
arts school is especially well
known for music. The young
artists who train here can be
seen in stimulating programs
in two auditoriums. Juilliard
also incorporates the School
for American Ballet, which is
the training ground for the
New York City Ballet. Dance
aficionados run to secure
tickets for the school's annual
workshop production in early
summer (tel 212/769-6600).
💷 Most are free except for opera
programs and dance workshops
🔲 66th Street (1)
🚌 M5, M7, M66, M104

KOSCIUSZKO FOUNDATION
Map 187 E16
15 East 65th Street
Tel 212/734-2130
www.kosciuszkofoundation.org
Programs featuring Polish
composers or artists.
💷 Varies 🔲 68th Street (6) 🚌 M1,
M2, M3, M4

MANHATTAN SCHOOL OF MUSIC
Off map 186 C12
Broadway at 122nd Street
Tel 212/749-2802 or 917/493-4428
www.msmnyc.edu
This institution with a world-
class reputation has a large
concert hall and several
smaller venues. The
programming is diverse—
orchestras, chamber
ensembles—and ticket prices
reasonable.
💷 Varies 🔲 125th Street (1) 🚌 M4,
M104

MERKIN CONCERT HALL
Map 186 C15
129 West 67th Street

*The Frick Collection is a beautiful
setting for music*

Tel 212/501-3330
www.ekcc.org
Part of the Kaufman Center,
national and international
chamber groups perform here.
You might find traditional
classical, new music or even a
group from Japan.
💷 $15–$45 🔲 66th Street (1) 🚌 M5,
M7, M104

MILLER THEATRE
Off map 186 C12
Columbia University, Broadway at 116th
Street
Tel 212/854-7799
www.millertheatre.com
Many cutting-edge classical
groups and composers are
presented here: John Zorn,

Julia Wolfe and John King,
for example.
💷 Varies 🔲 116th Street (1) 🚌 M104

NEW YORK PHILHARMONIC
Map 186 C16
Avery Fisher Hall, 10 Lincoln Center
Plaza
Tel 212/875-5656
www.newyorkphilharmonic.org
Established in 1842, this is the
oldest orchestra in the US.
Currently under the baton of
Lorin Maazel, the orchestra
performs more than 200
concerts annually. Dvorak's
New World Symphony was
premiered here in 1893.
💷 $25–$108 🔲 66th Street (1)
🚌 M5, M7, M66, M104

NEW YORK SOCIETY FOR ETHICAL CULTURE
Map 186 D16
2 West 64th Street at Central Park West
Tel 212/874-5210 or 866/468-7619
www.nysec.org
All kinds of cultural events are
held here, with lectures and
discussions often preceding
them.
🔲 66th Street (1) 🚌 M10

92ND STREET Y
Map 187 F13
Kauffman Concert Hall, 1395 Lexington
Avenue at 92nd Street
Tel 212/415-5500, 212/415-5740
www.92Y.org
The 92nd Street Y offers some
of the city's most varied
programming. It hosts music
recitals (Guarneri and Tokyo
string quartets, Janos Starker),
jazz, pop and folk, poetry and
literature readings (Thomas
Keneally, V. S. Naipaul), and
lectures on every conceivable
subject by contemporary
cultural leaders. A Jewish
cultural organization, it
celebrated its 133rd
anniversary in 2007.
💷 Varies 🔲 96th Street (6) 🚌 M96,
M98, M101, M102, M103

WEILL RECITAL HALL
Map 186 D17
881 Seventh Avenue
Tel 212/247-7800
www.carnegiehall.org
Small groups perform in this
250-seat hall in the Carnegie
Hall complex (▷ 192). Well
known for its Distinctive
Debuts Series.
💵 $20–$92 🚇 57th Street (N, Q, R,
W) 🚌 M6, M7, M57

ZANKEL HALL
Map 186 D17
881 Seventh Avenue
Tel 212/247-7800
www.carnegiehall.org
This 644-seat space in the
Carnegie Hall complex (▷ 192)
offers everything from early
music and popular song to Afro-
Cuban and other world music.
💵 $35–$90 🚇 57th Street (N, Q,
W) 🚌 M6, M7, M57

DANCE AND OPERA
ALVIN AILEY AMERICAN DANCE THEATER
Map 186 D17
405 West 55th Street at Ninth Avenue
Tel 212/405-9000
www.alvinailey.org
In 2005 this exciting black
modern dance company
opened a brand-new
permanent home with a 285-
seat theater and 12 studios.
Even if you don't go to a
performance, stop by to see
them working out in the first-
floor studios.
💵 $25–$110 🚇 Columbus Circle
(1, A, B, C, D), 57th Street/7th Avenue
(N, R, Q, W) 🚌 M11

AMATO OPERA THEATRE
Map 189 F22
319 Bowery at 2nd Street
Tel 212/228-8200
www.amato.org
The company has been putting
on tiny productions of five or
six operas annually since 1948.
Mignon Dunn and Jon Frederic
West performed here early in
their careers. Seats 107.
💵 $25–$35 🚇 Bleecker Street (6),
Lower East Side/Second Avenue (F, V)
🚌 M21, M103

AMERICAN BALLET THEATER
890 Broadway at 19th Street
Tel 212/477-3030
www.abt.org
This company performs
regularly at City Center
(see below) and at the
Metropolitan Opera House
(▷ 195) in the spring.

CITY CENTER
Map 186 D17
131 West 55th Street between Sixth and
Seventh avenues
Tel 212/247-0430 or 212/581-1212
www.citycenter.org
The exotic Moorish-style
building dating from 1922–24
is especially famous for dance
productions. The Dance

*The American Ballet Theatre
performs a wide range of work*

Theater of Harlem, Alvin Ailey
American Dance Theater, Paul
Taylor Dance Company,
American Ballet Theatre and
the San Francisco Ballet have
all performed here. The Gilbert
and Sullivan Players are also
residents. Originally a Shriner's
temple, the building was
converted by Mayor Fiorello
LaGuardia into a "people's
theater" in 1943.
💵 $10–$65 🚇 57th Street (N, Q, R,
W) 🚌 M5, M6, M7, M57

DANCE THEATER WORKSHOP
Map 188 D20
219 West 19th Street at Seventh Avenue
Tel 212/924-0077
www.dtw.org
In 1965 Jeff Duncan, Art
Bauman and Jack Moore
founded this choreographers'
collective, and it still promises
innovative performances here
and at other city venues. Many
famous dancers have begun
careers here—Bill T. Jones,
Mark Morris, Ann Carlson,
Eiko and Koma—plus such
theatrical talents as Bill Irwin,
Whoopi Goldberg and Paul
Zaloom.
💵 Varies 🚇 18th Street (1) 🚌 M14,
M20

DANCE THEATER OF HARLEM
Off map at 186 C13
Everett Center for the Performing Arts
466 West 152nd Street between
Amsterdam and St. Nicholas avenues
Tel 212/690-2800
www.dancetheatreofharlem.com
This exciting company presents
a series at the New York State
Theater and also has open
house every second Sunday of
each month. Their appearance
at the August street festival is
also fun. The repertory ranges
from classical to contemporary
works.
🎫 July at New York State Theater
💵 Varies 🚇 155th Street (C) 🚌 M18,
M100, M101

JOYCE SOHO
Map 189 E23
155 Mercer Street between Houston
and Prince streets
Tel 212/431-9233 or 212/334-7479
www.joyce.org
This theater offers cutting-edge
dance, often with an
alternative perspective.
Rehearsals are open to
the public.
💵 $8–$20 🚇 Prince Street (N, R, W)
🚌 M1, M6, M21

THE JOYCE THEATER
Map 188 D21
175 Eighth Avenue southwest corner of 19th Street
Tel 212/691-9740 or 212/242-0800
www.joyce.org
The city's premier dance venue hosts top international and domestic dance companies and showcases such important dance series as Altogether Different. Expect to see the Eliot Feld Ballet, Pilobolus Dance Theater and many others.
👆 Varies 🚇 23rd Street (C, E) 🚌 M20, M23

THE JUDSON MEMORIAL CHURCH
Map 189 E22
55 Washington Square South
Tel 212/477-0351
www.judson.org
For many decades this Baptist Church has nurtured avant-garde artists. It's most famous for the late Judson Poets Theater but it still hosts experimental dance series. Movement Research performs a regular series here.
👆 Varies 🚇 West 4th Street (A, C, E, F, S, V) 🚌 M5, M6, M8

THE KITCHEN
Map 188 C21
512 West 19th Street between Tenth and Eleventh avenues
Tel 212/255-5793
www.thekitchen.org
At this fixture of the downtown scene established in 1971, the careers of such artists as Philip Glass, Laurie Anderson, Eric Bogosian, Robert Mapplethorpe and Cindy Sherman were nurtured. It's still going strong.
👆 $5–$15 🚇 23rd Street (C, E) 🚌 M11, M23

LINCOLN CENTER FOR THE PERFORMING ARTS
Map 186 C16
Columbus Avenue between 62nd and 66th streets
Tel 212/875-5000 or 212/875-5456
www.lincolncenter.org
This huge complex is home to the Metropolitan Opera House, the New York State Theater, Avery Fisher Hall, the Vivian Beaumont and Mitzi E. Newhouse theaters, the New York Public Library of the Performing Arts, the Walter Reade movie theater and the Juilliard School. In summer there is dancing under the stars on the plaza as well as the Lincoln Center Festival,

The Metropolitan Opera House is a glamorous venue

a free event which presents hundreds of performing artists and companies of all kinds. For tours of the first three halls mentioned above call 212/875-5350 for reservations.
👆 Varies 🚇 66th Street (1) 🚌 M7, M11, M66, M104

MERCE CUNNINGHAM STUDIO
Map 188 D22
55 Bethune Street at Washington Street (11th floor)
Tel 212/255-8240
www.merce.org
The Studio Performance Series for Emerging Choreographers uses this large studio space from September to July.

It seats 99. Cunningham, now in his 80s, still teaches here.
👆 $15 🚇 14th Street (A, C, E), 14th Street (1, 2, 3) 🚌 M8, M11, M20

METROPOLITAN OPERA HOUSE
Map 186 C16
30 Lincoln Center Plaza between 63rd and 64th streets
Tel 212/362-6000
www.metopera.org
The Metropolitan Opera, which had its first season in 1883–84, moved to this building on the western side of Lincoln Center Plaza in 1966. Although modern, it is glamorous with its Chagall paintings, plush crimson carpeting, chandeliers and gold leaf. The back of each of the theater's 3,800-seats has a screen that shows subtitles during performances. Most productions are spectacular, with the best international stars. Season-ticket holders snap up most of the best seats (and the best-priced seats) but individual tickets are usually available. Beginning in May the American Ballet Theatre performs a traditional repertory plus more modern pieces by such choreographers as James Kudelka and Twyla Tharp.
👆 $26–$215, standing room $15–$20 🚇 66th Street (1) 🚌 M5, M7, M11, M66, M104

NEW YORK GRAND OPERA
154 West 57th Street, Suite 125
Tel 212/245-8837
www.newyorkgrandopera.org
Founded in 1973, this company performs fully staged operas with full orchestra at Carnegie Hall and also gives free performances in Central Park. It is still directed by its founder, Vincent La Silva.
👆 $20–$60 (Summer in Central Park free)

NEW YORK STATE THEATER
Map 186 C16
20 Lincoln Center Plaza at 63rd Street
Tel 212/870-5570
www.nycballet.com
www.nycopera.com
This 2,792-seat auditorium is home to the New York City Opera and the New York City Ballet. The New York City Opera is famous for its emphasis on the ensemble rather than soloists, and many prefer its stimulating productions over those of the Met. The New York City Ballet began in 1933, and is still going strong under artistic director Peter Martins. The company performs for 23 weeks in the State Theater and then moves upstate to Saratoga.
🎭 City Opera $32–$110 (standing room only $12), NY Ballet $30–78 🚇 50th Street (1, 9) 🚌 M5, M7, M11, M66, M104

STREB ACTION INVENTION LAB
Off map 189 G23 (Brooklyn)
51 North First Street between Wythe and Kent, Williamsburg, Brooklyn
Tel 718-384-6491
www.strebusa.org
Harry Houdini and Evel Knievel inspire Elizabeth Streb's daring energetic stunt-like "Popaction" dancing in which she crashes through glass and leaps from ledges. She performs at this 200-seat theater and supper club and also in Grand Central and at the Joyce Theater and the Kitchen.
🎭 Varies 🚇 Bedford Avenue (L)

Comedy, Poetry and the Spoken Word

BARNES & NOBLE
Map 188 E21
33 East 17th Street at Union Square and other locations
Tel 212/253-0810
www.bn.com
Barnes & Noble bookstores regularly sponsor readings, discussions and signings with numerous authors; the biggest names are most likely to appear at the Union Square branch.
🎭 Free 🚇 14th Street/Union Square (L, N, Q, R, W, 4, 5, 6) 🚌 M1, M2, M3, M6, M7, M14

BOWERY POETRY CLUB
Map 189 F22
308 Bowery between Bleecker and East 1st streets
Tel 212/614-0505 or 212/206-1515
www.bowerypoetry.com
All kinds of poets and performance artists play here. There are shows almost every night, and weekend lunchtimes performances, too.
🎭 $5–$15 🚇 Bleecker Street (6) Broadway/Lafayette (F, S, V) 🚌 M21, M103

CAROLINE'S ON BROADWAY
Map 186 D17
1626 Broadway between 49th and 50th streets
Tel 212/757-4100
www.carolines.com
First opened by Caroline Hirsch as a cabaret in Chelsea

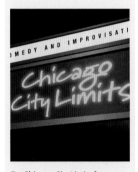

Try Chicago City Limits for improvised comedy

in 1981, the club gained a name throughout the 1980s and 1990s for its comedy bookings. Now in its glitzy Times Square venue, it presents live entertainment 365 nights a year. Jerry Seinfeld and Rosie O'Donnell did their early stand-up here.
🎭 Nightly, check program 🎫 $15–$45, plus 2-drink minimum 🚇 50th Street (1) 🚌 M10, M20, M50

CHICAGO CITY LIMITS
Map 186 D17
318 West 53rd Street at Eighth Avenue
Tel 212/888-5233
www.chicagocitylimits.com
This comedy revue company relocated to New York from Chicago in 1979. The resident troupe puts on two-hour improv shows. Don't sit in the front row if you're worried about being heckled. Soft drinks served.
🎭 Wed–Sun 🎫 $15 (plus 2-drink minimum) 🚇 50th Street (C, E) 🚌 M11

COMEDY CELLAR
Map 188 E22
117 MacDougal Street between West 3rd and Bleecker streets
Tel 212/254-3480
www.comedycellar.com
A cave-like venue that features nationally known comedians—Seinfeld, Stewart, Williams et al.
🎭 Nightly, check program 🎫 $10–$15, plus 2-drink minimum 🚇 West 4th Street (A, C, E, F, S, V) 🚌 M5, M6

DANGERFIELD'S
Map 187 F16
1118 First Avenue between East 61st and 62nd streets
Tel 212/593-1650
www.dangerfields.com
Rodney Dangerfield is no longer a regular presence, but this classic seedy club, established in 1969, has hosted many a legend, from Jay Leno and Jim Carrey to Jackie Mason, Tim Allen and Andrew Dice Clay.
🎭 Sun–Thu 8.45, Fri 8.30, 10.30, Sat. 8,

10.30, 12.30am $12.50–$20, no minimum 🚇 59th Street (4, 5, 6) 🚌 M15, M57

DONNELL MEDIA CENTER
Map 187 E17
New York Public Library, 20 West 53rd Street between Fifth and Sixth avenues
Tel 212/621-0609
www.nypl.org
Cultural events and readings.
🎫 Free 🚇 53rd Street/Fifth Avenue (E, V) 🚌 M1, M2, M3, M4, M5, M6, M7

THE DUPLEX
Map 188 D22
61 Christopher Street at Seventh Avenue South
Tel 212/255-5438
www.theduplex.com
A launching pad for Woody Allen, Joan Rivers and Rodney Dangerfield. The tradition continues in the upstairs cabaret room. Piano bar downstairs.
🕐 Nightly, check program 🎫 Cover varies, plus 2-drink minimum 🚇 Christopher Street/ Sheridan Square (1) 🚌 M8, M20

GOTHAM COMEDY CLUB
Map 188 D20
208 West 23rd Street between 7th and 8th avenues
Tel 212/367-9000
www.gothamcomedyclub.com
Old and new hands on the comedy scene play this upscale, elegant club in the Flatiron District, which opened in 1996.
🎫 Varies 🚇 23rd Street (1) 🚌 M14, M20

HOUSING WORKS USED BOOK CAFÉ
Map 189 F23
126 Crosby Street at Jersey Street
Tel 212/334-3324
www.housingworks.org
This bookstore with a gallery has become a major literary hub, attracting hipsters to readings, parties and events. Every third Friday of the month, there's an acoustic music concert. All monies support the homeless with HIV and AIDS.

🕐 Mon–Fri 10–9, Sat–Sun 12–7 (readings/events vary) 🎫 Free–$20 🚇 Prince Street (N, R), Broadway-Lafayette (F, S, V), Bleecker Street (6) 🚌 M1

NEW SCHOOL
Map 188 E21
Tishman Hall, 66 West 12th Street between Fifth and Sixth avenues
Tel 212/229-5488
www.nsu.newschool.edu
This prestigious university stages concerts, lectures and other performances including readings by writers such as Edmund White, poetry, film shows and discussions.
🚇 14th Street (F, V) 🚌 M5, M6, M7, M14

Enjoying a good book at Poets House

NEW YORK PUBLIC LIBRARY
Map 188 E18
Fifth Avenue between 41st and 42nd streets
Tel 212/930-0855
www.nypl.org
In addition to exhibitions, the library also sponsors lectures by leading writers and critics. They are usually held in the Celeste Bartos Forum.
🎫 Varies 🚇 42nd Street (B, D, F, V), Grand Central (4, 5, 6) 🚌 M1, M2, M3, M4, M42

92ND STREET Y
Map 187 F13
1395 Lexington Avenue at 92nd Street
Tel 212/415-5500
www.92Y.org
This major cultural force in the city has four performance spaces, programming everything from lectures given by heavy hitters like Bill Gates and Bill Clinton to readings sponsored in the Unterberg Poetry Center.
🎫 $16–$50 🚇 96th Street (6) 🚌 M96, M98, M101, M102, M103

NUYORICAN POETS CAFÉ
Map 189 G22
236 East 3rd Street between Avenues B and C
Tel 212/505-8183
www.nuyorican.org
Originally a platform for Puerto Rican poets and artists, the café is still famous for its Wednesday and Friday night poetry slams. Expect to see theater, screenplay readings and even Latin jazz. Take a cab there and back.
🕐 Tue–Sat 7–12, Sun 4–12 🎫 Varies 🚇 Lower East Side/Second Avenue (F, V) 🚌 M9, M21

PEOPLE'S IMPROV THEATER
Map 188 E19/20
154 West 29th Street between Sixth and Seventh avenues
Tel 212/563-7488
www.thepit-nyc.com
Improvisation here comes with caustic social commentary and audience participation.
🎫 Varies 🚇 28th Street (1) 🚌 M5, M6, M7, M20

THE POETRY PROJECT
Map 189 F21
St. Mark's Church-in-the-Bowery
131 East 10th Street at Second Avenue
Tel 212/674-0910
www.poetryproject.com
This legendary outpost in the East Village, which hosted W. H. Auden, Allen Ginsberg and many others, has readings most Mondays, Wednesdays and Fridays.
🎫 Varies 🚇 Astor Place (6), First Avenue (L) 🚌 M8, M15

WHAT TO DO

POETS HOUSE
Map 189 F23
72 Spring Street between Crosby and
Lafayette streets
Tel 212/431-7920
www.poetshouse.org
This 45,000-volume poetry
library has regular readings
and lectures.
🎫 Free–$7 🚇 Spring Street (6),
Spring Street (C, E) 🚌 M1

QUEENS COLLEGE
Music Building
Tel 718/997-4646
www.qc.edu/readings
The college offers regular

readings by international poets
and writers. No credit cards.
🎫 Varies 🎫 $15 🚇 Main Street (7)
and bus Q 25/34 (best to call for
directions)

STAND-UP NEW YORK
Map 186 C14
236 West 78th Street at Broadway
Tel 212/595-0850
www.standupny.com
Audiences here can be hard,
but comics at this typical
comedy club may emerge as
the stars of tomorrow.
🎫 Cover varies, 2-drink minimum
🚇 79th Street (1) 🚌 M79, M104

UPRIGHT CITIZENS BRIGADE THEATRE
Map 188 D20
307 West 26th Street between Eighth
and Ninth avenues
Tel 212/366-9176
www.ucbtheatre.com
The city's hippest and most
affordable comedy club. Expect
manic, original and inventive
improv-style sketches at the
150-seat theater.
🎫 Daily (show times vary) 🎫 Most
shows $5–$8 🚇 23rd Street (C, E)

Contemporary Live Music

WHAT TO DO

BLUES, COUNTRY, FOLK, REGGAE AND WORLD

ASIA SOCIETY
Map 187 F15
725 Park Avenue at East 70th Street
Tel 212/288-6400
www.asiasociety.org
The downstairs auditorium
showcases arts and culture—
dance, film, lectures and
music—from Asia. Ravi Shankar
made his American debut at
the Asia Society.
🎫 Varies 🚇 68th Street (6) 🚌 M1,
M2, M3, M4, M72

B. B. KING BLUES CLUB AND GRILL
Map 188 D18
237 West 42nd Street
Tel 212/997-4144
www.bbkingblues.com
Little Richard and Roberta
Flack, among others, have
all entertained at this large
bi-level club. On Sunday
a gospel choir shakes up the
Sunday brunch from 1.30
onward. Dance floor.
🎫 $10–$90 🚇 42nd Street/Times
Square (N, Q, R, S, W, 1, 2, 3, 7)
🚌 M10, M20, M42, M104

BITTER END
Map 189 E22
147 Bleecker Street at Thompson Street
Tel 212/673-7030
www.bitterend.com
The cradle of the antiwar folk

You'll find the craic at the Irish Arts Center

music scene in the 1960s, the
Bitter End is much more rock-
oriented today. Performances
every night.
🎫 $5–$15 🚇 West 4th Street (A, C, E,
F, V, S) 🚌 M5, M6, M21

IRISH ARTS CENTER
Map 186 C17
553 West 51st Street between Tenth and
Eleventh avenues
Tel 212/757-3318
www.irishartscenter.org
Comedy and music with a
Celtic-Gaelic flavor are
performed here usually the
second Sunday each month.
🎫 Varies 🚇 50th Street (C, E)
🚌 M11, M50

JAPAN SOCIETY
Map 187 F18
333 East 47th Street between First and
Second avenues
Tel 212/832-1155
www.japansociety.org
Traditional and contemporary
Japanese music concerts
and cultural events are held
in the 278-seat Lila Acheson
Wallace Auditorium.
🎫 Varies 🚇 51st Street (6) 🚌 M15,
M27, M50

LION'S DEN
Map 189 E22
214 Sullivan Street between Bleecker and
West 3rd streets
Tel 212/477-2782
www.cegmusic.com
Folk and rock artists are the
staples here.
🎫 Nightly (show times vary) 🎫 $8–$20
🚇 West 4th Street (A, C, E, F, S, V),
Bleecker Street (6) 🚌 M5, M6, M21

PADDY REILLY'S MUSIC BAR
Off map 188 F19
519 Second Avenue at 29th Street
Tel 212/686-1210
The Celtic house band, the
Prodigals, plays Friday nights.
Saturday is open mike night,
and visitors make an attempt
to play the bodhrán and the
uillean pipes.
🎫 Daily 11am–4am 🎫 $5–$15
🚇 28th Street (6) 🚌 M15

RODEO BAR
Map 188 F20
375 Third Avenue at East 27th Street
Tel 212/683-6500
www.rodeobar.com
This Southern-style roadhouse serves up Tex-Mex food and margaritas, along with nightly live music including bluegrass, country, rockabilly and alt-country.
🕐 Daily 11.30am–2am (music Mon–Tue 9–12, Wed 10–12, Thu 10–1, Fri–Sat 10.30–1.30 🎵 Free 🚇 28th Street (6) 🚌 M101, M102, M103

TERRA BLUES
Map 189 E22
149 Bleecker Street between LaGuardia Place and Thompson Street
Tel 212/777-7776
www.terrablues.com
At this second-floor club, acoustic acts warm up the crowd for the nightly blues show. The bar has a good selection of bourbons.
🕐 Nightly at 7pm, blues show 10pm 🎵 $5–$15, plus 2-drink minimum 🚇 West 4th Street (A, C, E, F, S, V) 🚌 M5, M6

TOWN HALL
Map 188 D18
123 West 43rd Street between Sixth Avenue and Broadway
Tel 212/840-2824 (recording) and 212/997-6661 (Mon–Sat 12–6)
www.the-townhall-nyc.org
This 1,500-seat theater, founded in 1921 by the suffragist League for Political Education, offers eclectic programming with Broadway songs, cabaret, opera, pop performances and world music as well as lectures and readings. McKim, Mead and White designed the Georgian-style building.
🎵 Free–$75 🚇 42nd Street/Times Square (N, Q, R, S, W, 1, 2, 3, 7), 42nd Street (B, D, F, V) 🚌 M5, M6, M7, M42

VILLAGE UNDERGROUND
Map 189 E22
130 West 3rd Street between Sixth Avenue and MacDougal Street
Tel 212/777-7745
www.thevillageunderground.com
A subterranean club with a good line-up of artists ranging from salsa bands to blues artists. Sunday is open-mic night.
🎵 Varies 🚇 West 4th Street (A, C, E, F, S, V) 🚌 M5, M6

WORLD MUSIC INSTITUTE
49 West 27th Street, Suite 930
Tel 212/545-7536
www.worldmusicinstitute.org
This organization sponsors world music concerts and

The Town Hall offers a wide range of performances

series at venues around town (Symphony Space, Cooper Union, Town Hall).

JAZZ AND CABARET
ARTHUR'S TAVERN
Map 188 D22
57 Grove Street between Seventh Avenue South and Bleecker Street
Tel 212/675-6879
www.arthurstavernnyc.com
This funky down-home bar has jazz most nights—usually traditional Dixieland.
🎵 Free 🚇 Christopher Street/Sheridan Square (1) 🚌 M8, M20

BEMELMANS BAR
Map 187 E14
Carlyle Hotel, 35 East 76th Street
Tel 212/744-1600
www.thecarlyle.com
The murals and the sophistication of the scene make this a classic New York experience.
🕐 Daily 11am–2am (entertainment from 5.30 usually) 🎵 $20–$25 at table, $10 at bar; no minimum 🚇 77th Street (6) 🚌 M1, M2, M3, M4

BIRDLAND
Map 188 D18
315 West 44th Street between Eighth and Ninth avenues
Tel 212/581-3080
www.birdlandjazz.com
Perhaps the most elegant and comfortable jazz club in town. Charlie Parker inspired the original Birdland, which opened in 1949, and he was its first headliner. Expect to hear everyone from Roy Haynes and Lee Konitz to Diana Krall and Nicholas Payton.
🕐 Shows daily, times vary 🎵 $20–$50 plus $10 minimum 🚇 42nd Street (A, C, E) 🚌 M10, M11, M20, M42

BLUE NOTE
Map 188 E22
131 West Third Street at Sixth Avenue
Tel 212/475-8592
www.bluenotejazz.com
Tiny and ultra-expensive, the Blue Note is always jammed with fans grooving to the sounds of contemporary leaders in jazz, blues, Latin and R & B. It also sponsors a Latin Jazz Festival.
🕐 Daily at 8pm and 10.30pm (and 12.30am weekends) 🎵 $20–$65 at tables, $40–45 at bar, plus $5 minimum 🚇 West 4th Street (A, C, E, F, S, V) 🚌 M5, M6

CAFÉ CARLYLE
Map 187 E14
Carlyle Hotel, 35 East 76th Street at
Madison Avenue
Tel 212/744-1600
www.thecarlyle.com
Though the legendary Bobby
Short has passed away, his
spirit lives on through the
music, from Cole Porter to
Bessie Smith entertaining café
society in high style. On
Monday night, Woody Allen
occasionally shows up with his
clarinet and the Eddy Davis
New Orleans Jazz Band.
◉ Sets: Tue–Sat 8.45pm and 10.45pm
🍷 $95, no minimum ◎ 77th Street (6)
🚌 M1, M2, M3, M4

CAFÉ PIERRE
Map 187 E16
Fifth Avenue at 61st Street
Tel 212/838-8000
www.tajhotels.com
Kathleen Landis and Nancy
Winston play and sing jazz and
cabaret standards, along with
customer requests.
◉ Tue–Thu 8.30–11.30, Fri–Sat
8.30–12.30 🍷 Free, $25 minimum
◎ 59th Street/Fifth Avenue (N, R, W)
🚌 M1, M2, M3, M4

CORNELIA STREET CAFÉ
Map 188 D22
29 Cornelia Street between Bleecker and
West 3rd streets
Tel 212/989-9319
www.corneliastreetcafe.com
This subterranean space hosts
everything from structured free
jazz and cabaret to poetry and
performance art.
🍷 Free–$15 ◎ West 4th Street (A, C,
E, F, S, V) 🚌 M5, M6, M21

COTTON CLUB
Off map 186 C12
656 West 125th Street between
Broadway and Riverside Drive
Tel 212/663-7980
www.cottonclub-newyork.com
Although its heyday was from
1923 to 1935 (then on 142nd
Street), this famous Harlem
landmark still has blues, jazz
and gospel acts that seem
straight out of the 1920s.
Monday night is swing night.

◉ Mon, Thu–Fri 8– 2, Sat–Sun
noon–2am 🍷 $15–$40 ◎ 125th
Street (1) 🚌 M104, Bx 15

DETOUR
Map 189 F21
349 East 13th Street between First and
Second Avenues
Tel 212/533-6212
www.jazzatdetour.com
This tiny casual no-cover jazz
bar is the place to hear young
emerging musicians and
singers playing traditional
and experimental jazz.
◉ Sun–Thu 4–2 (music 9–12.30),
Fri–Sat 4–4 (music 10–1.30) 🍷 2-drink
minimum ◎ 14th Street/Union Square
(L, N, Q, R, W, 4, 5, 6), First Avenue (L)
🚌 M14, M15

The Cotton Club is a New York
institution

DON'T TELL MAMA
Map 186 D18
343 West 46th Street between Eighth
and Ninth avenues
Tel 212/757-0788
www.donttellmama.com
Diverse singers and cabaret
artists perform here nightly.
🍷 None–$40, plus 2-drink minimum
◎ 42nd Street (A, C, E) 🚌 M11, M20

DUPLEX PIANO BAR AND
CABARET
Map 188 D22
61 Christopher Street at 7th Avenue
Tel 212/255-5438
www.theduplex.com
One of the city's best piano
bars, it's been around since
the 1950s and was where

performers including Woody
Allen tried out their cabaret
material. These days, most
nights see artists performing,
with open-mic sessions and a
Saturday karaoke.
◉ Daily 4–4 🍷 Most shows $7–$20
cover and 2-drink minimum
◎ Christopher Street-Sheridan Square
(1), 4th Street-Washington Square (A,
B, C, D, E, F, V)

FEINSTEIN'S AT THE REGENCY
Map 187 E16
Regency Hotel, 540 Park Avenue at East
61st Street
Tel 212/339-4095
www.feinsteinsattheregency.com
It's lush, elegant and exclusive.
Michael Feinstein plays on
occasion. Dinner is available.
◉ Shows Tue–Sat, usually at 8.30
🍷 $50–$75, plus $40 minimum
◎ Lexington/63rd Street (F), 59th
Street (4, 5, 6), 59th Street (N, R, W)
🚌 M1, M2, M3, M4, M57

IRIDIUM
Map 186 D17
1650 Broadway at 51st Street
Tel 212/582-2121
www.iridiumjazzclub.com
Guitar legend Les Paul plays
every Monday night at this chic
good-looking club. Top R&B and
jazz names appear, plus there
are Cuban jazz nights twice a
month. On Sunday there's a
jazz brunch buffet from 11 to 3,
with shows at 12.30 and 2.30.
◉ Sun–Thu 5–midnight (sets at 8 and
10), Fri–Sat 7pm–2am (sets at 8, 10 and
11.30) 🍷 $25–$95 ($5 minimum at bar,
$10 at table) ◎ 49th Street (N, R, W),
50th Street (1) 🚌 M6, M7, M50

JAZZ GALLERY
Map 189 F23
290 Hudson Street between Dominick
and Spring streets
Tel 212/242-1063
www.jazzgallery.org
Opened in 1995, this
exhibition and performance
space is used for jazz-oriented
and jazz-influenced art,
literature, drama and music.
◉ Times vary, check program
🍷 $12–$65 ◎ Spring Street (C, E),
Houston Street (1) 🚌 M20, M21

WHAT TO DO

JAZZ AT LINCOLN CENTER
Map 186 D16
Time Warner Center at Broadway and
60th Street
Tel 212/258-9800 or 212/721-6500
www.jazzatlincolncenter.org
Top-drawer jazz artists give
performances in the 1230-seat
Rose Theater, the 300- to 600-
seat Allen Room (whose 50-
foot-high (15m) glass wall
overlooks Columbus Circle) and
the more intimate Dizzy's Club
Coca-Cola, commemorating
Dizzy Gillespie.
🕐 Varies 🎟 Varies $30–$150; club has
cover and minimum 🚇 59th Street
(1) 🚌 M5, M104

JAZZ STANDARD
Map 188 F20
116 East 27th Street between Park
Avenue South and Lexington Avenue
Tel 212/576-2232
www.jazzstandard.com
The Union Square Café's
Danny Myers established this
popular downstairs venue with
food from his ground-floor
restaurant Blue Smoke. It's a
sleek, comfortable place for
music and a meal.
🕐 Daily 6.30–3 (show times vary)
🎟 $15–$30 🚇 28th Street (6) 🚌 M1,
M101, M102, M103

JOE'S PUB
Map 189 F22
Public Theater, 425 Lafayette Street
between Astor Place and East 4th Street
Tel 212/539-8770 or 212/539 8778
www.joespub.com
A favorite cabaret club of many
New Yorkers, named after
Public Theater founder Joe
Papp. It's comfortable the way
a club should be, with couches
and tables. DJs spin during
Late Night at Joe's.
🕐 Daily 6–4 (show times vary)
🎟 $10–$40, plus 2-drink
minimum 🚇 Astor Place (6)
🚌 M1, M8

LENOX LOUNGE
Off map 187 E12
288 Lenox Avenue between 124th and
125th streets
Tel 212/427-0253
www.lenoxlounge.com

This long-time Harlem hang-
out for musicians has jazz
every night except Tuesday.
🕐 Wed–Mon (show times vary)
🎟 Free–$20 🚇 125th Street (2, 3)
🚌 M7, M102

LOLA'S JAZZ CAFE
Off map in Brooklyn
613 Fifth Avenue, Brooklyn, between
Prospect and 17th
Tel 718/499-4530
A cheap and basic Puerto
Rican place that offers a mix of
live jazz and Latin nights.
🕐 Daily 4-4
🎟 No cover charge
🚇 Prospect Avenue (M, R)

*Jazz aficionados are spoilt for
choice*

OAK ROOM
Map 188 E18
Algonquin Hotel, 59 West 44th Street
between Fifth and Sixth avenues
Tel 212/419-9331
www.algonquinhotel.com
By nurturing such artists as
Steve Ross, Michael Feinstein,
Harry Connick, Jr. and Diana
Krall, this room led a revival of
cabaret. Dinner is available
before the first show.
🕐 Mon 8pm, Tue–Thu 9pm, Fri–Sat
9pm and 11.30pm, Sun noon
🎟 $60–75, plus 2-drink minumum,
dinner packages 🚇 42nd Street (B, D,
F, V) 🚌 M1, M2, M3, M4, M5, M6, M7

ST. PETER'S CHURCH
Map 187 F17
Citicorp Center, 619 Lexington Avenue
at 54th Street
Tel 212/935-2200
www.saintpeters.org
The regularly held jazz vespers
at this Lutheran church every
Sunday at 5pmat Citicorp
Center are well known among
New Yorkers and musicians,
along with the Wednesday jazz
at 1pm.
🎟 Donation 🚇 53rd Street/Lexington
Avenue (E, V) 🚌 M57, M98, M101,
M102, M103

SCHOMBURG CENTER FOR
RESEARCH IN BLACK CULTURE
Off map 187 E12
515 Malcolm X Boulevard at 135th Street
Tel 212/491-2200
www.nypl.org
This African-American cultural
archive sponsors an annual
Women's Jazz Festival and a
performance of Langston
Hughes' *Nativity* in December.
🎟 Varies 🚇 135th Street (B, C)
🚌 M7

SHOWMAN'S JAZZ CLUB
Off map 186 D12
375 West 125th Street between St.
Nicholas and Morningside avenues
Tel 212/864-8941
In the 1940s and 50s,
musicians often dropped in
here after hours to jam or just
hang out. Today musicians still
frequent the place and you
might find Grady Tate, George
Benson or Ed Bradley whiling
away the hours.
🕐 Mon–Thu 8.30pm–12.30am, Fri–Sat
10.30pm–3.30am 🎟 Free, 2-drink
minimum 🚇 125th Street (A, B, C, D)
🚌 M3

SMALL'S

Map 188 C22

183 West 10th Street between West 4th Street and Seventh Avenue South

Tel 212/252-5091

www.smallsjazzclub.com

This just may be the least expensive, quality jazz club in the city. It's named appropriately; the downstairs space is narrow and spare. The focus is on the music, and there are no distractions such as a bar or food. The musicians jam into the wee hours, with many dropping in from other clubs after hours. Several big names got their break here, notably Zaid Nasser, Grant Stewart, Jason Lindner and Ari Roland.

🕐 Daily 7pm–late 🎟 Cover $20 (includes one drink) 🚇 14th Street (1, 2, 3) 🚌 M20

SMOKE

Off map 186 C12

2751 Broadway between 105th and 106th Streets

Tel 212/864-6662

www.smokejazz.com

Intimate and comfortable with its plush couches, red velvet barstools and heavy drapes, this club was opened in 1999. It has headlined great jazz artists including organist Dr. Lonnie Smith and trombonist Slide Hampton, but it is also a good place to see local artists.

🕐 Daily 9pm, 11pm, 12.30am 🎟 Sun–Thu free, but $15 minimum, weekends cover varies $20–$25 🚇 103 Street (1) 🚌 M104

SWEET RHYTHM

Map 188 D22

88 Seventh Avenue South between Grove and Bleecker streets

Tel 212/255-3626

www.sweetrhythmny.com

The late Gil Evans played here when the place was called Sweet Basil. It's a casual spot where mainstream jazz artists play sets nightly.

🎟 $12–$25, plus $10 minimum 🚇 Christopher Street/Sheridan Square (1), West 4th Street (A, C, E, F, S, V) 🚌 M8, M20

TISHMAN AUDITORIUM

Map 188 E21

New School, 66 West 12th Street between Fifth and Sixth avenues

Tel 212 229-5488

www.newschool.edu

The New School's Afro-Cuban Jazz Orchestra under Bobby Sanabria plays here.

🕐 Varies 🚇 14th Street (F, V) 🚌 M2, M3, M5, M6

VILLAGE VANGUARD

Map 188 D21

178 Seventh Avenue at West 11th Street

Tel 212/255-4037

www.villagevanguard.com

Founded by Max Gordon in 1935, it's still the premier jazz club in the city, presided over

Jazz addicts can track down an after-hours jam

by Lorraine Gordon since her husband died in 1989. The Vanguard is intimate, has terrific acoustics and features top-flight artists. All the great names have played here— Coleman Hawkins, Lester Young and Thelonious Monk in the 40s, John Coltrane in the 60s, Keith Jarrett in the 70s, and Miles Davis and Bill Evans across the decades. Nowadays evenings often morph into a vibrant jam session.

🕐 Daily from 8pm (sets Sun–Thu 9 and 11, Fri–Sat 9, 11 and sometimes 12.30) 🎟 Cover varies, plus $10 minimum 🚇 14th Street (1, 2, 3) 🚌 M14, M20

ZINC BAR

Map 189 E22

90 West Houston Street between LaGuardia Place and Thompson Street

Tel 212/477-8337

www.zincbar.com

Music-lovers and musicians come to this casual, tiny bar to hear newcomers as well as such famous names as George Benson and Max Roach. There's usually Brazilian music on Saturdays and Sundays.

🕐 Daily 6pm–3.30am (show times vary) 🎟 Cover varies 🚇 West 4th Street (A, C, E, F, S, V), Houston Street (1), Bleecker Street (6) 🚌 M5, M6, M21

ROCK AND POP

AARON DAVIS HALL/ HARLEM STAGE

Off map 186 D12

City College of New York, West 135th Street and Convent Avenue

Tel 212/281-9240

www.harlemstage.org

Harlem's principal center for the performing arts presents established and emerging artists of color in music, dance, theater and multimedia performances. The Harlem Stage is across the street from the three-theater Aaron Davis Hall.

🎟 Varies 🚇 137th Street/Broadway (1) 🚌 M4, M5

APOLLO THEATER

Off map 186 D12

253 West 125th Street between Frederick Douglass Boulevard and St. Nicholas Avenue

Tel 212/531-5305

www.apollotheater.com

Originally a vaudeville theater, the Apollo has been a venue for black entertainers since 1934. Everyone from Duke Ellington and Billie Holiday to Aretha Franklin and Stevie Wonder have performed here. The Wednesday Amateur Night Competition is famous, drawing crowds who register their approval or disapproval with gusto. Today the entertainment ranges from musicians and singers to musicals, and there are Historic Tours, too.

🎟 Varies 🚇 125th Street (A, B, C, D), Lenox (1, 2, 3) 🚌 M104

ARLENE GROCERY

Map 189 G23

95 Stanton Street between Ludlow and Orchard streets

Tel 212/995-1652

www.arlenesgrocery.com

This former bodega is one of the best rock clubs in the city. The bar is pleasant, and the back room casually comfortable. It's the place to hear up-and-comers.

🕐 Daily 6pm–4am 🎟 Varies 🚇 Lower East Side/Second Avenue (F, V) 🚌 M15, M21

BEACON THEATRE

Map 186 C15

2124 Broadway at 74th Street

Tel 212/465-6500

www.beacontheatre.com

Many different artists perform here, from the likes of Sinead O'Connor and David Gray to modern ballet.

🎟 $33–$90 🚇 72nd Street (1, 2, 3) 🚌 M72, M104

BOWERY BALLROOM

Map 189 F23

6 Delancey Street between Bowery and Chrystie streets

Tel 212/533-2111

www.boweryballroom.com

When Patti Smith came out of retirement, it was to this rollicking tri-level venue in a 1929 Beaux Arts building that she returned. The club opened in 1997 and has comfortable lounges, good sound systems, a large stage and excellent sight lines. Beth Orton, Soul Asylum, Chris Robinson, David Byrne and Counting Crows are just a few of the bands that have played here.

Many legendary artists have performed at the Apollo Theater

🎟 $13–$35 🚇 Delancey/Essex (F, J, M, Z) 🚌 M103

CBGB DOWNSTAIRS LOUNGE

Map 189 F22

315 Bowery at Bleecker Street

Tel 212/982-4052

www.cbgb.com

Ever since it opened in 1973, this dark, funky place has been the home of underground rock (despite the fact that the name stands for "country bluegrass blues"). Here New Yorkers grooved to the Ramones, Patti Smith and all of the most important punk and post-punk bands from Blondie to Television and the Talking Heads. Sunday night, there's jazz in the downstairs lounge.

🎟 $7–$10 🚇 Bleecker Street (6) 🚌 M21, M103

COOPER UNION GREAT HALL

Map 189 F22

Seventh Street at Third Avenue

Tel 212/353-4195 or 212/279-4200

www.cooper.edu/ce

Everything from fado (Portuguese folk music) and contemporary classical music to Afro-Brazilian drum groups and samba bands can be heard in this hall at a private tuition-free college for the Advancement of Science and Art. Abraham Lincoln spoke here in 1860.

🎟 Free–$25 🚇 Astor Place (6), 8th Street (N, R, W) 🚌 M8, M101, M102, M103

KNITTING FACTORY

Map 189 E24

74 Leonard Street between Broadway and Church Street

Tel 212/219-3132

www.knittingfactory.com

Innovative owner Michael Dorf opened this club in TriBeCa in 1987 to headline local and international bands playing experimental music— free jazz, rock and even klezmer (a mix of eastern European Jewish music with other styles). Its dedicated musical audience comes to three performance spaces: the Main Space, the smaller Old Office and Alterknit Theater, which hosts a weekly poetry open mike, and the Tap Bar. The bar has plenty of beers on tap and free shows at midnight. The club also sponsors festivals and operates a record label.

🎟 $10–$30 🚇 Franklin Street (1) 🚌 M1, M6

MADISON SQUARE GARDEN
Map 188 D19
4 Penn Plaza
Tel 212/465-6741
www.thegarden.com
Located on top of Penn Station, this arena hosts sports events, concerts and other entertainment. Bob Dylan, Madonna, Michael Jackson, the Rolling Stones, Elton John and many other big star tours stop here.
🚇 34th Street/Penn Station (A, C, E, 1, 2, 3) 🚌 M10, M16, M20, M34

MAKOR
Map 186 D15
200 Hudson Street between Vestry and Desbrosses streets
Tel 212/601-1000
www.92Y.org
This venue, associated with a Jewish community center, offers an eclectic mix of musical entertainment ranging from rap to blues and gypsy to klezmer. It's strong on world music and brings in such performers as Nigerian Kofo the Wonderman and Maria del Mar Bonet from Mallorca.
🎫 $15–$30 🚇 Canal Street (1, A, C, E) 🚌 M6, M20

MERCURY LOUNGE
Map 189 G22
217 East Houston Street between First Avenue and Avenue A
Tel 212/260-4700
www.mercuryloungenyc.com
This is a regular stop on the downtown music scene. Bands—both local and international—perform back to back in one raucous room. You might find Holly Go Lightly, who sang with punk Brit Billy Childish, doing garage rock, for example. The adjacent lounge is slightly more serene.
🕐 Daily 8pm–3am 🎫 $8–$20 🚇 Lower East Side/Second Avenue (F, V) 🚌 M14, M21

ROSELAND BALLROOM
Map 186 D17
239 West 52nd Street between Broadway and Eighth Avenue
Tel 212/247-0200
www.roselandballroom.com
The original opened at 51st Street in 1919, but moved here in 1956. Once a legendary ballroom featuring the bands of Fletcher Henderson and Tommy Dorsey, today it hosts rock concerts and occasional sporting events.
🎫 $25–$27.50 🚇 50th Street (1), 50th Street (C, E) 🚌 M6, M7, M10, M20, M50

Latin American rhythms at Sounds of Brazil (SOB's)

SOB'S
Map 189 D23
204 Varick Street at Houston Street
Tel 212/243-4940
www.sobs.com
Since 1982 this club (Sounds of Brazil) has been at the forefront of Afro-Latino music. The featured band might play hip-hop and rap or driving Latin salsa with Haitian, reggae and Bhangra music, too.
🎫 $10–$20, plus $20 minimum 🚇 Houston Street (1) 🚌 M20, M21

SOUTHPAW
Off map 189 G25
125 Fifth Avenue between Sterling and St. John's Place, Park Slope, Brooklyn
Tel 718/230-0236
www.spsounds.com
This club designed for rock shows has great acoustics, a good-size stage and a terrific sound system.
🎫 Varies 🚇 Fourth Avenue (F, M, R, W)

SYMPHONY SPACE
Off map at 186 C12
2537 Broadway at 95th Street
Tel 212/864-5400
www.symphonyspace.org
Since 1978 this alternative space occupying a renovated movie theater has been offering eclectic programming in two theaters, the Peter Jay Sharp Theatre and the Leonard Nimoy Thalia. It's known for its free shows, Wall to Wall 12-hour marathons celebrating particular artists (Joni Mitchell, for example); for its Face the Music and Dance, which pairs musicians with choreographers; and for its Selected Shorts, an evening of major actors reading short stories. Companies that perform regularly include the New Amsterdam Symphony Orchestra, the Gilbert and Sullivan Players and the Manhattan Chamber Orchestra. Many world music artists, including guitarist Djelimady Tounkara from Mali and Indian tabla player Zakir Hussain, also perform here under the auspices of the World Music Institute.
🎫 $18–$50 🚇 96th Street (1, 2, 3) 🚌 M96, M104

WHAT TO DO

Theater

No fee applies when you buy your tickets at the box office; most open Monday to Saturday from 10am to 8pm and Sunday from 11am to 6.30pm. Standing Room Only tickets, which are sometimes available, go on sale when the box office opens on the day of the performance. Note the curtain times for each new production.

BROADWAY THEATERS

On Broadway, ticket prices range from $25 to $105 for major Broadway musicals and from $50 to $90 for dramas and comedies.

AL HIRSCHFELD
Map 188 D18
302 West 45th Street between Eighth and Ninth avenues
Tel 212/239-6200
Named for a theatrical caricaturist, this Moorish-style theater was built in 1924 and has lavish interiors. Avoid the side seats.
Tue–Sat 8, matinees Wed, Sat–Sun 2 42nd Street/Eighth Avenue (A, C, E) M6, M7, M10, M11, M42, M104

AMBASSADOR THEATRE
Map 188 D17
219 West 49th Street between Broadway and Eighth Avenue
Tel 212/239-6200
www.shubertorganization.com
Opened in 1921, this 1,125-seat auditorium is wider than it is deep, so viewing is good but with a mezzanine overhang.
Thu–Sat 8, Sun 7, Mon 8, Tue 7, matinees Sat–Sun 2 50th Street/Seventh Avenue (1), 49th Street (N, R) M6, M7, M10, M27, M50, M104

AMERICAN AIRLINES
Map 188 D18
227 West 42nd Street between Seventh and Eighth avenues
Tel 212/719-1300
www.roundabouttheatre.org
This restored 1918 theater

with 750 seats is now the home of the Roundabout Theatre Company, founded in 1965 to perform the classics and new plays at affordable prices.
Tue–Sat 8, matinees Wed, Sat–Sun 2 42nd Street/Times Square (N, Q, R, S, W, 1, 2, 3, 7) M6, M7, M10, M42, M104

AUGUST WILSON THEATRE
Map 186 D17
245 West 52nd Street between Broadway and Eighth Avenue
Tel 212/239-6200
The Theater Guild commissioned this striking theater with its Tuscan-style facade, and it opened in 1925.

The American Airlines theater has been impressively renovated

Tue–Sat 8, matinees Wed, Sat 2, Sun 3 50th Street (1), 50th Street (C, E) M6, M7, M10, M27, M50, M104

BELASCO
Map 188 E18
111 West 44th Street between Broadway and Sixth Avenue
Tel 212/239-6200
www.shubertorganization.com
Named after the bishop of Broadway David Belasco, this gem of a theater with 1,018 seats has some gorgeous Tiffany lamps and lovely murals by Everett Shinn. Avoid the side orchestra if you can.
Tue–Sat 8, matinees Wed, Sat 2, Sun 3 42nd Street/Times Square

(N, R, S, W, 1, 2, 3, 7), 42nd Street/Sixth Avenue (B, D, F) M5, M6, M7, M10, M42, M104

BERNARD B. JACOBS THEATRE
Map 188 D18
242 West 45th Street between Broadway and Eighth Avenue
Tel 212/239-6200
Laurence Olivier starred in *The Entertainer* on this stage, which opened in 1927.
Tue–Sat 8, matinees Wed 2, Sun 3 42nd Street/Times Square (N, Q, R, S, W, 1, 2, 3, 7), 42nd Street/Eighth Avenue (A, C, E) M6, M7, M10, M42, M104

BILTMORE THEATRE
Map 186 D18
261 West 47th Street between Broadway and Eighth Avenue
Tel 212/239-6200
This landmark theater (now with 650 seats) opened in 1925 and hosted such winners as *Hair* and Neil Simon's *Barefoot in the Park*. Recently it became the Broadway home of the Manhattan Theatre Club.
Tue–Sat 8, Sun 7, Sat, Sun 2 50th Street (C, E), 50th Street (1) M10, M20

BOOTH
Map 188 D18
222 West 45th Street between Broadway and Eighth Avenue
Tel 212/239-6200
www.shubertorganization.com
Numerous hits have played at this Italianate 781-seat theater dating to 1913 and named after actor Edwin Booth.
Mon, Wed, Fri–Sat 8, Tue 7, matinees Wed and Sat 2, Sun 3 42nd Street/ Times Square (N, R, S, W, 1, 2, 3, 7) M6, M7, M10, M42, M104

BROADHURST
Map 188 D18
235 West 44th Street between Broadway and Eighth Avenue
Tel 212/639-6200
www.shubertorganization.com
Named after Anglo-American playwright George Broadhurst, this theater was built by the Shuberts and has welcomed

WHAT TO DO

star-studded casts since opening in 1918. Seats 1,186. ⓦ Tue–Sat 8, matinees Wed, Sat 2, Sun 3 🚇 42nd Street/ Times Square (N, R, S, W, 1, 2, 3, 7) 🚌 M6, M7, M10, M42, M104

BROADWAY

Map 186 D17
1681 Broadway between 52nd and 53rd streets
Tel 212/239-6200
www.shubertorganization.com
This 1,752-seat theater was built as a movie house in 1924. Avoid the back of the house if you can. ⓦ Tue–Sat 8, matinees Wed, Sat 2, Sun 3 🚇 50th Street/Eighth Avenue (C, E), 50th Street/Seventh Avenue (1) 🚌 M6, M7, M10, M27, M50, M104

BROOKS ATKINSON

Map 186 D18
256 West 47th Street between Broadway and Eighth Avenue
Tel 212/307-4100
www.brooksatkinsontheater.com
Built in 1926, this ornate theater is named for longtime *New York Times* theater critic Brooks Atkinson. With 1,086 seats, you may feel you're too far from the stage if you sit in the rear mezzanine. ⓦ Tue–Sat 8, matinees Wed, Sat 2, Sun 3 🚇 50th Street/Eighth Avenue (C, E), 50th Street/Seventh Avenue (1) 🚌 M10, M27, M50, M104

CIRCLE IN THE SQUARE (UPTOWN)

Map 188 D17
1633 Broadway at 50th Street
Tel 212/239-6200
Opened in 1972, this theater is in the same building as the Gershwin theater. All 681 seats have good sight lines. ⓦ Tue–Sat 8, matinees Wed, Sat 2, Sun 3 🚇 50th Street/ Eighth Avenue (C, E), 50th Street/Seventh Avenue (1) 🚌 M6, M7, M10, M27, M50, M104

CORT

Map 188 E17
138 West 48th Street between Sixth and Seventh avenues
Tel 212/239-6200
www.shubertorganization.com

Named for producer John Cort, this 1,084-seat theater was modeled on the Petit Trianon and built in 1912. All seats have good sight lines. ⓦ Tue–Sat 8, matinees Wed, Sat 2, Sun 3 🚇 47th–50th streets/Rockefeller Center (B, D, F, V) 🚌 M6, M7, M10, M27, M50, M104

ETHEL BARRYMORE THEATRE

Map 188 D18
243 West 47th Street between Seventh and Eighth avenues
Tel 212/239-6200
Ethel Barrymore starred in *The Kingdom of God* to open this theater in 1928. Fred Astaire gave his last stage performance here in *The Gay*

The Hilton Theater puts on major musical productions

Divorcée in the 1930s. ⓦ Tue–Sat 8, matinees Wed, Sat–Sun 2 🚇 50th Street (C, E), 50th Street (1), 49th Street (N, R, W) 🚌 M10, M20, M104

EUGENE O'NEILL

Map 186 D17
230 West 49th Street between Broadway and Eighth Avenue
Tel 212/239-6200
Opened in 1926, the O'Neill was named for the great playwright in 1959. ⓦ Tue 7, Wed–Sat 8, matinees Wed, Sat 2, Sun 3 🚇 50th Street/Eighth Avenue (C, E), 50th Street/Seventh Avenue (1) 🚌 M6, M7, M10, M27, M50, M104

GERALD SCHOENFELD THEATER

Map 188 D18
236 West 45th Street between Broadway and Eighth Avenue
Tel 212/239-6200
Drama and comedy from Noel Coward's *Present Laughter* to the Royal Shakespeare Company's *Nicholas Nickleby* have played at this 1918 theater. Seats 1,078. ⓦ Wed–Sat 8, Mon 8, Tue 7, matinees Wed, Sat 2, Sun 3 🚇 42nd Street/Times Square (N, Q, R, S, W, 1, 2, 3, 7), 42nd Street/Eighth Avenue (A, C, E) 🚌 M6, M7, M10, M42, M104

GERSHWIN

Map 186 D17
222 West 51st Street between Broadway and Eighth Avenue
Tel 212/307-4100
www.gershwin-theater.com
Owned by the Broadway producers the Nederlanders, the Gershwin opened in 1972. The auditorium is on the second floor. It was renamed in 1983 after George and Ira. ⓦ Tue 7, Wed–Sat 8, matinees Wed, Sat 2, Sun 3 🚇 50th Street/Eighth Avenue (C, E), 50th Street/Seventh Avenue (1) 🚌 M6, M7, M10, M27, M50, M104

HELEN HAYES

Map 188 D18
240 West 44th Street between Seventh and Eighth avenues
Tel 212/944-9450 or 212/239-6200
This small Colonial Revival-style theater was built in 1912 to house productions of new and experimental theater. ⓦ Tue–Sat 8, matinees Wed, Sat 2, Sun 3 🚇 42nd Street/Times Square (N, Q, R, S, W, 1, 2, 3, 7), 42nd Street/Eighth Avenue (A, C, E) 🚌 M6, M7, M10, M42, M104

HILTON THEATER

Map 188 D18
213 West 42nd Street between Seventh and Eighth avenues
Tel 212/556-4750 or 212/307-4100
The Lyric (1903) and the Apollo (1920) were renovated and combined to create this

WHAT TO DO

1,839-seat house ideal for spectacular musicals. Most seats have good sight lines.
🕐 Tue–Sat 8, matinees Wed, Sat 2, Sun 3 🚇 42nd Street/Times Square (N, Q, R, S, W, 1, 2, 3, 7), 42nd Street/Eighth Avenue (A, C, E) 🚌 M6, M7, M10, M42, M104

IMPERIAL
Map 188 D18
249 West 45th Street between Broadway and Eighth Avenue
Tel 212/239-6200
www.shubertorganization.com
Gypsy, Fiddler on the Roof and *Les Misérables* played at this 1923 theater. Seats 1,421.
🕐 Mon–Sat 8, matinees Wed, Sat 2 🚇 42nd Street/Times Square (N, Q, R, S, W, 1, 2, 3, 7), 42nd Street/Eighth Avenue (A, C, E) 🚌 M6, M7, M10, M42, M104

JOHN GOLDEN THEATRE
Map 188 D18
252 West 45th Street between Broadway and Eighth Avenue
Tel 212/239-6200
www.shubertorganization.com
A small theater, named for producer John Golden and opened in 1927.
🕐 Tue–Sat 8, matinees Sat, Sun 2 🚇 42nd Street/Times Square (N, Q, R, S, W, 1, 2, 3, 7), 42nd Street/Eighth Avenue (A, C, E) 🚌 M6, M7, M10, M42, M104

LONGACRE
Map 188 D17
220 West 48th Street between Broadway and Eighth Avenue
Tel 212/239-6200
www.shubertorganization.com
Named for Longacre Square, today's Times Square, this 1,095-seat theater opened in 1913. Orchestra seats have the best sight lines.
🕐 Tue–Fri 8, Sat 5 and 9, Sun 3 and 7 🚇 50th Street/Seventh Avenue (1), 49th Street (N, R), 47th–50th streets/Rockefeller Center (B, D, F, Q) 🚌 M6, M10, M27, M42, M50, M104

LUNT-FONTANNE
Map 188 D18
205 West 46th Street between Broadway and Eighth Avenue

Tel 212/575-9200 or 212/307-4747
http://luntfontannetheatre.com
Designed by Carrère and Hastings in 1910, the theater was gutted in 1958. It seats 1,475 and was the New York home of *The Sound of Music*.
🕐 Tue–Wed 7, Thu–Sat 8, Sun 6.30, matinees Wed 2, Sat 2, Sun 1 🚇 42nd Street/Times Square (N, Q, R, S, W, 1, 2, 3, 7), 50th Street/Seventh Avenue (1, 9), 50th Street/Eighth Avenue (C, E) 🚌 M6, M10, M27, M42, M50, M104

LYCEUM
Map 188 D18
149 West 45th Street between Broadway and Sixth Avenue
Tel 212/239-6200
www.shubertorganization.com

The Music Box has a long history

Built in 1903 in Beaux Arts style, it's the oldest theater still in use on Broadway.
🕐 Tue–Sat 8, matinees Wed, Sat 2, Sun 3 🚇 49th Street (N, R), 47th–50th streets/Rockefeller Center (B, D, F) 🚌 M5, M6, M7, M10, M42, M104

MAJESTIC
Map 188 D18
245 West 44th Street between Broadway and Eighth Avenue
Tel 212/239-6200
www.shubertorganization.com
This 1,607-seat theater opened in 1927 and has hosted hits from *Carousel* to *Phantom of the Opera,* currently the longest-running show on Broadway.

🕐 Mon–Sat 8, matinees Wed, Sat 2 🚇 42nd Street/Times Square (N, Q, R, S, W, 1, 2, 3, 7), 42nd Street/Eighth Avenue (A, C, E) 🚌 M6, M7, M10, M42, M104

MARQUIS
Map 188 D18
1535 Broadway between 45th and 46th streets
Tel 212/382-0100 or 212/307-4100
www.marquistheatre.org
One of the newest large theaters on Broadway, with extra comforts, including well-raked seating. Seats 1,595.
🕐 Tue 7, Wed–Sat 8, matinees Wed, Sat 2, Sun 3 🚇 42nd Street/Times Square (N, Q, R, S, W, 1, 2, 3, 7) 🚌 M6, M7, M10, M27, M42, M50, M104

MINSKOFF
Map 188 D18
200 West 45th Street between Seventh and Eighth avenues
Tel 212/ 307-4100
www.minskofftheatre.vom
This Nederlander theater, built in 1973, is rather impersonal. An escalator takes you to the fourth-floor orchestra.
🕐 Tue 7, Wed–Sat 8, matinees Wed, Sat 2, Sun 3 🚇 42nd Street/Times Square (N, Q, R, S, W, 1, 2, 3, 7) 🚌 M6, M7, M10, M42, M104

MUSIC BOX
Map 188 D18
239 West 45th Street between Broadway and Eighth Avenue
Tel 212/239-6200
www.shubertorganization.com
Note the plaque, just inside the lobby, commemorating Irving Berlin, who built this theater in 1921 with producer Sam Harris to house his Music Box Revues.
🕐 Tue–Sat 8, matinees Sat 2, Sun 3 🚇 42nd Street/Times Square (N, Q, R, S, W, 1, 2, 3, 7), 42nd Street/Eighth Avenue (A, C, E) 🚌 M6, M7, M10, M42, M104

NEDERLANDER
Map 188 D18
208 West 41st Street between Seventh and Eighth avenues
Tel 212/921-8000 or 212/307-4100
http://nederlandertheatre.org
When *Rent* moved from the

East Village, it came to this theatre, and *Who's Afraid of Virginia Woolf?* opened here. Seats 1,189. Avoid side seats. Mon–Tue, Thu–Sat 8, matinees Sat, Sun 2 42nd Street/Times Square (N, Q, R, S, W, 1, 2, 3, 7) M6, M7, M10, M27, M42, M50, M104

NEIL SIMON
Map 186 D17
250 West 52nd Street between Broadway and Eighth Avenue
Tel 212/757-8646 or 212/307-4100
www.neilsimontheatre.com
This ornate theater, opened in 1927, has been home to many musicals, including *Porgy and Bess, Funny Face* and *Hairspray*. Seats 1,334.
Tue 7, Wed–Sat 8, matinees Wed, Sat 2, Sun 3 50th Street/Eighth Avenue (C, E), 50th Street/Seventh Avenue (1) M6, M7, M10, M27, M50, M104

NEW AMSTERDAM
Map 188 D18
214 West 42nd Street between Seventh and Eighth avenues
Tel 212/282-2900 or 212/307-4747 or 212/282-2907 for tours
www.disneyonbroadway.com
Florence Ziegfeld commissioned this art nouveau beauty in 1903. In 1997 the Walt Disney Company restored the place with its murals, stucco, tiles and woodwork, and installed *The Lion King* for a run. Avoid side seats.
Wed–Sat 8, Sun 6.30, matinees Wed, Sat 2, Sun 1. Tours Mon 9.30–5.30, Tue, Thu–Sat 9.30–11.30 42nd Street/Times Square (N, Q, R, S, W, 1, 2, 3, 7), 42nd Street/Eighth Avenue (A, C, E) M6, M7, M10, M42, M104

PALACE
Map 188 D18
1564 Broadway between 46th and 47th streets
Tel 212/730-8200 or 212/307-4747
www.nederlander.org
The Palace opened as a vaudeville house in 1913, and such legends as Bob Hope, Sophie Tucker, Jimmy Durante and the Marx

Brothers all entertained here. The Nederlanders restored it in 1965.
Tue–Sat 8, matinees Wed, Sat 2, Sun 3 50th Street (1), 49th Street (N, R) M7, M10, M27, M50, M104

RICHARD ROGERS
Map 188 D18
226 West 46th Street between Broadway and Eighth Avenue
Tel 212/221-1211
Guys and Dolls and other hits have played at this Renaissance Revival theater, built in 1924. Named for the composer, it seats 1,400.
Tue–Sat 8, matinees Wed, Sat 2, Sun 3 42nd Street/Times Square (N, Q, R, S, W, 1, 2, 3, 7), 42nd Street/

The New Amsterdam is an art nouveau gem

Eighth Avenue (A, C, E), 50th Street (1, 9) M10, M27, M50, M104

ST. JAMES
Map 188 D18
246 West 44th Street between Seventh and Eighth avenues
Tel 212/239-5800
Oklahoma!, The King and I, Hello Dolly and *The Producers* have all played in this Beaux Arts theater of 1927. Its mezzanine hangs over the orchestra.
Tue 7, Wed–Sat 8, matinees Wed, Sat 2, Sun 3 42nd Street/Times Square (N, Q, R, S, W, 1, 2, 3, 7), 42nd Street/Eighth Avenue (A, C, E) M6, M7, M10, M42, M104

SHUBERT
Map 188 D18
225 West 44th Street between Seventh and Eighth avenues
Tel 212/239-6200
www.shubertorganization.com
This theater, opened in 1913, is the cornerstone of the Shubert family's empire.
Mon–Tue, Thu–Sat 8, Sun 7, matinees Sat, Sun 2 42nd Street/Times Square (N, Q, R, S, W, 1, 2, 3, 7), 42nd Street/Eighth Avenue (A, C, E) M6, M7, M10, M42, M104

STUDIO 54
Map 186 D17
254 West 54th Street between Broadway and Eighth Avenue
Tel 212/239-6200
This former discotheque is now a 920-seat theater. *Cabaret* has played here.
Tue–Sat 8, Sun 7, matinees Sat, Sun 2 Seventh Avenue (B, D, E), 57th Street (N, R, Q) M6, M7, M27, M50, M57

VIVIAN BEAUMONT THEATER
Map 186 C16
150 West 65th Street
Tel 212/362-7600
This is categorized as a Broadway theater despite its address. Its deep-thrust stage allows for innovative directing.
Tue–Sat 8, matinees Wed, Sat 2, Sun 3 66th Street (1) M5, M7, M66, M104

WALTER KERR
Map 186 D17
219 West 48th Street between Broadway and Eighth Avenue
Tel 212/239-6200
Named after the famous *New York Times* critic, this is an ideal house for serious drama and classic comedy. Seats 947.
Tue–Sat 8, matinees Wed, Sat 2, Sun 3 50th Street/Eighth Avenue (C, E), 50th Street/Seventh Avenue (1) M7, M10, M27, M50, M104

WINTER GARDEN
Map 186 D17
1634 Broadway between 50th and 51st streets
Tel 212/563-5544
www.shubertorganization.com

The building dates to 1885 when it served as an auction hall and stable. The Shuberts made it into a theater in 1910. Al Jolson first appeared here in blackface. Seats 1,482.

🕐 Wed–Sat 8, matinees Wed, Sat 2, Sun 3 🚇 50th Street/Eighth Avenue (C, E), 50th Street/Seventh Avenue (1), 49th Street (N, R, W) 🚌 M6, M7, M10, M27, M50, M104

OFF-BROADWAY THEATERS

Off-Broadway theaters have 500 seats or fewer, and are usually either in the East or West villages or along 42nd Street between Eighth and Eleventh avenues. Here you'll see showcases, experimental plays, musicals in development and innovative revivals. Several Broadway hits have emerged from these venues. Ticket prices range from $25 to $65.

ACTOR'S PLAYHOUSE
Map 188 D22
100 Seventh Avenue South between Bleecker and West Fourth streets
Tel 212/463-0060 or 212/239-6200
This small downstairs venue, which has been around for 40 years, presents musical revues, often with a gay theme.
🕐 Varies, check programs
🚇 Christopher Street/Sheridan Square (1) 🚌 M20

BOUWERIE LANE
Map 189 F22
330 Bowery at Bond Street
Tel 212/677-0060
The Jean Cocteau Repertory Company (1971) presents five to seven masterworks from Euripides to Samuel Beckett between August and June at this beautiful old bank building. Seats 140.
🚇 Broadway-Lafayette (F, V, S) 🚌 M21, M103

BROOKLYN ACADEMY OF MUSIC (BAM)
Off map 189 G25
30 Lafayette Avenue
Tel 718/636-4100
www.bam.org
New York's premier progressive cultural complex is in Brooklyn. It incorporates several performance spaces—the Howard Gilman Opera House, seating 2,100; the 1,000-seat Harvey Lichtenstein Theater (entrance at 651 Fulton Street); a café; and a four-screen film complex.
🚇 DeKalb Avenue (B, D, N, Q, R) 🚌 M51

Bouwerie Lane specializes in repertory productions

CHERRY LANE
Map 188 D22
38 Commerce Street between Hudson and Bedford streets
Tel 212/989-2020
www.cherrylanetheater.org
In 1924 Edna St. Vincent Millay and others turned a warehouse into a theater. Today the Cherry Lane Alternative continues the theater's tradition of producing emerging playwrights.
🕐 Varies, check program
🚇 Christopher Street/Sheridan Square (1) 🚌 M20, M21

DARYL ROTH THEATER
Map 188 F21
101 East 15th Street at Union Square
Tel 212/375-1110
www.darylroththeater.com
Pulitzer Prize-winning Daryl Roth owns this theater in an old bank building. The space is inherently dramatic.
🚇 14th Street/Union Square (L, N, Q, R, W, 4, 5, 6) 🚌 M1, M2, M3, M6, M7, M14

JULIA MILES THEATER
Map 186 C17
424 West 55th Street
Tel 212/765-1706, tickets 212/757-3900
www.womensproject.org
Founded in 1978 by Julia Miles, the Women's Project Theatre is the nation's pre-eminent women's theater company. Seats 199.
🕐 Varies, see program 🚇 59th Street (A, B, C, D, 1) 🚌 M11, M57

MANHATTAN ENSEMBLE THEATRE
Map 189 E23
55 Mercer Street between Broome and Grand streets
Tel 212/925-1900
www.met.com
Home to the Manhattan Ensemble, founded by David Fishelson, this theater presents new plays that are often by well-known playwrights.
🚇 Canal Street (J, M, N, Q), Spring Street (C, E) 🚌 M1, M6

MANHATTAN THEATRE CLUB
261 West 47th Steet
Tel 212/581-1212 (tickets) or 212/399-3000 (info)
www.manhattantheatreclub.com
Founded in 1970 to perform new plays, this company is based at the Biltmore (▷ 205).
🚇 57th Street (N, Q, R, W), 57th Street (F) 🚌 M5, M6, M7

MINETTA LANE
Map 188 E22
18 Minetta Lane
Tel 212/420-8000
This Greenwich Village theater is a major off-Broadway player.
🚇 West 4th Street (A, C, E, F, S, V) 🚌 M5, M6, M8

WHAT TO DO

MITZI NEWHOUSE THEATER

Map 186 C16
150 West 65th Street
Tel 212 362-7600
www.lct.org
Spalding Gray performed
Swimming to Cambodia (1996)
at this Lincoln Center theater.
Its 299 seats are steeply raked.
◷ Tue–Sat 8, matinees Wed, Sat 2,
Sun 3 🚇 66th Street (1) 🚌 M5, M7,
M66, M104

THE NEGRO ENSEMBLE COMPANY

Map 188 D18
303 West 42nd Street at Eighth Avenue
Tel 212-582-5860
www.negroensemblecompany.org
Founded in 1967, this group
holds workshops for actors
and playwrights; it also
mounts productions.
🚇 42nd Street (A, C, E) 🚌 M10, M20,
M42

NEW YORK THEATRE WORKSHOP

Map 189 F22
79 East 4th Street between Second
Avenue and Bowery
Tel 212/780-9037 or 212/460-5475
www.nytw.org
A significant player on the
Manhattan theater scene.
Rent began life here, and
the workshop has staged Caryl
Churchill and Athol Fugard.
◷ Varies, see program 🚇 Broadway-
Lafayette (F, S, V), Bleecker Street (6)
🚌 M1, M21

THE ONTOLOGICAL HYSTERIC THEATER AT ST. MARKS

Map 189 F21
131 East 10th Street between Second
and Third avenues
Tel 212/420-1916
www.ontological.com
An important home for the
avant garde. Richard Foreman
presents his 40th-
anniversary production
here in 2008.
🚇 Astor Place (6), Eighth Street
(N, R, W) 🚌 M8, M15

PLAYWRIGHTS HORIZONS THEATER

Map 188 C18
416 West 42nd Street between Ninth
and Tenth avenues
Tel 212/564-1235
www.playwrightshorizons.org
This company is dedicated to
the production of new
American plays and musicals.
The main stage seats 198 and
the studio 96.
🚇 42nd Street (A, C, E) 🚌 M11, M42

PUBLIC THEATER

Map 189 F22
425 Lafayette Street between Astor
Place and East Fourth Street
Tel 212/539-8500 or 212/967-7555
www.publictheater.org
In 1967 producer Joe Papp got
the city to lease him the old
Astor Library and converted it

*Radio City was saved from
demolition in 1979*

into five theater spaces.
◷ Varies, see program 🚇 8th Street
(N, R, W), Astor Place (6) 🚌 M1, M8

RADIO CITY MUSIC HALL

Map 187 E17
1260 Sixth Avenue at 50th Street
Tel 212/247-4777
www.radiocity.com
This theater with plenty of art
deco paraphernalia was
spectacularly refurbished in
1999 to the tune of $70
million. It has seats for 5,882
in the orchestra and on
three mezzanines.
◷ One-hour tours daily 11–3
🎫 Tours: adult $17, child (under 12)
$10 🚇 47th-50th streets/Rockefeller
Center (B, D, F, V) 🚌 M5, M6, M7

SECOND STAGE THEATER

Map 188 D18
307 West 43rd Street between Eighth
and Ninth avenues
Tel 212/787-8302
www.2st.com
Dutch architect Rem Koolhaas
helped revamp the old bank
building that is home to this
company. Seats 299.
◷ Varies, see program 🚇 79th Street
(1) 🚌 M79, M104

SHAKESPEARE IN THE PARK

Map 186 D14
Delacorte Theater, 81st Street (West
Side), 79th Street (East Side)
Tel 212/539-8500
www.publictheater.org
The Public Theater sponsors
this summer festival in Central
Park at the Delacorte Theater.
Line up for free tickets from
noon onwards.
◷ Summer only Tue–Sun 🚇 79th
Street (1) 🚌 M1, M2, M3, M4, M79,
M104

THEATER FOR THE NEW CITY

Map 189 F21
155 First Avenue between 9th and 10th
streets
Tel 212/254-1109
www.theaterforthenewcity.net
Thought-provoking, often
politically inspired dramas
are the repertory of this
community-oriented company,
founded in 1970.
◷ Varies, see program 🚇 Astor Place
(6) 🚌 M8, M15

VINEYARD THEATRE

Map 188 F21
108 East 15th Street between Union
Square and Irving Place
Tel 212/353-3366, 212/353-0303
www.vineyardtheatre.org
Located in a residential
tower, this off-Broadway
theater has staged Pulitzer
Prize-winning plays before
they went to Broadway.
Seats 120.
◷ Varies, see program 🚇 14th
Street/Union Square (L, N, Q, R, W, 4, 5,
6) 🚌 M14, M101, M102, M103

WHAT TO DO

YORK (THEATRE AT ST. PETER'S)
Map 187 F17
619 Lexington Avenue at 54th Street
Tel 212/935-5824
The material presented at the modern performing space in this church at Citicorp Center is often experimental and challenging. Seats 147.
🕐 Varies, see program 🚇 51st Street (6), Fifth Avenue/53rd Street (E, V) 🚌 M98, M101, M102, M103

OFF-OFF-BROADWAY
These small theaters seat 100 or fewer, offer contemporary or innovative productions of traditional works, and often feature actors who don't belong to Actors Equity, the professional union.
Performances range from the mundane to the inspiring, and ticket prices from $10 to $55.

BLEECKER STREET THEATRE
Map 189 F22
45 Bleecker Street between Bowery and Lafayette Street
Tel 212/253-9983 or 212/307-4100
www.45bleecker.com
Home of the Culture Project, which produces eclectic works by contemporary playwrights. Main space seats 199 plus 45 below seats.
🕐 Varies, see program 🚇 Bleecker Street (6), Broadway/ Lafayette (F, S, V) 🚌 M1, M21, M103

CENTER STAGE/NY
Map 188 E20
48 West 21st Street between Fifth and Sixth avenues, fourth floor
Tel 212/513-1080
www.labtheater.org
Thirteen actors founded the Labyrinth Repertory Company in 1992 to enable members to write, direct and act. Now it has 60 international members, who produce annual productions here.
🕐 Varies 🚇 23rd Street (N, R, W), 23rd Street (F, V) 🚌 M2, M3, M5, M6, M7

CLASSICAL THEATRE OF HARLEM
Off map 186 D12
Harlem School of the Arts Theater, 645 St. Nicholas Avenue near 141st Street
Tel 212/926-4100 or 212/564-9983
www.classicaltheatreofharlem.org
This company, founded in 1988, has been recognized outside Harlem only recently. It has garnered acclaim for recent productions of Genet's *The Blacks* and Euripides' *The Trojan Women*.
🚇 145th Street (A, B, C)

FLEA THEATER
Map 189 E24
41 White Street between Broadway and Church Street

Shakespeare in the Park is a popular summer festival

Tel 212/226-2407
www.theflea.org
Home to the Bat Theater Company, which presents works by playwrights who are breaking new boundaries—either society's or their own.
🚇 Canal Street (A, C, E) 🚌 M1, M6

LA MAMA EXPERIMENTAL THEATER CLUB
Map 189 F22
74A East 4th Street between Second Avenue and Bowery
Tel 212/475-7710
www.lamama.org
One of the most famous off-off-Broadway theaters was founded in 1961 by Ellen Stewart to nurture new playwrights. It has three theaters: the Annex, the First Floor and the Club, a cabaret space.
🕐 Varies 🚇 Astor Place (6) 🚌 M8, M15

THE MINT SPACE
Map 188 D18
311 West 43rd Street between Eighth and Ninth avenues
Tel 212/315-9434 or 212/315-0231
www.minttheater.org
Home of the Mint Theater, one of the most recognized companies off-off-Broadway. It performs stimulating plays, which may be drawn from foreign traditions. Seats 74.
🚇 42nd Street (A, C, E) 🚌 M11, M20, M42

PERFORMING GARAGE
Map 189 E23
33 Wooster Street at Grand Street
Tel 212/966-9796
www.thewoostergroup.org
Home to the Wooster Group, an Obie-winning troupe founded in 1975 by Jim Clayburgh, Willem Dafoe, Spalding Gray and others. The group produces and develops experimental entertainment and theater.
🚇 Canal Street (A, C, E) 🚌 M6

THEATRE AT ST. CLEMENTS
Map 188 C18
423 West 46th Street between Ninth and Tenth avenues
Tel 212/246-7277 or 212/279-4200
Playwrights such as David Mamet and Terrance McNally have premiered works here, and many famous actors appeared here early in their careers. The plays often focus on contemporary spiritual, moral and ethical issues. The space is in an Episcopalian church and seats 151.
🕐 Varies 🚇 42nd Street (A, C, E) 🚌 M11, M42

WHAT TO DO

NIGHTLIFE

New Yorkers take their nightlife very seriously. You can always find a "scene" somewhere in the city that never sleeps, with the party shifting from bar to dance club and back, and then to the Meatpacking District at dawn.

Some New York City clubs have a great deal of attitude. At the hottest dance clubs, there's a competition to get in, and people dress à la mode to ensure that they get past the velvet rope and the bouncer at the door. And there's always a VIP room and an A-list for guests (although you can often get on the list by calling in advance or going to www.sheckys.com or www.promony.com). So tough has it become to gain entry to the most fashionable clubs, that even a $1,000 bribe will not work. Hence PartyBuddys, tel 1/877-93-2839, www.partybuddys.com, which promises to shepherd visitors on a nightlife tour for a fee, starting at $350 per person. Still, there are plenty of more casual clubs available, especially the gay spots (see *Next*, *HX*, *Metro Source* and *Go* for listings), which are often a lot more fun.

There are bars to suit every taste. Great saloons with antique bars often have a lot of history attached. The King Cole Bar claims to have invented the Bloody Mary, while P. J. Clarke's has long been assocaited with Damon Runyon types. In swank hotel bars such as the St. Regis's King Cole or the Carlyle's Bemelman's you can lounge in luxury. Rooftop bars are spectacular trysting places. Specialty bars serve up every liquor (beer, wine, champagne, vodka and sake). You'll find an extensive gay scene catering to different crowds and ages, concentrated mainly in Chelsea and Greenwich Village. Many lounges now have DJs spinning music, but they don't allow dancing because they usually lack a cabaret license.

The city's nightlife hot spots are Harlem, Chelsea, the East and West villages, and the Lower East Side. There's also plenty of action across the East River in Williamsburg, which now draws its own crowd from Manhattan. Drinking age is 21 (always carry a picture ID). British visitors should note that whiskey is rye, not Scotch.

New York has bars and clubs to suit every taste

DJs are in action at many lounges

The Bar and Lounge Scene

In addition to the outstanding hotel bars listed below, you might want to drop in at the following: Thom's Bar at 60 Thompson Hotel (60 Thompson Street, tel 212/219-2000); The Whiskey Bar on the 7th floor of the W Hotel New York, Times Square (1567 Broadway at 47th Street, tel 212/930-7444); Underbar at W Hotel Union Square (201 Park Avenue South, tel 212/358-1560); the Monkey Bar at the Hotel Elysee (▷ 300), and the Rise Bar at the Ritz Carlton (Battery Park, tel 917/790-2525).

There is no cover for the bars listed here. Note, too, that there is a strict no-smoking law in the city, instituted in 2003. Only bars that derive 10 percent of their revenue from cigars can opt out of the law and allow smoking.

ANGEL'S SHARE
8 Stuyvesant Street (2nd floor) between 9th Street and Third Avenue
Tel 212/777-5415
Tucked away upstairs in a Japanese restaurant, this tiny bar is named for the alcohol that evaporates while whiskey is aging. The lychee daiquiri is delicious.
🕒 Daily 6pm–2.30am 🚇 Astor Place (6)

THE AUCTION HOUSE
300 East 89th Street between First and Second avenues
Tel 212/427-4458
Sotheby's meets New Orleans bordello at this wood-paneled, split-level lounge. Patrons sip cocktails on velvet sofas beneath gilt-framed portraits.
🕒 Daily 7.30–4 🚇 86th Street (4, 5, 6)

AUTOMATIC SLIM'S
733 Washington Street at Bank Street
Tel 212/645-8660
An outpost of the original Automatic Slim's in Memphis, the kid brother in the Meatpacking District brings a soulful Southern feel, especially late at night when the tables are pushed back and the dancing begins.
🕐 Tue–Wed 5.30–2, Thu–Sat 5.30–4
🚇 Christopher Street-Sheridan Square (1), 14th Street (A, C, E)

B BAR
40 East 4th Street at Bowery
Tel 212/475-2220
www.bbarandgrill.com
B Bar has cooled as a hot spot, but its Tuesday night extravaganza, Beige, still draws gay society and other beauties. Large outdoor summer patio.
🕐 Mon 11.30am–2am, Tue, Thu–Fri 11.30am–4am, Wed 11.30am–3am, Sat 10.30am–4am, Sun 10.30am–2am
🚇 Broadway/ Lafayette (F, S, V), Bleecker Street (6)

BARAZA
133 Avenue C between East 8th and 9th streets
Tel 212/539-0811
No wonder this place is crowded: Just look at the prices and taste the sunshine in the mojitos and caipirhinas, and listen to the merengue, salsa and Afro-Cuban rhythms.
🕐 Daily 8pm–4am 🚇 Astor Place (6), First Avenue (L)

BARRAMUNDI
67 Clinton Street between Rivington and Stanton streets
Tel 212/529-6900
Manhattanites enjoy the odd woodsy Adirondack accents. The martinis and caipirhinas taste fine, and the crowd is friendly.
🕐 Daily 6–4 🚇 Delancey/Essex (F, J, M, Z)

BEMELMANS BAR
Carlyle Hotel, 35 East 76th Street between Park and Madison avenues
Tel 212/744-1600
Named for the illustrator of the beloved Madeleine books, Ludwig Bemelmans, this intimate bar attracts the city's most upscale tipplers with first-class cocktails and perfect piano music from Tony De Sare or the Chris Gillespie Trio most evenings (9.30–1.30).
🕐 Mon–Sat 11am–1am, Sun 11am–midnight 💰 Fri–Sat $20–$25 ($10 at bar) 🚇 77th Street (6)

BLACK SHEEP PUB
428 Bergen Street at 5th Avenue
Tel 718/638-1109
www.blacksheepbrooklyn.com
The Irish owners pour a good pint of Guinness at this neighborhood bar that doesn't look too promising from the

Champagne in a luxurious setting at the Bubble Lounge

outside but is a lively place when you get through the doors. There's a pub quiz Wednesday nights, movies on Tuesday, sports on TV most other times, and a good price on beers and pitchers.
🕐 Mon–Thu 5pm–2am, Fri, Sun noon–2am, Sat noon–4am
🚇 Bergen Street (2, 3), Atlantic Avenue-Pacific Street (D, M, N, R)

THE BUBBLE LOUNGE
228 West Broadway between Franklin and White streets
Tel 212/431-3433
www.bubblelounge.com
This 1930s-style lounge celebrates champagne by serving more than 24 types by the glass and 350 by the bottle, amid luxurious red sofas, marble tables and chandeliers.
🕐 Mon–Thu 5–2, Fri–Sat 5–4
🚇 Franklin Street (1)

CAMPBELL APARTMENT
15 Vanderbilt Avenue in Grand Central Station (southwest corner)
Tel 212/953-0409
It's worth seeking out this quintessential New York bar. Originally designed as an office for wealthy businessman John W. Campbell, it's dark and richly decorated in a Renaissance style. Today it caters to suburbanites en route to their homes in Connecticut and Westchester County.
🕐 Mon–Sat 3pm–1am, Sun 3–11pm
🚇 42nd Street/Grand Central (4, 5, 6, S)

COMMON GROUND
206 Avenue A between 12th and 13th streets
Tel 212/228-6231
www.commongroundnyc.com
A few blocks north of Tompkins Square Park is this bar that looks like a bar should, with wooden paneling, shelves filled with books, and even chandeliers giving it a hint of Victorian London. Nothing Victorian about the patrons, though, a mix of office workers and locals, enjoying either the bar snacks or the very tasty main plates on offer. Wednesday is trivia night, and there's an open-mic night on Sunday.
🕐 Mon–Wed 4–2, Thu–Fri 4–4, Sat 12–4, Sun 12–2 (kitchen closes midnight)
🚇 1st Avenue (L)

CRIME SCENE BAR AND LOUNGE
310 Bowery at Bleecker Street
Tel 212/477-1166
http://crimescenebar.com
If you like a bar with character then the Crime Scene fits the bill, not only for its yellow police-tape decor and walls painted with handcuffs, but for the real mix of people who

drink here. Thursday night is Rock Star Karaoke night and Sundays sees entertainment open-mic from 6pm–midnight. There's a pool table too, bar snacks and full-on meals, and cocktails with names like Disorderly Conduct.

🕐 Mon–Sat 3pm–4am
Ⓜ Bleecker Street (6), Lower East Side-2nd Avenue (F, V)

D.B.A.
41 First Avenue between East 2nd and 3rd streets
Tel 212/475-5097

Serious drinkers appreciate the massive selection of single malts (100) and beers (20 on tap) at this old-fashioned friendly bar. The backyard garden is great in summer.

🕐 Daily 1pm–4am Ⓜ Lower East Side/Second Avenue (F, V)

DECIBEL
240 East 9th Street between Second and Third avenues
Tel 212/979-2733
www.sakebardecibel.com

Subterranean, funky and cramped, this Japanese bar has a huge selection of sake. Take a booth and experiment.

🕐 Mon–Sat 8–2.50am, Sun 8–0.50am
Ⓜ Astor Place (6)

DIVINE BAR
244 East 51st Street between Second and Third avenues
Tel 212/319-9463

A young professional singles crowd turns this long tapas bar into late-night Madrid. Flights of the 60 wines are available along with 40 different beers.

🕐 Mon–Wed 5–2, Thu–Fri 5–3, Sat 7–3
Ⓜ 51st Street (6), Lexington/53rd Street (E, V)

ELAINE'S
1703 Second Avenue between East 88th and 89th streets
Tel 212/534-8103

The writers, actors, politicians and socialites who gather here have their own tables, but everyone is welcome. Look for Kathleen Turner, Barbara Walters, Candace Bushnell,

Gay Talese, Woody Allen and many others.

🕐 Mon–Sat 6–2, Sun 5–1 Ⓜ 86th Street (4, 5, 6)

ENOTECA I TRULLI
122 East 27th Street between Park Avenue South and Lexington Avenue
Tel 212/481-7372

This light and airy wine bar offers some 50 wines by the glass at the marble bar. Accompany them with some first-class cured meats, cheeses and olives from I Trulli next door.

🕐 Mon–Sat 5–12, Sun 5–10 Ⓜ 28th Street (6)

Tempting drinks are on offer at Happy Ending

EUGENE
27 West 24th Street between Fifth and Sixth avenues
Tel 212/462-0999
www.eugenenyc.com

The razzle-dazzle of this club-lounge—fluted columns, red-velvet club chairs, a glassed-in dining room—appeals to an international jet-set crowd.

🕐 Thu–Sat 10pm–4am Ⓜ 23rd Street (F, N, R, V)

FAT CAT BILLIARDS
75 Christopher Street at 7th Avenue
Tel 212/675-6056
http://fatcatmusic.org/

For a New York experience it's hard to beat going into a basement bar and playing

pool. The Fat Cat has 21 tables, along with seven ping-pong tables, three shuffleboard tables and three foosball (table football) machines. A good range of beers too, from around the world, and live music including jazz and salsa every night of the week.

🕐 Mon–Thu 2pm–5am, Fri–Sat noon–5am Ⓟ Pool $5 per hour, $3 cover on music nights Ⓜ Christopher Street-Sheridan Square (1), 4th Street–Washington Square (A, B, C, D, E, F, V)

FLANNERY'S BAR
205 West 14th Street at 7th Avenue
Tel 212/229-Tel 2122
www.flannerysny.com

Flannery's has been one of New York's best Irish bars for over 20 years now, with a winning mix of drink, music, sports and conversation. There are DJs twice a week, darts tournaments Wednesday and Saturday, and a rock and blues jam with the house band on Sundays—bring your guitar.

🕐 Mon–Sat 8pm–4am, Sun noon–4am
Ⓟ $5 cover on darts nights Ⓜ 14th Street (1, 2, 3, A, C, E), 8th Avenue (L)

FLUTE
205 West 54th Street between Seventh Avenue and Broadway
Tel 212/265-5169
www.flutebar.com

Perfect, if pricey, for an after-theater celebration, this gilt-and-mirror subterranean bar serves 20 champagnes by the glass. Snag one of the private curtained alcoves.

🕐 Sun–Wed 5–2, Thu 5–3, Fri–Sat 5–4
Ⓜ Seventh Avenue (B, D, E)

GLASS
287 Tenth Avenue between West 26th and 27th streets
Tel 212/904-1580

This sleek modernist space is fun and futuristic—worthy of the arty neighborhood. Check out the two-way mirrors in the bathrooms, and other visual tricks.

🕐 Wed–Sat 10pm–4am Ⓜ 28th Street (1)

WHAT TO DO

GRACE

114 Franklin Street between West Broadway and Church Street
Tel 212/343-4200
Wall Streeters and politicos cozy up to the long mahogany bar for apple martinis and tangerine margaritas in this lofty elegant space.
🕐 Daily 11.30am–4am 🚇 Franklin Street (1)

GUTTER

200 North 14th Street at Wythe Avenue, Brooklyn
Tel 718/387-3585
www.thegutterbrooklyn.com
Gutter is a new bar with an old 1950s kind of a feel, and eight bowling lanes. Vintage bowling memorabilia decorates the bar, which looks out over the bowling lanes and also has twelve craft beers on draft, but you can get pitchers too.
🕐 Mon–Thu 4–4, Fri–Sun noon–4am
🎳 $7 a game for bowling 🚇 Nassau Avenue (G), Bedford Avenue (L)

HAPPY ENDING

302 Broome Street between Eldridge and Forsythe streets
Tel 212/334-9676
This duplex lounge still reveals traces of its former life as a massage parlor, from the bellybutton-level showerheads to the tiled sauna alcoves and the circular booths (which used to be tubs). Innovative drinks.
🕐 Tue 10–4, Wed–Sat 7–4
🚇 Delancey/Essex (F, J, M, Z)

HUDSON BARS

Hudson Hotel, 356 West 58th Street between Eighth and Ninth avenues
Tel 212/554-6000
The two bars are central to this hipster hotel. In the Hudson, a long ornate table serves as the bar. Late at night, the backlit floor becomes a dance floor. In the Library, there are leather chairs, ottomans and a fireplace.
🕐 Hudson Sun–Wed 4–1.30, Thu–Sat 4–3; Library Sun–Wed noon–1am, Thu–Sat noon–2.30am 🚇 59th Street/Columbus Circle (A, B, C, D, 1)

IL POSTO ACCANTO

190 East 2nd Street between Avenues A and B
Tel 212/228-3562
A friendly wine bar. Order appetizers to go with one of 30 Italian wines by the glass.
🕐 Tue–Sun 6–2 🚇 Lower East Side/Second Avenue (F, V)

KING COLE BAR

St. Regis Hotel, 2 East 55th Street between Fifth and Madison avenues
Tel 212/753-4500
Named for the 1906 Maxfield Parrish mural *Old King Cole*, this bar claims to have invented the Bloody Mary. Excellent cognacs, grappas and single malts.

Enjoy a cocktail in one of New York's many bars

🕐 Sun–Thu 12–2, Fri–Sat 11.30am–2am 🚇 Fifth Avenue/53rd Street (E, V)

KUSH LOUNGE

191 Chrystie Street between Stanton and Rivington streets
Tel 212/677-7328
www.kushlounge.com
Exotic Moroccan-inspired decor sets the stage for the hip crowd at this seductive lounge, with its private alcoves and sunken hookah lounge. Global music spins on the turntable most nights.
🕐 Mon–Fri 7–4, Sat 8–4
🚇 Lower East Side/2nd Avenue (F, V), Bowery (J, M, Z)

THE LEVEE

Tel 212 Berry Street at Metropolitan Avenue, Brooklyn
Tel 718/218-8787
www.theleveenyc.com
New Yorkers who know their beer rate this place, which has a few dozen bottled ales as well as six draft brews. The Texan owner has made sure there's a friendly Southern feel, and there's a jukebox, pinball and pool table, and a basic bar menu to help soak up the beer. No frills but a great place to kick back.
🕐 Daily noon–4am
🚇 Bedford Avenue (L)

LEVEL V

675 Hudson Street at 14th Street
Tel 212/699-2410
This basement lounge at Vento is the latest hotspot in the meatpacking district. Black leather couches, glass tables and dramatic lighting set the scene for a chic and coiffed young crowd. VIPs are ushered into the private vaulted brick stalls. Best to reserve.
🕐 Wed–Sun 9–4, Tue 6–4 🚇 14th Street (A, C, E), Eighth Avenue (L)

LUKE'S BAR AND GRILL

1394 Third Avenue between 79th and 80th streets
Tel 212/249-7070
www.lukesbarandgrill.com
The bar and grill are equal partners at Luke's, which opened in 1990 and is the kind of respectable bar that appeals to families as well as young professionals. They serve typical bar food, with great burgers, and there's a wide stock of good beers, which becomes more evident when the restaurant closes about midnight/1am.
🕐 Mon–Fri 11.30am–4am, Sat–Sun 10am–4am 🚇 77th Street (6)

LUNA PARK

Union Square Park between Broadway and 17th Street
Tel 212/475-8464
The quintessential Manhattan summer scene, this open-air

bar/restaurant occupies the northern end of Union Square Park. Decent Mediterranean fare, too.

🕐 May–Sep Sun–Wed 12–12, Thu–Sat noon–1am 🚇 14th Street/Union Square (L, N, Q, R, W, 4, 5, 6)

MARIE'S CRISIS
59 Grove Street
Tel 212/243-9323
A mixed crowd of gays and straights gather around the upright piano and sing along to Broadway show tunes at this downstairs bar.

🕐 Daily 4–4 🚇 Christopher Street/ Sheridan Square (1)

MARION'S CONTINENTAL
354 Bowery between East 4th and Great Jones streets
Tel 212/475-7621
www.marionsnyc.com
A steady clientele gathers for reasonably priced martinis and theme nights. On Monday, for example, the Pontani Sisters cavort around as if they were in the Ziegfeld Follies.

🕐 Mon–Sat 5.30–2, Sun noon–2am 🚇 Broadway/Lafayette (F, S, V), Bleecker Street (6)

MERC BAR
151 Mercer Street between Houston and Prince streets
Tel 212/966-2727
www.mercbar.com
The ultra-hip have moved on, but this bar has comfortable seating, seductive lighting and groovy music. The front banquettes are great for people-watching in summer.

🕐 Sun–Tue 5–2, Wed–Sat 5–4 🚇 Broadway/Lafayette (F, S, V), Bleecker Street (6)

METROPOLITAN MUSEUM ROOF GARDEN
Metropolitan Museum of Art, 1000 Fifth Avenue at 82nd Street
Tel 212/277-8888
Classy all the way. What better accompaniment to a drink than a view of the sun setting over Central Park? The balcony bar is chic with its chamber music and jazz groups.

🕐 Roof Garden May–Oct Tue–Thu, Sun 9.30–5.15, Fri–Sat 9.30–8; Balcony Bar Fri–Sat 4–8 🚇 86th Street (4, 5, 6), 77th Street (6)

MORGANS BAR
Morgans Hotel, 237 Madison Avenue between East 37th and 38th streets
Tel 212/726-7755
www.morganshotel.com
This basement hideaway draws more than its fair share of celebrities. Sink into the leather chairs and enjoy the candlelight and well-made cocktails. Go after 10 to catch the place at its best.

🕐 Mon–Thu 5–1, Fri 5–2, Sat 6–2 🚇 33rd Street (6)

You can lounge in luxury in the city's finest bars

Ñ
33 Crosby Street between Broome and Grand streets
Tel 212/219-8856
A tiny narrow bar serving sangria with tasty tapas. Good sherry and Spanish wines.

🕐 Sun–Thu 5–2, Fri–Sat 5–4 🚇 Spring Street (6)

THE PARK
118 Tenth Avenue between West 17th and 18th streets
Tel 212/352-3313
This gargantuan complex with an attractive outdoor courtyard hosted J Lo's birthday bash.

🕐 Mon–Tue 11–2, Wed 11–3, Thu–Fri 11–4, Sat 10–4, Sun 10–2 🚇 14th Street (A, C, E), Eighth Avenue (L)

PEN TOP BAR
Peninsula Hotel, 700 Fifth Avenue at 55th Street
Tel 212/903-3097
Who can resist an invitation to a well-dressed outdoor rooftop bar in the heart of Manhattan? You'll pay for the privilege, but that's what makes memories.

🕐 Mon–Thu 4–midnight, Fri–Sat 4–1, Sat 3–10 🚇 Fifth Avenue/53rd Street (E, V), 51st Street (6)

PRAVDA
281 Lafayette Street between Houston and Prince streets
Tel 212/226-4944
Caviar and other Russian snacks accompany the vodka at this classy lounge. Sixty-five vodkas are available, many infused with ingredients like ginger, mango or horseradish.

🕐 Sun–Wed 5–1, Thu 5–2, Fri–Sat 5–3 (closed Sun, Jul–Aug) 🚇 Broadway/ Lafayette (F, S, V), Bleecker Street (6)

RAINBOW GRILL BAR
30 Rockefeller Plaza at 49th Street between Fifth and Sixth avenues
Tel 212/632-5000
www.rainbowroom.com
You can spend a fortune dining and dancing at the Rainbow Room—or head to this bar for cocktails among the starlit towers of Midtown. Jackets required.

🕐 Sun–Thu 5–midnight, Fri–Sat 5–1, dining and dancing selected Fri–Sat 🚇 47th–50th Streets (B, D, F, V)

RUBYFRUIT
531 Hudson Street between Charles and West 10th streets
Tel 212/929-3343
Couches and antique chairs are clustered around the fireplace in the upstairs bar, which attracts an over-35 crowd. There is a convivial restaurant downstairs.

🕐 Daily 3pm–4am 🚇 Christopher Street (1)

RUSSIAN VODKA ROOM
265 West 52nd Street between Broadway and Eighth Avenue
Tel 212/307-5835
A huge selection of flavored

vodkas, apple-cinnamon and horseradish, for example, are poured into martinis or drunk straight, the preference of the Russians who gather at this old-fashioned basement bar. Inexpensive menu.

🕐 Tue–Thu 4–2, Fri–Sat 4–3, Sun–Mon 4–1 🚇 50th Street (C, E)

ST. ANDREW'S

120 West 44th Street between Broadway and Sixth Avenue
Tel 212/840-8413
www.standrewsnyc.com

Scotch-lovers crowd the front bar at this traditional pub-style restaurant. Here they select their favorites from about 175 or so single malts. Go early or late to avoid the crush.

🕐 Daily 11.30am–4am 🚇 42nd Street (B, D, F, V)

SAKAGURA

211 East 43rd Street between Second and Third avenues
Tel 212/953-7253
www.sakagura.com

In the basement of a high-rise building, this bar seems lifted from Japan. Shelves are lined with 200 different types of sake, and you can order flights of four selections.

🕐 Mon–Thu noon–2.30, 6–midnight, Fri noon–2.30, 6–1, Sat 6–2, Sun 6–11 🚇 42nd Street/Grand Central (4, 5, 6)

STAR LOUNGE

Hotel Chelsea, 222 West 23rd Street between Seventh and Eighth avenues
Tel 212/255-4646

In the basement of the Hotel Chelsea, the Star Lounge is the new cool bar in the spot long occupied by the Serena Bar. The two rooms are dark and small, with regular DJ sessions.

🕐 Tue–Sat 6–4 🚇 23rd Street (1)

SLIPPER ROOM

167 Orchard Street at Stanton Street
Tel 212/253-7246
www.slipperroom.com

The name captures the mood of this lounge, where aspiring cabaret artists entertain.

🕐 Daily 8–4 🚇 Lower East Side/Second Avenue (F, V)

STONEWALL INN

53 Christopher Street between Seventh Avenue South and Waverly Place
Tel 212/463-0950
www.stonewall-place.com

It's nondescript, but this place has acquired near-mythic status for the gay movement. Here in 1969 some transvestites, using their stilettos, took a stand against the police.

🕐 Mon–Sat 3pm–4am, Sun noon–4am 🚇 Christopher Street/Sheridan Square (1)

SUGARCANE

245 Park Avenue South between 19th and 20th streets
Tel 212 475-9377

A night on the town, New York style

The gimmick at this Latino lounge is the "Cocktail Tree," a sampler holding the entire drinks menu. The DJ spins Brazilian-Caribbean sounds.

🕐 Mon–Wed 5.45–1, Thu–Sat 5.45–2, Sun 5.45–midnight 🚇 23rd Street (6), 23rd Street (N, R, W)

SWIFT HIBERNIAN LOUNGE

34 East 4th Street between Bowery and Lafayette Street
Tel 212/260-3600

Numerous brews are on tap at this slice of Dublin named for satirist Jonathan Swift.

🕐 Daily noon–4am 🚇 Broadway/Lafayette (F, S, V), Bleecker Street (6)

TAO

42 East 58th Street between Madison and Park avenues
Tel 212/888-2288
www.taorestaurant.com

A large golden Buddha presides over this loft space, which is so crowded with good-looking singles after work that it made it into an episode of *Sex and the City*.

🕐 Wed–Fri 11.30am–1am, Sat 5–1, Sun 5–midnight, Mon–Tue 11.30am–midnight, 🚇 Fifth Avenue/59th Street (N, R, W), 59th Street (4, 5, 6)

TEMPLE BAR

332 Lafayette Street between Houston and Bleecker streets
Tel 212/925-4242

This ultra-expensive bar attracts models and their coterie. A beautiful scene.

🕐 Mon–Thu 5–1, Fri–Sat 5–2 🚇 Broadway/Lafayette (F, S, V), Bleecker Street (6)

TOP OF THE TOWER

Beekman Tower, 3 Mitchell Place on First Avenue at 49th Street
Tel 212/980-4796

This 26th-floor eyrie is neither overhyped nor overpriced—a miracle considering how romantic the place is and how bewitching the views are.

🕐 Sun–Thu 5–1, Fri–Sat 5–2 🚇 51st Street (6), 53rd Street/Lexington (E, V)

THE TOWNHOUSE

236 East 58th Street at Second Avenue
Tel 212/754-4649
www.townhouseny.com

Upscale professionals gather around the piano here.

🕐 Sun–Wed 4–3, Thu–Sat 4–4 🚇 59th Street (4, 5, 6)

XUNTA

174 First Avenue between East 10th and 11th streets
Tel 212/614-0620

On Thursdays flamenco and guitar music provide the atmosphere for sangria and tapas at this lively bar. Good selection of sherries.

🕐 Mon–Thu 5–12 Fri 5–2, Sat 1pm–2am, Sun 1–12 🚇 14 Street (L), Lower East Side/Second Avenue (F, V)

Traditional Old New York

BRIDGE CAFÉ
279 Water Street between Dover Street and Peck Slip
Tel 212/227-3344
www.eatgoodinny.com
In New York they don't come much older than the Bridge Café, a tavern that was first opened in 1794 and still feels it. The bright red wood-framed building stands in the shadow of the Brooklyn Bridge, which was built almost a century later. With a colorful history as a brothel and a speakeasy, today the tavern has a fine bar menu and makes a terrific spot for a Sunday brunch.
🕐 Mon–Thu 11.45am–midnight, Fri 11.45am–1am, Sat 5pm–1am, Sun 11.45am–1am 🚇 Fulton St.-Broadway/Nassau (2, 3, 4, 5, A, C, J, M, Z)

CHUMLEY'S
86 Bedford Street between Barrow and Grove streets
Tel 212/675-4449
Originally opened in 1922 as a speakeasy, the bar attracted writers (note their book jackets on the walls), who have been replaced by locals and students.
🕐 Mon–Thu 4–midnight, Fri 4–2, Sat 11am–2am, Sun 11am–midnight 🚇 Christopher Street/Sheridan Square (1)

EAR INN
326 Spring Street between Greenwich and Washington streets
Tel 212/226-9060
This 1817 bar near the Hudson River used to cater to sailors and stevedores and now attracts writers and artists.
🕐 Daily noon–4am 🚇 Spring Street (C, E), Canal Street (1)

FANELLI CAFE
94 Prince Street at Mercer Street
Tel 212/226-9412
www.fanellicafe.com
Step through the etched-glass doors and you could be in London. A few artists still gather here, and you can get pub food in the back room.

🕐 Sun–Thu 10am–1.30am, Fri–Sat 10am–4am 🚇 Prince Street (N, R)

JOE ALLEN
326 West 46th Street between Eighth and Ninth avenues
Tel 212/581-6464
www.joeallenrestaurant.com
It's really a restaurant, but the bar is ideal for a pre- or post-theater drink. American menu.
🕐 Mon–Tue, Thu noon–11.45, Wed, Sun 11.30–11.45, Fri noon–midnight, Sat 11.30–midnight 🚇 42nd Street (A, C, E)

LANDMARK TAVERN
626 Eleventh Avenue at the southeast

Enjoy a drink in a literary setting at Chumley's

corner of 46th Street
Tel 212/247-2562
www.thelandmarktavern.org
The Landmark Tavern is worthy of its name, since it opened in 1868. The mahogany bar, antique mirrors and tile floor provide a historic patina. The traditional pub fare is good.
🕐 Daily 11.30am–3am (kitchen closes at 11pm) 🚇 42nd Street (A, C, E), 50th Street (C, E)

McSORLEY'S OLD ALE HOUSE
15 East 7th Street between Second and Third avenues
Tel 212/473-9148
McSorley's, established in 1854, became infamous for refusing to admit women

until 1970. The walls are plastered with old newspaper clippings. Students are the main patrons.
🕐 Mon–Sat 11am–1am, Sun 1–1 🚇 Astor Place (6), 8th Street (N, R)

OLD TOWN BAR
45 East 18th Street between Broadway and Park Avenue
Tel 212/529-6732
www.oldtownbar.com
At this authentic hang-out, dating from 1892, look for the private booths. Tiled floors, a long mirrored bar, pressed-tin ceiling and original gas lamps complete the look. No jukebox, conversation reigns.
🕐 Mon–Fri 11.30am–1am, Sat–Sun noon–1am 🚇 14th Street/Union Square (L, N, Q, R, W, 4, 5, 6)

P.J. CLARKE'S
915 Third Avenue at 55th Street
Tel 212/317-1616
www.pjclarkes.com
A tiny building overshadowed by skyscrapers, the bar played a major role in Billy Wilder's 1945 film *The Lost Weekend.*
🕐 Daily 11.30am–4am 🚇 59th Street (4, 5, 6)

PETE'S TAVERN
129 East 18th Street at Irving Place
Tel 212/473-7676
The writer O'Henry supposedly wrote *The Gift of the Magi* in a beer-stained booth here. In summer, snag a sidewalk table if you can.
🕐 Mon–Fri 10.30–3am, Sat–Sun 11–3am 🚇 14th Street/Union Square (L, N, Q, R, W, 4, 5, 6)

WHITE HORSE TAVERN
567 Hudson Street at 11th Street
Tel 212/989-3956
Dylan Thomas, Brendan Behan and Jack Kerouac all slaked their thirst here. In summer, the benches and picnic tables make perfect perches for Village people-watching.
🕐 Daily 11–3am 🚇 Christopher Street/ Sheridan Square (1), 14th Street (A, C, E)

Clubs

New York has loads of attitude, and it is on display at its worst at the entrances to dance clubs. At a few places, the henchmen at the door are rude and obnoxious. At many clubs, as the week gets closer to the weekend the door policies get stricter. In some places, the action doesn't warm up until after midnight.

49 GROVE
49 Grove Street at Bleecker Street
Tel 212/727-1100
In the deep-purple lounge downstairs at 49 Grove you'll find comfortable couches to sink right into while bottles or cocktails are brought to your table as the city's fashion crowd and other celebrities mingle and schmooze. The music is hip-hop, house, funk, garage and the prices are seriously high, even by New York club standards.
⏰ Thu–Sat 10pm–4am 🚇 Christopher Street-Sheridan Square (1), 4th Street-Washington Square (A, B, C, D, E, F, V)

APT
419 West 13th Street between Ninth Avenue and Washington Street
Tel 212/414-4245
www.aptwebsite.com
You must be on the A-list to snag one of the sofas in the upstairs apartment-style lounge (with a big bed as well as coffee tables). The sleek basement lounge is more accessible, but you still need to look good at this designer nightlife spot.
⏰ Mon–Sat 7pm–4am 💲 $0–$20 🚇 14th Street (A, C, E), Eighth Avenue (L)

BAKTUN
418 West 14th Street between Ninth Avenue and Washington Street
Tel 212/206-1590
www.baktun.com
A plain but vibrant club, especially at the weekly Saturday drum 'n bass party, when club kids trance in to the double-sided video screens. Live instrumental and electronic music, plus special events (kodo drummers from Japan) are featured other nights.
⏰ Mon, Wed–Sat 9–4 💲 Varies 🚇 14th Street (A, C, E)

BUNGALOW 8
515 West 27th Street between 10th and 11th avenues
Tel 212/629-3333
The challenge here is to get through the doors, as you either have to be a celebrity or be able to drop the right

New York's hottest clubs have a lot of attitude

name. Inside it's surprisingly small, which is another reason they keep people out, but it's definitely kudos to say you've been to Bungalow 8.
⏰ Daily 11pm–4am 🚇 28th Street (1), 23rd Street (C, E)

CAIN
544 West 27th Street between 10th and 11th avenues
Tel 212/947-8000
www.cainnyc.com
If you can get through the door of this exclusive Chelsea nightspot, it's like being out in Africa with zebra-skin decor and the occasional drummer who accompanies the DJ. Wednesdays and Saturdays are the best nights, and make sure you can afford it as they like people to buy a bottle and chill out. There's no cover charge.
⏰ Tue–Sat 10.30pm–4am 🚇 23rd Street (C, E)

CHINA CLUB
268 West 47th Street between Broadway and Eighth Avenue
Tel 212/398-3800
www.chinaclubnyc.com
This glitzy spot has been pulsating and attracting celebrities for 25 years. Today, sports figures and music heavies still head to its VIP lounge especially on Monday nights. Other nights are dedicated to house, salsa, merengue and R & B.
⏰ Mon, Thu–Sat 10pm–3am 💲 $20–$25 🚇 49th Street (N, R, W), 50th Street (1)

CIELO
18 Little West 12th Street between Ninth Avenue and Washington Street
Tel 212/645-5700
www.cieloclub.com
Tough to get into unless you're beautiful or famous since it only accommodates 300 standing. It's comfortable, with a small sunken dance floor (throbbing at 2am) and intimate nooks. Latin-flecked house and tribal and hot guest DJs attract the crowds.
⏰ Mon 9.30–3.30, Wed 10.30–4, Thu–Sat 11–4, Sun 10–4 💲 $15–$30 🚇 14th Street (A, C, E)

CLUB SHELTER
20 West 39th Street between Fifth and Sixth avenues
Tel 212/719-4479
www.clubshelter.com
Upstairs the ultimate garage party has been playing for more than a decade. Downstairs is LoverGirlNYC, a major lesbian event.
⏰ Sat 11pm–noon 💲 $20–$25 🚇 42nd Street (B, D, F, V), Fifth Avenue (7)

DIRTY DISCO
248 West 14th Street between 7th and 8th avenues
Tel 212/488-2525
Taking over the space where the infamous 2i's was, on the edge of the Meatpacking District, the club is split across two levels with a tiny dance floor. Despite the high drink prices it gets packed, and the music's a mix of rock, house, 70s disco and 80s hip-hop.
🕐 Mon 10pm–4am, Thu–Sat 11pm–4am 💲 $15 cover 🚇 14th Street (1, 2, 3, A, C, E), 8th Avenue (L)

ELEMENT
225 East Houston Street at Essex
Tel 212/254-2200
www.elementny.com
Opened in 2006 in a former bank building (and once the studio of artist Jasper Johns), by 2007 Element was already being acclaimed as one of the city's best dance clubs in an online poll. Attractions include a powerful sound system and a huge hardwood dance floor that throbs to disco, soul, reggae and anything else the DJs can pump out.
🕐 Thu–Sun 10pm–4am 🚇 Lower East Side-Second Avenue (F, V)

THE GRAND
41 East 58th Street at Madison Avenue
Tel 212/308-9455
www.thegrandnyc.com
The bright red and plush purple suede couches, the black walls and chandeliers can't fail to impress at the aptly named Grand, which has its quota of celebs but appeals more widely with its affordable ($15) cocktails and relaxed atmosphere.
🕐 Thu–Sat 10pm–3am 💲 $20–$30 🚇 59th Street (4, 5, 6), Lexington Avenue-59th Street (N, R, W)

HOME
532 West 27th Street between 10th and 11th avenues
Tel 212/273-3700
www.homeguesthouse.com
Long banquettes run the length of some of the walls of this Chelsea nightclub, which oozes style and atmosphere with its low lights, red wood floors, candles and couches. If the rock and pop music is too staid, you can move down the street to the sister club, the Guest House, for house music.
🕐 Tue–Sun 10pm–4am 🚇 28th Street (1), 23rd Street (C, E)

LOTUS
409 West 14th Street between Ninth and Tenth avenues
Tel 212/243-4420
www.lotusnewyork.com
European jet-setters flock to this chic supper club with attitude, attracted by the international DJs and the luxe

New York's clubs offer an eclectic range of music

balcony lounge and basement dance club. It's tough to get past the fu dogs at the door. Make a dinner reservation and bring the platinum.
🕐 Dinner Tue–Sat 7–11; club Tue–Sat 10–4 💲 $20 🚇 14th Street (A, C, E)

MARQUEE
289 Tenth Avenue between 26th and 27th streets
Tel 646/473-0202
www.marqueeny.com
This club has a lot of buzz and attracts a celebrity crowd who appreciate its plush comforts, French elegance (glittering contemporary chandeliers, velvet banquettes), cabaret room and good sightlines for watching the scene. Baby Tuesday caters to the fashion industry. The crowd is mainly straight, but there's a smattering of fashion-conscious gays too. Hip hop, house, funk and soul are the main musical themes.
🕐 Tue–Sat 10pm–4am 💲 Cover $20 🚇 23rd Street (C, E)

PIANOS
158 Ludlow Street between Stanton and Rivington streets
Tel 212/505-3733
www.pianosnyc.com
Don't expect piano entertainment at this bi-level bar—the name is a relic of a previous occupant. Go for the alternative music on Friday, Sunday and Monday.
🕐 Daily 3pm–4am 💲 $8–$10 🚇 DeLancey/Essex Street (F, J, M, Z)

THE PLUMM
246 West 14th Street between 7th and 8th avenues
Tel 212/675-1567
www.theplumm.com
Many New Yorkers think the Plumm's got it right, with a strict but not-too-strict door policy, affordable drinks and something happening every night, making it especially popular early in the week when many places are closed. There are two floors with a bar, DJs and music on each one, and occasional live gigs by big-name acts, often unannounced. No wonder people like The Plumm.
🕐 Daily 10pm–4am 🚇 14th Street (1, 2, 3, A, C, E), 8th Avenue (L)

SWING 46
349 West 46th Street between Eighth and Ninth avenues
Tel 212/262-9554
www.swing46.com
At this 1940s-style jazz club, you can lindy and jitterbug to top-notch live bands. Friday and Saturday is always swing. The management provides lessons to neophytes.
🕐 Sun–Thu 5–12, Fri–Sat 9–1 💲 $12–$15 🚇 42nd Street (A, C, E)

WHAT TO DO

SPORTS AND ACTIVITIES

New York City is a major sports destination, whether you fancy watching a game of baseball, football, basketball, ice hockey or tennis. If you want to take part in something yourself, try jogging in Central Park or working out at one of the many gyms.

Local and regional rivalries drive the professional sports scene. In baseball it's the Yankees (Bronx) versus the Mets (Queens). In addition, whenever the Yankees play the Red Sox, it's a grudge game because Boston has never forgiven New York for stealing Babe Ruth. The biggest sports are football (Giants and Jets) and basketball (Knicks and New Jersey Nets). Ice hockey has fanatical fans too, supporting the Rangers,

Islanders and New Jersey Devils, making for internecine rivalries between Manhattan, Long Island and New Jersey. Most seats are sold in advance by subscription to corporations and individuals. Tickets are available without fee at the box office; there's an extra fee for phone and online orders. Agencies like TicketMaster (tel 212/307-7171 or www.ticketmaster.com) usually charge a fee of from $4 to $8 per ticket. Tickets to any of these sports are tough to get and/or expensive, but you can always take a seat in one of the many raucous sports bars around town and see the action there, or at the large ESPN Zone in Times Square.

The major sports seasons are: baseball April–end October; basketball November–end April; soccer March–end October; football and ice hockey September–end April.

Despite the American women's global success in soccer, women's professional sports struggle for audience

support, although such teams as basketball's Liberty have loyal fans.

New Yorkers also enjoy a variety of exercise and activities. They go to the gym, walk, run, cycle, skate, rollerblade and play tennis, softball and street basketball. Equestrians can ride in Central Park. They have also rediscovered the waterfront and now enjoy kayaking and sailing from several downtown piers. The more sedentary count bowling and pool as sports.

Basketball is one of the city's biggest sports

Many New Yorkers exercise in Central Park

BASEBALL

BROOKLYN CYCLONES
Keyspan Park, 1904 Surf Avenue between 17th and 19th streets, Coney Island
Tel 718/449-8497
www.brooklyncyclones.com
This minor-league club has the fans cheering, because going to the game here is the way baseball used to be. Sitting in the bleachers at this waterfront stadium is just the ticket, especially for old Dodgers fans.
🎟 $5–$12 (single tickets available mid-Apr) 🚇 Stillwell Avenue/Coney Island

(W) 🚌 B36, B64, B74 (Stillwell/Surf Avenue)

NEW YORK METS
Shea Stadium , Roosevelt Avenue at 126th Street, Flushing, Queens
Tel 718/507-8499
www.mets.com
When the Brooklyn Dodgers left New York in 1957, the Mets in effect replaced them. Even though they haven't won a championship since 1986 and often finish at the bottom of their league, they continue to draw fans. You can usually get tickets unless they're

playing the Yankees or the Boston Red Sox. Shea Stadium, right underneath the landing path to LaGuardia airport, is noisy.
🎟 $8–$60 🚇 Willets Pt/Shea Stadium (7) 🚢 On Sat–Sun only: New York Waterway (tel 800/533-3779) operates from the South Street Seaport, East 34th Street or East 90th Street for $18 round-trip. Reservations recommended.

NEW YORK YANKEES

Yankee Stadium, East 161st Street and River Avenue, the Bronx
Tel 212/307-1212 for tickets, 718/579-4531 for tours
www.yankees.com

Since the Yankees began playing in 1903 as the New York Highlanders, they've racked up 26 World Championships. Tickets are tough to get for certain games (opening day, games against the Mets, the play-offs, the series) but not for other games. Even if you don't go to a game, take the one-hour tour to see the dugout, clubhouse and scoreboard operations before the New Yankee Stadium opens in 2009.

🖐 $8–$90 🚇 161st Street/Yankee Stadium (C, D, 4) 🚢 New York Waterway (tel 800/533-3779) operates from the South Street Seaport, East 34th Street or East 90th Street for $18 round-trip. Reservations recommended.

STATEN ISLAND YANKEES

Richmond County Bank Ballpark at St. George
Tel 718/720-9265 or 718/720-9200
www.siyanks.com

This minor-league team plays in a stadium overlooking the harbor. It's fun to take the trip on the Staten Island Ferry.

🖐 $9–$11 🚇 South Ferry (1) to Staten Island Ferry 🚢 Staten Island Ferry

BASKETBALL

NEW JERSEY NETS

Continental Airlines Arena, East Rutherford, N.J.
Tel 201/935-3900 or 1800-7NJNETS
www.nba.com/nets

This Atlantic Division basketball team has been on a winning streak thanks to All-star point guard Jason Kidd, Vince Carter and Richard Jefferson.

🖐 $10–$1,414 🚌 NJ Transit bus from 42nd Street/Port Authority Bus Terminal at Eighth Avenue

NEW YORK KNICKS

Madison Square Garden, 2 Pennsylvania Plaza, Seventh Avenue between West 31st and 33rd streets
Tel 212/465-5867 or 212/465-6741 (Madison Square Garden), 212/307-7171 for tickets
www.nba.com/knicks

The Knicks are the city's hottest ticket. This team and the Boston Celtics are the only charter members of the NBA left. Walt Frazier, Bill Bradley and Willis Reed made them golden in the 1970s, and Patrick Ewing helped them to the play-offs in 1994 and 1999. Since Ewing left, they have struggled. Today Allan Houston is the guy to watch. The Knicks City Dancers

Visit Larry and Jeff's to explore the city on two wheels

are pure Americana. Spike Lee is just one of the celebrity fans in attendance. For tours, call 212/465-5802.

🖐 $10–$3,000 🚇 34th Street/Penn Station (A, C, E, 1, 2, 3) 🚌 M20, M34

NEW YORK LIBERTY

Madison Square Garden, 2 Pennsylvania Plaza, Seventh Avenue between West 31st and 33rd streets
Tel 212/564-9622
www.nyliberty.com

The team, launched in summer 1997, has become a star in the Women's National Basketball Association (WNBA) and has played in WNBA finals.

🖐 $10–$69.50 🚇 34th Street/Penn Station (A, C, E, 1, 2, 3) 🚌 M20, M34

BICYCLING

LARRY & JEFF'S

1400 3rd Avenue between 79th and 80th streets
Tel 212/794-2929
www.bicyclesnyc.com

This store rents road and mountain bikes and is conveniently close to Central Park.

🕐 Daily 10–7 (until 8 during daylight savings) 🖐 $30 day (3hrs 30mins or more) 🚇 86th Street (4, 5, 6) 🚌 M15, M86

BIRDWATCHING

CHARLES A. DANA DISCOVERY CENTER

Central Park, 110th Street between Fifth and Lenox avenues
Tel 212/860-1370
www.centralparknyc.org or www.centralpark.com

Exhibits relate to the natural life in the park, and the center sponsors related activities in the park. For ranger-led activities call 1-866-NYCHAWK.

🕐 Tue–Sun 10–5 🖐 Free 🚇 Central Park North (2, 3) 🚌 M4

NEW YORK CITY AUDUBON SOCIETY

Tel 212/691-7483
www.nycaudubon.org

The New York City Audubon Society allows visitors to join its birdwatching walks in Central Park for a small fee.

BOWLING

BOWLMOR LANES

110 University Place between 12th and 13th streets
Tel 212/255-8188
www.bowlmor.com

This funky bowling alley has 42 lanes with automatic scoring. At Monday's Night Strike (10pm–3am), DJs spin music as you bowl.

🕐 Sun 11–midnight, Tue–Wed 11am–1am, Thu 11am–2am, Fri–Sat11am–3.30am, Mon 11am–2am 🖐 $8.45–$9.95 per game (shoe rental $5.50) 🚇 14th Street/Union Square (L, N, Q, R, W, 4, 5, 6) 🚌 M3

WHAT TO DO

LEISURE TIME

625 Eighth Avenue at West 42nd Street (2nd floor)
Tel 212/268-6909
www.leisuretimebowl.com

Cocktails are prominently advertised at the entrance to this 30-lane alley in the Port Authority Bus Terminal. Sports bar and video arcade.

🕐 Sun 1–11pm, Mon–Thu 10am–midnight, Fri 10am–1am, Sat 1pm–1am 💷 $6.50–$9.50 per game (shoe rental $5) 🚇 42nd Street (A, C, E) 🚌 M20, M42

CRICKET

VAN CORTLANDT PARK

Van Cortlandt Park, Park South and Bailey Avenue

The Caribbean communities brought cricket to the city and this is the best place to find a cricket game in progress.

🕐 Dawn–dusk in summer 💷 Free 🚇 242nd Street (1)

FOOTBALL

NEW YORK GIANTS

Giants Stadium, The Meadowlands, East Rutherford, N.J.
Tel 201/935-8111 or 201/935-8222 for tickets www.giants.com or www.meadowlands.com

Also known as the Big Blue Wrecking Crew, its fans are maniacally loyal and tickets are impossible to get. The team won their first NFL title in 1927; their golden years were in the late 1950s and 1960s when Frank Gifford, Roosevelt Brown and Sam Huff were in the line-up. The team made it to the Super Bowl in 2003.

💷 Single tickets unavailable 🚌 NJ Transit bus from 42nd Street/Port Authority Bus Terminal at Eighth Avenue

NEW YORK JETS

Giants Stadium, The Meadowlands, East Rutherford, N.J.
Tel 516/560-8100 or 516/560-8200
www.newyorkjets.com or www.meadowlands.com

This American Football League team has been playing since 1960, but only gained credibility after they drafted Joe Namath in 1965 and won

the Super Bowl in 1969. They moved to Giants Stadium in 1984. Tickets are hard to come by—you have to wait 15 years for season tickets.

💷 Season ticket only 🚌 NJ Transit bus from 42nd Street/Port Authority Bus Terminal Eighth Avenue

GOLF

VAN CORTLANDT GOLF COURSE

Tel 718/543-4595
www.nycgovparks.org

The oldest public golf course in the US is not exactly grade A, but it will do. Eighteen holes, 6,122 yards, with clubhouse and snack bar.

🕐 Dawn–dusk 💷 $16.75–$39.50 plus

New Yorkers are fanatical about football

$8 for non-NY residents 🚇 242nd Street (1)

HORSE RACING

AQUEDUCT

108th Street and Rockaway Boulevard, Ozone Park, Queens
Tel 718/641-4700
www.nyra.com

This racetrack, which opened in 1894, is only 30 minutes by train from Times Square.

🕐 Mid-Oct to early May Wed–Sun 1pm post time 💷 $1–$4 🚇 Aqueduct Racetrack (A)

BELMONT PARK

2150 Hempstead Turnpike and Plainfield Avenue , Elmont, Queens
Tel 516/488-6000

www.nyra.com

This beautiful 430-acre (174ha) racecourse is the largest in North America. In June, it hosts the Belmont Stakes, the third leg of the Triple Crown.

🕐 May–end Jul, Sep–end Oct Wed–Sun, 1pm post time 💷 $2–$5 🚆 Long Island Railroad's *Pony Express* from Penn Station

THE MEADOWLANDS

East Rutherford, New Jersey
Tel 201/935-8500
www.meadowlands.com

Trotters run from January through August and thoroughbreds from September through December at this track.

🕐 Wed–Sat, 7.30pm post time 💷 $1–$5 🚌 Transit bus from 42nd Street/Port Authority bus terminal at Eighth Avenue

YONKERS RACEWAY

Yonkers, New York
Tel 914/968-4200
www.yonkersraceway.com

One of the premier harness racing tracks in the nation is in the city, just north of the Bronx. The track celebrated its centennial in 1999. The most illustrious race run here is the Night of Champions, with a $1.2 million purse.

🕐 Wed–Sun, 7.40pm post time 💷 $2.25–$4.25 🚇 Woodlawn (4) and Beeline 20 bus

HORSEBACK RIDING

BRONX EQUESTRIAN CENTER

9 Shore Road, Bronx
Tel 718/885-0551
www.bronxequestriancenter.com

Located near the lovely Pelham Bay park, there's a chance here to go trail-riding through the woods or enjoy pony and hay wagon rides too.

🕐 Daily 9am–dusk 💷 Lessons $40 per half-hour, trail rides from $30 per hour, $5 for three pony rides 🚇 Phone for directions.

WHAT TO DO

ICE HOCKEY

NEW JERSEY DEVILS
Prudential Center, 165 Mulberry Street, Newark, NJ
Tel 973/757-6000
www.newjerseydevils.com or www.meadowlands.com
The Devils, who have won the Stanley Cup only twice, are currently the premier hockey team in the metro region, thanks largely to brilliant goalie Martin Brodeur and some experienced overseas players. Tickets are easily available.
🚺 $10–$200 🚂 NJ Transit train from Penn Station New York at 34th Street/7th Avenue to Penn Station New Jersey

NEW YORK ISLANDERS
Nassau Coliseum, Long Island
Tel 516/794-4100
www.newyorkislanders.com
Tickets to contests of this Long Island team are easier to come by than tickets to Rangers games, even though the Islanders won four straight Stanley Cups between 1980 and 1983. The two teams have an edgy rivalry.
🚺 $19–$75 🚂 LIRR to Hempstead then bus, or Westbury and cab

NEW YORK RANGERS
Madison Square Garden,
2 Pennsylvania Plaza, Seventh Avenue between West 31st and 33rd streets
Tel 212/465-4459, 212/307-7171 for tickets, 212/465-6225 for guest relations, 212/465-5802 for tours and 212/465-6741 for the Garden
www.newyorkrangers.com or www.thegarden.com
The Rangers may have the highest payroll in the National Hockey League, but they haven't made the play-offs for several seasons. They won their last Stanley Cup in 1993–94. Yet tickets are virtually impossible to get. The institutionalized violence on the ice rarely extends into the stands, but it's wise not to cheer the other team.
🚺 $40–$1,000 🚇 34th Street/Penn Station (A, C, E, 1, 2, 3) 🚌 M20, M34

JOGGING

CENTRAL PARK RESERVOIR
This 1.6-mile (2.6km) gravel path is the favorite track for Upper West Siders and Upper East Siders.
🚺 Free 🚇 86th Street (4, 5, 6), 86th Street (B, C) 🚌 M1, M2, M3, M4, M10, M86

KAYAKING

DOWNTOWN BOATHOUSE
Pier 96, Clinton Cove Park at 56th Steeet
Tel 646/613-0375
www.downtownboathouse.org
This organization offers free kayaking trips and instruction on the Hudson River from several locations.

Central Park is a great place for joggers

🕐 Mid-May to mid-Oct 🚺 Free 🚇 Columbus Circle (1) 🚌 M20

MANHATTAN KAYAK COMPANY
Pier 66, 26th Street and 12th Avenue
Tel 212/924-1788
www.manhattankayak.com
This company offers instruction and over 30 local tours for beginners, intermediates and advanced paddlers. Longer tours go to the Verrazano Bridge and farther.
🕐 Mid-Apr to end Oct 🚺 Tours $40–$250 🚇 8th Avenue (C, E) then M23 bus 🚌 M23

NEW YORK KAYAK COMPANY
Pier 40 at Houston Street
Tel 212/924-1327

www.nykayak.com
This company offers classes and guided tours, which last two or three hours.
🕐 Tours early May to mid-Oct 🚺 Classes: $50 per hr; tours: $100–$150 🚇 Houston Street (1) 🚌 M21

POOL

PRESSURE
110 University Place between 12th and 13th streets
Tel 212/352-1161
www.pressurenyc.com
This bubble on the roof of Bowlmor Lanes is the ultimate pool hall/multimedia lounge. It has 21 tables, plus a huge bar/lounge and one 21ft and three 16ft movie screens.
🕐 Fri–Sat 9pm–3am 🚺 $26 per hr 🚇 14th Street/Union Square (L, N, Q, R, W, 4, 5, 6) 🚌 M2, M3, M14

SLATE
54 West 21st Street between Fifth and Sixth avenues
Tel 212/989-0096
www.slate-ny.com
This is one of the city's best billiard-pool halls, with 31 tables.
🕐 Daily 11–4 🚺 $7–$17 per hr 🚇 23rd Street (N, R, W), 23rd Street (F, V) 🚌 M2, M3, M5, M6, M7

ROWING

LOEB BOATHOUSE
Central Park near East 72nd Street and Park Drive North
Tel 212-517-2233
www.thecentralparkboathouse.com
Weather permitting, you can rent bicycles and rowboats for use on the lake year round.
🕐 Daily 10am–dusk 🚺 Bicycles $9–$20 per hr, rowboats $10 per hr 🚇 68th Street (6), 72nd Street (B, C) 🚌 M1, M2, M3, M4, M10

RUNNING

NEW YORK MARATHON
New York Road Runners Club, 9 East 89th Street at Fifth Avenue
Tel 212/860-4455
www.nyrr.org
Thirty thousand athletes compete in this marathon, watched by 2.5 million

WHAT TO DO

spectators. The finish line is in Central Park.

⏱ First Sun in Nov

BLADES BOARD & SKATE

120 West 72nd Street at Columbus Street
Tel 212/787-3911
www.blades.com

This is the most convenient of these stores to Central Park, where you can rent in-line skates. There's also a branch at Chelsea Piers.

⏱ Mon–Sat 10–8, Sun 10–6
💲 Rentals $21.65 for 24 hr 🚇 72nd Street (1, 2, 3) 🚌 M7, M11, M72

EMPIRE SKATE CLUB

Tel 212/774-1774
www.empireskate.org

The club sponsors group skates, skating events and tours. Year-round skates include the Sunday morning roll from Columbus Circle at 11am and the Tuesday night skate from Blades at 120 West 72nd Street at 8pm.

⏱ Daily 6.30am–dusk 💲 Club membership $25 (you don't have to be a member to join group skates)

ROCKEFELLER CENTER ICE RINK

1 Rockefeller Center Plaza, Fifth Avenue between 49th and 50th streets
Tel 212/332-7654
www.rapatina.com/IceRink/

It's dreamlike to glide on this legendary rink under the golden statue of Prometheus. Live DJ Thursday 7–11pm.

⏱ Oct–late Apr several sessions daily, phone or visit website for timings
💲 Mon–Thu $5 lunch, $10 otherwise Fri–Sun and holidays $14; under 11 and seniors Mon–Thu $7.50, Fri–Sun and holidays $8.50, skate rental $7
🚇 47th–50th streets/Rockefeller Center (B, D, F, V) 🚌 M1, M2, M3, M4, M50

WOLLMAN RINK

Central Park at 62nd Street
Tel 212/439-6900
www.wollmanskatingrink.com

You can skate against the backdrop of the Manhattan skyline at this romantic outdoor rink—or, in summer, roller skate or blade.

⏱ Mon–Tue 10–2.30, Wed–Thu 10–10, Fri–Sat 10am–11pm, Sun 10–9 💲 Adult $9.50–$12, skate rental $5 🚇 59th Street/Fifth Avenue (N, R, W) 🚌 M5

RED BULL NEW YORK

Giants Stadium, Continental Airlines Arena
Tel 1-888-4METROTIX
www.metrostars.com

Despite the US soccer team qualifying for the 2006 World Cup, soccer has failed to capture the imagination of the American public. Perhaps the MetroStars changing their

The city offers a wide range of skating options

name to Red Bull New York and the move to the Red Bull Stadium in 2008 will help.

💲 $20–$75 🚇 NJ Transit bus from 42nd Street/Port Authority Bus Terminal at Eighth Avenue

CHELSEA PIERS

Piers 59–62 between 17th and 23rd streets
Tel 212/336-6000 or 212/336-6400 for golf, 212/336-6500 for field house, 212/336-6100 for Skyrink
www.chelseapiers.com

This is the city's ultimate sports facility, where many sports are catered to. There's also a four-tiered golf driving range, basketball and sand volleyball courts, and a huge gym.

⏱ Daily 6am–midnight 💲 Day passes available for different activities at various prices 🚇 23rd Street (C, E) 🚌 M23

DEPARTMENT OF PARKS AND RECREATION

830 Fifth Avenue at 64th Street
Tel 212/360-8111 or 212/408-0243 for pool information
www.centralparknyc.org

The best tennis courts are: Central Park and 93rd Street (tel 212/280-0205), 30 hard courts; Riverside Drive and 96th Street (tel 212/496-2006), eight clay courts; Riverside Drive and 119th Street (tel 212/496-2006), eight hard courts.

⏱ Tennis courts: early Apr–late Nov daily 6.30am–dusk 💲 Tennis $7 pass for one hour of play obtainable at office above or at Central Park courts 🚇 Fifth Avenue/59th Street (N, R, W) 🚌 M1, M2, M3, M4

U.S. OPEN TENNIS CHAMPIONSHIP

USTA National Tennis Center, Flushing Meadows–Corona Park, Queens
Tel 718/760-6200 or 516/354-2590
www.usopen.org or
www.usta.com

This two-week tournament is one of four in tennis' Grand Slam. Tickets to any session admit you to major matches played in Arthur Ashe stadium, and also to other courts. You can see more tennis if you buy daytime tickets, since many of the outer courts are not used at night. Tickets go on sale at the end of April; most are sold via subscription and what remain are usually in the stratosphere—but that's less an issue for day sessions, when most of the action is on the outer courts.

⏱ Late Aug–end Sep 💲 Varies enormously 🚇 Willetts Pt/Shea Stadium (7) 🚂 LIRR to Shea Stadium

WHAT TO DO

HEALTH AND BEAUTY

Almost every neighborhood in New York has a selection of health clubs with fitness equipment, classes and assorted frills—sometimes a pool. Massages, nutrition consultations and personal trainers may be available by appointment. Most offer day passes for visitors for a price (anywhere from $20 to $50). It's best to go at off-peak hours–between 12 and 2 and from 5 till 8 the clubs may be so crowded you have to sign up to use the machines.

The city has always had yoga studios and fancy hair salons, but it has seen an enormous growth of day spas and other pampering facilities. Some are world-class, like La Prairie in the Ritz; others cater to New Age constituencies, while still others hustle passers-by for a quick back massage. The Brazilian nail salons are considered extra-special.

HEALTH CLUBS

ASPHALT GREEN
555 East 90th Street between York and East End avenues
Tel 212-369-8890
www.asphaltgreen.org

Swimming is just one of the fitness options at Asphalt Green

This 5.5-acre (2.25ha) sports complex has Manhattan's only Olympic-size pool. It also has indoor and outdoor running tracks, fields for team sports, a large rooftop terrace with views of the East River, and a multi-level fitness center with 50-plus exercise classes.
🕐 Mon–Fri 5.30am–10pm, Sat–Sun 8–8 ✋ Day pass $25 🚇 96th Street (6) 🚌 M15, M31, M86

BALLY TOTAL FITNESS
641 Avenue of the Americas at 19th Street
Tel 212/645-4565
www.ballyfitness.com

This national chain has several facilities in Manhattan.
The Sixth Avenue club has more than 70 pieces of cardiovascular equipment, 73 pieces of resistance-training equipment, personal trainers and classes in yoga, Pilates and kwando.
🕐 Mon–Thu 5.30–11, Fri 5.30–10, Sat 9–8, Sun 9–7 ✋ 30-day trial membership $19 🚇 18th Strreet (1) 🚌 M5, M6, M7

CHELSEA PIERS
Piers 59–62 at 23rd Street and the Hudson River
Tel 212/336-6000
www.chelseapiers.com
The city's ultimate sports complex, built on four Hudson River piers, has facilities for 21 sports. In summer, the beach, sundecks, large pool and kayaking layout are inviting. There's a climbing wall as well as 200-meter and quarter-mile tracks, an ice rink, and rows of cardiovascular, circuit and strength-training equipment. There are courts for basketball, indoor sand volleyball and touch football, plus a boxing ring, golf driving range and batting cages. Some 125 classes a week offer everything from aerobics to yoga. Other facilities include a sports medicine clinic, café and spa.
🕐 Daily 6am–midnight ✋ Day passes available 🚇 23rd Street (C, E) 🚌 M23

CRUNCH FITNESS
54 East 13th Street between Broadway and University Place
Tel 212/475-2018
www.crunch.com
Crunch, which has 15 locations in the city, is

The Greenhouse Spa is one of the city's finest

the very popular premier brand of Bally Fitness. Each place has whimsy and pop style. The instructors are first rate, and the studio is known for its innovative classes, from street stomp to cycle karaoke.
🕐 Mon–Fri 6am–10pm, Sat–Sun 8–8 ✋ Day pass $24 🚇 14th Street/Union Square (L, N, Q, R, W, 4, 5, 6) 🚌 M1, M2, M3, M5

EQUINOX FITNESS CLUB

521 Fifth Avenue at 44th Street
Tel 212 972-8000
www.equinoxfitness.com
All 17 Equinox clubs in Manhattan are sleek and sophisticated and almost invariably offer spinning, Pilates, yoga, cardio-boxing and cardio machines.
🕐 Mon–Thu 5.30am–10pm, Fri 5.30am–8pm 💲 Day pass $35 🚇 42nd Street/Grand Central (4, 5, 6) 🚌 M1, M2, M3, M4, M5

NEW YORK HEALTH AND RACQUET CLUB

24 East 13th Street between Fifth Avenue and University Place
Tel 212/924-4600
www.nyhrc.com
The ten Manhattan branches of this chain offer sports, equipment and classes from tai chi and karate to aqua-cise. Each branch has a pool, and the one at 57th and Lexington comes complete with a full spa. Members have access to a beach and tennis club in New Rochelle, as well as a yacht docked at 23rd Street.
🕐 Mon–Fri 6am–11pm, Sat–Sun 8am–9pm 💲 Day pass $50 🚇 14th Street/Union Square (L, N, Q, R, W, 4, 5, 6) 🚌 M1, M2, M3, M5

NEW YORK SPORT CLUBS

128 Eighth Avenue at 16th Street
Tel 212/627-0065
www.nysc.com
This chain has close to 100 locations around town, mostly aerobic studios with cardio-fitness machines and free weights, plus a full program of exercise classes—cardio-kick-boxing, step, abs, Pilates and yoga. Massage treatments are usually available, too.
🕐 Mon–Thu 6am–11pm, Fri 6am–10pm, Sat–Sun 8am–9pm 💲 Day pass $25 🚇 18th Street (1) 🚌 M20

SPORTS CLUB/LA

330 East 61st Street between First and Second avenues
Tel 212/355-5100
45 Rockefeller Plaza
Tel 212/218-8600
www.TheSportsClubLA.com
The spectacular 61st Street location of this urban country club occupies 150,000 square feet (13,500sq m) and offers 50 fitness classes, five squash courts, two basketball courts, a climbing wall,weights, and a cardio deck with more than 200 machines. There's even rooftop tennis and golf.
🕐 Mon–Fri 5am–11pm, Sat–Sun 7am–9pm 💲 Day pass $35 with member only 🚇 59th Street (4, 5, 6) 🚌 M15

Stretch your muscles while enjoying great views at Clay

ACQUA BEAUTY BAR

7 East 14th Street near 5th Avenue
Tel 212/620-4329
www.acquabeautybar.com
Treatments include an Indonesian 'ritual of beauty', an Adlay (Asian wheat) body scrub and an indulgent Garden of Eastern Delights, combining a mist facial with a shiatsu massage. You can still get a Swedish massage and French manicure or pedicure, though.
🕐 Mon, Thu 10–9, Tue–Wed, Fri 10–8, Sat–Sun 10–7 💲 Facial $95–$225, manicure $12–$22, massage $90–$100 🚇 Union Square-14th Street (L, N, Q, R, W)

CLAY

25 West 14th Street between Fifth and Sixth avenues
Tel 212/206-9200
www.insideclay.com
Sleek, serene and minimal, Clay combines bodywork therapies with exercise (weights, cardio-boxing, yoga). The fireside lounge and rooftop deck are bonuses.
🕐 Mon–Thu 5.30am–11pm, Fri 5.30am–10pm, Sat–Sun 8–9 💲 Massage $110–$185 🚇 14th Street/Union Square (L, N, Q, R, W, 4, 5, 6) 🚌 M2, M3, M5, M14

CORNELIA DAY RESORT

663 Fifth Avenue between 52nd and 53rd streets
Tel 212/871-3050
www.cornelia.com
New York's weather and urban ambience does not lend itself to outdoor pampering. That may be changing with the rooftop massages here and the underwater shiatsu massage in the watsu pool. It offers a full range of spa services—facials, algae wraps and massages.
🕐 Mon–Sat 9am–10pm, Sun 9am–7pm 💲 Facial $175, massage from $150 🚇 5th Avenue/53rd Street (E, V) 🚌 M1, M2, M3, M4

GREAT JONES SPA

29 Great Jones Street at Lafayette
212/505-3185
www.greatjonesspa.com
The Great Jones Spa blends organic principles (a raw food café) with unashamed indulgence. They provide a kind of feng shui for the body, and the facilities are as impressive as the ambience is relaxing. There are water cures and waxing, acupuncture and detoxifying as well as the usual range of spa treatments.
🕐 Mon 4–10pm, Tue–Sun 9am–10pm 💲 Manicure $25–$40, facial $130–$295, massage $130–$210 🚇 Bleecker Street (6)

J. SISTERS
35 West 57th Street between Fifth and Sixth avenues
Tel 212/750-2485
www.jsisters.com

In 1987, seven Brazilian sisters opened a nail salon for "serious" Brazilian-style manicures and pedicures. They have now branched out to provide superb bikini waxing, facials and massage.

⊙ Tue, Fri–Sat 9–5.30, Wed–Thu 9–7.30 🅼 Manicure $45–$55, pedicure $65–$75, facial $60–$90 🆁 57th Street (F), 59th Street/Fifth Avenue (N, R, W) 🚌 M1, M2, M3, M4, M5, M6, M7, M57

JENIETTE
58 East 13th Street between University Place and Broadway
Tel 212/529-1616
www.jeniette.com

Since 1979 this East Village salon has been providing good manicures, pedicures facials and massage at much lower prices than uptown. It uses Dinur products.

⊙ Mon, Wed, Sat 10–7, Tue, Thu–Fri 10–8, Sun 11–6 🅼 Manicure $11–$20, facial $65, massage $75–$170 🆁 14th Street/Union Square (L, N, Q, R, W, 4, 5, 6) 🚌 M1, M5, M6, M14

LE PETIT SPA
140 East 34th Street between Lexington and Third avenues
Tel 212/685-0773
www.lspafumerie.com

This small salon inside the Spafumerie offers a full array of treatments. Fit in a mini facial or body polish when you're in a rush.

⊙ Daily 10–8 🅼 Facial $80–$120, massage $90–$110 🆁 33rd Street (6) 🚌 M98, M101, M102, M103, M34

MARIO BADESCU
320 East 52nd Street between 1st and 2nd avenues
Tel 212/758-1065
www.mariobadescu.com

You might expect Mario Badescu, whose clients include Sharon Stone, Kate Moss and P Diddy, to charge an arm and a leg to treat your hands and your feet, but his

prices are very reasonable and if you want one spa session in New York, book it here.

⊙ Mon–Tue, Fri 8.3–6 (in Jul–Aug and Dec Tue 8.30–8.30), Wed–Thu 8.30–8.30, Fri 8.30–6, Sat 8.30–5, Sun 10–5 🅼 Facial $65, manicure $15, pedicure $25, massage $70 🆁 51st Street (6), Lexington Avenue-53rd Street (E, V)

OASIS DAY SPA
108 East 16th Street near Union Square, 2nd floor
Tel 212/254-7722
www.nydayspa.com

Candlelight and soft music enhance popular spa, offering 15 massage treatments.

⊙ Mon–Fri 10am–10.15pm, Sat–Sun 9am–9.15pm 🅼 Facial $65–$200,

Feel the stress ebb away at Oasis Day Spa

massage $65–$185 🆁 14th Street/Union Square (L, N, Q, R, W, 4, 5, 6) 🚌 M1, M2, M3

PAUL LABRECQUE SALON AND SPA
171 East 65th Street between Lexington and Third avenues
Tel 212/988-7816
www.paullabrecque.com

London-trained Labrecque has coiffed the rich and famous for decades. The ultimate facial at this attractive salon provides five levels of hydration. It also offers sensual body treatments and massage treatments (Thai, Reiki, rolfing, phyto-essence and acupuncture).

⊙ Mon–Fri 8am–9pm, Sat 9–8, Sun 10–8 🅼 Facial $75–$185+, massage $70–$165 🆁 68th Street (6) 🚌 M98, M101, M102, M103

RESCUE BEAUTY LOUNGE
34 Gansevoort Street between Hudson and Greenwich streets, second floor
Tel 212/206-6409
www.rescuebeauty.com

Rescue takes a medical approach to pampering, maintaining hospital standards of cleanliness. This is the place to get the ultimate manicure or pedicure.

⊙ Tue–Fri 11–8, Sat–Sun 10–6 🅼 Manicure $28–$65, pedicure $48–$120, facial $85–$225 🆁 14th Street (A, C, E), Eighth Avenue (L) 🚌 M11, M20

SOHO SANCTUARY
119 Mercer Street near Prince Street
Tel 212/334-5550
www.sohosanctuary.com

This spa and yoga studio achieved a reputation when Julia Roberts made frequent visits. It offers facials, body wraps and massage.

⊙ Tue–Fri 10–9, Sat 10–4, Sun 12–6, Mon 3–9 🅼 Facial $125–$250, massage $125–$210 🆁 Prince Street (N, R, W) 🚌 M1, M6

SPAS IN HOTELS
Many hotels in the city have spas and fitness centers. Below are two of the best.

AFFINIA SPA AND WELLNESS CENTER
Benjamin Hotel, 125 East 50th Street between Lexington and Third avenues, third floor
Tel 212/715-2517
www.affiniaspa.com

Treatments available include aromatherapy massage, reflexology and hydrotherapy.

LA PRAIRIE SPA
Ritz Carlton, 50 Central Park South at Sixth Avenue
Tel 212/521-6135
www.ritzcarlton.com

Treatments include detoxification, shiatsu massage and exfoliation.

WHAT TO DO

CHILDREN'S NEW YORK

With its towering buildings, vibrant streets, sights and sounds, New York is wonderful for kids. Even a ride on the subway is exciting. A few of the family-friendly institutions are listed below. Also check the Sports and Activities section and the Shopping section (especially Niketown and the Disney Store). In addition, many seasonal events appeal to kids—performances of the Big Apple Circus and the *Nutcracker* at Christmas as well as the Radio City Christmas Spectacular; the Ringling Brothers' circus in spring; and the parades and fairs that take place throughout the year. As you research your visit, it's worth calling concert halls and museums in advance to find out what special events will be on while you're in town; reserve ahead for those that interest you.

FILM, TV, THEATER AND MUSIC

BACKSTAGE AT LINCOLN CENTER
Tel 212/875-5350
www.lincolncenter.org

Theater tailor-made for children at the New Victory

These one-hour tours take you backstage to the shops where the sets and costumes are made and to rehearsal rooms and storage areas.
🎦 Daily at 10.30, 12.30, 2.30, 4.30. Reservations recommended 🎟 Adult $13.50, child (under 12) $6 🚇 66th Street (1) 🚌 M5, M7, M104

LITTLE ORCHESTRA SOCIETY
Avery Fisher Hall, Lincoln Center, Broadway and West 65th Street
Tel 212/971-9500
www.littleorchestra.org
This company organizes two family concert series: Happy Concerts (children aged 6 to 12) and the Lollipops (tots

aged 3 to 5) at the Kaye Playhouse at Hunter College.
🎟 From $27–$99 🚇 66th Street (1, 9) 🚌 M5, M7, M104

LOEWS IMAX THEATER
1998 Broadway and 68th Street
Tel 212/336-5020
For some kids, the 3-D IMAX experience is too intense; those who tolerate it are usually enthralled. The screen is eight stories high. Programming changes roughly every two months.
🎟 Varies 🚇 66th Street (1, 9) 🚌 M5, M7, M104

NBC STUDIO TOUR
30 Rockefeller Plaza, 49th Street between Fifth and Sixth avenues
Tel 212/664-7174
www.nbc.com
Take one of the 70-minute tours of the NBC network's studios where *The Today Show* and *Saturday Night Live* are produced. Visitors peek into studios and also see how shows are made. The tour ends in a theater with a demonstration of HD TV.
🎦 Mon–Thu 8.30–4.30, Fri–Sat 9.30–5.30, Sun 9.30–4.30. Reservations recommended 🎟 Adult $18.50, child (6–12) $15.50 (under 6 not admitted) 🚇 47th–50th streets/Rockefeller Center (B, D, F, V) 🚌 M1, M2, M3, M4, M5, M6, M7

NEW VICTORY THEATER
229 West 42nd Street between Broadway and Eighth Avenue
Tel 212/223-3020

www.newvictory.org
The city's first theater designed for family programming is an intimate space and a must. All types of theater take place here. Every show is age rated from 4 to 12-plus, but shows here suit all ages.
🎟 $12.50–$35 🚇 42nd Street/Times Square (N, Q, R, S, W, 1, 2, 3, 7) 🚌 M6, M7

PAPER BAG PLAYERS
225 West 99th Street, between Broadway and Amsterdam
Tel 212/663-0390 or 800/777-2247 (box office)
www.paperbagplayers.org
The members of this beloved troupe make their costumes

Liberty Helicopters offer a view with a difference

and sets out of cardboard and paper bags and perform offbeat plays and revues.
🎦 Phone for details, as they tour regularly 🎟 $10–$30 🚇 68th Street (6) 🚌 M1, M2, M3, M4, M98, M101, M102, M103

TADA THEATER AND DANCE ALLIANCE
15 West 28th Street at Sixth Avenue
Tel 212/252-1619
www.tadatheater.com
Young professionals aged 8 to 17 put on entertaining shows and revues at this theater company-and-school.
🎟 Adult $18, child $8 🚇 23rd Street (F, V) 🚌 M5, M6, M7

THEATREWORKS USA
Lucille Lortel Theatre, 121 Christopher Street between Hudson and Bleecker
Tel 212/647-1100
www.theatreworksusa.org
This group puts on plays and musicals for children based on such favorites as *The Lion, the Witch and the Wardrobe* and *Charlotte's Web.*
🕐 Call for details 💷 $25
🚇 Christopher St–Sheridan Square (1)
🚌 M8, M20

THE "TODAY SHOW"
NBC Studios, Rockefeller Plaza
Kids may enjoy crowding against the barriers for a chance to be seen on nationwide TV. Just show up at dawn at the corner of 49th Street and Rockefeller Plaza.
🕐 Mon–Fri 7–10 💷 Free
🚇 47th–50th streets/Rockefeller Center (B, D, F, V) 🚌 M1, M2, M3, M4

YOUNG PEOPLE'S CONCERTS
Lincoln Center
Tel 212/875-5656 or 212/721-6500
www.newyorkphilharmonic.org or www.lincolncenter.org
Sponsored by the New York Philharmonic, these concerts introduce kids to great artists and great music. Children can attend demonstrations and workshops given by members of the orchestra. There's also a program for teens.
🕐 Four Saturdays during the year
💷 $6–$25 🚇 66th Street (1) 🚌 M5, M7, M104

MUSEUMS AND ATTRACTIONS
AMERICAN MUSEUM OF THE MOVING IMAGE
35th Avenue at 36th Street, Astoria, Queens
Tel 718/784-0077
www.movingimage.us
The permanent exhibit traces the process of making, producing and distributing movies and TV programs. Children enjoy the interactive exhibits and making their own short animations.
🕐 Wed–Thu 11–5, Fri 11–8, Sat–Sun 11–6.30 💷 Adult $10, child (5–18) $5,

under 5 free 🚇 Broadway (N), Steinway Street (R, G) 🚌 Q66, Q101 or Queens Artlink

AMERICAN MUSEUM OF NATURAL HISTORY
▷ 68–72

BROOKLYN MUSEUM OF ART
▷ 153

CHILDREN'S MUSEUM OF MANHATTAN
212 West 83rd Street between Broadway and Amsterdam Avenue
Tel 212/721-1234
www.cmom.org
The Children's Museum of Manhattan was designed to be a first museum experience

Educational fun at the Children's Museum of Manhattan

for kids from 10 months to 10 years old. It has plenty of sensory exhibits, plus a regular schedule of sing-alongs and other wonderful programs.
🕐 Tue–Sun 10–5 💷 Adults and children $9 🚇 86th Street (1), 81st Street (B, C) 🚌 M7, M11, M79, M104

CHILDREN'S MUSEUM OF THE ARTS
182 Lafayette Street between Broome and Grand streets
Tel 212/274-0986
Children aged from 1 to 11 are welcome at this playground-cum-museum, which offers all kinds of hands-on art projects.

🕐 Wed, Fri–Sun 12–5, Thu 12–6
💷 $9, child (under 1) free 🚇 Spring Street (6), Prince Street (N, R) 🚌 M1

CONEY ISLAND
▷ 152

ELLIS ISLAND
▷ 90–93

EMPIRE STATE BUILDING
▷ 94–96

FORBES MAGAZINE GALLERIES
▷ 99

GUGGENHEIM MUSEUM
▷ 110–111

INTREPID SEA, AIR AND SPACE MUSEUM
▷ 101

MADAME TUSSAUD'S
234 West 42nd Street between Eighth and Seventh avenues
Tel 800/246-8872
www.madame-tussauds.com
The New York version of this famous London waxworks museum opened in 2000. It has the usual collection of lifelike figures (here, geared to a New York audience, you'll see such luminaries as Joan Rivers, Woody Allen and Michael Jordan).
🕐 Sun–Thu 10–8, Fri–Sat 10–10
💷 Adult $29, child (4–12) $23, under 4 free 🚇 42nd Street (A, C, E), 42nd Street/Times Square (N, Q, R, S, W, 1, 2, 3, 7) 🚌 M5, M6, M7, M42

METROPOLITAN MUSEUM OF ART
▷ 114–119

MUSEUM OF THE CITY OF NEW YORK
▷ 123

MUSEUM OF COMIC AND CARTOON ART
594 Broadway (4th floor) between Houston and Prince
Tel 212/254-3511
www.moccany.org
Adults seeking to relive their childhoods and older kids who love their super heroes enjoy

coming here. The museum aims to promote the art of telling stories through pictures. Exhibits are dedicated to the works of such seminal figures as Harvey Kurtzman, founder of *MAD* magazine, or are theme-oriented like the recent Infinite Canvas exhibit, which explored the world of web-based comics.

🕐 Fri–Mon 12–5 🎫 $3, under 12 free 🚇 Broadway-Lafayette (B, D, F, V, 6), Prince Street (N, R, W) 🚌 M1, M6

MUSEUM OF MODERN ART
▷ 125

NEW YORK HALL OF SCIENCE
47-01 111th Street at 48th Avenue, Flushing Meadows–Corona Park, Queens
Tel 718/699-0005
www.nyscience.org
This museum was one of the first hands-on science museums in the US. The entire basement is filled with interactive exhibits. Permanent exhibits demonstrate biology, chemistry and physics, and special shows explore such topics as Optical Illusions. There's also a large outdoor science playground.

🕐 Sep–Mar Tue–Thu 9.30–2, Fri 9.30–5, Sat–Sun 10–6; Apr–Jun Mon–Thu 9.30–2, Fri 9.30–5, Sat–Sun 10–6; Jul–Aug and hol weekends Mon–Fri 9.30–5, Sat–Sun 10–6 🎫 Adult $11, child (2–17) $8 (free Sep–Jun Fri 2–5, Sun 10–11) 🚇 111th Street (7) 🚌 Q23, Q48

NEW YORK TRANSIT MUSEUM
Boerum Place and Schermerhorn Street, Brooklyn Heights
Tel 718/694-1600
www.mta.nyc.ny.us/mta/museum
Vintage subway cars and interactive exhibits tell the story of the city's public transportation.

🕐 Tue–Fri 10–4, Sat–Sun noon–5 🎫 Adult $5, child (3–17) $3, under 3 free 🚇 Borough Hall (2, 3, 4, 5), Hoyt Street (A, C, G), Jay Street (F)

PALEY CENTER FOR MEDIA
▷ 126

SONY WONDER TECHNOLOGY LAB
Sony Plaza, East 56th Street between Madison and Fifth avenues
Tel 212/833-8100
www.sonywondertechlab.com
Interactive exhibits on four floors here demonstrate the latest in communications, robotics, medical technology and entertainment. It's not as much of a hard sell as you might expect. Reservations are needed and can be made two weeks in advance.

🕐 Tue–Sat 10–5, Sun noon–5 🎫 Free 🚇 Fifth Avenue/53rd Street (E, V), Fifth Avenue/59th Street (N, R, W) 🚌 M1, M2, M3, M4

The New York Transit Museum is perfect for would-be drivers

SOUTH STREET SEAPORT MUSEUM AND MARKET-PLACE
▷ 134–135

STATUE OF LIBERTY
▷ 136–137

TIMES SQUARE
▷ 138–140

PARKS AND GARDENS
BROOKLYN BOTANIC GARDEN
▷ 152

CENTRAL PARK
▷ 78–83

NEW YORK BOTANICAL GARDEN
Kazimiroff (Southern) Boulevard at 200th Street, Bronx
Tel 718/817-8700
www.nybg.org
This lovely retreat with 250 acres (101ha) has two special areas for kids—the 8-acre (3-ha) Adventure Garden, and the Family Garden. The conservatory is beautiful and so are the many specialty gardens.

🕐 Tue–Sun 10–6 🎫 Prices vary with exhibitions. Grounds only adults $6, child (2–12) $1 🚇 Bedford Park Boulevard (B, D, 4) then walk, or take Bx 26 bus 🚌 Bx 19, Bx 26 🚉 Botanical Garden Station (Metro North)

WAVE HILL
675 West 249th Street at Independence Avenue, Bronx
Tel 718-549-3200
www.wavehill.org
The setting of this park in the toney Riverdale section of the Bronx is spectacular. So are the beautiful gardens and greenhouses. On weekends, there's often a Family Art Project scheduled.

🕐 Tue–Sun 9–5.30 (Oct 15–Apr 14 until 4.30) 🎫 Adult $6, child $2, under 6 free (free Tue and mornings on Sat) 🚇 231st Street (1, 9), then Bx 7 or Bx 10 🚌 Bx 7, Bx 10 🚉 Riverdale (Metro North, tel 212/532-4900)

TOY STORE
FAO SCHWARZ
767 Fifth Avenue between 58th and 59th streets
Tel 212/644-9400
www.fao.com
This is the toy store to end all toy stores. It's a fantasyland for kids and adults alike, with departments dedicated to everything from antique and classic toys to magic sets.

🕐 Mon–Wed 10–7, Thu–Sat 10–8, Sun 11–6 🚇 Fifth Avenue/59th Street (N, R, W) 🚌 M1, M2, M3, M4

WHAT TO DO

TRIPS AND TOURS

CIRCLE LINE CRUISES

Pier 83, West 42nd Street and Hudson
River
Tel 212/563-3200
www.circleline42.com
Circling around Manhattan in a
boat is the best way to grasp
the contours of the island and
the extraordinary city piled high
upon it. Depending on the
attention span of your kids, you
can opt for the two-hour
afternoon trip or the three-hour
version. The narration can be
great or mediocre, but the fresh
air, the passing craft and the
sights make it fun. The same
company also runs day-long
tours up the Hudson River.
🕐 Call for departure times and schedules. Operates Thu–Mon only in winter
💲 $12–$29.30 plus $1 fuel surcharge
🚇 42nd Street (A, C, E) then M42
🚌 M42, M50

LIBERTY HELICOPTERS

West 30th Street and Twelfth Avenue
Tel 212/967-6464
www.libertyhelicopters.com
Helicopters take off from the
heliport on tours from 2 to 17
minutes hovering above the
city and the Hudson River. If
you can afford it, why not?
💲 $69 (5 min), $119 (10 min), $186
(15 min) 🚇 34th Street (A, C, E)
🚌 M11, M34

MADISON SQUARE GARDEN

4 Penn Plaza, Seventh Avenue between
West 31st and 34th streets
Tel 212/465-5800 (tours) or 212/465-
6741 (information)
www.thegarden.com
One-hour tours go to the locker
rooms, the luxury boxes and the
sports bar and restaurant of this
vast 20,000-seat arena, home
to the Knicks and Liberty
basketball teams and to the
Rangers hockey team. Or just
see a game or special event.
The Westminster Dog Show and
the Westminster Cat Show are
sure-fire hits.
🕐 Daily 11–3 💲 Adult $17, child
(2–12) $12, under 2 free 🚇 34th Street
(A, C, E), 34th Street/Penn Station (1, 2,
3) 🚌 M10, M20, M34

ROOSEVELT ISLAND TRAM

Second Avenue at 60th Street
Tel 212/832-4555
www.rioc.com
Kids who have never ridden a
cable-car at a ski resort will get
a kick out of this aerial
tramway trip across the East
River and back.
🕐 Sun–Thu 6am–2am, Fri–Sat
6am–3.30am 💲 $2
🚇 59th Street (4, 5, 6) 🚌 M15, M57

STATEN ISLAND FERRY

Whitehall Terminal, 1 Whitehall Street
Tel 718/727-2508 or 718/815-2628
www.siferery.com
The view from the decks of the
harbor, the Statue of Liberty
and the Lower Manhattan

*Spectacular views from the
Staten Island ferry*

skyline is stunning—and free.
🕐 Daily 💲 Free 🚇 South Ferry
(1), Whitehall Street (N, R, W) 🚌 M1,
M6, M15

YANKEE STADIUM
▷ 158

WILDLIFE ATTRACTIONS

BRONX ZOO
▷ 157

CENTRAL PARK ZOO

Fifth Avenue and 64th Street
Tel 212/439-6500
www.wcs.org
A perfectly sized zoo for kids,
this Manhattan classic is
populated by youngsters'
favorites—sea lions, polar

bears, monkeys, pandas,
penguins and tropical birds.
The Tisch Children's Zoo is
great for little ones, with fish,
birds and llamas, pigs and
other domestic animals.
🕐 Daily 10–5 (Sat, Sun and holidays
until 5.30) 💲 Adult $8, child (3–12) $3,
under 3 free 🚇 Fifth Avenue (N, R),
68th Street (6) 🚌 M1, M2, M3, M4

NEW YORK AQUARIUM

Surf Avenue and West 8th Street, Coney
Island, Brooklyn
Tel 718-265-3400
www.nyaquarium.com
There are daily dolphin and
sea lion shows in summer at
this small park, which also
houses penguins, walruses,
Beluga whales, sharks and
seals—300 species in all. Most
exhibits are outside. In the
Discovery Center kids can pick
up starfish, crabs and other
small sea creatures.
🕐 Memorial Day–Labor Day, Mon–Fri
10–6, Sat–Sun 10–7; Apr–Memorial Day
and Labor Day–Oct 31 Mon–Fri 10–5,
Sat–Sun 10–5.30; Nov–Mar daily
10–4.30 💲 Adult $12, child (2–12) $8,
under 2 free 🚇 Stillwell Avenue (D),
8th Street (F, Q) 🚌 From Manhattan,
call 718/330-1234

CONCERTS FOR KIDS

The following venues offer
musical and performing
arts series or single
performances for families
at various times of year:
Brooklyn Center for the
Performing Arts at Brooklyn
College (tel 718-951-4500,
www.brooklyncenter.com);
Carnegie Hall, Seventh
Avenue and 57th Street
(tel 212/247-7800,
www.carnegiehall.org);
Metropolitan Opera, Lincoln
Center (tel 212/769-7008,
www.lincolncenter.org);
Jazz at Lincoln Center
(tel 212/258-9800,
www.jalc.org); Chamber
Music Society, Lincoln
Center (tel 212/875-5788, www.
chambermusicsociety.org).

FESTIVALS AND EVENTS

Note that the Convention & Visitors Bureau often has information about these events. Call 212/484-1222 or check www.nycvisit.com. Other useful websites are www.nyc.com and www.nyctourist.com.

JANUARY

NEW YORK ARMORY ANTIQUES SHOW

The city's most prestigious antiques fair in the Seventh Regiment Armory.
☎ 212/472-1180 (during show only); 212/484-1222
www.itinerantantiquesshow.com

FEBRUARY

CHINESE NEW YEAR

Depends on the lunar calendar
Firecrackers blast and dragon and lion dancers sashay through

Independence Day sees a spectacular firework display

the streets of Chinatown.
☎ 212/484-1222
www.chinatown-online.com

WESTMINSTER KENNEL DOG SHOW

Dates vary
About 2,500 canines strut their stuff at Madison Square Garden.
☎ 212/213-3165
www.westminsterkennelclub.org

MARCH

ST PATRICK'S DAY PARADE

March 17
Bagpipers and bands, politicians and New York's finest march down Fifth

Avenue from 86th to 44th streets celebrating the patron saint of Ireland.
☎ 212/484-1222
www.saintpatricksdayparade.com

MARCH–APRIL

EASTER PARADE

Depending on when Easter falls
People with a bent for fashion stroll down Fifth Avenue between 49th and 57th streets showing off their often wacky and wonderful hats.

NEW YORK INTERNATIONAL AUTO SHOW

Late March/early April
Heaven for car enthusiasts.
Jacob Javits Convention Center
☎ 800/282-3336
www.autoshowny.com, www.javitscenter.com

APRIL

MACY'S FLOWER SHOW

Last two weeks
More than 30,000 varieties of flower are arrayed in the store in celebration of spring.
☎ 212/494-4495

CHERRY BLOSSOM FESTIVAL

Late April, depending on when trees flower
A range of traditional Japanese activities and performances take place against a backdrop of gorgeous pink cherry blossoms in the Brooklyn Botanic Garden.
☎ 718/623-7200
www.bbg.org

MAY

NINTH AVENUE INTERNATIONAL FOOD FESTIVAL

Second or third weekend
Between 37th and 57th streets, Ninth Avenue is lined with

stands selling food of all kinds. Musical entertainment, too.
☎ 212/484-1222

FLEET WEEK

Third week
The tall ships and aircraft carriers sail in a majestic parade into New York Harbor and up the Hudson River. The festival includes military demonstrations, tugs of war and cooking fests, and culminates in a Memorial Day celebration. The best part is the posses of sailors roaming New York City streets in their crisp white uniforms.
☎ 212/245-0072
www.fleetweek.com

Macy's Flower Show is a riot of color

WASHINGTON SQUARE

Outdoor Art Exhibit Memorial Day weekend
The streets around Washington Square are lined with artists, photographers and craftspeople selling their work.
☎ 212/982-6255
www.nycgv.com

JUNE

BELMONT STAKES

First weekend in June
The last leg of the Triple Crown is run at Belmont on Long Island.
☎ 516/488-6000
www.nyra.com

PUERTO RICAN DAY PARADE

Second weekend in June

The city is awash with Puerto Rican flags.

☎ 718/401-0404

www.nationalpuertoricandayparade.org

LESBIAN AND GAY PRIDE PARADE

Last Sunday in June

The flamboyant parade from 52nd Street to Greenwich Village, via Fifth Avenue, is the culmination of a week of gay-oriented celebrations.

☎ 212/807-7433

www.nycpride.org

JULY

INDEPENDENCE DAY HARBOR FESTIVAL AND FIREWORKS

July 4

New York City celebrates the nation's birth with a festival in Lower Manhattan and some spectacular fireworks launched from barges on the East River.

☎ 212/484-1222

AUGUST

HARLEM WEEK

Most of August

A host of Harlem events—film, jazz and food festivals among them—start mid-July and the "week" runs into September.

☎ 212/862-8477 or 212/484-1222

www.harlemdiscover.com

LINCOLN CENTER OUT-OF-DOORS FESTIVAL

Over 100 free performances on the plazas at Lincoln Center, including music, dance, theatricals and more.

212/546-2656

www.lincolncenter.org

SEPTEMBER

WEST INDIAN PARADE AND CARNIVAL

Labor Day

Thousands flock to Brooklyn to see the dancers and bands sashaying along to reggae, soca and calypso. Caribbean food adds to the festivities.

☎ 212/484-1222

www.carnaval.com

FEAST OF SAN GENNARO

Eleven days in mid-September

The patron saint of Naples is paraded down Mulberry Street at this fiesta, with all kinds of Italian food and street entertainment.

☎ 212/226-6427

www.sangennaro.org

NEW YORK FILM FESTIVAL

17 days in late September or early October

The Film Society of Lincoln Center organizes this major film festival. The hub is the Walter Reade Theatre.

☎ 212/875-5600

www.filmlinc.com

Harlem Week runs throughout August

OCTOBER

BLESSING OF THE ANIMALS

First Sunday

At churches throughout the city, animals are blessed on St. Francis Day. The biggest event takes place at the Cathedral of St. John the Divine. People bring their pets.

☎ 212/316-7490

www.stjohndivine.org

HALLOWEEN PARADE

What started as an impromptu procession of drag queens in Greenwich Village has become a huge event with big-name sponsors. The costumes are amazing, but line up early to get a glimpse.

☎ 212/484-1222

www.halloween-nyc.com

NOVEMBER

NEW YORK CITY MARATHON

First weekend

Thousands of runners thunder across the Queensborough Bridge into Manhattan and race for the finish in Central Park.

☎ 212/860-4455

www.nyrrc.org

MACY'S THANKSGIVING DAY PARADE

Last Thursday

Families line the route from 77th Street and Central Park West to Herald Square to see the immense helium balloons.

☎ 212/484-1222

DECEMBER

LIGHTING OF THE CHRISTMAS TREE

Usually the first week in December

It's a media event, usually starring popular singers. Stake out your place early—or avoid the area altogether because crowds make it impossible to get through.

Rockefeller Center

☎ 212/332-6868

www.rockefellercenter.com

RADIO CITY SPECTACULAR

Through December 30

Busloads of revelers come to the city to see the Rockettes kick up a storm in their stylish chorus line for this seasonal show, which always includes a Parade of the Wooden Soldiers.

☎ 212/247-4777

www.radiocity.com

NEW YEAR'S EVE CELEBRATION

December 31

Times Square fills with thousands of partyers who show up to watch the ball drop announcing the official start of the next year.

WHAT TO DO

New York is best explored on foot and this section describes 10 walks that take in the most interesting parts of the city. The locations of the walks are marked on the map on the inside front cover of the book.

These pages also give suggestions for excursions outside the city center.

Out and About

42ND STREET TO THE UN HEADQUARTERS

This walk along 42nd Street is architecturally fascinating, taking you past some of the finest buildings in the city, including nine designated landmarks. It's a great stroll for families. Times Square is exciting, surprising and lots of fun, with its flashing billboards, electronic news and stock tickers, theater marquees and posters. The walk ends at the United Nations complex in a quiet, peaceful spot alongside the East River.

THE WALK

Distance: 1.5 miles (2.4km)
Allow: 2 hours
Start at 42nd Street/Port Authority subway
End at United Nations Building, 46th Street and First Avenue

HOW TO GET THERE

Subway: A
Bus: M15, M27, M42, M50

Leave the 42nd Street/Port Authority subway station and turn right, then proceed to the corner of West 42nd Street and Eighth Avenue.

❶ Times Square and 42nd Street are famous today for their theaters, giant neon advertisements and megastores. Look back toward Ninth Avenue and you will catch a glimpse of an older side of the area: Holy Cross Church, one of its oldest buildings, dates from 1887.

Face east toward Seventh Avenue and you'll see the gleaming spire of the Chrysler Building in the distance. Walk east toward it, passing the AMC 25-screen multiplex, formerly the Empire Theater, on your right. Next door is Madame Tussaud's and next to that the Candler Building.

❷ The Candler Building was named for a salesman for the Coca-Cola Company, which built this white terracotta tower in 1914. Two doors farther east is the New Amsterdam Theater, lavishly restored by the Walt Disney Company with an out-standing art nouveau foyer.

To see the building directly opposite, the New Victory Theater, you will need to cross this very busy street. So continue east to the traffic lights and use the cross-walk. The New Victory Theater, once known as Minsky's, was built in 1899 by Oscar Hammerstein I.

Restoration in 1995 has retained the beautiful old-fashioned interior. Continue east along West 42nd Street on this side of the street. Two doors east of the New Victory is the Reuters Building, and just east of that, Times Square (▷ 138–140), the triangle created by 42nd Street, Seventh Avenue and Broadway.

❸ The 25-story tower at No. 1 Times Square became the home of the *New York Times* on December 31, 1904; the inaugural fireworks display was almost outshone by the illuminated globe lowered from the roof to herald the New Year. Almost 100 years later, the globe is still lowered every New Year's Eve, and for many New Yorkers and visitors Times Square is still the place to celebrate the holiday. The tower now functions as an office block.

On the southeast corner of West 42nd Street and Broadway, on the right, is the former Knickerbocker Hotel, commissioned by Colonel John Jacob Astor. The songwriter George M. Cohan lived here for a time. Now condominiums, there is talk of returning it to its original use.

Continue east along 42nd Street, crossing Broadway and Sixth Avenue (now officially known as Avenue of the Americas).

❹ The flashy glass building leaning away from traffic on the north side of 42nd Street, 41 West 42nd Street, is the W. R. Grace Building, built in 1974 by architects Skidmore, Owings and Merrill.

Cross to the south side of the street and Bryant Park. Bryant Park sits on top of the subterranean stacks of the New York Public Library. During the World's Fair of 1853, the first to be held on United States soil, the park was the site of the Crystal Palace. To reach the library, continue east along 42nd Street to Fifth Avenue. The library rises ahead of you on the southwest corner of 42nd Street and Fifth Avenue.

❺ The majestic Beaux Arts New York Public Library (▷ 127) is guarded by two stone lions, Patience and Fortitude, who sit at the base of an imposing front stairway. Inside the building, the marble entrance area on the ground floor and the usually packed second-floor Main Reading Room are well worth a look.

Return to 42nd Street and continue along east, crossing Madison Avenue. On your left at Park Avenue is Grand Central Terminal. Cross the street and plunge in.

❻ Inside Grand Central Terminal (▷ 102–104), the ceiling in the Main Concourse, decorated with the constellations of the zodiac, and the Dining Concourse downstairs, are a treat.

Back on 42nd Street, continue east to Lexington Avenue and the Chanin Building (on the southwest corner). Named for the brothers who developed the Times Square Theater District, the building has an art deco bas-relief on the facade, the work of Edward Trumbull. Continue to the northwest corner for the Chrysler Building.

❼ The Chrysler Building (▷ 85) is one of the world's great 20th-century buildings— completed in 1929. Around the 30th floor a brick frieze depicts hubcaps and there are 9ft (3m)-high pineapples and giant stainless-steel radiator caps. The art deco foyer is made of African marble and chrome.

OUT AND ABOUT

Neon signs in Times Square

The magnificent Chrysler Building (above); flags from all over the world fly outside the United Nations Building (above right)

Continue to 220 East 42nd Street and you'll come to the Daily News Building.

8 The Daily News Building (▷ 87) was until 1995 the home of America's first tabloid newspaper.

Cross Second Avenue and continue on 42nd Street until you come to an area with steps on both sides of the street. These lead to the charming Tudor City apartments. From the top of the steps there's a splendid view of the United Nations Building, the East River and, beyond it, the borough of Queens. Turn left onto Tudor City Place, then right onto 43rd Street. Here, steps

lead down to Ralph Bunche Park. Cross United Nations Plaza (as First Avenue is called here) and turn left.

9 At the United Nations Headquarters (▷ 144), view the General Assembly lobby (foyer) and stroll through the gardens. The entrance to the complex is on 46th Street. John D. Rockefeller, Jr. donated the $8.5 million needed for the site.

WHEN TO GO
Crowds will not be out in full force if you begin your walk on a weekday morning before 10. If you wish to visit the United Nations Building at the end of

the walk, arrive early—the last tour begins at 4.45pm.

WHERE TO EAT
The Dining Concourse at Grand Central Terminal, 42nd Street at Park Avenue, is just the place to refuel; for variety at affordable prices, it can't be beaten. The Oyster Bar & Restaurant (tel 212/490-6650), on the same level, offers excellent seafood, but at higher prices.

PLACES TO VISIT
Madame Tussaud's Wax Museum
✉ 234 West 42nd Street
☎ 212/512-9600 or 800/246-8872
🕐 Sun–Thu 10–8, Fri–Sat 10–10
🎟 Adults $29, child (4–12) $23

OUT AND ABOUT

NORTHEAST CORNER OF CENTRAL PARK TO GRANT'S TOMB

This northeast corner of Central Park boasts beautiful gardens, commissioned by parks commissioner Robert Moses in 1936. You will also find a pretty pond, meandering paths, woods and picturesque waterfalls. Just outside the park is the largest church in the United States, the Cathedral Church of St. John the Divine. Nearby is Grant's Tomb, where the great Civil War general Ulysses S. Grant lies in rest.

THE WALK

Distance:	2 miles (3.2km)
Allow:	2 hours
Start at	Fifth Avenue and 105th Street
End at	122nd Street and Riverside Drive

HOW TO GET THERE

Bus: M4 to Madison Avenue and 104th Street; walk one block west to Fifth Avenue

Leave Madison Avenue by turning left onto East 105th Street, and walk one block west to the entrance gate of the Conservatory Garden, across the street from El Museo del Barrio (▷ 87) on Fifth Avenue.

❶ The Conservatory Garden—actually a complex of gardens — is at its best in July and August. As you enter, go straight toward the Classical fountain in the area known as the Italian Garden. Walk to your left to tour the maze-like English Garden. To the right of the Italian Garden is the lovely French Garden, with the charming Untermeyer Fountain (also called "Three Dancing Maidens"). Go past this fountain and the walk through the gate toward the pond on your right, whose Dutch name, Harlem Meer, means "little sea."

Skirt around the pond, keeping to the right, with the pond on your left.

❷ The Charles A. Dana Discovery Center, halfway around the pond, displays natural history exhibits in a Victorian-style building.

Continue around the pond and keep to the right of the Lasker Pool and ice-skating rink. Take the path up some steps, then down a few steps, then to the right and walk under the Huddlestone Arch. Still keeping right, with a pretty little waterfall on your left, walk about 300 yards (273m), and you'll come to a very small rustic wooden bridge on your left. Cross the bridge, keeping to the right and you'll come to the Glenspan Arch. There's a small waterfall beyond the arch and a small pool is just beyond that. Ahead of you, a couple of paths lead to Central Park West, which you can see. The path to the right takes you out to 103rd Street and Central Park West.

On Central Park West, leave the park, turn right and follow the busy street, past Strangers Gate on the right, to Frederick Douglass Circle. Cross Central Park West at

110th Street and continue left around the circle until you come to the traffic lights. Cross 110th Street and immediately turn left. You are now in Harlem. Continue west on 110th Street for two blocks to Amsterdam Avenue, passing the entrance to Morningside Park. Turn right and walk north to 111th Street and the Cathedral Church of St. John the Divine.

❸ The enormous Cathedral Church of St. John the Divine (▷ 67) is well worth exploring. The Peace Fountain in the Children's Sculpture Garden depicts a bronze Michael the Archangel slaying the devil.

Leaving the cathedral, cross to the west side of Amsterdam Avenue and follow 112th Street west one block to Broadway. Tom's Restaurant, familiar to fans of the TV show "Seinfeld," is on the right. If you are tired and do not want to continue, catch a bus on the west side of Broadway or take the M4 to Midtown East or the M104 to Midtown West. To continue the walk, go north up Broadway to 122nd Street, passing Columbia University (▷ 77), New York City's oldest institution of higher learning, on your right. Turn left onto 122nd Street and walk two blocks west, passing the Manhattan School of Music on your left, to Riverside Drive. Riverside Church is on your left.

❹ From its 392ft (119m) tower, Riverside Church (▷ 126) offers a magnificent view across the Hudson River.

❺ Nearby is the General Grant National Memorial (▷ 99), where Grant and his wife, Julia,

The "Three Dancing Maidens" Fountain in the French Garden, part of the Conservatory Garden

OUT AND ABOUT

The map shows a walking route from the Northeast Corner of Central Park to Grant's Tomb, with the following numbered stops:

1. Conservatory Garden
2. Charles A Dana Discovery Center
3. Cathedral Church of St John the Divine
4. Riverside Church
5. General Grant National Memorial

Locations marked include: Hudson River, Riverside Church, General Grant National Memorial, Columbia University, 116th Street Columbia University, Morningside Park, Cathedral Church of St John the Divine, Frederick Douglas Circle, 110th Street Cathedral Parkway, 110th Street (Central Park North), 103rd Street, The Pool, The Loch, Central Park, Harlem Meer, Lasker Pool & Rink, Frawley Circle, El Museo del Barrio, Museum of the City of New York

0 — 200 m
0 — 200 yds

Cathedral of St. John the Divine (top); Columbia University is one of the most prestigious colleges in the US (above)

rest side by side in two black sarcophagi. The Gaudí-style mosaic benches and tables surrounding the tombs are a good spot for a picnic.

From here you can walk back to Broadway and get the M4 or M104 bus downtown.

WHEN TO GO

Do this walk when the weather is pleasant and you want to have a quiet stroll away from crowds. Although the park is generally safe by day and is patroled, this is not a walk to do alone. Pack a picnic to enjoy along the way.

WHERE TO EAT

Tom's Restaurant, 2880 |Broadway at 112th Street (tel 212/ 864-6137).

PLACES TO VISIT

General Grant National Memorial
✉ Riverside Drive at West 122nd Street
☎ 212/666-1640
🕐 Daily 9–5

Riverside Church
✉ 490 Riverside Drive
☎ 212/870-6700
🕐 Daily 7am–10pm, Claremont Avenue entrance

The tranquil waterfall at Glenspan Arch (above right); the facade of Ulysses S. Grant's majestic tomb

OUT AND ABOUT

GREENWICH VILLAGE: IFC CENTER TO WASHINGTON SQUARE

Some of the country's finest literature and most radical ideas have developed in the area covered by this stroll. From the revolutionary Thomas Paine, who decried taxation without representation in colonial times, to the Stonewall rioters, whose protests sparked the gay liberation movement beginning in 1969, Village people have long been at the forefront of liberalism in America.

THE WALK

Distance: 1.9 miles (3km)

Allow: 2 hours

Start/End at West 4th Street/ Washington Square subway station

HOW TO GET THERE

Subway: A, C, E, F trains

Bus: M5, M6

Leave the subway on Avenue of the Americas (6th Avenue), cross the avenue at West 4th Street and position yourself in front of the IFC Center. Turn to your left (as you face the theater) and head along the avenue to Carmine Street. Turn right.

1 Along Carmine Street you pass first the Unoppressive, Non-Imperialist Bargain Books store on the left and then the House of Oldies Rare Records (on the right), both worth a browse.

Continue to Seventh Avenue South, cross it, and turn right. At St. Luke's Place (also called Leroy Street), go left. On your left you will pass J. J. Walker Park, once a graveyard, which locals claim is the resting place of the lost son of Louis XVI and Marie Antoinette. The brick and brownstone houses along this street date from the 1850s. Theodore Dreiser wrote *An American Tragedy* while he was living at No. 16. At Hudson Street, turn right, and walk two blocks to Barrow Street where you turn left.

2 On Barrow Street, take a look at the pretty garden behind the Church of St. Luke-in-the-Fields, built in 1822. The gate is on your right just before you reach Greenwich Street.

Backtrack along Barrow Street to Hudson Street, and stop for a snack or light lunch at the popular Belgian café, Petite

Abeille. Go across Hudson Street to 81 Barrow Street, where a plaque gives some architectural history of the area. Continue heading east on Barrow, then turn right onto Commerce Street. To the right at the bend in Commerce Street is the Cherry Lane Theater.

3 Cherry Lane Theater, an Off-Broadway venue, was founded in 1924 by the Pulitzer Prize-winning poet Edna St. Vincent Millay. Samuel Beckett's *Waiting for Godot* and *Endgame* both premiered here, as have plays by Edward Albee, David Mamet and many others.

Continue east on Commerce Street for one block and then turn right on Bedford Street. Notice the first two houses on your right.

4 The Isaacs-Hendricks House, 77 Bedford Street, is the oldest in the West Village. The narrowest house in the city is at No. 75, which was home to Edna St. Vincent Millay in 1923–24. The actor Cary Grant also lived here when he was young.

Return along Bedford Street, past Chumley's, a famous speakeasy, which put in an appearance in Warren Beatty's *Reds* and Woody Allen's *Sweet and Lowdown*. John Steinbeck, Eugene O'Neill, e e cummings and F. Scott Fitzgerald are among past patrons whose book jackets hang on the walls. It's great for drinks or dinner. When you reach Grove Street, turn left.

5 The pretty, leafy Grove Court, 10–12 Grove Street, was once dubbed "Ale Alley" because of the original Irish tenants' fondness for a brew.

Return to the corner of Grove and Bedford streets. The oldest

wooden house in the Village stands at 17 Grove Street. Continue one block roughly north on Bedford Street to Christopher Street, and turn right.

6 The long-established McNulty's Rare Teas and Choice Coffee Shop is at 109 Christopher Street, and from its looks it hasn't changed much since it opened in 1895. Go in and enjoy the aroma.

Continue east on Christopher Street and cross Seventh Avenue South.

7 Tiny Christopher Park, which was part of a tobacco farm from 1633 to 1638, is to your right. Stop for a rest on the bench next to George Segal's sculpture *Gay Liberation*, then look behind you at the Stonewall Bar and Club, where gay resistance to police arrests provoked the Stonewall Riot in 1969, the start of the gay rights movement. There's a modest plaque on the building. Christopher Street is also called Stonewall Place from the park up to Greenwich Avenue.

Walk along the Stonewall side of Christopher Street to Greenwich Avenue, and turn left. Go north one block, turn right onto West 10th Street and you'll come to Patchin Place; No. 4 was famously the home of e e cummings. Continue on West 10th Street one block east.

8 The ornate landmark Jefferson Market Library, at 425 Sixth Avenue, is a former courthouse built in 1877. The tower originally served as a fire-watching lookout.

Continue on West 10th Street, crossing Avenue of the Americas, until you come to Fifth Avenue.

OUT AND ABOUT

St. Luke's Place (left); Grove Court (above); George Segal's Gay Liberation *statue (right)*

Rare records to be explored on Carmine Street, Greenwich Village

Turn right and walk four blocks south on Fifth, through Washington Memorial Arch.

9 The original wooden arch was erected in 1889, in honor of George Washington 100 years after his inauguration. The marble Stanford White arch you see now was erected in 1895. The residential Washington Mews, on the east side of Fifth Avenue just north of the arch, were originally built as carriage houses for the wealthy residents of the fine town houses on Washington Square Park south of the arch. In the mews, John Dos Passos lived at No. 14A and Sherwood Anderson at No. 54. Washington Square Park, the focus of Greenwich Village, was once a potter's field and was the site of public executions until the 1800s.

Walk straight through the park to Washington Square South and turn right. This becomes West 4th Street, and ahead are the entrances to the subway on Avenue of the Americas.

WHEN TO GO

If you want to visit shops along the way, it is best to do this walk between 10 and 5 Monday to Saturday.

WHERE TO EAT

Petite Abeille, 466 Hudson Street (tel 212/741-6479, open 24 hours).
Chumley's, 86 Bedford Street (tel 212/675-4449).

SOHO'S PUCK BUILDING TO THE SOHO GRAND HOTEL

If you enjoy gallery-hopping or architecture, put this walk at the top of your list. SoHo, *S*outh of *Ho*uston (pronounced *how-stun*), a landmark district famous for the prefabricated cast-iron facades of its buildings, is full of galleries where some of the city's most interesting contemporary artists show their work.

THE WALK

Distance:	2 miles (3.2km)
Allow:	1.5 to 2 hours
Start at	Broadway/Lafayette subway station
End at	Canal Street subway station

HOW TO GET THERE

Subway:	F and downtown 6
Bus:	M6

Leave the Broadway/Lafayette Street subway and turn right (south) on Lafayette.

❶ The restored Puck Building is at 295 Lafayette Street. Don't miss the statue of Puck, decorated with gold leaf, above the door. Here the satirical magazine *Puck* was published, in German (1876–96) and in English (1877–1918). A plaque on the Houston Street side of the building relates its history. With its complex brickwork, the building was instantly revered as a prime example of New York commercial design.

Continue south along Lafayette, and turn right on Prince Street, then left on Broadway.

❷ The Little Singer Building at 561 Broadway was designed by Ernest Flagg. It was very avant-garde in 1904 with its curled steel, recessed glass and textured terracotta. It suggested the next great architectural step: replacing cast-iron floor supports with steel–the basis of the modern skyscraper.

Walk two blocks south to the corner of Broadway and Broome. Look across Broadway to the northeast corner of Broome and Broadway.

❸ The Haughwout Building, dating from 1857, is SoHo's oldest cast-iron beauty. Cast-iron facades were ornate, stylish, cheap, easy to assemble

and recyclable. The Haughwout Building architect based the facade on a window arch from a Venice library, repeating it 92 times. The first Otis elevator was installed here, inaugurating an era of ever-higher buildings.

Turn right onto Broome Street and right again onto Mercer Street. Go north on Mercer.

❹ Stop for drinks at Bar 89, two doors down–and make sure you check out the now-you-see-through-them-now-you-don't doors on the toilet facilities on the mezzanine.

Continue to Prince Street and turn left (west), then go left again onto Greene Street, where there are more cast-iron buildings.

❺ Many of these structures started out as warehouses. By 1962, a lot of them had been abandoned, and there were plans to raze the neighborhood in order to accommodate a highway, but the area was saved from demolition when residents protested. Rents were low here at the time so many artists, attracted to the huge, light-filled spaces, set up their homes and studios here; by the 1970s, artists had

almost completely taken over. Landmark designation for the neighborhood came in 1973. As you walk south on Greene Street, watch for Nos. 72–76, known as the King of Greene Street, with cast-iron Corinthian columns, and Nos. 28–30, the Queen of Greene Street, with a Second Empire roof.

Return along Greene to Grand Street and turn right. Walk one block west to Wooster Street and turn right. On the corner of Broome and Wooster streets, a shop called Vintage New York has more than 200 wines for you to sample, all from New York State.

❻ On Wooster Street, the Peter Blum Gallery at No. 99 is worth a visit. Exhibiting artists here work in a variety of media, with paintings, drawings, sculptures, photographs and cartoons on display. Nearby at No. 18 is the fashionable Deitch Projects in a huge loft. At No. 141, the innovative New York Earth Room exhibits great mounds of earth.

When you reach West Houston Street, turn left and walk one block west to West Broadway, where you turn left again and walk south all the way down to Canal Street.

❼ Just north of Canal Street is the SoHo Grand Hotel. Have a look at the postmodern industrial interiors, then join the hip crowds at the bar.

Continue south on West Broadway, and turn right at Canal Street. You'll see the Canal Street station for A, C and E subway lines two blocks along and, two blocks beyond that, the 1 and 2 subway stations.

The gold Puck statue outside the building of the same name

OUT AND ABOUT

Cast-iron buildings on
Greene Street (above); the
Little Singer Building (right)

WHEN TO GO

To make the most of this walk,
go when the art galleries are
open, generally Tuesday to
Sunday from 10 to 6.

WHERE TO EAT

Bar 89, 89 Mercer Street
(tel 212/274-0989).

PLACES TO VISIT

New York Earth Room

✉ 141 Wooster Street

☎ 212/473-8072

🕐 Wed–Sun noon–3, 3.30–6

💲 Free

Take some time to people-watch
at a café in SoHo (left);
West Broadway is a typical
SoHo thoroughfare (above)

BOWLING GREEN TO SCHERMERHORN ROW

New York City began here in the 17th century, so if you are interested in the city's history, this is the walk for you. From Bowling Green to South Street Seaport, this area encompasses some of the city's greatest treasures.

THE WALK

Distance:	2.5 miles (4km)
Allow:	2 to 2.5 hours
Start at	Bowling Green subway station
End at	Fulton Street subway station (A, 2, 3)

HOW TO GET THERE

Subway:	4, 5
Bus:	M6

Leave Bowling Green station, and you'll see Battery Park ahead of you. Taking the path to the right, walk toward Castle Clinton.

❶ Castle Clinton (tel 212/ 344-7220, Mon–Sun 8.30–5) was the immigrant clearing center before Ellis Island. You'll pass a temporary memorial to the victims of the World Trade Center, *The Sphere*, a sculpture which once stood between the towers as a symbol of world peace and is now a symbol of hope. In 1850, P. T. Barnum brought Europe's greatest soprano, Jenny Lind, to Castle Clinton, securing international stardom for both "the Swedish nightingale" and for himself as her promoter. Inside the gate to your right, a small museum displays dioramas depicting the castle's various uses from fort and entertainment center to ticket office for boat trips to the Statue of Liberty (▷ 136–137) and Ellis Island Immigration Museum (▷ 90–93).

Leave through the gate straight ahead and walk to your right, keeping to the path as it veers left past Slip 6.

❷ In the water, just beyond Slip 6, is the site of the *American Merchant Mariners Memorial*, a sculpture of a sinking ship by Marisol, dedicated to all merchant mariners

who have served the United States from the Revolutionary War to the present day.

Turn back and walk east past the ferries to Slip 3. Walk up the steps to your left.

❸ Albino Manca's sculpture of a bronze eagle with a funeral wreath, the *East Coast Memorial*, honors the memory of all the people who died in American waters during World War II.

Take the path west back toward Castle Clinton and turn right at the east gate. Walk past the Hope Garden to the point where Battery Place, Broadway and State Street meet. This small park is Bowling Green, where a statue of King George III was torn down by fervent nationalists in 1776.

❹ The imposing neoclassical US Custom House on the right houses the National Museum of the American Indian. The rotunda inside the Great Hall is well worth viewing.

Pass Bowling Green and walk north on Broadway, passing Arturo DiModica's bronze *Charging Bull* on your right. Continue past this symbol of stockmarket prosperity to Trinity Church, on your left.

❺ Trinity Church is historic (▷ 142–143). Many famous people are buried in the church-yard, including statesman Alexander Hamilton, steamboat inventor Robert Fulton and Captain James Lawrence, whose last words

("Don't give up the ship") are now legendary.

As you leave the churchyard, cross to the east side of Broadway and continue east on famous Wall Street, straight ahead.

❻ Wall Street (▷ 146–147) is where you will find the New York Stock Exchange, now closed to the public, halfway down the street on your right. No. 40 is the Trump Building. The Museum of American Financial History is at No. 48.

Walk east on Wall Street to William Street and go left, then left again onto Pine Street.

❼ On Pine Street, steps lead up to the Chase Manhattan Plaza, where sculptor Jean Dubuffet's *Group of Trees* takes center stage. Below the plaza is Isamu Noguchi's sunken sculpture garden.

Return to William Street by descending the steps to the right of the *Group of Trees*. Turn left to view the four abstract metal sculptures in Louise Nevelson Plaza. Across the street from the largest sculpture is the Federal Reserve Bank, designed to look like a Florentine palazzo. Just past the bank is Maiden Lane. Here turn left onto Maiden Lane, then right onto Nassau Street, and then right again onto John Street. At No. 44 is the United Methodist Church, with a fine Palladian front window. Continue east on John Street for five blocks, then left onto Water Street.

❽ The South Street Seaport Historic District (▷ 134–135) is full of boutiques and restaurants, more shopping mall than historic, but the atmosphere is festive and it's fun to be on the water; you have fine views of the East River, Brooklyn Bridge

The Sphere, a memorial to the World Trade Center tragedy, temporarily in Battery Park

OUT AND ABOUT

Playing chess is one way to spend your lunch-hour on Wall Street (above); the American flag flies outside many buildings on Wall Street (above right)

Brooklyn Bridge (▷ 74–75).

Fun is the watchword at South Street Seaport

and the river craft. At the northern end of Water Street is Manhattan's oldest saloon, the Bridge Café, dating from 1847, where you can have a drink and a meal.

Turn right (east) onto Dover Street, then right again onto Front Street. When you get to Beekman Street, turn left to the city's former fish market, Fulton Street Market. Go across South Street and walk to the end of Pier 17, and go up the steps for a spectacular view of Brooklyn Bridge (▷ 74–75). Then head toward South Street, cross over

and continue straight ahead along Fulton Street.

9 Schermerhorn Row, the Federal-style buildings along this street, were built as warehouses or counting houses in the early 1800s and named for the developer.

Continue west on Fulton Street to William Street and the subway station.

WHEN TO GO

To fully appreciate the bustle of Wall Street it is best to do this walk on weekdays.

WHERE TO EAT

Bridge Café, 279 Water Street (tel 212/227-3344), or any of the eateries at South Street Seaport.

PLACES TO VISIT

National Museum of the American Indian
www.nmai.si.edu
✉ 1 Bowling Green
☎ 212/514-3700
🕐 Mon–Wed, Fri–Sun 10–5, Thu 10–8
🎫 Free

OUT AND ABOUT

CITY HALL PARK TO WASHINGTON SQUARE PARK

Starting out from City Hall Park, you'll walk past the famous Woolworth Building, the world's tallest building until 1930 when the Chrysler Building spired even higher. Beyond lies Ground Zero, the site of the World Trade Center. You'll continue to SoHo and what remains of once-bustling Little Italy.

THE WALK

Distance:	3 miles (4.8km)
Allow:	2 to 2.5 hours
Start at	Park Place subway station
End at	West 4th Street/Washington Square

HOW TO GET THERE

Subway:	2, 3
Bus:	M6

When you leave Park Place subway station, City Hall and its park are on your left at the northern end of City Hall Park.

❶ The principal designer of City Hall (▷ 77) was a Frenchman, Joseph François Mangin, who also worked on the place de la Concorde in Paris. This mini-palace is where the mayor and city council have their offices. A wrought-iron fence keeps the rest of us out. In the park in front of City Hall is a statue of Nathan Hale, a spy for Washington's army, hanged by the English in 1776. Just before his execution he uttered his famous last words of regret that he had "but one life to lose for my country." The same area was the site of the 1863 Draft Riots (▷ 33). Behind City Hall facing

Chambers Street is the old Tweed Courthouse, now the Department of Education. In 1872, when Boss Tweed (▷ 33) ran the city and milked taxpayers of millions of dollars, the estimated cost of constructing the courthouse was $250,000. But by the time Tweed paid off friends and lined his own pockets to the tune of some $10 million, the tab was $14 million. Tweed died penniless in jail in 1878. Across Broadway is Cass Gilbert's Woolworth Building (▷ 144), between Park Place and Barclay Street, a skyscraper with lavish Gothic ornamentation and an amazingly rich lobby.

Continue south down Broadway.

❷ St. Paul's Chapel, on Broadway between Fulton and Vesey streets, is Manhattan's only remaining pre-Revolution building. George Washington worshiped here during the two years that New York was the nation's capital, and inside you can see his pew.

Turn right on Fulton Street and continue west.

❸ Along the fence protecting the site of the World Trade Center (now known as Ground Zero, ▷ 108) at the end of Fulton Street, on Church Street, photos, flags, candles, flowers, teddy bears and other memorials to the victims of the tragedy can still be seen. Alongside the memorial, people sell T-shirts, photographs and hats to anyone willing to buy such reminders of the 9/11 disaster. Reconstruction on this site is already underway. If you wish to have a closer look,

The glistening Woolworth Building was built in 1913

cross Church Street to the viewing wall.

Turn right on Church Street.

❹ At the corner of Church and Barclay streets is the Church of St. Peter, founded in 1785, and New York's oldest Catholic parish church.

Turn right on Park Place and you'll see City Hall Park ahead. Walk east through the park to get a good view of Brooklyn Bridge. Take Park Row to Centre Street and walk north to the US Courthouse.

❺ The US Courthouse, designed by architect Cass Gilbert, is on the corner of Centre Street and Foley Square.

A little farther north are the criminal courts. As you approach Canal Street, the proximity to Chinatown becomes obvious: Open-fronted shops sell everything from Chinese lanterns to refrigerator magnets and made-in-China trinkets. When you reach the corner of Centre Street and Canal Street, turn right. Walk two blocks east, then turn left on Mulberry Street and walk north.

❻ You are now in the heart of Little Italy (▷ 109), with a handful of Italian restaurants and cafés. Two blocks north, at 195 Grand Street, is Ferrara, founded in 1892, with strong coffee and sweet pastries.

Continue north on Mulberry Street to Prince Street, and turn left.

❼ On the southeast corner of Prince Street and Broadway is Dean & DeLuca, a temple to food and cuisine offering beautiful displays of the finest pastries, meats, fish and produce, plus good coffee at

OUT AND ABOUT

City Hall was completed in 1802 in the Federal style (above)

Chinatown canopies and Ground Zero memories (above)

the front counter. Cross Broadway and continue along Prince Street and turn right on West Broadway toward Houston Street.

As you cross Houston Street, West Broadway becomes LaGuardia Place.

8 Three blocks north is Washington Square Park. Once a hanging ground and a burial site for more than 10,000 unidentified paupers, this space became a public park in 1828.

After a rest in the park, you can catch a downtown train from West 4th Street/Washington Square back to Chambers Street near City Hall.

WHEN TO GO
The area around City Hall Park is at its liveliest on weekdays.

WHERE TO EAT
Ferrara, 195 Grand Street, between Mulberry and Mott streets (tel 212/226-6150).

Ferrara's, an Italian institution on Grand Street, where you can get great pastries and coffee (right)

MACY'S TO ROCKEFELLER CENTER

Some of New York's most striking sights are along this route—the Empire State Building, the Diamond District and Rockefeller Plaza, where you may be tempted to stop in at the NBC Experience Store to pick up a "Will & Grace," "Friends" or "Law & Order" T-shirt.

THE WALK

Distance: 3 miles (4.8km)
Allow: 2.5 hours
Start at 34th Street/Penn Station subway station
End at 34th Street/Herald Square

HOW TO GET THERE

Subway: 1, 2, 3
Bus: M10

Leave the 34th Street/Penn Station subway so you come out onto West 34th Street at Seventh Avenue (also known as Fashion Avenue).

❶ You are standing in front of Macy's, arguably New York's most famous department store. Encompassing two entire city blocks, this store is so big you could spend days here.

Head east on West 34th Street. Continue to Broadway, cross it and turn left onto Sixth Avenue (Avenue of the Americas), keeping to the right as you go through the intersection. Six blocks north on Sixth, past lots of shops and banks, is Bryant Park on your right, where you can rest or get a coffee in the park. Continue north past the park. At the corner of 43rd Street is the International Center of Photography (▷ 101).

❷ The Diamond District is concentrated on 47th Street between Fifth and Sixth avenues. Notice the diamond-motif street lights illuminating the corners. Millions of dollars worth of gems are traded daily in the businesses here.

Continue north on Sixth Avenue.

❸ At 49th Street you'll see the 70-story G. E. Building towers to the right at 30 Rockefeller Plaza. This building is the headquarters of General Electric and NBC (National Broadcasting Corporation) and is part of the Rockefeller Center (▷ 128–130), a city landmark. The ground floor of the building is worth visiting; note José Maria Sert's sepia murals depicting the progress of man. From Top of the Rock observation decks, on floors 67–70 of the G. E. Building there are spectacular views of the city.

Continue on Avenue of the Americas (Sixth Avenue) to 50th Street.

❹ Stop to admire the landmark art deco Radio City Music Hall (▷ 129), another city landmark and important element of the Rockefeller Center. Most famous for its Rockettes Christmas spectacular, it also hosts other music shows throughout the year. This was the world's largest indoor theater when it opened in 1932. Hour-long guided tours are worth the time and the money. The block-long entry, with its 24-carat-gold ceiling and two-ton glass chandeliers, is spectacular.

Just past Radio City, at 1290 Avenue of the Americas, is the AXA Financial Center. Stop in to view the foyer's magnificent multi-panel murals by Thomas Hart Benton depicting the nation's economic and social life on the eve of the Depression.

Back on Avenue of the Americas, go north a block to 52nd Street and turn right. The CBS Building, constructed in a dark granite in 1965, is on the corner of Avenue of the Americas and 52nd Street, a part of which is also known as Swing Street because of the many jazz clubs that flourished along here after the repeal of Prohibition.

❺ At 25 West 52nd Street is the Paley Center for Media (▷ 126). Next door at No. 21 is the 21 Club, a still-fashionable hangout, now a fine restaurant. Note the jockeys above the door.

At the corner of 52nd Street and Fifth Avenue, turn right and walk south a block.

❻ At St. Patrick's Cathedral (▷ 131), the largest Catholic cathedral in America, the flying buttresses and 330ft (100m) twin towers vie for your attention.

Turn left on 51st Street, and walk east past the cathedral toward Madison Avenue. Cross Madison Avenue.

❼ On the southeast corner of 51st and Madison is the New York Palace Hotel, which rises out of the Villard Houses, twin brownstone mansions built in 1884 by the Bavarian-born journalist, financier and railroad tycoon Henry Villard.

Continue walking east on 51st as far as Park Avenue. Turn left and walk one block north.

Macy's is the one everyone thinks of when they think stores

OUT AND ABOUT

8 The bronze-glass tower at 375 Park Avenue is the Seagram Building (▷ 141), a lively place in summer and a delight at Christmas with a tree and lights. Diagonally across the avenue is Lever House, built in 1952 with an avant-garde metal- and glass-curtain wall that reflects everything around.

Go left on East 53rd Street, walk west to Sixth Avenue and turn left again. Walk four blocks south.

9 The Rockefeller Center is a great place to shop, stop for a snack or just wander around.

From here you can take the subway to Herald Square.

WHEN TO GO
Avoid this walk on Sunday if you want to shop and visit St. Patrick's Cathedral. Monday to Saturday from 10 to 6 is best.

WHERE TO EAT
Rainbow Room in the Rockefeller Center (212/632-5000) or Rockefeller Center Café, 20 West 50th Street (212/332-7620)

PLACES TO VISIT
Paley Center for Media
✉ 25 West 52nd Street
☎ 212/621-6800
🕐 Tue–Sun noon–6, Thu until 8

Radio City Music Hall
✉ 1260 Sixth Avenue
☎ 212/247-4777
🕐 Daily 11–3
🎫 Hour-long behind-the-scenes tours every 30 min

Bryant Park is a pleasant green space to stop for a snack in summer (left)

Radio City Music Hall (top); St. Patrick's Cathedral (above)

Ice skating at the Rockefeller Center at Christmas

OUT AND ABOUT

[Map showing Midtown Manhattan: Museum of Modern Art, Museum of Arts and Design, Paley Center for Media, Radio City Music Hall, GE Building, Rockefeller Center, Diamond District, Seagram Building, New York Palace Hotel, St Patrick's Cathedral, Grand Central Terminal, International Center of Photography, Times Square, New York Public Library, Bryant Park, Morgan Library, Macy's, Empire State Building. Scale: 0–200 m, 0–200 yds]

CENTRAL PARK WEST HISTORIC DISTRICT

This walk begins with a quick look at the Dakota Building, where former Beatle John Lennon was shot in 1980, then stops at his memorial across the street in Central Park. In the 1960s, with private contributions of about $165 million, Upper West Side tenements were razed and the Lincoln Center was built in their stead, a very pleasant complex of pedestrian open spaces, theaters, concert halls, cinemas and museums. Many actors, actresses and movie directors work and live in the neighborhood—it's fun to see if you can spot any.

THE WALK

Distance:	1.5 miles (2.4km)
Allow:	1.5 to 2 hours
Start/End at	72nd Street subway station

HOW TO GET THERE

Subway:	B, C
Bus:	M10

Leave the 72nd Street subway at the corner of 72nd Street and Central Park West.

❶ The Dakota (▷ 87) is on the northwest corner of Central Park West and 72nd Street. Look at the front of the building on 72nd Street, where John Lennon was shot. His wife, Yoko Ono, still lives in the building.

Walk east across Central Park West and follow the path straight ahead to Strawberry Fields.

❷ Here there is a memorial to Lennon, a black-and-white mosaic called *Imagine*.

Go back to Central Park West, turn left, and walk south. Note the residential streets lined with 19th-century brownstones to your right. Turn left into the park at West 67th Street.

❸ Here, at Tavern on the Green, celebrities show up for gala events and film premieres and tourists come (and pay the price) to enjoy the seating on the leafy patio in summer. The Sheep Meadow, straight ahead, is a 15-acre (6ha) expanse created as part of the Olmsted and Vaux design for Central Park; at the time it reminded many city-dwellers of the rural landscapes they had left behind when they emigrated to the United States.

Return to Central Park West and go south for two blocks. Turn right on 65th Street to Columbus Avenue. Cross Broadway and Columbus Avenue. On the west of Broadway is the Lincoln Center.

❹ The Lincoln Center (▷ 112–113) includes Alice Tully Hall (on the northwest corner of 65th Street) and Avery Fisher Hall (on the southwest corner). Much of the movie *West Side Story* was shot in the tenements that once stood on this spot. Walk south from Avery Fisher about 300 yards (274m) to the Lincoln Center central plaza, with its fountain. On the south side of the plaza is the home of the New York City Ballet, the New York State Theater; rising over the plaza on the west is the Metropolitan Opera House with Austrian chandeliers and Marc Chagall murals visible through the glass facade. To the south of the Met is a pleasant open area where open-air concerts are held in summer and the Big Apple Circus holds forth over the year-end holidays. The pond sculpture, Henry Moore's *Reclining Figure*, and the Vivian Beaumont Theater lie to the north.

Go up the steps to the Juilliard School to the north, turn right then left down the steps to Broadway. Cross 66th Street, then cross Broadway to your right. Walk east on 66th to Columbus Avenue and turn left. On the right stands the contemporary ABC Building at No. 147 Columbus. Continue along Columbus to West 70th Street and turn left.

❺ At 135 West 70th, near the corner of 70th and Broadway is the Pythian Temple, now a condominium; designed by Thomas W. Lamb, and built in 1926, it was dedicated to Pythianism, the cult of the oracle at Delphi, and Assyrian sages still guard the entrance. Bill Haley and the Comets recorded "Rock Around the Clock" here in 1954. Across the street, at 154 West 70th Street, is Café Mozart, with extravagant cakes and pastries.

Continue west to Amsterdam Avenue then turn right. As you approach West 72nd Street, you'll see one of the few remaining old subway buildings from the early 1900s on your left and a pleasingly harmonious new structure, an expansion of the venerable subway station, across 72nd on the north side of the street. Cross West 72nd Street.

❻ The magnificent Beaux Arts Ansonia Building rises at 2109 Broadway between West 73rd and West 74th streets. Caruso, Stravinsky and Toscanini all lived at the Ansonia, and the sound-proofing between apartments and floors continues to attract distinguished musicians, singers and conductors.

Turn right on West 73rd Street; 18 row houses, between Nos. 248 and 272, are the earliest houses in the neighborhood, dating from 1885. Turn left on Central Park West.

❼ Designed in 1930 by architect Emery Roth, the towers of the San Remo Apartments at 145–146 Central Park West grace the skyline. Residents have included Paul Simon and Dustin Hoffman.

Continue north on Central Park West to 77th Street.

❽ The New-York Historical Society (▷ 126) is on the corner of 77th and Central Park West. The fascinating collections and unusual variety of gifts in the shop make this worth a stop.

Cross West 77th Street.

❾ The enormous American Museum of Natural History

OUT AND ABOUT

The fascinating American Museum of Natural History

The Dakota

Map labels

81st Street Museum of Natural History

C14

West 81st Street
West 80th Street
West 79th Street
West 78th Street
West 77th Street
West 76th Street
West 75th Street
West 74th Street
West 73rd Street
West 72nd Street
West 71st Street
West 70th Street
West 69th Street
West 68th Street
West 67th Street
West 66th Street
West 65th Street
West 64th Street

79th Street

Columbus Avenue
Amsterdam Avenue
BROADWAY
Columbus Avenue
Central Park West

American Museum of Natural History 9

New-York Historical Society 8

San Remo Apartments 7

Ansonia Building 6

The Dakota 1

72nd Street
72nd Street

Strawberry Fields 2

Pythian Temple 5

Lincoln Center 4

66th Street Lincoln Center
Juilliard School

Tavern on the Green 3

Central Park West
Central Park West

Olmsted Drive

The Lake

Central Park

The Sheep Meadow

65th Street Transverse Rd

0   200 m
0   200 yds

C15   E15
C16   D16   D14

N

OUT AND ABOUT

(▷ 68–72) is on your left. Go to the main entrance to admire the bronze statue of President Theodore Roosevelt seated upon a horse, then step inside to look at William Mackay's beautiful murals depicting events from Roosevelt's life in the Roosevelt Memorial Hall.

After leaving the museum, walk up Central Park West, and at the 81st Street traffic lights take the entrance to the park straight ahead of you. As soon as you enter, take the path immediately to your right and walk south along this path to West 72nd Street and back again to the 72nd Street subway station.

WHEN TO GO
This walk is very pleasant on Sunday afternoons. Most shops and restaurants are open then.

WHERE TO EAT
Café Mozart, 154 West 70th Street (tel 212/595-9797).

PLACES TO VISIT
American Museum of Natural History
✉ Central Park West at 79th Street
☎ 212/769-5100 ◔ Daily 10–5.45

New-York Historical Society
✉ 2 West 77th Street
☎ 212/873-3400
◔ Tue–Sat 10–6, Fri until 8, Sun 11–5.45

Sheep grazed in The Sheep Meadow until 1934

FORT TRYON PARK

Go to Fort Tryon Park for fresh air, a walk in the woods, spectacular views of the Hudson River from Manhattan's highest natural point, gardens and a medieval-style monastery.

THE WALK	
Distance: 1.5 miles (2.4km)	
Allow: 1.5 to 2 hours	
Start/End at Margaret Corbin Circle at 190th Street subway station	

HOW TO GET THERE	
Subway: A to 190th Street	
Bus: M4	

Leave the M4 bus at 190th Street rather than taking it to the Cloisters, the last stop. If you arrive by the A train, get off at 190th Street and take the elevator to street level and turn to your right as you come out of the station.

① One of the earliest battles of the American Revolutionary War was fought in Fort Tryon Park on November 16, 1776. General George Washington's troops were outnumbered 4,000 to 600 and lost to the British, who named the fort after the colonial governor, Sir William Tryon. Although the area around the park is known as Washington Heights, the British name for the fort was never changed.

John D. Rockefeller acquired the property in 1917 and in 1938 established the Cloisters, a branch of the Metropolitan Museum of Art, to house a large collection of medieval art. Frederick Law Olmsted, Jr., designed the gardens using more than 250 species of plant. Olmsted's stone walls, arches, terraces and stairs recall medieval Europe, making these 62 acres (25ha) a special spot.

Margaret Corbin Circle is named after a brave American woman who took over her husband's cannon after he was fatally wounded in the Fort Tryon battle, and who is the only woman buried at West Point. To your left, on the west side of the circle, stands a small stone building that was the gatehouse for the Billings estate. Cornelius K. G. Billings was a wealthy horseman from Chicago who spent more than $2 million building his Tryon Hill mansion between 1901 and 1905.

Make your way through the huge stone gateway ahead and onto the Promenade. Turn immediately to your left onto this walkway.

② The 3-acre (1.2ha) Heather Garden here enjoys a breathtaking view across the Hudson River to New Jersey's Palisades and the George Washington Bridge. With its many heathers, brooms, perennials and shrubs, this garden is one of the largest heather gardens on the east coast. By May, 5,000 bulbs are in full bloom, with more than 30 varieties of daffodils and tulips, and 1,000 lilies are in flower from June to September.

From the Heather Garden, return to the Promenade and follow it for about 300 yards (273m) to Linden Terrace.

③ In 1909, Billings erected a stela in Linden Terrace as a memorial to the Continental Army's defense of the site. Linden trees shade the pretty spot, and there are benches, parapets and splendid river views. At the northeast corner of the terrace, steps lead up to a flagpole. Standing here, you are on the highest natural point in Manhattan.

Return down the steps you have just come up to the Promenade, which veers to the left and down some stone steps. At the bottom of the steps continue along the path to your right.

④ You can see the Cloisters (▷ 86) straight ahead to the north. Stroll northward with the river on your left and, if you wish to have a quick look inside the museum, cross the road at the crosswalk (pedestrian crossing) on your right and continue along the path straight ahead. The entrance on your left leads to the gift shop, which sells Tiffany-like glass, art books, educational children's toys, videos and CDs to a background soundtrack of medieval music.

Continue north on the path you left to visit the Cloisters and stroll through the very pleasant woods and lawns. If you stay on the path closest to the road (Margaret Corbin Drive) that runs through the park, you'll come to the New Leaf Café.

⑤ The stunning location, trendy food and affordable prices of the New Leaf Café, an enterprise of actress Bette Midler's New York Restoration Project, make it a very pleasant rest stop. Proceeds support ongoing work in the park.

The path leads back to the park's main entrance at Margaret Corbin Circle.

WHEN TO GO	

It is best not to go on Mondays when the Cloisters and the restaurant are closed. Even if you do not spend time viewing the exhibits, a quick look at the Cloisters is well worthwhile.

WHERE TO EAT	

New Leaf Café, Fort Tryon Park (tel 212/568-5323; closed Mon).

PLACES TO VISIT	

The Cloisters
✉ Fort Tryon Park ☎ 212/923-3700
🕐 Mar–Oct Tue–Sun 9.30–5.15; rest of year Tue–Sun 9.30–4.45 💲 $20 adult, child (under 12) free

Margaret Corbin Circle, at the entrance to the park, is the start and finish of the walk (below); a blue jay in the park (below right)

OUT AND ABOUT

The impressive Cloisters (above); a walled walk around the park (below)

One of the many beautiful walkways that make up the Cloisters, which houses medieval European art (below)

Map labels:

B1

RIVERSIDE DRIVE

N

HIGHWAY 9A

HIGHWAY 9A

Margaret Corbin Drive

Arden St

BROADWAY

P

The Cloisters 4

Fort Tryon Park

Margaret Corbin Drive

Linden Terrace 3

New Leaf Café 5

Heather Garden 2

1

Margaret Corbin Circle

Bennett Ave

0   100 m
0   100 yds

B2

FORT TRYON PARK
THE CLOISTERS · HEATHER GARDEN · CAFE
City of New York Parks & Recreation

BROOKLYN HEIGHTS TO MANHATTAN

If Brooklyn were not part of New York City, it would be America's sixth-largest city. Historic Brooklyn Heights, with its many landmark churches, fine brownstones and leafy streets, remains one of the city's most distinguished residential areas. The walk across Brooklyn Bridge provides stunning views of Lower Manhattan.

THE WALK

Distance: 2.5 miles (4km)

Allow: 2 to 2.5 hours (allow time to enjoy the view of Manhattan from Brooklyn Bridge)

Start at High Street/Brooklyn Bridge subway station

End at Brooklyn Bridge/City Hall subway station

HOW TO GET THERE

Subway: A, C

Leave the High Street/Brooklyn Bridge subway station. As you come out of the station, you see Cadman Plaza Park, with its tall trees, paths and benches. On the right side of the park is Cadman Plaza West. Walk south on this street the length of the park.

1 Stop for a moment at the large stone monument on your left, dedicated to the Brooklyn men and women who fought during World War II. With its trees and benches, this park is a pleasant place to sit.

Continue on Cadman Plaza West, crossing Tillary Street. Pass the Korean War Veterans Plaza on your left and continue to the Federal Building and the Romanesque Revival US Post Office and Courthouse. Cross Johnson Street.

2 The enormous building on the left is the Supreme Court of New York. Pause to admire the statue of Christopher Columbus in front of the building and the bronze bust of Senator Robert F. Kennedy, the assassinated brother of President John F. Kennedy.

3 Straight ahead is an elaborate fountain and behind it is the

Greek Revival Brooklyn Borough Hall, built in 1848.

Just past Borough Hall is Joralemon Street. Walk west on Joralemon a block and a half to Sidney Place, on your left. Look down this little street to the big red church, St. Charles Borromeo Roman Catholic Church, built in 1849. Three blocks farther west on Joralemon, turn right on Hicks Street. Walk one block north.

4 Grace Church, at 254 Hicks Street, is one of many New York City churches designed by Richard Upjohn; it dates from 1849. Visit the charming entrance court off Hicks Street and cool off in the shade of the enormous elm tree.

Continue a block north on Hicks to Remsen Street, and turn right. Go one block east and cross Henry Street.

5 On your left is Richard Upjohn's Cathedral of Our Lady of Lebanon, the first round-arched, Early Romanesque Revival ecclesiastical building in the United States. Notice the medallions on the entrance doors. Originally the dining room doors on the French luxury liner *Normandie*, they were bought at an auction in 1945.

Continue another block east on Remsen, and turn left on Clinton Street. Walking north, as you cross Montague Street, look at St. Ann and the Holy Trinity Episcopal Church, a major work of James Renwick, Jr., on your left; it is one of the most important Victorian Gothic churches in the

The statue of Bobby Kennedy outside the Supreme Court of New York

United States. At the end of Clinton Street, turn left on Cadman Plaza West, left again on Clark Street and then right on Henry Street. Walk two blocks to Orange Street and turn left.

6 The Plymouth Church of the Pilgrims, built in 1849 on Orange Street between Henry and Hicks streets, was the center of anti-slavery sentiment during antebellum days. Abolitionist minister Henry Ward Beecher preached against slavery here. Abraham Lincoln worshiped here twice, and the building was a key part of the Underground Railroad, which helped get escaped slaves to freedom in the north. Beautiful stained-glass windows adorn this otherwise modest church, and in the courtyard next to it stands a bronze statue of Henry Ward Beecher by Gutzon Borglum, who sculpted the famous presidents' heads at Mount Rushmore.

Return to Henry Street and turn left. There are many cafés, restaurants and delis along here. At the traffic lights, turn right on Middagh Street and, at Cadman Plaza West, take the path ahead across the park. On your left is a plaque with information about the peregrine falcons that often roost here. At the fork in the path, keep left and you'll come to Washington Street. Turn left, and just before you come to the traffic lights at Prospect Street, go up the steps on your left.

7 You now leave Brooklyn Heights across Brooklyn Bridge (▷ 74–75), on the wide wooden pedestrian walkway. In 1883 Brooklyn Bridge became the world's longest suspension bridge, spanning the East River and connecting Brooklyn to Manhattan. This spectacular bridge, with its web of steel cables, remains as much a marvel today as it did when it was first built.

SENATOR ROBERT FRANCIS KENNEDY

NOVEMBER 20, 1925
JUNE 6, 1968

OUT AND ABOUT

Brooklyn Borough Hall (above); Hicks Street brownstones (above right); the Plymouth Church of the Pilgrims (right)

BROOKLYN BRIDGE 278

7

High Street Brooklyn Bridge

Plymouth Church of the Pilgrims 6

BROOKLYN

HEIGHTS

Cadman Plaza Park 1

Federal Building

TILLARY ST

US Post Office & Courthouse

Clark Street

Love Lane

Brooklyn Historical Society

Cathedral of Our Lady of Lebanon 5

St Ann and the Holy Trinity Episcopal Church

Brooklyn Borough Hall 3

Borough Hall

Supreme Court of New York 2

Grace Church 4

Rows of tulips brighten up Columbus Park

Vine Street, Middagh Street, Willow Street, Orange Street, Pineapple Street, Clark Street, Hicks Street, Henry Street, Monroe Place, Clinton Street, Columbia Heights, Pierrepont Street, College Place, Montague Street, Remsen Street, Grace Court, Joralemon Street, Garden Place, Sidney Place, Willow Place, Livingston Street, Schermerhorn Street, Court Street, Adams Street, Tillary Street, Johnson Street, Myrtle Av, Lawrence St, Jay Street, Concord Street, Sands St, High St, Pearl Street, Adams Street, McLaughlin Park

FURMAN ST

CADMAN PLAZA WEST

BROOKLYN-QUEENS EXPRESSWAY

H25
H27
J26

200 m
200 yds

OUT AND ABOUT

When you reach the other side of the bridge you'll see the Brooklyn Bridge City Hall subway, from where you can access lines 4, 5, 6 and J, M, Z.

WHEN TO GO
Any day of the week, morning or afternoon, but the walk across the bridge is especially romantic as the sun slowly sets behind Liberty Island and Lower Manhattan's city lights begin to twinkle.

WHERE TO EAT
Henry and Montague streets have a wide selection of cafés and restaurants.

COLUMBUS PARK

HUDSON RIVER VALLEY

The Hudson River flows 315 miles (508km) from the Adirondack Mountains to New York and out into the Atlantic. The splendor of this valley can be seen in the paintings by the Hudson River School artists of the 19th century, and still today the area is lovely, especially in the fall, when the colorful foliage brightens the shoreline.

BASICS

Historic Hudson Valley
☎ 914/631-8200
www.hudsonvalley.org

National Trust for Historic Preservation
☎ 914/631-4481

National Park Service
☎ 845/229-9115

HOW TO GET THERE

By train: Most of the valley north of New York City is easily visited by train. From Grand Central Terminal, take the Metro-North Hudson Line to the closest station; local taxis meet trains at most stations, or you can book one through Rivertowns Taxi (tel 914/478-2222).

By car: Follow the West Side Highway to the Henry Hudson Parkway and then the Saw Mill River Parkway (all one road, really, but with three different names). It's best to get specific directions from the Saw Mill by phoning each sight.

By river: The New York Waterway offers day-long excursions up the Hudson River, leaving from Pier 78 on Manhattan's west side (tel 1800/533-3779, www.newyorkwaterway.com).

HUDSON RIVER MUSEUM

The Hudson River Museum (511 Warburton Avenue, Yonkers, tel 914/963-4550; Wed–Sun noon–5, Fri noon–8) is built around a historic house and a modern addition. Collections encompass art and history, and there's a planetarium. At the Museum Café, you can have a light lunch with splendid views of the Hudson River and the Palisades in New Jersey. Take Metro-North to Yonkers, then grab a cab (about $5).

SUNNYSIDE TO LYNDHURST

Sunnyside, a National Historic Landmark, was the home of Washington Irving, who wrote *The Legend of Sleepy Hollow* and was America's first internationally known author. The cottage (tel 914/631-8200; Apr–end Oct Wed–Mon 10–5; Nov–Dec Sat–Sun 10–4) was built in the 18th century and enlarged by Irving in 1835. Guided tours of the house and grounds are available up to one hour before closing time. There is a visitor center, museum shop and seasonal café. From Grand Central Terminal, catch a train to Tarrytown, where taxis wait.

Lyndhurst, a spectacular Gothic Revival-style mansion (tel 914/631-4481; mid-Apr to end Oct Tue–Sun 10–5; rest of year Sat–Sun 10–4), was the home of railroad tycoon Jay Gould. The surrounding lawns have amazing Hudson River views. You can call a cab to take you to Sunnyside, or walk on the footpath.

PHILLIPSBURG MANOR AND KYKUIT

Phillipsburg Manor, on Route 9 in Sleepy Hollow, is a restored colonial farm once owned by the Phillips family (tel 914/631-3992; Apr–end Oct Wed–Mon 10–5; Nov–Dec Wed–Mon 10–4). Guided tours are available and houses and outbuildings like the barn and working grist mill are staffed by interpreters in costume who explain early Hudson River Valley life.

Kykuit is a National Trust Historic Site that was home to four generations of the wealthy Rockefeller family. The sumptuous mansion is filled with priceless antiques and works of art, and sculptures fill the beautifully landscaped gardens. Guided tours (mid-May to early Nov Wed–Mon 10–3) begin at Phillipsburg Manor; tickets go on sale at 9am and are issued on a first-come, first-served basis (children under 10 are not admitted).

VAN CORTLANDT MANOR

This 18th-century Hudson Valley mansion belonged to the Van Cortlandt family for more than 260 years. Pierre Van Cortlandt was the first lieutenant-governor of New York State. The house has original furnishings, and the kitchen is a tour highlight with its original hearth and beehive oven (tel 914/271-8981; Apr–end Oct Wed–Mon 10–5; Nov–end Dec Sat–Sun 10–4).

WEST POINT, FRANKLIN D. ROOSEVELT NATIONAL HISTORIC SITE TO VANDERBILT MANSION

Farther upstate, there are several other landmarks on the eastern banks of the Hudson, most notably West Point Military Academy. Nearby is Cold Spring,

A long wooden footbridge leads to Phillipsburg Manor

OUT AND ABOUT

a charming riverfront town known for its antiques shops and garrison, home to another 19th-century mansion Boscobel (tel 845/265-3638). Next stop would be Beacon, a riverfront town that is being revived with the help of such institutions as DIA Arts. Farther north are two sites associated with the Roosevelts. The best way to visit is by car.

Your first stop is the United States Military Academy at **West Point** (tel 845/938-2638). America's most respected academy has turned out some great generals, presidents and astronauts. The museum displays guns, uniforms, medals and flags from various conflicts, and the grounds are beautiful in their own right.

Franklin D. Roosevelt National Historic Site (tel 800/337-8474; daily 9–5) was the Depression-era president's birthplace. The house, library and museum have a large collection of family memorabilia. Franklin and his formidable wife, Eleanor, are buried in the rose garden; a white marble monument marks their graves.

From this point a shuttle bus will take you to the **Eleanor Roosevelt National Historic Site** (daily 9–5) in the grounds of the Roosevelt estate.

Vanderbilt Mansion (tel 800/337-8474; daily 9–5, visit by guided tour only), 2 miles

The Monument to the American Soldier in the US Military Academy at West Point (above); Sunnyside, where Irving got his inspiration to write The Legend of Sleepy Hollow *(right)*

(3.5km) north of the Roosevelt Historic Site, is a lavish Beaux Arts mansion that was designed by architects McKim, Mead and White for the grandson of railroad magnate Cornelius Vanderbilt. Inside you will see all the splendors money can buy, from Renaissance to rococo furniture and works of art. The gardens are exquisite, and there are several walking trails that skirt the river.

WHERE TO EAT

In Tarrytown there are three good places to find something to eat: Equus Restaurant, The Castle (tel 914/631-3646); Main Street Café, 24 Main Street (tel 914/524-9770); and Striped Bass, 236 Main Street (tel 914/366-4455).

Fall foliage surrounds the Victory Monument in the US Military Academy at West Point

OUT AND ABOUT

LONG ISLAND

Long Island is 125 miles (202km) long and between 12 and 23 miles (19 and 37km) wide. It lies east of New York City and is washed by the Atlantic Ocean on the south and Long Island Sound on the north. The rocky northern shoreline, scalloped with beaches, coves and bluffs, and sometimes called the Gold Coast, has attracted the affluent since the late 19th century. The Hamptons, at the east of the island, on the Atlantic shore, has become the playground of wealthy families, who have built fine summer houses and mansions. The delightful Atlantic-pounded beaches along the southern shore offer an escape from city heat in summer. The western part of the island, which consists of the Manhattan boroughs of Brooklyn and Queens, is densely populated, but the farther east you go, the more rural it becomes. Here are historic homes, fishing ports, historic whaling towns, museums and state parks.

BASICS

🛈 NYC & Company
☎ 212/484-1222
🕐 Mon–Fri 8.30–6, Sat–Sun 9–5
www.nyc.visit.com

HOW TO GET THERE

By train: Go to Pennsylvania Station on 7th Avenue between 31st and 33rd streets. From here catch a Long Island Railroad train to the town nearest the place of interest.

By car: From New York, travel from Manhattan east on the Long island Expressway (I-495). Buses and trains are often a better way to get to Long Island, but you usually need a car to get around the various sights, so it's best to take your own wheels.

OLD WESTBURY GARDENS AND SAGAMORE HILL HISTORIC SITE

Old Westbury Gardens (tel 516/333-0048) was the home of financier John S. Phipps (1874–1958), his wife Margarita and their four children. The Charles II-style manor house is furnished with English antiques and decorative arts. The surrounding 160 acres (64ha), with 88 breathtaking acres (36ha) of formal gardens, walkways, architectural follies and woodlands, are dotted with ponds and lakes. The gardens are between the Long Island Expressway and Jericho Turnpike (Route 25). By car, take Exit 39 (Glen Cove Road) off the I-495. Follow the service road east for 1 mile (1.5km), turn right on Old Westbury Road and continue for half a mile.

Sagamore Hill National Historic Site is northeast of Old Westbury, the home of President Theodore Roosevelt from 1885 until his death in 1919. The house is furnished as it was when he lived here (tel 516/922-4788; Memorial Day–Labor Day daily 10–4; rest of year Wed–Sun). Tours last half an hour and are offered on a first-come, first-served basis. They are limited in size, so arrive early if possible (by noon in summer they are often sold out). To get there by car, take Exit 41N (Oyster Bay) off I-495 onto Route 106 North. Travel for 4 miles (6km) to Route 25A, where you will turn right and travel 2.5 miles (4km) to the third traffic light. At the bottom of a long hill, turn left onto Cove Road and continue for

Sagamore Hill House (left); the Atlantic Ocean washes onto Robert Moses State Park on Fire Island (below), south of Long Island

OUT AND ABOUT

The Vanderbilt Museum at Centerport was built in 1910 by William K. Vanderbilt

1.5 miles (2.5km). Turn right onto Cove Neck Road for 1.5 miles (2.5km).

WALT WHITMAN BIRTHPLACE TO OLD BETHPAGE VILLAGE

Walt Whitman (1819–92) was one of America's finest poets and essayists. At his birthplace (tel 631/427-5240; Jun 15–Labor Day Mon–Fri 11–4, Sat–Sun 12–5; rest of year Wed–Fri 1–4, Sat–Sun 11–4), south of Sagamore Hill, you will see Whitman memorabilia, including photographs and excerpts from his writings and letters. To get there from I-495, take Exit 49N onto Route 110 North. Turn left onto Walt Whitman Road in Huntington Station. As the site is very popular with school groups, you may want to phone ahead.

Old Bethpage Village (tel 516/572-8400; Mar–end Oct Wed–Fri 10–4, Sat–Sun 10–5; Nov–Dec Wed–Sun 10–4) is an area of shops, farms, a one-room school-house, a church, gardens and homes filled with antiques, staffed by costumed interpreters explaining about life on Long Island in the 19th century. Special events are lively and fun.

The Theodore Roosevelt Sanctuary at Sagamore Hill

ORGANIZED TOURS

New York offers more tours than any city in the world. There are walking tours, bicycle tours, harbor tours, art and theater tours, behind-the-scenes tours, bus tours, limo tours, train tours, multilingual tours and special-interest tours such as ethnic, food and shopping tours. Some major bookstores have shelves of books about New York, many of them with self-guiding tours themed around everything from nature to literary history. The list of tour operators below is a small sample of what's available.

Details: www.nycvisit.com (click on Visitors, Things To Do and Tours)

BICYCLE TOURS

CENTRAL PARK BICYCLE TOURS
203 West 58th Street
Tel 212/541-8759
www.centralparkbiketour.com
Rent a bicycle and ride around Central Park with a knowledgeable guide for two hours. Tours daily at 10am, 1pm and 4pm
Adult $40, child (under 16) $20. Rental only: $20 for 2 hours, $25 for 3 hours, $40 all day

BUS TOURS

ON LOCATION TOURS
Tel 212/209-3370
www.screentours.com
Coaches depart from different locations. Reservations are recommended. New York TV Tour is a 3 to 3.5-hour tour to 40 locations; "Sex and the City" Tour is a 4-hour tour; the "Sopranos" Tour is 4 hours.
New York TV tour: adult $34, plus $2 ticket fee. "Sex and the City" tour: $37. "Sopranos" tour: $40

HELICOPTER TOURS
Helicopters leave from the Downtown Manhattan Heliport at Pier 6 and South Street and from the VIP Heliport at West 30th Street.

LIBERTY HELICOPTER TOURS
Tel 212/967-2099
www.libertyhelicopters.com
Fly over Manhattan's skyscrapers, New York Harbor and the five boroughs.
$69, 5–7 min; $186, 15–17 min

RIVER TOURS

CIRCLE LINE
Tel 212/563-3200
www.circleline42.com
Cruises from the Circle Line (Pier 83 at West 42nd Street/12th Avenue or Pier 16, South Street Seaport at Fulton Street and East River) are worth every penny. Take the 3-hour Full Island cruise, the 2-hour Semi-Circle cruise, 75-minute Liberty cruise, or a combination of packages. Combos are more expensive. Cruises with live music (adults only) operate from May to September. In spring and fall remember that it's at least 10 degrees colder on the water—and more when you consider wind chill in a moving boat.
Adult $20–$29.50, child under 12 $12–$17. Cruises $35–$50

WALKING TOURS
Here are a few that are highly recommended. Call ahead for up-to-date schedules.

BIG APPLE GREETER
Tel 212/669-8159
www.bigapplegreeter.org
A free public service. The guides—volunteer New Yorkers—are matched with visitors according to language and interests. Give at least a week's advance notice (longer during peak season).

BIG ONION WALKING TOURS
Tel 212/439-1090
www.bigonion.com
Two-hour tours. Guides have degrees in American history. No reservations necessary.
Adult $15, child $10

GRAND CENTRAL PARTNERSHIP
Tel 212/883-2420
www.grandcentralpartnership.org
Free tours of Grand Central Terminal every Friday lunchtime at 12.30. Just show up outside Grand Central Terminal at Philip Morris at 42nd Street and Park Avenue.

THEMED WALKING TOURS

MUNICIPAL ARTS SOCIETY
Tel 212/439-1049
www.mas.org
Architectural tours of Grand Central Terminal and other sites, including Ground Zero, Madison Avenue, Rockefeller Center and Martin Luther King Boulevard in Harlem. Guides are professional architects, historians, educators and writers.
Adult $15

NEW YORK GALLERY TOURS
Tel 212/946-1548
www.nygallerytours.com
Ten modern art galleries in two hours in Chelsea, SoHo and other locations.
Adult $20

PATRIOT TOURS
Tel 718/717-0963
www.patriottoursnyc.com
Historical walking tours of Lower Manhattan specializing in the people, stories, sites and events of the Revolutionary War and Civil War eras.
Adult $20

OUT AND ABOUT

Eating and Staying

EATING OUT IN NEW YORK

You can dine around the world in New York City and you can spend a pittance or a fortune or somewhere in between. The choice is yours. Some New Yorkers dine out every night, others save the top-class choices for special occasions. Dining trends change from season to season. The biggest news is British chef Gordon Ramsay's first US restaurant winning two Michelin stars.

RESERVATIONS, DRESS CODES AND OTHER NOTES

In general, it's wise to make a reservation for dinner, especially on weekends. Indeed, top-class restaurants require reservations and will ask you to provide a telephone number for confirmation. If you want a table at Jean-Georges, Le Bernardin, Gordon Ramsay or similar, call well in advance. Sometimes, at these "famous" restaurants, it can be tough to get through even to the reservation desk. Just keep trying. If you're on your own and want to eat on the run, you may be able to eat at the bar in one of these fancy restaurants. Note that some restaurants do not take reservations for parties under six people. In Midtown, luncheon reservations are essential.

The United States is a more casual culture than most and strict dress codes have disappeared. Nonetheless a few places still do require a jacket and tie at dinner so remember to ask when making a reservation. In general, casual smart is the way to go.

Smoking is not allowed in public spaces period. The majority of restaurants have full bars; some sell beer and wine only, and a few have no liquor but will allow you to bring your own. At premier restaurants, there will be a substantial corkage fee if you bring your own wine.

Vegetarians will find a welcome. Many of the top-class dining rooms offer vegetarian menus, and even fast-food joints are offering more healthful options on their menus these days.

Breakfast may be served all day at coffee shops and diners. Otherwise, the normal breakfast hours are from 7 to 11am. Lunch usually runs from 11.30am to 2 or 2.30pm and dinner from 5pm to 10 or 11pm, depending on the day of the week. Most top-class restaurants close for lunch on Saturday and Sunday. Many restaurants offer brunch on Sunday or both Saturday and Sunday.

TAXES, TIPPING AND OTHER FINANCIAL CONSIDERATIONS

A sales tax of 8.375 percent will be added to your dining bill. Americans tip more generously than most other nationalities. The minimum (with good service) is 15 percent; many people double the tax for a 16.75 percent tip. Many restaurants offer prix-fixe menus, which often provide good value. In January and late June, a special promotion offers a three-course menu at reduced rates for lunch and dinner at numerous restaurants; this promotion is often extended so it's always worth checking if it's available.

DESSERT AND COFFEE

Greenwich Village has been famous for its coffeehouses since the 1950s. Of the few that remain Caffe Reggio (119 MacDougal Street, tel 212/475-9557) is one of the best, a genuine Italian coffeehouse where you can idle away an afternoon over a few espressos. Le Gamin (132 West Houston at Sullivan Street tel 212/475-1543) is a similar French version. Palacinka (28 Grand Street, tel 212/625-0362) is a small, busy café attracting an artsy SoHo crowd for the restaurant's namesake Eastern European crepes bathed in chocolate, or fresh fruit sauces. The Paris-inspired Payard Patisserie & Bistro (1032 Lexington Avenue, tel 212/717-5252) displays the creations of former Restaurant Daniel pastry chef, François Payard. The pastry case displays all kinds of gems plus handmade chocolates; sorbets are also available. Crowds make their way to the tiny storefront Magnolia Bakery (401 Bleecker Street, tel 212/462-2572) to taste the cupcakes iced with thick ultrasweet buttercream. In the East Village, Veniero's (342 East 11th Street, tel 212/674-7070) has been making and selling delicious Italian pastries for aeons.

EATING

TRADITIONAL AMERICAN FOOD

The United States of America is a nation of immigrants. Traditional American food has evolved out of the traditions of the immigrant populations—German, Jewish, Italian, Scandinavian, Latino, Asian—plus Native American and African-American. Each group has contributed its ingredients and techniques to the current food scene. The Germans brought sauerkraut, sausages and pumpernickel; the Hungarians goulash and stuffed cabbage; the Cubans black bean soup and Cuban cuisines, most notably Southern, Cajun, Southwestern and Tex-Mex.

DRINKS

The New York bar scene is extremely varied. Bars range from cheap dives charging a few dollars for a drink to luxury lounges charging anywhere from $10 for a cocktail. Despite the campaign against drinking and driving, most bars offer happy hours when they charge half price for drinks or offer two for the price of one.

sandwiches; the Irish corned beef and cabbage; the Japanese sushi and teriyaki; the Jews chopped liver pastrami and knishes; the Greeks kebabs; the Lebanese baba ganoush and falafel; the Mexicans salsa, tacos and refried beans; the Moroccans couscous; the Russians blinis and caviar; the Spanish tapas, chorizo and paella; the Swedes gravlax; and the Welsh leek and potato pie. Many of these dishes (or American modifications) have become common fare on all-American menus at standard American restaurants and even at lowly diners. The United States also boasts some distinctive regional

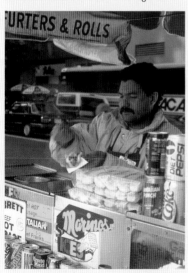

Hot dogs from a Manhattan street vendor

Note that American bartenders expect to be tipped (at least 10 percent). As far as drinks go, international beers and microbrews are readily available; cocktails are in vogue and every day brings a new concoction to light. Food is always available. It ranges from burgers and wings to more sophisticated fare. Most bars open from mid-morning to anywhere from 1am to 4am. Note that the drinking age is 21; expect to be "carded" (to show a photo ID), so carry an identification with photo. Buy wine and liquor at a liquor store; supermarkets sell beer only.

SOME NEW YORK DINING INSTITUTIONS

New York does have some unique dining institutions. The most famous is the deli. Among delis, the most traditional is the Jewish deli, which sells a variety of smoked fish and meats, plus items such as bagels, pastrami and corned beef sandwiches, chopped liver, pickles and knishes. The word deli is also used for small neighborhood grocery stores, often operated by Korean merchants. They sell coffee, bagels, sandwiches, salads and other grocery items.

The coffeeshop/diner is another traditional dining haven. It will have counters and stools as well as table service. Here people secure endless cups of coffee, and breakfast, lunch or dinner selections taken from a vast (usually laminated) menu. The city has plenty of fast-food outlets too (McDonald's, etc). Look for street vendors too. They sell everything from hot salty pretzels to soups, hot dogs and ethnic snacks. The other dining establishment that is endemic to New York is the pizza parlor. The most visible coffee vendor is Starbucks, which seems to be on every corner, but there are plenty of independent cafés, especially in the West and East villages.

EATING

LATE NIGHT/24-HOUR

Despite New York's reputation as a 24/7 town, it's not that easy to find food in the wee hours. Among tried-and-true late-night oases, the hip but strangely unpretentious Blue Ribbon (97 Sullivan Street, tel 212/274-0404) draws clubbers and workers, including many chefs for sesame-glazed catfish, tofu ravioli, paella, and oysters on the half shell. It's open from 4pm to 4am daily.

The Coffee Shop (29 Union Square West, tel 212/243-7969), which looks like what you'd expect, is like nothing you'd find in Peoria with its Brazilian ownership and varied fare.

At Empire Diner (210 Tenth Avenue, tel 212/243-2736), you'll pay for the stylish chrome-and-black art deco setting as well as for the classic egg dishes, sandwiches and meat loaf. It's open around the clock except on Tuesday. In the Meatpacking District, Florent (69 Gansevoort Street, tel 212/989-5779) serves bistro-style food to night owls, clubbers and meat-market workers—onion soup, blood sausage, steak frites and the usual breakfast favorites.

Singles can almost always eat at the bar in Manhattan. If the place is full, or if you want to eat on the run, just ask.

EATING

Bagel
An unsweetened dense eggless bread cooked in water and then baked. It's shaped with a hole in the middle.

Boston baked beans
Navy beans flavored with molasses and salt pork

Chicken-fried steak
Batter-dipped steak

Chowder
Thick soup traditionally made with clams or corn

Cobbler
Fruit pie topped with a biscuit-style crust

Egg cream
A thick drink made with chocolate syrup, milk and seltzer

Eggplant
Aubergine

Eggs over easy
Fried eggs that have been turned over so they are cooked through

Eggs sunnyside up
Fried eggs that have not been turned over

French toast
Bread coated with beaten eggs and sautéed. Served with maple syrup.

Grits
Corn kernels with the bran and germ removed

The famous Oyster Bar in Grand Central Terminal

Hero
An extra-large long roll

Key lime pie
Made with a special lime variety from Florida

London broil
A particular cut of flank steak

Lox
Cured salmon

Meat loaf
Ground beef, turkey and pork

combined with breadcrumbs and egg and baked

New York cheesecake
Jewish-style dense and creamy cake, which may be plain or topped with fruit

On the rocks
With ice

Pot roast
Braised beef

Pretzel
An elongated biscuit, which is shaped and twisted into a knot. It's sprinkled with coarse salt and sold warm from carts on the street.

Salisbury steak
A beef patty

Scotch
Scottish whiskey

Stack of pancakes
Three or four thick batter cakes served with maple syrup

Sub
Short for submarine; another name for an extra-large long roll

Straight up
No ice

Waldorf salad
Apples, celery and walnuts in mayonnaise; first created at the Waldorf Astoria

Whiskey
American rye

RESTAURANTS BY CUISINE

The restaurants listed alphabetically on pages 270 to 290 are grouped here by cuisine.

American contemporary
Annisa
Aureole
Blue Hill
Blue Ribbon Bakery
Cafe Gray
Compass
Craft and Craftbar
Cru
Devin Tavern
Eleven Madison Park
Etats-Unis
Gotham Bar & Grill
Gramercy Tavern
The Harrison
Hudson River Café
Ouest
Per Se
Prune
Red Cat
River Café
Sarabeth's
Tasting Room
Tavern on the Green
Town
Union Square Café
Veritas
WD-50

American regional
Mesa Grill

American traditional
'21' Club

Asian
Ruby Foo's
Spice Market

Barbecue
Blue Smoke
Virgil's Real Barbecue

Burgers
Corner Bistro

Caribbean
Maroons
Negril Village

Chinese
Dim Sum Go Go
Shun Lee Palace

Continental
Four Seasons

Deli
Barney Greengrass
Katz's Deli

Eclectic
Spotted Pig

French
Aix
Artisanal
Balthazar
Bouley
Brasserie
Café Boulud
Chanterelle
Daniel
DB Bistro Moderne
Fleur de Sel
Gordon Ramsay at the London
Jean-Georges
Métisse
Montrachet
Odeon
Paradou
Pastis

Greek
Estiatorio Milos
Molyvos
Periyali

Indian
Banjara
Dawat
Devi
Diwan
Hampton Chutney
Tabla
Tamarind

Italian
Babbo
Bar Pitti
Bread

Cesca
Felidia
Fiamma Osteria
Gnocco
Gonzo
I Coppi
L'Impero
Lupa
Naples 45
Peasant

Japanese
Bond Street
Masa
Nobu
Sugiyama
Sushi Yasuda
Taka
Tomoe Sushi

Korean
Cho Dang Gol
Woo Lae Oak

Latin American
Calle Ocho
Pio Pio

Malaysian
Nyonya

Mediterranean
Picholine

Mexican
Crema Restaurant
Dos Caminos
Hell's Kitchen
La Palapa
Maya
Mesa Grill
Mi Cocina
Pampano
Rosa Mexicano
Sueños
Zarela

Middle Eastern
Persepolis

Noodle shops
Big Wong King

Pizza
John's Pizzeria Pizza
Otto Enoteca Pizzeria

Russian
Uncle Vanya Café

Scandinavian
Aquavit
Good World Bar and Grill

Seafood
Aquagrill
Blue Fin
Esca
Estatorio Milos
Grand Central Oyster Bar
Le Bernardin
Mermaid Inn
Oceana
Pearl Oyster Bar

Soul
Amy Ruth's
Londel's

Spanish
Bolo
Casa Mono
Pintxos
Pipa

Steak
Mark Joseph Steakhouse
Peter Luger Steakhouse
Strip House

Thai
Holy Basil
Pam Real Thai
Vong

Vegetarian
Angelica Kitchen

Vietnamese
Le Colonial
Nam

HOTELS WITH EXCEPTIONAL DINING ROOMS

Four Seasons
Hotel Wales
Le Parker Meridien
Mandarin Oriental
Mark
Mercer Hotel
New York Palace

Ritz-Carlton (Central Park South)
Royalton
Sherry Netherland
Surrey
Trump International Hotel
W-NY

RESTAURANT LOCATOR

↑ Hudson River Café
↑ Métisse
Amy Ruth's, ↑
Londel's

UPPER WEST SIDE

Aix
Barney Greengrass
Ouest
Calle Ocho
Ruby Foo's
Cesca
Compass
Tavern on the Green
Picholine
Rosa Mexicano
Jean-Georges (Trump International Hotel)
Cafe Gray, Masa, Per Se
Sugiyama
Molyvos
Uncle Vanya Café
Est Mil
Gord Rams
Le Bernardin
Pam Real Thai
Blue Fin (W Times Square Hotel)
Hell's Kitchen

West 95th Street
West 94th Street
West 93rd Street
West 92nd Street
West 91st Street
West 90th Street
West 89th Street
West 88th Street
West 87th Street
West 86th Street
West 85th Street
West 84th Street
West 83rd Street
West 82nd Street
West 81st Street
West 80th Street
West 79th Street
West 78th Street
West 77th Street
West 76th Street
West 75th Street
West 74th Street
West 73rd Street
West 72nd Street
West 71st Street
West 70th Street
West 69th Street
West 68th Street
West 67th Street
West 66th Street
West 65th Street
West 64th Street
West 63rd Street
West 62nd Street
West 61st Street
West 60th Street
West 59th Street
West 58th Street
WEST 57TH STREET
West 56th Street
West 55th Street
West 54th Street
West 53rd Street
West 52nd Street
West 51st Street
West 50th Street
West 49th Street
West 48th Street
West 47th Street
West 46th Street
West 45th Street

Riverside Drive
Riverside Park
Hudson River
Highway 9A
West End Avenue
Broadway
Amsterdam Avenue
Columbus Avenue
Central Park West
Ansonia Building
San Remo Apartments
The Dakota
American Museum of Natural History
New-York Historical Society
81st Street Museum of Nat Hist
86th Street
79th Street
72nd Street
Freedom Place
West 69th Street
West 68th Street
Riverside Boulevard
64th Street Lincoln Center
Juilliard School
Lincoln Center
Museum of Biblical Art
Columbus Circle
57th Street
De Wit Clinton Park
12th Av.
11th Avenue
10TH AVENUE
9th Avenue
8th Avenue
7th Avenue
Broadway
Intrepid Sea, Air and Space Museum
Strawberry Fields
The Lake
The Sheep Meadow
CENT PA
Ce Pa Rese
79th Street Tran
268
Car Hal

B
C
D

13
14
15
16
17

RESTAURANT LOCATOR

269

The prices given are for a
two-course lunch (L) for one
person and a three-course à
la carte dinner (D) for one
person. The wine price is the
starting price for a bottle of
wine.

AIX

Map 266 C13
2398 Broadway at 88th Street
Tel 212/874-7400
www.aixnyc.com
Didier Virot has brought
robust Provençal cuisine
to the Upper West Side at
this tri-level restaurant. He
adds his twists to such dishes
as pistou, which is enhanced
with lemon cream, or foie
gras sautéed with almonds,
marinated in Calvados and
vanilla and served in
cinnamon reduction. Desserts
are innovative (apple-rosemary
brioche with honey Calvados
sauce, anyone?).
🕐 Sun–Thu 5.30–10.30, Fri–Sat
5.30–11
🍴 D $60, Wine $32
🚇 86th Street (1)
🚌 M104

AMY RUTH'S

Off map 266 D12
113 West 116th Street between
Malcolm X Boulevard and Adam
Clayton Powell Jr. Blvd
Tel 212/280-8779
It's named for the owner's
grandmother, who taught
her Southern-style cooking.
Most items on the menu are
named for someone, such
as the Reverend Al Sharpton
(chicken and waffles). At
dinner, look for lusty Southern
fried chicken, oxtail stew
and fried or baked catfish.
No alcohol.
🕐 Mon–Thu 7.30am–11pm, Fri–Sun
24hrs
🍴 L $17, D $22
🚇 116th Street (2, 3, B, C)
🚌 M3, M7, M116

ANGELICA KITCHEN

Map 269 F21
300 East 12th Street between First and
Second avenues
Tel 212/228-2909
www.aangelicakitchen.com
This plain, 60s-like spot proves
that vegetarian cuisine does
not have to be bland. Go for
the hearty soups, excellent
chili or tasty noodle dishes and
sandwiches. No alcohol.

No credit cards.
🕐 Daily 11.30–10.30
🍴 L $15, D $20
🚇 14th Street/Union Square (4, 5, 6, L,
N, Q, R, W)
🚌 M14, M15

ANNISA

Map 268 D22
13 Barrow Street between Bleecker and
West 4th streets
Tel 212/741-6699
www.annisarestaurant.com
At this minimalist restaurant
Chef Anita Lo cooks coherent
fusion cuisine. For appetizers,
oysters might arrive with
three root vegetables, while
roasted kabocha squash
and maiiake mushrooms
could be combined with
bitter chocolate. Smoked
lamb hominy is enriched
with chili and lime. No credit
cards.

🕐 Mon–Sat 5.30–10, Sun 5.30–9.30
🍴 D $55, Wine $27
🚇 West 4th Street (A, C, E, F),
Christopher Street/Sheridan Square (1)
🚌 M20, M21

AQUAGRILL

Map 269 E23
210 Spring Street at Sixth Avenue
Tel 212/274-0505
www.aquagrill.com
Every day brings a fresh
selection of seafood—cod,
halibut, grouper, monkfish,
tuna—which can be prepared
to your specifications,
roasted, poached or grilled,
or served in such dishes
as sea bass with smoked

pepper and crispy bacon in
thyme vinaigrette. Star of the
show is the oyster bar, which
offers about 24 varieties.
Prices are fair.
🕐 Mon–Thu noon–3, 6–10.45, Fri
noon–3, 6–11.45, Sat noon–3.45,
6–11.45, Sun noon–3.45, 6–10.30
🍴 L $30, D $50, Wine $27
🚇 Spring Street (C, E)
🚌 M6

AQUAVIT

Map 267 E17
65 East 55th Street between Madison
and Park avenues
Tel 212/307-7311
www.aquavit.org
In a sleek modern space, Chef
Marcus Samuelsson creates
contemporary interpretations
of Swedish–Scandinavian
cuisine: Oysters come
with a mango-curry sorbet;
mushroom broth is poured
over delicately smoked arctic
char. There's a wide selection
of aquavits, plus 250 wines
(15 by the glass). Jackets are
required in the dining room,
but the front café is more
casual and offers more
traditional Scandinavian fare.
🕐 Mon–Thu noon–2.30, 5.30–10.30,
Fri noon–2.30, 5.15–10.45, Sat
noon–2.30, 5–10.45, Sun 5.30–10.30
🍴 L $35, D $82, Wine $45
🚇 Fifth Avenue (E, V)
🚌 M1, M2, M3, M4, M5, M6, M7

ARTISANAL

Map 268 E19
2 Park Avenue at 32nd Street
Tel 212/725-8585
www.artisanalbistro.com
This gem is all about cheese,
and the quality of the
250 varieties in the walk-in
cheese vault is astonishing,
ranging from cabecou de
Rocamadour to callu
de cabreddu. Savor them
straight or in a fondue.
Not to worry if you don't
eat cheese: Escargots, moules
and main dishes such as
crisp skate wing with blood

EATING

orange Grenobloise and steak frites complete the menu. Some 170 wines are available by the glass.

🕐 Mon–Thu 11.45–11, Fri–Sat 11.45–midnight, Sun 11–10
🍽 L $40, D $50, Wine $32
🚇 33rd Street (6)
🚌 M1

AUREOLE

Map 267 E16
34 East 61st Street between Madison and Park avenues
Tel 212/319-1660
www.aureolerestaurant.com

Aureole's chef/owner Charlie Palmer is one of the most highly regarded talents on the American culinary scene. This elegant Upper East Side town-house with a grand staircase and towers of wine, liquor and flowers, is made for special occasions. Palmer uses ultra-fresh ingredients in such signature dishes as slow-poached Maine lobster with heirloom tomatoes, which is served with lemon-verbena-infused consommé, and seared Hudson Valley foie gras. The wine list features 600 selections, 25 by the glass. In summer, sit in the courtyard.

🕐 Mon–Fri noon–2.30, 5.30–11, Sat 5–11
🍽 L $46, D $95, Wine $45
🚇 59th Street (4, 5, 6), 59th Street/Fifth Avenue (N, R, W)
🚌 M1, M2, M3, M4

BALTHAZAR

Map 269 F23
80 Spring Street between Broadway and Lafayette Street
Tel 212/965-1414
www.balthazarny.com

Keith McNally has cloned a classic Paris brasserie with smoky gilded mirrors, tile floor, red-leather banquettes and a vast 27ft (8m) bar. Bistro fare includes the seafood platter piled high with oysters, clams, shrimp and scallops; chicken

---

BABBO

Map 268 E22
110 Waverly Place between MacDougal Street and Sixth Avenue
Tel 212/777-0303
www.babbonyc.com

With his ponytail and orange clogs, Mario Batali has a lust for life that's infectious and an originality that is breathtaking. At Babbo, his flagship restaurant, the welcome is warm and the food some of the freshest and lustiest anywhere. Try the handmade beef cheek ravioli or the prosciutto with spicy fig jam. The deep all-Italian wine list is a revelation.

🕐 Mon–Sat 5.30–11, Sun 5–11
🍽 D $65, Wine $25
🚇 West 4th Street (A, C, E, F, S, V)
🚌 M5, M6

paprika; and skate in brown butter. The place is crowded and vibrant and loaded with celebrity cachet. Bread and pastries come from the adja-cent bakery. The 300-selection wine list is totally French.

🕐 Mon–Thu 7.30–11.30, noon–5, 5.45–1, Fri 7.30–11.30, noon–5, 5.45–2, Sat 8–4, 5.45–2, Sun 8–4, 5.30–midnight
🍽 L $30, D $40, Wine $26
🚇 Prince Street (N, R), Spring Street (6)
🚌 M1, M5

BANJARA

Map 269 F22
97 First Avenue at 6th Street
Tel 212/477-5956

Sixth Street is lined with Indian restaurants, but Banjara is the best of the lot. Northern Indian cuisine is the specialty. The tandoori dishes are particularly good with their fine smoky flavor. Also appealing are the pasanda lamb, cooked in a yogurt-based curry sauce, and the palak ghost—lamb cooked in a purée of spinach, tomatoes, ginger and cumin seeds.

🕐 Daily 12–12
🍽 L $20, D $30, Wine $19
🚇 Astor Place (6)
🚌 M8, M15

BAR PITTI

Map 269 E22
268 Sixth Avenue between Bleecker and Houston streets
Tel 212/982-3300

Actors, writers, fashion

---

designers and Village residents gather at this European-style boîte. In summer, the sidewalk dining affords great people-watching and the chance to observe the comings and goings next door at celebrity hot spot Da Silvano. Your best bet is to select one of the reliable meat, fish or pasta chalkboard specials. Otherwise, choose one of the typical pastas, perhaps spaghetti with clam sauce. No credit cards.

🕐 Daily noon–midnight
🍽 L $25, D $35, Wine $30
🚇 West 4th (A, C, F, S, V), Houston Street (1)
🚌 M5, M6

BARNEY GREENGRASS

Map 266 C13
541 Amsterdam Avenue between West 86th and 87th streets
Tel 212/724-4707
www.barneygreengrass.com

An Upper West Side tradition since 1929, Barney Greengrass is frantic on weekends, when locals come to feast on huge platters of smoked fish—whitefish, sable, sturgeon and lox—or sandwiches made

with similar contents, plus fresh caviar, chopped herring salad, cheese blintzes, borscht and other such specialties. During the week, it's less frenzied. Credit cards are taken on bills of $25 or more only.

🕐 Tue–Fri 8.30–4, Sat–Sun 8.30–5
🍽 L $15, D $20
🚇 86th Street (1)
🚌 M7, M86, M104

BIG WONG KING

Map 269 F24
67 Mott Street between Bayard and Canal streets
Tel 212/964-0540

At this Manhattan restaurant you're guaranteed a cheap, tasty meal. Don't expect any decor, tablecloth or efficient

EATING

service. You're here for
noodles (with duck, chicken,
shrimp), congee and other
standard Cantonese dishes.
No credit cards.

🕒 Daily 8.30am–9pm
🍴 L $15, D $20
🚇 Canal Street (J, M, N, Q, R, W, Z, 6)
🚌 M1

BLUE FIN
Map 268 D18
W Times Square Hotel
1567 Broadway at 47th Street
Tel 212/918-1400
www.Brguestrestaurants.com
The vast, theatrical Blue Fin
made a culinary and design
splash when it opened in
2002. It offers the freshest
fish, prepared simply in such
dishes as salmon in a warm
bacon sherry vinaigrette,
or poached halibut in
ancho-chili-and-vegetable
broth. Sushi is available on
the first floor of the two-story
space, which has a dramatic
floating staircase that looks
out over a school of black
fish suspended from the
ceiling against an undulating
ocean-like white wall. There
are 600 wines on the list,
30 by the glass.

🕒 Daily 7–11, 11.30–4, Sun–Mon
5–midnight, Tue–Thu 5–12.30,
Fri–Sat 5–1
🍴 L $36, D $60, Wine $28
🚇 49th Street (N, R, W), 50th Street (1)
🚌 M10, M20, M27, M104

BLUE HILL
Map 268 E22
75 Washington Place, between
MacDougal and Sixth Avenue
Tel 212/539-1776
www.bluehillnyc.com
Candlelight and extravagant
bouquets set the inviting
tone of this below-ground
dining room. It's named for
a farm in Massachusetts
where the chef finds his
seasonal, locally grown
ingredients. Expect corn shoots

in June, squash and apples
in fall. The menu offers six
appetizers and seven entrées—
say, fall mushrooms braised
and steamed with fingerling
potato tart, followed by
roasted trout with a pistou
of vegetables with puréed
basil, or poached duck
with a stew of organic carrots
with toasted spices. Desserts
are enticing.

🕒 Mon–Sat 5.30–11, Sun 5.30–10
🍴 D $55, Wine $35
🚇 W 4th Street (A, C, E, F, S, V)
🚌 M5, M6

BLUE RIBBON BAKERY
Map 269 D22
35 Downing Street at Bedford Street
Tel 212/337-0404
www.blueribbonrestaurants.com
Refreshing sandwiches made
with house-baked breads and
tasty small plates draw crowds
at lunch, while such dinner
entrées as New Orleans barbecue shrimp and filet mignon
with tomato, onion and water-
cress salad and potato cake

draw night-time customers.
There are so many small
plates—mushroom ravioli,
sweet sopressata, smoked
red trout—you could eat
for two months without
repetition. Cheese lovers
appreciate the choice of goat,
cow and sheep cheeses.
Extensive wine list.

🕒 Mon–Thu noon–midnight, Fri
noon–2am, Sat 11.30am–2am, Sun
11.30am–midnight
🍴 L $25, D $50, Wine $28
🚇 Houston Street (1)
🚌 M20

BLUE SMOKE
Map 268 F20
116 East 27th Street between Park
Avenue South and Lexington Avenue
Tel 212/447-7733
www.bluesmoke.com
The secret of barbecue is
slow cooking and well-
blended spices. Danny Meyer

studied it for three years and
traveled 62,000 miles before
opening this rustic red-hot
restaurant. Barbecue addicts
drool over the rib sampler.
Eight beers are on tap, while
the 50-selection wine list
pairs well with the food.
A good jazz room downstairs
shares the interesting upstairs
menu.

🕒 Mon–Wed 11.30–11, Thu–Fri
11.30–1am, Sat noon–1am, Sun
noon–11pm
🍴 L $25, D $36, Wine $27
🚇 23rd Street (6)
🚌 M1, M101, M102, M103

BOLO
Map 268 E20
23 East 22nd Street between Broadway
and Park Avenue
Tel 212/228-2200
www.bolorestaurant.com
The contemporary Spanish
cuisine shines here against an
understated decor. Chef Bobby
Flay knows how to successfully
assemble contrasting and
complementary flavors—
anchovies in sour orange,
clams in saffron and tomato
among the tapas, and rioja-
glazed tuna or pork tenderloin
with caramelized date sauce
among the more substantial
dishes. Good selection of
wines (13 by the glass) and
spectacular array of sherries.

🕒 Mon–Fri noon–2.30, Sun–Thu
5.30–10, Fri–Sat 5.30–11
🍴 L $24, D$50, Wine $24
🚇 23rd Street (N, R, W, 6)
🚌 M1, M2, M3, M6, M7

BOND STREET
Map 269 F22
6 Bond Street between Broadway and
Lafayette Street
Tel 212/777-2500
The buzz has lessened at this
sleek Japanese spot in a
SoHo brownstone, but the
glistening sushi and sashimi
are as beautiful as ever.
Among the appetizers, expect
seared duck with shitake and
truffle glaze, or monkfish filet
with spicy-and-sour salsa.
Desserts are innovative
Japanese. Traditional tatami
rooms are upstairs; downstairs
there's a fashionable lounge
serving exotic saketinis.

🕒 Tue–Sat 6–11.30, Sun–Mon 6–10.30
🍴 D $45, omakase $60–$100,
Wine $35
🚇 Broadway/Lafayette (F, S, V)
🚌 M1, M5, M6

EATING

BOULEY

Map 269 E24
120 West Broadway at Duane Street
Tel 212/964-2525
www.bouley.net

David Bouley made his name in 1987 when he opened the original Bouley. This gem is his encore. The dining rooms are gorgeous: One is in Venetian stucco with a fireplace; the other has crimson vaulted ceilings and glazed walls hung with Impressionist paintings.

The exquisitely prepared cuisine makes occasional Asian references, as in the chilled lobster with Serrano ham, mango and artichoke, in a Thai curry dressing. Don't miss the Valrhona chocolate soufflé.
🕐 Daily 11.30–3, 5–11.30
🍴 L $55, D $75, Wine $45
🚇 Chambers Street (A, C, E, 1, 2, 3)
🚌 M6, M20

BRASSERIE

Map 267 F17
100 East 53rd Street between Park and Lexington avenues
Tel 212/751-4840
www.patinagroup.com

From its theatrical entrance ramp to its buzzing bar, Brasserie is one very cool room and so very New York. The French-Mediterranean menu is satisfying, ranging as it does from salad Niçoise and burgers (with oyster mushrooms, bacon and roasted onions) to duck cassoulet and rice-crusted black sea bass in lemongrass and lime broth. Great sushi and a raw bar, too.
🕐 Mon–Thu 7–10, 11.30–5.30, 5.30–midnight, Fri 7–10, 11.30–5.30, 5.30–1am, Sat 11–3.30, 5.30–10
🍴 L $40, D $50, Wine $30
🚇 53rd Street/Lexington Avenue (E, V), 51st Street (6)
🚌 M1, M2, M3, M4, M98, M101, M102, M103

BREAD

Map 269 F23
20 Spring Street between Elizabeth and Mott streets
Tel 212/334-1015

This small casual café makes delicious paninis, soups, salads and daily plates. Try the gazpacho in summer and the prosciutto di Parma with truffle oil, bruschetta, spicy shrimp salad, and delicious bread and tomato soup in winter. There is a choice of wines with 12 wines sold by the glass.
🕐 Sun–Thu 10.30–midnight, Fri-Sat 10.30–1am
🍴 L $15, D $25
🚇 Spring Street (6), Bowery (J, M, Z), Grand Street (S)
🚌 M1

CAFÉ BOULUD

Map 267 E15
20 East 76th Street between Fifth and Madison avenues
Tel 212/772-2600
www.danielnyc.com

Many diners consider this casually smart 1930s-style Parisian neighborhood restaurant their favorite Daniel Boulud restaurant. Three Daniel muses inspire the menu—classics, seasons and ethnic cuisines. You will find a pot au feu and a good bouillabaisse; and entrées inspired by Tuscany, Morocco, Vietnam, Spain and the Caribbean. The 450 wine selections are categorized by varietal.
🕐 Tue–Sat noon–2.30, 5.45–11, Sun 11.30–2.30, 5.45–11, Mon 5.45–11
🍴 L $40, D $60, Wine $25
🚇 77th Street (6)
🚌 M1, M2, M3, M4, M79

CAFE GRAY

Map 266 D16
10 Columbus Circle 3rd floor
Tel 212/823-6338

Despite the views of Central Park, the room is not worthy of the cuisine prepared by Swiss-born Gray Kunz, formerly of Lespinasse. He is a consummate artist able to draw on techniques from around the world to create such dishes as lamb chops on carrots melding orange, lemon, cumin and cayenne or branzino in a verbena flavored bouillon.
🕐 Sun–Thu 5–10, Fri-Sat 5–11.30
🍴 L $40, D $60, Wine $40
🚇 59th Street/Columbus Circle (A, B, C, D, 1)
🚌 M5, M7, M10, M20, M104

CALLE OCHO

Map 266 D14
446 Columbus Avenue between West 81st and 82nd streets
Tel 212/873-5025
www.calleochonyc.com

Calle Ocho has brought a limited menu of very good Latin cuisine to the Upper West Side. Start with one of the refreshing ceviches (say,

lobster with lemon, lime and jalapeño) or appetizers like arepa with spicy braised short ribs. Fish and meat dishes are tasty, both the coffee-glazed tuna or the basil chimichurri chicken with roasted almond sauce.
🕐 Mon–Thu 6–11, Fri 6–midnight, Sat 5–midnight, Sun 11.30–3, 5–10
🍴 D $45, Wine $22
🚇 81st Street (B, C)
🚌 M7, M11, M79

CASA MONO

Map 268 F21
52 Irving Place at 17th Street
Tel 212/253-2773
www.casamononyc.com

Mario Batali has turned to Spain for inspiration at this small tapas bar reminiscent of those found in Barcelona and Madrid. It's crowded and noisy and the dishes invite experimentation. There might be bacalao croquettes with orange flavored aioli, cockles with scrambled eggs and Serrano ham, or oxtails with piquillo peppers along with more substantial dishes and great artisanal cheeses. Affordable wine and sherry selection.

🕒 Daily noon–midnight
🍴 L $25, D $36, Wine $30
🚇 14th Street/Union Square L, N, Q, R, W
🚌 M1, M2, M3, M6, M7, M101, M102, M103

CESCA
Map 266 C15
164 West 75th Street (at Amsterdam Avenue)
Tel 212/787-6300
www.cescanyc.com
Popular casual Italian trattoria turning out some very fine cuisine. Settle into a velvet-covered booth and order the veal meatballs in broth or the roasted oysters under a spicy tomato zabaglione and crisp pancetta. It's tasty, relaxing and eminently affordable.

🕒 Mon–Thu 5–11, Fri–Sat 5–11.30, Sun 12–3, 5–10
🍴 D $45, Wine $25
🚇 72nd Street (1, 2, 3)
🚌 M7, M11, M104

CHANTERELLE
Map 269 E24
2 Harrison Street at Hudson Street
Tel 212/966-6960
www.chanterllenyc.com
The presentation of the superb food is simply exquisite at this ultra-spacious classic. The menu changes monthly, but the cuisine is always full-flavored. Conclude with one of the luscious desserts—molten vanilla cake with spring strawberries, for example.

🕒 Thu–Sat noon–2.30, 5.30–11, Sun–Wed 5.30–11
🍴 L $35, 3-course prix fixe $42, D 3-course prix fixe $98, tasting $128, Wine $30
🚇 Franklin Street (1)
🚌 M20

CHO DANG GOL
Map 268 E19
55 West 35th Street between 5th and 6th avenues
Tel 212/695-8222
www.chodanggolny.com
This popular Korean place in the Midtown West area makes its own tofu daily, but it's not a vegetarian restaurant. The tasty tofu (they really know how to cook it) can be mixed with pork, squid and octopus, among other things, with a

casserole being the house specialty. Korean wine is served, but most people opt for sake. Sweet-lovers should note there are no desserts.

🕒 Daily 11.30–10.30
🍴 L $30 D $30 Wine $14
🚇 34th St. Herald Square (B, D, F, N, Q, R, V, W), 34th St. Penn Station (1, 2, 3)
🚌 M5, M6, M7, M16, M34

COMPASS
Map 266 C15
208 West 70th Street at Amsterdam Avenue
Tel 212/875-8600
www.compassrestaurant.com
Chef Neil Annis worked at Bouley and with Alain Ducasse in Paris before taking charge of the Compass kitchen. Here he has maintained its traditions of serving fine contemporary American cuisine with influences (just like New York itself) from all over the world. Dishes like Corn Risotto and Rack of Berkshire Pork with Italian Prune show how the kitchen brings these tastes together superbly.

🕒 Mon–Thu 5–11, Fri-Sat 5–12, Sun 11.30–2.30, 5–10
🍴 D $55 Prix Fixe 3-course menu $35 Wine $24
🚇 72nd Street (1, 2, 3)
🚌 M5, M7 M104

CORNER BISTRO
Map 268 D21
331 West 4th Street between Jane Street and Eighth Avenue
Tel 212/242-9502
www.cornerbistro.ypguides.net

The distressed graffiti-covered tables and booths at this plain West Village bar remain the best place in town to grab burgers. Made with 8oz (225g) hunks of ground chuck, they come plain or topped with bacon or blue cheese. Other sandwiches and chili are also available. Good jukebox and beer. No credit cards.

🕒 Mon–Sat 11.30am–4am, Sun

noon–4am
🍴 L $10, D $15
🚇 14th Street (A, C, E)
🚌 M14, M20

CRAFT AND CRAFTBAR
Map 268 E20
43 East 19th Street between Broadway and Park Avenue South
Tel 212/780-0880
www.craftrestaurant.com
When Tom Colicchio conceived Craft he wanted diners to create their own dishes from a menu that was essentially not any more than a list of ingredients. This is still the focus, but the chef now supplies more direction with superb results. Most dishes are roasted (striped bass, quail) or braised (red snapper, short ribs). Desserts can be perfect fresh fruits, intense sorbets or decadent confections like the toffee steamed pudding. The cheeses are stunning. The leather, copper and steel, and plain wood furnishings and fittings recall the Arts and Crafts movement. Casual Craftbar takes a similar focus-on-the-ingredients approach to sandwiches, fried oysters and braised dishes.

🕒 Mon–Fri noon–2, Mon–Thu 5.30–10, Fri–Sat 5.30–11, Sun 5–9
🍴 L $50, D $65, Wine $28
🚇 23rd Street (N, R, W), 23rd Street (6)
🚌 M1, M2, M3, M6, M7

CREMA RESTAURANTE
Map 268 E21
111 West 17th Street between 6th and 7th avenues
Tel 212/ 691-4477
www.cremarestaurante.com
Julieta Ballasteros has been voted among the top two Mexican chefs in New York six years in a row, by Zagat. Her Chelsea restaurant combines the zingy flavors of Mexico with the subtlety of fine French cuisine, with dishes such as a casserole of cheese and Mexican chorizo served with corn tortillas. Leave room for unusual desserts like the pumpkin cheesecake.

🕒 Tue–Wed, Sun 12–11, Thu–Sat noon–midnight
🍴 L $25 D $45 Wine $22
🚇 18th Street (1), 14th Street (F, V)
🚌 M5, M6, M7, M20

EATING

DB BISTRO MODERNE

Map 268 E18

55 West 44th Street between Fifth and Sixth avenues

Tel 212/391-2400

www.danielnyc.com

This most casual and contemporary of Boulud's restaurants, with its carved wood furniture, beaded curtains and fabric-wrapped ceiling panels, is a great Theater District choice. It's famous for its $27 sirloin burger—a fistful of ground sirloin wrapped around red wine-braised short ribs with truffle and foie gras, served with tomato confit and fresh horseradish. Other delights include: roast salmon with honeyed eggplant (aubergine) and stuffed zucchini (courgette) flowers; Muscovy duck breast with blood orange jus. Extensive wine list.

🕐 Mon–Fri 7–10, 12–2.30, Mon 5–10, Tue 5–11, Wed–Thu 5.15–11, Fri 5–11.30, Sat 8–11, 12–2.30, 5–11.30, Sun 8–11, 5–10

🍴 L $45, D $60, Wine $25

🚇 42nd Street/Grand Central (S, 4, 5, 6, 7), 42nd Street (B, D, F, V)

🚌 M1, M2, M3, M4, M42

CRU

Map 268 E22

24 Fifth Avenue at Ninth Street

Tel 212/529-1700

www.cru-nyc.com

The 3,000-selection wine list (50 by the glass) is a gift to wine lovers to be accompanied by some carefully prepared contemporary European cuisine in elegant surroundings. Start with crudo or appetizers, which will supply such delights as fluke with mango and caviar or tuna with caper espresso and olives praline. Entrees are equally exciting, even revelatory—just try the silky poussin baked in buttermilk and finished with orange paprika carrots and chanterelles and parsley root.

🕐 Mon–Sat 5.30–11 (closed Mon in Aug)

🍴 D $78, Wine $36

🚇 8th Street (N, R, W)

🚌 M2, M3, M5, M8

DANIEL

Map 267 E16

60 East 65th Street at Park Avenue

Tel 212/288-0033

www.danielnyc.com

Lyons-born chef Daniel Boulud opened this restaurant in 1993. It has all the romance of an Italian Renaissance palazzo, and dining here is a joyous experience. Signature dishes include the creamy oyster velouté with lemongrass and caviar, roast squab stuffed with foie gras and black truffle, and chocolate fondant with nougatine. Warm madeleines,

home-made chocolates and petits fours conclude the meal. The predominantly French wine list offers more than 1,600 selections. Jacket and tie required.

🕐 Mon–Sat 5.45–11

🍴 D 3-course prix fixe $98, tasting menus $165–$185, Wine $30

🚇 63rd Street/Lexington (F), 68th Street (6)

🚌 M1, M2, M3, M4, M66

DAWAT

Map 267 F16

210 East 58th Street between Second and Third avenues

Tel 212/355-7555

www.restaurant.com/dawat

Cookbook author Madhur Jaffrey consults on the menu at this comfortable Indian, aptly named "invitation to feast." The spices are skillfully blended to subtle effect in such dishes as shrimp in coconut sauce flavored with

curry leaves and smoked tamarind; chicken tikka; and baby goat in cardamom sauce. Appealing rice and vegetarian specialties.

🕐 Mon–Sat 11.30–3, 5.30–11, Sun 5.30–11

🍴 L $60, D $65, Tasting menus $45, $65, $75, Wine $19

🚇 59th Street/Lexington Avenue (6)

🚌 M15, M57, M98, M101, M102, M103

DEVI

Map 268 E21

8 East 18th Street between Fifth Avenue and Broadway

Tel 212/691-1300

www.devinyc.com

Antique palace doors, etched colored glass lanterns, and raw silk will transport you to India in a minute. And so will the food, which draws inspiration from street food and from good regional cuisine. Goan shrimp are cooked with balchao, a vinegar based sauce; fishes are baked in banana leaf to retain their flavor; Manchurian cauliflower is a fiery mixture of tomato sauce with scallions and chilies. All are redolent with cilantro (coriander), mint, tamarind and coconut.

🕐 Mon–Sun 5.30–11

🍴 D $45 3 courses, $65 6-course tasting menu, Wine $35

🚇 14th Street/Union Square (L, N, Q, R, W, 4, 5, 6)

🚌 M2, M3, M5, M6, M7

DEVIN TAVERN

Map 269 E24

363 Greenwich Street between Franklin and Harrison streets

Tel 212/334-7337

www.devintavern.com

The rather ordinary name conceals an extraordinarily good menu of mostly simple dishes superbly done. The decor of this TriBeCa place echoes the cuisine with a kind of rustic elegance, and the menu offers entrées such as Long Island Duck Breast and Pepper Crusted Venison. Other options like the Lobster Club Sandwich and Stone Peach Melba show where the kitchen's coming from, and it succeeds admirably.

🕐 Mon–Thu 12–3, 5.30–11, Fri 12–3, 5.30–12, Sat 5.30–12, Sun 11–4, 5.30–9

🍴 L $25, D $50, Wine $25

🚇 Franklin Street (1), Chambers (A, C)

🚌 M20

DIM SUM GO GO

Map 269 F24

5 East Broadway between Catherine and Oliver streets

Tel 212/732-0797

At this small, modernist restaurant you can find the latest in Chinese cuisine: updated dim sum, presented in bamboo steamers or on pupu platters. Expect jicama and lotus root dumplings, crabmeat stuffed in green spinach dough, wood mushrooms and carrot dumplings. Pork buns and shrimp dumplings are the kitchen's nod to tradition.

🕐 Daily 10am–11pm

🍴 L $23, D $27

🚇 East Broadway (F), Canal Street (J, M, N, R, Q, W, Z, 6)

🚌 M9, M15, M22

DIWAN

Map 267 F16

148 East 48th Street between Lexington and Third avenues

Tel 212/593-5425

This uptown Indian trendsetter serves more than traditional dishes like vindaloos, chicken murgh and tandoori. You can also expect butter chicken, apricot Cornish hens, lamb in almond sauce, and sea bass with fenugreek sauce.

🕐 Mon–Thu 11.30–2.30, 5–10.30, Fri 11.30–2.30, 5–11, Sat–Sun 5–11

🍴 L $24, D $40, Wine $20

🚇 51st Street (6)

🚌 M50, M98, M101, M102, M103

DOS CAMINOS

Map 268 E20

373 Park Avenue South between 26th and 27th streets

Tel 212/294-1000

www.brguestrestaurants.com

This is as far from an enchilada hut as you can get. The space is celebratory, the bar stocks 150 tequilas, and the fare covers all the bases—guacamole made tableside; shrimp, scallop and tuna ceviche; chicken mole; and pan-roasted snapper with pineapple-passion fruit sauce. Desserts run to ice creams and sorbets such as guava-mango sorbet.

🕐 Daily 11.30–4, Sun–Tue 5–11, Wed–Thu 5–11.30, Fri–Sat 5–12.30am

🍴 L $25, D $40, Wine $32

🚇 28th Street (6)

🚌 M1

ELEVEN MADISON PARK

Map 268 E20

11 Madison Avenue at 24th Street

Tel 212/889-0905

www.elevenmadisonpark.com

This dramatic dining space, once the brokers' hall of the Metropolitan Life insurance company, is worthy of the cuisine created by Daniel Humm. The fish dishes are fragrant and moist (seared Arctic char in black truffle vinaigrette), and meat dishes robust (grilled hanger steak in shallot sauce).

Appetizers include seared foie gras in a sauternes coulis. The international wine list leans to the French, and there are 36 options by the glass.

🕐 Daily 11.30–2, Sun–Thu 5.30–10, Fri–Sat 5.30–10.30

🍴 L $45, D $82, Wine $35

🚇 23rd Street (6)

🚌 M1, M2, M3

ESCA

Map 268 D18

402 West 43rd Street at Ninth Avenue

Tel 212/564-7272

www.esca-nyc.com

Esca, another star in Mario Batali's firmament, prepares fish Southern Italian style. The menu changes daily, but you might find Mediterranean sea bass in sea salt or Amalfi-style fritto misto, with crispy scrod, skate, calamari, steamers, oysters and shrimp. Appetizers run to crispy Neapolitan-style eel and juicy morsels from a serious raw bar.

🕐 Mon–Sat noon–2.30, Mon 5–10.30, Tue–Sat 5–11.30, Sun 4.30–10.30

🍴 L $35, D $50, Wine $28

🚇 42nd Street (A, C, E)

🚌 M11

ESTIATORIO MILOS

Map 266 D17

125 West 55th Street between Sixth and Seventh avenues

Tel 212/245-7400

www.milos.ca

Some 19 selections of fish are priced by the pound and range from pompano and monkfish to tuna and swordfish. Your choice will be filleted at the table. Appetizers lean to the briny, like calamari stuffed with three types of cheese and fresh mint. Honey, nuts and yogurt come to the fore in the traditional sweets.

🕐 Mon–Sat noon–3, 5.30–11, Sun 5–11

🍴 L 3-course prix fixe $35, D $67, Wine $40

🚇 57th Street (F), 57th Street (N, Q, R, W)

🚌 M10, M20

ETATS-UNIS

Map 267 F14

242 East 81st Street between Second and Third avenues

Tel 212/517-8826

www.etatsunisrestaurant.com

French though the motif maybe, this is still an American neighborhood restaurant. The bistro-style menu changes daily. Look for veal in Riesling with shitake and oyster mushrooms, and a charcoal-grilled swordfish in sweet red pepper purée. Desserts are delicious and there is a good selection of cheeses.

🕐 Daily 6–10

🍴 D $65, Wine $28

🚇 77th Street (6)

🚌 M15, M79, M98, M101, M102, M103

EATING

FOUR SEASONS

Map 267 F17

99 East 52nd Street between Park and Lexington avenues

Tel 212/754-9494

www.fourseasonsrestaurant.com

Titans and moguls have regular tables at this modernist power restaurant designed by Philip Johnson and Mies van der Rohe. When it opened in 1959, it helped launch the city's food revolution. The square bar at the center of the rosewood-paneled Grill Room is a great cocktail spot. The pièce de résistance is the Pool Room, with a large fountain as centerpiece. Chef Christian Albin's signature dish is roast duck, which is carved table-side. The soufflés are justly famous. First-rate wine list.

Ⓣ Mon–Fri noon–2.15, 5–9.30, Sat 5–11.30

Ⓕ L $70, D $100, Wine $45

Ⓢ 51st Street (6), Fifth Avenue/53rd Street (E, V)

Ⓑ M50, M98, M101, M102, M103

FELIDIA

Map 267 F16

243 East 58th Street between Second and Third avenues

Tel 212/758-1479

www.lidiasitaly.com

Owner Lidia Bastianich is a tireless promoter of Italian cuisine and Felidia is a top Italian restaurant. The Istrian wedding pillows, stuffed with rum, raisins and three cheeses, are a signature dish, but chef Fortunato Nicotra has added regional dishes, such as roasted goose ravioli. The wine list offers great Italian labels.

Ⓣ Mon–Thu noon–2.30, 5–11, Fri noon–2, 5–11.30, Sat 5–11.30

Ⓕ L $40, 3-course prix fixe $29.50, D $55, Wine $30

Ⓢ 59th Street (4, 5, 6)

Ⓑ M15, M57, M98, M101, M102, M103

FIAMMA OSTERIA

Map 269 E23

206 Spring Street between Sixth Avenue and Sullivan Street

Tel 212/653-0100

www.brguestrestaurants.com

An Italian bistro with attitude, this bi-level restaurant is as much about Hollywood styling as it is about food. Red wine braised octopus and corona beans with olives and peppers, stracci with rabbit Bolognese and other exceptional pastas, plus veal chops perfumed with sage and served with caramelized sweet and sour cipollini onions are some of the beguiling dishes.

Ⓣ Mon 6–10, Tue–Thu 6–11, Fri 6–midnight, Sat 5.30–midnight

Ⓕ L $36, D $65, Wine $35

Ⓢ Spring Street (C, E)

Ⓑ M6

FLEUR DE SEL

Map 268 E20

5 East 20th Street between Broadway and Fifth Avenue

Tel 212/460-9100

www.fleurdeselnyc.com

It may look unassuming but the food is not at this French gem. Many dishes have surprising elements. Imagine venison in a beet licorice sauce, sea bass with Malbec wine sauce or rack of lamb with horseradish crème and rosemary jus. Desserts are equally thrilling.

Ⓣ Daily noon–2, Mon–Sat 5.30–10.30, Sun 5–9

Ⓕ L prix fixe $29, D prix fixe $76,

6-course $89, Wine $48

Ⓢ 23rd Street (N, R, W)

Ⓑ M2, M3, M5, M6, M7

GNOCCO

Map 269 G21

337 East 10th Street between A and B avenues

Tel 212/677-1913

www.gnocco.com

No prizes for guessing the house specialty here—delicious home-made gnocco which are fried and served with either a sauce or a cold meat plate and not to be confused with gnocchi. Either way these, and the other fresh pasta dishes, are Italian cooking at its best. The intimate dining room conceals a lovely garden dining area out back, and the service is relaxed and amiable Italian-style.

Ⓣ Mon–Fri 5pm–midnight, Sat–Sun noon–midnight

Ⓕ L $20, D $40, Wine $28

Ⓢ Astor Place (6), First Avenue (L)

Ⓑ M8, M9, M14a

GONZO

Map 268 D21

140 West 13th Street between Sixth and Seventh avenues

Tel 212/645-4606

Gonzo may be moderately priced, but the rustic food is very good, made with ultra-fresh ingredients and served to a hip lively crowd in a comfortable setting. Start your meal with a plate of sliced meats and cheeses or cicchetti, such as beet and Gorgonzola salad, or chickpea and sun-dried tomato spread. The pastas and pizzas are inventive. Among entrées, the Venetian calf's liver is superb.

Ⓣ Mon–Thu 5.30–11, Fri 5.30–midnight, Sat 5–midnight, Sun 5–10.30

Ⓕ D $40, Wine $28

Ⓢ 14th Street

Ⓑ M5, M6, M20

GOOD WORLD BAR AND GRILL

Map 269 G24

3 Orchard Street between Canal and Division streets

Tel 212/925-9975

www.goodworldbar.com

Distinctive Swedish cuisine is served in this lively, refreshing dining room. Here, several kinds of herring are offered, along with gravlax, Swedish meatballs and game in season. A Swedish-interpreted burger comes with capers and beets.

Ⓣ Daily 11–4am

Ⓕ L $25, D $40, Wine $28

Ⓢ East Broadway (F), Grand Street (S)

Ⓑ M15

GORDON RAMSAY AT THE LONDON

Map 266 D17
The London NYC Hotel, 151 West 54th Street between 6th and 7th avenues
Tel 212/ 468-8888
www.gordonramsay.com

All eyes were on the UK's star chef Gordon Ramsay when he moved into the London NYC Hotel in 2006, wondering if he could succeed in the Big Apple too. In 2007 he won two Michelin stars, which answered the doubters. You'll need to book two months ahead—exactly two months ahead, as tables go as soon as they're available, with diners longing to try Ramsay's supreme ability to combine flavors and let every single one shine through in dishes like his baked fluke with almond bread, celery hearts, Concord grapes and champagne velouté.

🕐 Daily 12–2.30, 5.30–11
🍽 L Prix Fixe 3-course $45 D $90, 7-course Menu Prestige $120 W $43
🚇 7th Avenue (B, D, E), 57th Street (N, Q, R, W)
🚌 M6, M7

GOTHAM BAR & GRILL

Map 268 E21
12 East 12th Street between Fifth Avenue and University Place
Tel 212/620-4020
www.gothambarandgrill.com

Unique among Manhattan celebrity chefs, Alfred Portale has not yet created his own mini-chain. This may be why his fresh-tasting, dramatically presented contemporary cuisine continues to excite even after more than 20 years. Rack of lamb is Portale's signature dish, but you can't go wrong with the truffle crusted halibut with verjus sauce or the Snake River Farms pork with caramelized cipollini onions. The warm apple and mango tartes tatin and the warm Gotham chocolate cake are sublime. Extra-special tea selections.

🕐 Mon–Fri noon–2.15, Mon–Thu 5.30–10, Fri 5.30–11, Sat 5–11, Sun 5–10
🍽 L $35, D $70, Wine $40
🚇 14th Street/Union Square (L, N, Q, R, W, 4, 5, 6)
🚌 M2, M3, M5

GRAMERCY TAVERN

Map 268 E20
42 East 20th Street between Broadway and Park Avenue South
Tel 212/477-0777
www.gramercytavern.com

Danny Meyer's stellar restaurant, under Executive Chef Michael Anthony, still shines. Both the main dining room (a warren of several cozy rooms) and the more casual tavern in the front are striking and comfortable. The truly warm hospitality and the seamless service make this one of the city's top tables. You can't go wrong on this menu, which offers a seared foie gras paired with a rhubarb tart, arugula and

sherry vinegar, and a roasted monkfish wrapped with pancetta. Twenty-five wines from the superb list are available by the glass. Desserts are equally as delightful as the main dishes.

🕐 Dining room: Mon–Fri noon–2, Sun–Thu 5.30–10, Fri–Sat 5.30–11; Tavern: Sun–Thu noon–11, Fri–Sat noon–midnight
🍽 L $35, 3-course prix fixe $36, D 3-course prix fixe $82, tasting menu $110; Tavern L $30, D $40, Wine $24
🚇 23rd Street (N, R, W)
🚌 M1, M2, M3, M6, M7

GRAND CENTRAL OYSTER BAR

Map 268 E18
Grand Central Terminal, 42nd Street and Park Avenue
Tel 212/490-6650
www.oysterbarny.com

You don't have to love oysters to love this legendary room in the lower level of Grand Central. Since it opened in 1913 the Guastavino-tiled space has starred in many a movie. Today, it's jammed at lunch and busy in the early evening with people

sampling the 20–30 fresh fish choices, or slurping down oysters in a dozen varieties, all flown in daily. The chowders and chowderlike panroasts are famous.

🕐 Mon–Fri 11.30–9.30, Sat noon–9.30
🍽 L $35, D $45, Wine $26
🚇 42nd Street/Grand Central (4, 5, 6)
🚌 M1, M2, M3

HAMPTON CHUTNEY

Map 269 F23
68 Prince Street between Crosby and Lafayette streets
Tel 212/226-9996
www.hamptonchutney.com

South Indian dosas and uttapas are the specialties of this counter-style eatery. The classic dosa is filled with spiced potato here, but many Western-inspired variations are offered, from avocado, tomato, arugula and jack cheese, to tuna with cilantro-chutney dressing. Good sandwiches on black, sourdough and other breads, too. Chai and lassi are the choice drinks.

🕐 Daily 11–9
🍽 $12
🚇 Prince Street (N, R), Broadway/Lafayette (F, S, V), Spring Street (6)
🚌 M1, M6

THE HARRISON

Map 269 E24
355 Greenwich Street at Harrison Street
Tel 212/274-9310
www.theharrison.com

With its tufted leather banquettes and weathered wood paneling, this friendly, inviting restaurant is the kind of neighborhood spot where people drop in regularly. The food is brimming with flavor; the skillet calf's liver comes with bacon, onion and potato strudel in a rich sherry sauce; while sautéed skate is redolent of treviso, pancetta and preserved lemon. The spicy

EATING

French fries are superb.

🕐 Mon–Thu 5.30–11, Fri–Sat 5.30–11.30, Sun 5–10
🍴 D $45, Wine $25
🚇 Franklin Street (1)
🚌 M20

HELL'S KITCHEN
Map 268 D18
679 Ninth Avenue between West 46th and 47th streets
Tel 212/977-1588

Here, a contemporary interpretation of Mexican cuisine uses prime American ingredients. Start with calamari in smoked chipotle broth, or chayote and portobello mushroom roll with chipotle pepper sauce. The strong exotic drinks from the bar match the interesting and robust flavors.

🕐 Tue–Fri 11.30–3, Sun–Tue 5–11, Wed–Sat 5–midnight
🍴 L $20, D $37, Wine $24
🚇 42nd Street (A, C, E)
🚌 M11

HOLY BASIL
Map 269 F22
149 Second Avenue between East 9th and 10th streets
Tel 212/460-5557
www.holybasilrestaurant.com

This is one of the city's best Thai restaurants. Here, the kitchen balances the flavors

of sweet and salt associated with the cuisine. The stars are the fish dishes, such as the whole crisp fish, which you can order in red chili sauce or a delicious tamarind sauce. Wine selections pair well with the food.

🕐 Mon–Thu 5–11.30, Fri 5–midnight, Sat 4–midnight, Sun 4–11
🍴 D $30, Wine $23
🚇 Astor Place (6)
🚌 M15

JEAN-GEORGES
Map 266 D16
Trump International Hotel Tower
1 Central Park West between 60th and 61st streets
Tel 212/299-3900
www.jean-georges.com

Jean-Georges Vongerichten is the toast of the town. Thoroughly French, he has developed a signature cuisine that is intensely flavored and highly textured, based on vegetable and fruit essences, oils, vinaigrettes and broths. Stellar examples are the peekytoe crab and English pea fondue with rhubarb gelée and shiso purée, and the veal tenderloin with fricasee of mushrooms, fava beans, and Meyer lemon with liquid Parmesan. It's hard to snag a table here, so consider dining in the less formal Nougatine at the same address. There's a 700-plus-strong wine list. Terrace dining in summer.

🕐 Mon–Thu 12–2.30, 5.30–11, Fri 12–2.30, 5.15–11, Sat 5.15–11, closed Sun
🍴 L $45, 3-course $20 (in Nougatine), 2-course $24; D $60, 4-course prix fixe $95, 7-course prix fixe $125, Wine $22
🚇 59th Street/Columbus Circle (A, C, B, D, 1)
🚌 M7, M10, M20

HUDSON RIVER CAFÉ
Map 266 B13 (off map)
[697 West 133rd Street at 12th Avenue
Tel 212/ 491-9111
http://hudsonrivercafe.com

There's live jazz every Wednesday and Sunday evening, and brunch on Saturdays and Sundays, all adding to the easy-going feel of the Hudson River Café. The menu doesn't try to be over-fancy, and the prices are reasonable, especially the wine, but dishes like the steamed mussels in fresh

herbs, chardonnay and Dijon mustard, and filet mignon in a brandy mustard sauce keep customers coming back.

🕐 Mon–Fri 5pm–midnight, Sat 11–3, 5–12, Sun 11–3, 5–10
🍴 D $50, Wine $25
🚇 125th Street (1)
🚌 M5

I COPPI
Map 269 G22
432 East 9th Street between First Avenue and Avenue A
Tel 212/254-2263
www.icoppinyc.com

This restaurant is like a piece of Tuscany in Manhattan. Wood tables and rush-seated chairs create a rustic charm accompanied by music from the opera and floral bouquets. Tuna carpaccio is paper-thin and spiked with green peppercorn sauce; sliced pears with Gorgonzola and stracchino cheese make for a perfect salad. Among the secondi, there might be grilled wild boar, or wild striped bass with caper and black olives. The wine list leans to Italy.

🕐 Mon–Thu 5–11, Fri 5–11.30, Sat 11.30–3, 5–10, Sun 11.30–4, 5–10.30
🍴 D $50, Wine $25
🚇 Astor Place (6)
🚌 M8, M14, M15

L'IMPERO
Off map 268 F18
45 Tudor City Place (access from East 41st Street)
Tel 212/599-5045
www.limpero.com

Tucked away in Tudor City, L'Impero is a lovely hideaway. The dining rooms are comfortable and seductively lit, the service gracious, and the food extremely good and even affordable. Taste the roasted lobster with chickpeas, the extraordinary pastas (farfalle with sweetbreads, bitter greens, chanterelles and shallots or the duck and foie gras agnolotti), and delicious secondi like the roast capretto. The wine list is excellent and fairly priced.

🕐 Mon–Thu noon–2.30, 5.30–10.30, Fri noon–2.30, 5–11.30, Sat 5–11.30
🍴 L $40, D $55, Wine $30
🚇 42nd Street/Grand Central (4, 5, 6)
🚌 M15, M27, M42, M50

EATING

JOHN'S PIZZERIA PIZZA

Map 268 D22

278 Bleecker Street between Sixth and Seventh avenues

Tel 212/243-1680

www.johnspizzerianyc.com

The pizza served at this John's Pizzeria is frequently touted as the best in the city, and it is extraordinarily good indeed. Note that this is not a pizza parlor; slices are not available. Instead, take a booth and order a whole pie loaded with toppings—more than 50 are available. No credit cards.

🕐 Mon–Sat 11.30–11.30, Sun noon–11.30

🍴 L $20, D $30, Wine $18

🚇 West 4th Street (A, C, E, F, S, V), Christopher Street/Sheridan Square (1)

🚌 M5, M20

KATZ'S DELI

Map 269 G22

205 East Houston Street between Ludlow and Orchard streets

Tel 212/254-2246

www.katzdeli.com

The site of the hilarious climactic scene in *When Harry Met Sally* is the last remaining deli in what was once a thriving Jewish neighborhood. Opened in 1888, it upholds deli traditions: nondescript surroundings and immense knishes and pastrami sandwiches. Credit cards accepted on bills of $20 and more only.

🕐 Sun, Wed–Thu 8am–10.45pm, Mon–Tue 8am–9.45pm, Fri–Sat 8am–2.45am

🍴 L $15, D $20

🚇 Lower East Side/Second Avenue (F, V)

🚌 M14, M15, M21

LA PALAPA

Map 269 F22

77 St. Mark's Place between First and Second avenues

Tel 212/777-2537

www.lapalapa.com

At this dark and sultry Mexican, cookbook author Diana Kennedy is the inspiration for much of the cooking, which reveals the complex flavors of epazote, cactus pads, avocado leaves and numerous chilies. The balance is always right, whether in the shrimp with red mole sauce, or the baked cod with guajillo, garlic and achiote barbecue sauce. Meat dishes are also well spiced. Then there are the extras—pinto beans with smoked bacon and chayotes in spicy cream.

🕐 Mon–Fri noon–midnight, Sat–Sun 11am–midnight

🍴 L $20, D $35, Wine $26

🚇 Astor Place (6)

🚌 M8, M15

LE COLONIAL

Map 267 F16

149 East 57th Street between Lexington and Third avenues

Tel 212/752-0808

www.lecolonialnyc.com

The bamboo-and-fans French colonial ambience is a perfect backdrop for the Vietnamese cuisine at this striking spot. Start with chao tom (grilled shrimp wrapped around sugarcane with angel-hair noodles, lettuce, mint and peanut dipping sauce) or the delicious steamed ravioli with chicken and mushrooms. The steamed sea bass dishes are outstanding.

LE BERNARDIN

Map 266 D17

155 West 51st Street between Sixth and Seventh avenues

Tel 212/489-1515

www.le-bernardin.com

Le Bernardin, the best seafood restaurant in the city, may also be the best restaurant in the city. The teak-paneled room is spacious and comfortable, the service discreet and precise, and the food exquisite. Chef Eric Ripert's dishes are designed to show off the flavor and texture of the specific type of fish. Cod is served in a sage and garlic broth, halibut poached in lemongrass and coconut, and monkfish oven roasted and served with lemon-paprika sauce. Signature appetizers—tuna carpaccio; a scallop wrapped in a cabbage leaf with foie gras and truffles and steamed; and black bass ceviche topped with coriander, mint, jalapeños and tomatoes—are all gems. Desserts are equally inspirational.

🕐 Mon–Fri noon–2.30, Mon–Thu 5.30–10.30, Fri–Sat 5.30–11

🍴 L prix fixe $64, D 3-course prix fixe $107, Wine $50

🚇 47th–50th streets/Rockefeller Center (B, D, F, V), 49th Street (N, R, W)

🚌 M5, M6, M7

🕐 Mon–Fri noon–2, Sun–Mon 5.30–10.30, Tue–Thu 5.30–11, Fri–Sat 5.30–11.30

🍴 L $30, D $37, Wine $38

🚇 59th Street (4, 5, 6), 59th Street/Lexington Avenue (N, R, W)

🚌 M57, M98, M101, M102, M103

LONDEL'S

Off map 266 D12

2620 Frederick Douglass Boulevard between 139th and 140th streets

Tel 212/234-6114

www.londelsrestaurant.com

The South has given the United States its most distinctive cuisine, and this restaurant serves some of the best, from the Southern fried chicken and barbecue back ribs to the blackened catfish. Order collard greens or candied yams on the side, and bread pudding with rum sauce. You'll have had a feast. Live music on

EATING

Friday and Saturday.
- ⏰ Tue–Sat 11.30am–midnight
- 🍴 L $18, D $30, Wine $25
- Ⓜ 145th Street (A, B, C, D)
- 🚌 M10

LUPA
Map 269 E22
170 Thompson Street between Bleecker and Houston streets
Tel 212/982-5089
www.luparestaurant.com

Lupa, beloved Food Channel host Mario Batali's moderately priced restaurant, has the feel of a casual Roman trattoria. The cuisine starts with ultra-fresh staples, many of which are made on the premises, notably the pasta, sausages and cheeses featured as appetizers. The simple, intense main dishes range from a classic saltimbocca to bucatini all' amatriciana, made with bacon, onions and cilantro. Side dishes such as the braised escarole and the cauliflower with capers are worthy, too.
- ⏰ Daily noon–midnight
- 🍴 L $27, D $35, Wine $21
- Ⓜ West 4th Street (A, C, E, F, S, V)
- 🚌 M5, M6, M21

MARK JOSEPH STEAKHOUSE
Map 269 F25
261 Water Street at Peck Slip
Tel 212/277-0020
www.markjosephsteakhouse.com
Those who have had enough of Peter Luger's sawdust-on-the-floor style claim that this sleek and more modern meat specialist is the city's best steakhouse. The porterhouse is the choice cut. Add a salad and an order of the hash-brown potatoes, finish with the apple galette or a slice of pecan pie.
- ⏰ Mon–Fri 11.30–10, Fri 11.30–11, Sat 5–11
- 🍴 L $30, D $60, Wine $30
- Ⓜ Broadway-Nassau (A, C), Fulton Street (J, M, Z, 2, 3, 4, 5)
- 🚌 M9, M15

MAROONS
Map 268 D21
244 West 16th Street between Seventh and Eighth avenues
Tel 212/206-8640
www.maroonsnyc.com
Southern and Jamaican flavors are the draw at this small, unassuming restaurant. This is one place you can find fried green tomatoes, luscious fried chicken, fiery Jamaican jerk chicken and other regional delights.
- ⏰ Tue–Sun 11.30–3.30, daily 5.30–midnight
- 🍴 L $25, D $35, Wine $21
- Ⓜ 18th Street (1), 14th Street (A, C, E)
- 🚌 M20

MASA
Map 266 D16
Time Warner Center
10 Columbus Circle 4th Floor
Tel 212/823-9800
www.masanyc.com
Currently the Holy Grail of dining in Manhattan. Here, sushi chef Masa (from Tokyo via Los Angeles) holds forth behind his hinoki counter creating whatever he has selected as the freshest and best from around the world. It seats only 26 (10 at the sushi bar) and sushi lovers swear it is nirvana.
- ⏰ Tue–Fri noon–1.30, Mon–Sat 6–9.30
- 🍴 $400 prix fixe ($100 penalty for cancellations within 48 hours of reservation), Wine $40
- Ⓜ 59th Street/Columbus Circle (A, B, C, D, 1, 9)
- 🚌 M5, M7, M10, M20, M104

MAYA
Map 267 F16
1191 First Avenue between East 64th and 65th streets
Tel 212/585-1818
www.modernmexican.com
Sophisticated Mexican cuisine is the draw here. The chile relleno stuffed with seafood and gouda cheese is a palate-pleasing combination and the guacamole, served in the stone pestle in which it's made, is among the best in the city. The pork tenderloin marinated with onion-orange salsa is ultra tender and richly flavored. A winner. No credit cards.
- ⏰ Tue–Thu 5–11, Fri–Sat 5–11.30, Sun–Mon 5–10
- 🍴 D $42, Wine $32
- Ⓜ Lexington Avenue/63rd Street (F), 68th Street (6)
- 🚌 M15

MERMAID INN
Map 269 F22
96 Second Avenue between 5th and 6th streets
Tel 212/674-5870
www.themermaidnyc.com
This is the closest that Manhattan can come to a seafood shack complete with ocean paraphernalia and navigational charts. The menu opens with a small selection of raw shellfish and follows with everything from chowder and spaghetti fra diavolo to zaruela brimming with lobster tail, cod and squid. No desserts are available, except what the house provides for free.
- ⏰ Mon–Sat 6–1
- 🍴 D $35, Wine $28
- Ⓜ Astor Place (6), Eighth Street (N, R, W)
- 🚌 M15, M103

MESA GRILL
Map 268 E21
102 Fifth Avenue between 15th and 16th streets
Tel 212/807-7400
www.mesagrill.com

When Bobby Flay opened this restaurant in 1991, he introduced New Yorkers to the spices of the Southwest, and the place continues to excite. The red walls recall Sedona rock, the shrimp and fresh corn with black pepper tamale is hot off the grill, and the cactus pear margaritas cool the heat. Follow the cornmeal-crusted oysters and mango habanero sauce with sixteen-spice chicken in cilantro-pumpkin seed sauce. Brunches are distinctive as well—it's not everywhere you'll find tequila-smoked-salmon quesadilla.
- ⏰ Mon–Fri noon–2.30, Sat 11.30–2.30, Sun 11.30–3, Sun–Thu 5.30–10.30, Fri–Sat 5–11
- 🍴 L $25, D $48, Wine $26
- Ⓜ 14th Street/Union Square (L, N, Q, R, W, 4, 5, 6)
- 🚌 M2, M3, M5, M14

EATING

MÉTISSE

Map 266 C13 (off map)
239 West 105th Street at Broadway
Tel 212/666-8825
www.metissefrenchbistro.com

Wednesdays here are popular nights with live French gypsy jazz music and half-price bottles of wine, though Métisse buzzes on other nights too with diners taking advantage of the French bistro dishes such as *coq au vin* and *steak frites*. The atmosphere and decor are both French bistro too, and the wine list is predominantly French—and affordable, even without the half-price offer.

🕐 Mon 4–10.30, Tue–Thu 11–10.30, Fri 11–11, Sat 10.30–11, Sun 10.30–10
🍽 L $20 and 3-course prix fixe $16.95, D $35 and 3-course prix fixe $19.95, Wine $28
🚇 103rd Street (1)
🚌 M60, M104

MI COCINA

Map 268 D21
57 Jane Street at Hudson Street
Tel 212/627-8273
www.micocinany.com

Mi Cocina was one of the city's first restaurants to offer authentic regional Mexican cuisine. Start with the shrimp in spicy chile adobo or the corn tamale filled with guajillo chile sauce and Mexican white cheese. To follow, there are rich mole-coated chicken enchiladas or lighter dishes like the chicken marinated with lime, oregano and blue agave tequila. The brightly painted rooms decked with folk art strike just the right note, and the small garden courtyard is romantic on a summer evening.

🕐 Mon–Thu 4.30–10.45, Fri 4.30–11.45, Sat 11–3.30, 4.30–11.45, Sun 11–3.30, 4.30–10.45
🍽 D $40, Wine $25
🚇 14th Street (A, C, E)
🚌 M20

MOLYVOS

Map 266 D17
871 Seventh Avenue between West 55th and 56th streets
Tel 212/582-7500
www.molyvos.com

This large space with a café, a bar and two dining rooms, brings Greece to Manhattan. The Greek dips and spreads are irresistible, including the garlicky roasted eggplant (aubergine) purée and the

tzatziki, a blend of yogurt, cucumber, garlic, mint, dill and lemon. Also outstanding are the cold meze such as grilled baby octopus with olives, fennel, lemon and oregano, and fava beans mashed with olive oil. Marinated lamb shanks, whole grilled fish and rabbit stew are traditional main courses. The 165-bottle wine list includes more than 50 Greek wines; 10 are available by the glass.

🕐 Mon–Thu 12–3, 5.30–11.30, Fri–Sat 12–3, 5–midnight, Sun noon–11
🍽 L $30, D $43, Wine $32
🚇 Seventh Avenue (B, D, E), 57th Street (N, R, Q, W)
🚌 M10, M20

MONTRACHET

Map 269 E24
239 West Broadway between Walker and White streets
Tel 212/219-2777
www.myriadrestaurantgroup.com

The focus is on the plate in this spare, minimal classic. Chef Chris Gesualdi expresses his distinctive style in such dishes as roasted salmon with Riesling and magret of duck with verjus and huckleberries. Appetizers range from lobster and corn soup to foie gras with oxtail and candied root vegetables. Chocolate and fruit are the core dessert ingredients.

🕐 Mon–Thu 5.30–10.30, Fri noon–2.30, 5.30–11, Sat 5.30–11
🍽 L $40, D $60, tasting menus $85 and $105, Wine $30

🚇 Canal Street (A, C, E), Franklin Street (1)
🚌 M6, M20

NAM

Map 269 E24
110 Reade Street at West Broadway
Tel. 212 267 1777
www.namnyc.com

Nam stands out for its style and for its authentic and often unique dishes. Particularly alluring are the appetizers. Banh xeo, for example, is a crepe filled with mushrooms, bean sprouts, coconut-flavored rice, shrimp and chicken; ca tim nuong—simple but addictive—consists of grilled Asian eggplant (aubergine) with ginger, lime, garlic and a little chili. Among the many main dishes, crisp red snapper and chicken with chile lemongrass sauce make excellent dinner choices.

🕐 Mon–Fri noon–2, Sun–Thu 5.30–10, Fri–Sat 5.30–11
🍽 L $22, D $28, Wine $28
🚇 Chambers Street (1)
🚌 M20

NAPLES 45

Map 268 E18
Met Life Building, 200 Park Avenue at East 45th Street (entrance on 45th)
Tel 212/972-7001
www.rapatina.com/naples45

Authentic Neopolitan pizzas emerge piping hot from the wood-fired ovens, as do the fish of the day. The menu showcases southern Italian cooking with a good range of fish, chicken and steak dishes—and vegetarians won't leave unsatisfied, either. The *piccoli piatti*, or small plates, are popular appetizers, especially the steamed mussels and veal meatballs.

🕐 Mon–Fri 7.30am–10pm
🍽 L $30, D $40, Wine $22
🚇 Grand Central 42nd Street (4, 5, 6, 7, S)
🚌 M1, M2, M3, M4, M101, M102, M103, M98

NEGRIL VILLAGE

Map 269 E22
70 West 3rd Street between La Guardia Place and Thompson Street
Tel 212/477-2804
www.negrilvillage.com

The neo-Caribbean dishes sit wonderfully on the tongue at this sultry restaurant. It's hard to choose between the succulent curried goat, and

EATING

such specialties as the ackee and the saltfish. Tropical desserts include key lime cheesecake with mango coulis. The downstairs rum lounge pours 50 different rums.

🕐 Daily 11am–3.30pm, Sun–Thu 5–11pm, Fri–Sat 5pm–3.30am

🍴 L $22, D $40, Wine $20

🚇 West 4th Street (A, C, E, F, S, V)

🚌 M5, M21

NYONYA
Map 269 F23
194 Grand Street between Mott and Mulberry streets
Tel 212/334-3669
Malaysian cuisine draws on many different Asian cooking traditions—Chinese, Indian, Thai and Malay. You can sample some of the country's appealing, sometimes spicy dishes at this plain favorite. You have a wide choice of rice, noodle, casserole and other dishes; start with a roti (Indian pancake) or the satays, and follow with a fiery sambal or a curry made with lemongrass, chili and coconut milk. No credit cards.

🕐 Sun–Thu 11am–11.30pm, Fri–Sat 11am–midnight

🍴 L $20, D $25

🚇 Grand Street (S)

🚌 M1

OCEANA
Map 267 E17
55 East 54th Street between Madison and Park avenues
Tel 212/759-5941
www.oceanarestaurant.com
With its nautical interior, Oceana is something like a streamlined yacht, even though it's in a handsome town house. The French-Asian cuisine is bold and often surprising, as exemplified by, for example, the loup de mer accompanied by a tamarind and wasabi sauce, and the salmon roulade, which is stoked up with smoked bacon and peppered green apple and served in a red wine and olive sauce. The international wine

NOBU
Map 269 E24
105 Hudson Street between Franklin and North Moore streets
Tel 212/219-0500
www.myriadrestaurantgroup.com
Celebrities flock to Drew Nieporent's TriBeCa hotspot for the artistic sushi and sashimi fashioned by chef Nobu Matsuhisa. If you can afford it, choose the omakase menu, which will deliver the chef's inspirations for the day. Or choose from baby abalone, live scallop or sashimi drizzled with garlic and ginger-flavored olive oil. Masu sake is served in small cedar cups with salted rims; finish with green tea crème caramel. Reservations are hard to come by; the next best thing is to drop in to Next Door Nobu.

🕐 Mon–Fri 11.45–2.15, 5.45–10.45, Sat–Sun 5.45–10.15

🍴 L $28, D $50, omakase $100, $120 or $150, Wine $34

🚇 Franklin Street (1)

🚌 M20

list offers 1,100 selections, 15 by the glass.

🕐 Mon–Fri noon–2.30, Mon–Fri 5.30–10.30, Sat 5–10.30

🍴 L 3-course prix fixe $48, D 3-course prix fixe $78, Wine $35

🚇 53rd Street/Fifth Avenue (E, V)

🚌 M1, M2, M3, M4

ODEON
Map 269 E24
145 West Broadway between Thomas and Duane streets
Tel 212/233-0507
www.theodeonrestaurant.com
In the early 1980s this cafeteria-turned-hip-bistro was the incubator of the downtown scene. Odeon still has Venetian blinds on the windows and chrome stools at the bar, but nowadays it caters to neighborhood residents as well as downtown celebrities, with

a typical bistro menu of onion soup gratinée, moules and steak frites. This is a great late-night stop.

🕐 Mon–Fri noon–2am, Sat–Sun 9am–2am

🍴 L $28, D $42, Wine $18

🚇 Chambers Street (A, C, E), Chambers Street (1, 2, 3)

🚌 M6, M20

OTTO ENOTECA PIZZERIA
Map 269 E22
1 Fifth Avenue at 8th Street
Tel 212/995-9559
www.ottopizzeria.com
Mario Batali continues to apply his genius to educating the average American palate to real Italian cuisine and wine. Here, the arena is pizza, which you can have with marinara, or—a better idea—in one of the combinations dreamed up by Mario, such as topped with porcini and taleggio or with tomato, fennel, bottarga (silver mullet roe), pecorino and mozzarella. The wine card is extraordinary, and the gelati are the best in the city, period.

🕐 Daily 11.30am–midnight

🍴 L $18, D $27, Wine $20

🚇 West 4th Street (A, C, E, F, S, V)

🚌 M2, M3, M5

OUEST
Map 266 C14
2315 Broadway between West 83rd and 84th streets
Tel 212/580-8700
www.ouestny.com
This lively, entertaining restaurant helped raise the Upper West Side's culinary reputation with Tom Valenti's fresh seasonal menu. Settle into one of the cherry-red booths and order the luscious short ribs, one of the braised or roasted meats such as the roast free-range chicken with garlic jus, or a fish dish such as seared tuna with white bean purée, black olive-lemon compote and red pepper coulis. The nightly specials attract crowds, especially on Monday, when the kitchen turns out the chef's signature braised lamb shanks. Desserts are Italian-inspired.

🕐 Mon–Thu 5–11, Fri–Sat 5–midnight, Sun 11–2, 5–10

🍴 D $55, Wine $29

🚇 86th Street (1, 9)

🚌 M104

EATING

PAMPANO

Map 267 F17
209 East 49th Street between 2nd and 3rd avenues
Tel 212/751-4545
www.modernmexican.com

Placido Domingo loved to eat and so he helped open this restaurant where chef Richard Sandoval, who hails from Mexico City, via California, produces great contemporary Mexican using such exciting ingredients as huitlacoche, epazote, pomegranate, queso blanco and every conceivable kind of pepper. The chile rellenos are roasted not fried and stuffed with seafood and tart manchego. Start with any one of the great ceviches and continue with one of the terrific seafood dishes. Meat lovers are out of luck although the lamb in adobo orange sauce is tasty. The outdoor terrace is as close to the beach as you can get in midtown Manhattan.

🕐 Mon–Fri 11.30–2.30, Mon–Wed 5–10, Thu–Sat 5–10.30, Sun 5–9.30
🍽 L $30, D $51, Wine $32
🚇 51st Street (6)
🚌 M15, M27, M50, M101, M102, M103

PAM REAL THAI

Map 266 C17
404 West 49th Street between Ninth and Tenth avenues
Tel 212/333-7500
www.pamrealthai.com

At this authentic Thai, none of the sweet, sour and salt dishes have been compromised to suit a more timid palate. The traditional favorites are all available: superb hot and milder curries, fiery salads made with green papaya, ground pork with lime dressing, noodle dishes and, best of all, duck with chili sauce and lime leaves. Bring your own bottle. No credit cards.

🕐 Sun–Thu 11.30–11, Fri–Sat 11.30–11.30
🍽 L $15, D $20
🚇 50th Street (C, E, 1, 9)
🚌 M11, M50

PARADOU

Map 268 C21
8 Little West 12th Street between 9th Avenue and Washington Street
Tel 212/463-8345
www.paradounyc.com

A taste of Provence in the Meatpacking District, Paradou is equally popular with workers, shoppers and in the evening with lovers of good hearty French cooking. The garden gives a country feel right in the heart of the city, and with dishes such as cassoulet, duck *magret* and venison *pot au feu* on the menu, you could almost be in Provence.

🕐 Mon–Wed 6–12, Thu–Fri 6–1, Sat noon–1am, Sun noon–10pm
🍽 D $45, Wine $32
🚇 14th Street (A, C, E), 8th Avenue (L)
🚌 M11, M14a

PASTIS

Map 268 D21
9 Ninth Avenue at Little 12th Street
Tel 212/929-4844

At Pastis, you could just as easily be on Paris' rue St Denis around the corner from Les Halles. Every detail rings true: the zinc bar, the smoky mirrors, the tiles and the French ads. Then there are the *plats* (dishes)—onion soup gratinée, croque monsieur, skate *au beurre noir*, steak and moules frites, and, at breakfast, wonderful brioche and egg dishes. Owner Keith McNally's heritage shows through in the fish and chips and the beans on toast. Wine is served in tumblers. Expect lines, and look out for celebrities in summer.

🕐 Mon–Wed 8am–1am, Thu 8am–2am, Fri 8am–2.45am, Sat 10am–2.45am, Sun 10am–1am
🍽 L $30, D $35, Wine $18
🚇 14th Street (A, C, E)
🚌 M11, M14

PEARL OYSTER BAR

Map 268 E22
18 Cornelia Street
Tel 212/691-8211
www.pearloysterbar.com

The fiercely loyal patrons of this spot with a marble bar don't mind lining up for New England favorites such as oysters, creamy chowder and

PER SE

Map 266 D16
Time Warner Center, 10 Columbus Circle 4th Floor
Tel 212/823-9335

The room has urban chic and fine views, but diners come to taste the superlative cuisine of Thomas Keller, whom many consider America's finest chef. He arrived from the Napa Valley with his famous French Laundry. The menu changes daily, but diners can expect perfectly prepared dishes right down to the finest details. His "oysters and pearls" (oysters, tapioca and osetra caviar) and his "macaroni and cheese" (lobster mascarpone in a lobster broth topped with a wheel of crisp Parmesan) are legendary signature dishes. The wine list has 500 selections to pair with the exquisite food. It's hard to snag one of the 16 tables.

🕐 Fri–Sun 11.30–1.30, daily 5.30–10
🍽 Prix fixe tasting menus $250, Wine $40
🚇 59th Street/Columbus Circle (A, B, C, D, 1)
🚌 M5, M7, M10, M20, M104

the fried oyster sandwiches doused in rémoulade sauce. The pièce de résistance is the delicious lobster roll encased in a toasted bun.

🕐 Mon–Fri noon–2.30, Mon–Sat 6–11
🍽 L $30, D $40, Wine $28
🚇 West 4th Street (A, C, E, F, S, V)
🚌 M5, M6, M20

PEASANT

Map 269 F23
194 Elizabeth Street between Prince and Spring streets
Tel 212/965-9511
www.peasantnyc.com

EATING

This cozy storefront has become a popular chef's hang-out. As the name suggests it produces bold rustic Italian cuisine from its wood-fired ovens. Wood-roasted sardines, roasted clams and really fine pizzas are carefully prepared. The grilled fishes are flavored with the best olive oil, lemon and herbs and cooked to perfection.

🕐 Tue–Sat 6–11, Sun 6–10
🍴 D $40, Wine $20
🚇 Bowery (J, M, Z), Spring Street (6)
🚌 M1, M6

PERIYALI
Map 268 E20
35 West 20th Street between Fifth and Sixth avenues
Tel 212/463-7890
www.periyali.com
This was the first authentic Greek restaurant to open in Manhattan, and it has remained a premier Greek destination. The ambience is warm and appealing (white plaster, dark wood beams and attractive displays of appetizers). Everything is carefully prepared, from the fragrant avgolemono soup to the grilled lamb chops with fresh rosemary.

🕐 Mon–Fri noon–3, Mon–Fri 5.30–11, Fri–Sat 5.30–11.30
🍴 L $30, D $40, Wine $32
🚇 23rd Street (N, R, W)
🚌 M2, M3, M5, M6, M7

PERSEPOLIS
Map 267 F15
1407 Second Avenue between 73rd and 74th streets
Tel 212/535-1100
www.persepolisnyc.com
Thai chef San Sethachutkul had to master the art of Persian cooking when he took over the kitchens at Persepolis, but there is a similarity in the way the cuisines blend and contrast flavors. The Vermont lamb shank served with almond, raisin and herb couscous is just one example of this Middle Eastern cuisine at its finest, followed by typical desserts like roasted pineapple or baklava.

🕐 Sun–Thu noon–11, Fri–Sat noon–midnight
🍴 L $20 3-course Prix fixe, D $35, Wine $24
🚇 Lexington Avenue (6)
🚌 M15

PETER LUGER STEAKHOUSE
Off map 269 G25
178 Broadway between Bedford and Briggs streets, Williamsburg, Brooklyn
Tel 718/387-7400
www.peterluger.com
Many people will tell you that this old-fashioned beer hall-style restaurant serves the city's best steak. The meat itself is carefully selected, aged on the premises and cooked to perfection. All the traditional cuts are available, but the most fun is the porterhouse, which is sliced tableside. Don't miss the creamed spinach and mashed potatoes. No credit cards.

🕐 Mon–Thu 11.45–9.45, Fri–Sat 11.45–10.45, Sun 12.45–9.45
🍴 L $40, D $60, Wine $27
🚇 Marcy Ave (J, M, Z)

PICHOLINE
Map 266 D16
35 West 64th Street between Central Park West and Broadway
Tel 212/724-8585
www.picholinenyc.com
The Mediterranean cuisine at Picholine is superb. Among the entrees, the licorice-lacquered squab is exquisite, perfectly complemented by foie gras, glazed turnips and spiced rhubarb marmalade. The wild mushroom and duck risotto is a perennial favorite. It's easy to fill up with delicious entrees and main courses—but be sure to save room for one more course. Picholine also has one of the city's most fabulous cheese trays.

🕐 Mon–Thu 5–11, Fri–Sat 5–11.45, Sun 5–9
🍴 D $80, tasting menu $120, Wine $45
🚇 66th Street (1)
🚌 M10, M20

PINTXOS
Off map 269 D23
510 Greenwich Street between Canal and Spring streets
Tel 212/343-9923
Pintxos are Basque tapas, and this unassuming restaurant offers 18 of them—and they are your best bet here, even though the menu also offers eight or so meat and fish entrees. Look for spicy chorizo, Basque anchovies, stuffed mussels and white asparagus, which all go wonderfully well with the available wines.

🕐 Mon–Thu 11.30–10, Fri 11.30–11, Sat 4.30–11

🍴 L $25, D $30, Wine $22
🚇 Spring Street (C, E), Houston Street (1)
🚌 M20

PIO PIO
Map 267 F13
1746 First Avenue between East 90th and 91st streets
Tel 212/426-5800
This is the Peruvian version of the Boston Chicken chain. Order a quarter, half or whole chicken, marinated in secret spices. Then add some ceviche tostones, red beans or yuca frita and a beer, and you've got yourself a tasty meal. Amex credit cards only.

🕐 Daily 11–11
🍴 L $15, D $35, Wine $25
🚇 86th Street (4, 5, 6)
🚌 M15

PIPA
Map 268 E21
ABC Carpet and Home, 38 East 19th Street between Broadway and Park Avenue South
Tel 212/677-2233
Nuevo Latin king Douglas Rodriguez does Spanish at this lively restaurant, whose name means "great time." You can make a meal of the tapas—succulent fried oysters with banana-and-lentil salad, horseradish aioli and crispy bacon; shrimp with garlic oil and chilies; or sautéed chorizo. Follow up with a rice, meat or fish dish, or perhaps a paella. The white or red sangria are perfect accompaniments, or go for one of the rum drinks.

🕐 Mon–Thu noon–11, Fri noon–midnight, Sat 11am–midnight, Sun 11–10.30
🍴 L $20, D $40, Wine $32
🚇 4th Street/Union Square (L, N, Q, R, W, 4, 5, 6)
🚌 M1, M2, M3, M6, M7

EATING

PRUNE

Map 269 F22
54 East 1st Street between First and
Second avenues
Tel 212/677-6221
www.prunerestaurant.com
Everything is meticulously
prepared at this small,
idiosyncratic restaurant. Dinner
entrées might include roast
duck with green olives, or
whole grilled fish with fennel
oil and salt. Order one of the

carefully prepared vegetable
accompaniments. Choose,
perhaps, between the roast
beets or the bitter greens salad
with oil and lemon juice to
complement the beautifully
presented dishes.
🕐 Mon–Thu 11.30–3.30, 6–11, Fri
11.30–3.30, 6–midnight, Sat 10–3.30,
6–midnight, Sun 10–3.30, 5–10
🍴 L $24, D $55, Wine $27
🚇 Lower East Side/Second Avenue
(F, V)
🚌 M15, M21

RED CAT

Map 268 C20
227 Tenth Avenue between West 23rd
and 24th streets
Tel 212/242-1122
www.theredcat.com
A downtown art crowd packs
this vivacious, inviting bistro
a narrow crimson room
illuminated by large Moroccan
lanterns. The contemporary
kitchen puts plenty of flavor
into its creations—take, for
example, the crisp skate wing
in caper brown butter, or the
calves' liver au poivre. Tasty
Parmesan fries spiked with
mustard aioli are one of the
most popular side orders.
Desserts are eclectic but
equally delicious. The wine
list is carefully chosen, and
17 selections are available
by the glass.
🕐 Mon–Thu 5–11, Fri–Sat 5–midnight,
Sun 4.30–10.30
🍴 D $40, Wine $24
🚇 23rd Street (C, E)
🚌 M11, M23

RIVER CAFÉ

Map 269 G25
1 Water Street at Old Fulton Street,
Brooklyn
Tel 718/522-5200
www.rivercafe.com
Opened in 1977, this old-timer
tucked on a barge under the
Brooklyn Bridge is still one
of the city's most romantic
restaurants, with magical views
of the river and downtown
Manhattan skyline. A dynasty
of great American chefs from
Larry Forgione to the current
Brad Steelman have made the
kitchen famous. Nowadays you
might start with the tuna
tartare with coconut sauce,
then go on to the rack of
lamb with lavender flower
glaze or the sautéed black
sea bass with turmeric
coconut sauce. The chocolate
Brooklyn Bridge remains a
signature dessert. There are
500 selections on the wine list.
🕐 Mon–Sat noon–3, 5.30–10, Fri–Sat
noon–3, 5.30–11, Sun 11.30–3, 5.30–10
🍴 L $40, D 3-course prix fixe $95,
Wine $20
🚇 High Street (A, C), York Street (F)

ROSA MEXICANO

Map 266 D16
61 Columbus Avenue at West 62nd
Street NE corner
Tel 212/977-7700
www.rosamexicano.com
A waterfall studded with
sculptures of Acapulco-style
divers, among other decorative
notes, sets a flashy scene at
this authentic Mexican. The
guacamole, which is made
at the table, is fragrant with

cilantro (coriander) and
oregano, and the menu offers
unusual regional dishes such
salmon al guajillo, beef short
ribs marinated in lime and beer
and *budin Azteca*, a flavorsome
tortilla pie.
🕐 Mon–Fri noon–3, Sat–Sun
11.30–2.30, Tue–Sat 5–11.30, Sun 4–10,
Mon 5–10

🍴 L $25, D $42, Wine $23
🚇 59th Street/Columbus Circle (A, B,
C, D, 1)
🚌 M5, M7, M11, M104

RUBY FOO'S

Map 266 C14
2182 Broadway at 77th Street
Tel 212/724-6700
www.brguestrestaurants.com
This, the original Ruby Foo's,
made a big splash when it
opened in 1996 on the Upper
West Side with its dramatic
staircase and red lacquer walls.
The pan-Asian cuisine was the
other big draw then and now,
ranging from dim sum and
sushi to hot-and-sour shrimp
with water chestnuts and
coconut sticky rice, and seven-
flavored beef with ginger
mashed potatoes and chile-
lime salsa. Have fun.
🕐 Sun–Mon 11.30–11, Tue–Thu
11.30–11.30, Fri–Sat 11.30–12.30am
🍴 L $25, D $40, Wine $26
🚇 79th Street (1)
🚌 M104

SARABETH'S

Map 267 E13
1295 Madison Avenue between East
92nd and 93rd streets
Tel 212/410-7335
Sarabeth Levine is most
famous for her luscious
baking and breakfasts, but
that does not mean that she
can't turn out equally wonderful lunch and dinner fare.
Try her short ribs in zinfandel
or her hazelnut-crusted sea
bass, and you'll be a fan.
At breakfast, don't miss the
cinnamon French toast or
the pumpkin waffles—and
plan on a light lunch
afterwards.
🕐 Mon–Sat 8am–11pm, Sun
8am–9.30pm
🍴 L $20, D $40, Wine $25
🚇 96th Street (6)
🚌 M1, M2, M3, M4

EATING

SHUN LEE PALACE

Map 267 F17
155 East 55th Street between Lexington and Third avenues
Tel 212/371-8844
www.shunleepalace.com

It's still the best Chinese restaurant in the city, even though it's been around since 1972. It may be expensive, but the dining rooms are comfortable and elegant and the Shanghai, Szechuan and Cantonese cuisine is beautifully presented. Besides such traditional dishes as crispy sea bass Hunan style and lobster in black bean sauce, you will find such extraordinary specialties as Grand Marnier prawns and red cooked short ribs Hang Chow style. There's a branch near the Lincoln Center at 43 West 65th Street between Central Park West and Columbus Avenue (tel 212/595-8895)—a good bet for a leisurely meal or a pre-concert snack.

⏰ Mon–Sat noon–11.30, Sun noon–11
🍴 L $40, D $50, Wine $40
🚇 Lexington Avenue/53rd Street (E, V), 51st Street (6)
🚌 M57, M98, M101, M102, M103

SPICE MARKET

Map 268 D21
403 West 13th Street at Ninth Avenue
Tel 212/675-2322
www.jean-georges.com

Expect a sensual experience. Beguiling and theatrical are the only words to describe this Southeast Asian space swathed in teak lit by silk lanterns, and dotted with palm trees. It's Jean-Georges Vongrichten's stage for exciting spicy street food. Roll the spring rolls in lettuce with fresh mint and cilantro (coriander) and dip them in sweet lime and rice vinegar broth, sample the fiery pork vindaloo or the black pepper shrimp with pineapple.

⏰ Sun–Thu noon–midnight, Fri–Sat noon–1am
🍴 L $30, D $40, Wine $28
🚇 14th Street (A, C, E, L)
🚌 M11

SPOTTED PIG

Map 268 D22
314 West 11th Street at Greenwich Street
Tel 212/620-0393
www.thespottedpig.com

It may have Mario Batali as part owner, but it is the chef April Bloomfield who is drawing crowds at this small "gastro pub." She comes most recently from London's River Cafe and delivers some gutsy cuisine—veal kidneys, lamb with salsa verde, roast cod with parsley sauce and her beloved gnudi (gnocchi with sheep's milk ricotta and brown butter and sage). Note though that the menu changes constantly at this lively ongoing party.

⏰ Mon–Fri noon–2am, Sat–Sun 11am–2am
🍴 L $20, D $40, Wine $32
🚇 Christopher Street (1), 14th Street (A, C, E, L)
🚌 M11, M20

STRIP HOUSE

Map 269 E21
13 East 12th Street between Fifth Avenue and University Place
Tel 212/328-0000
www.theglaziergroup.com

Recalling a 19th-century bordello with its tufted leather banquettes and swathe of velvet, this place serves up juicy succulent beef, notably the New York strip. Other cuts are available along with a couple of fish dishes, wild striped bass with artichokes, pancetta and basil sauce, for example.

⏰ Mon–Thu 5–11.30, Fri–Sat 5–midnight, Sun 5–11
🍴 D $60, Wine $35
🚇 14th Street/Union Square (L, N, Q, R, W, 4, 5, 6)
🚌 M2, M3, M5

SUEÑOS

Map 268 D21
311 West 17th Street between 8th and 9th avenues
Tel 212/243-1333
www.suenosnyc.com

Owner and executive chef Sue Torres opened Sueños in 2003 with the aim of serving traditional Mexican cooking with a contemporary twist, and the *New York Times* said she produces the most exciting Mexican food in the city. The menu does feature familiar dishes like tortillas, quesadillas and guacamole, but re-invented and served alongside entrées such as tamarind-glazed steak. The decor is as colorful as the dishes and the cocktails.

⏰ Sun–Wed 5–11, Thu–Sat 5–midnight
🍴 D $40, 3-course prix fixe $30, Wine $22
🚇 14th Street (A, C, E), 8th Avenue (L)
🚌 M11, M14d, M20

SUGIYAMA

Map 266 D17
251 West 55th Street between Broadway and Eighth Avenue
Tel 212/956-0670
www.sugiyama-nyc.com

Here, the seasons inform chef Nao Sugiyama's Kaiseki cuisine. You have a choice of various 5-, 6-, or 8-course dinners and post- or pre-theater. Each includes an appetizer, sashimi, soup, a sizzling dish on hot stone and dessert. The selection of sake by the glass and by the bottle is extensive.

⏰ Tue–Sat 5.30–11.45
🍴 D $52–$175, $32 pre-theater, Wine $28
🚇 59th Street/Columbus Circle (A, B, C, D, 1)

SUSHI YASUDA

Off map 268 F18
204 East 43rd Street between Second and Third avenues
Tel 212/972-1001
www.sushiyasuda.com

Here owner Naomichi Yasuda displays his artistry, selecting the best fish, evaluating its texture, masterfully cutting it to release the best flavor, and cooking and seasoning the rice to perfection. Then he crafts a meal for the individuals who sit down at his sushi bar, according to their tastes and experience, and to the size of their mouths. It's custom-made perfection, but naturally it comes at a high price. For a delightful meal request one of his eight tuna specialties or one of the eel pieces for which he is renowned.

🕐 Mon–Fri noon–2.15, 6–10.15, Sat 6–10.15, closed Sun
🍴 L $80, D $100, Wine $18 (sake)
🚇 42nd Street/Grand Central (S, 4, 5, 6, 7)

TAKA
Map 268 D22
61 Grove Street between Bleecker and Seventh Avenue South
Tel 212/242-3699

Takako Yoneyama is a female sushi master, rare in a culture that has denied women such a role because their body temperature is one degree higher than a man's. At this atypical restaurant with Western-style paintings and bentwood chairs, she wields her knives creatively and delivers a bento box containing sushi, sashimi, shumai and other small dishes that's a real bargain.

🕐 Tue–Sun 5–11
🍴 D $35
🚇 Christopher Street/Sheridan Square (1)
🚌 M20

TAMARIND
Map 268 E20
41–43 East 22nd Street between Broadway and Park Avenue South
Tel 212/674-7400
www.tamarinde22.com
The dining room of this Indian restaurant is sleek, modern and comfortable (although noisy), the cuisine fresh and the wine list expansive. The flavor of the restaurant's namesake fruit infuses many of the wonderful dishes, such as

SPECIAL
TABLA
Map 268 E20
11 Madison Avenue at 25th Street
Tel 212/889-0667
Danny Meyer's Tabla delivers a superb dining experience with its plush decor, gracious service and fragrant cuisine. In the sensual coral and jade jewel box of a room upstairs, the menu offers Bombay native Floyd Cardoz's dishes, which use the spices of South India—tamarind, kokum, clove, cinnamon and black pepper. Goan-spiced crab cake, rice-flaked black bass, and duck samosa, set off by shaved fennel, almonds and dried fruit chutney are just a few favorites. The sorbets are packed with flavor. The wine selections pair beautifully with the food (16 by the glass). On the ground floor, the informal and very affordable Bread Bar serves a selection of tandoori dishes and small plates of superb Indian breads.

🕐 Mon–Fri 12–2, Sun–Wed 5.30–10, Thu–Sat 5.30–10.30
🍴 L $35, 3-course prix fixe $32, D 3-course prix fixe $64, tasting menu $92, Wine $35
🚇 23rd Street (N, R, W), 23rd Street (6)
🚌 M2, M3

the shrimp cooked in coconut sauce flavored with curry leaves and smoked tamarind, but there are other flavors as well—the she-crab soup with sweet spices, ginger and saffron is another winner. The lamb vindaloo is authentically spiced, as are many of the vegetarian dishes. Some are refreshingly new—*bhindi do piazza*, which is okra flavored with brown onions and dried mango, for example. Even the desserts shine.

🕐 Daily 11.30–3, Sun–Thu 5.30–11.30, Fri–Sat 11.30–midnight
🍴 L $24, D $40, Wine $30
🚇 23rd Street (N, R), 23rd Street (6)
🚌 M1, M2, M3, M6, M7

TASTING ROOM
Map 269 F22
72 East 1st Street between First and Second avenues
Tel 212/358-7831
www.thetastingroomnyc.com
This small restaurant offers just a dozen jewel-like tasting dishes. Based on seasonal vegetables, fish and meat, they range from chilled venison consommé to seabass escabeche with red onion, saprasata and sherry vinaigrette. Every dish has a surprise element, like the candied fennel that comes with the brown butter-lemon tart. The 300 American wines, 10 by the glass, include some hard-to-find selections.

🕐 Mon–Fri 3pm–1am, Sat–Sun 10am–1am
🍴 D $50, Wine $28
🚇 Lower East Side/Second Avenue (F, V)
🚌 M15

TAVERN ON THE GREEN
Map 266 D16
Central Park West at 67th Street
Tel 212/873-3200
www.tavernonthegreen.com
Visitors are drawn to this bauble of a restaurant at the edge of Central Park, shaded by stately trees outlined after dark by thousands of twinkling fairy lights. The view from the Crystal Room and the summer dining terrace creates a certain magical, festive look. Against all odds, the Tavern delivers a memorable dining experience—despite its stature as a prime visitor destination, despite its size, and despite the breadth of its menu, which ranges from prime rib with Yorkshire pudding to sautéed

rainbow trout in brown butter sauce. The wine list boasts 1,000 selections, a 1975 Chateau Petrus among them. From May to mid-October you can dance under the stars in the garden areas from 9pm.

🕐 Mon–Fri 11.30–3, Sun–Thu 5–10, Fri–Sat 5–10.30, Sat–Sun 10–3
🍴 L $40, prix fixe $39, D $65, Wine $32
🚇 66th Street (1)
🚌 M10

TOMOE SUSHI
Map 269 E22
172 Thompson Street between Bleecker and Houston streets
Tel 212/777-9346
Around the corner from New York University, this plain sushi parlor does a brisk trade among students and other sushi aficionados, drawn by its reasonable prices. About 30 different sushi choices and 30 varieties of maki rolls are available, along with traditional hot dishes and noodles.

🕐 Mon 5–11, Tue–Sat 1–3, 5–11, Sun 5–10
🍴 L $25, D $30
🚇 West 4th Street (A, C, E, F, S, V)
🚌 M5, M6, M21

TOWN
Map 267 E17
Chambers Hotel
15 West 56th Street between Fifth and Sixth avenues
Tel 212/582-4445
www.townnyc.com
Strands of crystal beads suspended in the two-story loft space in this stylish subterranean dining room swathed in suede and blond wood sparkle magically. Chef Geoffrey Zakarian's fusion cuisine sparkles, too. Start with the fragrant octopus fricassée in lemongrass broth, or the lobster bisque, zapped with ginger, coconut and wood sorrel. Zakarian poaches

or roasts his fish to retain moisture, glazing swordfish with mushroom tapenade and serving with smoked tomato and marjoram coulis, for instance; the venison is simply slow-roasted to exquisite tenderness. Desserts are show-stoppers.

🕐 Mon–Fri 7–10.30am, 12–2.30, 5.30–1am, Sat 7–10, 5.30–1am, Sun 7–10.30, 11–2.30, 5.30–9.30
🍴 L $45, 3-course prix fixe $26, D 4-course prix fixe $71, Wine $36
🚇 53rd Street/Fifth Avenue (E, V)
🚌 M1, M2, M3, M4, M57

'21' CLUB
Map 267 E17
21 West 52nd Street between Fifth and Sixth avenues
Tel 212/582-7200
www.21club.com
The hamburger makes head-lines for its price ($30 and climbing), but this storied locale is about so much more than the sandwich. Two college students opened it as a speakeasy in Greenwich Village in 1920; it was frequented by Humphrey Bogart, F. Scott Fitzgerald and Joe Di Maggio after relocating to this town house in 1929. Old-fashioned and masculine, it purveys fist-size medallions of beef flambéed with cognac and Dijon, chicken hash and Dover sole, along with newer, lighter dishes like black sea bass in champagne sauce. The daily special ice creams, gussied up or plain, are the choice desserts, and the wine cellar is renowned. Jacket and tie required.

🕐 Mon–Fri noon–2.30, Mon–Thu 5.30–10, Fri–Sat 5.30–11
🍴 L $60, D $80, Wine $30
🚇 47th–50th streets (B, D, F, V)
🚌 M1, M2, M3, M4, M5, M6, M7

UNCLE VANYA CAFE
Map 266 D17
315 West 54th Street between Eighth and Ninth avenues
Tel 212/262-0542
Russian home cooking starts at this plain storefront restaurant: hearty borscht, beef dumplings with sour cream, stuffed cabbage rolls and beef Stroganoff with kasha. It's all good and filling and costs very little. Try one of the Georgian wines, if

you dare.
🕐 Mon–Thu noon–11, Fri–Sat noon–midnight
🍴 L $20, D $25, Wine $25
🚇 50th Street (C, E)
🚌 M10, M11, M20

UNION SQUARE CAFÉ
Map 268 E21
21 East 16th Street between Fifth Avenue and Union Square West
Tel 212/243-4020
www.unionsquarecafe.com
Union Square Café remains a darling of the downtown publishing industry because it delivers on every aspect of the dining experience from the comfortable but not-too-fussy setting to the warm but thoroughly professional service. Michael Romano's bold Tuscan cuisine is thoughtfully imaginative and always flavorful. The meats and fishes are grilled to perfection and enhanced with just the right combination of ingredients. Try the grilled salmon with Meyer lemon citronette, or the organic chicken with mustard-cognac sauce.
The signature warm banana tart with honey-vanilla ice cream and macadamia brittle is perfect. There is also a 200-plus international wine list.

🕐 Daily noon–2, Sun–Thu 5.30–10, Fri–Sat 5.30–11
🍴 L $35, D $50, Wine $22
🚇 14th Street/Union Square (L, N, Q, R, W, 4, 5, 6)
🚌 M2, M3, M5, M7

VERITAS
Map 268 E20
43 East 20th Street between Broadway and Park Avenue South
Tel 212/353-3700
www.veritas-nyc.com
With 2,700 selections, Veritas has the most comprehensive wine list in the city. And the kitchen offers some gutsy cuisine to go with the wines.

Expect pepper-crusted venison with Armagnac or juniper, or braised veal in Barolo reduction. Even a dish like red snapper brings a surprise—here it arrives in Thai red curry nage. Hot chocolate and doughnuts is the signature dessert.

🕐 Mon–Sat 5.30–10.30, Sun 5–10
🍴 D 3-course prix fixe $82, Wine $15
🚇 23rd Street (N, R), 23rd Street (6)
🚌 M1, M2, M3, M6, M7

VIRGIL'S REAL BARBECUE
Map 268 D18
152 West 44th Street between Sixth Avenue and Broadway
Tel 212/921-9494
www.virgilsbbq.com
The aroma of hickory wood smoke alone is enough

to draw you into this vast barbecue emporium. Here, the huge platters of Memphis-style barbecue or fried chicken arrive with grits or mashed potatoes and biscuits and gravy. Po'boys, also known as hero sandwiches, round out the southern-style menu.

🕐 Sun–Mon 11–11, Tue–Fri 111.30am–midnight, Sat 11am–midnight
🍴 L $30, D $40, Wine $20
🚇 42nd Street/Times Square (N, Q, R, S, W, 1, 2, 3, 7), 42nd Street (B, D, F, V)
🚌 M5, M6, M7

VONG
Map 267 F17
200 East 54th Street at Third Avenue
Tel 212/486-9592
When Jean-Georges launched his French-Asian cuisine, it was revolutionary. Today, it's just plain beautiful, and the explosive flavors still dance on the tongue. Vongerichten worked in

Thailand, Hong Kong and Singapore in the 1980s, and the flavors of lemongrass, cilantro (coriander), ginger and coconut milk changed his life.

🕐 Mon–Fri noon–2.30, 6–11, Sat 5–11, Sun 5.30–9
🍴 L $50, 3-course prix fixe $28, D $60, tasting menu $68, 3-course pre-theater $38, Wine $32
🚇 53rd Street/Lexington Avenue (F, V), 51st Street (6)
🚌 M98, M101, M102, M103

WD-50
Map 269 G23
50 Clinton Street between Stanton and Rivington streets (east side of the street)
Tel 212/477-2900
www.wd-50.com
Wylie Dufresne made the

Lower East Side a dining destination when he cooked at 71 Clinton Street. Now he has his own place, a sleek postmodern dining room where he mixes exciting but harmonious flavor combinations—octopus with celery pesto, pineapple and almonds, striped bass with passion fruit. Desserts are also creative.

🕐 Mon–Sat 6–11, Sun 6–10
🍴 D $55, Wine $40
🚇 Delancey (F), Essex (J, M, Z)
🚌 M9, M21

WOO LAE OAK
Map 269 E23
148 Mercer Street between Houston and Prince streets
Tel 212/925-8200
www.woolaeoaksoho.com
Here, you'll find a stylized American version of Korean cuisine. Start with the hot Dungeness crab wrapped in spinach crepes, or tuna tartare served over Korean pear.

Among the selections for the on-the-table barbecue there are 17 meats, fishes and vegetables, including ostrich, squid and tripe. Among other dishes, short ribs are swathed in sweet soy sauce, and then there are soups, casseroles and rice dishes. Don't forget the kimchi—the pickle dishes that are a perennial presence on the Korean table.

🕐 Sun–Thu noon–10.30, Fri–Sat noon–11.30
🍴 L $15, D $45, prix fixe $40 and $50, Wine $34
🚇 Broadway/Lafayette (F, S, V), Prince Street (N, R), Bleecker Street (6)
🚌 M1, M5

ZARELA
Map 267 F17
953 Second Avenue between 50th and 51st streets
Tel 212/644-6740
www.zarela.com
Don't be fooled by the festive ambience of this restaurant, for it offers some of the most authentic regional Mexican cuisine in the city. Whether or not you are looking for northern fajitas and flautas, or Oaxacan moles and coastal Veracruz-style dishes, you will find it here along with rare seasonal specialties.

🕐 Mon–Fri noon–3, Mon–Thu 5–11, Fri–Sat 5–11.30, Sun 5–10
🍴 L $23, prix fixe $29.95, D $35, prix fixe $42, Wine $21
🚇 Lexington/53rd Street (E, V), 51st Street (6)
🚌 M15

EATING

MAJOR RESTAURANT CHAINS

New York is a good place for eclectic and unusual eating, but there are also plenty of tried-and-tested chains, where you know exactly what you're getting and how much you'll have to pay.

	Price range ($–$$$)	Alcohol	Child menu	Takeout	Phone number	Website
RESTAURANTS						
Baluchi's	$$	Yes	No	Yes	212/594-5533	www.baluchis.com
Burritoville	$	No	Yes	Yes	212/563-9010	www.burritoville.com
California Pizza Kitchen	$$	Yes	Yes	Yes	800/919-3227	www.californiapizzakitchen.com
Lemongrass Grill	$$	Yes	No	Yes	718/399-7100	www.lemongrassgrill.org
Patsy's Pizzeria	$$	Yes	No	Yes	212/688-5916	www.patsyspizzeria.com
Pizza Hut	$	Some	Yes	Yes	972/338-7700	www.pizzahut.com
Pizzeria Uno	$$	Yes	Yes	Yes	866/600-8667	www.pizzeriauno.com
TGI Friday's	$$	Yes	Yes	Yes	972/662-5400	www.Fridays.com
Two Boots Pizzeria	$	Some	Yes	Yes	212/777-2668	www.twoboots.com
Xando Cosi	$	Yes	Yes	Yes	847/444-3200	www.xandocosi.com
Zen Palate	$$	No	No	Yes	212/614-9291	www.zenpalate.com

SANDWICHES AND FAST FOOD						
Au Bon Pain	$	No	No	Yes	617/423-2100	www.aubonpain.com
Burger King	$	No	Yes	Yes	305/378-3000	www.burgerking.com
Cosí Sandwich Bar	$	Yes	No	Yes	847/444-3200	www.getcosi.com
Kentucky Fried Chicken	$	No	Yes	Yes	800/225-5532	www.kfc.com
Le Pain Quotidien	$	No	No	Yes	212/625-9009	www.painquotidien.com
Little Pie Company	$	No	No	Yes	212/414-2324	www.littlepiecompany.com
McDonald's	$	No	Yes	Yes	800/244-6227	www.mcdonalds.com
Pret à Manger	$	No	No	Yes	646/728-0750	www.pretamanger.com
Subway	$	No	Yes	Yes	203/877-4281	www.subway.com
Wendy's	$	No	Yes	Yes	614/764-3100	www.wendys.com

COFFEE SHOPS						
Dean and DeLuca	$	No	No	Yes	877/826-9246	www.deananddeluca.com
Krispy Kreme Donuts	$	No	No	Yes	800/457-4779	www.krispykreme.com
Starbucks	$	No	No	Yes	800/782-7282	www.starbucks.com

STAYING IN NEW YORK

Traditionally the priciest hotels in New York have been relatively traditional, formal places. However the last two decades have seen a number of ultra-chic hotels open around the city, offering guests luxurious amenities in modern, stylish settings. The restaurants, lounges and bars in these places also attract trendy New Yorkers, as well as visitors to the city. There are plenty of hotel rooms, but it is hard to find a comfortable room under $150. If money is no object, reserve a room at the Carlyle or the Four Seasons.

Accommodation in New York ranges from cutting-edge luxury with impeccable service to less expensive options in local neighborhoods

For less expensive options, check out the inexpensive chains—Red Roof, Super 8 and others. The city also has some bed-and-breakfasts, which charge less than the average hotel and provide good-value extras. Hostels are the least expensive lodging options (see the box on the opposite page).

It used to be that all the best hotels were in Midtown but that has changed dramatically. Now, there are first-class luxury hotels downtown in SoHo, Greenwich Village and the Financial District. Still, there are more bargains away from Midtown. New York City hotels range in size from vast 2,000-room monstrosities to smaller establishments with 250 rooms or less. If you stay at a large convention hotel, expect to find crowded lobbies, more lines and slower service. Most hotels have similar amenities. The average hotel room comes with air conditioning, private bathroom, cable TV, telephone, coffeemaker, hairdryer, iron and ironing board. The level of luxury and the quality and range of the service are the real distinctions between hotels. Top-class hotel rooms boast luxe fabrics and linens (Frette, Pratesi), high-tech electronics and telephony, and high staff-to-guest ratios, which guarantees prompt, courteous service. Space is at a premium in Manhattan, so expect rooms to be on the small side. Double-glazed windows, which are usually standard, help reduce noise. Most hotels have complimentary coffee/tea service, and newspapers either in the lobby or delivered to your room.

Today there is no such thing as a standard rack rate. Prices fluctuate with customer demand. To get the best rate on a hotel room, always call the hotel directly and ask for the best available rate and what special discounts are available. Alternatively, go online to such discount services as hotels.com, quikbook.com or hoteldiscounts.com to secure the best rates. Winter (Jan–end Feb) and summer (Jul–end Aug) are the least expensive seasons. Depending on the hotel, weekend rates may be higher or lower than midweek. Parking charges of $35 and up will add substantially to any bill. Note, too, that 13.625 percent will be added to your bill, as well as additional occupancy taxes of a dollar or two which are charged for each night's stay.

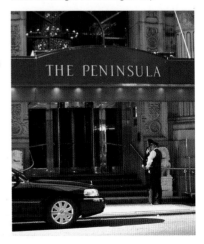

The Peninsula is a luxurious choice on Fifth Avenue

HOSTELS IN NEW YORK

BIG APPLE HOSTEL (Map 296 D18)
119 West 45th Street between Sixth and Seventh avenues,
10036, tel 212/302-2603, www.bigapplehostel.com

CHELSEA CENTER HOSTEL (Map 296 D19)
313 West 29th Street between Eighth and Ninth avenues,
10031, tel 212/643-0214, www.chelseacenterhostel.com

CHELSEA INTERNATIONAL HOSTEL
(Map 296 D20)
251 West 20th Street between Seventh and Eighth avenues,
10011, tel 212/647-0010, www.chelseahostel.com

HOSTELLING INTERNATIONAL
(Off map 294 C12)
891 Amsterdam Avenue at 104th Street, tel 212/932-2300,
www.hinewyork.org

WEST SIDE YMCA (Map 294 D16)
5 West 63rd Street between Central Park West and
Broadway, 10023, tel 212/630-9600, www.ymcanyc.org

WHITEHOUSE (Map 297 F22)
340 Bowery between 2nd and Great Jones streets, 10012,
tel 212/477-5623, www.whitehousehotelofny.com

HOTELS BY AREA

The hotels are listed alphabetically on pages 298–309. Here they are listed by area.

LOWER EAST SIDE
Off-SoHo Suites

GREENWICH VILLAGE/MEAT MARKET/CHELSEA
Abingdon Guest House
Chelsea
Chelsea Lodge
Hotel Gansevoort
Inn on 23rd Street
Larchmont
Maritime Hotel
Washington Square

SOHO/TRIBECA
Cosmopolitan Hotel-Tribeca
Hotel Azure
Mercer
SoHo Grand
Tribeca Grand

UNION SQUARE/FLATIRON DISTRICT/GRAMERCY PARK
Gershwin
Giraffe
Inn at Irving Place
Union Square Inn

MADISON SQUARE PARK/ MURRAY HILL
Avalon
Grand Union
Hotel Chandler
Marcel

Morgans
70 Park Avenue
Thirty Thirty
Wolcott

MIDTOWN WEST/THEATER DISTRICT
Algonquin
Americana Inn
Belvedere
Blakely
Broadway Inn
Casablanca
Dream Hotel
Hudson
Le Parker Meridien
Mansfield
Michaelangelo
Moderne
Muse
Ritz Carlton
Royalton
Shoreham
Travel Inn
Warwick
Wyndham

LINCOLN CENTER/UPPER WEST SIDE
Beacon
Excelsior
Hotel Roger Williams
Lucerne
Mandarin Oriental

Newton
On the Ave
Trump International Hotel and Tower

MIDTOWN EAST
Beekman Tower
Benjamin
Edison
Elysee
Four Seasons
Hotel 57
Kimberly
Library
Metro
Millennium UN Plaza
New York Palace
Peninsula
St. Regis
Sherry-Netherland
Waldorf-Astoria Hotel And Towers
W-New York

UPPER EAST SIDE
Affinia Gardens
Carlyle
Gracie Inn
Lowell
Pierre
Plaza Athenée
The Pod
Surrey
Wales

STAYING

HOTEL LOCATOR

B **C** **D**

West 95th Street

Newton

Hostelling International

West 93rd Street

UPPER WEST

West 92nd Street

SIDE

West 91st Street

West 90th Street

West 89th Street

West 88th Street

West 87th Street

86th Street

West 86th Street

86th Street

CENTR PARK

West 85th Street

West 84th Street

Riverside Park

West 83rd Street

West 82nd Street

81st Street Museum of Nat Hist

Excelsior

West 81st Street

Cen

Lucerne

West 80th Street

American Museum of Natural History

West 79th Street

79th Street

West 78th Street

On The Ave

West 77th Street

New-York Historical Society

West 76th Street

West 75th Street

San Remo Apartments

Beacon

West 74th Street

Ansonia Building

West 73rd Street

The Dakota

West 72nd Street

72nd Street

72nd Street

Strawberry Fields

The Lake

West 71st Street

West 70th Street

West 69th Street

Freedom Place

West 69th Street

West 68th Street

Riverside Boulevard

West 68th Street

The Sheep Meadow

West 67th Street

66th Street Lincoln Center

Juilliard School

West 66th Street

West 65th Street

Tavern on the Green

65th

West 64th Street

Lincoln Center

West 64th Street

West Side YMCA

West 63rd Street

West 63rd Street

Museum of Biblical Art

West 62nd Street

62nd Street

West 61st Street

West 61st Street

Trump International Hotel & Tower

West 60th Street

59th Street Columbus Circle

COLUMBUS CIRCLE

West 59th Street

West 59th Street

Mandarin Oriental

Central

West 58th Street

Hudson

57th Street

Car Hall

WEST 57TH STREET

West 56th Street

Moderne

Le M Bla

West 55th Street

Dream Hotel

West 54th Street

West 53rd Street

7th Avenue

West 52nd Street

West 51st Street

WJ Hotel

The Michelangelo

West 50th Street

50th Street

49th Street

West 49th Street

59th Street

Belvedere

West 48th Street

West 47th Street

Edison

BROADWAY

Broadway Inn

West 46th Street

Big Ap Hos

294

B Intrepid Sea, Air and Space Museum

West 46th Street

C **D**

HOTEL LOCATOR

ABINGDON GUEST HOUSE
Map 296 D21
13 Eighth Avenue at West 12th Street, 10014
Tel 212/243-5384
www.abingdonguesthouse.com
Located in two historic three-story red-brick town houses above a coffee shop in Greenwich Village, the guest house is unmarked. The nine rooms are individually decorated and well furnished with antiques. Amenities include private bath (with hairdryer), cable TV and free Wi-Fi. The patio garden is a bonus.
$199–$279
9
14th Street (A, C, E), Christopher Street/Sheridan Square (1)
M20, M14

AFFINIA GARDENS
Map 295 F16
215 East 64th Street, between Second and Third avenues, 10021
Tel 212/355-1230
www.affinia.com
The suites at this well-located hotel have fully equipped kitchens, grocery shopping service and guest laundry. There's also a fitness center.
Doubles and suites from $250
131
68th Street (6)
M15, M72, M98, M101, M102, M103

ALGONQUIN
Map 296 E18
59 West 44th Street between Fifth and Sixth avenues, 10036
Tel 212/840-6800
www.algonquinhotel.com
It's famous for being the place where in the 1920s Robert Benchley, Dorothy Parker and the rest of the *Vanity Fair/New Yorker* crowd gathered regularly for lunch at the Round Table. The rooms are moderate in size and furnished with reproductions of American antiques. The wood-paneled Oak Room is the city's best cabaret, and there's a fitness center.
$209–$499, suite from $309
150 rooms, 24 suites

42nd Street (B, D, F, V)
M5, M7, M42

AMERICANA INN
Map 296 E18
69 West 38th Street between Fifth and Sixth avenues, 10018
Tel 212/840-6700
www.theamericanainn.com
Rooms here are bright, modern and comfortable, if plainly decorated. They are equipped with cable TV and telephone. All rooms share a bath, and each floor has a kitchenette.
$85–$95
50
42nd Street (B, D, F, V)
M5, M6, M7

AVALON
Map 296 E19
16 East 32nd Street at Madison Avenue, 10016
Tel 212/299-7000
www.theavalonny.com

This small hotel is near the Empire State Building and has traditionally furnished rooms. Executive suites have fax, Bose radio and cordless phone. Complimentary breakfast and evening champagne are set out in the mahogany-paneled library off the lobby.
Double from $269, suite from $315, including breakfast
70 rooms, 30 suites
33rd Street (6)
M1, M2, M3, M4, M34

BEACON
Map 294 C15
2130 Broadway between 74th and 75th streets, 10023
Tel 212/787-1100
www.beaconhotel.com
Less than 10 blocks from the Lincoln Center and close to Central Park, this 25-story hotel offers good value. Guests can save money using the kitchenette with stove, microwave and

refrigerator. Amenities include TV, telephone and hairdryer. Fitness center.
$235–$325, suite from $295
120 rooms, 110 suites
72nd Street (1, 2, 3)
M7, M11, M104

BEEKMAN TOWER
Map 295 F17
3 Mitchell Place (East 49th Street and First Avenue), 10017
Tel 212/355-7300
www.thebeekmanhotel.com
This all-suite hotel, in a 1928 art deco building near the UN, has accommodations that include bedroom, sitting room and fully equipped kitchen. The deluxe suites have such extras as VCRs and two-line phones. The bar/restaurant on the top floor is one of the most romantic aeries in the city. Fitness center on-premises.

$209–$440, 2-bedroom suite from $350
174 suites
51st Street (6)
M15

BELVEDERE
Map 294 D17
319 West 48th Street between Eighth and Ninth avenues, 10036
Tel 212/245-7000
www.belvederehotelnyc.com
The most expensive hotel in the Empire Hotel group, the Belvedere has handsome sizable rooms with kitchenettes fitted with microwave, refrigerator

and coffeemaker. Executive rooms are also available. On premises, the Churrascaria Plataforma is a Brazilian steakhouse.

💵 $219–$289
🛏 400 rooms and suites
🚇 50th Street (C, E)
🚌 M11, M20, M50

BENJAMIN

Map 295 F17
125 East 50th Street at Lexington Avenue, 10022
Tel 212/715-2500
www.thebenjamin.com

Conveniently situated in Midtown, this Manhattan Suites hotel offers good-looking rooms and excellent facilities in a handsome 1927 building. The rooms are furnished with mahogany pieces. Guests can select from a ten-type pillow menu. The Affinia Spa and Wellness Center (▷ 228) is a bonus. Restaurant and bar.

💵 Doubles from $359, suites from $429
🛏 209
🚇 51st Street (6)
🚌 M50, M98, M101, M102, M103

BLAKELY

Map 294 D17
136 West 55th Street between Sixth and Seventh avenues, 10019
Tel 212/245-1800
www.blakelyny.com

The rooms are handsome with a traditional English flavor conveyed in foxhunt

prints and cherry furnishings. Amenities include full kitchenettes with microwave and mini-fridge plus the latest in tech—flat screen TVs, DVD/CD players, cordless phones and complimentary WiFi. Comforts run to Frette bathrobes and Penhaligon toiletries. Restaurant-bar and fitness center.

💵 $225–$345, suite from $325
🛏 58 rooms, 55 suites
🚇 57th Street (N, Q, R, W), 57th Street (F)
🚌 M5, M6, M7, M57

BROADWAY INN

Map 296 D18
264 West 46th Street between Broadway and Eighth Avenue, 10036
Tel 212/997-9200
www.broadwayinn.com

In the Theater District, this cozy small hotel could be found in London or any other European city. The second-floor lobby welcomes guests to a comfortable hearth and book-lined aerie. The rooms vary in size, but it's one of the few places in town where a solo traveler can rent a single room—and save money doing so. They are basically decorated and have such amenities as cable TV, telephone and hairdryer. Suites have extras such as a refrigerator and microwave. Quietest rooms are in the back. No elevator.

💵 $225, suite from $299, including breakfast
🛏 30 rooms, 11 suites
🚇 42nd Street (A, C, E), 42nd Street/Times Square (N, Q, R, S, W, 1, 2, 3, 7)
🚌 M6, M7, M20, M27, M104

CASABLANCA

Map 296 D18
147 West 43rd Street between Sixth and Seventh avenues, 10036
Tel 212/869-1212
www.casablancahotel.com

CARLYLE

Map 295 E14
35 East 76th Street between Madison and Park avenues, 10021
Tel 212/744-1600
www.thecarlyle.com

This is a striking art deco building. The rooms boast large bathrooms and every conceivable amenity. The public areas are classics, particularly Bemelman's Bar with its charming murals and the café where Bobby Short plays. Facilities include fitness center and pool.

💵 $700, suites from $1.050
🛏 181 rooms and suites
🚇 77th Street (4, 5)
🚌 M1, M2, M3, M4

Close to the Theater District, the boutique-style Casablanca is small and personal and offers stylish, modern, well-equipped rooms. The public areas have a Moroccan feel with tiles and rattan chairs.

💵 Doubles from $299, suites from £449
🛏 40 rooms, 8 suites
🚇 42nd Street/Times Square (N, Q, R, S, W, 1, 2, 3, 7, 9), 42nd Street (B, D, F, V)
🚌 M6, M7, M10, M20

STAYING

CHELSEA

Map 296 D20
222 West 23rd Street between Seventh and Eighth avenues, 10011
Tel 212/243-3700
www.chelseahotel.com

Many artists and bohemians have stayed or lived here since it opened in 1884, including Mark Twain and Dylan Thomas. The rooms vary in size and decor. Serena's, the bar opened by Serena Bass, attracts a Brit-pack crowd.

🛏 $235, suites from $350
ℹ 375 rooms (250 permanent residents)
🚇 23rd Street (C, E), 23rd Street (1)
🚌 M20, M23

CHELSEA LODGE

Map 296 D20
318 West 20th Street between Eighth and Ninth avenues, 10001
Tel 212/243-4499
www.chelsealodge.com
In very fashionable Chelsea, this small hotel occupies

a handsome red-brick town house, which has been lovingly restored by the owners. The rooms are decorated in plain American country style with patterned wallpaper and eclectic furnishings. Most have hardwood floors and small TVs, plus sink and shower. Toilet is in the hall.

🛏 $129
ℹ 22
🚇 23rd Street (C, E)
🚌 M11, M20

COSMOPOLITAN HOTEL–TRIBECA

Map 297 E24
95 West Broadway at Chambers Street, 10007
Tel 212/566-1900
www.cosmohotel.com

This hotel has a great downtown location and good-looking rooms. They're all furnished with industrial-style carpeting and Scandinavian-style pieces, but they have private bath, TV and telephone.

🛏 $75–$190
ℹ 125
🚇 Chambers Street (1, 2, 3), Chambers Street (A, C)
🚌 M20

DREAM HOTEL

Map 294 D17
210 West 55th Street between Broadway and Seventh Avenue
Tel 212/247-2000
www.dreamny.com
From the minute you enter the lobby you know that this hotel is all about design. A crystal boat is suspended from the ceiling and an enormous aquarium dominates the space. The rooms are dramatically furnished with blue satin headboards and lit blue too. Bathrooms are hip-minimalist. The rooms have the latest tech amenities—plasma TV, iPod with Bose speakers. Lounges are found in the lobby, on the rooftop and underground. Plus Deepak Chopra has located an Ayurvedic center here.

🛏 Doubles from $259, suite from $519
ℹ 204 rooms and 16 suites
🚇 7th Avenue (B, D, E), 57th Street/7th Avenue (N, Q, R, W)
🚌 M10, M20

EDISON

Map 296 D18
228 West 47th Street between Broadway and Eighth Avenue, 10036
Tel 212/840-5000.
www.edisonhotelnyc.com
Theater patrons appreciate this art deco 1931 hotel in the center of the Theater District. The entrance lobby is somewhat bland but functional. The rooms are moderately priced and have cable TV and telephone. Restaurant and bar too.

🛏 Doubles from $195, suites from $255
ℹ 900 rooms and suites
🚇 50th Street (C, E), 50th Street (1)
🚌 M6, M7, M20, M27, M104

ELYSÉE

Map 295 E17
60 East 54th Street, 10022
Tel 212/753-1066
www.elyseehotel.com

This little gem of a hotel, built in 1926, has comfortable rooms decorated with fine French antique reproductions and luxurious fabrics. Bathrooms are marble and brass. The Monkey Bar, named for its murals, was once home to such regulars as Tallulah Bankhead. Guests have use of a nearby sports club.

🛏 Doubles from $295, suites from $425, including Continental breakfast and wine and cheese (weekday evenings)
ℹ 86 rooms, 15 suites
🚇 53rd Street/Fifth Avenue (E, V), 51st Street (6)

EXCELSIOR

Map 294 D14
45 West 81st Street between Columbus Avenue and Central Park West, 10024
Tel 212/362-9200
www.excelsiorhotelny.com
One of the few hotels on the Upper West Side, near the Natural History Museum, the Excelsior offers spotless modern rooms equipped

STAYING

with cable TV, dual-line phone with data port, and such niceties as bathrobes. Small, decently equipped exercise room.

🛏 $169–$269, suite from $259
ℹ️ 199 rooms and suites
🚇 81st Street (B, C)
🚌 M7, M11, M10, M79

GERSHWIN
Map 296 E20
7 East 27th Street between Fifth and Madison avenues, 10016
Tel 212/545-8000
www.gershwinhotel.com
The Gershwin attracts young budget travelers, who stay in plain doubles or dormitory-style rooms with 10 beds. Rooms have cable TV and phone. On weekends, live bands play in the Gallery Lounge.

🛏 $119, suite from $249, dorm for two $53, women only dorm $43, coed dorm $33
ℹ️ 130 rooms, 6 suites

SPECIAL
FOUR SEASONS
Map 295 E16
57 East 57th Street between Madison and Park avenues, 10022
Tel 212/758-5700
www.fourseasons.com

The service at this hotel is legendary; staff are trained to cater to a guest's every whim. I. M. Pei designed the 53-story building, which opened in 1993. The rooms, averaging 600sq feet (55sq m) are the largest in the city and include a dressing area. The suites have walk-in closets and balconies with grand city views. The large fitness center contains a full spa, and the restaurant and bar are both top-of-the-line.

🛏 $675, suite from $1,250
ℹ️ 305 rooms, 63 suites
🚇 59th Street (4, 5, 6)
🚌 M1, M2, M3, M4

🚇 28th Street (N, R, W)
🚌 M2, M3

GIRAFFE
Map 296 F20
365 Park Avenue South between 26th and 27th streets, 10016
Tel 212/685-7700
www.hotelgiraffe.com
A small boutique hotel in the

Flatiron neighborhood evokes the 1920s and 1930s. Each floor has only seven rooms, decorated in glamorous colors and materials. Many have balconies. On-premises restaurant, plus access to a nearby health club.

🛏 $329–$399, suite from $425, including breakfast and wine and cheese (weekday evenings)
ℹ️ 52 rooms, 21 suites
🚇 23rd Street (6)
🚌 M1

GRACIE INN
Map 295 G14
502 East 81st Street between York and East End avenues, 10028
Tel 212/628-1700
www.thegracieinn.com
Slightly off the beaten track, near the mayor's mansion, this inn attracts long-term guests to 12 apartments in a five-story building. Each has a kitchenette, plus TV and phone with data port. The penthouses have waterbeds, whirlpool tubs and sundecks. Wireless and DVD on request. Breakfast delivered to your room is a welcome indulgence.

🛏 Studio $139–$179, 1-bedroom suite from $189
ℹ️ 12 rooms, 2 suites
🚇 77th St (6)
🚌 M15, M31, M79

GRAND UNION
Map 296 E19
34 East 32nd Street between Madison and Park avenues, 10016
Tel 212/683-5890
www.hotelgrandunion.com
This old-fashioned hotel in

the trend-setting Flatiron neighborhood has clean basic rooms that are equipped with small refrigerators and phones with data ports. Coffee shop.

🛏 $157.50–$250
ℹ️ 95
🚇 33rd Street (6)
🚌 M1, M2, M3, M34

HOTEL 57
Map 295 F17
130 East 57th Street at Lexington, 10022
Tel 212/753-8841
www.habitatny.com
Little wonder that travelers love this place. It has a great location, and the contemporary rooms are clean, comfortable and attractively decorated after a makeover. All have cable TV and telephone with data port.

🛏 $295, suite from $465
ℹ️ 205 rooms and suites
🚇 59th Street (4, 5, 6)
🚌 M59, M98, M101, M102, M103

HOTEL AZURE
Map 297 E24
120 Lafayette Street at Canal Street, 10013
Tel 212/925-4378
www.hotelazure.com
The Azure is a compact (28 rooms on five floors) boutique hotel in the SoHo district, which is smoke-free. Room rates include a complimentary newspaper and bottled water, as well as breakfast. All rooms are simple but bright and modern, with lots of blue and white, and all have free high-speed internet, direct-dial phones with voice mail and 32-inch flat-screen TVs with cable.

🛏 $303-$400 including breakfast
ℹ️ 28
🚇 Canal Street (4, 5, 6)

STAYING

HOTEL CHANDLER

Map 296 E19
12 East 31st Street between Fifth and Madison avenues, 10016
Tel 212/889-6363
www.hotelchandler.com
This 14-floor boutique hotel in the Murray Hill neighborhood occupies a 1903 Beaux Arts building, which has been carefully renovated and decorated in retro style. Rooms are small but chic, with CD and DVD, free high-speed internet, personal phone number and flat-screen TV. The 12:31 bar attracts a hip after-work crowd. There is a fitness room with sauna.

💵 $345–$510, suite from $595
🛏 120 rooms, 8 suites
🚇 33rd Street (6)
🚌 M2, M3, M5

HOTEL GANSEVOORT

Map 296 D21
18 Ninth Avenue at 13th Street
Tel 212/206-6700
www.hotelgansevoort.com
This meat-packing district hotel adopts South Beach style with such dramatic features as heated rooftop pool, kaleidoscopic illuminated glass columns that change color and mood, and a Japanese restaurant with a fetching outdoor courtyard bar-dining area. Rooms are decorated in minimalist style and hues (fabric headboards, stainless-steel sinks), and feature the latest amenities—plasma TVs and complimentary WiFi. Spa and fitness center occupy a lower level.

💵 Doubles from $395, suite from $625
🛏 167 rooms, 20 suites
🚇 14th Street (A, C, E)
🚌 M11

HOTEL ROGER WILLIAMS

Map 296 E19
131 Madison Ave at 31st Street, 10016
Tel 212/448-7000
www.rogerwilliamshotel.com
In 1997 Unique Hotels Group renovated this fine old hotel (1928). They transformed the lobby, lining it with limestone and coating the fluted columns with zinc. In the good-size rooms they installed sleek contemporary maple furnishings, shoji window screens, and such amenities as VCRs, CD players, 27-in TVs, and three phones. Bathrooms

have hairdryers, Frette robes and Aveda toiletries. Cappuccino and espresso are available 24 hours. There's also a fitness studio.

💵 $245–$385, suite from $500
🛏 183 rooms, 2 suites
🚇 33rd Street (6)
🚌 M1, M2, M3

HUDSON

Map 294 D16
356 West 58th Street between Eighth and Ninth avenues, 10019
Tel 212/554-6000
www.hudsonhotel.com
The Hudson is Ian Schrager's and Philippe Starck's latest "hotel as on-going party". Guests arrive in the ivy-draped lobby via escalators encased in a chartreuse-green tube. Starck trademarks include oversized chairs and other objects like the 500-gallon watering can in the garden courtyard. The rooms are small and furnished with minimalist stainless-steel pieces, plus the latest technical amenities. The Library lounge has plenty of leather, a hearth and a dramatically lit antique billiard table. A long gilded table serves as a bar in the lounge, which converts into a dance club at night. Landscaped roof terrace a bonus.

💵 Doubles from $259, suites from $389
🛏 1,000 rooms, 11 suites
🚇 59th Street/Columbus Circle (A, B, C, D, 1) 🚌 M1, M20, M57

INN AT IRVING PLACE

Map 296 F21
56 Irving Place between East 17th and 18th streets, 10003
Tel 212/533-4600
www.InnatIrving.com
These two 1834 town houses have plenty of ersatz atmosphere. Rooms have fireplaces and four-poster beds dressed with Frette linens, plus antique reproductions. Amenities include two-line telephones with data port, VCRs and CD players. Guests sit on tufted chairs around the fireplaces in Lady Mendl's at afternoon tea. Lounge, too.

💵 $415–625
🛏 12 rooms and suites
🚇 14th Street/Union Square (L, N, Q, R, W, 4, 5, 6) 🚌 M1, M2, M3, M14

LE PARKER MERIDIEN

Map 294 D17
118 West 57th Street between Sixth and Seventh avenues, 10019
Tel 212/245-5000
www.parkermeridien.com

The rooms in this French hotel are furnished with sleek modernist pieces and contain the latest amenities—32-inch TV, ergonomic chairs, fax, DVD, CD player and free high-speed internet access. Hip bistro-style Seppi's serves Mediterranean fare, while Norma's luxury all-day break-fast is famous. Jack's Lounge produces exotic cocktails. There is an excellent 42nd-floor fitness center with a rooftop jogging track.

💵 $255–$660, suite from $580
🛏 600 rooms, 100 suites
🚇 57th Street (N, Q, R, W)
🚌 M6, M7, M57

INN ON 23RD STREET

Map 296 D20
131 West 23rd Street between Sixth and Seventh avenues, 10011
Tel 212/463-0330
www.innon23rd.com
If you prefer a bed-and-breakfast, then this inn in a 19th-century town house (with an elevator!) has much to offer. The Fisherman family has furnished it with family heirlooms and eclectic pieces. The rooms have such modern amenities as dual-line phone (local calls are free). Bathrooms are small. Guest amenities include an inviting second-floor library and an honor bar with liquor, wine and beer, plus a microwave.

💵 $189–$269, suite from $329, including breakfast
🛏 14
🚇 23rd Street (F, V), 23rd Street (1)
🚌 M5, M6, M7, M20, M23

STAYING

LIBRARY

Map 296 E18

299 Madison Avenue at 41st Street,
10017

Tel 212/983-4500

www.libraryhotel.com

It's not just the design concept that book lovers appreciate at this boutique property, it's also the service. Each floor of the hotel is dedicated to a subject category from the Dewey Decimal system and each room has a collection of art and books related to a sub-category. The decor is modern and minimalist. Amenities include multi-line phones and free WiFi. Refreshments are served in the second-floor, book-lined Reading Room. There's also an American Bistro and Wine Bar and complimentary passes to a nearby fitness center.

💷 $325–$425, suite from $415, including breakfast and afternoon wine and cheese

🛏 52 rooms, 8 suites

🚇 Grand Central/42nd Street (S, 4, 5, 6, 7)

🚌 M1, M2, M3, M4, M42

KIMBERLY

Map 295 F17

145 East 50th Street between Third and Lexington avenues, 10022

Tel 212/702-1600

www.kimberlyhotel.com

This small personal hotel in Midtown has a European flavor. Originally built in 1985 as an apartment house, it has large rooms with fully equipped kitchens. Some rooms have balconies; they all have three dual-line phones and high-speed internet access. Guests also have membership at the New York

Health and Racquet Clubs.

💷 Doubles from $259, suites from $299

🛏 26 rooms, 158 suites

🚇 51st Street (6)

🚌 M50, M98, M101, M102, M103

LARCHMONT

Map 297 E21

27 West 11th Street between Fifth and Sixth avenues, 10011

Tel 212/989-9333

www.larchmontHotel.com

This is a great buy on an extra-quiet side street in Greenwich Village. It has plenty of character and appeals to European travelers who don't mind shared bathrooms (bathrobe and slippers provided). The rooms are attractively decorated, ultra clean and well equipped with air conditioning, cable TV and telephone.

💷 $109–$135, including breakfast

🛏 58

🚇 14th Street (F, V), Sixth Avenue (L)

🚌 M2, M3, M5, M6

LOWELL

Map 295 E16

28 East 63rd Street between Madison and Park avenues, 10021

Tel 212/838-1400

www.lowellhotel.com

This little-known hotel, in an elegant 1920s town house, draws a regular clientele. The rooms are furnished with antiques and the suites are spectacular, with fireplaces and large garden terraces. There's 24-hour room service and

MANDARIN ORIENTAL

Map 294 D16

80 Columbus Circle at West 60th Street, 10023

Tel 212/805-8800

www.mandarinoriental.com

This hotel soars majestically above Columbus Circle commanding views of Central Park, the Hudson River and the Manhattan skyline from floors 35 through 54 of the new Time Warner Center. Rooms are sumptuously furnished and designed. Bathrooms have deep tubs and glass wall showers plus flat panel TVs. Room service can be ordered from Asiate an Asian-inspired fine dining restaurant. MO Bar (on the 35th floor) has been attracting a lot of buzz. Facilities include a two-story spa, and a fitness center with 75-foot lap pool. The hotel has access to all of the facilities in the Time Warner Center.

💷 Doubles from $895, suites from $2,400

🛏 202 rooms, 46 suites

🚇 59th Street (A, B, C, D, 1, 9)

🚌 M5, M7, M10, M104

concierge, and also two restaurants and fitness center.

💷 $665–$750, suite from $980

🛏 23 rooms, 47 suites

🚇 59th Street (4, 5)

🚌 M1, M2, M3, M4

LUCERNE

Map 294 C14

201 West 79th Street between Broadway and Amsterdam Avenue, 10024

Tel 212/875-1000

www.thelucernehotel.com

This hotel, in a 1903 landmark building, is a bargain. Rooms are spacious enough for queen or king beds, and have marble bathrooms. The suites have sitting areas as well as kitchenette with refrigerator and microwave. Facilities include a decent fitness center.

💷 $195–$330, suite from $225, including breakfast

🛏 142 rooms, 42 suites

🚇 79th Street (1)

🚌 M7, M11, M79

STAYING

MANSFIELD

Map 296 E18

12 West 44th Street between Fifth and Sixth avenues, 10036

Tel 212/277-8700

www.mansfieldhotel.com

Occupying a 1904 Beaux-Arts building with many original features, the hotel is convenient for the theater and Midtown shopping. The elegantly furnished rooms have sleigh beds with steel mesh headboards, metal and fabric armoires, plus free WiFi. Nearby health club.

🛏 Doubles from $319, suites from $419, including breakfast

🛌 100 rooms, 24 suites

🚇 42nd Street (B, D, F, V)

🚌 M1, M2, M3, M4, M5, M42

MARCEL

Map 296 F20

201 East 24th Street between Second and Third avenues, 10011

Tel 212/696-3800

www.nychotels.com

The rooms at this hotel are serene and minimal. Sheathed in blond wood and furnished in taupe, they have such modern clever design accents as high hats over the beds. They also have exceptional amenities for the price: dual-line phones with data ports and CD players, for instance. On-premises restaurant.

🛏 $135–$249

🛌 135 rooms and suites

🚇 23rd Street (6)

🚌 M15, M23, M101, M102, M103

MARITIME HOTEL

Map 296 D21

363 West 16th Street at Ninth Avenue

Tel 212/242-4300

www.themaritimehotel.com

In Chelsea and close to nightlife central, the Meatpacking District, this hotel was formerly the headquarters of the Maritime Union. In keeping with that history, the rooms are small and cabin-like with teak paneling and port-hole windows. Furnishings are modern and the rooms feature the latest technology—flat panel TVs and high-speed internet access. It has two attention-grabbing restaurants. Matsura is a dramatic basement supper-club style Japanese restaurant; there's also a Mediterranean café with a large outdoor terrace garden landscaped with

METRO

Map 296 E19

45 West 35th Street between Fifth and Sixth avenues, 10001

Tel 212/947-2500

www.hotelmetronyc.com

This has to be one of the best-value hotels in the city. It has a good Midtown location and plenty of art deco style. The rooms are nicely decorated with good-looking beds, nightstands and chairs and equipped with cable TV, and phone with data port. The marble bathrooms have hairdryers. Guests can relax in the library, which actually has books, or on the rooftop garden terrace. The sleek Metro Grill provides room service.

🛏 $295–$450, suite from $375, including breakfast

🛌 179 rooms and suites

🚇 34th Street (B, D, F, N, Q, R, V, W)

🚌 M2, M3, M5, M6, M7

magnolia trees and lily pond.

🛏 $245–$315

🛌 120 rooms, 4 suites

🚇 14th Street (A, C, E)

🚌 M11

MERCER

Map 297 E23

147 Mercer Street between Prince and Spring streets, 10012

Tel 212/966-6060

www.mercerhotel.com

The Hollywood crowd loves this East Coast version of Andre Balaz's Château Marmont. The SoHo location is ultra-hip, but the place is discreet, comfortable and tranquil. The loft-style rooms are spacious and minimalist. Christian Liaigre used neutral colors, glass, fabrics like linen, and rich woods from Africa. Extras include a mini-bar stocked by Dean and DeLuca and three telephones including a portable. If that's not enough, then the Mercer Kitchen under star chef Jean Georges Vongerichten is the clincher. Access to a nearby fitness center is provided.

🛏 $595–$820, suite from $1,500

🛌 75 rooms and suites

🚇 Prince St (N, R, W)

🚌 M1, M6

THE MICHAELANGELO

Map 294 D17

152 West 51st Street between 6th and 7th avenues, 10019

Tel 212/765-0505

www.michelangelohotel.com

The boutique Michaelangelo hotel is in Midtown Manhattan, a block west of Radio City Music Hall and convenient for Broadway's theater district. It's the only US property of an Italian hotel chain, and the Italian influences are everywhere: the friendliness of the staff, the Italian marble in the reception and in guest bathrooms, and in the Limoncello restaurant. All the rooms are very spacious by New York standards and feature high-speed internet, CD players, voice mail and large whirlpool bathtubs.

🛏 $395, suites from $595 including breakfast

🛌 178 rooms and suites

🚇 49th Street (N, R)

🚌 M1, M2

MILLENNIUM UN PLAZA

Off map 295 G18

1 UN Plaza at 44th Street and First Avenue, 10017

Tel 212/758-1234

www.millenniumhotels.com

Across the street from the UN, this flashy hotel attracts international diplomats and other wealthy visitors. Many of the rooms, which are located from the 28th floor and up, have splendid views of the skyline and the East River. They are well equipped with two-line phones with data port and printer/fax/copier. Traditional rooms feature mahogany and cherry furnishings, while more classicly furnished rooms with their blond woods look more contemporary. The fitness center has indoor pool and tennis court. The Ambassador Grill and lounge serves contemporary American cuisine.

🛏 Doubles from $229, suites from $359

🛌 382 rooms, 45 suites

🚇 42nd Street/Grand Central (S, 4, 5, 6, 7)

🚌 M15, M27, M50

STAYING

MODERNE

Map 294 D17

243 West 55th Street between Broadway and Eighth Avenue, 10019

Tel 212/397-6767

www.nychotels.com

This small retro-style hotel in a fine location near Carnegie Hall is reliable. The rooms are sleekly decorated (padded high back bed, built-in nightstands, op art) and equipped with the latest gadgetry—VCR, CD player and telephone with data port—plus hairdryer and an extra phone in the bathroom.

🛏 Doubles from $135, suites from $185

🛎 29 rooms, 5 suites

🚇 Seventh Avenue (B, D, E), 59th Street/Columbus Circle (A, B, C, D, 1)

🚌 M10, M20, M104

MORGANS

Map 296 E19

237 Madison Avenue between East 37th and 38th streets, 10016

Tel 212/686-0300

www.morganshotelgroup.com

In 1984 Ian Schrager opened this hotel, his first in New York City. It's discreet (no nameplate visible) and more sedate than most. Minimalist furnishings decorate the rooms, which are ultra-comfortable with their club chairs, ottomans and window seats, and good looking, too, with suede headboards and bird's-eye maple cabinets. Bathrooms have whirlpool tubs and stainless-steel fixtures, granite floors and eye-catching black and white tile. The rooms also have the latest amenities. The dramatic cellar bar and the restaurant Asia de Cuba attract a fashion-conscious crowd. Residents have complimentary access to a nearby fitness club.

🛏 Doubles from $329, suites from $489

🛎 113 rooms and suites

🚇 33rd Street (6), 42nd Street/Grand Central (S, 4, 5, 6, 7)

🚌 M1, M2, M3, M4, M42, M34

THE MUSE

Map 296 D18

130 West 46th Street between 6th and 7th avenues, 10036

Tel 212/485-2400

www.themusehotel.com

Close to the Broadway theater district, the Muse pays homage to New York's performing arts with specially commissioned artworks in rooms and public areas. It's close by the Rockefeller Center too. The rooms and bathrooms are spacious and smartly decorated in contemporary style, with such amenities as in-room spa treatments, on-demand movies, high-speed internet. Some rooms have balconies with city views. The Muse has a complimentary 24-hour fitness center, daily paper delivery and evening wine receptions.

🛏 $439, suites from $629

🛎 181 rooms, 19 suites

🚇 42nd Street (B, D, F, V)

🚌 M6, M7, M20, M27, M104

NEWTON

Map 294 C13

2528 Broadway between 94th and 95th streets, 10025

Tel 212/678-6500

www.newyorkhotel.com

This reliable hotel caters to the workers in the entertainment industry who appreciate the value of the rooms here. They are equipped with cable TV and phone, and some have microwaves and refrigerators. WiFi access throughout.

🛏 $95–$160

🛎 98 rooms, 12 suites

🚇 96th Street (1, 2, 3)

🚌 M104

NEW YORK PALACE

Map 295 E17

455 Madison Avenue between 50th and 51st streets, 10022

Tel 212/888-7000

www.newyorkpalace.com

Six landmark brownstones designed by McKim, Mead and White make up the core of this luxury hotel. Owner Sultan of Brunei has spent lavishly on the decor of the public areas and the guest rooms. Several gorgeous Louis Comfort Tiffany windows and alabaster sculptures by Saint-Gaudens grace the interiors.

The accommodations are located in a 55-story tower. Business travelers appreciate the executive amenities: fax, three phones and spacious desk. The restaurant Istana offers an olive bar (30-plus), numerous sherries, and tapas at afternoon tea and contemporary American cuisine. Fitness center available.

🛏 $340–$595, suite from $1,000

🛎 806 rooms, 86 suites

🚇 51st Street (6)

🚌 M1, M2, M3, M4, M50

OFF-SOHO SUITES

Map 297 F23

11 Rivington Street between Chrystie and Bowery streets, 10002

Tel 212/979-9808

www.offsoho.com

It's pushing the envelope when the location is described as SoHo. It is, in fact, on the Lower East Side, the last of Manhattan's gentrified neighborhoods. Savvy travelers will appreciate the low prices of these suites, which have bedroom living/dining area. Ideal for two couples traveling

together, as each suite shares a kitchen and bath. They are well equipped with cable TV, telephone, modular jack, VCR and minibar. Fitness center available.

🛏 $179–$239, quads $289–$379

🛎 38 suites

🚇 Bowery (J, M, Z)

🚌 M103

ON THE AVE

Map 294 C14
2178 Broadway at 77th Street, 10024
Tel 212/362-1100
www.pntheave-nyc.com

A few blocks from the Natural History Museum, this small hotel built in 1922 is part of the Citylife Hotel Group, which has rescued and refurbished several historic buildings in Manhattan. The rooms, furnished in sleek modern style (duvets on beds, retro chairs), feature vibrant paintings by Alfonso Muñoz. Amenities include two phones. The three floors of penthouse suites have fine views.

🏨 Doubles from $299, suites from $459
ℹ 250 rooms, 16 suites
Ⓜ 79th Street (1)
🚌 M79, M104

PENINSULA

Map 295 E17
700 Fifth Avenue at 55th Street, 10019
Tel 212/956-2888
www.peninsula.com

This small hotel in a beautiful 23-story 1902 Beaux Arts building has a premier location, luxurious interiors and superb service. The rooms contain the latest amenities: fax, hands-free telephone, TV in the bathroom, free WiFi, free "Water Bar," and bedside electronic control of all the electrical systems. The furnishings are luxurious and made even more so by the moodlighting. The Pen-Top Bar & Terrace is ideal for summertime trysts and Fives is an inviting bar/restaurant overlooking Fifth Avenue. Large outstanding fitness center, too, with an indoor pool, sundeck and spa.

🏨 $775–£1,125, suites from $1,275
ℹ 185 rooms, 54 suites
Ⓜ 59 Street/Fifth Avenue (E, V)
🚌 M1, M2, M3, M4, M57

PIERRE

Map 295 E16
Fifth Avenue at 61st Street, 10021
Tel 212/838-8000
www.tajhotels.com

Overlooking Central Park, this 41-story hotel, built in 1930, is the quintessence of luxury, service and refinement. Named after the son of Jacques Pierre, owner of the Hotel Anglais in Monte Carlo, it is currently under Four Seasons management and offers the same premier service. Both the rooms and the public areas are traditionally decorated with antiques. Trompe-l'oeil work decorates the Rotunda, where breakfast, afternoon tea and cocktails are served, and the marble, etched glass, silk and satin of the Café Pierre are extravagant. Even the fitness center is elegant.

🏨 $420–$645, suite from $750
ℹ 200 rooms, 51 suites
Ⓜ 59th Street/Fifth Avenue (N, R, W)
🚌 M1, M2, M3, M4

PLAZA ATHÉNÉE

Map 295 E16
37 East 64th Street at Madison Avenue, 10065
Tel l212/734-9100
www.plaza-athenee.com

The hotel is a luxurious touch of European sophistication on a quiet, tree-lined street just one block from Central Park. All rooms are furnished with antique-style European furniture with Belgian linens and writing desks. All rooms also include CD players, high-speed internet access, in-room movies, and two-line speaker phones, while some of the suites have their own dining rooms with indoor atriums and outdoor balconies.

🏨 Rooms $695-$1,150, suites from $1620
ℹ 114 rooms and 35 suites
Ⓜ Lexington Avenue (F)
🚌 MI, M2, M3, M4

RITZ CARLTON

Map 295 E16
50 Central Park South, 10019
Tel 212/308-9100
www.ritzcarlton.com

On the corner of Sixth Avenue and Central Park, this sparkling 33-story hotel has magnificent views. The lobby sets an opulent tone with its limestone walls, inlaid onyx floor and Samuel Halpert paintings. The rooms are luxuriously decorated in soft shades with brocade drapes and other plush fabrics. Room amenities include flat-screen TVs, DVDs and multi-line cordless phones. Park-view rooms have telescopes for birdwatching. Bathrooms have deep tubs with neck pillows, Frederic Fekkai toiletries and Frette candles. Pratesi linens and Bang and Olufsen stereos grace the suites. The Ritz Carlton is famous for its exceptional service, which here even extends to complimentary Burberry trench coats. The modern Restaurant Atelier offers innovative French cuisine. The Star Lounge specializes in elegant afternoon tea and classic cocktails. The full service La Prairie spa (▷ 228) is the first to open in the US. Fitness center, too. Note that Ritz Carlton also has another hotel overlooking the Statue of Liberty at Battery Park (tel 212/344-0800).

🏨 $525–$995, suite from $1,495
ℹ 259 rooms, 47 suites
Ⓜ 59th Street/Fifth Avenue (N, R, W), 57th Street (F)
🚌 M5, M6, M7

STAYING

ST. REGIS
Map 295 E17
2 East 55th Street at Fifth Avenue, 10022
Tel 212/753-4500
www.stregis.com

Colonel John Jacob Astor IV conceived this beautiful 1904 Beaux Arts style hotel. The hallmarks of luxury, marble, gold leaf, tapestries and Louis XVI furniture are joined by the latest in technical wizardry. The service—each floor has 24-hour butler service—is also extraordinary. Suites have CD player/stereo, flat-screen TV, MP3 player, and high-speed internet. The King Cole Bar is famous for the 1932 murals painted by Maxfield Parrish and for the creation of the first Bloody Mary in 1934 (originally called the "Red Snapper"). Tea in the Astor Court is one of the city's best. Remède spa and a fitness center.

🛏 $660–$750, suite from $1,200
🛈 182 rooms, 74 suites
🚇 Fifth Avenue/53rd Street (E, V)
🚌 M1, M2, M3, M4

THE POD HOTEL
Map 296 F17
230 East 51st Street, between Second and Third avenues, 10022
Tel 212/355-0300
www.thepodhotel.com
If space is not a factor, then the new Pod Hotel (previously the Pickwick Arms) is New York's version of the increasing world trend for providing simple but small rooms for travelers on a budget or in a hurry. Designed like ships' cabins to maximize storage space, they still manage to provide bathrooms, safes, TVs, free Wi-Fi and iPod docking stations. Some single rooms have shared bathrooms.

🛏 $149 twin bunk room, $249 double

🛈 348
🚇 51st Street (6)
🚌 M15, M50, M98, M101, M102, M103

ROYALTON
Map 296 E18
44 West 44th Street between Fifth and Sixth avenues, 10036
Tel 212/869-4400
www.royaltonhotel.com
The first hotel conceived by Ian Schrager, the late Steve Rubell and Philippe Starck became an instant sensation and a magnet for the city's movers and shakers. Some even dubbed their Brasserie 44 the Condé Nast cafeteria. The rooms are sleekly decorated

in contemporary minimalist style using trendy materials like slate, steel and glass. Bathrooms have oval tubs, and rooms come equipped with plasma TVs, CD and DVD players, and WiFi. Bar 44 is a pleasant place for a drink. The fitness center is open 24 hours.

🛏 Doubles from $289, suites from $499
🛈 165 rooms, 3 suites
🚇 42nd Street (B, D, F, V)
🚌 M1, M2, M3, M4

70 PARK AVENUE
Map 296 E19
70 Park Avenue at 38th Street
Tel 212/973-2400
www.70parkave.com
In the quiet Murray Hill neighborhood, Kimpton's first property in New York City has been designed in contemporary style, but with comfort in mind, even though the rooms are on the small side. Guests can select their own pillows and blankets. Deep soaking tubs invite repose in the bathrooms. Yoga mats and a 24-hour yoga channel are also available. Tech equipment runs to 42-inch flat panel TVs, DVD/CD players and KioPhones that can be used

SOHO GRAND
Map 297 E23
310 West Broadway between Canal and Grand streets, 10013
Tel 212/965-3000
www.sohogrand.com
Since the CEO of Hartz pet food owns this stylish downtown hotel, it puts out a welcome mat for animals. It was a pioneer, too, when it opened in art-oriented SoHo. A cast-iron staircase studded with coke-bottle glass leads up to the vibrant lobby. Cool tones create the ambience in the rooms, but there are plenty of guest comforts—bathrobes, Frette linens and velvet drapes, plus DVD and WiFi. Restaurant, two bars and fitness center.

🛏 $339–$599, suite $3,500
🛈 363 rooms and suites
🚇 Canal Street (A, C, E)
🚌 M5

for e-mail and web surfing. Pets are welcome. The Silverleaf Tavern offers contemporary American fare.

🛏 Doubles from $325, suites from £1,000
🛈 205 rooms and suites
🚇 Grand Central/42nd Street (4, 5, 6, 7)
🚌 M1, M2, M3, M4, M42

SHERRY-NETHERLAND
Map 295 E16
781 Fifth Avenue between 59th and 60th streets, 10022
Tel 212/355-2800
www.sherrynetherland.com
This hotel is unique because it's a building cooperative, which means that the owners individually decorate their units, and that the number of guest rooms fluctuates between 100 and 150. It's also one of the best situated and most opulent cooperatives. The building dates from 1927 and much of its luxury detailing was taken from a nearby Vanderbilt mansion that was being torn down. It has plenty of genuine European style so it's not surprising that Harry Cipriani chose to open a restaurant here. There is a bar and fitness center for guests.

🛏 $425–$600, suite from $650
🛈 150 rooms and suites
🚇 59th Street/Fifth Avenue (N, R, W)
🚌 M1, M2, M3, M4

STAYING

SHOREHAM

Map 295 E17

33 West 55th Street between Fifth and Sixth avenues, 10019

Tel 212/247-6700

www.shorehamhotel.com

This mid-size Midtown hotel, right behind the Museum of Modern Art, has been imaginatively updated and now boasts the latest looks and the most up-to-date technology and amenities in the rooms. Mesh headboards shimmer above the beds. The decor includes plenty of aluminum, plus entertainment musts such as plasma TVs and DVDs. Choice rooms are in the back. Restaurant and bar available.

Doubles from $359, suites from $569, including Continental breakfast

143 rooms, 31 suites

53rd Street/Fifth Avenue (E, V)

M1, M2, M3, M4, M5, M6, M7

SURREY

Map 295 E15

20 East 76th Street at Madison Avenue, 10021

Tel 212/288-3700

www.affinia.com

The Surrey's large suites with kitchenettes and dining area are attractively decorated and well equipped, with dual-line phones, WiFi, irons and bathrobes. Another reason to stay here? Eminent chef Daniel Boulud's Café Boulud is on the premises. Facilities include a fitness center.

$324–$963

132 suites

77th St (6)

M1, M2, M3, M4, M79

THIRTY THIRTY

Map 296 E19

30 East 30th Street between Madison and Park avenues, 10016

Tel 212/689-1900

www.thirtythirty-nyc.com

On the edge of the burgeoning Flatiron District in a refurbished 1902 building, this hotel is decent value. The rooms sport the latest minimal look, but they are small and exhibit some European-style solutions—TVs suspended on the walls and very limited furnishings. Still, they do have such conveniences as telephone with data port and hairdryer. Superior rooms have 27-inch TVs. Bathrooms

are tiled and have glass shower doors.

$200–$299

235 rooms and suites

33rd Street (6)

M1, M101, M103

TRAVEL INN

Map 296 C18

515 West 42nd Street between Tenth and Eleventh avenues, 10036

Tel 212/695-7171

www.newyorkhotel.com

The great benefits of this Manhattan hotel are the outdoor pool and the free parking. The rooms are simple but comfortable, with data port and voicemail.

$105–$250

160

42nd Street (A, C, E)

M42, M11

TRIBECA GRAND

Map 297 E24

2 Avenue of the Americas at White Street, 10013

Tel 212/519-6600

www.tribecagrand.com

With its luxurious 98-seat private screening room, this hotel, close to SoHo and the Village, caters to the independent film crowd. The lobby opens to a dramatic atrium lounge/restaurant. The rooms are modern and come with such gadgets as wireless keyboards, a bathroom TV with waterproof remote, Bose radio and fax/printer. Bliss and Kiehl products in the bathroom and the Dean & DeLuca snacks are alluring extras. The business center is exceptionally well equipped, and the workstations have flat-panel screens. Hartz owns the place, so pets are welcome. Fitness center.

Doubles from $339, suite from $699

203 rooms

Franklin Street (1)

M6

TRUMP INTERNATIONAL HOTEL AND TOWER

Map 294 D16

1 Central Park West at Columbus Circle, 10023

Tel 212/299-1000

www.trumpintl.com

You have to admire Donald Trump for taking one of the worst buildings in the country, recognizing its strengths, and transforming it into such a stylish hotel. The location is

superb, with breathtaking views of Central Park and easy access to the Lincoln Center and Midtown. The rooms, located between the third and 17th floors, are stylish, and each has plasma TV, VCR, CD AND DVD; suites have whirlpool tubs and even telescopes. The restaurant Jean-Georges is another draw. Excellent fitness center with lap pool and spa.

Doubles from $595, suites from $845

38 rooms, 129 suites

59th Street/Columbus Circle (A, B, C, D, 1, 9)

M10, M20

UNION SQUARE INN

Map 297 F21

209 East 14th Street between Second and Third avenues

Tel 212/614-0500

www.unionsquareinn.com

Even though most rooms are small with wall pegs for closets and only showers in the tiled bathrooms, this place is attractive and modern and offers decent value. No elevator. Coffeeshop.

$119–$159, including breakfast

41

14th Street/Union Square (L, N, Q, R, W, 4, 5, 6)

M14, M15, M101, M102, M103

WALDORF-ASTORIA HOTEL AND TOWERS

Map 295 F17

301 Park Avenue between 49th and 50th streets, 10022

Tel 212/355-3000

www.waldorfastoria.com or

The Waldorf opened in 1931 to rave reviews. The largest hotel in the world at the time, it remains monumental—some would say overwhelming. The Towers, which occupy the 28th to 42nd floors, have a separate entrance and the most luxurious rooms. The clubby Bull and Bear is popular for steaks, while Peacock Alley is famous for its afternoon tea. Oscar's is a very chic coffeeshop and

Inagiku is authentically Japanese. Large fitness center; excellent business center.

🛏 Waldorf $239–$629, suite from $349; Waldorf Towers $399–$799, suite from $599

🛏 1,049 rooms, 197 suites (Waldorf), 79 rooms, 101 suites (Towers)

🚇 51st Street (6)

🚌 M1, M2, M3, M4, M50

WALES

Map 295 E13
1295 Madison Avenue between 92nd and 93rd streets, 10128
Tel 212/876-6000
www.waleshotel.com

The Hotel Wales is a study in old-fashioned luxury in a nine-story building on the quiet Upper East Side near Museum Mile and Central Park. The rooms are traditional with plush chairs and half-poster beds, with VCRs and CD player. Sarabeth's Kitchen, with yummy breakfast pastries and teas, and Joanna's Italian Restaurant are bonuses. Small fitness studio.

🛏 Doubles from $286, suite from $386, including breakfast

🛏 46 rooms, 42 suites

🚇 96th Street (6)

🚌 M1, M2, M3, M4, M96

WARWICK

Map 295 E17
65 West 54th Street at Sixth Avenue, 10019
Tel 212/247-2700
www.warwickhotelny.com

William Randolph Hearst built this impressive hotel in 1927

as his East Coast hideaway and guest facility. Many a movie celebrity settled into residence here, including Cary Grant. The large rooms have such rare amenities as walk-in closets and extra-large marble bathrooms, plus modern ones such as high-speed internet and two dual-line phones. They are furnished in English style with Asian accents. Facilities include a restaurant, bar and fitness center.

🛏 $220–$425, suite from $385

🛏 359 rooms, 67 suites

🚇 57th Street (F)

🚌 M5, M6, M7, M57

WASHINGTON SQUARE

Map 297 E22
103 Waverly Place between Fifth and Sixth avenues, 10011
Tel 212/777-9515
www.washingtonsquarehotel.com

On the northwest corner of Washington Square Park, this small hotel has a casual bohemian air. The rooms are small, basic and unimaginative, but the price is right. They do have cable TV and telephone with data port. Facilities include an attractive restaurant-lounge (with occasional jazz) and exercise room.

🛏 $150–$210, including breakfast

🛏 160

🚇 West 4th Street (A, C, E, F, S, V)

🚌 M5, M6, M8

WOLCOTT

Map 296 E19
4 West 31st Street between Fifth Avenue and Broadway, 10001
Tel 212/268-2900
www.wolcott.com

Close to the Empire State Building, this hotel has comfortable rooms decorated in an old-fashioned style (candy-stripe wallpaper, patterned bed cover, wing chair). The amenities you can expect in the rooms include cable TV, telephone with data port,

hairdryer and air conditioning. There is a fitness room.

🛏 Doubles from $200, suite add $20

🛏 144 rooms, 23 suites

🚇 28th Street (N, R, W), 34th Street/Herald Square (B, D, F, N, Q, R, V, W)

🚌 M2, M3, M5, M6, M7

W-NEW YORK

Map 295 F17
541 Lexington Avenue between East 49th and 50th streets, 10022
Tel 212/755-1200
www.whotels.com

W is the hip Starwood Hotels chain. Here, as elsewhere in the group, the lobby is a living room space, where you can relax on ottomans or play board games. Natural elements are always evident, too: pots of grass, waterfalls, polished chunks of tree trunk as coffee tables and bouquets of grasses and seedpods, for example. Rooms are modern and equipped with Web TV, two-line phones, VCRs and CD players. Good food and beverage outlets polish the image—Rande Gerber's Whiskey Blue and Drew Nieporent's Heartbeat Restaurant. The spa and fitness center is a standout.

🛏 $239–$550, suites from $1,000

🛏 647 rooms, 67 suites

🚇 51st Street (6)

🚌 M50, M101, M102, M103

WYNDHAM

Map 295 E16
42 West 58th Street between Fifth and Sixth avenues, 10019
Tel 212/753-3500

This place is a great value. It's a quirky hotel relying on its good word-of-mouth and a great Midtown location, a block from Central Park and a short walk from both the Lincoln Center and the Theater District. The decor is old-fashioned, as is the service and the attitude. Suites come with pantries, refrigerators and walk-in closets. All rooms have cable TV and telephone.

🛏 $179–$399, suite from $250

🛏 140

🚇 57th Street (F), 59th Street/Fifth Avenue (N, R, W)

🚌 M1, M2, M3, M4, M5, M6, M7

STAYING

MAJOR HOTEL CHAINS

Company	Description	Number of Hotels in Manhattan	Contact Number and Website
Best Western	Decent quality, budget accommodation	4	602/957-4200; www.bestwestern.com
Clarion Hotels	A Choice Hotels International brand. It's moderately priced and offers full amenities	2	301/592-5000 www.clarionhotel.com
Comfort Inn	Strictly budget. Rooms-only; no extras (restaurants, for example). Owned by Choice Hotels International	4	301/592-5000; 800/228-5150 www.comfortinn.com
Courtyard Marriott	A moderately priced Marriott brand that appeals to business travelers	3	301/380-3000 www.courtyard.com
Crowne Plaza	The second-tier full-service brand of Intercontinental	2	770/604-2000; 0870/400-9670 www.crowneplaza.com
Days Inns/Hotels	Decent-quality budget accommodations	1	800/329-7466 www.daysinn.com
Doubletree Suites	Hilton's all-suite hotel	2	310/278-4321; www.doubletree.com
Embassy Suites	Another Hilton all-suite hotel; trademark is complimentary breakfast and evening hors d'oeuvres	1	800/362-2779 www.embassysuites.com
Four Points	Starwood's budget brand	1	800/640-8100; www.fourpoints.com
Hampton Inn	Hilton's moderately priced brand	4	800/426-7866; www.hamptoninn.com
Hilton	International full-service hotel chain	4	800/445-8667; www.hilton.com
Holiday Inn/ Holiday Inn Express	Consistent good-value accommodations. Express is the budget line. Owned by Intercontinental	4	770/604-2000 www.holiday-inn.com
Howard Johnson	Moderately priced accommodations	3	800/446-4656; www.hojo.com
Hyatt	International full-service hotel chain	2	312/750-1234; 888/591-1234; www.hyatt.com
La Quinta	Budget chain	1	866/725-1661; 800/642-4241 www.lq.com
Marriott Hotels	The premier brand of this international chain	3	301/380-3000; 888/236-2427 www.marriott.com
Quality Inn Hotels	Decent-quality hotels for business and leisure travelers. Owned by Choice Hotels	2	301/592-5000; 800/4choice www.qualityinn.com
Radisson	Full-service international chain	1	888/201-1718; www.radisson.com
Ramada Inns	Full-service moderately priced hotel chain. Ramada Limited brand lacks in-house dining	2	800/272-6232 www.ramada.com
Red Roof Inns	Modern, high-quality budget accommodations	1	800/567-7720 www.redroof.com
Renaissance	Marriott's moderately priced full-service brand	1	301/380-3000; 888/236-2427 www.renaissancehotels.com
Sheraton	Owned by Starwood, Sheraton offers good-quality modern full-amenity hotels	3	914/640-8100; 800/325-35353 www.sheraton.com
W Hotels	The hip brand owned by Starwood Hotels	5	914/640 8100; www.whotels.com
Westin	This Starwood's brand appeals to business travelers	2	914/640-8100; 800/937-8461 www.starwood.com

STAYING

Planning

BEFORE YOU GO

GEOGRAPHY

New York City is in the northeast United States. Four of the five boroughs that comprise New York City are islands. Manhattan, the most populous, is bordered on the east by the East River and on the west by the Hudson River. The narrow Harlem River separates it from the Bronx to the north, and Long Island Sound separates it from Long Island to the south. The city has a waterfront of 578 miles (930km). The Bronx is the only borough on the mainland and it is bounded by water to the south, east and west. The surrounding landscape is flat, although the highest point, at Todt Hill on Staten Island, is the highest point on the Atlantic coast south of Maine at 409ft (124m).

During the Ice Age, most of New York State was covered by glaciers, with southern Long Island and Staten Island being the exceptions. The movement of the glaciers produced nine distinct physiographic regions.

The four seasons are very distinct in this region, and New Yorkers endure, without too many complaints, the cold, damp winters and hot, humid summers.

DAYLIGHT HOURS

Be aware of the number of daylight hours you have when planning your days out in and around the city. There are some areas, away from central tourist areas, that are best avoided after dark.

TEMPERATURE

![Average temperature per day per night chart]

Average temperature per day per night

°F 90 / 60 / 32 / 0 — °C 32 / 15 / 0 / -18

J F M A M J J A S O N D

Average no. of days above 65°F below 32°F

30 / 20 / 10 / 0

J F M A M J J A S O N D

RAINFALL

Average rainfall

in 5 / 4 / 3 / 2 / 1 / 0 — mm 127 / 102 / 76 / 51 / 25 / 0

J F M A M J J A S O N D

AVERAGE SUNRISE/SUNSET TIMES		
	SUNRISE	SUNSET
Jan	7.15	4.45
Feb	6.50	5.30
Mar	6.10	6.00
Apr	5.15	6.30
May	4.30	7.00
Jun	4.30	7.30
Jul	4.35	7.30
Aug	5.00	7.00
Sep	5.30	6.00
Oct	5.30	5.20
Nov	6.35	4.45
Dec	7.15	4.30

Carl Schurz Park (above); cooling off at a fire hydrant (left)

TEMPERATURE

Below left are the average daily maximum and minimum temperatures for New York City. Precipitation in December, January, February and March can fall in the form of snow.

WINTER

The city's average annual snowfall is 29.2 inches (74cm), most of it falling in January and February. However, even after heavy snowfall, plows quickly remove the snow and disruptions are minimal. The strong winds, more pronounced as you approach the East or Hudson rivers, makes it feel colder than it really is.

SUMMER

In July and August, the hottest months, humidity can be as high as 90 percent, the sun can be fierce, and everyone feels lethargic and sticky. Avoid these months if you suffer from the heat. If you do decide to visit then, make sure to wear sunscreen during the day both in the city and at the beaches.

THE BEST TIME TO VISIT

The most pleasant time to visit, and therefore the most expensive, as it is peak season, is May to early June and September to mid-November.

From May to early June, the days are delightfully comfortable and the evenings cool; showers are always a possibility. From September to late October, days are still warm but evenings start getting cooler. The leaves change to gold and red in mid- to late October, which is very pretty but

PLANNING

not as spectacular as in New England, farther north. By November, days are much cooler and there is more rain and wind.

TIME ZONES

New York is on Eastern Standard Time, five hours behind GMT. Daylight Saving Time, four hours behind GMT, is from early April to late October. An easy way to remember this is: In April, the clocks "spring" ahead one hour, and in October they "fall" behind one hour.

TIME ZONES

CITY	TIME DIFFERENCE	TIME AT NOON IN NEW YORK
Amsterdam	+6	6pm
Berlin	+6	6pm
Brussels	+6	6pm
Chicago	-1	11am
Dublin	+5	5pm
Johannesburg	+7	7pm
London	+5	5pm
Madrid	+6	6pm
Montreal	0	noon
Paris	+6	6pm
Perth, Australia	+13	1am
Rome	+6	6pm
San Francisco	-3	9am
Sydney, Australia	+15	3am
Tokyo	+14	2am

DOCUMENTATION FOR NON-US VISITORS

SECURITY

Since 9/11, security in the US has been stepped up. Restrictions are tight on what baggage you can check in and what you can carry on board, both for domestic and international flights (see www.tsa.gov for the latest information). Expect your belongings to be searched at airports, at museums and at the entryways of many office buildings. Prohibited items may be confiscated. If you are carrying bottled water, you may be asked to take a sip of it, or, more likely, dispose of it altogether. Co-operation will facilitate easy access. For the most up-to-date information on security in and around the city visit the city's official tourism office at www.nycvisit.com.

VISA AND PASSPORT REQUIREMENTS

Canadian citizens, like all other nationalities, must have a machine-readable passport to enter the United States. Non-resident foreign visitors must show their machine-readable passport, their visa if required, and their round-trip ticket when entering the United States. Upon entry, expect to be fingerprinted and photographed.

For up-to-date information on visa requirements and how to obtain one, it is vital that you contact the American embassy in your home country months before your journey. Passport and visa requirements can change at short notice so always check before you travel.

CUSTOMS ALLOWANCES

Visitors arriving in New York from outside the country are required to fill in a Customs Declaration before landing in the United States, and they must declare everything except personal effects, which include either 200 cigarettes or 50 cigars or 2.2lbs (1kg) of smoking tobacco, providing you are 21 or older. You may also bring in 1 liter (33.8fl oz) of alcohol.

Visitors are not allowed to bring in any fruits, vegetables, plants, meat or meat products, firearms or ammunition.

If you have any questions, telephone the Customs Information Line on 202/354-1000 or contact your nearest United States consulate or embassy before departing, or

visit www. customs.ustreas.gov and click on "Travel." If you are bringing more than $10,000 into the country, you must declare it on the customs form given to passengers during your inbound flight. You may bring in only $100 worth of gifts duty free, however.

WHAT YOU CAN TAKE HOME

If you buy expensive items, you can often avoid paying New York City's 8.375 percent sales tax by having the items shipped back to your home. Ask when making the purchase, but before paying. Because rules vary for each country, contact the customs service in your country by telephone or check its website.

PLANNING

US EMBASSIES AND CONSULATES ABROAD

COUNTRY	ADDRESS	WEBSITE
Australia	Moonah Place, Yarralumla ACT 2600, tel 61 2 6214 5600	http://canberra.usembassy.gov
Canada	490 Sussex Drive, Ottawa, ON K1N 1G8, tel 1 800 283-4356 or 613 238-5335	http://ottawa.usembassy.gov
France	2 avenue Gabriel, 75382 Paris, tel 33 1 43 12 22 22	http://france.usembassy.gov
Germany	Neustädtische Kirchstr. 4-5, 10117 Berlin, Federal Republic of Germany tel 030 2385 174	http://berlin.usembassy.gov
Ireland	42 Elgin Road, Ballsbridge, Dublin 4, tel 353 1 668 8777	http://dublin.usembassy.gov
Italy	via Vittorio Veneto 119/A, 00187 Roma, tel 39 06 46741	http://italy.usembassy.gov
New Zealand	29 Fitzherbert Terrace, Thorndon, Wellington, tel 644 462 6000	http://wellington.usembassy.gov
Spain	Calle Serrano 75, 28006 Madrid, tel 91 587 2200	http://madrid.usembassy.gov
South Africa	PO Box 9536, Pretoria 0001, 877 Pretorius St, Pretoria, tel 27 12 43 4000	http://pretoria.usembassy.gov
UK	24 Grosvenor Square, London, W1A 1AE, tel 020 7499-9000	http://london.usembassy.gov

TRAVEL INSURANCE

The US does not have reciprocal healthcare arrangements with other countries. Ensure you purchase full travel insurance in your country before departing. Check that it covers cancellations, lost luggage and medical expenses up to at least $1 million, including dental care. Medical costs in the US are high, so make sure you have good medical coverage. The cost of insurance depends on your age, health, type and length of your trip. One-year coverage is very economical if you are planning more than one trip per year. Family coverage is also good value if you are traveling with a spouse and children.

PRACTICALITIES

CLOTHING

Casual clothing is acceptable in restaurants, museums and attractions throughout New York City. In summer, men must wear a shirt to enter most restaurants, although only a handful of the city's restaurants require men to wear a jacket and tie. Of course, there is no shortage of stores where you can buy any clothing that you may have forgotten to bring with you. In public places, you will be expected to wear shoes (no bare feet), and men are expected to remove their hats in churches.

Comfortable walking shoes are a must. In winter, you will need a hat or earmuffs, scarf, gloves or mittens, boots, a sweater and a warm coat or jacket. If you want to go ice skating or sledding in Central Park, you can either bring your own gear or rent skates once you're there.

In spring, bring a sweater and a spring coat or jacket. In summer, prepare for hot, humid weather, and be sure to bring a sun hat or cap and sunglasses. In the fall, pack a sweater and a light jacket or coat as well as lighter clothes in case of warm weather. Rainwear and an umbrella, however, are a must all year round.

SHOPPING

Don't overpack. Shopping in New York is fun, and you can readily find anything you may need—umbrella vendors seem to materialize on almost every significant street corner when it rains (you can pick an umbrella up for just $5), and you can readily acquire sunglasses on the street on fine days.

Clothes, accessories, electronic equipment and many other items come in wider selections than in most of the rest of the United States and are cheaper than in many European countries.

For every shopper, bargain-hunting can be rewarding. Be aware, however, that the "Going out of business" sales advertised on posters at electronic equipment stores in the Theater District are bogus—these "sales" are a come-on to attract naïve customers. Before buying, get the model number of the product you want and check other retailers' prices online or you will almost certainly pay too much; if you're spending a significant sum of money, it's better to patronize a reputable specialist retailer. In vintage and second-hand shops it is always worthwhile to ask for a better price—sometimes you will get it.

Keep in mind that many stores close on public holidays; SoHo is fairly closed on Mondays and the Lower East Side is shuttered on Saturdays and very slow on Friday afternoons.

MEASUREMENTS

If you are more used to metric measurements than imperial, the conversion table below will be very useful.

CONVERSION CHART		
FROM BY	TO	MULTIPLY
Inches	Centimeters	2.54
Centimeters	Inches	0.3937
Feet	Meters	0.3048
Meters	Feet	3.2810
Yards	Meters	0.9144
Meters	Yards	1.0940
Miles	Kilometers	1.6090
Kilometers	Miles	0.6214
Acres	Hectares	0.4047
Hectares	Acres	2.4710
Gallons	Liters	4.5460
Liters	Gallons	0.2200
Ounces	Grams	28.35
Grams	Ounces	0.0353
Pounds	Grams	453.6
Grams	Pounds	0.0022
Pounds	Kilograms	0.4536
Kilograms	Pounds	2.205
Tons	Tonnes	1.0160
Tonnes	Tons	0.9842

The chart below indicates how UK and European clothing and shoe sizes compare with those in the US

UK	Europe	US	
36	46	36	
38	48	38	
40	50	40	SUITS
42	52	42	
44	54	44	
46	56	46	
48	58	48	
7	41	8	
7.5	42	8.5	
8.5	43	9.5	SHOES
9.5	44	10.5	
10.5	45	11.5	
11	46	12	
14.5	37	14.5	
15	38	15	
15.5	39/40	15.5	SHIRTS
16	41	16	
16.5	42	16.5	
17	43	17	
8	36	6	
10	38	8	
12	40	10	
14	42	12	DRESSES
16	44	14	
18	46	16	
20	46	18	
4.5	37.5	6	
5	38	6.5	
5.5	38.5	7	SHOES
6	39	7.5	
6.5	40	8	
7	41	8.5	

VOLTAGE AND ADAPTERS

The power supply in the US is 110/120 volts AC (60 cycles). American plugs have two-prong flat pins, so you will need an adapter if you have plugs with two round pins, or three pins.

It is best to buy an adapter before departing or in the airport shop as they can be difficult to find in the US, although some department stores and pharmacies stock them. You will also need a voltage transformer for European appliances.

COMFORT AND ETIQUETTE
Public restrooms

Restrooms are normally labeled "Women" and "Men" or use a male/female symbol. You may notice that they are labeled in Spanish as well as English in airports, some restaurants and clubs. Public restrooms are found in visitor centers (▷ 324) and in Grand Central Terminal (▷ 102–104), but New Yorkers stop in hotels, large bookstores, department stores or cafés— theoretically restrooms in eating places are for patrons only, but in some restaurants it's an option. Restrooms in public buildings are wheelchair-accessible and may offer facilities for baby-changing. Restrooms in most parts of the city are clean and well supplied with soap, hand-dryers and paper. A few in Chinatown are substandard.

Traveling with children

New York is family-friendly for the most part, with special discounts for children, special prices for meals and plenty of attractions to keep them happy. Many hotels let kids stay for free and most museums do not charge for young children. Look for special things to do in the "Weekend" section of the Friday New York Times, New York magazine's "Cue" section and in Time Out New York. Special performances can sell out or fill up early, so expect to plan ahead. For baby-sitting services there's the Baby Sitters' Guild (tel 212/682-0227 or www.babysittersguild.com).

Laundry services

Most hotels either offer laundry services or will recommend one. Before you make your reservation, check what the hotel offers.

Smoking

When smoking in New York was banned in all public places, including restaurants, clubs, bars and anywhere an employee may be exposed to a patron's smoke, it was very controversial. Today it is widely accepted. People who want to smoke must go outside. There is no smoking on buses, subways or trains, but you may smoke in the privacy of your hotel room—providing it is a designated smoking room.

Dealing with beggars

It is your choice whether to give money to beggars. If you would prefer not to, simply keep on moving if a beggar approaches you on the street and asks for money. Don't make eye contact and don't engage in conversation. On the subway, you may come across beggars who deliver a monologue about their hard times and about how your donation will help their family. Again, if you prefer not to give, don't make eye contact, and shake your head "no" if you are approached personally.

On subways

If all seats are taken, move to the center of the subway car so you don't block the doors. If a senior citizen, an adult with a young child, a pregnant woman or person with a disability gets on and there are no available seats, offer yours. It's the civilized thing to do, and your fellow passengers —at least the civilized ones—will admire you for it.

GAY AND LESBIAN NEW YORK

The Stonewall Riot on Christopher Street in Greenwich Village is credited with starting the gay liberation movement in New York City in 1969. Today, gay and lesbian visitors will find New York an easy place to visit. The West Village, especially Christopher Street, is full of shops, restaurants and services with a gay orientation, as is Chelsea, on Eighth Avenue from 16th to 23rd streets.

Finding help

● The International Gay & Lesbian Travel Association (tel 800/448-8550 or 954/776-2626, www.iglta.org) is a specialist travel agency.
● Lesbian, Gay, Bisexual & Transgender Community Center (208 West 13th Street, between Seventh and Eighth avenues, tel 212/620-7310, www.gaycenter.org) is an excellent source of information on what's happening in the city and where to stay.
● Gay and Lesbian Switchboard (www.glnh.org) offers peer counseling and information on events.

What's happening

For current gay and lesbian nightlife, pick up a copy of Metro, Go, HX, New York Blade, Next and Village Voice, all of them free publications. Time Out New York, available at all street news-stands and many other retail outlets, has an excellent section on what's on for gay and lesbian visitors.

St. Patrick's Cathedral, with its two spires, is dwarfed by Midtown skyscrapers

PLACES OF WORSHIP

With its rich cultural mix, this city of immigrants offers a place to worship for every kind of belief. Listings in newspapers note the topic of the current week's theme. For the most extensive list of churches, temples, synagogues and mosques, look in the *Yellow Pages*.

PLACES OF WORSHIP	
Baptist	Abyssinian Baptist Church (132 Odell Clark Place at West 138th Street between Adam Clayton Powell Boulevard and Lenox Avenue, tel 212/862-7474).
Buddhist	New York Buddhist Church (Riverside Drive between 105th and 106th streets, tel 212/678-0305; www.newyorkbuddhistchurch.org).
Greek Orthodox	Holy Trinity Greek Orthodox Cathedral (319 East 74th Street tel 212/288-3215; www.thecathedral.goarch.org).
Interfaith	Cathedral of St. John the Divine (1047 Amsterdam Avenue at 112th Street, tel 212/316-7490; www.stjohndivine.org).
Jewish	Temple Emanu-El (1 East 65th Street at Fifth Avenue, tel 212/744-1400; www.emanuelnyc.org) is reform.
Muslim	Mosque of Islamic Brotherhood (130 West 113th Street, tel 212/662-4100; www.mosqueofislamicbrotherhoodinc.org)
Roman Catholic	St. Patrick's Cathedral (960 Madison Avenue, tel 212/753-2261; www.saintpatrickscathedral.org).

MONEY

TAXES

In New York City an 8.375 percent sales tax is added at the cash register. You will pay this on most purchases, except on clothing and footwear. The hotel tax is 13.25 percent, plus $2 per room per night. The parking garage tax is 18.25 percent.

TIPPING

You must tip people in the service sector because their livelihood depends on tips. Employers pay them a minimum wage, in most cases, and expect tips to make up the rest of their income. If you tip less than expected, you are sending a message that the service was less than satisfactory.

- **In restaurants**, tip waiters, waitresses and bartenders at least 15 percent of the bill—to figure it out quickly just double the 8.375 percent sales tax listed on the bill. Tip 20 percent in expensive restaurants, and always round up for good service. The head waiter in upscale restaurants expects 5 percent and the cloakroom attendant expects $1 when they give you back your coat.
- **In taxis**, tip the driver 15 to 20 percent, more if the journey is short.
- **In hotels**, tip the bellboy $1 or $2 for each suitcase he carries up to your room or down to the lobby. The chambermaid expects $2 for a few nights' stay. The hall porter expects $1 or $2 for getting you a taxi.
- **At the airport or train station**, tip the porter who transports your luggage $1 or $2 per bag.

FOR NON-US VISITORS
Changing money

If you are coming from outside the United States, change money before you leave home so that you can pay taxis, trains or buses on arrival. The commission at airport bureaux de change is higher than in most banks. Dollar bills of a higher denomination than $20 may not be accepted by taxi drivers, so it is best to always have small bills available. There are bureaux de change throughout Manhattan, but you get better service in banks and at the visitor center in Times Square (▷ 324). There are ATMs all over the city. Expect to pay up to $3 per transaction if you are using a bank other than your own.

- **American Express Travel Services** has many offices in the city, including one on the mezzanine level at Macy's in Herald Square (tel 212/695-8075).
- **Travelex** has a number of offices (tel 212/679-4365 or www.travelex.com).
- **Chase Manhattan Bank** (tel 212/935-9935 or www.chase.com) has more than 400 branches with bureaux de change.

How to get money

Most people use credit cards to pay for hotels, restaurant meals and shopping. However, some restaurants and other establishments accept only cash. If you rent a car, a credit card will be essential. MasterCard, Visa and American Express are the cards most often accepted (but Amex occasionally is not accepted). Diner's Club and Carte Blanche are accepted by most restaurants and many hotels, but not all. Discover, enRoute, Eurocard and JCB are also often accepted, but not always.

Traveler's checks in US dollars, although less common than in

MONEY VOCABULARY	
$	dollar
¢	cent
a penny	1 cent
a nickel	5 cents
a dime	10 cents
a quarter	25 cents
a half dollar	50 cents
5 bucks	5 dollars

PLANNING

the past, remain a safe way to carry money. Keep a copy of the serial numbers separate from the checks and record the ones you cash, so that any lost or stolen checks can be replaced quickly. Checks from American Express (tel 800/528-4800 or www.americanexpress.com) are the most widely accepted. Most restaurants and large stores will accept traveler's checks as payment but will ask to you to produce your passport. Most banks will cash them, but charge between 1 percent and 4 percent on the value for doing so. American Automobile Association members can avoid fees by purchasing checks from an AAA office.

Stolen credit cards or traveler's checks
If your credit card is stolen, report the theft to the bank so that charges can be blocked. Also notify the police. The bank's toll-free number is usually on the back of the credit card. It's a good idea to photocopy the front and

back sides of everything in your wallet, or at least write down the numbers you need to report the card lost, and carry this information separately.

Exchange rates
For the latest market conversion rates, visit www.oanda.com or www.x-rates.com.

MONEY-SAVING TIPS
● CityPass (tel 707/256-0490, www.citypass.com) is a book of tickets to six attractions and will

10 EVERYDAY ITEMS AND HOW MUCH THEY COST	
Takeout sandwich	$6
Bottle of water	$2
Cup of tea or coffee	$1
Pint of beer	$6
Glass of wine	$10
Daily newspaper	25c–$1.25
Roll of camera film	$8
20 cigarettes	$7.75
An ice cream	$2.50
A gallon of fuel (petrol)	$2

save you hours of waiting in line at attractions, as well as 50 percent on admission to the American Museum of Natural History (▷ 68–72), Empire State Building (▷ 94–96), Guggenheim Museum (▷ 110–111), Metropolitan Museum of Art (▷ 114–119) and MoMA (▷ 125), as well as on two-hour Circle Line harbor cruises (▷ 232). The CityPass costs $65 ($49 for ages 12–17) and can be purchased at any attraction. It is good for nine days once you begin using it.

BANKNOTES AND COINS

Local currency One US dollar is worth 100 cents. Paper bills come in denominations of $1, $5, $10, $20, $50 and $100. Bills are all the same size and color, so look carefully at the numbers on them before handing them over. Each type of coin is a different size, so they are easier to differentiate (coins and bills are not shown actual size).

1 cent
penny

5 cents
nickel

10 cents
dime

25 cents
quarter

50 cents

Dollar

Coin images courtesy United States Mint.

(Money-Saving Tips continued)

● **New York Pass** (250 West 49th Street, New York 10019, tel 877/714-1999, www.newyorkpass.com) an all-inclusive passport to New York City that gets you admission to and discounts at more than 40 attractions. The New York Pass can be purchased at Madame Tussaud's (234 West 42nd Street), the Empire State Building's Skyride (350 Fifth Avenue) or online. Passes cost $65 ($45 children 2–12) for one day, or you can buy them for two ($95/75), three ($120/95) or seven ($155/120) days.

● **"Pay-what-you-wish"** is the admission scheme adopted by some attractions; a suggested admission is posted, but you decide how much you actually pay. Some museums are free one day a week or for a couple of evening hours. To save on museum admission prices, visit during the hours given in the table above.

● **The Official NYC Guide** (810 Seventh Avenue, New York 10019, tel 800/NYC-VISIT or 212/397-8222, www.nycvisit.com) is published by NYC & Company, the city's official tourism marketing organization, and contains discount vouchers for hotels, stores, restaurants, cruises and museums. Buy the book online, or pick up a copy from one of the visitor centers.

MUSEUM ADMISSION	PAY-WHAT-YOU-WISH	FREE
American Folk Art Museum		Fri 5.30–7.30pm
Bronx Zoo	All day Wed	
Brooklyn Botanic Garden		Sat 10–noon, All day Tue
Guggenheim Museum	Fri 5.45–7.45pm	
Jewish Museum		Sat 11–5.45
MoMA		Fri 4–8pm
Museum of Arts and Design	Thu 6–8pm	
New York Botanical Garden		All day Wed, Sat 10–noon
Whitney Museum of American Art	Fri 6–9pm	

The New York Pass can bring you substantial savings on many attractions

HEALTH

New York City has some of the best hospitals and doctors in the country, so if you should be in need of care, you have come to the right place. But make sure you have full insurance (▷ 314).

INOCULATIONS
If you are arriving in the United States from Canada or from a European Union member country, you will probably not need inoculations. However, check with your travel agent or with a US consulate or embassy (▷ 314). All visitors to the United States are advised to be fully immunized against tetanus and diptheria.

WHAT TO TAKE
If you will be in New York during the summer, make sure to have sunscreen, which you can easily purchase from any pharmacy upon arrival. You should bring any medication you require with you and, if it is prescription medicine, pack it in your in-flight baggage. Take copies of your prescription to be on the safe

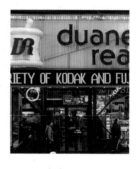

A New York pharmacy

side. If the bag in which you are carrying medication gets lost or stolen, the copy of the prescription will make it easier to get a replacement.

If you require medication containing habit-forming drugs or narcotics, such as some cough medicines, diuretics, heart drugs, tranquilizers, sleeping pills, anti-depressants, stimulants, etc., make sure they are properly labeled and that you have a prescription or written statement from your doctor confirming that you are taking these under a

doctor's direction and that you require them while traveling.

If you suffer from heart problems, epilepsy or diabetes, it is a good idea to wear a Medic Alert Identification Tag so that the doctor can easily get access to your medical records through the 24-hour hotline in case of an emergency. You can get this tag by phoning 888/633-4298 or visit www.medicalert.org.

DRINKING WATER
The tap water in New York is safe to drink, as is water from public water fountains. However, bottled water is sold throughout the city in stores, restaurants and vending machines.

BUYING MEDICATIONS
The 24-hour pharmacies listed opposite are all located in convenient places.

Travelers from abroad may require a prescription in the United States to purchase certain medications, such as birth control pills, inhalers and codeine, that they can buy over the counter in their own country.

PLANNING

HEALTHY FLYING

● Visitors from Europe, Australia or New Zealand may be concerned about the effect of a long-haul flight on their health. The most widely publicized concern is deep vein thrombosis (DVT). Misleadingly labeled "economy class syndrome," DVT is when a blood clot forms in the body's deep veins, particularly in the legs. The clot can move around the bloodstream and can be fatal.

● You are most at risk if you are elderly, pregnant, using the contraceptive pill, smoke or are overweight. If you think you are at increased risk of DVT, see your doctor before departing. Flying increases the likelihood of DVT because passengers are often seated in a cramped position for long periods of time and may become dehydrated.

● Other health hazards for flyers are airborne diseases and bugs spread by the air-conditioning system on board. These hazards are largely unavoidable but if you have a serious medical condition, seek advice from a doctor before flying.

To minimize risk:
Drink water (not alcohol)
Don't stay immobile for hours at a time
Stretch and exercise your legs periodically
Do wear elastic flight socks, which support veins and reduce the chances
of a clot forming

EXERCISES

1 ANKLE ROTATIONS	2 CALF STRETCHES	3 KNEE LIFTS

Lift feet off the floor. Draw a circle with the toes, moving one foot clockwise and the other counterclockwise	Start with heel on the floor and point foot upwards as high as you can. Then lift heels high keeping balls of feet on the floor	Lift leg with knee bent while contracting your thigh muscle. Then straighten leg pressing foot flat to the floor

Pharmacies are generally open from 9am to 5pm and can be recognized by signs in the window—either a mortar and pestle or a caduceus (a staff with two entwined snakes and two wings at the top, which symbolize a physician).

FINDING A DOCTOR

If you need to find a doctor in New York, contact any one of the health services listed below. They are reputable healthcare providers accustomed to treating visitors.

DOCS at New York Healthcare (55 East 34th Street between Park and Madison avenues, tel 212/252-6001) is a walk-in medical center for non-emergency cases. New York University Downtown Hospital (tel 212/312-5000) offers referrals. N.Y. Hotel Urgent Medical Services (952 Fifth Avenue between 76th and 77th streets, tel 212/737-1212, www.travelmd.com) was set up by a New York City doctor to treat visitors. Whether you need a prescription, a medical examination or a dentist, a specialist will come to your hotel

room. He or she will produce appropriate identification. The hotel visit fee is $350 to $400, with higher rates at night and on weekends. You can also go to the office for a fee of $175–$200—either drop in or phone for an appointment. Emergency rooms (ER rooms) in

some hospitals have walk-in clinics where you can go for non-emergencies (and pay a slightly lower rate than in the emergency area), but you will probably have to wait for a long time. Or you can always ask the hotel staff to suggest a doctor.

IF YOU HAVE TO GO TO THE HOSPITAL

Before you go, phone your travel insurance company's emergency number to find out which hospitals accept your insurance. You will need to show your insurance card at the hospital

PHARMACIES OPEN 24 HOURS		
NAME	**ADDRESS**	**TELEPHONE**
Duane Reade	224 West 57th Street/Broadway	212/541-9708
Duane Reade	485 Lexington Avenue/47th Street	212/682-5338
Duane Reade	2025 Broadway/70th Street	212/579-9955
Rite Aid	408 Grand Street/Clinton	212/529-7115

PLANNING

before any treatment will be given.

INSURANCE FOR NON-US VISITORS

Although you are not required to have health insurance in order to visit the United States, it would be extremely unwise not to. The US does not have reciprocal health agreements with other countries and the cost of healthcare is very high, whether you need a doctor's visit or dental care or have a medical emergency. An emergency room visit usually carries a minimum charge of $500, and that's before you begin receiving treatment. Make sure that you have a good insurance policy that covers all healthcare, including dental care (▷ 314).

(▷ 314)

OPTICIANS

Lenscrafters has several Midtown locations. Go to 542 Fifth Avenue at 45th Street, tel 212/302-4882
www.lenscrafters.com

Cohen's Optical has numerous locations in Manhattan, including
2561 Broadway tel 212/666-2615 and 2 West 14th Street tel 212/989-3937
www.cohensfashionoptical.com

ALTERNATIVE MEDICINE

Alternative medical treatments are widely available in New York City.

American Academy of Medical Acupuncture
www.medicalacupuncture.org
Chiropractic Federation of New York
64 East 34th Street,
tel 212/532-0185
North American Society of Homeopaths
www.homeopathy.org

Chinatown offers a wide selection of herbal and alternative treatments, including acupuncture. You will find, among others:

Grand Meridian Herbs, Acupuncture and Massage
211 Grand Street, New York 10013,
tel 212/965-1503
Kamwo Herbs
209 Grand Street, New York 10013,
tel 212/966-6370
Zon Foo Acupuncture and Medical
36 East Broadway, 2nd Floor, New York 10002, tel 212/925-2501

COMMUNICATIONS

TELEPHONE CHARGES
Public pay phones

Local calls cost 25 cents for the first three minutes. Even if you are making a local call, one that has the 212 or 646 area code, you must still dial 1, then the area code, before the seven-digit number. This includes calls from Manhattan to other boroughs, (area codes 718 and 347).

All calls that are not local are so-called long-distance calls, which cost more; for these, you again have to dial 1 followed by the area code and seven-digit number.

Paying by card

Prepaid calling cards, sold at many convenience stores and news-stands in various denominations, are the easiest and probably the cheapest way to phone home.

Public pay phones throughout New York City take phonecards. Airport public telephones all accept MasterCard, Visa and American Express.

TELEPHONES AND NON-US VISITORS
Telephone numbers

Local and long-distance calls: dial 1 + area code + 7-digit number

Word telephone numbers: Some numbers are made easy to remember by using the letters on the dial rather than the numbers, for example, 1-800/WHITNEY. Find the letters on the dial to call these numbers.

Toll-free numbers

There is no charge for telephone

COUNTRY CODES FROM THE UNITED STATES

Dial 011 followed by the country code, the city code, then the telephone number

Australia	(011) 61
Belgium	(011) 32
France	(011) 33
Germany	(011) 49
Greece	(011) 30
Ireland	(011) 353
Italy	(011) 39
Netherlands	(011) 31
New Zealand	(011) 64
Spain	(011) 34
Sweden	(011) 46
United Kingdom	(011) 44

numbers with area codes 800, 888 and 877. The 911 emergency number is also free.

High-toll numbers

Telephone numbers with area codes 700 and 900 are chat lines, dating services or other specialized services that can charge anywhere between 95¢ and $15 per minute.

Cell phones and laptops

If your cell phone is not equipped to make calls from the US, you may as well leave it at home. If you plan to use a laptop while traveling, make sure that the battery is fully charged before you leave home. At airport

Public pay phones can be an economical way to keep in touch

PLANNING

Mail boxes are blue

security, you may be asked to take the laptop out of the case. Security officers may ask you if it is yours, if it is new and if anyone else has been using it. Make sure that you have an adapter for your laptop, and a converter for voltage if necessary, if it does not have a US two-prong, flat-pin plug and does not work on 110/120 volts. If you plan to use it a lot, bring an extra battery.

EMAIL
Go to www.mail2web.com and type in your email address and password to retrieve your email from any web browser. You can also open a free email account

via www.hotmail.com or www.mail.yahoo.com.
You can check your email from most hotel lobbies, at internet cafés or Kinko's copy shops (www.kinkos.com), which are found throughout the city.

Alternatively, use the free terminals at the Times Square Information Center at 1560 Broadway (▷ 324).

CYBER-CAFÉS
There are more and more of these around town (see below for two well-known cafés).

POST OFFICES
The main post office is at 441 Eighth Avenue between 31st and 33rd streets (tel 212/330-3002). Throughout the city there are numerous branches, which are listed in the *Yellow Pages*. Most branches are open Monday to Friday 8, 9 or 10am to 6pm. A few open Saturday 9am to 4pm.

POSTAGE RATES
A regular letter costs:
Within the US, minimum of 41 cents
Across the border to Canada or Mexico, minimum of 69 cents
Overseas, minimum of 90 cents

CYBER CONNECTIONS	
Kinko's	**Cybercafé**
60 West 40th Street	250 West 49th Street at Broadway/
Tel 212/921-1060	8th Avenue
www.kinkos.com	Tel 212/333-4109
Daily 24 hours	Mon–Fri 8am–11pm, Sat–Sun 1–11pm
Also at many other locations	

FINDING HELP

The crime rate in New York has plummeted over the past 10 years and it is now one of the safest large cities in the United States. However, it is big and crowded, and crimes do occur, so always be aware of your surroundings and people around you. If someone does try to steal your property, let them take it, then report the crime to the police.

PERSONAL SECURITY
● Do not keep all your money, credit cards and traveler's checks in the same place.
● Do not carry large sums of money with you. Use the

hotel safe if you have brought valuables or have large amounts of cash.
● Do not walk alone at night

in deserted areas, and do not go into parks after dark unless there is a concert and a large crowd is already there.
● If someone "falls" in front of you, be aware that this may be a ploy to distract you while an accomplice picks your pocket.
● Wear shoulder bags and cameras over one shoulder and across your front—in bandolier style. Do not let your handbag dangle from the back of your chair in restaurants; put it on your lap rather than risk making it an easy target.

OBEY THE LAWS
● Drinking laws are strictly enforced in New York. It is against the law to drive with an open container of alcohol in the car and also, of course, to drive while intoxicated.

New York City policeman

PLANNING

LOST AND FOUND TELEPHONE NUMBERS

MTA for buses or trains
212/424-4343

Taxi and Limousine
Commission for taxis
311

Police property clerk
(lost for more than 48 hours)
646/610-5100

LEGAL AGE	
To purchase tobacco	18 years
To gamble or play the lottery	18 years
To purchase/consume alcohol	21 years
To rent a car	25 years

● Smoking in all public places, such as restaurants, museums, on public transportation or in public offices, is illegal in New York. You must smoke outside—as you will see many New Yorkers doing.

IF YOU ARE ARRESTED

● Remember that New York has been on high alert at different times since 9/11 and that even when these alerts are not in effect, there is a high police presence in the streets, at public places, in airports and at other metropolitan locations. Never joke about matters of security—it's a crime.
● Visitors from abroad need to be aware that the police can arrest you if you break the law, if they have a strong suspicion that you have been involved in a crime, or if your behavior or activities make them suspect that you are involved in criminal activities.

If you are arrested, you have the right to remain silent, to make a telephone call, and you have the right to contact a lawyer. Anything you say can be used as evidence against you. Your best option is to contact your embassy or consulate (see below) and ask for their assistance.

CONSULATES FOR VISITORS FROM OVERSEAS	
Australia	212/351-6500
Canada	212/596-1628
Ireland	212/319-2555
New Zealand	212/832-4038
United Kingdom	212/745-0200

EMBASSIES FOR VISITORS FROM OVERSEAS			
COUNTRY	ADDRESS	TELEPHONE	WEBSITE
Australia	1601 Massachusetts Avenue, NW, Washington DC 20036	202/797-3000	www.austemb.org
Canada	501 Pennsylvania Avenue, NW, Washington DC 20001	202/682-1740	www.canadianembassy.org
Ireland	2234 Massachusetts Avenue, NW, Washington DC 20008	202/462-3939	www.irelandemb.org
New Zealand	37 Observatory Circle NW, Washington DC 20008	202/328-4800	www.nzembassy.com/usa
United Kingdom	3100 Massachusetts Avenue, NW, Washington DC 20008	202/588-6500	www.britainusa.com

MEDIA

At the newspaper stands on many streets throughout the city, you can buy newspapers in English, Spanish and, at some, a few other languages, as well as a wide variety of magazines.

NEWSPAPERS
● *The New York Times* is the city's most widely read daily (www.nytimes.com), published seven days a week. The Sunday edition includes a magazine and special sections for sports, travel, real estate, etc.
● The *Daily News* is a tabloid published seven days a week and offers a large quantity of Sunday supplements.
● The *New York Post* is another tabloid published daily.
● The *Wall Street Journal* is the much-respected New York-based national financial newspaper.
● The *New York Observer* is the pink-hued weekly full of media and political gossip.

Taking the time out to sit and watch the world go by—and possibly to log on to the internet

MAGAZINES
● *The New Yorker* (www.new yorker.com) is a national literary and news magazine with New York listings and reviews; published every Monday.
● *New York Magazine* (www.newyorkmetro.com), published every Monday, is a good source of information on restaurants, theaters, movies, books, art, television and bargains around town.
● *The Village Voice* (www. villagevoice.com) is published weekly every Tuesday, with extensive listings of music, clubs, arts and entertainment.
● *Time Out* (www. timeoutnewyork.com) is a very good comprehensive weekly magazine with plenty of listings on just about everything going on around town.

To buy newspapers from other countries, go to **Universal News & Magazines** (234 West 42nd Street between Seventh and

MAJOR RADIO STATIONS	
www.nyradioguide.com	
AM:	
Sports	620 (WSNR)
News and Talk	820 (WNYC feeds from NP Rand; the BBC World Service)
Multi-ethnic	930 (WPAT)
News	1130 (WBBR)
News around the clock	880 and 1010 (WINS)
FM:	
Classic and talk	93.9 (WYNC-FM)
Classical	96.3 (WQXR, the radio station of the New York Times)
Top 40	108.3 (also known as Z-100).

NATIONAL TV STATIONS
2 (CBS)
4 (NBC)
5 (Fox)
7 (ABC)
9 and 11 (independent)
13 (PBS)

Eighth avenues, tel 212/221-1809; www.universalnewsusa.com) and nine other locations around Manhattan.

Number 9 West 57th Street (right); billboard for one of New York's radio stations (below)

MAJOR TV STATIONS
On cable, NY1 is all about New York, and more than 50 stations on cable, available in most hotels, supply movies, weather updates and home shopping. If you're traveling with kids, ask whether the Disney Channel is available.

OPENING TIMES AND PUBLIC HOLIDAYS

New York never sleeps. The working week is Monday through Friday, 9am to 5pm, but some banks are open on Saturday mornings and many stores are open longer hours; most stores are open all weekend. Some pharmacies are open 24/7, as are some coffee shops and bureaux de change.

Always phone in advance if timing is critical or if you're making a detour to visit a particular place.

PUBLIC HOLIDAYS
On public holidays many museums, some restaurants and all public office buildings close. New Year's Day, Christmas and Thanksgiving are the biggest, most widely celebrated holidays, when most New York businesses grind to a halt. Airports and train stations are particularly busy in the period leading up to these holidays, when many New Yorkers travel out of town to be with family or friends. However,

it is also a time when the city is festive and celebrations are enjoyed by visitors as well as New Yorkers (for a list of parades ▷ 324). Much of the city closes down or slows during the Jewish High Holidays—Rosh Hashanah and Yom Kippur—in September and early October.

OPENING HOURS			
	OPEN	CLOSED	COMMENTS
Stores	Mon–Sat, 10–7 Sun noon–6		Many closed Sun Upper East Side, Sat Lower East Side
Banks	Mon–Fri 9.30–3.30	Sat–Sun	Some close at 3, some open Sat morning
Offices	Mon–Fri 9–5	Sat–Sun	
Museums	Tue–Sun		Some open Mon or close another day
Galleries	Tue–Sat 10–6	Mon	
Doctors	Mon–Fri 9–5	Sat–Sun	▷ 319
Pharmacies	Daily 9–7 or 9–9		Shorter hours and Sun closing in commercial neighborhoods, some 24hrs
Grocery stores	Daily 7am–9pm		As above
Restaurants	Daily (see listings)	Some close one day a week	Many serve until 11pm or midnight, a few between 4pm and 5.30pm

PUBLIC HOLIDAYS
January 1
New Year's Day
3rd Monday in January
Martin Luther King Day
3rd Monday in February
Presidents' Day
Last Monday in May
Memorial Day
July 4
Independence Day
1st Monday in September
Labor Day
2nd Monday in October
Columbus Day
November 11
Veterans' Day
4th Thursday in November
Thanksgiving Day
December 25
Christmas Day

PLANNING

TOURIST INFORMATION

EVENTS AND PARADES

Lively events worth planning a trip around take place throughout the year. If you are in New York during a parade, don't miss it. The two biggest are the St. Patrick's Day Parade and the Macy's Thanksgiving Day Parade, which is televised nationwide. The crowd scene is almost as entertaining as the parade. Check local listings for dates, times and parade routes, and plan to show up early for either of them to get a choice viewing spot.

TOURIST OFFICES

Major visitor centers, listed below, are well worth visiting on your first or second day. Many brochures offer discount vouchers, which will save you a few dollars at attractions or restaurants. In addition, most hotels offer a good selection of maps and free brochures.

Times Square Information Center

(1560 Broadway between 46th and 47th streets, tel 212/768-1560, www.timessquarenyc.org, daily 8–8)

This is New York's central tourist office and has free brochures, maps, helpful staff, a Broadway Ticket Center and a Metropolitan Transportation Authority that sells MetroCards (▷ 43), as well as providing ATMs, currency-exchange machines and free internet. It's worth visiting even if

New York's marathon goes from Staten Island to Central Park

EVENTS	PARADES
January or early February	**January**
Chinese New Year in Chinatown	Three Kings' Day
April–October	Martin Luther King Day Parade
Baseball season	**March**
May	St. Patrick's Day
Ninth Avenue International Food Festival	Greek Independence Day Parade
June	(parade of circus animals
Metropolitan Opera park concerts,	to Madison Square Garden)
Museum Mile celebration	**March or April**
July	Easter Parade, Fifth Avenue between
Independence Day fireworks over the	44th and 59th streets
East River	**June**
July–August	Puerto Rican Day Parade
Shakespeare in the Park	Lesbian and Gay Pride
August–September	**October**
Lincoln Center Out-of-Doors Festival;	Columbus Day Parade
Harlem Week	Halloween Parade in Greenwich Village
September	**November**
Feast of San Gennaro, in Little Italy	Macy's Thanksgiving Day
September–October	
New York Film Festival	
Early November	
New York Marathon	
December	
Tree lighting at Rockefeller Center,	
New Year's Eve celebrations	

you think you don't need to. Some of the free walking tours start from here.

NYC & Company Visitor Information Center

(810 Seventh Avenue between 52nd and 53rd streets, tel 212/484-1222, Mon–Fri 8.30 to 6, Sat–Sun 9–5)

Smaller than the Times Square complex, this information center has free brochures and leaflets. The interactive terminal with touch-screen access to visitor information is extremely useful. Buy advance tickets to major attractions here and your CityPass (▷ 317), and pick up a copy of the *Official New York City Guide*.

The center provides an ATM (cashpoint), plus telephones that are directly connected to American Express offices.

Lower East Side Visitors Center

(261 Broome Street between Orchard and Allen streets, tel 888/825-8374 or 212/226-9010, www.lowereastsideny.com, daily 10–4)

Provides pamphlets covering local shopping, dining and nightlife entertainment.

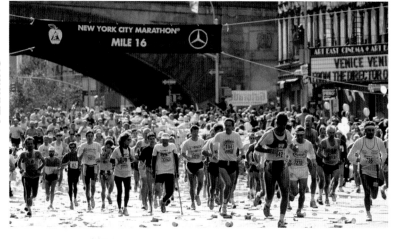

PLANNING

BOOKS, MAPS, MOVIES AND TELEVISION

BOOKS
Non-fiction
The Historical Atlas of New York City: Eric Homberger, Henry Holt and Company, New York, 1998
A fascinating book on the history of New York, always a pleasure to read. Excellent graphics, maps and photographs.

New York City (A Short History): George J. Lankevich, New York University Press, New York, 2002
A fascinating look at New York's political and social history from the first settlers to the election of Mayor Michael Bloomberg.

New York: Songs of the City: Nancy Groce, Watson-Guptill Publications, New York, 1999
A delightful musical journey through New York's five boroughs, with anecdotes and facts about people in the music industry, lyrics of old tunes about New York, and beautifully reproduced music sheet covers and posters.

Fiction
Novelists and short-story writers have always been attracted to New York, and many American classics have been set here. For short stories pick up O. Henry's *The Voice of the City* (1908) or Damon Runyon's *Guys and Dolls* (1932). Novels such as F. Scott Fitzgerald's *The Beautiful and the Damned* (1922), John Dos Passos's *Manhattan Transfer* (1925), J. D. Salinger's *The Catcher in the Rye* (1951) and Truman Capote's *Breakfast at Tiffany's* (1958) are all popular reads. More recent novels include Tom Wolfe's *Bonfire of the Vanities* (1987) and *The New York Trilogy* (1988) by Paul Auster.

MAPS AND OTHER PUBLICATIONS
Fodor's *New York City* Fodor's shows you the way on and off the beaten path, with detailed reviews and expert inside track knowledge.

Fodor's *Gold Guide to New York City* Information on where to go, what to see and how to get there, written by New York City-based shopping experts,

restaurant critics and other specialists. It includes detailed descriptions of hundreds of restaurant and hotel choices, information on sights, and listings of stores and sports opportunities. Useful web links and Smart Travel Tips help in planning.

AIA Guide to New York City: Norval White & Elliot Willensky, Three Rivers Press, New York, 2000
The American Institute of Architects' guide to parks and buildings in all five boroughs is a treasure of architectural knowledge and opinion. With structures arranged in geographical order, it's fun to have as you amble around town, but it's hefty.

Guide to New York City Landmarks: John Wiley & Sons, Inc. 1998
This guide to the city's landmarks and historic districts is ideal for walking tours.

MOVIES
New York has been the setting of great movies by some great directors. Why not watch a few of them before you visit?

42nd Street (1933), Hal Wallis
King Kong (1933), Merian C. Cooper
Guys and Dolls (1955), Samuel Goldwyn
Breakfast at Tiffany's (1961), M. Jurrow, R. Shepherd
West Side Story (1961), Robert Wise

The place for literary bargains

Mean Streets (1973), Martin Scorsese
Taxi Driver (1976), Martin Scorsese
New York, New York (1977), Martin Scorsese
Saturday Night Fever (1977), John Badham
Manhattan (1979), Woody Allen
Broadway Danny Rose (1984), Woody Allen
The Cotton Club (1984), Francis Ford Coppola
Desperately Seeking Susan (1985), Susan Seidelman
Radio Days (1987), Woody Allen
When Harry Met Sally (1989), Rob Reiner
A Bronx Tale (1993), Robert De Niro
Pollock (2000), Ed Harris
Gangs of New York (2002), Martin Scorsese
The Devil Wears Prada (2006), David Franke

TELEVISION
High drama, farce and comedy are played out on the streets of New York daily, and on the screens in people's homes throughout the world when they tune into the following popular TV shows set in or about New York City. Many of them can also be seen on video or DVD.

Friends (now in rerun)
Law & Order
NYPD Blue (now in rerun)
Seinfeld (now in rerun)
Sex and the City (now in rerun)
Will & Grace

PLANNING

USEFUL WEBSITES

ACCOMMODATIONS
● **All New York Hotels**
www.allnewyorkhotels.net
Search for a hotel (including
discount hotels) by name or
criteria
● **Hotel Conxions**
www.hotelconxions.com
Finds great deals on city hotels
● **Manhattan Bed and
Breakfast**
www.bedandbreakfast.com/
manhattan-new-york.html lists
inns and bed-and-breakfast
options in Manhattan
● **Room Connection**
www.RoomConnection.com
A central reservation service for
hotels in New York City
● **YMCA Guest Rooms**
www.ymcanyc.org Main YMCA
site with links to YMCAs around
Greater New York

BROADWAY AND
OFF-BROADWAY TICKETS
● **Playbill's Online Theater
Club**
www.playbillclub.com
A membership club that gives
discounts to top shows
● **TeleCharge**
www.telecharge.com
● **Theater Direct International**
www.broadway.com
● **TheaterMania**
www.theatermania.com
● **Ticketmaster**
www.ticketmaster.com

MONEY
● **Travelex Worldwide Money**
www.travelex.com

NEW YORK CITY
INFORMATION
● **Alliance for Downtown New
York**
www.downtownny.com
Everything you need to know
about Downtown, including links
to a free bus service and an
interactive map
● **The Bronx Tourism Council**
www.ilovethebronx.com
● **Brooklyn Tourism Council**
www.brooklynX.org
● **Citysearch**
www.newyork.citysearch.com
Attractions, events, hotels, real
estate, restaurants and
shopping
● **Customs information for
entering New York City**
www.customs.ustreas.gov

● **New York Convention &
Visitors Bureau**
www.nycvisit.com
● **Times Square Business
Improvement District**
www.timessquarebid.org
The official site for Times Square
and what's going on there

NEWS, REVIEWS AND
WHAT'S ON
● **New York Metro**
www.nymetro.com
New York magazine and Metro
TV website
● **New York Today**
www.nytoday.com
The *New York Times* site, a guide
for New Yorkers and visitors to
what's on and what to do
● **The *New York Times***
www.nytimes.com
● ***The New Yorker***
www.newyorker.com
● ***New York Press***
www.nypress.com
A free weekly newspaper
● ***Time Out New York***
www.timeoutnewyork.com
● ***Village Voice***
www.villagevoice.com
A culturally hip publication

RADIO
New York City is the United
States's top radio outlet. The
radio dial is literally cacophonous,
and if you live in an area without
a similar level or choice, just
turning on the radio and flipping
the dial is an experience. A few
top stations are:
● **WYNC-FM 93.9 (820-AM)**
www.wnyc.org
● **1010 WINS-AM Radio**
www.1010wins.com

Keeping in touch is easy

● **WBGO-FM 88.3 Radio**
www.wbgo.org
● **WQXR-FM 96.3**
www.wqxr.com
New York Times radio station,
with classical music
● **WFAN-AM 660**
www.wfan.com
Sports and news talk
● **WOR-AM 710**
www.wor710.com
Venerable NYC talk radio

TRANSPORTATION
● **Airports**
www.newyorkairports.com
● **Trains**
www.amtrak.com
● **Airtrain Newark**
www.airtrainnewark.com
An on-airport service and shuttle
from Newark Liberty International
Airport Train Station to Newark
Liberty Airport
● **American Automobile
Association**
www.aaa.com
● **Subways and buses**
www.mta.info

GENERAL
● **The Baby Sitters' Guild**
www.babysittersguild.com
For child care at any time
● **Smart Pages**
www.smartpages.com
Telephone numbers in the U.S.
● **Weather**
www.weather.com or
www.cnn.com/weather
A comprehensive weather
service

GLOSSARY FOR NON-US VISITORS

You will see signs in Spanish throughout the city, especially in subways, and hear a wide variety of languages in various neighborhoods. But the New York vocabulary also has its idiosyncrasies, as you will see below.

arugula	rocket (salad)
automated teller machine (ATM)	cashpoint
Band-Aid/bandage	plaster
bill	banknote
car (on a train)	carriage
cart	trolley
check (restaurant)	bill
cilantro	coriander
cookie	biscuit
cot	camp bed
counterclockwise	anticlockwise
crib	cot
crosswalk	zebra crossing
day care	crèche
desk clerk	receptionist
dessert	pudding
diaper	nappy
directory assistance	directory enquiries
eggplant	aubergine
elevator	lift
emergency room (hospital)	casualty
faucet	tap
flashlight	torch
french fries	chips
gas	petrol
gas station	garage
hood (car)	bonnet
house trailer/RV	caravan
Jello™	jelly
jelly	jam
license plate	number plate
liquor store	off-licence
long-distance bus	coach
mail	post
main street	high street
one-way ticket	single ticket
pants	trousers
panty-hose	tights
parking lot	car park
pavement	road surface, usually referring to the street
pharmacy	chemist
phone booth	phone box
potato chips	crisps
private school	public school
public holiday	bank holiday
pull-off	lay-by
rent	hire
restrooms	toilets
round-trip ticket	return ticket
row houses	terrace
sidewalk	pavement
soccer	football
soda	fizzy soft drink
street musician	busker
stroller	pushchair/buggy
sweater	jumper, jersey
takeout	takeaway
taxi stand	taxi rank
two-lane highway	dual carriageway
traffic circle	roundabout
truck	lorry
trunk (car)	boot
underpass	subway
underpants (men's)	pants
undershirt	vest
vacation	holiday
vest	waistcoat
washcloth	face flannel
wharf/pier	quay
yard (residential)	garden
zucchini	courgette

NEW YORK GLOSSARY

balcony	gallery
brownstones	four- and five-story 19th-century row houses originally faced with cheap brown sandstone
checkroom	cloakroom
crosstown	an east–west direction across the city
downtown	a direction south of any point
first balcony	dress circle
jaywalking	crossing the street illegally, or not at the crosswalk
orchestra seats	stalls
upstate	the state of New York north of New York City
uptown	a direction north of any point

BUILDING FLOOR NUMBERING

The first floor in America is the ground floor to British visitors, the second floor is the first floor, and so on. This is worth watching out for when visiting museums, galleries and other public buildings.

NEW YORK NEIGHBORHOODS

New York is divided into the five boroughs of Manhattan, Brooklyn, the Bronx, Queens and Staten Island, each with their own distinct character.

MANHATTAN
Attractions, many of them world famous, line the streets of Manhattan, the area stretching from Battery Park at its tip to Harlem in the north, beyond Central Park.

Financial District
The oldest part of the city and the nexus of the securities industry anchored by the New York Stock Exchange and Wall Street. It's still primarily a business district, although residents have moved in over the last decade.

Battery Park City
A 92-acre (35ha) complex, built on landfill from the creation of the World Trade Center in 1974. It includes housing, commercial and retail space, plus a marina and the Museum of Jewish Heritage.

TriBeCa
It means *Tri*angle *Be*low *Ca*nal and is defined by Canal and Barclay streets and Broadway and the Hudson River. In 1980, the Odeon restaurant opened and pioneer residents followed, settling into the warehouses and manufacturing buildings. It now has the highest real-estate values in the city and plenty of celebrity cachet. Home to TriBeCa Film Studios, it's still a mixed-use neighborhood of gritty warehouse lofts, loft-style restaurants and low-end retail.

Civic Center
The focal point of City government, incorporating the courts, police and immigration. City Hall is at the center of the area. It's dwarfed by the nearby Municipal Building, designed by McKim, Mead and White.

Chinatown
In the 1840s, Chinatown was just eight blocks. Today it includes about 30 blocks, from Kenmare and Delancey streets to East Broadway and Worth Street, and from Broadway to Allen Street. Shop for fish, meat, vegetables and herbal remedies or dine in the many affordable restaurants.

Little Italy
Very little of this once vibrant community survives. Most of the Italians have moved to the suburbs and Chinese residents have replaced them. It consists largely of Mulberry Street, which is lined with tourist-oriented restaurants, plus one or two genuine delis.

NoLita
It stands for *No*rth of *Li*ttle *Ita*ly. The narrow streets around St. Patrick's Cathedral, once the heart of the Italian community, are now lined with hip designer boutiques.

SoHo
In 1973 the 20 blocks between Houston, Canal, West Broadway and Broadway were designated a Historic District, protecting the best stock of cast-iron buildings in the city. Artists had already begun reclaiming the manufacturing and warehouse spaces and pioneering a loft lifestyle. Today the artists and most of the art galleries have moved on; the area is now an ultra-expensive, chic shopping mall crowded with non-residents on weekends.

Bowery
A long street connecting Chinatown to the East Village, it was once the city's Skid Row, lined with flophouses and numerous stores selling kitchen supplies and lighting fixtures. Today it is being gentrified.

Lower East Side
The traditional gateway for every wave of immigrants, from the Jewish and the Italians to the Puerto Ricans, this was the last Manhattan neighborhood to be updated. Today, young professionals and artists occupy the tenements and congregate at the clubs and bars along Orchard, Clinton and other streets. Remnants of the Puerto Rican community survive, and so does the bargain bazaar on Sunday along Orchard Street. The boundaries stretch from 14th Street to Fulton and Franklin and from the East River to Broadway, incorporating Chinatown, Little Italy and the East Village neighborhoods.

Greenwich Village/West Village
This area stretches from 14th to Houston streets and from the Hudson River to Bowery and Fourth Avenue. Originally a poor neighborhood housing the workers and stevedores who worked the waterfront, it became a bohemia around 1900, attracting a mixture of artists, writers and anarchists. Today, it's a mixed neighborhood. The gay population has mostly moved to Chelsea, and now "successful" singles and families occupy the town houses and apartments. Small boutiques line the west end of Bleecker Street. The southern section around Bleecker Street and Sixth Avenue still has an Italian flavor.

Meatpacking District
Sandwiched between the West Village and Chelsea around 14th Street, this gritty neighborhood is being redeveloped. Restaurants, bars, clubs and stores are opening and hotels too.

NoHo
Between SoHo and Greenwich Village (from Houston to Eighth Streets and Mercer to Bowery/Third Avenue), this youth-oriented neighborhood has plenty of fashionable shopping, bars and restaurants. The acronym stands for *No*rth of *Ho*uston.

East Village
This was originally an extension of the Lower East Side, settled by Jewish and Ukrainian/Polish communities. In the 1960s and 70s it became the center of the counter-culture. It has been rapidly redeveloped and is now filled with restaurants, bars and a young street scene.

Alphabet City
It refers to avenues A, B, C and D between Houston and 14th streets. In the 1970s, First Avenue marked the DMZ and the streets east of First were considered dangerous drug supermarkets. Gentrification

PLANNING

began in 1983 when Operation Pressure Point started cleaning up the drug trade, and buildings on Tompkins Square became co-ops. Today young professionals occupy the tenement apartments; there's a thriving dining and bar scene, including a substantial number of gay bars and clubs. The original Hispanic population has been dispersed.

Gramercy Park
This genteel and dignified neighborhood radiating from the eponymous gated garden square remains primarily residential. It stretches from 18th to 23rd streets and from Park Avenue South to Third Avenue.

Union Square/Flatiron District
This hot new neighborhood leading south from the Flatiron Building on 22nd Street and around Madison Square has plenty of bars, restaurants and clubs. The Green Market at Union Square is a must on Saturday. The former Ladies' Mile along Sixth Avenue between 15th and 24th streets is now occupied by large national chain stores. The boundaries go from 14th to 23rd streets and from Park to Sixth avenues.

Chelsea
Today Chelsea is the center of the gay community and the new focus for contemporary art anchored by numerous warehouse/ garage galleries around and along 24th Street. It has a lively club and restaurant scene. The boundaries stretch from 14th to 30th streets and from Sixth Avenue to the Hudson River.

Murray Hill
A quiet residential neighborhood between 34th and 40th streets between Madison and Third avenues. It is becoming increasingly commercial on the fringes. The Morgan Library and the Episcopalian church, where the Roosevelts worshiped, set the tone.

Midtown
The commercial heart of the city between 34th and 59th streets on the West Side and from 40th to 59th streets on the East Side. It includes major attractions, shops, restaurants, theaters, TV studios, Nasdaq and corporate offices.

Times Square/ Theater District
The old peep shows, hookers and junkies have been displaced, and the area around 42nd Street and Broadway is now occupied by an array of major corporations and national chain stores—Condé Nast, Reuters, ESPN Zone, Toys R-Us and many others, who share the area with new hotels, clubs and theaters.

Clinton/Hell's Kitchen
Real-estate developers have rediscovered this neighborhood from 42nd to 59th streets between Eighth Avenue and the Hudson River. It was formerly known as Hell's Kitchen and was the site of slaughterhouses, freight yards and factories.

Upper East Side
It stretches from 59th to 96th streets from Fifth Avenue to the East River. The section from 59th to 78th streets between Fifth and Park avenues is often referred to as the Gold Coast, where those who can afford it live. Farther east it was not always elegant, but it became more so in 1956 when the Third Avenue El was demolished and Madison Avenue became an ultra-chic shopping street. Today it is filled with private clubs, consulates, art galleries, restaurants and fine residences. Museum Mile extends along Fifth Avenue from 81st Street north past the Metropolitan Museum of Art.

Yorkville
High-rise apartments line the streets of what was formerly the German section between Lexington and Third avenues on 86th Street.

Carnegie Hill
Between 86th and 96th streets between Fifth and Third avenues, this is primarily a low-key wealthy residential district, anchored by the Carnegie mansion (now the Cooper-Hewitt National Design Museum). The area is home to such prestigious private schools as Dalton, Spence and Horace Mann, plus the Guggenheim and the Jewish Museum.

East Harlem/Spanish Harlem
From 96th to 142nd streets, between Park Avenue and the East River, this area is still home to El Barrio, the community

established by the Puerto Ricans, who first arrived at the end of World War I and increased in numbers after World War II. Today it's a mixed neighborhood of Italians, African-Americans and Hispanics.

Lincoln Square
The square is the area around the Lincoln Center. Wealthy individuals, many of them successful performers, occupy the towers, and the area buzzes with bars, restaurants and stores. The ABC and CNN studios are a major presence.

Upper West Side
Broadway cuts right through this section that extends from 59th to 125th streets between the Hudson River and Central Park West. The blocks around 72nd Street were the center of an old German/East-European, primarily Jewish, liberal intellectual community. In the 1970s and 80s, Columbus and Amsterdam avenues were gentrified and the old single-room occupancy hotels returned to handsome residences. Today, it's often referred to as a Manhattan suburb, because of its family orientation, although it has become more fashionable recently, as new chic restaurants have opened. Central Park West is lined with expensive cooperatives overlooking Central Park. Notable attractions include the American Museum of Natural History .

Morningside Heights
Columbia University dominates this neighborhood, along with Barnard, Teachers College, the Cathedral of St. John the Divine and the Union Theological and Jewish Theological seminaries.

Harlem
Stretching from 110th Street to the Harlem River and from Fifth to St. Nicholas avenues, Harlem is the city's most famous black community. Originally a suburb for the wealthy, it was settled in the late 19th century by Jewish immigrants from Germany. When the subway arrived in the early 20th century, most of the black community moved in from midtown Manhattan and also from the southern states, and it drew black artists, writers and musicians. In the 1920s the Harlem Renaissance brought

whites and blacks together to the clubs, theaters and jazz joints. Later it became a blighted community, destroyed by the riots of the 1960s. Today it has been rediscovered by the middle classes and increasingly by whites in search of reasonably priced houses. The restaurants and churches attract visitors.

Washington Heights/Inwood
This is the last stop in Manhattan. It has been home to many different immigrant groups. Today, it's largely a Dominican community, although young professionals are moving in. It's also home to the Cloisters.

BROOKLYN
With the highest population of the five boroughs (2.5 million), Brooklyn is a healthy rival to Manhattan. It's full of world-class museums, spacious parks, landmark buildings and lively neighborhoods.

Greenpoint
This is an old Polish neighborhood where young professionals have moved because of its proximity to Manhattan.

Williamsburg
Primarily a Jewish and African-American neighborhood, recently it has been discovered by the young and hip. It's now reminiscent of 1950s Greenwich Village.

DUMBO
One developer alone has created this neighborhood (Down Under the Manhattan Bridge Overpass) by renting to artists and musicians. It's likely to become the next "hot" neighborhood à la SoHo.

Brooklyn Heights
This is a former premier residential neighborhood. The Promenade has magnificent views of the Manhattan skyline.

Cobble Hill
This is another affluent residential neighborhood where the streets are lined with elegant brownstones. Atlantic Avenue supports a major Middle Eastern community.

Prospect Park
The Brooklyn Botanic Gardens are in Prospect Park and the Brooklyn Museum of Art is adjacent to the gardens.

Carroll Gardens
Fine brownstones made this primarily Italian neighborhood an attractive residential area for those who could not afford to buy in Manhattan.

Fort Greene
After it was designated a historic district in 1978, professionals started buying the handsome brownstones. It's home to the Brooklyn Academy of Music.

Park Slope
Brooklyn's "alternative" village on the western edge of Prospect Park. The main commercial streets are 7th and 5th avenues.

Crown Heights
The city's largest West Indian community, plus a thriving Hasidic Jewish community.

Brighton Beach/Coney Island
Often called Little Odessa due to its Russian Jewish community, Brighton Beach has a boardwalk, clubs, restaurants and stores servicing the Russian community.

Next door, Coney Island was the city's great blue-collar playground from the late 1890s to the early 1930s. In the 1960s it became drug infested and dangerous. Today it is being revived. It's home to the New York Aquarium.

QUEENS
An international melting pot, Queens has the most diverse population of the five boroughs, and is also the largest. Named for Queen Catherine of Braganza, Charles II's wife, it is a good place to go to sample ethnic life and cuisine.

Astoria
The old Greek neighborhood has survived. Astoria was also a film-making area and some of the studios have been revived, including one that houses the American Museum of the Moving Image.

Long Island City
This is Queens' most industrialized area. The gritty waterfront area is being revamped.

Forest Hills
This wealthy, largely Jewish enclave, only a short commute from Manhattan, has handsome apartment houses, and good restaurants and social services.

Jackson Heights
This is a major South American and Indian enclave on 82nd Street.

Corona, Shea Stadium and Flushing Meadows Park
The stadium is the home of the Mets. The park has the National Tennis Center, the New York Hall of Science and the Queens Museum of Art. Corona is mainly a Dominican, Colombian and Mexican community.

Flushing Meadows
This is an area populated by Chinese, Koreans, Vietnamese, Malaysians and Japanese.

THE BRONX
The Bronx was once an expensive retreat for the wealthy. Development in the 1920s brought more well-heeled residents, then it got a reputation as a crime-laden area, and now has been turned into a much more tourist-friendly borough, with plenty of attractions and beautiful parks.

Fordham
The Bronx Zoo and the New York Botanical Garden are in this neighborhood. Arthur Avenue is a colorful Italian area.

Riverdale
The most desirable residential neighborhood in the borough and the location of Wave Hill, an 1843 estate once home to Mark Twain and Teddy Roosevelt and now a public garden and cultural center.

Van Cortlandt Park and Woodlawn Cemetery
Many famous people are buried at Woodlawn, including F. W. Woolworth, Irving Berlin and Duke Ellington. Van Cortlandt Park is a delightful space with forests and hills to explore.

City Island
New Yorkers come to this historic fishing community for fresh fish.

STATEN ISLAND
Staten Island is more than twice the size of Manhattan. Its residents are largely blue collar, still living a fairly autonomous, rural life away from busy Manhattan. Attractions include Alice Austen House, Snug Harbor Cultural Center and Historic Richmond Town.

PLANNING

332-333   UPPER WEST SIDE

Central Park

334-335   UPPER EAST SIDE

Mill Rock

Carl Schurz Park

Franklin D Roosevelt Island

John Jay Park

LONG ISLAND CITY

QUEENSBORO

QUEENS

Hudson

336-337   THEATER DISTRICT

338-339   MIDTOWN

East

CHELSEA

STUYVESANT TOWN

EAST VILLAGE

340-341   ALPHABET CITY   342-343

SOHO

LITTLE ITALY

LOWER EAST SIDE

WILLIAMSBURG BRIDGE

East River Park

TRIBECA

EAST SIDE   East

MANHATTAN BRIDGE

FINANCIAL DISTRICT

344-345

BATTERY PARK CITY

BROOKLYN HEIGHTS

CONNECTICUT

NEW YORK

346-347

Newark   New York

NEW JERSEY

New York's Outer Boroughs

─────	Main road
─────	Other road
⋯⋯⋯	Minor road/path
▬▬▬	Railway
▰	Park
▰	Important building
●	Featured place of interest
	Subway station:
●	1, 2, 3
●	4, 5, 6
●	7
●	A, C, E
●	B, D, F
●	L
●	M, J, Z
●	N, R, Q, W
●	S (42 St Shuttle)
●	V (0530-2300 Mon-Fri)
▰	Railway station
🅿	Parking

332-345   0 — 300 m / 0 — 250 yds

346-347   0 — 8 km / 0 — 5 m

Maps

West 93rd Street

West 92nd Street

UPPER WEST

West 91st Street

SIDE

West 90th Street

West 89th Street

West 88th Street

West 87th Street

West 86th Street

86th
Street

West 85th Street

West 84th Street

West 83rd Street

West 82nd Street

West 81st Street

West 80th Street

Riverside
Park

West End Avenue

BROADWAY

Amsterdam Avenue

Riverside Drive

HIGHWAY 9A

West 79th Street

79th
Street

West 78th Street

West 77th Street

West 76th Street

Hudson River

BROADWAY

West 75th Street

West 74th Street

Ansonia
Building

West 73rd Street

West 72nd Street

Riverside Drive

72nd Street

West 71st Street

West 70th Street

West 69th Street

West
69th
Street

Freedom

West
68th
Street

West 68th Street

Riverside Blvd

Place

West 67th Street

66th Street
Lincoln Center

West 66th Street

Juilliard School

West 65th Street

West 64th Street

Lincoln
Center

West End Avenue

West 63rd Street

West 62nd
Street

West 61st Drive

Amsterdam Avenue

West 62nd Stree

West 61st Street

West 60th Street

West 59th

West 59th Street

Central
Park
Reservoir

Jewish
Museum

East 93rd Street

East 92nd Street

East 91st Street

Cooper-Hewitt
National Design Museum

East 90th Street

National
Academy
of Design

PARK AVENUE

13

Guggenheim
Museum

East 88th Street

East 87th Street

86th
Street

86th Street Transverse Road

East 86th Street

86th
Street

Neue
Galerie

CENTRAL PARK

East 85th Street

East 84th Street

East 83rd Street

5th Avenue

The Metropolitan
Museum of Art

East 82nd Street

81st Street
Museum of Nat Hist

Central Park

East 81st Street

East 80th Street

14

Turtle Pond

East 79th Street

79th Street Transverse Road

East 78th Street

PARK AVENUE

American Museum
Natural History

Central Park West

Drive

East 77th Street

77th
Street

New-York
Historical Society

5th Avenue

East 76th Street

334

The
Lake

East 75th Street

Whitney Museum
of American Art

Conservatory
Water

East 74th
Street

The Dakota

East 73rd Street

72nd
Street

Strawberry
Fields

East 72nd Street

15

Olmsted Drive

East 71st Street

Frick
Collection

Asia Society
and Museum

East 70th Street

East Drive

East 69th Street

Madison Avenue

68th Street
Hunter College

The
Sheep
Meadow

East 68th Street

West

East 67th Street

Drive

Tavern on
the Green

East 66th Street

65th Street Transverse Road

East 65th Street

West 64th Street

East 64th Street

16

West
63rd Street

Center Drive

Park

Ice
Rink

FIFTH

East 63rd Street

East 62nd Street

um of
d Art

Drive

AVENUE

East 61st Street

st 61st Street

North

The
Pond

East 60th Street

PARK AVENUE

333

59th Street
Columbus Circle

D

337

E

333

COLUMBUS
CIRCLE

Central

Park

South

5th Avenue

East 59th Street

Jewish Museum

E

F

East 92nd Street

East 91st Street

East 91st Street

Cooper-Hewitt National Design Museum

National Academy of Design

East 90th Street

East 90th Street

East 89th Street

13

Guggenheim Museum

East 88th Street

East 88th Street

East 87th Street

East 87th Street

86th Street

East 86th Street

East 86th Street

Neue Galerie

East 85th Street

East 85th Street

East 84th Street

East 84th Street

The Metropolitan Museum of Art

East 83rd Street

East 83rd Street

East 82nd Street

East 82nd Street

14

East 81st Street

East 81st Street

East 80th Street

East 80th Street

East 79th Street

East 79th Street

East 78th Street

East 78th Street

East 77th Street

77th Street

East 77th Street

East 76th Street

East 76th Street

333

East 75th Street

East 75th Street

Whitney Museum of American Art

East 74th Street

East 74th Street

Conservatory Water

East 73rd Street

East 73rd Street

East 72nd Street

East 72nd Street

15

East 71st Street

East 71st Street

Frick Collection

Asia Society and Museum

East 70th Street

East 70th Street

East 69th Street

East 69th Street

68th Street Hunter College

East 68th Street

East 68th Street

East 67th Street

East 67th Street

FIFTH

East 66th Street

East 66th Street

AVENUE

East 65th Street

East 65th Street

East 64th Street

East 64th Street

16

Lexington Avenue 63rd Street

East 63rd Street

East 63rd Street

East 62nd Street

East 62nd Street

East 61st Street

East 61st St

Lexington Avenue

Mount Vernon Hotel Museum and Garden

334

E

East 60th Street

East 60th Street

HIGHWAY

5th Avenue

59th Street

338

F

East 59th Street

East 59th Street

Avenue labels: 5th Avenue, PARK AVENUE, Madison Avenue, Lexington Avenue, 3rd Avenue, 2nd Avenue, 1st Avenue, York Avenue

East Drive

North

332

West 59th Street

West 58th Street

WEST 57TH STREE

West 56th Street

West 55th Street

West 54th Street

De Witt Clinton Park

West 53rd Street

West 52nd Stree

West 51st Street

West 50th Street

West 49th Street

West 48th Street

West 47th Street

Intrepid Sea, Air and Space Museum

West 46th Street

West 46th Street

West 45th Stree

West 44th Stree

West 43rd Stree

WEST 42ND STREE

West 41st Street

West 40th Stree

West 39th Stree

HIGHWAY 495

West 38th Stree

West 37th Stree

Jacob K Javits Convention Center

West 36th Stree

West 35th Stree

West 34th Stree

West 33rd Street

West 31st Street

West 30th Stree

West 29th Stree

West 28th Stree

Chelsea Park

West 27th Street

West 26th Stree

Hudson River

12th Av

12th Avenue

12TH AVENUE

12th Avenue

11th Avenue

11th Avenue

11th Avenue

9A

10TH AVENUE

10TH AVENUE

10TH AVENUE

DYER AVENUE

340

16

17

18

19

20

B

C

B

C

5th Avenue

16

E East Street

59th Street

334

F

East 59th Street

East Street

East 58th Street

East 58th Street

STREET **EAST 57TH** **STREET**

East 57th Street

Trump Tower

Street East 56th Street

West 56th Street

5th Avenue

PARK AVENUE

Lexington Avenue

3rd Avenue

2nd Avenue

1st Avenue

Sutton Place

Street East 55th Street

East 55th Street

PARK AVENUE

Street East 54th Street

East 54th Street

5th Avenue / 53rd Street

Street East 53rd Street

17

Lexington Avenue

East 53rd Street

FRANKLIN DELANO ROOSEVELT DRIVE

Seagram Building

Street East 52nd Street

East 52nd Street

Paley Center for Media

St Patrick's Cathedral

Municipal Art Society

51st Street

East 51st Street

Rockefeller Plaza

Street East 50th Street

Mitchell Pl

MIDTOWN

East 49th Street

East 49th Street

MANHATTAN

Street East 48th Street

East 48th Street

Street East 47th Street

East 47th Street

Street East 46th Street

East 46th Street

United Nations Headquarters

Street East 45th Street

East 45th Street

5th Avenue

Madison Avenue

Vanderbilt Avenue

PARK AVENUE

Lexington Avenue

3rd Avenue

2nd Avenue

United Nations Plaza

Street East 44th Street

East 44th Street

Grand Central Terminal

18

East 43rd Street

Chrysler Building

East 43rd Street

Tudor City Place

5th Avenue

337

Grand Central 42nd Street

EAST 42ND **STREET**

STREET EAST STREET

Chanin Building

Daily News Building

495

New York Public Library

East 41st Street

East 41st Street

Street East 40th Street

East 40th Street

TUNNEL

Street East 39th Street

East 39th Street

TUNNEL

Street East 38th Street

East 38th Street

ENTRANCE

EXIT

Street East 37th Street

Morgan Library

PARK AVENUE

East 36th Street

East 36th Street

STREET

Street East 35th Street

STREET

East 35th Street

STREET **EAST 34TH** **STREET**

EAST 34TH **STREET**

19

Empire State Building

East 33rd Street

33rd Street

East 33rd Street

FDR DRIVE SERVICE ROAD

Street East 32nd Street

East 32nd Street

Street East 31st Street

East 31st Street

5th Avenue

East 30th Street

Lexington Avenue

3rd Avenue

2nd Avenue

1st Avenue

East 30th Street

Little Church Around the Corner

East 29th Street

East 29th Street

Anew Street

East 28th Street

East 28th Street

20

East 27th Street

28th Street

Mt Carmel Place

East 27th Street

338

E East 26th Street

342

F East 26th Street

Main Street

22n.

West Road

East Road

Vernon Boulevard

43rd

43rd Street

11th Street

12th Street

Street

Street

9th Street

10th Street

44th Avenue

13th Street

21ST STREET

22nd St

45th Road
Court House Square

44th Road

17

44th Drive

45th Avenue

45th Avenue

45th Road

46th Avenue

QUEENS

21st Street
(Van Alst)

46th Road

5th Street

47th Avenue

JACKSON AVENUE

21ST STREET

47th Road

Vernon

49th Ave

50th Av

18

495

48th Avenue

Gantry
Plaza
State Park

P

Center Blvd

49th Avenue

Vernon Boulevard

Vernon Boulevard
Jackson Avenue

11TH STREET

50th Avenue

Avenue

QUEENS MIDTOWN TUNNEL

2nd Street

51st Avenue

Borden

Avenue

53rd Avenue

54th Avenue

East River

2nd Street

Ash Street

Box Street

Commercial Street

Clay Street

Manhattan Street

Street

Dupont Street

19

Eagle Street

Franklin Street

Freeman Street

Ave

Green Street

Street

West Street

Huron Street

India St

20

Java

336

C

West 26th Street

West 25th Street

West 24th Street

10TH AVENUE

West 23rd Street

West 22nd Street

Chelsea
Waterside Park

20

West 21st Street

P

West 20th Street

11TH AVENUE

West 19th Street

West 18th Street

West 17th Street

West 16th Street

P

West 15th Street

9A

WEST 14TH STREET

21

West   Washington   13t

Little West 12th Street

Bloomfield
Street   10TH AVENUE   Gansevoort

Street

Horatio   Street

Gansevoort
Street   WEST STREET   Jane   Street

Hudson River   West 12

Bethun

Ban

22

23

20

terside
ple

e Drive

op

uyvesant
al

Avenue C Loop

oop

Avenue C

East 16th
Street

East 15th Street

21

East River

SERVICE DRIVE

EAST 14TH STREET

East 13th Street

Avenue D

East 12th Street

Szold Place

East 11th Street

East 10th Street

East 9th Street

East 8th Street

East 7th Street

East 6th Street

East 5th Street

East 5th Walk

FRANKLIN DELANO ROOSEVELT DRIVE

FRANKLIN DELANO ROOSEVELT DRIVE

Avenue B

Avenue D

East 4th Street

East 4th Walk

East 3rd Street

Avenue D

East 3rd
Street

Louis Street

East
River
Park

22

Mangin Street

Baruch Place

Avenue B

Avenue C

EAST HOUSTON STREET

Hamilton
Fish Park

Columbia

Attorney Avenue

Stanton Street

Baruch Drive

Franklin D Roosevelt Drive

eet

Suffolk Street

Clinton Street

Attorney Street

Ridge Street

Pitt Street

Rivington Street

Street

WILLIAMSBURG BRIDGE APPROACH

Columbia Street

23

LOWER
EAST SIDE

Ridge Street

Pitt Street

Willett Street

Broome

Columbia Street

Broome Street

Lewis Street

Franklin D Roosevelt Drive

Suffolk Street

Street

Street

Street

Grand Street

Jackson Street

ed Park

Henry

Madison Street

Cherry Street

Corlears Hook

G

Grand Street
STREET
Street
Street
BOWERY
STREET
Hester Street
Elizabeth St
Canal Street
Division Street
Street
Street
Division Street
East Broadway
Broadway
Market Street
Street
Henry Street
Street
P
Oliver Street
James Place
James Street
Madison Street
Catherine Street
Monroe Street
Street
Street
Catherine Slip
Cherry Street
Water Street
Catherine Slip
Street
Saint
Mills Road
of the Finest
Street
Peck Slip
Water Street
Front Street
SOUTH STREET
Fulton Street Market
P
Front Street
Front Street
P

Seward Park

G 343

Street
Broadway
East Broadway
Clinton Street
Jefferson Street
Street
Monroe St
Rutgers Street
Cherry Street
Rutgers Park
South Street
Rutgers Slip
Falcon Drive
Street
PIKE STREET
Market Slip
Street

FRANKLIN DELANO ROOSEVELT DRIVE

MANHATTAN BRIDGE

East River

BROOKLYN BRIDGE

South Street Seaport

H

Madison Street
Cherry Street
Corlears Hook Park
Monroe Street
Gouverneur Street
Montgomery Street
Water Street
Street

24

25

Pearl Street
John Street
Plymouth Street
Water St
York Street

Plymouth Street
Street
Washington St
Adams St
Main Street
New Dock Street
Empire-Fulton Ferry State Park
Water Street
Front Street
York Street
P
278

OLD FULTON STREET
Doughty Street
Vine Street
Middagh Street
Willow Street
Hicks Street
Columbia Street
Orange Street
Pineapple Street
Clark Street
Heights Street
Pierrepont Street
Montague Street
Remsen Street
Grace Court
Grace Court Aly
Grace Church
Joralemon Street
Columbia Pl
Willow Place
State Street

Plymouth Church of the Pilgrims
BROOKLYN
HEIGHTS

CADMAN PLAZA WEST
High Street Brooklyn Bridge
Cadman Plaza
Cadman Plaza Park

Clark Street
College Place
Henry Street
Love Lane
Monroe Place
Clinton Street
Street
Brooklyn Historical Society
Cathedral of Our Lady of Lebanon
Street
Hunts Lane
Hicks Street
Carden Place
Street

FURMAN ST

BROOKLYN-QUEENS EXPRESSWAY

26

27

H 345

ATLANTIC AVENUE

23 Pequannock

Pompton Lakes

Wyckoff

Westwood

Hacken Pascac

202 23

208

Ridgewood

17

Oradel Reservo

Pequannock Township

Hawthorne

Glen Rock

Paramus

Dumont

Wayne

507

New Milfc

Montville 202

Lincoln Park

Naaktp

Passaic

Fair Lawn

20

River Edge

Bergenfiel

Passaic

Kockaw

23

PATERSON

Totowa

4

19

Elmwood Park

Saddle Brook

Hackensack

Teaneck

80

West Paterson

46

Garfield

Lodi

80

4

West Caldwell

Little Falls

159

Cedar Grove

23

Clifton

Passaic

Hasbrouck Heights

46

Ridgefield Park

93

Palisade Park

280

Verona

3

21

Wallington

17

120

Hackensack

Cliffside Park

Fairvie

577

Montclair

Nutley

7

Rutherford

Livingston

10

Bloomfield

Belleville

Passaic

17

Lyndhurst

3

95

501

North Bergen

West New Yor

495

MAI

West Orange

NEW   **JERSEY**

Orange

East Orange

South Orange

North Arlington

21

Kearny

7

95

Secaucus

Weehawke

Union City

Hoboken

Hudson

Maplewood

Harrison

Summit

24

Millburn

Irvington

NEWARK

124

78

21

JERSEY CITY

78

LOWE MANHATTAN

Springfield

82

Union

Hillside

27

Newark International

95

440

169

Ellis Island Museum

478

New York Transit Museum

Statue of Liberty

Cranford

28

Roselle Park

439

I

81

Waterfront Museum

Westfield

Roselle

ELIZABETH

Bayonne

Scotch Plains

Clark

Rahway

22

Linden

440

Newark Bay

Upper New York Bay

Kill Van Kull

PORT RICHMOND

Snug Harbor Cultural Center

The Narrows

278

Colonia

Rahway

95

CLIFTON

Garibaldi Meucci Museum

Alice Austen House

Iselin

Avenel

Carteret

278

Lower New York Bay

Woodbridge

9

SOUTH BEACH

Fords

95

184

35

Arthur Kill

440

STATEN ISLAND

Jacques Marchais Museum of Tibetan Art

Historic Richmond Town

OAKWOOD

Gateway National Recreation Area

Great Kills Harbor

ANNADALE

TOTTENVILLE

Perth Amboy

Conference House

Raritan Bay

Raritan

Port Chester
Captain Harbor
CONNECTICUT
120
287
127
Rye
Harrison
Scarsdale
Mamaroneck
Long Island Sound
Eastchester
100
22
Milton Harbor
Bronx River
YONKERS
87
Tenafly
9
Mount Vernon
New Rochelle
1
95
87
Hudson
New York Botanical Garden
Pelham Park
Glen Cove
WASHINGTON HEIGHTS
glewood
9W
Fort Lee
BAYCHESTER
Hart Island
City Island
Long Island Sound
Bronx Zoo
678
695
Eastchester Bay
BRONX
Yankee Stadium
I 895
Port Washington
101
HARLEM
87
SOUNDVIEW
25A
278
Central Park
Rikers Island
Westchester Creek
678
295
DOUGLASTON
ATTAN
LaGuardia
ASTORIA
Flushing
North New Hyde Park
25
Westbury
Long Island City
Queens Museum of Art
New York Hall of Science
Flushing Meadows
25A
495
258
Mineola
East River
25
Garden City
Uniondale
24
ELMHURST
278
QUEENS
25
QUEENS VILLAGE
Floral Park
Hempstead
102
GLENDALE
24
Franklin Square
WILLIAMS-BURG
JAMAICA
Elmont
West Hempstead
NEW YORK
878
North Valley Stream
ST ALBANS
Brooklyn Museum
Valley Stream
Roosevelt
Brooklyn Botanic Garden
EAST NEW YORK
878
Lynbrook
Rockville Centre
Baldwin
Prospect Park
27
John F Kennedy International
ROSEDALE
East Rockaway
FLATBUSH
Spring Creek Park
Jamaica Bay
Woodmere
Oceanside
Canarsie Beach Park
Powell Creek
BROOKLYN
Gateway National Recreation Area
Head of Bay
East Rockaway Channel
Garrett Lead
HEEPSHEAD BAY
Bergen Beach Park
Far Rockaway
Broad Channel
Middle Bay
oney land
BRIGHTON BEACH
Long Beach
Atlantic Beach
Rockaway Beach
Rockaway Point

The following indexes list hotels, restaurants and cafés, stores, theaters and music and dance venues.

ACKNOWLEDGMENTS

Abbreviations for the credits are as follows:

AA = AA World Travel Library, **t** (top), **b** (bottom), **c** (center), **l** (left), **r** (right)

UNDERSTANDING NEW YORK

5 AA/C Sawyer; **8tl** AA/C Sawyer; **8tr** AA/S McBride; **8ctr** AA/C Sawyer; **8cbr** AA/R Elliott; **8br** AA/P Kenward; **9tl** Jean-Georges; **9cl** Photodisc; **9bl** AA/D Corrance; **9cr** AA/T Souter; **9b** AA/C Sawyer; **10tl** AA/C Sawyer; **10cl** AA/C Sawyer; **10bl** AA/P Kenward; **10tr** AA/D Corrance; **10cr** AA/C Sawyer; **10br** AA/C Sawyer.

LIVING NEW YORK

11 AA/P Kenward; **12/3bg** AA/C Sawyer; **12tl** AA/C Sawyer; **12/3t** AA/C Sawyer; **12c** AA/R Elliott; **12cr** AA/C Sawyer; **12cl** AA/P Kenward; **12bl** AA/C Sawyer; **13tr** AA/R Elliott; **13cl** AA/C Sawyer; **13c** AA/R Elliott; **13cr** AA/R Elliott; **13br** AA/C Sawyer; **14/5bg** AA/C Sawyer; **14tl** AA/S McBride; **14tc** AA/C Sawyer; **14tr** AA/S McBride; **14c** AA/R Elliott; **14cl** AA/C Sawyer; **14bl** AA/C Sawyer; **14/5c** AA/S McBride; **15tl** AA/C Sawyer; **15cl** AA/C Sawyer; **15tr** AA/R Elliott; **15cr** AA/C Sawyer; **16/7bg** AA/C Sawyer; **16tl** AA/D Corrance; **16tr** AA/S McBride; **16c** AA/E Rooney; **16cr** AA/C Sawyer; **16br** AA/D Corrance; **16/7c** AA/C Sawyer; **17tl** AA/C Sawyer; **17tr** AA/C Sawyer; **17cl** AA/C Sawyer; **17c** AA/C Sawyer; **17cr** AA/R Elliott; **18/9bg** AA/C Sawyer; **18tl** AA/C Sawyer; **18tc** AA/C Sawyer; **18tr** AA/C Sawyer; **18cl** AA/D Corrance; **18cr** AA/S McBride; **18cbl** AA/R Elliott; **18bl** AA/C Sawyer; **19tl** AA/P Kenward; **19tr** AA/C Sawyer; **19cl** AA/C Sawyer; **19cr** Getty Images; **20/1bg** AA/C Sawyer; **20tl** AA/C Sawyer; **20tr** AA/C Sawyer; **20cl** AA/C Sawyer; **20cr** AA/D Corrance; **20cr** AA/D Corrance/ © ARS, NY and DACS, London 2008; **20bc** AA/C Sawyer; **21tl** The Kobal Collection; **21tc** AA/C Sawyer; **21c** AA/R Elliott; **21r** AA/P Kenward; **22/3bg** AA/C Sawyer; **22tl** AA/C Sawyer; **24tr** AA; **22cl** Nova Development Corp; **22cr** Getty Images; **22b** AA/D Corrance; **22/3t** Nova Development Corp; **23cl** Getty Images; **23tc** AA/C Sawyer; **23tr** AA/C Sawyer; **23c** Nova Development Corp; **24bg** AA/C Sawyer; **24l** Getty Images; **24tc** Federal Reserve Board, Washington, D.C; **24tr** AA/C Sawyer; **24cr** AA/C Sawyer.

THE STORY OF NEW YORK

25 Illustrated London News; **26/7bg** AA; **26cl** Mary Evans Picture Library; **26cr** Corbis; **26bl** Corbis; **26/7b** AA; **26/7c** Mary Evans Picture Library; **27l** Mary Evans Picture Library; **27c** AA; **27br** Mary Evans Picture Library; **28/9bg** AA; **28cl** Mary Evans Picture Library; **28cr** Mary Evans Picture Library; **28bl** AA/R Elliott; **28/9** Representation of the Terrible Fire of New York in 1776 (engraving) by French School th(18th century), Museum of the City of New York, USA/Bridgeman Art Library; **29cl** AA; **29c** Mary Evans Picture Library; **29bl** AA; **29br** Mary Evans Picture Library; **30/1bg** New York Looking South from Union Square, pub. by John Bachman, 1849 (litho) by C Bachman (19th century), Museum of the City of New York, USA/Bridgeman Art Library; **30cl** View of the Ruins after the Great Fire in New York, Dec. 16th & 17th 1835, engraved by W I Bennett, pub. by L P Glover, by Bernardo Belottto Canaletto (1720-80), Museo di Goethe, Rome, Italy/Bridgeman Art Library; **30c** Hulton Archives/Getty Images; **30cr** Mary Evans Picture Library; **30/1** New York Looking South from Union Square, pub. by John Bachman, 1849 (Litho) by C Bachman (19th century), Museum of the City of New York, USA/Bridgeman Art Library; **31cl** Hulton Archives/Getty Images; **31c** Hulton Archives/Getty Images; **31bl** AA/C Sawyer; **31br** Hulton Archives/Getty Images; **32/3bg** AA; **32c** Illustrated London News; **32cr** Mary Evans Picture Library; **32bl** AA; **33cl** Illustrated London News; **33c** AA; **33bl** Hulton Archives/Getty Images; **33br** AA/R Elliott; **34/5bg** AA/C Sawyer; **34cl** AA/C Sawyer; **34cr** AA/C Sawyer; **34bl** Hulton Archives/Getty Images; **34br** Mary Evans Picture Library; **34/5** AA/C Sawyer; **34cl** Mary Evans Picture Library; **35c** Hulton Archives/Getty Images; **35bc** AA/R Elliott; **35br** AA/C Sawyer; **36/7bg** AA/R Elliott; **36cl** AA/P Kenward; **36cr** Corbis; **36bl** AA/R Elliott; **36/7** AA/R Elliott; **37cl** Corbis; **37c** Hulton Archives/Getty Images; **37cr** Hulton Archives/Getty Images; **3br** AA/C Sawyer; **38bg** AA/C Sawyer; **38c** Getty Images; **38cr** AA/S McBride; **38bl** AA/C Sawyer; **38br** AA/C Sawyer.

ON THE MOVE

39 AA/C Sawyer; **40/1** Digital Vision; **42t** Digital Vision; **42b** NY Airport Service; **43t** AA/S L Day; **43b** AA/C Sawyer; **44/5** AA/S L Day; **44** AA/C Sawyer; **46/7** AA/S L Day; **46** AA/C Sawyer; **47c** AA/R Elliott; **47b** AA/S McBride; **48/9** AA/C Sawyer; **48tr** AA/C Sawyer; **48br** AA/C Sawyer; **49tl** AA/C Sawyer; **50** AA/C Sawyer; **51t** AA/D Corrance; **51cr** AA/D Corrance; **51br** AA/C Sawyer; **52/3** Digital Vision; **52** AA/E Rooney; **53t** AA/C Sawyer; **53b** AA/C Sawyer; **54/5** AA/C Sawyer; **54cr** AA/C Sawyer; **54b** AA/C Sawyer; **55** Courtesy of Greyhound Lines, Inc; **56t** AA/C Sawyer; **56c** AA/N Sumner.

THE SIGHTS

57 AA/C Sawyer; **62l** AA/R Elliott; **62r** AA/C Sawyer; **63l** AA/D Corrance; **63r** AA/R Elliott; **64l** AA/C Sawyer; **64r** AA/C Sawyer; **65l** AA/C Sawyer; **65r** AA/D Corrance; **66l** AA/C Sawyer; **66r** AA/C Sawyer; **67tl** Downtown Alliance; **67tr** AA/C Sawyer; **67bl** Asia Society & Museum/Frank Oudeman; **68** AA/C Sawyer; **69t** American Museum of Natural History; **69cr** AA/C Sawyer; **69c** American Museum of Natural History; **69r** D Finnin/American Museum of Natural History; **69b** American Museum of Natural History; **70t** AA/R Elliott; **70cl** American Museum of Natural History; **70c** American Museum of Natural History; **70cr** American Museum of Natural History; **70bl** American Museum of Natural History; **72** D Finnin/American Museum of Natural History; **73t** AA/C Sawyer; **73cr** AA/C Sawyer; **73br** AA/C Sawyer; **74t** AA/C Sawyer; **74cl** AA/C Sawyer; **74cr** AA/C Sawyer; **75** AA/D Corrance; **76t** Don Perdue; **76cl** Don Perdue; **77tl** AA/C Sawyer; **77tc** AA/C Sawyer; **77tr** Dahesh Museum of Art; **78t** AA/E Rooney; **78cl** AA/C Sawyer; **78c** AA/C Sawyer; **78cr** AA/C Sawyer; **79t** AA/S McBride; **79br** AA/S McBride; **80tl** AA/S McBride; **80tr** AA/S McBride; **80c** AA/S McBride; **80cr** AA/S McBride; **82** AA/D Corrance; **83l** AA/S McBride; **83c** AA/C Sawyer; **83r** AA/C Sawyer; **84t** AA/C Sawyer; **84l** AA/S McBride; **85t** AA/C Sawyer; **85cr** AA/C Sawyer; **85br** AA/S McBride; **86t** AA; **86l** AA/C Sawyer; **87tl** AA/C Sawyer; **87tc** AA/D Corrance; **87tr** AA/C Sawyer; **88t** AA/C Sawyer; **88cl** AA/C Sawyer; **88c** AA/S McBride; **88cr** AA/C Sawyer; **88bl** AA/S McBride; **89** AA/C Sawyer; **90** AA/C Sawyer; **91** Corbis; **92t** By courtesy of the Ellis Island Immigration Museum; **92cl** By courtesy of the Ellis Island Immigration Museum; **92c** Corbis; **92cr** AA/R Elliott; **92bl** AA/S McBride; **94** AA/C Sawyer; **95** AA/C Sawyer; **95cl** AA/C Sawyer; **95cr** AA/S McBride; **96** AA/C Sawyer; **97t** AA P Kenward; **97r** Federal Hall; **98t** AA/C Sawyer; **98cl** AA/C Sawyer; **99tl** AA/C Sawyer; **99tc** AA/C Sawyer; **99tr** AA/C Sawyer; **100t** Frick Collection; **100cl** Frick Collection; **101tl** AA/C Sawyer; **101tc** AA/C Sawyer; **101tr** AA/R G Elliott; **102** AA/S McBride; **103t** AA/S McBride; **103cl** AA/S McBride; **103c** AA/S McBride; **103cr** AA/S McBride; **104tl** AA/S McBride; **104tr** AA/S McBride; **105t** AA/S McBride; **105cl** AA/C Sawyer; **105c** AA/S McBride; **105cr** AA/C Sawyer; **106** AA/S McBride; **107cl** AA/C Sawyer; **107c** AA/P Kenward; **107cr** AA/S McBride; **107b** AA/C Sawyer; **108t** AA/C Sawyer; **108cl** AA/C Sawyer; **109tl** Jewish Museum; **109tc** AA/C Sawyer; **109tr** Lower East Side Tenement Museum; **110t** AA/C Sawyer; **110cl** AA/S McBride; **110c** Flask, Glass and Fruit, 1877 by Paul Cezanne (1839-1906) Solomon R Guggenheim Museum, New York, USA/Bridgeman Art Library; **110cr** AA/C Sawyer; **111t** Robert Harding Picture Library; **111br** Jeanne Hebuterne in a Yellow Jumper, 1918-19 (oil on canvas) by Amedeo Modigliani (1884-1920), Solomon R Guggenheim Museum, New York, USA/Bridgeman Art Library; **112t** AA/P Kenward; **112cl** AA/C Sawyer; **112c** Lincoln Center/Steve J Sherman; **112cr** AA/E Rooney; **113** AA/P Kenward; **114t** AA/C Sawyer; **114cl** AA/C Sawyer; **114c** Lady at the Tea Table, 1885 (oil on canvas) by Mary Stevenson Cassatt (1844-1926), Metropolitan Museum of Art, New York, USA/Bridgeman Art Library; **114cr** AA/R Elliott; **115** AA/R Elliott; **116** AA/D Corrance; **118** Corbis; **119t** AA/D Corrance; **119cl** AA; **119c** The Dance Lesson, c 1879 (pastel) by Edgar Degas (1834-1917) Metropolitan Museum of Art, New York, USA/Bridgeman Art Library; **119cr** AA/C Sawyer; **120tl** AA/R G Elliott; **120tc** Mount

Vernon Hotel Museum; **120tr** Museum of American Financial History; **121t** AA/R Elliott; **121cr** AA/C Sawyer; **122t** © Photo SCALA, Florence,The Pierpont Morgan Library, 2001; **122cl** AA/C Sawyer; **123tl** Museum of the Chinese in Americas; **123tr** Museum of Arts and Design; **124tl** AA/R Elliott; **124tc** Maika, Neue Galerie, © Christian Schad Stiftung Aschaffenburg/VG Bild-Kunst, Bonn and DACS, London 2008; **124tr** AA/R Elliott; **125t** © Photo SCALA, Florence, Museum of Modern Art, 2003; **125cr** Museum of Modern Art/©2005 Timothy Hursley; **126tl** Courtesy of the NY City Police Museum; **126tc** New York Historical Society; **126tr** AA/C Sawyer; **127t** AA/R Elliott; **127cr** AA/C Rooney; **128t** AA/S McBride; **128cl** AA/S McBride; **128c** AA/S McBride; **128cr** AA/C Sawyer; **129** AA/C Sawyer; **130tl** AA/C Sawyer; **130cl** AA/C Sawyer; **130r** AA/C Sawyer; **130bl** AA/S McBride; **131tl** AA/S McBride; **131tc** AA/C Sawyer; **131tr** AA/C Sawyer; **132t** AA/S McBride; **132cl** S McBride; **132c** AA/C Sawyer; **132cr** AA/C Sawyer; **132bl** AA/C Sawyer; **133** AA/C Sawyer; **134t** AA/C Sawyer; **134cl** AA/S McBride; **134cr** AA/C Sawyer; **134bl** South Street Seaport; **135t** AA/C Sawyer; **135b** AA/C Sawyer; **136t** AA/E Rooney; **136cl** AA/C Sawyer; **136c** AA/E Rooney; **136cr** AA/P Kenward; **136bl** AA/R Elliott; **137** AA/C Sawyer; **138** AA/C Sawyer; **139** AA/C Sawyer; **140tl** AA/C Sawyer; **140cl** AA/C Sawyer; **141tl** AA/C Sawyer; **141tc** AA/C Sawyer; **141tr** AA/C Sawyer; **142t** AA/C Sawyer; **142cl** AA/P Kenward; **142c** AA/C Sawyer; **142cr** AA/C Sawyer; **143** AA/P Kenward; **144tl** AA/C Sawyer; **144tc** AA/C Sawyer; **144tr** AA/C Sawyer; **145t** AA; **145r** AA/C Sawyer; **146** AA/C Sawyer; **147t** AA/C Sawyer; **147cl** AA/C Sawyer; **147c** AA/C Sawyer; **147cr** AA/C Sawyer; **148/9** AA/R Elliott, ©ADAGP, Paris and DACS, London 2008; **148c** Whitney Museum of American Art View 2/Jeff Goldberg, Esto; **148bl** AA/R Elliott; **150cl** AA/P Kenward; **150cr** Whitney Museum of American Art View 1/Jeff Goldberg, Esto; **150b** Corbis; **151** Railroad Crossing, 1922-23 by Edward Hopper (1882-1967) Whitney Museum of American Art, New York, USA/Bridgeman Art Library; **152tl** AA/R Elliott; **152tr** AA/C Sawyer; **152b** Brooklyn Historical Society; **153t** The Peaceable Kingdom, c 1840-45) by Edward Hicks (1780-1849), Brooklyn Museum of Art, New York, USA/Bridgeman Art Library; **153cr** AA/C Sawyer; **154tl** AA/R Elliott; **154tc** AA/C Sawyer; **154tr** AA/C Sawyer; **154bl** NY Transit Museum; **155tl** NY Hall of Science; **155tc** AA/C Sawyer; **155tr** Waterfront Museum/Frank Zimmerman; **155c** AA/R Elliott; **156tl** Garibaldi Meucci Museum; **156tc** AA/C Sawyer; **156tr** AA/C Sawyer; **156bl** Historic Richmond Town; **157t** AA/R Elliott; **157cr** Bronx Zoo; **158t** Getty Images; **157l** Photodisc.

WHAT TO DO

159 Photodisc; **164t** AA/M Jourdan; **164cl** Screaming Mimi's; **164c** AA/C Sawyer; **165/5c** AA/C Sawyer; **165cl** AA/C Sawyer; **165cr** AA/C Sawyer; **166cl** AA/S McBride; **166cr** AA/S McBride; **166b** Me & Ro; **167cl** AA/C Sawyer; **167c** Jimmy Choo; **167cr** AA/C Sawyer; **168** AA/C Sawyer; **169t** AA/M Jourdan; **169c** AA/K Paterson; **170t** AA/M Jourdan; **170** AA/R G Elliott; **171t** AA/M Jourdan; **171c** AA/C Sawyer; **172t** AA/M Jourdan; **172c** AA/C Sawyer; **173t** AA/M Jourdan; **173c** AA/C Sawyer; **174t** AA/M Jourdan; **174c** Kirna Zabete; **175t** AA/M Jourdan; **175c** Mark Bulkin; **176t** AA/M Jourdan; **176c** AA/C Sawyer; **177t** AA/M Jourdan; **177c** AA/C Sawyer; **178t** AA/M Jourdan; **178c** AA/P Kenward; **179t** AA/M Jourdan; **179c** Broadway Panhandler; **180t** AA/M Jourdan; **180c** Eye Candy; **181t** AA/M Jourdan; **181c** Jimmy Choo; **182t** AA/M Jourdan; **183t** AA/M Jourdan; **184t** AA/M Jourdan; **184c** AA/C Sawyer; **185t** Digital Vision; **185cl** Digital Vision; **185c** Digital Vision; **190t** AA/C Sawyer; **190c** AA/S Collier; **191t** AA/C Sawyer; **191c** Jonathan B Ragle; **192t** Digital Vision; **192c** AA/C Sawyer; **193t** Digital Vision; **193c** Frick Collection/John Bigelow Taylor; **194t** Digital Vision; **194c** AA/P Kenward; **195t** Digital Vision; **195c** AA/C Sawyer; **196t** Brand X Pics; **196c** Chicago City Limits; **197t** Brand X Pics; **197c** Michael Moran; **198t** Brand X Pics; **198c** AA/C Coe; **199c** © Bob Colton/Black Star; **199t** Brand X Pics; **200c** AA/C Sawyer; **201t** Digital Vision; **201c** Digital Vision; **202t** Digital Vision; **202c** Digital Vision; **203t** Digital Vision; **203c** AA/C Sawyer; **204t** Digital Vision; **204c** Sob's; **205t** AA/C Sawyer; **205c** American Airlines Theatre; **206t** AA/C Sawyer; **206cc** AA/C Sawyer; **207t** AA/C

Sawyer; **207c** AA/C Sawyer; **208t** AA/C Sawyer; **208c** AA/C Sawyer; **209t** AA/C Sawyer; **209c** Bowerie Lane; **210/1t** AA/C Sawyer; **210c** AA/P Kenward; **211c** Carol Rosegg; **212t** AA/T Souter; **212cl** Brand X Pics; **212cr** Brand X Pics; **213t** AA/T Souter; **213c** Bubble Lounge; **214t** AA/T Souter; **214c** Happy Ending; **215t** AA/T Souter; **215c** Photodisc; **216t** AA/T Souter; **216c** Photodisc; **217t** AA/T Souter; **217c** Photodisc; **218t** Piano's; **218c** AA/C Sawyer; **219t** Piano's; **219c** Brand X Pics; **220t** Piano's; **220c** Brand X Pics; **221t** Photodisc; **221cl** AA/P Kenward; **221cr** AA/C Sawyer; **222t** Photodisc; **222c** AA/C Sawyer; **223t** Photodisc; **223c** Photodisc; **224t** Photodisc; **224c** AA/R G Elliott; **225t** Photodisc; **225c** AA/P Kenward; **226t** Photodisc; **226cl** Asphalt Green; **226cr** Greenhouse Spa; **227t** Photodisc; **227c** Clay; **228t** Photodisc; **228c** Oasis Day Spa; **229t** AA/R G Elliott; **229cl** New Victory Theatre; **229cr** Liberty Helicopters; **230t** AA/R G Elliott; **230c** Children's Museum of Manhattan; **231t** AA/R G Elliott; **231c** Steve Williams © 2003; **232t** AA/R G Elliott; **232c** AA/C Sawyer; **233t** AA/S L Day; **233cl** AA/S L Day; **233cr** AA/P Kenward; **234t** AA/S L Day.

OUT AND ABOUT

235 AA/P Kenward; **237tl** AA/C Sawyer; **237tc** AA/C Sawyer; **237tr** AA/C Sawyer; **237cr** AA/C Sawyer; **238** AA/N Lancaster; **239t** AA/C Sawyer; **239ct** AA/R Elliott; **239cb** AA/N Lancaster; **239b** AA/N Lancaster; **241tl** AA/N Lancaster; **241tr** AA/C Sawyer; **241cr** AA/C Sawyer; **241bl** AA/N Lancaster; **242** AA/C Sawyer; **243tl** AA/C Sawyer; **243tr** AA/C Sawyer; **243bc** AA/C Sawyer; **243br** AA/C Sawyer; **244** AA/C Sawyer; **245tl** AA/C Sawyer; **245tr** AA/C Sawyer; **245cr** AA/C Sawyer; **245br** AA/E Rooney; **246** AA/R Elliott; **247tr** AA/C Sawyer; **247ctr** AA/C Sawyer; **247cbr** AA/C Sawyer; **247br** AA/C Sawyer; **248** AA/C Sawyer; **249tr** AA/C Sawyer; **249c** AA/S McBride; **249cr** AA/C Sawyer; **249b** AA/C Sawyer; **251tl** AA/C Sawyer; **251tr** AA/C Sawyer; **251b** AA/C Sawyer; **252/3** AA/N Lancaster; **253tr** AA/P Kenward; **253ctr** AA/C Sawyer; **253cb** AA/C Sawyer; **253b** AA/N Lancaster; **254** AA/N Lancaster; **255tl** AA/N Lancaster; **255tr** AA/N Lancaster; **255c** AA/C Sawyer; **255b** AA/N Lancaster; **256** AA/R Elliott; **257t** AA/R Elliott; **257c** AA/R Elliott; **257b** AA/R Elliott; **258c** AA/R Elliott; **258/9** AA/R Elliott; **259t** AA/R Elliott; **259c** AA/R Elliott; **260l** AA/C Sawyer; **260c** AA/C Sawyer; **260r** AA/C Sawyer.

EATING AND STAYING

261 AA/C Sawyer; **262l** AA/C Sawyer; **262cl** AA/P Kenward; **262cr** AA/C Sawyer; **262r** AA/P Kenward; **263l** AA/C Sawyer; **263c** AA/C Sawyer; **263r** AA/R Elliott; **263bl** AA/R Elliott; **264l** AA/C Sawyer; **264c** AA/C Sawyer; **264r** AA/D Corrance; **264cb** AA/S McBride; **270l** AA/S Collier; **270r** AA/S Collier; **270b** AA/S Collier; **271r** AA/S McBride; **272l** AA/M Langford; **272r** AA/S Collier; **273c** AA/T Harris; **276bc** AA/S Collier; **276r** Photodisc; **277l** AA/S Collier; **278r** AA/S McBride; **279l** AA/S Collier; **280tl** AA/S McBride; **280bl** AA/S McBride; **281l** AA/S Collier; **281r** AA/S Collier; **282l** AA/S Collier; **284l** AA/S McBride; **284r** AA/S McBride; **285** ImageState; **286r** AA/C Sawyer; **287l** AA/S Collier; **287r** AA/S Collier; **288l** AA/S Collier; **288r** AA/S Collier; **288br** AA/S McBride; **289l** AA/J Ranken; **289r** AA/S Collier; **290cl** AA/S Collier; **291t** AA/S McBride; **291c** AA/S McBride; **291b** AA/N Lancaster; **292l** AA/C Sawyer; **292cl** AA/C Sawyer; **292cr** AA/C Sawyer; **292r** AA/C Sawyer; **292b** AA/C Sawyer; **293l** AA/C Sawyer; **293cl** AA/C Sawyer; **293cr** AA/C Sawyer; **293r** AA/C Sawyer; **299tr** AA; **299br** AA/C Sawyer

PLANNING

311 AA/C Sawyer; **312t** AA/C Sawyer; **312c** AA/E Rooney; **316** AA/C Sawyer; **317** MRI Banker's Guide to Foreign Currency, Houston USA; **318t** Leisure Pass North America LLC; **318b** AA/C Sawyer; **320** AA/C Sawyer; **321t** AA/C Sawyer; **321b** AA/C Sawyer; **322** AA/S Collier; **323tr** AA/P Kenward; **323cr** AA/R Elliott; **324** AA/E Rooney; **325** AA/R Elliott; **326** AA/S Collier.

Project editor
Betty Sheldrick

Interior design
David Austin, Glyn Barlow, Alan Gooch, Kate Harling, Bob Johnson,
Nick Otway, Carole Philp, Keith Russell

Additional interior design work
Jo Tapper, Nautilus Design

Picture research
Carol Walker

Cover design
Tigist Getachew

Internal repro work
Susan Crowhurst, Ian Little, Michael Moody

Production
Helen Brown, Lyn Kirby

Mapping
Maps produced by the Mapping Services Department of AA Publishing

Main contributors
Coleen Degnan-Veness, Marilyn Wood

Copy editors
Sheila Hawkins, Sarah Hudson, Jo Perry

Updater
Donna Dailey

Revision management
Bookwork Creative Associates Ltd

See It New York City
ISBN 978-1-4000-0691-5
Third Edition

Color separation by Keenes, UK
Printed and bound by Leo, China
10 9 8 7 6 5 4 3 2 1

Special Sales: This book is available for special discounts for bulk purchases for sales promotions or
premiums. Special editions, including personalized covers, excerpts of existing books, and corporate
imprints, can be created in large quantities for special needs. For more information, write to Special
Markets/Premium Sales, 1745 Broadway, MD 6-2, New York, NY 10019 or e-mail
specialmarkets@randomhouse.com.

A03306
Mapping in this title produced from New York data © Tele Atlas N. V. 2003
Relief map images supplied by Mountain High Maps ® Copyright © 1993 Digital Wisdom, Inc
Weather chart statistics supplied by Weatherbase © Copyright 2003 Canty and Associates, LLC
Transport map © Communicarta Ltd, UK

Important Note: Time inevitably brings changes, so always confirm prices, travel facts,
and other perishable information when it matters. Although Fodor's cannot accept
responsibility for errors, you can use this guide in the confidence that
we have taken every care to ensure its accuracy.

Fodor's Key to the Guides

AMERICA'S **GUIDEBOOK LEADER** PUBLISHES GUIDES FOR **EVERY KIND OF TRAVELER**. CHECK OUT OUR MANY SERIES AND FIND YOUR **PERFECT MATCH**.

GOLD GUIDES

Built for today's travelers with unique graphics and maps for easy planning and advice on quintessential local experiences, along with Fodor's Choice rated hotels, restaurants, and sights to guarantee an exceptional vacation.

EXPLORING GUIDES

Splendid color photography paired with exquisitely written articles on history, culture, art, and architecture; suggested walks and excursions; and full-color maps allow you to experience a destination like a well-informed local.

COMPASS AMERICAN GUIDES

Long-time resident writers and photographers reveal the culture and character of American cities, states, and regions through intelligently written essays, literary excerpts, and stunning color imagery.

AROUND THE CITY WITH KIDS

68 great ideas for family fun in and around the city, hand-picked by resident parents, with age-appropriate ratings, entertaining trivia, and nearby kid-friendly snack spots.

SEE IT GUIDES

Colorful and practical, these illustrated guides feature smart writing on history and culture, rich photography, *and* practical travel information. Complete dining and restaurant reviews, exact admission fees, kid-friendly ratings, and everything from sightseeing and shopping, to nightlife, performing arts, and outdoor activities.

25 BEST

Compact city guides of must-see sights and the best dining, shopping, and activities; with a detailed, full-size street map conveniently built-in so you can confidently navigate the city.

FLASHMAPS

Easy-to-follow maps perfect for residents or visitors who want to quickly locate restaurants, shops, museums, movie theaters, subway and bus routes, and more.

LANGUAGES FOR TRAVELERS

All the words and phrases you need for greeting locals, dining out, and getting around in a handy phrasebook along with two CDs for pronunciation practice.

Available at bookstores everywhere.
For a complete list of more than 300 guidebooks,
visit **Fodors.com/shop**.

Dear Traveler

From buying a plane ticket to booking a room and seeing the sights, a trip goes much more smoothly when you have a good travel guide. Dozens of writers, editors, designers, and cartographers have worked hard to make the book you hold in your hands a good one. Was it everything you expected? Were our descriptions accurate? Were our recommendations on target? And did you find our tips and practical advice helpful? Your ideas and experiences matter to us. If we have missed or misstated something, we'd love to hear about it. Fill out our survey at www.fodors.com/feedback or e-mail us at seeit@fodors.com. Or you can snail mail to the See It Editor at Fodor's, 1745 Broadway, New York, New York 10019. We'll look forward to hearing from you.

Tim Jarrell
Publisher